A GUIDE TO
CHILDREN'S LITERATURE
ABOUT THE NEEDS AND PROBLEMS
OF YOUTH AGED 2-15

To Brett, Brian, and Troy —
May they always find friends in books.

CONTENTS

CONDENSED SUBJECT INDEX

Use this Condensed Subject Index to search easily through the more than 450 topics. To locate a book, turn to the desired subject in the Subject Index; titles of relevant books are listed under each subject.

C

Camp Experiences
See also: *Separation anxiety*

Canada

Cancer
See also: *Hospital, going to; Leukemia; Surgery*

Cardiac Conditions
See also: *Surgery: heart*

Careers
Dancer
Planning. *See also: Education; Work, attitude toward*
Singer

Catholic, Roman
See: *Roman Catholic*

Cerebral Palsy
See also: *Birth defects; Brain injury*

Change
Accepting
New Home. *See also: Life style: change in; Moving*
Resisting

Chemical Dependency
See: *Alcoholism; Drugs; Reality, escaping*

Chicano
See: *Mexican-American*

Chicken Pox

See: *Communicable diseases: chicken pox*

Child Abuse

See also: *Cruelty*

Childbirth

See also: *Pregnancy; Sibling: new baby*

Children's Home, Living in

See also: *Adoption; Foster home; Orphan*

Chinese-American

Choice Making

See: *Decision making*

Chores

See also: *Job; Responsibility*

Cigarettes

See: *Smoking*

Cigars

See: *Smoking*

Classmate Relationships

See: *School: classmate relationships*

Cleanliness

See: *Baths, taking of*

Cleft Lip/Palate

See also: *Birth defects; Speech problems; Surgery*

Cooperation

See also: *Helping; Neighbors/Neighborhood; Sharing/Not sharing*

in Play

in Work

Coping

See: *Problem solving; Resourcefulness*

Copying

See: *Honesty/Dishonesty; Imitation*

Courage, Meaning of

See also: *Encouragement; Fear*

Courtesy

See: *Etiquette*

Cousin

See: *Relatives*

Crazy

See: *Mental illness*

Creativity

See also: *Curiosity; Fantasy formation; Imagination; Problem solving; Resourcefulness*

Crime/Criminals

See also: *Accidents: hit and run; Death: murder; Delinquency, juvenile; Detention home, living in; Guilt, feelings of; Parole; Prostitution; Rape; Stealing; Vandalism*

Crippled

See: *Birth defects; Deformities; Handicaps; Limbs, abnormal or missing; Paralysis; Quadriplegia; Wheelchair, dependence on*

Cruelty

See also: *Child abuse; Violence*

Cults

Cultural/Ethnic Groups

See: *Specific group (e.g. Afro-American; Puerto Rican-American)*

Curiosity

See also: *Creativity*

D

Danger

See: *Risk, taking of*

Dating

See: *Boy-girl relationships: dating; Sex*

Daydreaming

See also: *Fantasy formation; Magical thinking; Nightmares; Reality, escaping; Wishes*

Deafness

See also: *Muteness*

I

Ideals

See: *Identification with others; Values/Valuing*

Identification with Others

See also: *Imitation; Leader/Leadership; Values/Valuing*

Adults

Peers. *See also: Friendship*

Story characters

Identity, Search for

See also: *Adoption*

Illegitimate Child

See: *Unwed mother: child of*

Illnesses

See also: *Communicable diseases; Doctor, going to; Hospital, going to; Mental illness; Surgery*

Amyotrophic Lateral Sclerosis. *See: Amyotrophic Lateral Sclerosis*

Asthma. *See: Asthma*

Being ill

Cancer. *See: Cancer*

Cardiac conditions. *See: Cardiac conditions*

Diabetes. *See: Diabetes*

Individuation

See: *Autonomy; Dependence/Independence; Separation anxiety*

Infant

See: *Sibling: new baby*

Inferiority, Feelings of

See also: *Shyness*

Inhibition

See: *Inferiority, feelings of; Shyness*

Initiative, Taking

See: *Autonomy; Leader/Leadership; Work, attitude toward*

Injuries

See: *Accidents; Doctor, going to; Fractures; Hospital, going to; Surgery; Sutures*

Insanity

See: *Mental illness*

Insecurity

See: *Security/Insecurity*

Institutions/Institutionalization

See: *Children's home, living in; Detention home, living in; Mental hospital, living in; Nursing home, living in; Schools, private*

Integration

See also: *Prejudice; School*

Job

See also: *Baby-sitting; Chores; Money: earning; Responsibility; Work, attitude toward*

Judgment, Effect of Emotions on

Justice/Injustice

See also: *Blame; Guilt, feelings of*

Juvenile Delinquency

See: *Delinquency, juvenile*

Juvenile Detention

See: *Detention home, living in*

K

Killing

See: *Death: murder; Violence; War*

Kissing

See: *Boy-girl relationships; Sex*

L

Language Problems

See: *Communication; Speech problems*

Laziness

See: *Chores; Responsibility: avoiding; School: achievement/underachievement; Work, attitude toward*

Mental Retardation

See also: *Brain injury; Education: special; Learning disabilities*

Down's Syndrome. *See: Down's Syndrome*

Mexican-American

Middle Child

See: *Sibling: middle*

Migrant Workers

Minding

See: *Discipline, meaning of*

Minority Groups

See: *Differences, human; Prejudice*

Misunderstandings

See: *Communication: misunderstandings*

Mixed Marriage

See: *Marriage: interracial; Marriage: interreligious*

Money

Earning. *See also: Job*

Management

Mongoloid

See: *Down's Syndrome*

Moral Values

See: *Values/Valuing: moral/ethical*

Native American

Nature

Appreciation of

Living in harmony with

Respect for

Naughty Child

See: *Discipline, meaning of*

Negative Attitude

See: *Inferiority, feelings of; Shame*

Neglect

See: *Chores; Job; Parental: negligence; Responsibility: neglecting*

Neglected Child

See: *Abandonment; Deprivation, emotional; Parental: negligence*

Negro

See: *Afro-American*

Neighbors/Neighborhood

See also: *Cooperation*

Nervous Breakdown

See: *Mental illness*

Neurosis

See: *Mental illness*

Physical Handicaps

See: *Handicaps*

Planning

See: *Careers: planning; Problem solving; Responsibility*

Play

See also: *Fantasy formation; Imaginary friend; Imagination; Peer relationships; Reality, escaping; Sharing/Not sharing*

Poliomyelitis

See also: *Braces on body/limbs; Paralysis; Wheelchair, dependence on*

Popularity

See: *Boy-girl relationships; Friendship; Peer relationships*

Poverty

See also: *Differences, human; Ghetto; Prejudice: social class*

Power Struggle

See: *Parent/Parents: power struggle with*

Practical Jokes/Pranks

See also: *Teasing*

Pregnancy

See also: *Abortion; Childbirth; Unwed mother*

Prejudice

See also: *Differences, human; Hatred; Hostility; Integration; Ostracism; Rejection*

Self-Esteem

See also: *Guilt, feelings of; Self, attitude toward*

Self-Identity

See: *Identity, search for*

Self-Image

See: *Self, attitude toward*

Self-Improvement

Self-Reliance

See: *Dependence/Independence*

Self Respect

See: *Self, attitude toward: respect*

Selfishness/Unselfishness

See: *Egocentrism; Giving, meaning of; Sharing/Not sharing*

Senility

See: *Age: senility*

Separation, Marital

See also: *Divorce*

Separation Anxiety

See also: *Anxiety; Camp experiences; Homesickness; Hospital, going to; Loneliness; Loss: feelings of; School: entering; Schools, private*

Separation from Loved Ones

See also: *Abandonment; Homesickness; Hospital, going to; Loneliness; Loss: feelings of; Mourning, stages of; Moving*

Sex

See also: *Boy-girl relationships*

Attitude toward

Premarital. *See also: Prostitution; Unwed mother*

Sex Role

See: *Gender role identity*

Sexism

See: *Prejudice: sexual*

Sexuality

See: *Gender role identity; Prejudice: sexual*

Shame

See also: *Embarrassment; Guilt, feelings of*

Sharing/Not Sharing

See also: *Cooperation; Egocentrism; Play*

Shoplifting

See: *Stealing: shoplifting*

Showing Off

See: *Attention seeking; Boasting*

Shyness

See also: *Inferiority, feelings of*

Size
See: *Height; Weight control*

Skipping School
See: *School: truancy*

Sleep
See: *Bedtime; Nightmares*

Slum
See: *Ghetto; Poverty*

Smoking
See also: *Drugs; Marijuana*

Social Class
See: *Poverty; Prejudice: social class; Wealth/Wealthy*

Sorrow
See: *Death; Mourning, stages of; Separation from loved ones*

Speech Problems
See also: *Cleft lip/palate*
Stuttering

Sports/Sportsmanship
See also: *Competition; Little League*

Status
See: *Peer relationships; Prejudice: social class*

Stealing
See also: *Crime/Criminals; Delinquency, juvenile*
Shoplifting

Unwanted Child

See: *Abandonment; Rejection: parental*

Unwed Mother

See also: *Pregnancy; Sex: premarital*

Child of

V

Values/Valuing

See also: *Differences, human; Identification with others*

Aesthetic

Materialistic

Moral/Ethical

Vandalism

See also: *Crime/Criminals; Delinquency, juvenile*

Vanity

See: *Pride/False pride*

Violence

See also: *Aggression; Cruelty; Death: murder; Delinquency, juvenile; Rape; War*

Visiting

Visual Impairment

See also: *Blindness; Glasses, wearing of*

W

War

See also: *Violence*

War Orphan

See: *Orphan*

Wealth/Wealthy

See also: *Differences, human*

Weight Control

See also: *Appearance*

Overweight

Wheelchair, Dependence on

See also: *Amputee; Multiple sclerosis; Paralysis; Poliomyelitis; Prosthesis; Quadriplegia*

Wishes

See also: *Daydreaming; Fantasy formation; Magical thinking*

Withdrawal

See: *Reality, escaping*

Womanliness

See: *Gender role identity: female*

Women's Rights

See also: *Gender role identity: female; Prejudice: sexual*

Work, Attitude Toward
  See also: *Careers: planning; Job; Responsibility*

Working Mother
  See: *Parent/Parents: mother working outside home*

Worries
  See: *Anxiety; Fear*

Y

Youngest Child
  See: *Sibling: youngest*

SUBJECT INDEX

To locate a book through the
Subject Index, find the desired
subject; titles of relevant books
are listed under each subject.

A

Abandonment

See also: *Loss: feelings of; Rejection; Separation from loved ones*
Coleman, William Laurence. ORPHAN JIM: A NOVEL.
Ages 13 and up. 158
Kerr, M. E., pseud. IS THAT YOU, MISS BLUE?
Ages 11-14. 379
LeShan, Eda J. WHAT'S GOING TO HAPPEN TO ME? WHEN PARENTS SEPARATE OR DIVORCE.
Ages 8 and up. 402

Abortion

See also: *Pregnancy*
Beckman, Gunnel. MIA ALONE.
Ages 12 and up. 46

Absent Parent

See: *Divorce: of parents; Parental: absence*

Accidents

See also: *Guilt, feelings of; Hospital, going to*
Cate, Dick. FLYING FREE.
Ages 8-10. 124
Haar, Jaap ter. THE WORLD OF BEN LIGHTHART.
Ages 10-13. 287
Wolde, Gunilla. BETSY AND THE DOCTOR.
Ages 3-7. 697

Airplane

Rivera, Geraldo. A SPECIAL KIND OF COURAGE: PROFILES OF YOUNG AMERICANS.
Ages 12 and up. 544

Accidents (cont.)

Automobile
Cook, Marjorie. TO WALK ON TWO FEET.
Ages 11-14. 177
Kingman, Lee. HEAD OVER WHEELS.
Ages 12 and up. 383
Nicholson, William G. PETE GRAY: ONE-ARMED
MAJOR LEAGUER.
Ages 9-12. 479

Fractures. *See: Fractures*

Hit and run. *See also: Crime/Criminals*
Hinton, Nigel. COLLISION COURSE.
Ages 11 and up. 315

Achievement

See: *Competition; School:
achievement/underachievement; Success*

Addiction

See: *Alcoholism; Drugs; Marijuana; Peer relationships:
peer pressures; Smoking*

Adolescence

See: *Maturation; Menstruation; Puberty*

Adoption

See also: *Children's home, living in; Identity, search
for; Orphan*
Pursell, Margaret Sanford. A LOOK AT
ADOPTION.
Ages 3-7. 523
Rivera, Geraldo. A SPECIAL KIND OF COURAGE:
PROFILES OF YOUNG AMERICANS.
Ages 12 and up. 544

Afro-American (cont.)

Age

See also: *Grandparent; Great-grandparent*

Aging

Age (cont.)

Green, Phyllis. MILDRED MURPHY, HOW DOES YOUR GARDEN GROW?
Ages 9-11. 263

Mathis, Sharon Bell. THE HUNDRED PENNY BOX.
Ages 8-10. 445

Pevsner, Stella. KEEP STOMPIN' TILL THE MUSIC STOPS.
Ages 9-12. 509

Raynor, Dorka. GRANDPARENTS AROUND THE WORLD.
Ages 4 and up. 528

Simmons, Anthony. THE OPTIMISTS OF NINE ELMS.
Ages 8-11. 600

Wittman, Sally. A SPECIAL TRADE.
Ages 2-5. 693

Senility

Johnston, Norma. IF YOU LOVE ME, LET ME GO.
Ages 12 and up. 354

Johnston, Norma. THE SWALLOW'S SONG.
Ages 12 and up. 357

Majerus, Janet. GRANDPA AND FRANK.
Ages 12 and up. 440

Tolan, Stephanie S. GRANDPA — AND ME.
Ages 10-13. 655

Wilkinson, Brenda Scott. LUDELL AND WILLIE.
Ages 12 and up. 681

Aggression

See also: *Anger; Hatred; Hostility; Name-calling; Revenge; Teasing; Violence*
Carle, Eric. THE GROUCHY LADYBUG.
Ages 3-7. 113

Ambivalence, Feelings of (cont.)

Herman, Charlotte. THE DIFFERENCE OF ARI STEIN.
Ages 9-12. 312

LeShan, Eda J. WHAT'S GOING TO HAPPEN TO ME? WHEN PARENTS SEPARATE OR DIVORCE.
Ages 8 and up. 402

Rodowsky, Colby F. WHAT ABOUT ME?
Ages 11-13. 556

Smith, Doris Buchanan. DREAMS & DRUMMERS.
Ages 10-12. 612

Sobol, Harriet Langsam. MY BROTHER STEVEN IS RETARDED.
Ages 7-10. 618

Spence, Eleanor. THE DEVIL HOLE.
Ages 10-14. 619

Vigna, Judith. ANYHOW, I'M GLAD I TRIED.
Ages 3-6. 661

Amputee

See also: *Hospital, going to; Limbs, abnormal or missing; Prosthesis; Surgery; Wheelchair, dependence on*

Cook, Marjorie. TO WALK ON TWO FEET.
Ages 11-14. 177

Nicholson, William G. PETE GRAY: ONE-ARMED MAJOR LEAGUER.
Ages 9-12. 479

Rivera, Geraldo. A SPECIAL KIND OF COURAGE: PROFILES OF YOUNG AMERICANS.
Ages 12 and up. 544

Amyotrophic Lateral Sclerosis

Dixon, Paige, pseud. MAY I CROSS YOUR GOLDEN RIVER?
Ages 12 and up. 202

Anger

See also: *Aggression; Depression; Hatred; Hostility; Tantrums*

Alexander, Anne. TO LIVE A LIE.
Ages 9-12. 7

Barkin, Carol and Elizabeth James. SOMETIMES I HATE SCHOOL.
Ages 5-7. 34

Conaway, Judith. I'LL GET EVEN.
Ages 4-7. 170

Dobrin, Arnold. GILLY GILHOOLEY: A TALE OF IRELAND.
Ages 5-8. 203

Grohskopf, Bernice. SHADOW IN THE SUN.
Ages 10 and up. 281

Hapgood, Miranda. MARTHA'S MAD DAY.
Ages 3-6. 293

Kingman, Lee. HEAD OVER WHEELS.
Ages 12 and up. 383

Kroll, Steven. THAT MAKES ME MAD!
Ages 4-7. 389

Riley, Susan. WHAT DOES IT MEAN? ANGRY.
Ages 3-6. 539

Schlein, Miriam. I HATE IT.
Ages 4-7. 575

Sharmat, Marjorie Weinman. I'M NOT OSCAR'S FRIEND ANYMORE.
Ages 3-7. 586

Terris, Susan Dubinsky. THE CHICKEN POX PAPERS.
Ages 10-12. 640

Tester, Sylvia Root. FEELING ANGRY.
Ages 3-6. 643

Williams, Barbara Wright. JEREMY ISN'T HUNGRY.
Ages 4-7. 684

Animals (cont.)

Responsibility for

Aaron, Chester. SPILL.
  Ages 12-14. 1
Bunting, Anne Evelyn. MAGIC AND THE NIGHT RIVER.
  Ages 5-9. 96
Cleaver, Vera and Bill Cleaver. DUST OF THE EARTH.
  Ages 12 and up. 139
Dexter, Pat Egan. ARROW IN THE WIND.
  Ages 10-13. 200
Holmes, Efner Tudor. AMY'S GOOSE.
  Ages 8-11. 330
Renner, Beverly Hollett. THE HIDEAWAY SUMMER.
  Ages 10-13. 531
Skorpen, Liesel Moak. BIRD.
  Ages 6-8. 606
Skorpen, Liesel Moak. MICHAEL.
  Ages 4-8. 609

Anxiety

See also: *Fear; Separation anxiety*
Beckman, Gunnel. MIA ALONE.
  Ages 12 and up. 46
Corcoran, Barbara. THE FARAWAY ISLAND.
  Ages 10-13. 179
Harris, Dorothy Joan. THE SCHOOL MOUSE.
  Ages 6-8. 294
Marshall, James. GEORGE AND MARTHA — ONE FINE DAY.
  Ages 3-6. 442
Valencak, Hannelore. A TANGLED WEB.
  Ages 9-11. 659

Apathy

See: *Depression*

Appalachia
Cleaver, Vera and Bill Cleaver. TRIAL VALLEY.
Ages 12 and up. 141

Appearance

See also: *Height; Weight control*

Body concept. *See: Self, attitude toward: body concept*

Concern about
Danziger, Paula. THE PISTACHIO
PRESCRIPTION: A NOVEL.
Ages 11-13. 190
Girion, Barbara. THE BOY WITH THE SPECIAL
FACE.
Ages 5-8. 249
Perl, Lila. THE TELLTALE SUMMER OF TINA C.
Ages 10-13. 503
Tobias, Tobi. JANE, WISHING.
Ages 6-9. 651

Deformities. *See: Deformities*

Freckles. *See: Freckles*

Glasses. *See: Glasses, wearing of*

Hair. *See: Hair style, importance of*

Appendectomy
See: *Hospital, going to*

Appetite
See: *Weight control*

Apple Polishing
See: *Attention seeking*

Approach-Avoidance Conflict
See: *Ambivalence, feelings of*

Arguing

Barkin, Carol and Elizabeth James. ARE WE STILL BEST FRIENDS?
Ages 4-7. 31
Blue, Rose. SEVEN YEARS FROM HOME.
Ages 8-12. 59
Burningham, John Mackintosh. THE FRIEND.
Ages 2-5. 104
Erskine, Jim. THE SNOWMAN.
Ages 3-6. 219
Madison, Winifred. MARINKA, KATINKA AND ME (SUSIE).
Ages 7-10. 438
Platt, Kin. CHLORIS AND THE WEIRDOS.
Ages 11 and up. 516

Artificial Limbs

See: *Prosthesis*

Asthma

Danziger, Paula. THE PISTACHIO PRESCRIPTION: A NOVEL.
Ages 11-13. 190
Wilkinson, Brenda Scott. LUDELL.
Ages 10-14. 680

Athletics

See: *Competition; Sports/Sportsmanship*

Attention Seeking

See also: *Boasting*
Brandenberg, Franz. I WISH I WAS SICK, TOO!
Ages 3-7. 73
Delaney, Ned. RUFUS THE DOOFUS.
Ages 4-6. 195
Rodowsky, Colby F. P.S. WRITE SOON.
Ages 10-12. 555

Baby-Sitter (cont.)

Klein, Norma. BLUE TREES, RED SKY.
Ages 7-10. 384
Vestly, Anne-Catharina. AURORA AND
SOCRATES.
Ages 8-10. 660
Wells, Rosemary. STANLEY & RHODA.
Ages 4-7. 678

Baby-Sitting

See also: *Job; Sibling: older*
Greenberg, Barbara. THE BRAVEST BABYSITTER.
Ages 4-8. 265

Involuntary
Carlson, Natalie Savage. MARIE LOUISE'S
HEYDAY.
Ages 3-6. 116
Greenfield, Eloise. GOOD NEWS.
Ages 5-6. 271

Watson, Pauline. CURLEY CAT BABY-SITS.
Ages 5-8. 675
Williams, Barbara Wright. JEREMY ISN'T
HUNGRY.
Ages 4-7. 684

Baths, Taking of
Barrett, Judith. I HATE TO TAKE A BATH.
Ages 4-6. 37

Battered Child

See: *Child abuse*

Beauty, Personal

See: *Appearance*

Bedtime
Barrett, Judith. I HATE TO GO TO BED.
Ages 4-6. 36

Bedtime (cont.)

Crowe, Robert L. CLYDE MONSTER.
Ages 3-6. 186
Low, Joseph. BENNY RABBIT AND THE OWL.
Ages 4-7. 419
Marzollo, Jean. CLOSE YOUR EYES.
Ages 2-5. 444
Tobias, Tobi. CHASING THE GOBLINS AWAY.
Ages 4-7. 650

Belonging

See also: *Clubs; Gangs: membership in; Loneliness;
Peer relationships; Rejection*
Bailey, Pearl. DUEY'S TALE.
Ages 12 and up. 29
Chandler, Edna Walker. INDIAN PAINTBRUSH.
Ages 9-11. 126
Coatsworth, Elizabeth Jane. MARRA'S WORLD.
Ages 8-11. 150

Delaney, Ned. RUFUS THE DOOFUS.
Ages 4-6. 195
Johnston, Norma. THE SANCTUARY TREE.
Ages 12 and up. 356
Kent, Deborah. BELONGING: A NOVEL.
Ages 11-14. 375
Madison, Winifred. CALL ME DANICA.
Ages 10-13. 435
Miles, Betty. LOOKING ON.
Ages 11-14. 457
Moncure, Jane Belk. A NEW BOY IN
KINDERGARTEN.
Ages 4-7. 463
Reiss, Johanna. THE JOURNEY BACK.
Ages 10-14. 530
Rosen, Winifred. HENRIETTA, THE WILD
WOMAN OF BORNEO.
Ages 4-7. 560
Simon, Norma. ALL KINDS OF FAMILIES.
Ages 5-8. 602

Belonging (cont.)

Valencak, Hannelore. A TANGLED WEB.
Ages 9-11. 659

Best Friend

See: *Friendship: best friend*

Bias

See: *Prejudice*

Birth Defects

See also: *Cerebral palsy; Cleft lip/palate; Learning disabilities; Limbs, abnormal or missing*
Viscardi, Henry. THE PHOENIX CHILD: A STORY OF LOVE.
Ages 13 and up. 665

Bizarre Thoughts/Behavior

See: *Mental illness*

Black

See: *Afro-American*

Blame

See also: *Guilt, feelings of; Justice/Injustice*
Burch, Robert Joseph. THE WHITMAN KICK.
Ages 12 and up. 100
Low, Joseph. MY DOG, YOUR DOG.
Ages 4-6. 421

Blindness

See also: *Education: special; Pets: guide dog; Visual impairment*
Gill, Derek Lewis Theodore. TOM SULLIVAN'S ADVENTURES IN DARKNESS.
Ages 10-14. 247

Blindness (cont.)

Haar, Jaap ter. THE WORLD OF BEN
LIGHTHART.
Ages 10-13. 287
Hocken, Sheila. EMMA AND I.
Ages 12 and up. 324
Kent, Deborah. BELONGING: A NOVEL.
Ages 11-14. 375
Little, Jean. LISTEN FOR THE SINGING.
Ages 10-14. 413
Nelson, Mary Carroll. MICHAEL NARANJO: THE
STORY OF AN
AMERICAN INDIAN.
Ages 9-12. 476
Petersen, Palle. SALLY CAN'T SEE.
Ages 5-8. 506
Resnick, Rose. SUN AND SHADOW: THE
AUTOBIOGRAPHY OF A WOMAN WHO
CLEARED A PATHWAY TO THE SEEING
WORLD FOR THE BLIND.
Ages 12 and up. 532

Wolf, Bernard. CONNIE'S NEW EYES.
Ages 9 and up. 703
Wosmek, Frances. A BOWL OF SUN.
Ages 7-9. 710

Boarding Schools

See: *Schools, private*

Boasting

See also: *Attention seeking*
Duvoisin, Roger Antoine. PETUNIA'S TREASURE.
Ages 5-8. 212
Rodowsky, Colby F. P.S. WRITE SOON.
Ages 10-12. 555
Sharmat, Marjorie Weinman. I'M TERRIFIC.
Ages 4-7. 587

Body Concept

See: *Name-calling; Self, attitude toward: body concept*

Boy-Girl Relationships

See also: *Friendship; Peer relationships; Sex*
Alexander, Anne. CONNIE.
Ages 10-13. 6
Angell, Judie. RONNIE AND ROSEY.
Ages 11 and up. 20
Bach, Alice. A FATHER EVERY FEW YEARS.
Ages 11-13. 27
Brancato, Robin Fidler. BLINDED BY THE LIGHT.
Ages 11-14. 70
Brancato, Robin Fidler. WINNING.
Ages 12 and up. 72
Branscum, Robbie. JOHNNY MAY.
Ages 9-12. 77
Bridgers, Sue Ellen. HOME BEFORE DARK.
Ages 12 and up. 81
Burch, Robert Joseph. THE WHITMAN KICK.
Ages 12 and up. 100

Carlson, Dale Bick. TRIPLE BOY.
Ages 13 and up. 115
Cleaver, Vera and Bill Cleaver. TRIAL VALLEY.
Ages 12 and up. 141
Cohen, Barbara Nash. BITTER HERBS AND HONEY.
Ages 11-13. 153
Colman, Hila Crayder. SOMETIMES I DON'T LOVE MY MOTHER.
Ages 12 and up. 166
Corcoran, Barbara. AXE-TIME, SWORD-TIME.
Ages 11 and up. 178
Danziger, Paula. THE PISTACHIO PRESCRIPTION: A NOVEL.
Ages 11-13. 190
Dodd, Wayne. A TIME OF HUNTING.
Ages 11-14. 204

Boy-Girl Relationships (cont.)

Boy-Girl Relationships (cont.)

Mazer, Norma Fox. DEAR BILL, REMEMBER ME?
AND OTHER STORIES.
Ages 12 and up. 449
Miles, Betty. LOOKING ON.
Ages 11-14. 457
Peck, Richard. ARE YOU IN THE HOUSE
ALONE?
Ages 12 and up. 500
Platt, Kin. CHLORIS AND THE WEIRDOS.
Ages 11 and up. 516
Reynolds, Pamela. WILL THE REAL MONDAY
PLEASE STAND UP.
Ages 11-14. 533
Scoppettone, Sandra. THE LATE GREAT ME.
Ages 12 and up. 579
Steptoe, John Lewis. MARCIA.
Ages 12 and up. 621
Wilkinson, Brenda Scott. LUDELL AND WILLIE.
Ages 12 and up. 681

Braces on Body/Limbs

See also: *Limbs, abnormal or missing; Poliomyelitis*
Rodowsky, Colby F. P.S. WRITE SOON.
Ages 10-12. 555

Bragging

See: *Boasting*

Brain Injury

See also: *Cerebral palsy; Learning disabilities; Mental
retardation*
Goldreich, Gloria. SEASON OF DISCOVERY.
Ages 11-13. 256
Melton, David. A BOY CALLED HOPELESS.
Ages 10 and up. 451

Bravery

See: *Courage, meaning of*

Broken Bones

See: *Fractures; Surgery*

Brother

See: *Sibling*

Bully

See also: *Harassment*

Being bothered by
Degens, T. THE GAME ON THATCHER ISLAND.
  Ages 11-14. 193
Meddaugh, Susan. TOO SHORT FRED.
  Ages 6-8. 450
Robinson, Charles. NEW KID IN TOWN.
  Ages 4-7. 548

Fear of
Leigh, Bill. THE FAR SIDE OF FEAR.
  Ages 10-14. 398

C

Camp Experiences

See also: *Separation anxiety*
Angell, Judie. IN SUMMERTIME IT'S TUFFY.
  Ages 11-13. 19
Cone, Molly Lamken. CALL ME MOOSE.
  Ages 9-11. 174
Jones, Ron. THE ACORN PEOPLE.
  Ages 10 and up. 360
Shaw, Richard. SHAPE UP, BURKE.
  Ages 10-14. 593

Change (cont.)

New Home. *See also: Life style: change in; Moving*

Change (cont.)

Chetin, Helen. HOW FAR IS BERKELEY?
Ages 11-13. 128

Cleaver, Vera and Bill Cleaver. DUST OF THE EARTH.
Ages 12 and up. 139

Corcoran, Barbara. MAKE NO SOUND.
Ages 10-13. 181

Garrigue, Sheila. BETWEEN FRIENDS.
Ages 9-12. 243

Green, Phyllis. MILDRED MURPHY, HOW DOES YOUR GARDEN GROW?
Ages 9-11. 263

Irion, Ruth Hershey. THE CHRISTMAS COOKIE TREE.
Ages 8-10. 345

Isadora, Rachel. THE POTTERS' KITCHEN.
Ages 4-8. 347

Jacobson, Jane. CITY, SING FOR ME: A COUNTRY CHILD MOVES TO THE CITY.
Ages 6-10. 349

Keats, Ezra Jack. THE TRIP.
Ages 4-7. 368

Lingard, Joan. A PROPER PLACE.
Ages 12 and up. 407

Prather, Ray. NEW NEIGHBORS.
Ages 4-7. 522

Sachs, Marilyn. DORRIE'S BOOK.
Ages 9-12. 566

Spence, Eleanor. THE DEVIL HOLE.
Ages 10-14. 619

Yep, Laurence Michael. DRAGONWINGS.
Ages 12 and up. 712

Resisting

Alexander, Anne. TO LIVE A LIE.
Ages 9-12. 7

Change (cont.)

Bunting, Anne Evelyn. HIGH TIDE FOR
  LABRADOR.
  Ages 9-11. 95
Chandler, Edna Walker. INDIAN PAINTBRUSH.
  Ages 9-11. 126
Colman, Hila Crayder. THAT'S THE WAY IT IS,
  AMIGO.
  Ages 11-13. 168
Gonzalez, Gloria. GAUCHO.
  Ages 10-13. 257
Greene, Constance Clarke. I AND SPROGGY.
  Ages 9-11. 267
Johnston, Norma. THE SANCTUARY TREE.
  Ages 12 and up. 356
Mack, Nancy. I'M NOT GOING.
  Ages 4-8. 427
O'Dell, Scott. ZIA.
  Ages 10 and up. 486
Pollowitz, Melinda. CINNAMON CANE.
  Ages 10-12. 519

Sachs, Marilyn. DORRIE'S BOOK.
  Ages 9-12. 566
Strete, Craig Kee. PAINT YOUR FACE ON A
  DROWNING IN THE RIVER.
  Ages 12 and up. 629
Uchida, Yoshiko. JOURNEY HOME.
  Ages 12-14. 657
Watson, Wendy McLeod. MOVING.
  Ages 3-6. 677

Chemical Dependency

See: *Alcoholism; Drugs; Reality, escaping*

Chicano

See: *Mexican-American*

Chicken Pox

See: *Communicable diseases: chicken pox*

Child Abuse

See also: *Cruelty*
Anderson, Mary Quirk. STEP ON A CRACK.
  Ages 12 and up. 18
Bauer, Marion Dane. FOSTER CHILD.
  Ages 11-13. 42
Hunt, Irene. THE LOTTERY ROSE.
  Ages 11 and up. 337
Mazer, Harry. THE WAR ON VILLA STREET: A
NOVEL.
  Ages 11-13. 448
Roberts, Willo Davis. DON'T HURT LAURIE!
  Ages 10-14. 545
Ruby, Lois. ARRIVING AT A PLACE YOU'VE
NEVER LEFT.
  Ages 12 and up. 564

Childbirth

See also: *Pregnancy; Sibling: new baby*

Dragonwagon, Crescent. WIND ROSE.
  Ages 4-8. 208

Children's Home, Living in

See also: *Adoption; Foster home; Orphan*
Hunt, Irene. THE LOTTERY ROSE.
  Ages 11 and up. 337
Viscardi, Henry. THE PHOENIX CHILD: A STORY
OF LOVE.
  Ages 13 and up. 665

Chinese-American

Pinkwater, Manus. WINGMAN.
  Ages 9-12. 513
Yep, Laurence Michael. CHILD OF THE OWL.
  Ages 11 and up. 711
Yep, Laurence Michael. DRAGONWINGS.
  Ages 12 and up. 712

Clubs (cont.)

Myers, Walter Dean. FAST SAM, COOL CLYDE, AND STUFF.
Ages 11-14. 469
Perl, Lila. THE TELLTALE SUMMER OF TINA C.
Ages 10-13. 503

Commune

See also: *Life style*
Rich, Louise Dickinson. SUMMER AT HIGH KINGDOM.
Ages 12 and up. 536
Shaw, Richard. THE HARD WAY HOME.
Ages 11-13. 592

Communicable Diseases

See also: *Illnesses*

Chicken Pox

Galbraith, Kathryn Osebold. SPOTS ARE SPECIAL!
Ages 4-7. 241
Terris, Susan Dubinsky. THE CHICKEN POX PAPERS.
Ages 10-12. 640
Wolde, Gunilla. BETSY AND THE CHICKEN POX.
Ages 3-7. 696

Communication

Importance of
Baldwin, Anne Norris. A LITTLE TIME.
Ages 9-11. 30
Barkin, Carol and Elizabeth James. SOMETIMES I HATE SCHOOL.
Ages 5-7. 34
Brooks, Jerome. THE TESTING OF CHARLIE HAMMELMAN.
Ages 10-13. 84

Communication (cont.)

Lack of

Communication (cont.)

Communication (cont.)

Valencak, Hannelore. A TANGLED WEB.
Ages 9-11. 659
Watson, Pauline. DAYS WITH DADDY.
Ages 5-8. 676
Wood, Phyllis Anderson. WIN ME AND YOU
LOSE.
Ages 10-13. 709
Yep, Laurence Michael. DRAGONWINGS.
Ages 12 and up. 712
Zolotow, Charlotte Shapiro. WHEN THE WIND
STOPS.
Ages 5-7. 722

Rumor

Terris, Susan Dubinsky. TWO P'S IN A POD.
Ages 9-12. 641

Competition

See also: *Little League; Sports/Sportsmanship*

Bach, Alice. THE MEAT IN THE SANDWICH.
Ages 10-13. 28
Katz, Bobbi. VOLLEYBALL JINX.
Ages 9-11. 364
Knudson, R. Rozanne. ZANBANGER.
Ages 10-13. 387
Love, Sandra. MELISSA'S MEDLEY.
Ages 10-13. 418
Platt, Kin. RUN FOR YOUR LIFE.
Ages 9-12. 518

Compromise

See: *Communication; Cooperation*

Conflict

See: *Ambivalence, feelings of; Problem solving*

Conscience

See: *Guilt, feelings of*

Cooperation (cont.)

in Play

Bottner, Barbara. JUNGLE DAY OR, HOW I LEARNED TO LOVE MY NOSEY LITTLE BROTHER.
Ages 4-7. 62

Erskine, Jim. THE SNOWMAN.
Ages 3-6. 219

Knudson, R. Rozanne. ZANBANGER.
Ages 10-13. 387

Winthrop, Elizabeth. THAT'S MINE!
Ages 2-6. 691

in Work

Barkin, Carol and Elizabeth James. DOING THINGS TOGETHER.
Ages 4-7. 32

Blaine, Margery Kay. THE TERRIBLE THING THAT HAPPENED AT OUR HOUSE.
Ages 3-7. 56

Bradbury, Bianca. "I'M VINNY, I'M ME".
Ages 12 and up. 65

Cleaver, Vera and Bill Cleaver. DUST OF THE EARTH.
Ages 12 and up. 139

Dauer, Rosamond. BULLFROG BUILDS A HOUSE.
Ages 4-7. 191

Hunt, Irene. WILLIAM: A NOVEL.
Ages 12 and up. 338

Melton, David. A BOY CALLED HOPELESS.
Ages 10 and up. 451

Renner, Beverly Hollett. THE HIDEAWAY SUMMER.
Ages 10-13. 531

Coping

See: *Problem solving; Resourcefulness*

Copying

See: *Honesty/Dishonesty; Imitation*

Courage, Meaning of

See also: *Encouragement; Fear*

Brady, Mari. PLEASE REMEMBER ME: A YOUNG WOMAN'S STORY OF HER FRIENDSHIP WITH AN UNFORGETTABLE FIFTEEN-YEAR-OLD BOY.
Ages 12 and up. 68

Brancato, Robin Fidler. WINNING.
Ages 12 and up. 72

Bunting, Anne Evelyn. HIGH TIDE FOR LABRADOR.
Ages 9-11. 95

Christman, Elizabeth. A NICE ITALIAN GIRL.
Ages 12 and up. 132

Clyne, Patricia Edwards. TUNNELS OF TERROR.
Ages 10-12. 149

Coerr, Eleanor. SADAKO AND THE THOUSAND PAPER CRANES.
Ages 11 and up. 151

Cohen, Peter Zachary. BEE.
Ages 10-13. 157

Distad, Audree. THE DREAM RUNNER.
Ages 10-13. 201

Dixon, Paige, pseud. MAY I CROSS YOUR GOLDEN RIVER?
Ages 12 and up. 202

Fife, Dale. NORTH OF DANGER.
Ages 10-12. 227

Greenberg, Barbara. THE BRAVEST BABYSITTER.
Ages 4-8. 265

Greenwald, Sheila. THE SECRET IN MIRANDA'S CLOSET.
Ages 8-11. 274

Courage, Meaning of (cont.)

Courtesy

See: *Etiquette*

Cousin

See: *Relatives*

Crazy

See: *Mental illness*

Creativity

See also: *Curiosity; Fantasy formation; Imagination; Problem solving; Resourcefulness*
Byars, Betsy Cromer. THE CARTOONIST.
Ages 8-12. 107
Fife, Dale. WHO'LL VOTE FOR LINCOLN?
Ages 8-10. 229

Greenwald, Sheila. THE SECRET IN MIRANDA'S CLOSET.
Ages 8-11. 274
Holl, Adelaide Hinkle. SMALL BEAR BUILDS A PLAYHOUSE.
Ages 5-7. 326
Wosmek, Frances. A BOWL OF SUN.
Ages 7-9. 710
Yep, Laurence Michael. DRAGONWINGS.
Ages 12 and up. 712

Crime/Criminals

See also: *Accidents: hit and run; Death: murder; Delinquency, juvenile; Detention home, living in; Guilt, feelings of; Parole; Prostitution; Rape; Stealing; Vandalism*
Alter, Judy. AFTER PA WAS SHOT.
Ages 10-13. 11

Cultural/Ethnic Groups

See: *Specific group (e.g. Afro-American; Puerto Rican-American)*

Curiosity

See also: *Creativity*
Adler, David A. A LITTLE AT A TIME.
Ages 4-6. 2
Freschet, Berniece. LITTLE BLACK BEAR GOES FOR A WALK.
Ages 4-6. 236
Green, Phyllis. MILDRED MURPHY, HOW DOES YOUR GARDEN GROW?
Ages 9-11. 263
Zolotow, Charlotte Shapiro. WHEN THE WIND STOPS.
Ages 5-7. 722

D

Danger

See: *Risk, taking of*

Dating

See: *Boy-girl relationships: dating; Sex*

Daydreaming

See also: *Fantasy formation; Magical thinking; Nightmares; Reality, escaping; Wishes*
Cameron, Eleanor Butler. TO THE GREEN MOUNTAINS.
Ages 11 and up. 111
Madison, Winifred. BECKY'S HORSE.
Ages 10-12. 434
Merriam, Eve. UNHURRY HARRY.
Ages 5-8. 452

Death (cont.)

of Father

Death (cont.)

Angell, Judie. RONNIE AND ROSEY.
Ages 11 and up. 20
Bloch, Marie Halun. DISPLACED PERSON.
Ages 10-13. 57
Bradbury, Bianca. WHERE'S JIM NOW?
Ages 11-13. 67
Colman, Hila Crayder. SOMETIMES I DON'T
LOVE MY MOTHER.
Ages 12 and up. 166
Colman, Hila Crayder. THAT'S THE WAY IT IS,
AMIGO.
Ages 11-13. 168
Grimes, Nikki. GROWIN'.
Ages 9-11. 277
Gripe, Maria Kristina. THE GREEN COAT.
Ages 13 and up. 279
LeShan, Eda J. LEARNING TO SAY GOOD-BY:
WHEN A PARENT DIES.
Ages 12 and up. 401

Lutters, Valerie. THE HAUNTING OF JULIE
UNGER.
Ages 10-13. 425
Madison, Winifred. CALL ME DANICA.
Ages 10-13. 435

of Fiancé/Fiancée
O'Dell, Scott. KATHLEEN, PLEASE COME HOME.
Ages 12 and up. 485

of Friend
Aaron, Chester. SPILL.
Ages 12-14. 1
Distad, Audree. THE DREAM RUNNER.
Ages 10-13. 201
Goldreich, Gloria. SEASON OF DISCOVERY.
Ages 11-13. 256
Hunt, Irene. THE LOTTERY ROSE.
Ages 11 and up. 337
Moe, Barbara. PICKLES AND PRUNES.
Ages 10-13. 461

Death (cont.)

Holland, Isabelle. OF LOVE AND DEATH AND OTHER JOURNEYS.
Ages 11 and up. 329

Hunt, Irene. WILLIAM: A NOVEL.
Ages 12 and up. 338

Kaplan, Bess. THE EMPTY CHAIR.
Ages 10-14. 363

LeShan, Eda J. LEARNING TO SAY GOOD-BY: WHEN A PARENT DIES.
Ages 12 and up. 401

Mann, Peggy. THERE ARE TWO KINDS OF TERRIBLE.
Ages 9-12. 441

Peck, Richard. FATHER FIGURE: A NOVEL.
Ages 11 and up. 501

Murder. *See also: Crime/Criminals; Violence*
Rees, David. RISKS.
Ages 11 and up. 529

Roberts, Willo Davis. THE VIEW FROM THE CHERRY TREE.
Ages 9-12. 546

Ruby, Lois. ARRIVING AT A PLACE YOU'VE NEVER LEFT.
Ages 12 and up. 564

of Pet

Carrick, Carol. THE ACCIDENT.
Ages 4-8. 119

Cate, Dick. NEVER IS A LONG, LONG TIME.
Ages 9-11. 125

Hall, Lynn. FLOWERS OF ANGER.
Ages 10-12. 288

Hegwood, Mamie. MY FRIEND FISH.
Ages 4-8. 304

Thiele, Colin Milton. STORM BOY.
Ages 8-11. 646

Tobias, Tobi. PETEY.
Ages 6-9. 653

Decision Making (cont.)

Honig, Donald. HURRY HOME.
  Ages 7-9. 331
Lee, H. Alton. SEVEN FEET FOUR AND
  GROWING.
  Ages 9-12. 396
Myers, Walter Dean. IT AIN'T ALL FOR NOTHIN'.
  Ages 11-13. 470
Rice, Eve. NEW BLUE SHOES.
  Ages 3-5. 535
Sharmat, Marjorie Weinman. WALTER THE WOLF.
  Ages 4-7. 591
Snyder, Anne. MY NAME IS DAVY — I'M AN
  ALCOHOLIC.
  Ages 12 and up. 616
Townsend, John Rowe. NOAH'S CASTLE.
  Ages 11 and up. 656

Deformities

See also: *Limbs, abnormal or missing*

Viscardi, Henry. THE PHOENIX CHILD: A STORY
  OF LOVE.
  Ages 13 and up. 665

Delinquency, Juvenile

See also: *Crime/Criminals; Detention home, living in;*
  Gangs; Rebellion; Stealing; Vandalism; Violence
Ashley, Bernard. TERRY ON THE FENCE.
  Ages 12 and up. 25
Luger, Harriett Mandelay. THE ELEPHANT TREE.
  Ages 12 and up. 424
Murphy, Barbara Beasley. NO PLACE TO RUN.
  Ages 12 and up. 467
Platt, Kin. HEADMAN.
  Ages 13-19. 517

Dentist, Going to

Barnett, Naomi. I KNOW A DENTIST.
  Ages 6-8. 35

Dentist, Going to (cont.)

Rockwell, Harlow. MY DENTIST.
Ages 4-7. 552
Schalebin-Lewis, Joy. THE DENTIST AND ME.
Ages 4-7. 572
Ziegler, Sandra. AT THE DENTIST: WHAT DID CHRISTOPHER SEE?
Ages 4-7. 715

Dependability

See: *Responsibility: accepting*

Dependence/Independence

See also: *Autonomy*
Alter, Judy. AFTER PA WAS SHOT.
Ages 10-13. 11
Angell, Judie. RONNIE AND ROSEY.
Ages 11 and up. 20

Arrick, Fran. STEFFIE CAN'T COME OUT TO PLAY.
Ages 12 and up. 24
Bloch, Marie Halun. DISPLACED PERSON.
Ages 10-13. 57
Bradbury, Bianca. BOY ON THE RUN.
Ages 11-13. 64
Bruna, Dick. I CAN DRESS MYSELF.
Ages 2-4. 89
Bulla, Clyde Robert. SHOESHINE GIRL.
Ages 8-10. 93
Burch, Robert Joseph. TWO THAT WERE TOUGH.
Ages 9-11. 99
Cleaver, Vera and Bill Cleaver. QUEEN OF HEARTS.
Ages 10-13. 140
Coleman, William Laurence. ORPHAN JIM: A NOVEL.
Ages 13 and up. 158

Dependence/Independence (cont.)

Dependence/Independence (cont.)

Depression

Deprivation, Emotional

Determination (cont.)

Determination (cont.)

Robinet, Harriette. JAY AND THE MARIGOLD.
Ages 6-9. 547

Diabetes

Dolan, Edward Francis and Richard B.
Lyttle. BOBBY CLARKE.
Ages 10-12. 205

Diet/Dieting

See: *Weight control: overweight*

Differences, Human

See also: *Poverty; Prejudice; Self, attitude toward:
feeling different; Values/Valuing; Wealth/Wealthy*
Anders, Rebecca. A LOOK AT MENTAL
RETARDATION.
Ages 3-7. 16

Anders, Rebecca. A LOOK AT PREJUDICE AND
UNDERSTANDING.
Ages 3-7. 17
Brightman, Alan. LIKE ME.
Ages 3-8. 82
Friskey, Margaret Richards. RACKETY, THAT
VERY SPECIAL RABBIT.
Ages 3-5. 237
Herman, Charlotte. THE DIFFERENCE OF ARI
STEIN.
Ages 9-12. 312
Hurwitz, Johanna. THE LAW OF GRAVITY.
Ages 10-13. 341
Leigh, Frances. THE LOST BOY.
Ages 10-13. 399
Scoppettone, Sandra. HAPPY ENDINGS ARE ALL
ALIKE.
Ages 12 and up. 578
Simon, Norma. WHY AM I DIFFERENT?
Ages 4-8. 603

Divorce (cont.)

Pursell, Margaret Sanford. A LOOK AT DIVORCE.
Ages 3-7. 524

of Parents

Alexander, Anne. TO LIVE A LIE.
Ages 9-12. 7
Ames, Mildred. WHAT ARE FRIENDS FOR?
Ages 9-11. 12
Berger, Terry. HOW DOES IT FEEL WHEN YOUR PARENTS GET DIVORCED?
Ages 6-11. 50
Bradbury, Bianca. BOY ON THE RUN.
Ages 11-13. 64
Butler, Beverly Kathleen. A GIRL CALLED WENDY.
Ages 12 and up. 106
Caines, Jeannette Franklin. DADDY.
Ages 4-8. 110

Christopher, Matthew F. THE FOX STEALS HOME.
Ages 8-10. 133
Corcoran, Barbara. HEY, THAT'S MY SOUL YOU'RE STOMPING ON.
Ages 11-14. 180
Dexter, Pat Egan. ARROW IN THE WIND.
Ages 10-13. 200
Grollman, Earl A. TALKING ABOUT DIVORCE: A DIALOGUE BETWEEN PARENT AND CHILD.
Ages 7-10. 283
Hazen, Barbara Shook. TWO HOMES TO LIVE IN: A CHILD'S-EYE VIEW OF DIVORCE.
Ages 5-8. 302
Hunter, Evan. ME AND MR. STENNER.
Ages 10-13. 339
LeShan, Eda J. WHAT'S GOING TO HAPPEN TO ME? WHEN PARENTS SEPARATE OR DIVORCE.
Ages 8 and up. 402

Divorce (cont.)

Lisker, Sonia Olson and Leigh Dean. TWO SPECIAL CARDS.
Ages 6-9. 410
Madison, Winifred. THE GENESSEE QUEEN.
Ages 11 and up. 436
Meyer, Carolyn. C. C. POINDEXTER.
Ages 12 and up. 453
Newfield, Marcia. A BOOK FOR JODAN.
Ages 8-12. 478
Perry, Patricia and Marietta Lynch. MOMMY AND DADDY ARE DIVORCED.
Ages 3-6. 504
Pevsner, Stella. A SMART KID LIKE YOU.
Ages 10-13. 510
Platt, Kin. CHLORIS AND THE FREAKS.
Ages 11 and up. 515
Rogers, Helen Spelman. MORRIS AND HIS BRAVE LION.
Ages 4-7. 557

Sheffield, Janet N. NOT JUST SUGAR AND SPICE.
Ages 9-12. 594
Thomas, Ianthe. ELIZA'S DADDY.
Ages 4-7. 647
Wolitzer, Hilma. OUT OF LOVE.
Ages 10-13. 704
Wood, Phyllis Anderson. WIN ME AND YOU LOSE.
Ages 10-13. 709

Doctor, Going to

See also: *Fractures; Hospital, going to; Illnesses; Surgery; Sutures*
Wolde, Gunilla. BETSY AND THE DOCTOR.
Ages 3-7. 697

Doubt

See: *Inferiority, feelings of; Trust/Distrust*

Down's Syndrome

Baldwin, Anne Norris. A LITTLE TIME.
Ages 9-11. 30
Garrigue, Sheila. BETWEEN FRIENDS.
Ages 9-12. 243
Ominsky, Elaine. JON O.: A SPECIAL BOY.
Ages 4-7. 489
Rodowsky, Colby F. WHAT ABOUT ME?
Ages 11-13. 556

Dreams

See: *Daydreaming; Nightmares; Wishes*

Drinking

See: *Alcoholism*

Dropout, School

McKillip, Patricia A. THE NIGHT GIFT.
Ages 11 and up. 430

Drugs

See also: *Alcoholism; Marijuana; Reality, escaping; Smoking*

Abuse of

O'Dell, Scott. KATHLEEN, PLEASE COME HOME.
Ages 12 and up. 485

Dependence on

Taylor, Paula. JOHNNY CASH.
Ages 7-10. 638

Dyslexia

See: *Learning disabilities*

E

Eating Problems

See: *Weight control*

Ecology

See: *Nature*

Economic Status

See: *Poverty; Wealth/Wealthy*

Education

See also: *Careers: planning; School*

Special. *See also: Blindness; Handicaps; Learning disabilties; Mental retardation; Talents*

Gill, Derek Lewis Theodore. TOM SULLIVAN'S ADVENTURES IN DARKNESS.

Ages 10-14. 247

Gold, Phyllis. PLEASE DON'T SAY HELLO.

Ages 7 and up. 253

Heide, Florence Parry. SECRET DREAMER, SECRET DREAMS.

Ages 13 and up. 306

Melton, David. A BOY CALLED HOPELESS.

Ages 10 and up. 451

Resnick, Rose. SUN AND SHADOW: THE AUTOBIOGRAPHY OF A WOMAN WHO CLEARED A PATHWAY TO THE SEEING WORLD FOR THE BLIND.

Ages 12 and up. 532

Education (cont.)

Swarthout, Glendon Fred and Kathryn Swarthout. WHALES TO SEE THE. Ages 10-12. 632

Value of

Chukovsky, Kornei Ivanovich. THE SILVER CREST: MY RUSSIAN BOYHOOD. Ages 12 and up. 135

Cohen, Miriam. WHEN WILL I READ? Ages 4-6. 156

Ho, Minfong. SING TO THE DAWN. Ages 10-13. 320

Morrison, Bill. LOUIS JAMES HATES SCHOOL. Ages 5-7. 466

Ego Ideal

See: *Identification with others*

Egocentrism

See also: *Empathy; Sharing/Not sharing*

Williams, Barbara Wright. IF HE'S MY BROTHER. Ages 3-7. 683

Embarrassment

See also: *Shame*

Christopher, Matthew F. GLUE FINGERS. Ages 7-9. 134

Conaway, Judith. WAS MY FACE RED! Ages 4-7. 172

Leigh, Frances. THE LOST BOY. Ages 10-13. 399

Mack, Nancy. WHY ME? Ages 5-8. 429

Miles, Betty. JUST THE BEGINNING. Ages 10-12. 456

Miles, Betty. LOOKING ON. Ages 11-14. 457

Emotions (cont.)

Identifying

Empathy

Empathy (cont.)

Tolan, Stephanie S. GRANDPA — AND ME.
Ages 10-13. 655

Encouragement

See also: *Courage, meaning of*
Rice, Eve. NEW BLUE SHOES.
Ages 3-5. 535

Equal Rights

See: *Prejudice; Women's rights*

Equality

See: *Differences, human; Prejudice*

Escaping Reality

See: *Reality, escaping*

Eskimo

Griese, Arnold Alfred. THE WIND IS NOT A
RIVER.
Ages 9-12. 276
Houston, James A. FROZEN FIRE: A TALE OF
COURAGE.
Ages 10-13. 334

Ethnic Differences

See: *Prejudice: ethnic/racial*

Etiquette

Gordon, Shirley. CRYSTAL IS MY FRIEND.
Ages 6-9. 258
Hoban, Russell Conwell. DINNER AT ALBERTA'S.
Ages 5-7. 323

Exceptional Children

See: *Education: special; Learning disabilities; Mental retardation; Talents*

Exile

See: *Ostracism*

Expectancy, Power of

See: *Expectations*

Expectations

See also: *Peer relationships; peer pressures*
Cohen, Barbara Nash. BITTER HERBS AND HONEY.
Ages 11-13. 153
Cone, Molly Lamken. CALL ME MOOSE.
Ages 9-11. 174

Corcoran, Barbara. AXE-TIME, SWORD-TIME.
Ages 11 and up. 178
Etter, Les. GET THOSE REBOUNDS!
Ages 10-13. 220
First, Julia. MOVE OVER, BEETHOVEN.
Ages 10-13. 231
Griese, Arnold Alfred. THE WAY OF OUR PEOPLE.
Ages 9-12. 275
Hintz, Sandy and Martin Hintz. WE CAN'T AFFORD IT.
Ages 4-7. 317
Kerr, M. E., pseud. I'LL LOVE YOU WHEN YOU'RE MORE LIKE ME.
Ages 12 and up. 378
Neigoff, Mike. RUNNER-UP.
Ages 9-11. 474
Rabe, Berniece Louise. NAOMI.
Ages 12 and up. 527

Expectations (cont.)

Rock, Gail. A DREAM FOR ADDIE.
  Ages 9-12. 551
Schulman, Janet. JENNY AND THE TENNIS NUT.
  Ages 7-9. 577
Smith, Nancy Covert. JOSIE'S HANDFUL OF
  QUIETNESS.
  Ages 9-11. 614

Extended Family

See: *Family: extended*

F

Fairness

See: *Honesty/Dishonesty; Sharing/Not sharing*

Family

See also: *Grandparent; Great-grandparent;
Parent/Parents; Relatives; Sibling;
Stepbrother/Stepsister; Stepparent*

Extended
Mazer, Norma Fox. DEAR BILL, REMEMBER ME?
  AND OTHER STORIES.
  Ages 12 and up. 449
Simon, Norma. ALL KINDS OF FAMILIES.
  Ages 5-8. 602
Terris, Susan Dubinsky. THE CHICKEN POX
  PAPERS.
  Ages 10-12. 640

Relationships. *See also: Sibling: relationships*
Cate, Dick. FLYING FREE.
  Ages 8-10. 124

Family (cont.)

Unity. *See also: Communication: parent-child*

Family (cont.)

Family (cont.)

Hunt, Irene. WILLIAM: A NOVEL.
  Ages 12 and up. 338
Hutchins, Patricia. THE BEST TRAIN SET EVER.
  Ages 5-8. 342
Isadora, Rachel. THE POTTERS' KITCHEN.
  Ages 4-8. 347
Kerr, Judith. THE OTHER WAY ROUND.
  Ages 12 and up. 376
Kingman, Lee. HEAD OVER WHEELS.
  Ages 12 and up. 383
Little, Jean. LISTEN FOR THE SINGING.
  Ages 10-14. 413
Lowry, Lois. A SUMMER TO DIE.
  Ages 10-14. 423
Madison, Winifred. BECKY'S HORSE.
  Ages 10-12. 434
Melton, David. A BOY CALLED HOPELESS.
  Ages 10 and up. 451

Neville, Emily Cheney. GARDEN OF BROKEN GLASS.
  Ages 11-14. 477
Nolan, Madeena Spray. MY DADDY DON'T GO TO WORK.
  Ages 4-7. 480
Simon, Norma. ALL KINDS OF FAMILIES.
  Ages 5-8. 602
Taylor, Mildred D. ROLL OF THUNDER, HEAR MY CRY.
  Ages 10 and up. 636
Tobias, Tobi. JANE, WISHING.
  Ages 6-9. 651
Uchida, Yoshiko. JOURNEY HOME.
  Ages 12-14. 657
Wallace, Barbara Brooks. JULIA AND THE THIRD BAD THING.
  Ages 8-10. 673

Fantasy Formation

See also: *Creativity; Daydreaming; Imaginary friend; Imagination; Magical thinking; Play; Wishes*

Colman, Hila Crayder. THE SECRET LIFE OF HAROLD THE BIRD WATCHER.
Ages 8-10. 165

Lutters, Valerie. THE HAUNTING OF JULIE UNGER.
Ages 10-13. 425

Madison, Winifred. THE GENESSEE QUEEN.
Ages 11 and up. 436

Pinkwater, Manus. WINGMAN.
Ages 9-12. 513

Schick, Eleanor Grossman. NEIGHBORHOOD KNIGHT.
Ages 5-7. 573

Screen, Robert Martin. WITH MY FACE TO THE RISING SUN.
Ages 11 and up. 580

Valencak, Hannelore. A TANGLED WEB.
Ages 9-11. 659

Fat

See: *Weight control: overweight*

Father

See: *Communication: parent-child; Parent/Parents: single*

Fatso

See: *Weight control: overweight*

Fear

See also: *Anxiety; Courage, meaning of; Nightmares; Security/Insecurity*

Fear (cont.)

Berkey, Barry R. and Velma A. Berkey. ROBBERS, BONES & MEAN DOGS.
Ages 5-9. 51

Bloch, Marie Halun. DISPLACED PERSON.
Ages 10-13. 57

Clifton, Lucille. AMIFIKA.
Ages 4-7. 143

Conaway, Judith. SOMETIMES IT SCARES ME.
Ages 3-7. 171

Dragonwagon, Crescent. WILL IT BE OKAY?
Ages 3-7. 207

Griese, Arnold Alfred. THE WAY OF OUR PEOPLE.
Ages 9-12. 275

Heide, Florence Parry. GROWING ANYWAY UP.
Ages 12-14. 305

Leigh, Bill. THE FAR SIDE OF FEAR.
Ages 10-14. 398

Miles, Miska, pseud. AARON'S DOOR.
Ages 5-9. 458

Riley, Susan. WHAT DOES IT MEAN? AFRAID.
Ages 3-6. 538

Shanks, Ann Zane. OLD IS WHAT YOU GET: DIALOGUES ON AGING BY THE OLD AND THE YOUNG.
Ages 10 and up. 582

Shaw, Richard. SHAPE UP, BURKE.
Ages 10-14. 593

Showers, Paul. A BOOK OF SCARY THINGS.
Ages 3-6. 596

of Animals

Little, Lessie Jones and Eloise Greenfield. I CAN DO IT BY MYSELF.
Ages 5-7. 415

Low, Joseph. BOO TO A GOOSE.
Ages 5-8. 420

Tester, Sylvia Root. THAT BIG BRUNO.
Ages 3-7. 644

of Being lost. *See: Lost, being*

Fear (cont.)

of Darkness

Cleary, Beverly Bunn. RAMONA THE BRAVE.
Ages 7-10. 138

Conford, Ellen. EUGENE THE BRAVE.
Ages 5-7. 175

Crowe, Robert L. CLYDE MONSTER.
Ages 3-6. 186

Johnston, Tony. NIGHT NOISES: AND OTHER
MOLE AND TROLL STORIES.
Ages 4-7. 358

Low, Joseph. BENNY RABBIT AND THE OWL.
Ages 4-7. 419

Marzollo, Jean. CLOSE YOUR EYES.
Ages 2-5. 444

Tobias, Tobi. CHASING THE GOBLINS AWAY.
Ages 4-7. 650

Winthrop, Elizabeth. POTBELLIED POSSUMS.
Ages 4-6. 690

of Death. *See also: Illnesses: terminal; Surgery*

Clyne, Patricia Edwards. TUNNELS OF TERROR.
Ages 10-12. 149

Rabe, Berniece Louise. NAOMI.
Ages 12 and up. 527

of Physical harm

Arrick, Fran. STEFFIE CAN'T COME OUT TO
PLAY.
Ages 12 and up. 24

Bauer, Marion Dane. FOSTER CHILD.
Ages 11-13. 42

Cohen, Peter Zachary. BEE.
Ages 10-13. 157

Hunt, Irene. THE LOTTERY ROSE.
Ages 11 and up. 337

Kerr, Judith. THE OTHER WAY ROUND.
Ages 12 and up. 376

Lipsyte, Robert. ONE FAT SUMMER.
Ages 12-14. 409

Friendship (cont.)

Friendship (cont.)

Wilkinson, Brenda Scott. LUDELL.
  Ages 10-14. 680
Wittman, Sally. PELLY AND PEAK.
  Ages 4-8. 692
Young, Miriam Burt. TRUTH AND
  CONSEQUENCES.
  Ages 9-12. 714
Zolotow, Charlotte Shapiro. IT'S NOT FAIR.
  Ages 5-7. 718

Imaginary friend. *See: Imaginary friend*

Keeping friends

Hopkins, Lee Bennett. I LOVED ROSE ANN.
  Ages 6-9. 333
Sargent, Sarah. EDWARD TROY AND THE WITCH
  CAT.
  Ages 9-11. 569

Lack of

Albert, Louise. BUT I'M READY TO GO.
  Ages 11-14. 5
Valencak, Hannelore. A TANGLED WEB.
  Ages 9-11. 659
Zolotow, Charlotte Shapiro. THE UNFRIENDLY
  BOOK.
  Ages 4-8. 721

Making friends

Albert, Louise. BUT I'M READY TO GO.
  Ages 11-14. 5
Alexander, Anne. TO LIVE A LIE.
  Ages 9-12. 7
Brandenberg, Franz. NICE NEW NEIGHBORS.
  Ages 6-8. 74
Brown, Fern G. HARD LUCK HORSE.
  Ages 9-11. 85
Carrick, Malcolm. TRAMP.
  Ages 7-9. 122

Friendship (cont.)

Friendship (cont.)

Friendship (cont.)

Friendship (cont.)

Gender Role Identity (cont.)

Male

Colman, Hila Crayder. THAT'S THE WAY IT IS, AMIGO.

Ages 11-13. 168

Hooks, William Harris. DOUG MEETS THE NUTCRACKER.

Ages 8-11. 332

Isadora, Rachel. MAX.

Ages 4-7. 346

Peck, Richard. FATHER FIGURE: A NOVEL.

Ages 11 and up. 501

Simon, Marcia L. A SPECIAL GIFT.

Ages 10-13. 601

Vestly, Anne-Catharina. AURORA AND SOCRATES.

Ages 8-10. 660

Generation Gap

See: *Communication: lack of; Communication: parent-child*

Generosity

See: *Sharing/Not sharing*

German-American

Irion, Ruth Hershey. THE CHRISTMAS COOKIE TREE.

Ages 8-10. 345

Getting Along With Others

See: *Communication: parent-child; Cooperation: in play; Cooperation: in work*

Ghetto

See also: *Afro-American; Jewish; Poverty*

Glasses, Wearing of (cont.)

Delaney, Ned. TWO STRIKES, FOUR EYES.
Ages 5-8. 196
Neigoff, Mike. SOCCER HERO.
Ages 9-11. 475

Goals

Cohen, Miriam. WHEN WILL I READ?
Ages 4-6. 156
Distad, Audree. THE DREAM RUNNER.
Ages 10-13. 201
Love, Sandra. MELISSA'S MEDLEY.
Ages 10-13. 418
Sargent, Sarah. EDWARD TROY AND THE WITCH
CAT.
Ages 9-11. 569

God

See: *Religion*

Going Away

See: *Abandonment; Camp experiences; Hospital, going
to; Schools, private; Separation anxiety; Separation
from loved ones*

Going Steady

See: *Boy-girl relationships: dating*

Grandparent

See also: *Age; Family; Great-grandparent*
Shanks, Ann Zane. OLD IS WHAT YOU GET:
DIALOGUES ON AGING BY THE OLD AND
THE YOUNG.
Ages 10 and up. 582

Death of. *See: Death: of grandparent*

Illness of. *See: Illnesses: of grandparent*

Grandparent (cont.)

Living in child's home

Beckman, Gunnel. THAT EARLY SPRING.
Ages 12 and up. 47

Coatsworth, Elizabeth Jane. MARRA'S WORLD.
Ages 8-11. 150

Herman, Charlotte. OUR SNOWMAN HAD OLIVE EYES.
Ages 9-11. 313

Johnston, Norma. IF YOU LOVE ME, LET ME GO.
Ages 12 and up. 354

LeRoy, Gen. EMMA'S DILEMMA.
Ages 9-12. 400

Levy, Elizabeth. LIZZIE LIES A LOT.
Ages 9-11. 405

Palay, Steven. I LOVE MY GRANDMA.
Ages 4-7. 491

Pollowitz, Melinda. CINNAMON CANE.
Ages 10-12. 519

Talbot, Toby. DEAR GRETA GARBO.
Ages 11-13. 635

Tolan, Stephanie S. GRANDPA — AND ME.
Ages 10-13. 655

Living in home of

Cleaver, Vera and Bill Cleaver. QUEEN OF HEARTS.
Ages 10-13. 140

Colman, Hila Crayder. THE AMAZING MISS LAURA.
Ages 11-14. 161

Corcoran, Barbara. THE FARAWAY ISLAND.
Ages 10-13. 179

Corcoran, Barbara. HEY, THAT'S MY SOUL YOU'RE STOMPING ON.
Ages 11-14. 180

Härtling, Peter. OMA.
Ages 8-11. 296

Grandparent (cont.)

Johnston, Norma. THE SWALLOW'S SONG.
Ages 12 and up. 357
Lutters, Valerie. THE HAUNTING OF JULIE
UNGER.
Ages 10-13. 425
Maher, Ramona. ALICE YAZZIE'S YEAR.
Ages 9-12. 439
Majerus, Janet. GRANDPA AND FRANK.
Ages 12 and up. 440
Perl, Lila. THE TELLTALE SUMMER OF TINA C.
Ages 10-13. 503
Screen, Robert Martin. WITH MY FACE TO THE
RISING SUN.
Ages 11 and up. 580
Wilkinson, Brenda Scott. LUDELL.
Ages 10-14. 680
Wilkinson, Brenda Scott. LUDELL AND WILLIE.
Ages 12 and up. 681
Yep, Laurence Michael. CHILD OF THE OWL.
Ages 11 and up. 711

Love for

Adler, David A. A LITTLE AT A TIME.
Ages 4-6. 2
Bartoli, Jennifer. NONNA.
Ages 4-9. 38
Beckman, Gunnel. THAT EARLY SPRING.
Ages 12 and up. 47
Blue, Rose. THE THIRTEENTH YEAR: A BAR
MITZVAH STORY.
Ages 10-12. 60
Brandenberg, Franz. A SECRET FOR
GRANDMOTHER'S BIRTHDAY.
Ages 3-7. 75
Bunting, Anne Evelyn. MAGIC AND THE NIGHT
RIVER.
Ages 5-9. 96
Campbell, R. Wright. WHERE PIGEONS GO TO
DIE.
Ages 12 and up. 112

Grandparent (cont.)

Skorpen, Liesel Moak. MANDY'S
GRANDMOTHER.
Ages 4-7. 608
Talbot, Toby. DEAR GRETA GARBO.
Ages 11-13. 635
Vogel, Ilse-Margret. DODO EVERY DAY.
Ages 7-9. 666
Williams, Barbara Wright. KEVIN'S GRANDMA.
Ages 4-7. 685
Wood, Joyce. GRANDMOTHER LUCY IN HER
GARDEN.
Ages 4-8. 707
Yep, Laurence Michael. CHILD OF THE OWL.
Ages 11 and up. 711

Respect for

Babbitt, Natalie. THE EYES OF THE AMARYLLIS.
Ages 11-14. 26
Kerr, M. E., pseud. GENTLEHANDS.
Ages 11-14. 377

Great-Grandparent

See also: *Age; Family; Grandparent*
Knotts, Howard. GREAT-GRANDFATHER, THE
BABY AND ME.
Ages 5-8. 385
Pevsner, Stella. KEEP STOMPIN' TILL THE
MUSIC STOPS.
Ages 9-12. 509

Greed

Duvoisin, Roger Antoine. PETUNIA'S TREASURE.
Ages 5-8. 212
Ginsburg, Mirra. TWO GREEDY BEARS.
Ages 3-8. 248
Jones, Penelope. I DIDN'T WANT TO BE NICE.
Ages 4-7. 359

Grief

See: *Death; Depression; Loss: feelings of; Mourning, stages of; Separation from loved ones*

Growing Up

See: *Maturation*

Growth

See: *Height: short; Height: tall; Maturation*

Guide Dog

See: *Blindness; Pets: guide dog*

Guilt, Feelings of

See also: *Accidents; Blame; Crime/Criminals; Death; Depression; Justice/Injustice; Mourning, stages of; Self-esteem; Shame*

Bach, Alice. A FATHER EVERY FEW YEARS.
Ages 11-13. 27
Carlson, Dale Bick. TRIPLE BOY.
Ages 13 and up. 115
Christman, Elizabeth. A NICE ITALIAN GIRL.
Ages 12 and up. 132
Crawford, Charles P. LETTER PERFECT.
Ages 12 and up. 184
Farley, Carol J. THE GARDEN IS DOING FINE.
Ages 11 and up. 223
Feagles, Anita Macrae. THE YEAR THE DREAMS CAME BACK.
Ages 11-14. 225
Guest, Judith. ORDINARY PEOPLE.
Ages 13 and up. 285
Hassler, Jon. FOUR MILES TO PINECONE.
Ages 10-14. 297
Heide, Florence Parry. GROWING ANYWAY UP.
Ages 12-14. 305

H

Hair Style, Importance of
　Girion, Barbara. THE BOY WITH THE SPECIAL
　　FACE.
　　Ages 5-8. 249

Half Brother/Half Sister

　See: *Sibling: half brother/half sister*

Handicaps

　See also: *Education: special*
　Brown, Fern G. YOU'RE SOMEBODY SPECIAL
　　ON A HORSE.
　　Ages 10-13. 87
　Fanshawe, Elizabeth. RACHEL.
　　Ages 4-6. 222
　Jones, Ron. THE ACORN PEOPLE.
　　Ages 10 and up. 360

　Mack, Nancy. TRACY.
　　Ages 4-8. 428
　Pursell, Margaret Sanford. A LOOK AT PHYSICAL
　　HANDICAPS.
　　Ages 3-7. 525

Amputee. *See: Amputee*

Asthma. *See: Asthma*

Birth defects. *See: Birth defects*

Blindness. *See: Blindness*

Braces on body/limbs. *See: Braces on body/limbs*

Brain injury. *See: Brain injury; Cerebral palsy;
Learning disabilities; Mental retardation*

Cardiac conditions. *See: Cardiac conditions; Surgery:
heart*

Handicaps (cont.)

Cleft lip/palate. *See: Cleft lip/palate*

Deafness. *See: Deafness*

Deformities. *See: Deformities*

Down's Syndrome. *See: Down's Syndrome*

Limbs, abnormal or missing. *See: Limbs, abnormal or missing*

Multiple
Viscardi, Henry. THE PHOENIX CHILD: A STORY OF LOVE.
Ages 13 and up. 665

Muteness. *See: Muteness*

Paralysis. *See: Paralysis*

Prejudice. *See: Prejudice: toward handicapped persons*

Prosthesis. *See: Prosthesis*

Quadriplegia. *See: Quadriplegia*

Speech problems. *See: Speech problems*

Wheelchair. *See: Wheelchair, dependence on*

Harassment

See also: *Bully*
Hickman, Janet. THE STONES.
Ages 9-12. 314
Holland, Isabelle. DINAH AND THE GREEN FAT KINGDOM.
Ages 10-13. 328

Hard of Hearing

See: *Deafness*

Hatred

See also: *Aggression; Anger; Hostility; Prejudice*
Hunt, Irene. THE LOTTERY ROSE.
Ages 11 and up. 337

Honesty/Dishonesty (cont.)

Levy, Elizabeth. LIZZIE LIES A LOT.
  Ages 9-11. 405
Lexau, Joan M. I'LL TELL ON YOU.
  Ages 5-8. 406
McLenighan, Valjean. I KNOW YOU CHEATED.
  Ages 6-8. 431
Myers, Walter Dean. IT AIN'T ALL FOR NOTHIN'.
  Ages 11-13. 470
Nöstlinger, Christine. GIRL MISSING: A NOVEL.
  Ages 11 and up. 482
Rodowsky, Colby F. P.S. WRITE SOON.
  Ages 10-12. 555
Sharmat, Marjorie Weinman. A BIG FAT
  ENORMOUS LIE.
  Ages 3-7. 583
Wahl, Jan. WHO WILL BELIEVE TIM KITTEN?
  Ages 5-8. 671
Willard, Nancy. STRANGERS' BREAD.
  Ages 3-8. 682

Young, Miriam Burt. TRUTH AND
  CONSEQUENCES.
  Ages 9-12. 714

Hospital, Going to

See also: *Accidents; Amputee; Cancer; Doctor, going
to; Fractures; Illnesses; Leukemia; Mental hospital,
living in; Separation anxiety; Separation from loved
ones; Surgery*
Bruna, Dick. MIFFY IN THE HOSPITAL.
  Ages 2-5. 90
Singer, Marilyn. IT CAN'T HURT FOREVER.
  Ages 9-12. 604
Sobol, Harriet Langsam. JEFF'S HOSPITAL BOOK.
  Ages 2-7. 617
Wolde, Gunilla. BETSY AND THE DOCTOR.
  Ages 3-7. 697

Hospital, Going to (cont.)

Ziegler, Sandra. AT THE HOSPITAL: A SURPRISE FOR KRISSY.
Ages 3-6. 716

Hostility

See also: *Aggression; Anger; Hatred; Prejudice; Trust/Distrust*
Gerson, Corinne. PASSING THROUGH.
Ages 12 and up. 245
Paterson, Katherine Womeldorf. THE GREAT GILLY HOPKINS.
Ages 10-13. 494
Robison, Nancy. ON THE BALANCE BEAM.
Ages 8-10. 549
Stevenson, James. THE WORST PERSON IN THE WORLD.
Ages 4-8. 625

Strete, Craig Kee. PAINT YOUR FACE ON A DROWNING IN THE RIVER.
Ages 12 and up. 629

Human differences

See: *Differences, human*

Hyperactivity

Green, Phyllis. WALKIE-TALKIE.
Ages 10-13. 264

I

Ideals

See: *Identification with others; Values/Valuing*

Identification with Others

See also: *Imitation; Leader/Leadership;
Values/Valuing*

Adults
Gripe, Maria Kristina. THE GREEN COAT.
Ages 13 and up. 279
Miles, Betty. LOOKING ON.
Ages 11-14. 457

Peers. *See also: Friendship*
Degens, T. THE GAME ON THATCHER ISLAND.
Ages 11-14. 193

Story characters
Cone, Molly Lamken. CALL ME MOOSE.
Ages 9-11. 174

Identity, Search for

See also: *Adoption*

Ames, Mildred. WITHOUT HATS, WHO CAN
TELL THE GOOD GUYS?
Ages 9-12. 13
Angier, Bradford and Barbara Corcoran. ASK FOR
LOVE AND THEY GIVE YOU RICE PUDDING.
Ages 12-14. 21
Arkin, Alan. THE LEMMING CONDITION.
Ages 10 and up. 23
Bach, Alice. THE MEAT IN THE SANDWICH.
Ages 10-13. 28
Bailey, Pearl. DUEY'S TALE.
Ages 12 and up. 29
Bernays, Anne. GROWING UP RICH.
Ages 13 and up. 52
Bradbury, Bianca. BOY ON THE RUN.
Ages 11-13. 64
Branscum, Robbie. THE SAVING OF P.S.
Ages 9-12. 78
Bridgers, Sue Ellen. HOME BEFORE DARK.
Ages 12 and up. 81

Identity, Search for (cont.)

Brown, Fern G. JOCKEY — OR ELSE!
  Ages 9-12. 86
Budbill, David. BONES ON BLACK SPRUCE
  MOUNTAIN.
  Ages 10-13. 91
Bunting, Anne Evelyn. ONE MORE FLIGHT.
  Ages 10-13. 97
Butler, Beverly Kathleen. A GIRL CALLED
  WENDY.
  Ages 12 and up. 106
Charlip, Remy and Lilian Moore. HOORAY FOR
  ME!
  Ages 3-6. 127
Cohen, Barbara Nash. BITTER HERBS AND
  HONEY.
  Ages 11-13. 153
Colman, Hila Crayder. TELL ME NO LIES.
  Ages 10-12. 167

Cunningham, Julia Woolfolk. COME TO THE
  EDGE.
  Ages 9-13. 187
DeLage, Ida. AM I A BUNNY?
  Ages 3-6. 194
Distad, Audree. THE DREAM RUNNER.
  Ages 10-13. 201
Dunnahoo, Terry. WHO CARES ABOUT ESPIE
  SANCHEZ?
  Ages 10-12. 210
Etter, Les. GET THOSE REBOUNDS!
  Ages 10-13. 220
Gonzalez, Gloria. GAUCHO.
  Ages 10-13. 257
Greenwald, Sheila. THE SECRET IN MIRANDA'S
  CLOSET.
  Ages 8-11. 274
Gripe, Maria Kristina. THE GREEN COAT.
  Ages 13 and up. 279

Identity, Search for (cont.)

Windsor, Patricia. DIVING FOR ROSES.
Ages 13 and up. 687

Illegitimate Child

See: *Unwed mother: child of*

Illnesses

See also: *Communicable diseases; Doctor, going to;
Hospital, going to; Mental illness; Surgery*
Hunter, Kristin Eggleston. THE SURVIVORS.
Ages 12 and up. 340

Amyotrophic Lateral Sclerosis. *See: Amyotrophic
Lateral Sclerosis*

Asthma. *See: Asthma*

Being ill
Brandenberg, Franz. I WISH I WAS SICK, TOO!
Ages 3-7. 73

Hirsch, Linda. THE SICK STORY.
Ages 6-9. 319
Numeroff, Laura Joffe. PHOEBE DEXTER HAS
HARRIET PETERSON'S SNIFFLES.
Ages 4-7. 484

Cancer. *See: Cancer*

Cardiac conditions. *See: Cardiac conditions*

Diabetes. *See: Diabetes*

of Grandparent
Campbell, R. Wright. WHERE PIGEONS GO TO
DIE.
Ages 12 and up. 112
Cate, Dick. NEVER IS A LONG, LONG TIME.
Ages 9-11. 125
Pollowitz, Melinda. CINNAMON CANE.
Ages 10-12. 519

Hyperactivity. *See: Hyperactivity*

Illnesses (cont.)

Leukemia. *See: Leukemia*

of Parent
Bates, Betty. THE UPS AND DOWNS OF JORIE
  JENKINS.
  Ages 9-12. 41
Delton, Judy. IT HAPPENED ON THURSDAY.
  Ages 5-8. 197
Farley, Carol J. THE GARDEN IS DOING FINE.
  Ages 11 and up. 223
Holland, Isabelle. OF LOVE AND DEATH AND
  OTHER JOURNEYS.
  Ages 11 and up. 329
Honig, Donald. HURRY HOME.
  Ages 7-9. 331
Johnston, Norma. THE SANCTUARY TREE.
  Ages 12 and up. 356

of Sibling
Butler, Beverly Kathleen. A GIRL CALLED
  WENDY.
  Ages 12 and up. 106
Graber, Richard. A LITTLE BREATHING ROOM.
  Ages 10-14. 260
Wolde, Gunilla. BETSY AND THE CHICKEN POX.
  Ages 3-7. 696

Terminal. *See also: Fear: of death*
Blue, Rose. THE THIRTEENTH YEAR: A BAR
  MITZVAH STORY.
  Ages 10-12. 60
Brady, Mari. PLEASE REMEMBER ME: A YOUNG
  WOMAN'S STORY OF HER FRIENDSHIP WITH
  AN UNFORGETTABLE FIFTEEN-YEAR-OLD
  BOY.
  Ages 12 and up. 68

Illnesses (cont.)

Coerr, Eleanor. SADAKO AND THE THOUSAND
PAPER CRANES.
Ages 11 and up. 151
Farley, Carol J. THE GARDEN IS DOING FINE.
Ages 11 and up. 223
Lowry, Lois. A SUMMER TO DIE.
Ages 10-14. 423
Mann, Peggy. THERE ARE TWO KINDS OF
TERRIBLE.
Ages 9-12. 441
Mazer, Norma Fox. DEAR BILL, REMEMBER ME?
AND OTHER STORIES.
Ages 12 and up. 449
Moe, Barbara. PICKLES AND PRUNES.
Ages 10-13. 461
Ruby, Lois. ARRIVING AT A PLACE YOU'VE
NEVER LEFT.
Ages 12 and up. 564

Imaginary Friend

See also: *Fantasy formation; Imagination; Magical
thinking; Play*
Choate, Judith Newkirk. AWFUL ALEXANDER.
Ages 4-7. 130
Dauer, Rosamond. MY FRIEND, JASPER JONES.
Ages 3-6. 192
Greenfield, Eloise. ME AND NEESIE.
Ages 4-7. 272
Hazen, Barbara Shook. GORILLA WANTS TO BE
THE BABY.
Ages 3-5. 301
King, Cynthia. THE YEAR OF MR. NOBODY.
Ages 6-8. 381
Sachs, Marilyn. A DECEMBER TALE.
Ages 9-12. 565
Young, Michael. THE IMAGINARY FRIEND.
Ages 4-7. 713

Imagination

See also: *Creativity; Fantasy formation; Imaginary friend; Magical thinking; Play*

Babbitt, Natalie. THE EYES OF THE AMARYLLIS.
Ages 11-14. 26

Baylor, Byrd. HAWK, I'M YOUR BROTHER.
Ages 5-8. 45

Burningham, John Mackintosh. COME AWAY FROM THE WATER, SHIRLEY.
Ages 4-7. 103

Byars, Betsy Cromer. THE TV KID.
Ages 9-12. 109

Ewing, Kathryn. A PRIVATE MATTER.
Ages 8-10. 221

Galbraith, Kathryn Osebold. SPOTS ARE SPECIAL!
Ages 4-7. 241

Holland, Isabelle. DINAH AND THE GREEN FAT KINGDOM.
Ages 10-13. 328

Keats, Ezra Jack. THE TRIP.
Ages 4-7. 368

Low, Joseph. BENNY RABBIT AND THE OWL.
Ages 4-7. 419

Marzollo, Jean. CLOSE YOUR EYES.
Ages 2-5. 444

Numeroff, Laura Joffe. PHOEBE DEXTER HAS HARRIET PETERSON'S SNIFFLES.
Ages 4-7. 484

Paterson, Katherine Womeldorf. BRIDGE TO TERABITHIA.
Ages 9-12. 493

Pomerantz, Charlotte. THE MANGO TOOTH.
Ages 4-7. 521

Schick, Eleanor Grossman. NEIGHBORHOOD KNIGHT.
Ages 5-7. 573

Shimin, Symeon. I WISH THERE WERE TWO OF ME.
Ages 4-7. 595

Imitation

See also: *Identification with others*
Hinton, Susan Eloise. RUMBLE FISH.
Ages 12 and up. 316

Immigrants

See also: *Prejudice: ethnic/racial; Refugees*
Madison, Winifred. CALL ME DANICA.
Ages 10-13. 435
Yep, Laurence Michael. DRAGONWINGS.
Ages 12 and up. 712

Impatience

See: *Patience/Impatience*

Independence

See: *Dependence/Independence*

Independent Thinking

See: *Autonomy*

Indian, American

See: *Native American*

Individuality

See: *Autonomy*

Individuation

See: *Autonomy; Dependence/Independence; Separation anxiety*

Infant

See: *Sibling: new baby*

Inferiority, Feelings of

See also: *Shyness*
Byars, Betsy Cromer. THE CARTOONIST.
  Ages 8-12. 107
Cohen, Barbara Nash. BENNY.
  Ages 9-11. 152
Conaway, Judith. WILL I EVER BE GOOD
  ENOUGH?
  Ages 6-9. 173
Danziger, Paula. THE PISTACHIO
  PRESCRIPTION: A NOVEL.
  Ages 11-13. 190
Glass, Frankcina. MARVIN & TIGE.
  Ages 12 and up. 250
Grohskopf, Bernice. CHILDREN IN THE WIND.
  Ages 11-13. 280
Katz, Bobbi. VOLLEYBALL JINX.
  Ages 9-11. 364

Keats, Ezra Jack. LOUIE.
  Ages 3-7. 367
Keller, Beverly Lou. THE BEETLE BUSH.
  Ages 5-8. 369
Lipsyte, Robert. ONE FAT SUMMER.
  Ages 12-14. 409
Mazer, Harry. THE WAR ON VILLA STREET: A
  NOVEL.
  Ages 11-13. 448
Mazer, Norma Fox. DEAR BILL, REMEMBER ME?
  AND OTHER STORIES.
  Ages 12 and up. 449
Miles, Betty. JUST THE BEGINNING.
  Ages 10-12. 456
Neigoff, Mike. RUNNER-UP.
  Ages 9-11. 474
Perl, Lila. DUMB, LIKE ME, OLIVIA POTTS.
  Ages 9-12. 502
Perl, Lila. THE TELLTALE SUMMER OF TINA C.
  Ages 10-13. 503

Inferiority, Feelings of (cont.)

Rodowsky, Colby F. P.S. WRITE SOON.
Ages 10-12. 555
Swetnam, Evelyn. YES, MY DARLING
DAUGHTER.
Ages 9-12. 633
Udry, Janice May. HOW I FADED AWAY.
Ages 5-8. 658

Inhibition

See: *Inferiority, feelings of; Shyness*

Initiative, Taking

See: *Autonomy; Leader/Leadership; Work, attitude
toward*

Injuries

See: *Accidents; Doctor, going to; Fractures; Hospital,
going to; Surgery; Sutures*

Insanity

See: *Mental illness*

Insecurity

See: *Security/Insecurity*

Institutions/Institutionalization

See: *Children's home, living in; Detention home, living
in; Mental hospital, living in; Nursing home, living
in; Schools, private*

Integration

See also: *Prejudice; School*
Waldron, Ann Wood. THE INTEGRATION OF
MARY-LARKIN THORNHILL.
Ages 10-13. 672

Integration (cont.)

School busing
Blue, Rose. THE PREACHER'S KID.
Ages 9-12. 58

Internment

See also: *Prejudice: ethnic/racial*
Kerr, Judith. THE OTHER WAY ROUND.
Ages 12 and up. 376
Uchida, Yoshiko. JOURNEY HOME.
Ages 12-14. 657

Interracial marriage

See: *Marriage: interracial*

Intolerance

See: *Patience/Impatience; Prejudice*

Ireland
Lingard, Joan. A PROPER PLACE.
Ages 12 and up. 407

Isolation

See: *Loneliness; Ostracism; Peer relationships: avoiding others*

Israel
Hoban, Lillian Aberman. I MET A TRAVELLER.
Ages 10-12. 322

J

Jail

See: *Detention home, living in*

Jealousy (cont.)

Byars, Betsy Cromer. THE CARTOONIST.
Ages 8-12. 107
Hamilton, Virginia. ARILLA SUN DOWN.
Ages 12 and up. 291
Hazen, Barbara Shook. GORILLA WANTS TO BE
THE BABY.
Ages 3-5. 301
Ho, Minfong. SING TO THE DAWN.
Ages 10-13. 320
Kerr, M. E., pseud. LOVE IS A MISSING PERSON.
Ages 12 and up. 380
Rodowsky, Colby F. WHAT ABOUT ME?
Ages 11-13. 556
Rogers, Pamela. THE STONE ANGEL.
Ages 10-12. 558
Terris, Susan Dubinsky. AMANDA, THE PANDA,
AND THE REDHEAD.
Ages 5-7. 639
Tester, Sylvia Root. FEELING ANGRY.
Ages 3-6. 643

Winthrop, Elizabeth. A LITTLE DEMONSTRATION
OF AFFECTION.
Ages 12-16. 689
Wolde, Gunilla. BETSY AND THE CHICKEN POX.
Ages 3-7. 696

Jewish

See also: *Ghetto*
Bernays, Anne. GROWING UP RICH.
Ages 13 and up. 52
Blue, Rose. THE THIRTEENTH YEAR: A BAR
MITZVAH STORY.
Ages 10-12. 60
Cohen, Barbara Nash. BENNY.
Ages 9-11. 152
Cohen, Barbara Nash. BITTER HERBS AND
HONEY.
Ages 11-13. 153

Job (cont.)

Pfeffer, Susan Beth. KID POWER.
Ages 9-12. 511
Shaw, Richard. THE HARD WAY HOME.
Ages 11-13. 592

Judgment, Effect of Emotions on

Bernays, Anne. GROWING UP RICH.
Ages 13 and up. 52
Bunting, Anne Evelyn. HIGH TIDE FOR
LABRADOR.
Ages 9-11. 95
Christman, Elizabeth. A NICE ITALIAN GIRL.
Ages 12 and up. 132
Degens, T. THE GAME ON THATCHER ISLAND.
Ages 11-14. 193
Hinton, Nigel. COLLISION COURSE.
Ages 11 and up. 315
Leigh, Frances. THE LOST BOY.
Ages 10-13. 399

O'Dell, Scott. KATHLEEN, PLEASE COME HOME.
Ages 12 and up. 485
Platt, Kin. CHLORIS AND THE WEIRDOS.
Ages 11 and up. 516

Justice/Injustice

See also: *Blame; Guilt, feelings of*
Christman, Elizabeth. A NICE ITALIAN GIRL.
Ages 12 and up. 132
Colman, Hila Crayder. THE CASE OF THE
STOLEN BAGELS.
Ages 7-10. 162
Knudson, R. Rozanne. ZANBANGER.
Ages 10-13. 387
Samuels, Gertrude. ADAM'S DAUGHTER.
Ages 13 and up. 568
Taylor, Mildred D. ROLL OF THUNDER, HEAR
MY CRY.
Ages 10 and up. 636

Juvenile Delinquency

See: *Delinquency, juvenile*

Juvenile Detention

See: *Detention home, living in*

K

Killing

See: *Death: murder; Violence; War*

Kissing

See: *Boy-girl relationships; Sex*

L

Language Problems

See: *Communication; Speech problems*

Laziness

See: *Chores; Responsibility: avoiding; School: achievement/underachievement; Work, attitude toward*

Leader/Leadership

See also: *Identification with others; Responsibility: accepting*
Bunting, Anne Evelyn. SKATEBOARD FOUR. Ages 8-10. 98
Clyne, Patricia Edwards. TUNNELS OF TERROR. Ages 10-12. 149

Leader/Leadership (cont.)

Dolan, Edward Francis and Richard B.
Lyttle. BOBBY CLARKE.
Ages 10-12. 205

Dygard, Thomas J. WINNING KICKER.
Ages 11-14. 213

Fife, Dale. WHO'LL VOTE FOR LINCOLN?
Ages 8-10. 229

Leigh, Bill. THE FAR SIDE OF FEAR.
Ages 10-14. 398

Neigoff, Mike. SOCCER HERO.
Ages 9-11. 475

Sharmat, Marjorie Weinman. MAGGIE
MARMELSTEIN FOR PRESIDENT.
Ages 9-12. 588

Terris, Susan Dubinsky. TWO P'S IN A POD.
Ages 9-12. 641

Learning, Love of

See: *Education: value of*

Learning Disabilities

See also: *Birth defects; Brain injury; Education:
special; Mental retardation*

Albert, Louise. BUT I'M READY TO GO.
Ages 11-14. 5

Corcoran, Barbara. AXE-TIME, SWORD-TIME.
Ages 11 and up. 178

Pevsner, Stella. KEEP STOMPIN' TILL THE
MUSIC STOPS.
Ages 9-12. 509

Smith, Doris Buchanan. KELLY'S CREEK.
Ages 8-13. 613

Swarthout, Glendon Fred and Kathryn
Swarthout. WHALES TO SEE THE.
Ages 10-12. 632

Lesbianism

See: *Homosexuality: female*

Little League (cont.)

Loneliness

See also: *Belonging; Depression; Separation anxiety; Separation from loved ones*

Love, Meaning of (cont.)

Loyalty (cont.)

Nöstlinger, Christine. GIRL MISSING: A NOVEL.
Ages 11 and up. 482
Scoppettone, Sandra. HAPPY ENDINGS ARE ALL
ALIKE.
Ages 12 and up. 578
Singer, Marilyn. NO APPLAUSE, PLEASE.
Ages 10-12. 605

Lying

See: *Honesty/Dishonesty; Values/Valuing*

M

Magical Thinking

See also: *Daydreaming; Fantasy formation; Imaginary
friend; Imagination; Wishes*
Corcoran, Barbara. MAKE NO SOUND.
Ages 10-13. 181

Orgel, Doris. A CERTAIN MAGIC.
Ages 11-13. 490

Make-Believe

See: *Fantasy formation; Imaginary friend; Imagination;
Play*

Manliness

See: *Gender role identity: male*

Manners

See: *Etiquette*

Marijuana

See also: *Drugs; Smoking*
Hanlon, Emily. IT'S TOO LATE FOR SORRY.
Ages 11-14. 292

Maturation (cont.)

Maturation (cont.)

Maturation (cont.)

Menstruation

See also: *Puberty*
Branscum, Robbie. JOHNNY MAY.
Ages 9-12. 77
Greene, Constance Clarke. I KNOW YOU, AL.
Ages 11 and up. 268

Mental Hospital, living in

See also: *Hospital, going to; Mental illness*
Rivera, Geraldo. A SPECIAL KIND OF COURAGE:
PROFILES OF YOUNG AMERICANS.
Ages 12 and up. 544

Mental Illness

See also: *Depression; Illnesses; Mental hospital, living in; Reality, escaping*

of Adolescent
Anderson, Mary Quirk. STEP ON A CRACK.
Ages 12 and up. 18
Carlson, Dale Bick. TRIPLE BOY.
Ages 13 and up. 115
Guest, Judith. ORDINARY PEOPLE.
Ages 13 and up. 285
Levoy, Myron. ALAN AND NAOMI.
Ages 11-14. 404

of Child. *See also: Autism*
Heide, Florence Parry. SECRET DREAMER,
SECRET DREAMS.
Ages 13 and up. 306

of Parent
Roberts, Willo Davis. DON'T HURT LAURIE!
Ages 10-14. 545
Ruby, Lois. ARRIVING AT A PLACE YOU'VE
NEVER LEFT.
Ages 12 and up. 564

Moving (cont.)

Watson, Wendy McLeod. MOVING.
Ages 3-6. 677

Multiple Sclerosis

See also: *Wheelchair, dependence on*
Rivera, Geraldo. A SPECIAL KIND OF COURAGE:
PROFILES OF YOUNG AMERICANS.
Ages 12 and up. 544

Murder

See: *Death: murder*

Muteness

See also: *Deafness*
Beckwith, Lillian. THE SPUDDY: A NOVEL.
Ages 11 and up. 48
Heide, Florence Parry. SECRET DREAMER,
SECRET DREAMS.
Ages 13 and up. 306

N

Name, Dissatisfaction with

Gessner, Lynne. MALCOLM YUCCA SEED.
Ages 8-10. 246
Rice, Eve. EBBIE.
Ages 3-7. 534
Waber, Bernard. BUT NAMES WILL NEVER
HURT ME.
Ages 4-8. 668

Name-Calling

See also: *Aggression; Teasing*
Crayder, Dorothy. ISHKABIBBLE!
Ages 9-12. 185

Narcotic Habit

See: *Drugs*

Nature (cont.)

Ernst, Kathryn. MR. TAMARIN'S TREES.
Ages 5-8. 218
Gackenbach, Dick. DO YOU LOVE ME?
Ages 5-8. 238
Holmes, Efner Tudor. AMY'S GOOSE.
Ages 8-11. 330
Paulsen, Gary. THE FOXMAN.
Ages 11-14. 495
Thiele, Colin Milton. STORM BOY.
Ages 8-11. 646

Naughty Child

See: *Discipline, meaning of*

Negative Attitude

See: *Inferiority, feelings of; Shame*

Neglect

See: *Chores; Job; Parental: negligence; Responsibility: neglecting*

Neglected Child

See: *Abandonment; Deprivation, emotional; Parental: negligence*

Negro

See: *Afro-American*

Neighbors/Neighborhood

See also: *Cooperation*
Green, Phyllis. MILDRED MURPHY, HOW DOES YOUR GARDEN GROW?
Ages 9-11. 263
Mohr, Nicholasa. IN NUEVA YORK.
Ages 13 and up. 462

Nervous Breakdown

See: *Mental illness*

Neurosis

See: *Mental illness*

New Baby

See: *Sibling: new baby*

New Home

See: *Change: new home; Moving*

Nightmares

See also: *Daydreaming; Fear*
 Anderson, Mary Quirk. STEP ON A CRACK.
  Ages 12 and up. 18
 Kingman, Lee. HEAD OVER WHEELS.
  Ages 12 and up. 383

Nardine, Elisabeth. DAYDREAMS AND NIGHT.
 Ages 4-7. 472

Nursery School
 Rockwell, Harlow. MY NURSERY SCHOOL.
  Ages 3-5. 553
 Wolde, Gunilla. BETSY'S FIRST DAY AT
  NURSERY SCHOOL.
  Ages 2-5. 699

Nursing Home, Living in
 Clifford, Ethel Rosenberg. THE ROCKING CHAIR
  REBELLION.
  Ages 11-13. 142
 Shanks, Ann Zane. OLD IS WHAT YOU GET:
  DIALOGUES ON AGING BY THE OLD AND
  THE YOUNG.
  Ages 10 and up. 582

O

Obedience/Disobedience

See: *Discipline, meaning of*

Obesity

See: *Weight control: overweight*

Old Age

See: *Age*

One-Parent Home

See: *Parent/Parents: single*

Only Child

Hazen, Barbara Shook. WHY COULDN'T I BE AN
ONLY KID LIKE YOU, WIGGER.
Ages 4-7. 303

Holmes, Efner Tudor. AMY'S GOOSE.
Ages 8-11. 330
LeRoy, Gen. EMMA'S DILEMMA.
Ages 9-12. 400
Sachs, Marilyn. DORRIE'S BOOK.
Ages 9-12. 566

Operation

See: *Hospital, going to; Surgery*

Orphan

See also: *Adoption; Children's home, living in; Foster
home*
Bernays, Anne. GROWING UP RICH.
Ages 13 and up. 52
Bradbury, Bianca. "I'M VINNY, I'M ME".
Ages 12 and up. 65

Overweight

See: *Weight control: overweight*

P

Pain

See: *Accidents; Depression; Doctor, going to; Hospital, going to; Illnesses; Surgery; Sutures*

Paralysis

See also: *Poliomyelitis; Quadriplegia; Wheelchair, dependence on*
White, Paul. JANET AT SCHOOL.
   Ages 5-8. 679

Paranoid Thoughts

See: *Mental illness; Trust/Distrust*

Parent/Parents

See also: *Family; Parental*

Adoptive. *See: Adoption*

Communication with. *See: Communication: parent-child*

Deceased. *See: Death: of father; Death: of mother*

Divorce of. *See: Divorce: of parents*

Fighting between
Colman, Hila Crayder. NOBODY HAS TO BE A KID FOREVER.
   Ages 10-13. 164
Danziger, Paula. THE PISTACHIO PRESCRIPTION: A NOVEL.
   Ages 11-13. 190
Lagercrantz, Rose. TULLA'S SUMMER.
   Ages 8-11. 390

Parent/Parents (cont.)

Illness of. *See: Illnesses: of parent*

Interracial marriage. *See: Marriage: interracial*

Interreligious marriage. *See: Marriage: interreligious*

Mental illness of. *See: Mental illness: of parent*

Mother working outside home
Blaine, Margery Kay. THE TERRIBLE THING THAT HAPPENED AT OUR HOUSE.
Ages 3-7. 56
Cleary, Beverly Bunn. RAMONA AND HER FATHER.
Ages 7-10. 137
Klein, Norma. BLUE TREES, RED SKY.
Ages 7-10. 384
Love, Sandra. BUT WHAT ABOUT ME?
Ages 9-12. 417
Miles, Betty. JUST THE BEGINNING.
Ages 10-12. 456

Sawyer, Paul. MOM'S NEW JOB.
Ages 7-10. 570
Watson, Pauline. DAYS WITH DADDY.
Ages 5-8. 676

Power struggle with
Branscum, Robbie. THE THREE WARS OF BILLY JOE TREAT.
Ages 9-11. 79

Punitive
Graber, Richard. A LITTLE BREATHING ROOM.
Ages 10-14. 260

Reconciliation of. *See: Reconciliation, parental*

Remarriage of. *See also: Stepbrother/Stepsister; Stepparent*
Bates, Betty. BUGS IN YOUR EARS.
Ages 10-13. 40
Branscum, Robbie. THE SAVING OF P.S.
Ages 9-12. 78

Parent/Parents (cont.)

Respect for/Lack of respect for

Parent/Parents (cont.)

LeShan, Eda J. WHAT'S GOING TO HAPPEN TO
ME? WHEN PARENTS SEPARATE OR DIVORCE.
Ages 8 and up. 402

Matthews, Ellen. GETTING RID OF ROGER.
Ages 8-10. 446

Moe, Barbara. PICKLES AND PRUNES.
Ages 10-13. 461

Platt, Kin. CHLORIS AND THE WEIRDOS.
Ages 11 and up. 516

Sargent, Sarah. EDWARD TROY AND THE WITCH
CAT.
Ages 9-11. 569

Schick, Eleanor Grossman. NEIGHBORHOOD
KNIGHT.
Ages 5-7. 573

Slote, Alfred. MATT GARGAN'S BOY.
Ages 9-11. 611

Zindel, Paul. I LOVE MY MOTHER.
Ages 3-7. 717

Stepparent. *See: Parent/Parents: remarriage of;
Stepparent*

Substitute
Clark, Mavis Thorpe. IF THE EARTH FALLS IN.
Ages 11-14. 136
Härtling, Peter. OMA.
Ages 8-11. 296
Wilkinson, Brenda Scott. LUDELL.
Ages 10-14. 680
Wilkinson, Brenda Scott. LUDELL AND WILLIE.
Ages 12 and up. 681

Suicide of. *See: Suicide: of parent*

Unemployed
Nolan, Madeena Spray. MY DADDY DON'T GO
TO WORK.
Ages 4-7. 480

Unwed mother. *See: Unwed mother*

Parental

See also: *Parent/Parents*

Abandonment. *See: Abandonment*

Absence
Bawden, Nina Mary Kark. THE PEPPERMINT PIG.
Ages 9-14. 44
Clifton, Lucille. AMIFIKA.
Ages 4-7. 143
Elfman, Blossom. A HOUSE FOR JONNIE O.
Ages 12 and up. 215
Greene, Constance Clarke. I KNOW YOU, AL.
Ages 11 and up. 268
Hickman, Janet. THE STONES.
Ages 9-12. 314
Peck, Richard. FATHER FIGURE: A NOVEL.
Ages 11 and up. 501

Abuse. *See: Child abuse*

Alcoholism. *See: Alcoholism: of father; Alcoholism: of mother*

Control. *See also: Discipline, meaning of*
First, Julia. MOVE OVER, BEETHOVEN.
Ages 10-13. 231

Interference
Cone, Molly Lamken. CALL ME MOOSE.
Ages 9-11. 174
Pearson, Susan. THAT'S ENOUGH FOR ONE DAY, J. P.!
Ages 5-7. 499
Sachs, Marilyn. A SECRET FRIEND.
Ages 10-12. 567

Negligence. *See also: Deprivation, emotional*
Corcoran, Barbara. MAKE NO SOUND.
Ages 10-13. 181

Parental (cont.)

Overprotection
Angell, Judie. RONNIE AND ROSEY.
Ages 11 and up. 20
Bradbury, Bianca. BOY ON THE RUN.
Ages 11-13. 64
Burningham, John Mackintosh. COME AWAY
FROM THE WATER, SHIRLEY.
Ages 4-7. 103
Mazer, Norma Fox. DEAR BILL, REMEMBER ME?
AND OTHER STORIES.
Ages 12 and up. 449
Smith, Doris Buchanan. DREAMS & DRUMMERS.
Ages 10-12. 612
Talbot, Toby. DEAR GRETA GARBO.
Ages 11-13. 635
Wolitzer, Hilma. OUT OF LOVE.
Ages 10-13. 704

Rejection. *See: Rejection: parental*

Unreliability
Collier, James Lincoln. GIVE DAD MY BEST.
Ages 10-14. 159
Corcoran, Barbara. MAKE NO SOUND.
Ages 10-13. 181
Madison, Winifred. THE GENESSEE QUEEN.
Ages 11 and up. 436
Myers, Walter Dean. IT AIN'T ALL FOR NOTHIN'.
Ages 11-13. 470

Weakness
Stoutenburg, Adrien. WHERE TO NOW, BLUE?
Ages 10-12. 628

Parole

See also: *Crime/Criminals*
Samuels, Gertrude. ADAM'S DAUGHTER.
Ages 13 and up. 568

Parting

See: *Separation from loved ones*

Patience/Impatience

Delton, Judy. MY MOM HATES ME IN JANUARY.
Ages 3-6. 198
Merriam, Eve. UNHURRY HARRY.
Ages 5-8. 452

Patriotism

See also: *Loyalty*
Hickman, Janet. THE STONES.
Ages 9-12. 314

Peer Relationships

See also: *Belonging; Boy-girl relationships; Play*
Bach, Alice. THE MEAT IN THE SANDWICH.
Ages 10-13. 28

Conaway, Judith. WAS MY FACE RED!
Ages 4-7. 172
Hanlon, Emily. IT'S TOO LATE FOR SORRY.
Ages 11-14. 292
Hassler, Jon. FOUR MILES TO PINECONE.
Ages 10-14. 297
Kingman, Lee. BREAK A LEG, BETSY MAYBE!
Ages 12 and up. 382
Lee, H. Alton. SEVEN FEET FOUR AND
GROWING.
Ages 9-12. 396
Luger, Harriett Mandelay. THE ELEPHANT TREE.
Ages 12 and up. 424
Shaw, Richard. SHAPE UP, BURKE.
Ages 10-14. 593

Avoiding others

Albert, Louise. BUT I'M READY TO GO.
Ages 11-14. 5

Peer Relationships (cont.)

Pets (cont.)

Lexau, Joan M. I'LL TELL ON YOU.
Ages 5-8. 406
Low, Joseph. MY DOG, YOUR DOG.
Ages 4-6. 421
McNulty, Faith. MOUSE AND TIM.
Ages 5-7. 433
Zweifel, Frances William. BONY.
Ages 6-7. 723

Substitute for human relationship
Holland, Isabelle. ALAN AND THE ANIMAL KINGDOM.
Ages 10-13. 327
Holland, Isabelle. DINAH AND THE GREEN FAT KINGDOM.
Ages 10-13. 328
Iwasaki, Chihiro. WHAT'S FUN WITHOUT A FRIEND?
Ages 4-7. 348

Phobia

See: *Fear*

Physical Handicaps

See: *Handicaps*

Planning

See: *Careers: planning; Problem solving; Responsibility*

Play

See also: *Fantasy formation; Imaginary friend; Imagination; Peer relationships; Reality, escaping; Sharing/Not sharing*
Burningham, John Mackintosh. COME AWAY FROM THE WATER, SHIRLEY.
Ages 4-7. 103

Play (cont.)

Holl, Adelaide Hinkle. SMALL BEAR BUILDS A PLAYHOUSE.
Ages 5-7. 326
Isadora, Rachel. MAX.
Ages 4-7. 346

Poliomyelitis

See also: *Braces on body/limbs; Paralysis; Wheelchair, dependence on*
Rivera, Geraldo. A SPECIAL KIND OF COURAGE: PROFILES OF YOUNG AMERICANS.
Ages 12 and up. 544

Popularity

See: *Boy-girl relationships; Friendship; Peer relationships*

Poverty

See also: *Differences, human; Ghetto; Prejudice: social class*
Branscum, Robbie. JOHNNY MAY.
Ages 9-12. 77
Ho, Minfong. SING TO THE DAWN.
Ages 10-13. 320
Mohr, Nicholasa. IN NUEVA YORK.
Ages 13 and up. 462
Naylor, Phyllis Reynolds. WALKING THROUGH THE DARK.
Ages 12 and up. 473
Pinkwater, Manus. WINGMAN.
Ages 9-12. 513
Stoutenburg, Adrien. WHERE TO NOW, BLUE?
Ages 10-12. 628
Wilkinson, Brenda Scott. LUDELL.
Ages 10-14. 680

Poverty (cont.)

Wilkinson, Brenda Scott. LUDELL AND WILLIE.
Ages 12 and up. 681

Power Struggle

See: *Parent/Parents: power struggle with*

Practical Jokes/Pranks

See also: *Teasing*
Crawford, Charles P. LETTER PERFECT.
Ages 12 and up. 184
Gackenbach, Dick. HOUND AND BEAR.
Ages 4-6. 240

Pregnancy

See also: *Abortion; Childbirth; Unwed mother*
Christman, Elizabeth. A NICE ITALIAN GIRL.
Ages 12 and up. 132
Elfman, Blossom. A HOUSE FOR JONNIE O.
Ages 12 and up. 215

O'Dell, Scott. KATHLEEN, PLEASE COME HOME.
Ages 12 and up. 485

Prejudice

See also: *Differences, human; Hatred; Hostility;
Integration; Ostracism; Rejection*
Anders, Rebecca. A LOOK AT PREJUDICE AND
UNDERSTANDING.
Ages 3-7. 17

Ethnic/Racial. *See also: Immigrants; Internment;
Marriage: interracial; Refugees*
Blue, Rose. THE PREACHER'S KID.
Ages 9-12. 58
Butler, Beverly Kathleen. A GIRL CALLED
WENDY.
Ages 12 and up. 106
Cohen, Barbara Nash. BITTER HERBS AND
HONEY.
Ages 11-13. 153

Prejudice (cont.)

Prejudice (cont.)

Simon, Marcia L. A SPECIAL GIFT.
  Ages 10-13. 601
Slote, Alfred. MATT GARGAN'S BOY.
  Ages 9-11. 611

Social class. *See also: Poverty*
Chukovsky, Kornei Ivanovich. THE SILVER CREST:
  MY RUSSIAN BOYHOOD.
  Ages 12 and up. 135
Hamilton, Gail, pseud. TITANIA'S LODESTONE.
  Ages 11-13. 290
Hayes, Sheila. THE CAROUSEL HORSE.
  Ages 10-12. 300
Madison, Winifred. GETTING OUT.
  Ages 12 and up. 437
Paterson, Katherine Womeldorf. BRIDGE TO
  TERABITHIA.
  Ages 9-12. 493

Rich, Louise Dickinson. SUMMER AT HIGH
  KINGDOM.
  Ages 12 and up. 536
Smith, Nancy Covert. JOSIE'S HANDFUL OF
  QUIETNESS.
  Ages 9-11. 614

Premarital Sex

See: *Sex: premarital; Unwed mother*

Presents

See: *Giving, meaning of*

Pretending

See: *Fantasy formation; Imaginary friend; Imagination*

Pride/False Pride

Bunting, Anne Evelyn. MAGIC AND THE NIGHT RIVER.
Ages 5-9. 96

Fowler, Carol. DAISY HOOEE NAMPEYO.
Ages 11 and up. 233

Friskey, Margaret Richards. RACKETY, THAT VERY SPECIAL RABBIT.
Ages 3-5. 237

Greenfield, Eloise. GOOD NEWS.
Ages 5-6. 271

Hamilton, Virginia. ARILLA SUN DOWN.
Ages 12 and up. 291

Lampman, Evelyn Sibley. THE POTLATCH FAMILY.
Ages 11-13. 391

Little, Lessie Jones and Eloise Greenfield. I CAN DO IT BY MYSELF.
Ages 5-7. 415

Meddaugh, Susan. TOO SHORT FRED.
Ages 6-8. 450

Miles, Betty. JUST THE BEGINNING.
Ages 10-12. 456

Naylor, Phyllis Reynolds. WALKING THROUGH THE DARK.
Ages 12 and up. 473

Riley, Susan. WHAT DOES IT MEAN? SUCCESS.
Ages 3-6. 543

Rosenblatt, Suzanne. EVERYONE IS GOING SOMEWHERE.
Ages 4-6. 561

Sharmat, Marjorie Weinman. I'M TERRIFIC.
Ages 4-7. 587

Strete, Craig Kee. PAINT YOUR FACE ON A DROWNING IN THE RIVER.
Ages 12 and up. 629

Tobias, Tobi. ARTHUR MITCHELL.
Ages 7-10. 649

Pride/False Pride (cont.)

Wolf, Bernard. ADAM SMITH GOES TO SCHOOL.
Ages 4-7. 701

Priorities, Establishing

See: *Problem solving; Values/Valuing*

Prison

See: *Crime/Criminals; Delinquency, juvenile; Detention home, living in*

Privacy, Need for

Byars, Betsy Cromer. THE CARTOONIST.
Ages 8-12. 107
Dragonwagon, Crescent. WHEN LIGHT TURNS INTO NIGHT.
Ages 4-7. 206
Hayes, Geoffrey. BEAR BY HIMSELF.
Ages 4-6. 299

Marshall, James. GEORGE AND MARTHA — ONE FINE DAY.
Ages 3-6. 442

Private Schools

See: *Schools, private*

Problem Solving

See also: *Ambivalence, feelings of; Creativity; Decision making; Resourcefulness*
Anderson, Mary Quirk. STEP ON A CRACK.
Ages 12 and up. 18
Baldwin, Anne Norris. A LITTLE TIME.
Ages 9-11. 30
Bronin, Andrew. GUS AND BUSTER WORK THINGS OUT.
Ages 4-7. 83
Brown, Fern G. JOCKEY — OR ELSE!
Ages 9-12. 86

Problem Solving (cont.)

Psychosis

See: *Mental illness*

Puberty

See also: *Maturation; Menstruation*
Branscum, Robbie. JOHNNY MAY.
Ages 9-12. 77
Greene, Constance Clarke. I KNOW YOU, AL.
Ages 11 and up. 268
Rabe, Berniece Louise. NAOMI.
Ages 12 and up. 527

Puerto Rican-American

Gonzalez, Gloria. GAUCHO.
Ages 10-13. 257
Mohr, Nicholasa. IN NUEVA YORK.
Ages 13 and up. 462

Punishment

See: *Detention home, living in: Discipline, meaning of;*
Parent/Parents: punitive

Pupil-Teacher Relationships

See: *School: Pupil-teacher relationships*

Q

Quadriplegia

See also: *Paralysis; Wheelchair, dependence on*
Brancato, Robin Fidler. WINNING.
Ages 12 and up. 72
Kingman, Lee. HEAD OVER WHEELS.
Ages 12 and up. 383

R

Rage

See: *Aggression; Anger; Tantrums*

Rape

See also: *Crime/Criminals; Violence*
Peck, Richard. ARE YOU IN THE HOUSE ALONE?
Ages 12 and up. 500
Scoppettone, Sandra. HAPPY ENDINGS ARE ALL ALIKE.
Ages 12 and up. 578

Reality, Escaping

See also: *Daydreaming; Drugs; Mental illness; Play*
Byars, Betsy Cromer. THE TV KID.
Ages 9-12. 109

Heide, Florence Parry. GROWING ANYWAY UP.
Ages 12-14. 305
Levoy, Myron. ALAN AND NAOMI.
Ages 11-14. 404
Lutters, Valerie. THE HAUNTING OF JULIE UNGER.
Ages 10-13. 425
Pinkwater, Manus. WINGMAN.
Ages 9-12. 513
Rodowsky, Colby F. P.S. WRITE SOON.
Ages 10-12. 555

Rebellion

See also: *Delinquency, juvenile*
Bova, Benjamin William. CITY OF DARKNESS: A NOVEL.
Ages 12 and up. 63

Remarriage

See: *Parent/Parents: remarriage of; Stepparent*

Remorse

See: *Guilt, feelings of; Values/Valuing*

Report Cards

See: *School: achievement/underachievement*

Reputation

Colman, Hila Crayder. THE CASE OF THE
STOLEN BAGELS.
Ages 7-10. 162
Etter, Les. GET THOSE REBOUNDS!
Ages 10-13. 220

Resourcefulness

See also: *Creativity; Problem solving*

Bethancourt, T. Ernesto, pseud. NEW YORK CITY
TOO FAR FROM TAMPA BLUES.
Ages 10-14. 55
Bradbury, Bianca. "I'M VINNY, I'M ME".
Ages 12 and up. 65
Bulla, Clyde Robert. KEEP RUNNING, ALLEN!
Ages 4-6. 92
Clyne, Patricia Edwards. TUNNELS OF TERROR.
Ages 10-12. 149
Griese, Arnold Alfred. THE WIND IS NOT A
RIVER.
Ages 9-12. 276
Hocken, Sheila. EMMA AND I.
Ages 12 and up. 324
Houston, James A. FROZEN FIRE: A TALE OF
COURAGE.
Ages 10-13. 334
Hutchins, Patricia. HAPPY BIRTHDAY, SAM.
Ages 5-7. 343

Resourcefulness (cont.)

Jewell, Nancy. CHEER UP, PIG!
Ages 4-8. 353
Keller, Beverly Lou. THE BEETLE BUSH.
Ages 5-8. 369
Kellogg, Steven. MUCH BIGGER THAN MARTIN.
Ages 4-7. 374
Lattimore, Eleanor Frances. ADAM'S KEY.
Ages 7-9. 395
Lingard, Joan. A PROPER PLACE.
Ages 12 and up. 407
Meddaugh, Susan. TOO SHORT FRED.
Ages 6-8. 450
Neigoff, Mike. SOCCER HERO.
Ages 9-11. 475
Pape, Donna Lugg. SNOWMAN FOR SALE.
Ages 5-7. 492
Pfeffer, Susan Beth. KID POWER.
Ages 9-12. 511

Resnick, Rose. SUN AND SHADOW: THE AUTOBIOGRAPHY OF A WOMAN WHO CLEARED A PATHWAY TO THE SEEING WORLD FOR THE BLIND.
Ages 12 and up. 532
Sargent, Sarah. EDWARD TROY AND THE WITCH CAT.
Ages 9-11. 569
Schlein, Miriam. THE GIRL WHO WOULD RATHER CLIMB TREES.
Ages 4-8. 574

Respect

See: *Age: respect for; Grandparent: respect for; Parent/Parents: respect for/lack of respect for*

Responsibility

See also: *Chores; Job; Work, attitude toward*

Responsibility (cont.)

Accepting. *See also: Leader/Leadership*

Alter, Judy. AFTER PA WAS SHOT.
Ages 10-13. 11

Bach, Alice. A FATHER EVERY FEW YEARS.
Ages 11-13. 27

Bloch, Marie Halun. DISPLACED PERSON.
Ages 10-13. 57

Blue, Rose. THE THIRTEENTH YEAR: A BAR MITZVAH STORY.
Ages 10-12. 60

Bova, Benjamin William. CITY OF DARKNESS: A NOVEL.
Ages 12 and up. 63

Bradbury, Bianca. "I'M VINNY, I'M ME".
Ages 12 and up. 65

Bulla, Clyde Robert. SHOESHINE GIRL.
Ages 8-10. 93

Bunting, Anne Evelyn. SKATEBOARD FOUR.
Ages 8-10. 98

Choate, Judith Newkirk. AWFUL ALEXANDER.
Ages 4-7. 130

Cleaver, Vera and Bill Cleaver. QUEEN OF HEARTS.
Ages 10-13. 140

Cleaver, Vera and Bill Cleaver. TRIAL VALLEY.
Ages 12 and up. 141

Cohen, Peter Zachary. BEE.
Ages 10-13. 157

Collier, James Lincoln. GIVE DAD MY BEST.
Ages 10-14. 159

Colman, Hila Crayder. THE CASE OF THE STOLEN BAGELS.
Ages 7-10. 162

Francis, Dorothy Brenner. THE FLINT HILLS FOAL.
Ages 8-11. 234

Holland, Isabelle. ALAN AND THE ANIMAL KINGDOM.
Ages 10-13. 327

Responsibility (cont.)

Responsibility (cont.)

Avoiding
Dauer, Rosamond. MY FRIEND, JASPER JONES.
Ages 3-6. 192
Hinton, Nigel. COLLISION COURSE.
Ages 11 and up. 315
Lexau, Joan M. I'LL TELL ON YOU.
Ages 5-8. 406
Polushkin, Maria. BUBBA AND BABBA.
Ages 3-8. 520
Snyder, Anne. MY NAME IS DAVY — I'M AN
ALCOHOLIC.
Ages 12 and up. 616

Neglecting
Shaw, Richard. THE HARD WAY HOME.
Ages 11-13. 592

Retardation

See: *Mental retardation*

Revenge

See also: *Aggression*
Hall, Lynn. FLOWERS OF ANGER.
Ages 10-12. 288
Sharmat, Marjorie Weinman. MAGGIE
MARMELSTEIN FOR PRESIDENT.
Ages 9-12. 588

Rights

See: *Prejudice; Women's rights*

Risk, Taking of
Clyne, Patricia Edwards. TUNNELS OF TERROR.
Ages 10-12. 149
Conaway, Judith. I DARE YOU!
Ages 5-7. 169
Fife, Dale. NORTH OF DANGER.
Ages 10-12. 227

Running Away (cont.)

Thompson, Jean, pseud. I'M GOING TO RUN AWAY!
Ages 4-8. 648

Russia

Chukovsky, Kornei Ivanovich. THE SILVER CREST: MY RUSSIAN BOYHOOD.
Ages 12 and up. 135
Wallace, Barbara Brooks. JULIA AND THE THIRD BAD THING.
Ages 8-10. 673

S

Sadness

See: *Depression*

Schizophrenia

See: *Mental illness*

School

See also: *Education; Integration*

Achievement/Underachievement
Byars, Betsy Cromer. THE TV KID.
Ages 9-12. 109
Colman, Hila Crayder. ETHAN'S FAVORITE TEACHER.
Ages 7-9. 163
First, Julia. AMY.
Ages 8-11. 230
McKillip, Patricia A. THE NIGHT GIFT.
Ages 11 and up. 430

School (cont.)

Morrison, Bill. LOUIS JAMES HATES SCHOOL.
Ages 5-7. 466
Perl, Lila. DUMB, LIKE ME, OLIVIA POTTS.
Ages 9-12. 502
Smith, Doris Buchanan. DREAMS & DRUMMERS.
Ages 10-12. 612

Behavior

Allard, Harry. MISS NELSON IS MISSING!
Ages 5-8. 9
Colman, Hila Crayder. THE CASE OF THE
STOLEN BAGELS.
Ages 7-10. 162

Busing. *See: Integration: school busing*

Classmate relationships

Ames, Mildred. WHAT ARE FRIENDS FOR?
Ages 9-11. 12

Barkin, Carol and Elizabeth James. DOING
THINGS TOGETHER.
Ages 4-7. 32
Barkin, Carol and Elizabeth James. I'D RATHER
STAY HOME.
Ages 4-6. 33
Blue, Rose. THE PREACHER'S KID.
Ages 9-12. 58
Branscum, Robbie. THE THREE WARS OF BILLY
JOE TREAT.
Ages 9-11. 79
Cohen, Miriam. "BEE MY VALENTINE!"
Ages 5-7. 155
Cohen, Miriam. WHEN WILL I READ?
Ages 4-6. 156
Colman, Hila Crayder. ETHAN'S FAVORITE
TEACHER.
Ages 7-9. 163
Crayder, Dorothy. ISHKABIBBLE!
Ages 9-12. 185

Dropout. *See: Dropout, school*

School (cont.)

Entering. *See also: Separation anxiety*
Bram, Elizabeth. I DON'T WANT TO GO TO
SCHOOL.
Ages 3-5. 69
Brandenberg, Franz. SIX NEW STUDENTS.
Ages 5-7. 76
Burningham, John Mackintosh. THE SCHOOL.
Ages 3-5. 105
Greenfield, Eloise. ME AND NEESIE.
Ages 4-7. 272
Kantrowitz, Mildred. WILLY BEAR.
Ages 4-6. 362
Pearson, Susan. EVERYBODY KNOWS THAT!
Ages 4-7. 496
Wolf, Bernard. ADAM SMITH GOES TO SCHOOL.
Ages 4-7. 701

Fear of. *See: Fear: of school*

Negative experiences
Colman, Hila Crayder. THE CASE OF THE
STOLEN BAGELS.
Ages 7-10. 162
Hentoff, Nat. THIS SCHOOL IS DRIVING ME
CRAZY.
Ages 11-15. 311

Nursery. *See: Nursery school*

Phobia. *See: Fear: of school; Separation anxiety*

Pupil-teacher relationships
Allard, Harry. MISS NELSON IS MISSING!
Ages 5-8. 9
Barkin, Carol and Elizabeth James. SOMETIMES I
HATE SCHOOL.
Ages 5-7. 34
Brandenberg, Franz. SIX NEW STUDENTS.
Ages 5-7. 76

School (cont.)

Branscum, Robbie. THE THREE WARS OF BILLY JOE TREAT.
Ages 9-11. 79

Chandler, Edna Walker. INDIAN PAINTBRUSH.
Ages 9-11. 126

Cleary, Beverly Bunn. RAMONA THE BRAVE.
Ages 7-10. 138

Colman, Hila Crayder. THE CASE OF THE STOLEN BAGELS.
Ages 7-10. 162

Colman, Hila Crayder. ETHAN'S FAVORITE TEACHER.
Ages 7-9. 163

Elfman, Blossom. A HOUSE FOR JONNIE O.
Ages 12 and up. 215

Johnston, Norma. A MUSTARD SEED OF MAGIC.
Ages 12 and up. 355

Kelley, Sally. TROUBLE WITH EXPLOSIVES.
Ages 10-13. 373

Kent, Deborah. BELONGING: A NOVEL.
Ages 11-14. 375

Kerr, M. E., pseud. IS THAT YOU, MISS BLUE?
Ages 11-14. 379

Perl, Lila. DUMB, LIKE ME, OLIVIA POTTS.
Ages 9-12. 502

Pevsner, Stella. A SMART KID LIKE YOU.
Ages 10-13. 510

Pfeffer, Susan Beth. MARLY THE KID.
Ages 11-13. 512

Pollowitz, Melinda. CINNAMON CANE.
Ages 10-12. 519

Rock, Gail. ADDIE AND THE KING OF HEARTS.
Ages 9-12. 550

Wilkinson, Brenda Scott. LUDELL.
Ages 10-14. 680

Report cards. *See: School: achievement/underachievement*

School (cont.)

Transfer
Miller, Ruth White. THE CITY ROSE.
Ages 11-13. 460
Moncure, Jane Belk. A NEW BOY IN
KINDERGARTEN.
Ages 4-7. 463

Truancy
Morrison, Bill. LOUIS JAMES HATES SCHOOL.
Ages 5-7. 466

School Phobia

See: *Fear: of school; Separation anxiety*

Schools, Private

See also: *Separation anxiety*

Boys'
Hentoff, Nat. THIS SCHOOL IS DRIVING ME
CRAZY.
Ages 11-15. 311

Girls'
Kerr, M. E., pseud. IS THAT YOU, MISS BLUE?
Ages 11-14. 379

Secret, Keeping
Brandenberg, Franz. A SECRET FOR
GRANDMOTHER'S BIRTHDAY.
Ages 3-7. 75
Fife, Dale. NORTH OF DANGER.
Ages 10-12. 227
Townsend, John Rowe. NOAH'S CASTLE.
Ages 11 and up. 656

Security Blanket

See: *Transitional objects: security blanket*

Security/Insecurity

See also: *Deprivation, emotional; Fear; Trust/Distrust*
Anker, Charlotte. LAST NIGHT I SAW
ANDROMEDA.
Ages 9-11. 22
Byars, Betsy Cromer. THE PINBALLS.
Ages 10-13. 108
Corcoran, Barbara. THE FARAWAY ISLAND.
Ages 10-13. 179
Corcoran, Barbara. MAKE NO SOUND.
Ages 10-13. 181
Dragonwagon, Crescent. WILL IT BE OKAY?
Ages 3-7. 207
Hoban, Lillian Aberman. I MET A TRAVELLER.
Ages 10-12. 322
Holland, Isabelle. DINAH AND THE GREEN FAT
KINGDOM.
Ages 10-13. 328

Swetnam, Evelyn. YES, MY DARLING
DAUGHTER.
Ages 9-12. 633
Uchida, Yoshiko. JOURNEY HOME.
Ages 12-14. 657
Valencak, Hannelore. A TANGLED WEB.
Ages 9-11. 659

Seeing Eye Dog

See: *Blindness; Pets: guide dog*

Segregation

See: *Integration; Prejudice; School*

Seizures

See: *Cerebral palsy*

Self, Attitude Toward

See also: *Emotions; Self-esteem*

Accepting

Bailey, Pearl. DUEY'S TALE.
Ages 12 and up. 29
Bornstein, Ruth. LITTLE GORILLA.
Ages 2-5. 61
Brown, Marc Tolon. ARTHUR'S NOSE.
Ages 3-7. 88
Carle, Eric. THE MIXED-UP CHAMELEON.
Ages 4-8. 114
Greenwald, Sheila. THE SECRET IN MIRANDA'S
CLOSET.
Ages 8-11. 274
Herman, Charlotte. THE DIFFERENCE OF ARI
STEIN.
Ages 9-12. 312
Jeschke, Susan. SIDNEY.
Ages 4-7. 351

Lampman, Evelyn Sibley. THE POTLATCH
FAMILY.
Ages 11-13. 391
Lee, H. Alton. SEVEN FEET FOUR AND
GROWING.
Ages 9-12. 396
Little, Jean. STAND IN THE WIND.
Ages 8-11. 414
Meddaugh, Susan. TOO SHORT FRED.
Ages 6-8. 450
Pfeffer, Susan Beth. MARLY THE KID.
Ages 11-13. 512
Schulman, Janet. JENNY AND THE TENNIS NUT.
Ages 7-9. 577
Scoppettone, Sandra. HAPPY ENDINGS ARE ALL
ALIKE.
Ages 12 and up. 578
Screen, Robert Martin. WITH MY FACE TO THE
RISING SUN.
Ages 11 and up. 580

Self, Attitude Toward (cont.)

Sharmat, Marjorie Weinman. WALTER THE WOLF.
Ages 4-7. 591
Taylor, Paula. JOHNNY CASH.
Ages 7-10. 638
Vigna, Judith. EVERYONE GOES AS A PUMPKIN.
Ages 3-6. 663
Wittman, Sally. PELLY AND PEAK.
Ages 4-8. 692
Yep, Laurence Michael. CHILD OF THE OWL.
Ages 11 and up. 711

Blame. *See: Blame*

Body concept

Brooks, Jerome. THE TESTING OF CHARLIE
HAMMELMAN.
Ages 10-13. 84
Brown, Marc Tolon. ARTHUR'S NOSE.
Ages 3-7. 88

Confidence

Conaway, Judith. WILL I EVER BE GOOD
ENOUGH?
Ages 6-9. 173
Etter, Les. GET THOSE REBOUNDS!
Ages 10-13. 220
Gackenbach, Dick. HARRY AND THE TERRIBLE
WHATZIT.
Ages 4-7. 239
Johnston, Norma. IF YOU LOVE ME, LET ME GO.
Ages 12 and up. 354
Lattimore, Eleanor Frances. ADAM'S KEY.
Ages 7-9. 395
Mazer, Norma Fox. DEAR BILL, REMEMBER ME?
AND OTHER STORIES.
Ages 12 and up. 449
Richard, Adrienne. INTO THE ROAD.
Ages 12 and up. 537

Doubt. *See: Identity, search for; Inferiority, feelings of*

Self, Attitude Toward (cont.)

Embarrassment. *See: Embarrassment*

Feeling different. *See also: Differences, human*
Albert, Louise. BUT I'M READY TO GO.
Ages 11-14. 5
Chandler, Edna Walker. INDIAN PAINTBRUSH.
Ages 9-11. 126
Colman, Hila Crayder. THE SECRET LIFE OF HAROLD THE BIRD WATCHER.
Ages 8-10. 165
Cook, Marjorie. TO WALK ON TWO FEET.
Ages 11-14. 177
Hamilton, Gail, pseud. TITANIA'S LODESTONE.
Ages 11-13. 290
Herman, Charlotte. THE DIFFERENCE OF ARI STEIN.
Ages 9-12. 312
Hooks, William Harris. DOUG MEETS THE NUTCRACKER.
Ages 8-11. 332

Keller, Beverly Lou. THE GENUINE, INGENIOUS, THRIFT SHOP GENIE, CLARISSA MAE BEAN & ME.
Ages 10 and up. 372
Kingman, Lee. HEAD OVER WHEELS.
Ages 12 and up. 383
Le Guin, Ursula Kroeber. VERY FAR AWAY FROM ANYWHERE ELSE.
Ages 12 and up. 397
Lionni, Leo. A COLOR OF HIS OWN.
Ages 3-5. 408
Rosen, Winifred. HENRIETTA, THE WILD WOMAN OF BORNEO.
Ages 4-7. 560

Hatred. *See: Hatred*

Pity
Cook, Marjorie. TO WALK ON TWO FEET.
Ages 11-14. 177

Self-Esteem

See also: *Guilt, feelings of; Self, attitude toward*
Christopher, Matthew F. GLUE FINGERS.
Ages 7-9. 134
Friskey, Margaret Richards. RACKETY, THAT
VERY SPECIAL RABBIT.
Ages 3-5. 237
Mack, Nancy. WHY ME?
Ages 5-8. 429
Neigoff, Mike. RUNNER-UP.
Ages 9-11. 474
Pevsner, Stella. KEEP STOMPIN' TILL THE
MUSIC STOPS.
Ages 9-12. 509
Shaw, Richard. SHAPE UP, BURKE.
Ages 10-14. 593
Smith, Doris Buchanan. KELLY'S CREEK.
Ages 8-13. 613

Stevens, Carla McBride. PIG AND THE BLUE
FLAG.
Ages 6-8. 622
Udry, Janice May. HOW I FADED AWAY.
Ages 5-8. 658
Williams, Barbara Wright. SOMEDAY, SAID
MITCHELL.
Ages 3-6. 686

Self-Identity

See: *Identity, search for*

Self-Image

See: *Self, attitude toward*

Self-Improvement

Holland, Isabelle. DINAH AND THE GREEN FAT
KINGDOM.
Ages 10-13. 328

Self-Reliance

See: *Dependence/Independence*

Self Respect

See: *Self, attitude toward: respect*

Selfishness/Unselfishness

See: *Egocentrism; Giving, meaning of; Sharing/Not sharing*

Senility

See: *Age: senility*

Separation, Marital

See also: *Divorce*
Bach, Alice. A FATHER EVERY FEW YEARS.
Ages 11-13. 27

Beckman, Gunnel. MIA ALONE.
Ages 12 and up. 46
Beckman, Gunnel. THAT EARLY SPRING.
Ages 12 and up. 47
Cameron, Eleanor Butler. TO THE GREEN MOUNTAINS.
Ages 11 and up. 111
Colman, Hila Crayder. NOBODY HAS TO BE A KID FOREVER.
Ages 10-13. 164
Corcoran, Barbara. AXE-TIME, SWORD-TIME.
Ages 11 and up. 178
Greenfield, Eloise. TALK ABOUT A FAMILY.
Ages 8-10. 273
Gripe, Maria Kristina. THE GREEN COAT.
Ages 13 and up. 279
Heide, Florence Parry. WHEN THE SAD ONE COMES TO STAY.
Ages 8-11. 307

Sex (cont.)

Attitude toward

Shanks, Ann Zane. OLD IS WHAT YOU GET:
DIALOGUES ON AGING BY THE OLD AND
THE YOUNG.
Ages 10 and up. 582
Steptoe, John Lewis. MARCIA.
Ages 12 and up. 621

Premarital. *See also: Prostitution; Unwed mother*
Beckman, Gunnel. MIA ALONE.
Ages 12 and up. 46
Beckman, Gunnel. THAT EARLY SPRING.
Ages 12 and up. 47
Brancato, Robin Fidler. BLINDED BY THE LIGHT.
Ages 11-14. 70
Christman, Elizabeth. A NICE ITALIAN GIRL.
Ages 12 and up. 132
Peck, Richard. ARE YOU IN THE HOUSE
ALONE?
Ages 12 and up. 500

Snyder, Anne. MY NAME IS DAVY — I'M AN
ALCOHOLIC.
Ages 12 and up. 616
Steptoe, John Lewis. MARCIA.
Ages 12 and up. 621

Sex Role

See: *Gender role identity*

Sexism

See: *Prejudice: sexual*

Sexuality

See: *Gender role identity; Prejudice: sexual*

Shame

See also: *Embarrassment; Guilt, feelings of*

Sharing/Not Sharing (cont.)

Willard, Nancy. STRANGERS' BREAD.
Ages 3-8. 682

Shoplifting

See: *Stealing: shoplifting*

Showing Off

See: *Attention seeking; Boasting*

Shyness

See also: *Inferiority, feelings of*
Brooks, Jerome. THE TESTING OF CHARLIE
HAMMELMAN.
Ages 10-13. 84
Carrick, Malcolm. TRAMP.
Ages 7-9. 122
Corcoran, Barbara. THE FARAWAY ISLAND.
Ages 10-13. 179

Keller, Beverly Lou. FIONA'S BEE.
Ages 5-8. 371
Lee, H. Alton. SEVEN FEET FOUR AND
GROWING.
Ages 9-12. 396
Miles, Betty. ALL IT TAKES IS PRACTICE.
Ages 9-12. 454
Miller, Ruth White. THE CITY ROSE.
Ages 11-13. 460
Stolz, Mary Slattery. CIDER DAYS.
Ages 8-11. 626
Wold, Jo Anne. TELL THEM MY NAME IS
AMANDA.
Ages 5-8. 694

Sibling

See also: *Family*

Death of. *See: Death: of sibling*

Sibling (cont.)

Wolde, Gunilla. BETSY'S BABY BROTHER.
Ages 2-5. 698

Older. *See also: Baby-sitting*
Cleaver, Vera and Bill Cleaver. QUEEN OF
HEARTS.
Ages 10-13. 140
Clifton, Lucille. MY BROTHER FINE WITH ME.
Ages 5-8. 147
Hoban, Lillian Aberman. ARTHUR'S PEN PAL.
Ages 4-7. 321
Kaye, Geraldine. TIM AND THE RED INDIAN
HEADDRESS.
Ages 5-7. 365
Klein, Norma. BLUE TREES, RED SKY.
Ages 7-10. 384
Matthews, Ellen. GETTING RID OF ROGER.
Ages 8-10. 446
Peck, Richard. FATHER FIGURE: A NOVEL.
Ages 11 and up. 501

Peterson, Jeanne Whitehouse. I HAVE A SISTER —
MY SISTER IS DEAF.
Ages 4-7. 507
Supraner, Robyn. IT'S NOT FAIR!
Ages 3-7. 631
Williams, Barbara Wright. JEREMY ISN'T
HUNGRY.
Ages 4-7. 684

Rejection. *See: Rejection: sibling*

Relationships. *See also: Family: relationships*
Alexander, Martha G. I'LL BE THE HORSE IF
YOU'LL PLAY WITH ME.
Ages 3-6. 8
Bawden, Nina Mary Kark. THE PEPPERMINT PIG.
Ages 9-14. 44
Bottner, Barbara. JUNGLE DAY OR, HOW I
LEARNED TO LOVE MY NOSEY LITTLE
BROTHER.
Ages 4-7. 62

Sibling (cont.)

Sibling (cont.)

Sibling (cont.)

Ho, Minfong. SING TO THE DAWN.
Ages 10-13. 320
Miles, Betty. JUST THE BEGINNING.
Ages 10-12. 456
Pearson, Susan. MONNIE HATES LYDIA.
Ages 7-10. 498
Rosen, Winifred. HENRIETTA, THE WILD
WOMAN OF BORNEO.
Ages 4-7. 560
Stolz, Mary Slattery. CIDER DAYS.
Ages 8-11. 626
Stolz, Mary Slattery. FERRIS WHEEL.
Ages 8-11. 627
Vogel, Ilse-Margret. MY TWIN SISTER ERIKA.
Ages 6-10. 667

Stepbrother/Stepsister. *See: Parent/Parents:
remarriage of; Stepbrother/Stepsister*

Suicide of. *See: Suicide: of sibling*

Twins. *See: Twins*

Younger
Alexander, Martha G. I'LL BE THE HORSE IF
YOU'LL PLAY WITH ME.
Ages 3-6. 8
Hamilton, Virginia. ARILLA SUN DOWN.
Ages 12 and up. 291
Hinton, Susan Eloise. RUMBLE FISH.
Ages 12 and up. 316
Pearson, Susan. MONNIE HATES LYDIA.
Ages 7-10. 498
Zolotow, Charlotte Shapiro. MAY I VISIT?
Ages 4-7. 719

Youngest
Bulla, Clyde Robert. KEEP RUNNING, ALLEN!
Ages 4-6. 92
Corey, Dorothy. TOMORROW YOU CAN.
Ages 2-5. 182

Sports/Sportsmanship (cont.)

Dolan, Edward Francis and Richard B. Lyttle. BOBBY CLARKE.
Ages 10-12. 205

Dygard, Thomas J. WINNING KICKER.
Ages 11-14. 213

Etter, Les. GET THOSE REBOUNDS!
Ages 10-13. 220

Katz, Bobbi. VOLLEYBALL JINX.
Ages 9-11. 364

Knudson, R. Rozanne. FOX RUNNING: A NOVEL.
Ages 11 and up. 386

Knudson, R. Rozanne. ZANBANGER.
Ages 10-13. 387

Knudson, R. Rozanne. ZANBOOMER.
Ages 10-13. 388

Lee, H. Alton. SEVEN FEET FOUR AND GROWING.
Ages 9-12. 396

Lexau, Joan M. I'LL TELL ON YOU.
Ages 5-8. 406

Love, Sandra. MELISSA'S MEDLEY.
Ages 10-13. 418

Mazer, Harry. THE WAR ON VILLA STREET: A NOVEL.
Ages 11-13. 448

Neigoff, Mike. RUNNER-UP.
Ages 9-11. 474

Neigoff, Mike. SOCCER HERO.
Ages 9-11. 475

Nicholson, William G. PETE GRAY: ONE-ARMED MAJOR LEAGUER.
Ages 9-12. 479

Platt, Kin. RUN FOR YOUR LIFE.
Ages 9-12. 518

Robison, Nancy. ON THE BALANCE BEAM.
Ages 8-10. 549

Sports/Sportsmanship (cont.)

Slote, Alfred. THE HOTSHOT.
Ages 8-11. 610

Status

See: *Peer relationships; Prejudice: social class*

Stealing

See also: *Crime/Criminals; Delinquency, juvenile*
Ames, Mildred. WHAT ARE FRIENDS FOR?
Ages 9-11. 12
Anderson, Mary Quirk. STEP ON A CRACK.
Ages 12 and up. 18
Ashley, Bernard. TERRY ON THE FENCE.
Ages 12 and up. 25
Collier, James Lincoln. GIVE DAD MY BEST.
Ages 10-14. 159
Dahl, Roald. DANNY: THE CHAMPION OF THE
WORLD.
Ages 10 and up. 189

Hinton, Nigel. COLLISION COURSE.
Ages 11 and up. 315
McLenighan, Valjean. NEW WHEELS.
Ages 7-9. 432
Mohr, Nicholasa. IN NUEVA YORK.
Ages 13 and up. 462
Platt, Kin. RUN FOR YOUR LIFE.
Ages 9-12. 518
Rockwell, Thomas. THE THIEF.
Ages 8-10. 554
Ruby, Lois. ARRIVING AT A PLACE YOU'VE
NEVER LEFT.
Ages 12 and up. 564

Shoplifting
Dexter, Pat Egan. ARROW IN THE WIND.
Ages 10-13. 200

Stepbrother/Stepsister

See also: *Family; Parent/Parents: remarriage of*

Stepbrother/Stepsister (cont.)

Bates, Betty. BUGS IN YOUR EARS.
Ages 10-13. 40
Francis, Dorothy Brenner. THE FLINT HILLS
FOAL.
Ages 8-11. 234
Greene, Constance Clarke. I AND SPROGGY.
Ages 9-11. 267
LeShan, Eda J. WHAT'S GOING TO HAPPEN TO
ME? WHEN PARENTS SEPARATE OR DIVORCE.
Ages 8 and up. 402
Roberts, Willo Davis. DON'T HURT LAURIE!
Ages 10-14. 545
Thomas, Ianthe. ELIZA'S DADDY.
Ages 4-7. 647

Stepparent

See also: *Family; Parent/Parents: remarriage of*

Father

Bates, Betty. BUGS IN YOUR EARS.
Ages 10-13. 40
Clifton, Lucille. EVERETT ANDERSON'S NINE
MONTH LONG.
Ages 4-7. 145
Clifton, Lucille. EVERETT ANDERSON'S 1-2-3.
Ages 4-6. 146
Green, Phyllis. ICE RIVER.
Ages 8-10. 262
Hunter, Evan. ME AND MR. STENNER.
Ages 10-13. 339
LeShan, Eda J. WHAT'S GOING TO HAPPEN TO
ME? WHEN PARENTS SEPARATE OR DIVORCE.
Ages 8 and up. 402
Morey, Walter. YEAR OF THE BLACK PONY.
Ages 10-13. 465
Nöstlinger, Christine. GIRL MISSING: A NOVEL.
Ages 11 and up. 482

Stepparent (cont.)

O'Hanlon, Jacklyn. FAIR GAME.
Ages 11-13. 487
Platt, Kin. CHLORIS AND THE FREAKS.
Ages 11 and up. 515
Roberts, Willo Davis. DON'T HURT LAURIE!
Ages 10-14. 545

Mother

Bates, Betty. BUGS IN YOUR EARS.
Ages 10-13. 40
Francis, Dorothy Brenner. THE FLINT HILLS
FOAL.
Ages 8-11. 234
Kaplan, Bess. THE EMPTY CHAIR.
Ages 10-14. 363
LeShan, Eda J. WHAT'S GOING TO HAPPEN TO
ME? WHEN PARENTS SEPARATE OR DIVORCE.
Ages 8 and up. 402
Pevsner, Stella. A SMART KID LIKE YOU.
Ages 10-13. 510

Pfeffer, Susan Beth. MARLY THE KID.
Ages 11-13. 512
Reiss, Johanna. THE JOURNEY BACK.
Ages 10-14. 530
Wolitzer, Hilma. OUT OF LOVE.
Ages 10-13. 704

Stereotype

See: *Prejudice*

Stitches

See: *Doctor, going to; Sutures*

Stuttering

See: *Speech problems: stuttering*

Substitute Parent

See: *Parent/Parents: substitute*

Suicide (cont.)

of Sibling
Gerson, Corinne. PASSING THROUGH.
Ages 12 and up. 245

Superego

See: *Identification with others; Values/Valuing*

Superstition
Babbitt, Natalie. THE EYES OF THE AMARYLLIS.
Ages 11-14. 26
Delton, Judy. IT HAPPENED ON THURSDAY.
Ages 5-8. 197
Katz, Bobbi. VOLLEYBALL JINX.
Ages 9-11. 364
Wallace, Barbara Brooks. JULIA AND THE THIRD BAD THING.
Ages 8-10. 673

Surgery

See also: *Amputee; Cancer; Cleft lip/palate; Doctor, going to; Fear: of death; Hospital, going to; Illnesses; Sutures*
Sobol, Harriet Langsam. JEFF'S HOSPITAL BOOK.
Ages 2-7. 617
Viscardi, Henry. THE PHOENIX CHILD: A STORY OF LOVE.
Ages 13 and up. 665

Heart. *See also: Cardiac conditions*
Singer, Marilyn. IT CAN'T HURT FOREVER.
Ages 9-12. 604

Tonsillectomy
Bruna, Dick. MIFFY IN THE HOSPITAL.
Ages 2-5. 90
Ziegler, Sandra. AT THE HOSPITAL: A SURPRISE FOR KRISSY.
Ages 3-6. 716

Sutures

See also: *Doctor, going to; Surgery*
Wolde, Gunilla. BETSY AND THE DOCTOR.
Ages 3-7. 697

Sympathy

See: *Empathy*

T

Talents

See also: *Education: special*
Grimes, Nikki. GROWIN'.
Ages 9-11. 277

Artistic
Colman, Hila Crayder. THE AMAZING MISS LAURA.
Ages 11-14. 161
Fowler, Carol. DAISY HOOEE NAMPEYO.
Ages 11 and up. 233
Kingman, Lee. BREAK A LEG, BETSY MAYBE!
Ages 12 and up. 382
Madison, Winifred. GETTING OUT.
Ages 12 and up. 437
Nelson, Mary Carroll. MICHAEL NARANJO: THE STORY OF AN AMERICAN INDIAN.
Ages 9-12. 476
Pinkwater, Manus. WINGMAN.
Ages 9-12. 513
Rock, Gail. A DREAM FOR ADDIE.
Ages 9-12. 551
Rodowsky, Colby F. WHAT ABOUT ME?
Ages 11-13. 556

Trust/Distrust (cont.)

Swetnam, Evelyn. YES, MY DARLING
DAUGHTER.
Ages 9-12. 633

Trustworthiness

See: *Honesty/Dishonesty*

Truth

See: *Honesty/Dishonesty*

Twins

Fraternal
Goldreich, Gloria. SEASON OF DISCOVERY.
Ages 11-13. 256

Identical
Kingman, Lee. HEAD OVER WHEELS.
Ages 12 and up. 383

Vogel, Ilse-Margret. MY TWIN SISTER ERIKA.
Ages 6-10. 667

U

Uncle

See: *Relatives*

Unemployment

See: *Parent/Parents: unemployed*

Untruthfulness

See: *Honesty/Dishonesty*

Unwanted Child

See: *Abandonment; Rejection: parental*

Unwed Mother

See also: *Pregnancy; Sex: premarital*
Beckman, Gunnel. MIA ALONE.
  Ages 12 and up. 46
Christman, Elizabeth. A NICE ITALIAN GIRL.
  Ages 12 and up. 132
Elfman, Blossom. A HOUSE FOR JONNIE O.
  Ages 12 and up. 215
Johnston, Norma. A MUSTARD SEED OF MAGIC.
  Ages 12 and up. 355
Ruby, Lois. ARRIVING AT A PLACE YOU'VE
  NEVER LEFT.
  Ages 12 and up. 564
Windsor, Patricia. DIVING FOR ROSES.
  Ages 13 and up. 687

Child of
Colman, Hila Crayder. TELL ME NO LIES.
  Ages 10-12. 167

Glass, Frankcina. MARVIN & TIGE.
  Ages 12 and up. 250

V

Values/Valuing

See also: *Differences, human; Identification with
others*
Bethancourt, T. Ernesto, pseud. THE DOG DAYS OF
  ARTHUR CANE.
  Ages 11 and up. 54
Kerr, M. E., pseud. IS THAT YOU, MISS BLUE?
  Ages 11-14. 379

Aesthetic
Hooks, William Harris. DOUG MEETS THE
  NUTCRACKER.
  Ages 8-11. 332

Values/Valuing (cont.)

Materialistic

Bulla, Clyde Robert. SHOESHINE GIRL.
Ages 8-10. 93

Colman, Hila Crayder. AFTER THE WEDDING.
Ages 12 and up. 160

Gerson, Corinne. PASSING THROUGH.
Ages 12 and up. 245

Hayes, Sheila. THE CAROUSEL HORSE.
Ages 10-12. 300

Heide, Florence Parry. WHEN THE SAD ONE
COMES TO STAY.
Ages 8-11. 307

Kerr, M. E., pseud. LOVE IS A MISSING PERSON.
Ages 12 and up. 380

Naylor, Phyllis Reynolds. WALKING THROUGH
THE DARK.
Ages 12 and up. 473

Pfeffer, Susan Beth. KID POWER.
Ages 9-12. 511

Moral/Ethical

Alexander, Anne. CONNIE.
Ages 10-13. 6

Ashley, Bernard. TERRY ON THE FENCE.
Ages 12 and up. 25

Bach, Alice. THE MEAT IN THE SANDWICH.
Ages 10-13. 28

Blue, Rose. THE PREACHER'S KID.
Ages 9-12. 58

Blue, Rose. THE THIRTEENTH YEAR: A BAR
MITZVAH STORY.
Ages 10-12. 60

Colman, Hila Crayder. THE AMAZING MISS
LAURA.
Ages 11-14. 161

Crawford, Charles P. LETTER PERFECT.
Ages 12 and up. 184

Dodd, Wayne. A TIME OF HUNTING.
Ages 11-14. 204

Values/Valuing (cont.)

Vandalism

See also: *Crime/Criminals; Delinquency, juvenile*
Rockwell, Thomas. THE THIEF.
Ages 8-10. 554

Vanity

See: *Pride/False pride*

Violence

See also: *Aggression; Cruelty; Death: murder;
Delinquency, juvenile; Rape; War*
Degens, T. THE GAME ON THATCHER ISLAND.
Ages 11-14. 193

Visiting

Degens, T. THE GAME ON THATCHER ISLAND.
Ages 11-14. 193

Goldman, Susan. GRANDMA IS SOMEBODY
SPECIAL.
Ages 4-7. 255
Wolkstein, Diane. THE VISIT.
Ages 3-5. 706

Visual Impairment

See also: *Blindness; Glasses, wearing of*
Litchfield, Ada Bassett. A CANE IN HER HAND.
Ages 6-9. 412
Little, Jean. LISTEN FOR THE SINGING.
Ages 10-14. 413

W

War

See also: *Violence*

Weight Control (cont.)

Overweight

Brooks, Jerome. THE TESTING OF CHARLIE HAMMELMAN.
Ages 10-13. 84

Holland, Isabelle. DINAH AND THE GREEN FAT KINGDOM.
Ages 10-13. 328

Hurwitz, Johanna. THE LAW OF GRAVITY.
Ages 10-13. 341

Lipsyte, Robert. ONE FAT SUMMER.
Ages 12-14. 409

Miles, Betty. LOOKING ON.
Ages 11-14. 457

Neville, Emily Cheney. GARDEN OF BROKEN GLASS.
Ages 11-14. 477

Stevens, Carla McBride. PIG AND THE BLUE FLAG.
Ages 6-8. 622

Talbot, Charlene Joy. THE GREAT RAT ISLAND ADVENTURE.
Ages 10-13. 634

Winthrop, Elizabeth. POTBELLIED POSSUMS.
Ages 4-6. 690

Wheelchair, Dependence on

See also: *Amputee; Multiple sclerosis; Paralysis; Poliomyelitis; Prosthesis; Quadriplegia*

Cook, Marjorie. TO WALK ON TWO FEET.
Ages 11-14. 177

Fanshawe, Elizabeth. RACHEL.
Ages 4-6. 222

Fassler, Joan. HOWIE HELPS HIMSELF.
Ages 5-8. 224

Green, Phyllis. WALKIE-TALKIE.
Ages 10-13. 264

Grohskopf, Bernice. SHADOW IN THE SUN.
Ages 10 and up. 281

Wheelchair, Dependence on (cont.)

Kingman, Lee. HEAD OVER WHEELS.
   Ages 12 and up. 383
Mack, Nancy. TRACY.
   Ages 4-8. 428
White, Paul. JANET AT SCHOOL.
   Ages 5-8. 679

Wishes

See also: *Daydreaming; Fantasy formation; Magical thinking*
Clifton, Lucille. THREE WISHES.
   Ages 6-8. 148
Johnston, Tony. NIGHT NOISES: AND OTHER
   MOLE AND TROLL STORIES.
   Ages 4-7. 358
Tobias, Tobi. JANE, WISHING.
   Ages 6-9. 651

Withdrawal

See: *Reality, escaping*

Womanliness

See: *Gender role identity: female*

Women's Rights

See also: *Gender role identity: female; Prejudice: sexual*
Colman, Hila Crayder. NOBODY HAS TO BE A
   KID FOREVER.
   Ages 10-13. 164
Dygard, Thomas J. WINNING KICKER.
   Ages 11-14. 213
Gripe, Maria Kristina. THE GREEN COAT.
   Ages 13 and up. 279
Ho, Minfong. SING TO THE DAWN.
   Ages 10-13. 320

Work, Attitude Toward (cont.)

Work, Attitude Toward
  See also: *Careers: planning; Job; Responsibility*
   Klein, Norma. BLUE TREES, RED SKY.
    Ages 7-10. 384
   Shaw, Richard. THE HARD WAY HOME.
    Ages 11-13. 592

Working Mother
  See: *Parent/Parents: mother working outside home*

Worries
  See: *Anxiety; Fear*

Y

Youngest Child
  See: *Sibling: youngest*

AUTHOR
INDEX

To locate a book through the
Author Index, find the author's
name; titles are listed alphabetically under each author's name.

A

Aaron, Chester
SPILL. 1

Adler, David A.
LITTLE AT A TIME, A. 2

Adoff, Arnold
BIG SISTER TELLS ME THAT I'M BLACK. 3

Albert, Burton
MINE, YOURS, OURS. 4

Albert, Louise
BUT I'M READY TO GO. 5

Alexander, Anne
CONNIE. 6
TO LIVE A LIE. 7

Alexander, Martha G.
I'LL BE THE HORSE IF YOU'LL PLAY WITH ME. 8

Allard, Harry
MISS NELSON IS MISSING! 9

AUTHOR INDEX

AUTHOR INDEX

Byars, Betsy Cromer
CARTOONIST, THE. 107
PINBALLS, THE. 108
TV KID, THE. 109

C

Caines, Jeannette Franklin
DADDY. 110

Cameron, Eleanor Butler
TO THE GREEN MOUNTAINS. 111

Campbell, R. Wright
WHERE PIGEONS GO TO DIE. 112

Carle, Eric
GROUCHY LADYBUG, THE. 113
MIXED-UP CHAMELEON, THE. 114

Carlson, Dale Bick
TRIPLE BOY. 115

Carlson, Natalie Savage
MARIE LOUISE'S HEYDAY. 116
RUNAWAY MARIE LOUISE. 117

AUTHOR INDEX

AUTHOR INDEX

Miles, Betty
ALL IT TAKES IS PRACTICE. 454
AROUND AND AROUND — LOVE. 455
JUST THE BEGINNING. 456
LOOKING ON. 457

Miles, Miska, pseud.
AARON'S DOOR. 458

Milgram, Mary
BROTHERS ARE ALL THE SAME. 459

Miller, Ruth White
CITY ROSE, THE. 460

Moe, Barbara
PICKLES AND PRUNES. 461

Mohr, Nicholasa
IN NUEVA YORK. 462

Moncure, Jane Belk
NEW BOY IN KINDERGARTEN, A. 463

Montgomery, Elizabeth Rider
MYSTERY OF THE BOY NEXT DOOR, THE. 464

Moore, Lilian, joint author
See: Charlip, Remy

P

Paisley, Tom
See: Bethancourt, T. Ernesto, pseud.

Palay, Steven
I LOVE MY GRANDMA. 491

Pape, Donna Lugg
SNOWMAN FOR SALE. 492

Passailaigue, Thomas E.
See: Bethancourt, T. Ernesto, pseud.

Paterson, Katherine Womeldorf
BRIDGE TO TERABITHIA. 493
GREAT GILLY HOPKINS, THE. 494

Paulsen, Gary
FOXMAN, THE. 495

Pearson, Susan
EVERYBODY KNOWS THAT! 496
IZZIE. 497
MONNIE HATES LYDIA. 498
THAT'S ENOUGH FOR ONE DAY, J. P.! 499

AUTHOR INDEX

AUTHOR INDEX

370

TITLE
INDEX

To locate a book through the Title
Index, find the title of the book;
titles are listed alphabetically.

A

TITLE INDEX

D

DADDY
Caines, Jeannette Franklin. 110

DAISY HOOEE NAMPEYO
Fowler, Carol. 233

DANNY: THE CHAMPION OF THE WORLD
Dahl, Roald. 189

DAVID AND DOG
Hughes, Shirley. 335

DAYDREAMS AND NIGHT
Nardine, Elisabeth. 472

G

GAME ON THATCHER ISLAND, THE
Degens, T. 193

GARDEN IS DOING FINE, THE
Farley, Carol J. 223

GARDEN OF BROKEN GLASS
Neville, Emily Cheney. 477

GAUCHO
Gonzalez, Gloria. 257

GENESSEE QUEEN, THE
Madison, Winifred. 436

I

TITLE INDEX

430

M

S

V

W

PUBLISHERS/PRODUCERS DIRECTORY

A

Abelard-Schuman, Ltd.
10 East 53 Street
New York NY 10022

Abingdon Press
201 Eighth Avenue South
Nashville TN 37202

Ace Books
51 Madison Avenue
New York NY 10010

Addison-Wesley Publishing Company, Inc.
Jacob Way
Reading MA 01867

Albert Whitman & Company
See: Whitman (Albert) & Company

Alfred A. Knopf, Inc.
See: Knopf (Alfred A.) Inc.

American Guidance Service, Inc.
Publishers' Building
Circle Pines MN 55014

Arthur Barr Productions, Inc.
See: Barr (Arthur) Productions, Inc.

Atheneum Publishers
597 Fifth Avenue
New York NY 10017

Atlantic Monthly Press, The
8 Arlington Street
Boston MA 02116

Avon Books
959 Eighth Avenue
New York NY 10019

B

Ballantine Books, Inc.
201 East 50 Street
New York NY 10022

Bantam Books, Inc.
666 Fifth Avenue
New York NY 10019

Barr (Arthur) Productions, Inc.
3490 East Foothill Boulevard
Pasadena CA 91107

Beacon Press, Inc.
25 Beacon Street
Boston MA 02108

Bradbury Press, Inc.
2 Overhill Road
Scarsdale NY 10583

C

Carolrhoda Books, Inc.
241 First Avenue North
Minneapolis MN 55401

Charles Scribner's Sons
See: Scribner's (Charles) Sons

Childrens Press, Inc.
1224 West Van Buren Street
Chicago IL 60607

Child's World, Inc.
P.O. Box 681
Elgin IL 60120

Clarion Books
See: Houghton Mifflin Company

Collins (William) Publishers, Inc.
200 Madison Avenue
New York NY 10016

Collins-World
See: Collins (William) Publishers, Inc.

Coward, McCann & Geoghegan, Inc.
200 Madison Avenue
New York NY 10016

Creative Education
123 South Broad Street
Mankato MN 56001

Crowell (Thomas Y.) Company, Inc.
10 East 53 Street
New York NY 10022

Crown Publishers, Inc.
1 Park Avenue
New York NY 10016

D

Daniel Wilson Productions, Inc.
See: Wilson (Daniel) Productions, Inc.

David McKay Company, Inc.
See: McKay (David) Company, Inc.

Day (John) Company, Inc.
10 East 53 Street
New York NY 10022

Delacorte Press
1 Dag Hammarskjold Plaza
245 East 47 Street
New York NY 10017

Dell Publishing Company, Inc.
1 Dag Hammarskjold Plaza
245 East 47 Street
New York NY 10017

Dial Press, Inc., The
1 Dag Hammarskjold Plaza
245 East 47 Street
New York NY 10017

Dillon Press, Inc.
500 South Third Street
Minneapolis MN 55415

Disney (Walt) Productions
Educational Film Division
500 South Buena Vista Avenue
Burbank CA 91503

Dodd, Mead & Company, Inc.
79 Madison Avenue
New York NY 10016

Doubleday & Company, Inc.
245 Park Avenue
New York NY 10017

Dutton (E.P.) & Company, Inc.
2 Park Avenue
New York NY 10016

E

E.P. Dutton & Company, Inc.
See: Dutton (E.P.) & Company, Inc.

Educational Enrichment Corporation
357 Adams Street
Bedford Hills NY 10507

Elsevier/Nelson Books
2 Park Avenue
New York NY 10016

Encyclopaedia Britannica Films
425 North Michigan Avenue
Chicago IL 60611

Ericksson (Paul S.) Publisher, Inc.
Battell Building
Middlebury VT 05753

F

Farrar, Straus & Giroux, Inc.
19 Union Square West
New York NY 10003

Fawcett Book Group
1515 Broadway
New York NY 10036

Fawcett World Library
See: Fawcett Book Group

Follett Publishing Company
1010 West Washington Boulevard
Chicago IL 60607

Four Winds Press
50 West 44 Street
New York NY 10036

Franklin Watts, Inc.
See: Watts (Franklin) Inc.

Frederick Warne & Company, Inc.
See: Warne (Frederick) & Company, Inc.

G.P. Putnam's Sons
See: Putnam's (G.P.) Sons

G

Garrard Publishing Company
107 Cherry Street
New Canaan CT 06840

Golden Press
See: Western Publishing Company, Inc.

Greenwillow Books
105 Madison Avenue
New York NY 10016

Grosset & Dunlap, Inc.
51 Madison Avenue
New York NY 10010

H

Hanes Corporation
2000 West First Street
Winston-Salem NC 27104

Harcourt Brace Jovanovich, Inc.
757 Third Avenue
New York NY 10017

Harper & Row Publishers, Inc.
10 East 53 Street
New York NY 10022

Harvey House, Inc.
20 Waterside Plaza
New York NY 10010

Hastings House Publishers, Inc.
10 East 40 Street
New York NY 10016

Henry Z. Walck
See: Walck (Henry Z.) Inc.

Holiday House, Inc.
18 East 53 Street
New York NY 10022

Holt, Rinehart and Winston, Inc.
383 Madison Avenue
New York NY 10017

Houghton Mifflin Company
2 Park Street
Boston MA 02107

Human Sciences Press
72 Fifth Avenue
New York NY 10011

I

Illumination Films
665 Fifth Avenue
New York NY 10022

Independence Press
Drawer H H
Independence MO 64055

Instructional/Communications Technology, Inc.
10 Stepar Place
Huntington Station NY 11746

J

J.B. Lippincott Company
See: Lippincott (J.B.) Company

John Day Company, Inc.
See: Day (John) Company, Inc.

Julian Messner, Inc.
See: Messner (Julian) Inc.

K

Knopf (Alfred A.) Inc.
201 East 50 Street
New York NY 10022

L

Learning Corporation of America
1350 Avenue of the Americas
New York NY 10019

Lerner Publications Company
241 First Avenue North
Minneapolis MN 55401

Library of Congress
Washington, DC 20540

Lippincott (J.B.) Company
10 East 53 Street
New York NY 10022

Little, Brown and Company
34 Beacon Street
Boston MA 02106

Lothrop, Lee & Shepard Company
105 Madison Avenue
New York NY 10016

M

MacDonald-Raintree, Inc.
205 West Highland Avenue
Milwaukee WI 53203

McGraw-Hill Book Company
1221 Avenue of the Americas
New York NY 10020

McKay (David) Company, Inc.
750 Third Avenue
New York NY 10017

Macmillan Publishing Company, Inc.
866 Third Avenue
New York NY 10022

Martin Tahse Productions
See: Tahse (Martin) Productions

Messner (Julian) Inc.
1230 Avenue of the Americas
New York NY 10020

Methuen, Inc.
777 Third Avenue
New York NY 10017

Miller-Brody Productions
See: Random House, Inc., School Division

Morrow (William) & Company, Inc.
105 Madison Avenue
New York NY 10016

N

Nelson (Thomas) Inc.
See: Elsevier/Nelson Books

New American Library
1301 Avenue of the Americas
New York NY 10019

P

Pantheon Books
201 East 50 Street
New York NY 10022

Paramount Pictures Corporation
5451 Marathon Street
Hollywood CA 90038

Parents' Magazine Press
See: Four Winds Press

Paul S. Ericksson Publisher, Inc.
See: Ericksson (Paul S.) Publisher, Inc.

Penguin Books, Inc.
See: Viking Penguin, Inc.

Pocket Books, Inc.
1230 Avenue of the Americas
New York NY 10020

Phillips (S.G.) Inc.
305 West 86 Street
New York NY 10024

Platt & Munk Publishers
51 Madison Avenue
New York NY 10012

Prentice-Hall, Inc.
Englewood Cliffs NJ 07632

Putnam's (G.P.) Sons
200 Madison Avenue
New York NY 10016

R

Raintree Publishers, Ltd.
See: MacDonald-Raintree, Inc.

Random House, Inc.
201 East 50 Street
New York NY 10022

Random House, Inc.
School Division
400 Hahn Road
Westminster MD 21157

Rawson Publishers, Inc.
630 Third Avenue
New York NY 10017

Reader's Digest Press
200 Park Avenue
New York NY 10017

S

S.G. Phillips, Inc.
See: Phillips (S.G.) Inc.

St. Martin's Press, Inc.
175 Fifth Avenue
New York NY 10010

Scholastic Book Services
50 West 44 Street
New York NY 10036

Scribner's (Charles) Sons
597 Fifth Avenue
New York NY 10017

Seabury Press, Inc., The
See: Houghton Mifflin Company

Simon & Schuster, Inc.
1230 Avenue of the Americas
New York NY 10020

Society for Visual Education, Inc.
1345 West Diversey Parkway
Chicago IL 60614

T

Tahse (Martin) Productions
1041 North Formosa Avenue
Los Angeles CA 90046

Thomas Nelson, Inc.
See: Elsevier/Nelson Books

Thomas Y. Crowell Company, Inc.
See: Crowell (Thomas Y.) Company, Inc.

Tomorrow Entertainment
570 Lexington Avenue
New York NY 10022

V

Viking Penguin, Inc.
625 Madison Avenue
New York NY 10022

Viking Press, Inc., The
See: Viking Penguin, Inc.

W

Walck (Henry Z.) Inc.
750 Third Avenue
New York NY 10017

Walt Disney Productions
See: Disney (Walt) Productions

Warne (Frederick) & Company, Inc.
2 Park Avenue
New York NY 10016

Warner Books, Inc.
75 Rockefeller Plaza
New York NY 10019

Watts (Franklin) Inc.
730 Fifth Avenue
New York NY 10019

Western Publishing Company, Inc.
1220 Mound Avenue
Racine WI 53404

Westminster Press, The
925 Chestnut Street
Philadelphia PA 19107

Westport Communications
155 Post Road East
Westport CT 06880

Whitman (Albert) & Company
560 West Lake Street
Chicago IL 60606

William Collins Publishers, Inc.
See: Collins (William) Publishers, Inc.

William Morrow & Company, Inc.
See: Morrow (William) & Company, Inc.

Wilson (Daniel) Productions, Inc.
300 West 55 Street, 8th floor
New York NY 10019

X

Xerox Publishing Division
1200 High Ridge Road
Stamford CT 06905

DOES NOT CIRCULATE

NO I.L.L. 98

THE BOOKFINDER

Volume 2

Annotations of Books Published
1975 through 1978

A Guide to Children's Literature About the Needs and Problems of Youth Aged 2-15

Sharon Spredemann Dreyer, M.Ed.

American Guidance Service, Circle Pines, Minnesota 55014

International Standard Book Number 0-913476-46-3

Printed in the United States of America

CONTENTS

INTRODUCTION

A GUIDE TO
CHILDREN'S LITERATURE
ABOUT THE NEEDS AND PROBLEMS
OF YOUTH AGED 2-15

ACKNOWLEDGMENTS

The *Bookfinder* represents the talents and efforts of many people. The following persons, especially, are acknowledged with gratitude:

Caroljean Wagner, Head of the Central Youth Library, Milwaukee Public Library, was the chief consultant throughout the development of both volumes of the *Bookfinder.* Her expertise, dedication, and enthusiasm were applied to identifying, organizing, and evaluating materials.

Marianna Markowetz, Curriculum Librarian, University of Wisconsin-Milwaukee, and Ervin S. Yanke, Coordinator of Elementary Education, West Allis-West Milwaukee Public Schools, acted as consultants, contributing valuable suggestions and criticism as the concept of the *Bookfinder* was researched and developed.

Carl Malmquist, M.D., psychiatrist in private practice, Minneapolis, reviewed the *Bookfinder* as it was developed, and offered constructive suggestions for expansion and clarification of the Subject Index.

Jane Laswell, Librarian, Bowling Green, Kentucky, advised the author on proper indexing and was responsible for the arrangement and cross-referencing of the *Bookfinder* indexes and the Publishers/Producers Directory.

H. Reginald Laswell, Head of Library Automation and Technical Services, Western Kentucky University, Bowling Green, thoroughly researched the great amount of recent material about bibliotherapy and the psychology of reading.

Staff members at the Library for the Blind and Physically Handicapped, Milwaukee, Wisconsin, helped identify the books available in materials for blind and physically handicapped persons.

Many librarians made extra efforts to locate and lend the books reviewed and indexed in the *Bookfinder.* The staff at the Milwaukee Public Library was extraordinarily helpful, as were the staffs at the New Berlin Public Library, Frank Lloyd Wright Junior High School (West Allis), Oak Creek Public Library, all in Wisconsin, and the Western Kentucky University Library.

Children's book editors and subsidiary-rights departments of over 65 publishing companies graciously worked to identify which of the publications listed in the *Bookfinder* are also available in other printed or audiovisual media. They also supplied hundreds of books for review.

Sixteen people who participated in a field trial during the spring of 1974 — teachers, librarians, counselors, and psychologists from the Milwaukee metropolitan area — provided reactions and suggestions in the initial stages of the development of the *Bookfinder.* Participants were Carol Bahr, Shirley Conlon, Delma Erickson, Suzanne Felan, Dorothy Frana, Ruth George, Bernice Harper, Patricia Hoppe, Stanley Ladich, Marilee McMullen, Marianna Markowetz, Marion Pagenkipf, John Peters, John Ricci, Ellen Rubin, and Kathleen Rudes.

Professionals in sixteen field-test sites contributed valuable suggestions during the spring of 1976 to help refine the publication. They were:

Georgia Bouda, Children's Librarian, Mill Road Public Library, Milwaukee, Wisconsin.

Jim Bray, Children's Librarian, Rochester Public Library, Rochester, Minnesota.

Betty Charley, Children's Librarian, Minot Public Library, Minot, North Dakota.

Shirley Conlon, Librarian, Irving Elementary School, West Allis, Wisconsin.

Eleanore Donnelly, Coordinator of Branch Services, London Public Library and Art Museum, London, Ontario, Canada.

Suzanne Felan, Assistant Principal, Richfield Elementary School, Richfield, Wisconsin.

Ruth George, Children's Librarian, Atkinson Public Library, Milwaukee, Wisconsin.

Donna Goff, Director of Day Care Services, Child Development Centers of Minnesota, St. Paul, Minnesota.

Joseph Hallein, Chief Librarian/Lecturer, School of Library and Information Science, The University of Western Ontario, London, Ontario, Canada.

Kathleen Israel, Coordinator, Adult and Children's Services, Windsor Public Library, Windsor, Ontario, Canada.

Margaret E. Johnston, Coordinator of Boys and Girls Resources, Boys and Girls House, The Toronto Public Library, Toronto, Ontario, Canada.

Amy Kellman, Reviewer of Books for Children, *Teacher Magazine*, Pittsburgh, Pennsylvania.

Marilee McMullen, Librarian, Frank Lloyd Wright Junior High School, West Allis, Wisconsin.

John Ricci, Coordinator of Pupil Services, West Allis-West Milwaukee Public Schools, Wisconsin.

MaryLett Robertson, School Library Media Specialist, West Hills Elementary School, Knoxville, Tennessee.

Mary Claire Sherman, Coordinator, Library/Media Services, Juneau School District, Douglas, Alaska.

JoAnn Urlocker, Head of Central Children's Branch, London Public Library and Art Museum, London, Ontario, Canada.

Phillis M. Wilson, Director, Rochester Public Library, Rochester, Minnesota.

Everett Chard, Susan Busch, Sharon Franklin, Merille Glover, April Knudson, Patty Mamula, Judith Melquist, and Diane Wachter read and summarized hundreds of children's books.

Erik Wensberg, freelance editor, New York, edited all of the annotations. He is an artist with words.

Verona Ufford spent many hours on *Bookfinder* correspondence, and deciphered and typed all of the edited manuscript.

Finally, my gratitude and appreciation to the entire staff at American Guidance Service. No one has ever worked with a more cooperative, talented group of people. They truly dedicate themselves and their talents to producing quality educational materials.

AN INTRODUCTION
TO THE BOOKFINDER

Bookfinder 2 *begins where* Bookfinder 1 *leaves off, indexing and reviewing 723 children's books published from 1975 through 1978. It maintains the same easy indexing system and format, and offers new, incisive annotations.* Bookfinder 2 *expands the Subject Index to include contemporary topics — aging, harassment, prostitution, rape — reflected in recent children's literature. Widely reviewed and acclaimed by professionals and lay persons who work with children,* Bookfinder 1 *remains a vital reference for school and public libraries, churches, YMCAs, YWCAs, psychologists, psychiatrists, social service agencies, and other groups and individuals who work with children and young people.* Bookfinder 2 *is its perfect companion.*

Written words have influenced the attitudes, decisions, and behavior of humankind since the beginning of recorded history. An inscription over a library in ancient Thebes proclaimed it "the Healing Place of the Soul." The written word has also been credited with less benign effects: Abraham Lincoln once greeted Harriet Beecher Stowe, author of *Uncle Tom's Cabin,* as "the little lady who wrote the book that made this big war."

Books have an important role in everyday life. Through well-chosen books, readers may increase their self-knowledge and self-esteem, gain relief from unconscious conflicts, clarify their values, and better understand other people. By identifying with characters in books, people may come to realize that they are part of humanity, that they are not alone in their struggles with reality. Reading increases personal knowledge and invites readers to consider themselves objectively.

If children who are experiencing difficulties can read about others who have solved similar problems, they may see alternatives for themselves. By presenting possible solutions, books can help prevent some difficult situations from becoming full-blown problems. Through encountering frustrations and anxieties, hopes and disappointments, successes and failures in fictional situations, youngsters may gain insights applicable to situations they meet in real life. Both volumes of the *Bookfinder: A Guide to Children's Literature About the Needs and Problems of Youth* were developed with these effects in mind.

Bookfinder 2 is a reference work that describes and categorizes 723 current children's books according to more than 450 psychological, behavioral, and developmental topics of concern to children and young adolescents, aged 2 through 15. It is written primarily for parents, teachers, librarians, counselors, psychologists, psychiatrists, and other adults who want to identify books that may help children cope with the challenges of life. In short, the *Bookfinder* was created to fill the need for a way to match children and books.

Bibliotherapy

As people became aware that the written word could influence behavior, they began to develop ways to apply this power. During the first half of the nineteenth century, American doctors Benjamin Rush and John Minson Galt II recommended reading as part of the treatment for patients physically and/or mentally ill. During the early 1900s, French psychiatrist Pierre Janet believed that patients could be helped toward a better life through assigned readings. The term 'bibliotherapy' was first used by Samuel McChord Crothers in a 1916 *Atlantic Monthly* article. More recently, in the 1930s, Doctors Karl and William Menninger advocated the use of literature in the treatment of their patients. Publications by the two brothers encouraged others, both professional and lay people, to use literature to help solve problems and promote coping behavior.

Bibliotherapy, the use of reading material to help solve emotional problems and to promote mental health, was used with military personnel during both world wars and with civilians in rehabilitation hospitals, tuberculosis sanatoriums, and general hospitals. Schools have used books and stories as "social helpers" for over a century.

During the last 40 years, many theses and dissertations have been written about various aspects of bibliotherapy. One of the most significant, by Caroline Shrodes in 1949, was especially important in establishing the background for much of the recent research into the theory and practice of bibliotherapy and the psychology of reading. Bibliotherapy continues to grow in popularity, with more research being done, more articles and papers being published. A number of colleges and universities offer class work, conduct seminars, and provide practicum experiences for people interested in learning more about the process and practice, the methods and materials of bibliotherapy.

If youngsters who are experiencing difficulties can read about children who have encountered and solved similar problems, they may see hope for themselves. For example, young children suffering the loss of a loved one may feel comforted after Jennifer Bartoli's *Nonna* is read aloud and discussed with them. Older children may receive comfort after reading and discussing Earl Grollman's *Talking About Death* or Peggy Mann's *There Are Two Kinds of Terrible.* Children who feel responsible for their parents' divorce may come to terms with their feelings of guilt after reading Terry Berger's *How Does It Feel When Your Parents Get Divorced?* or Eda LeShan's *What's Going to Happen to Me? When Parents Separate or Divorce.* Children may also become better equipped for tomorrow's challenges by meeting similar challenges in today's reading. For example, children who read about Adam as he enters first grade in Bernard Wolf's *Adam Smith Goes to School* may find their own adjustment to a new school much easier. Children who have read Charlotte Herman's *Our Snowman Had Olive Eyes* or Toby Talbot's *Dear Greta Garbo* may adjust better when a grandparent moves in with the family.

Three main steps are usually present in the process of bibliotherapy:

1. **Universalization and identification.** From their reading, children come to see that they are not the only persons with particular fears, frustrations, worries, or living conditions. Recognizing similarities between themselves and fictional or biographical characters, they see themselves in those characters and thus may work out their problems vicariously.

Identification is not limited to a reader's identification of self with a story character. A child may also see his or her own mother, father, or other important person in the story. As a result, the child may develop a better understanding and appreciation of the real person.

Children may identify with characters in animal stories as well as with fictional human beings, when the animals have believable human characteristics. Children's reactions to James Marshall's picture books about George and Martha, two hippopotamuses, are examples. Children readily identify with these two animal friends who experience the same feelings, expectations, and companionship typical of childhood friendships.

When the parents, older siblings, and peers in a child's life are inappropriate models of behavior, characters in books may fill that child's need for an ego ideal.

2. **Catharsis.** A child who identifies with a fictional character lives through situations and shares feelings with that character. This vicarious experience may produce a release of tension or an imitation of the character's behavior. (When this happens, it is important that the child have someone with whom to discuss the reading, either individually or in a group.)

An advantage of reading as a therapeutic experience is that it does not force a child to participate. If the fictional situation becomes too intense, too stimulating, too painful, the reader can back off and assume the role of observer. Control rests with the reader, not with someone else. This sort of self-direction is reassuring and can help the child learn to look at problems objectively.

3. **Insight.** Through reading, children may become more aware of human motivations and of rationalizations for their own behavior. They may develop a more realistic view of their abilities and self-worth.

Because the written word tends to carry a special kind of authority, children who feel doubt and suspicion toward adults and peers tend to be less doubtful and suspicious of books. Authors of fiction generally become trusted, because they rarely impose judgment explicitly.

Thus books can become valuable companions to a developing child. Indeed, children often read beyond their tested reading levels in order to read about people faced with situations or problems similar to their own. Adults who want to help children locate the most appropriate and therapeutic books should find the *Bookfinder* a handy guide.

Using the Bookfinder

Annotations of 723 children's books are the heart of *Bookfinder 2*. There are three ways to locate annotations of particular books:

1. Locate the desired subject in the Subject Index. Under the subject heading, identify the most promising books listed. Then refer to the annotations section below to find summaries of those books.

2. Locate the author's name in the Author Index. Identify the desired book and then refer to the annotations for the book summary.

3. Locate the book title in the Title Index. Identify its author and then refer to the annotations for the book summary.

The *Bookfinder*'s split-page format allows the user to leave any of the three indexes open to a particular page while leafing through the annotations. For quick and easy reference, the annotations are arranged alphabetically by author's last name; they are also numbered sequentially.

Each annotation contains the following information:

1. The *bibliographic information* includes the author's complete name. Any pseudonyms are noted. Annotations of books that have been translated into English from another language name the translator and the language of the original publication. Information about illustrations and photographs includes the name of the artist and whether the illustrations or photographs are in black and white or in color. The name of the publisher appears for each book. (All publishers' addresses* are listed in the Publishers/Producers Directory, located after the indexes.) The book's original copyright date is listed; or, in the case of a translation, the date of the original United States copyright is listed. A book that has already gone out of print is indicated by "o.p." following the copyright date. Some out-of-print titles are included because many libraries already have them on their shelves, and it is always possible that an out-of-print title will be reprinted. Also indicated are the number of pages in the book. If the book's pages have not been numbered, the total number of printed pages is indicated by a number followed by the word "counted."

2. The *main subject heading,* or primary theme of the book, is printed in upper-case letters near the top of each annotation. Significant secondary themes are listed alphabetically in lower-case letters under the main subject heading.

3. The first paragraph of each annotation is a *synopsis* of the book. It introduces the main character and describes the plot and the character relationships that provide the main and secondary themes. Whenever possible, the main

---

*With cross-referencing to current names in cases where publishing companies have merged or changed their names.

character's name, sex, and age or grade level are mentioned in the first sentence of the synopsis. Race, culture, religion, and social class of the characters are indicated only when they are pertinent issues in the story. Each summary is carried through to the conclusion of the story.

4. The second paragraph of each annotation is usually a *commentary* that restates the book's main message and indicates strengths or limitations of the way the message is presented. Potential uses of the book may also be suggested. Literary merit, special qualifications of the author, sequels, and the significance of illustrations or photographs may be mentioned here. Points of special concern or interest (such as premeditated violence, explicit sex, controversial language) are also mentioned.

5. A *general reading level* is indicated at or near the end of the annotation. Often, children within the stated age range will be interested in and able to read the book independently or with minimal help. All of the books listed for preschool children, and many of the books listed for primary-age children, are read-aloud volumes.

6. The final element of each annotation is information about *other forms of the publication,* such as films, tapes, paperbound editions, and materials for blind or other physically handicapped people.

Application

The person who wants to use books to help children understand the challenges and problems of growing up need not be a professional counselor. Indeed, the main qualifications are an interest in and a concern for children and a willingness to become familiar with children's literature. Reading guidance can be a simple procedure. Of course, professional therapeutic skills are necessary if the child's problem is severe. But in general, the *Bookfinder* can be used to good effect by nearly everyone who works with children.

Parents are in an ideal position to use the *Bookfinder* to help their children cope with new situations. Consider the following examples: Four-year-old Timmy is scheduled to see the doctor for an examination; his symptoms indicate that surgery might be necessary. Timmy's parents tell him of the planned visit to the doctor but never mention the possibility of surgery or going to the hospital. They intend to wait until the doctor has made a definite diagnosis. But when Timmy tells his playmates about his appointment with the doctor, they eagerly embellish their own experiences and what they have heard about doctors, hospitals, and surgery. A very frightened little boy comes home and announces, "I may go to the doctor's office, but I'm not going to any hospital!" Acknowledging his fears, Timmy's parents refer to the *Bookfinder* for stories about hospitals. At Timmy's level of understanding, they find Harriet Langsam Sobol's *Jeff's Hospital Book,* which describes a young child's surgery and hospital stay. Timmy's parents read the book to him and candidly discuss the story and the photographs. Several days later, when Timmy's doctor does confirm the need for surgery, Timmy confidently tells his friends, "I'm going to the hospital to have an operation."

Another family has two children, both adopted — a five-year-old boy and a three-year-old girl. The parents want the children to know that they were adopted and have told them about their adoption several times. One day, with help from their parents and the *Bookfinder,* the children find Valentina Wasson's *The Chosen Baby* at the public library. The children ask their parents to read it aloud again and again; it is their favorite book, "about kids just like us." The boy eagerly shares the book with his friends, and both children learn to accept themselves and their situation.

A child can more easily understand and accept other difficult experiences — death of a loved person or pet, parental divorce, transfer to a new school, arrival of a new baby in the family, and various other fears — through reading about similar situations. The child's parents can use the

Bookfinder to find an appropriate book. In sharing that book and in expressing feelings about the story, family members can increase their understanding of themselves and others. This appreciation can, in turn, lead to stronger and more trusting relationships.

School and public librarians may find the *Bookfinder* useful for helping children find books to meet their individual needs, and for helping parents, teachers, and other professionals find materials appropriate for special needs of an individual or group. For example, an elementary school is about to include handicapped children in existing classes — mainstreaming. To help the students in the school understand the feelings and needs, the strengths and limitations of handicapped children, the librarian and teachers refer to the *Bookfinder* and identify appropriate books. Several of the books are read aloud and discussed in classes. Others are attractively displayed, encouraging students to do additional reading on their own. The insights the students derive from these books may increase their effectiveness in helping their handicapped classmates feel comfortable in the new surroundings.

Public librarians frequently have specific requests — from children, parents, teachers, and other adults who work with children — for books about particular concerns, attitudes, and developmental tasks. A librarian, sensing that some children have interests or concerns that they prefer not to talk about, puts a copy of the Bookfinder on top of the card catalog. A poster, mounted above it, invites students to peruse the index on their own, to find books of personal interest.

Librarians in children's hospitals have a special role as they work with medical professionals to meet the emotional and physical needs of sick children. Hospital librarians usually seek books that promote understanding and acceptance of hospital routines and medical procedures. Lengthy and depressing hospital confinement can be made brighter and more hopeful through carefully prescribed reading.

Teachers are in a good position to match books with children's needs and concerns. A kindergarten teacher who knows that one of her or his students has had a new baby join the family may see that child is having trouble adjusting. Consulting the *Bookfinder,* the teacher may choose Gunilla Wolde's *Betsy's Baby Brother* as a read-aloud story. The teacher can then invite the children to share their experiences with the class. They can compare their feelings with those of Betsy and consider some of the happy aspects of having a new baby at home. After such reading and discussion, a youngster is likely to become more patient and less jealous of the new sibling than before.

Teachers can often promote students' understanding of themselves and others through books, by reading aloud to the class or by encouraging independent reading. This reading can be enjoyable when books are chosen with reader interests and needs in mind. Then readers are likely to want to read more, and reading skills will probably improve in the process.

For example, a teacher has the class agree on one topic of interest — aging, fear, prejudice, sibling relationships — locate the topic in the *Bookfinder,* and select books to read individually. The teacher then chooses one especially pertinent book to read aloud to the class. After all the reading is completed, discussion and other activities are organized to integrate ideas from the children's varied reading experiences.

A teacher divides the class into small groups with each group first selecting a topic of interest, finding the topic in the *Bookfinder,* and then choosing a book (or books) to be read within the group. As the books are read, groups discuss them. When the reading is completed, each group prepares a culminating activity to present to the class.

The following are examples of thought-provoking activities that can follow the reading: role-playing, dramatization, mock interview with the book's main character, bulletin boards, recordings, films, filmstrips, supplemental reading lists, and radio and television programs related to the reading. Teachers can read open-ended stories. Or they can stop reading a story just short of the conclusion and ask the class to end the story. (The teacher should then finish reading the story to the class so students can compare their conclusion with the author's.)

Teachers who read aloud to their classes have many opportunities for discussing how a character felt about something or why the character made particular decisions. Good questions and discussions can broaden students' decision-making abilities and increase their understanding of other people.

A teacher who knows that a child has a problem might introduce the child to a book about "someone who was very much like you" or "someone who also . . . ." Or, to be more subtle, teachers can introduce, to the whole class, that book and other books the class might enjoy. If the teacher sees the troubled child reading one of the suggested books, the teacher might show a willingness to discuss the book with the child.

The school counselor can work with the teacher and the librarian to select books for special study units — for example, on friendship, courage, fear, or other pertinent topics. Counselors working with individual children or small groups of children can choose books to suit personal needs. For example, a new student is transferring into the school. The counselor consults the *Bookfinder,* selects several appropriate titles, and suggests that the new student might like to read about others who have experienced the same kind of change. Reading about someone else in the same situation may provide some hints for making the adjustment easier.

The school counselor can use the *Bookfinder* to help students in individual or group counseling select appropriate reading to be done between counseling sessions. Such reading can extend the counseling experience and serve as a point of reference for beginning the next counseling session.

The foregoing examples are meant to show how children might face everyday problems — as well as more severe problems — more confidently if they have also faced them vicariously, through books. The use of books to help children can be simple or complex, depending on the children's needs and on the confidence and background of the adults who want to help. Parents, teachers, librarians, and counselors and other mental health specialists may find the *Bookfinder* useful. So may nurses, providers of day care, scout leaders, recreation leaders, camp counselors, church youth leaders — and anyone else in a position to help youngsters expand their understanding, tolerance, and ability to cope with the challenges of life.

DEVELOPMENT OF THE BOOKFINDER

The *Bookfinder* was conceived in 1968 as a supplement to the author's thesis for the master's degree. The bibliography then included over 300 books for children ages 9 through 15. The need for easy access to children's literature about developmental problems became more apparent, and the author decided to update, expand, and reorganize the original bibliography.

Formal development of the *Bookfinder* was initiated in 1973. It began with an extensive new review of current children's literature.

Book Selection

All available bibliographies and children's book review sources were examined in the search for appropriate books. Children's book publishers submitted hundreds of books for the author to consider. Books familiar to the author, consultants, and field-trial participants were considered, as were books within the collection of the Central

Youth Library in Milwaukee. For *Bookfinder 2*, over 2500 books were reviewed in the selection process.

All of the books annotated in *Bookfinder 2* were published between 1975 and 1978. (*Bookfinder 1* covers books published through 1974.) Books published after 1978 are not included because they could not be reviewed properly before *Bookfinder 2* was printed. In addition, the selected books were required to be in print in hardbound form and to be available through ordinary means: libraries, bookstores, book jobbers, and publishers. (The paperbound *More Time to Grow* by Sharon Hya Grollman is also included because it is part of a series.)

Timeliness and appropriateness of content were other important criteria. Timely, "here and now" books are usually more helpful to children with problems than older books are, unless the older books speak to timeless issues. The selected books are, therefore, about the modern child or are so universal in appeal that the difference in time or place is unimportant.

The book plots and themes had to be carried through to resolution or presented completely enough to provoke thoughtful consideration or discussion. The characters had to be realistic. The problem faced by the characters had to be brought out clearly and explored without moralizing.

Artistic quality was also a consideration. Literary quality, although not the prime concern, had to be acceptable to the author of the *Bookfinder*. Where many books on a particular topic were available, only the best were selected for annotation. Illustrations or photographs also had to be of acceptable quality, appropriate to the story, and supportive of its message.

Despite the author's careful concern for proper book selection criteria, the selection of each book was necessarily a subjective process. Some users of the *Bookfinder* will disagree with the inclusion of some titles or will look in vain for some of their favorites.* But every user should find many pertinent and applicable books among the 723 entries, which represent more than 475 authors and 69 publishing companies.

Many picture books are included in the *Bookfinder*. They are not just cute stories; they have plots and characters that encourage reader identification. These books should help prepare young children for new experiences and new stages of development and help solve current problems.

About 60 percent of the books annotated in *Bookfinder 2* have main characters of the white middle class. This is a reflection on these authors' own choice of characters. A great effort was made to select books which are honest, realistic representations of people, and which treat characters' ethnic, religious, economic, or other social identity with intelligence and sensitivity.

The nature of existing children's literature is also reflected in the percentages of books included in *Bookfinder 2* for various age levels. About 35 percent of the books in *Bookfinder 2* are classified for ages 12 and up, 30 percent for ages 8 through 11, and 35 percent for ages 2 through 7.

The vast majority of the indexed books — about 90 percent — are fiction. About 10 percent are biography, and there are a few especially significant nonfiction publications.

Clues to meaningful book selection may come from knowledge of the child's home life, family, out-of-school activities, personal ambitions, and other interests. It is important also to consider the reader's vocabulary and comprehension levels, because children should not be forced to read beyond their skills. The reading should be a voluntary and pleasant experience — not another assignment.

---

*Bookfinder users are invited to send their comments and suggestions to the publisher: American Guidance Service, Inc., Publishers' Building, Circle Pines, Minnesota 55014.

Annotations

The first step in writing annotations was to categorize each book according to its main theme and any relevant sub-themes. For example, a subject heading *FRIENDSHIP: Best Friend* means that the plot of the book centers around the thoughts, feelings, and activities of people who regard themselves as best friends. Much care has been taken to ensure that the subject headings accurately indicate the content of the book.

What may appear as an obvious theme to some readers may seem less so to others. A concentrated effort has been made to define themes by asking, "Does this book offer enough information about a particular situation or problem to warrant recommending it to a child who is facing that situation or problem?" Beyond that guideline, only the user can determine whether a book is suitable for a specific child with a specific need. The *Bookfinder* was not developed to prescribe books for particular children; it was developed as a reference that categorizes and describes books as objectively as possible.

As the annotations were prepared, publishing information was carefully checked and rechecked for uniformity and accuracy. Discrepancies were found. Therefore, book titles with idiosyncratic capitalization have been given standard capitalization.

The original book publishers were asked to tell which of their publications listed in the *Bookfinder* are available in film, filmstrip, tape or cassette, record, paperbound, or large-print editions. If a book's subsidiary rights were retained by the author or the author's agent, there is no way that the book publisher would be aware of rights sold for other formats. Some books, therefore, may be available in other media not known to either the book's publisher or the *Bookfinder's* author. Although these are very recent materials, it is possible that some items may already be out of stock. Producers (addresses are included in the Publishers/ Producers Directory) should be contacted directly for further information. *Paperbound Books in Print* was also used to identify books available in paperbound form. Materials available for blind people — tapes, cassettes, talking books, Braille editions, and large-print volumes — were identified through the indexes and catalogs of the Library of Congress, Wisconsin Regional Library for the Blind and Physically Handicapped. (Most of these materials are available only through regional branches of the Library of Congress and can be obtained only by persons who are legally blind or physically handicapped. Questions regarding materials for blind and physically handicapped people should be directed to local public librarians, who can supply more information about the program and explain how to apply for service.)

Since descriptions of the plots, themes, and characters are meant to be of greatest service to the adult user, the book summaries have been written for adults. No deliberate attempt has been made to whet the reader's appetite. Nevertheless, a child with sixth-grade reading and comprehension skills could probably browse through the annotations and select books without adult assistance.

Subject Index

The Subject Index lists the primary and secondary themes of all the books in the *Bookfinder*. To compile the working Subject Index, the author, publisher, and project consultants identified over 600 topics they considered important to children and adolescents. Following final book selection for *Bookfinder 1*, the number of topics decreased to about 450. In the development of *Bookfinder 2*, some headings were deleted because no appropriate books were found to cover those themes in a significant manner. New headings were added, such as cults, hyperactivity, superstition, terminal illnesses, and importance of communication.

Field Test

Field testing of the *Bookfinder* took place during the spring of 1976 in six states — Alaska, Minnesota, North Dakota, Pennsylvania, Tennessee, and Wisconsin — and in the province of Ontario. Sixteen field-test sites provided information from four types of libraries: school, general public, college/consultant, and children's public. Each site was given a field-test version of the annotated bibliography, along with limited subject, author, and title indexes and 453 rough-draft annotations. Parents, counselors, teachers, librarians, and psychologists were asked to review this material, and their comments contributed to the refinement of the *Bookfinder*. Psychiatrists and supervising librarians also suggested ways to make the *Bookfinder* more useful.

BOOK SELECTION AIDS

For more help in finding appropriate children's books, the reader may want to use the following references, many of which include titles not found in the *Bookfinder*. *Bookfinder* titles that are included in these references are reviewed from various points of view or for purposes that may differ from the *Bookfinder*'s. Titles preceded by an asterisk (*) are more recent, and thus did not appear in the *Bookfinder 1* Book Selection Aids bibliography.

Altshuler, Anne. *Books That Help Deal with a Hospital Experience*, Rockville, Maryland: United States Department of Health, Education and Welfare, 1974. (Available through Superintendent of Documents, United States Government Printing Office, Washington, D.C. 20402)

This 22-page pamphlet is a comprehensive guide to children's literature about hospitals, illnesses, and the medical procedures children might encounter. A brief introduction explains how books can be used to reassure children facing what is often a traumatic experience. This pamphlet lists and annotates 49 books and pamphlets for preschool and elementary children, including pamphlets not indexed elsewhere, such as the Children's Hospital of Philadelphia publication *Michael's Heart Test*.

Association of Hospital and Institution Libraries. *Bibliotherapy: Methods and Materials*. Chicago: American Library Association, 1971.

The first 66 pages of this paperbound volume review the background and techniques of bibliotherapy, especially as it pertains to the hospital library. Extensive professional bibliographies are included. The second part of the book contains a well-annotated bibliography of literature for children in the middle grades through junior high school: Books for the Troubled Child and Adolescent. This bibliography is divided into such sections as Adjusting to Physical Handicaps, Sibling and Peer Relationships, The Value of Education and the Dropout, and Parents with Problems.

*Baskin, Barbara H. and Karen H. Harris. *Notes from a Different Drummer: A Guide to Juvenile Fiction Portraying the Handicapped*. New York: R. R. Bowker Company, 1977.

This guide to children's literature about mentally and/or physically handicapped people is divided into five main sections. The first four discuss handicapped people in society and literature, evaluate children's fiction and its application, and investigate patterns and trends in children's fiction, 1940-1975. A fifth section summarizes and evaluates 311 books written between 1940 and 1975. A broad-range reading level (e.g., YC — Young Child; MC — Mature Child) is given for each entry.

*Bernstein, Joanne E. *Books to Help Children Cope with Separation and Loss*. New York: R. R. Bowker Company, 1977.

The introduction to this reference describes how the bibliography was compiled, discusses separation and loss as they relate to children, and defines and explains bibliotherapy. The bibliography itself contains 438 titles, most of which are fiction, though some nonfiction is included. Each entry contains bibliographic information, reading interest and reading grade levels, and a comprehensive summary of plot. The entries are divided into three main categories — Learning to Face Separation, Coping with Tragic Loss, and "Who Will Take Care of Me?" Each of these is subdivided into more specific topics. The guide concludes with extensive professional bibliographies on separation and loss, and on bibliotherapy.

Eakin, Mary K., ed. *Good Books for Children, 3rd ed.: A Selection of Outstanding Books Published 1950-1965.* Chicago: The University of Chicago Press, 1966.

This publication indexes, reviews, and suggests grade levels for 1,391 children's books that were originally included and recommended in the *Bulletin of the Center for Children's Books.* Most of the books are for children in grades 4 through 9. Some of the topics included in the subject index are: adaptability, bedtime, exaggeration, houses, inventions, security, and value-building.

Feminists on Children's Media. *Little Miss Muffet Fights Back.* New York, 1971. (Available through Feminists on Children's Literature, P.O. Box 4315, Grand Central Station, New York 10017)

This 48-page pamphlet is a bibliography of children's literature selected for its "positive and nonstereotyped portrayal of girls and women." Each book is briefly annotated, and the collection is divided into fifteen categories, including Fiction, From the Past, Science Fiction, and Sex Education.

*Gillespie, John T. *More Junior Plots: A Guide for Teachers and Librarians.* New York: R. R. Bowker Company, 1977.

This guide describes 72 books for children aged 11 through 16 years. Books are arranged according to nine developmental goals related to adolescence. These include: Getting Along in the Family, Developing Lasting Values, Understanding Social Problems, Understanding Physical and Emotional Problems, Becoming Self-Reliant, and Developing a Wholesome Self-Image. Each entry includes bibliographic information, plot summary, discussion of themes within the book, techniques for "book talks," suggestions for other uses or activities (additional similar books are listed here), and information about the author.

*Gillis, Ruth J. *Children's Books for Times of Stress: An Annotated Bibliography.* Bloomington: Indiana University Press, 1978.

This is an index of 261 books published between 1932 and 1976 for children preschool age through age nine. (Many titles are from the 1970s.) Each entry includes bibliographic information, description of plot or contents, and an evaluation of the book. Each entry also lists professional sources where the book has been reviewed. Seven broad headings — Behavior, Family, Difficult Situations, New Situations, Self Concept, Friendship, and Emotions — are divided into subheadings.

Kircher, Clara J., ed. *Behavior Patterns in Children's Books: A Bibliography.* Washington, D.C.: The Catholic University of America Press, 1966.

This bibliography indexes and briefly annotates 507 books for children of preschool age through grade 9. Although many books in the bibliography are now out of print, this is a good reference for older library collections. Books are divided into 24 broad categories, including Little Problems of Small Children, Acceptance of Things as They Are, Making Friends, and Orphans and Adopted Children.

*Lass-Woodfin, Mary Jo, ed. *Books on American Indians and Eskimos: A Selection Guide for Children and Young Adults.* Chicago: American Library Association, 1978.

Reviews of 807 children's books written before 1977 are included in this reference. In addition to bibliographic information and estimated reading grade level, each entry has a summary of content, comments on possible uses, comments on strengths and weaknesses in "writing, accuracy, format, and feel," and a rating of Good, Adequate, or Poor. Two persons reviewed each book; where opinions differed, both points of view are included.

*McDonough, Irma, ed. *Canadian Books for Young People/Livres Canadiens Pour La Jeunesse.* Toronto: University of Toronto Press, 1978.

This revised index includes Canadian children's books (preschool age through age 9) written in English and/or French. All of these books were in print at the time the reference was printed. Each entry includes bibliographic information and an annotative sentence. The reference is divided into two sections: the first lists books in English; the second (written in French) lists books in French. Books are organized in such categories as Picture Books, Sports and Recreation, and Fiction: Stories, Fantasy, and Historical Fiction.

*Mills, Joyce White, ed. *The Black World in Literature: A Bibliography of Print and Non-Print Materials.* Atlanta, GA: School of Library Service of Atlanta University, 1975.

This 42-page booklet indexes and briefly annotates children's books published in 1974 and 1975 about black people in the United States and Africa. Each book is rated Highly Recommended, Recommended, or Not Recommended. Audiovisual titles are interfiled with book titles and briefly described, but not rated. The bibliography is divided into two sections: For Younger Children, ages 3-8; and For Older Children, ages 9-13. Nine subdivisions within these sections include Picture and Easy Books, Biography, Folklore, History, and Junior Fiction. A list of adult reference sources is included.

*Mills, Joyce White, ed. *The Black World in Literature: A Bibliography of Print and Non-Print Materials.* Vol. 2. Atlanta, GA: School of Library Service of Atlanta University, 1976.

This 45-page booklet indexes and briefly annotates children's books published in 1975 and 1976 about black people. It does not duplicate any entries from the 1975 edition (see above) but has the same format, subject headings, and rating system, and lists audiovisual materials and adult reference sources.

Reid, Virginia M., ed. *Reading Ladders for Human Relations.* 5th ed. Washington, D.C., American Council on Education, 1972.

This reference was compiled to help teachers, librarians, and other adults select appropriate reading material for children and young people. Books are briefly annotated, divided into age levels — primary, intermediate, junior, and senior — and arranged in four "Reading Ladders": Creating a Positive Self-Image, Appreciating Different Cultures, Living with Others, and Coping with Change. Each Ladder has several subheadings. The introduction contains an explanation of the purpose of this reference and suggestions for using books with children and young people to help promote the development of "positive human relationships."

Rollock, Barbara, ed. *The Black Experience in Children's Books.* New York: The New York Public Library, 1974.

This comprehensive bibliography of Black literature includes books for children and books to be shared by children and adults. It covers "a wide range of subjects reflecting the social, political, and economic contributions Blacks are making in this country (USA) and in the developing nations in Africa." Entries are briefly annotated.

*Spirit, Diana L. *Introducing More Books: A Guide for the Middle Grades.* New York: R. R. Bowker, 1978.

This reference includes plot summaries of 72 books and lists additional related materials for each entry for reading, viewing, and listening. Altogether, about 500 titles are mentioned. Books are listed according to nine developmental goals for children aged 8 through 14. Among these goals are: Understanding Social Problems, Understanding Physical and Emotional Problems, Developing Values, and Making Friends. Each entry includes bibliographic information and a paragraph of thematic analysis followed by material for discussion and other related materials.

Sutherland, Zena, ed. *The Best in Children's Books.* Chicago: The University of Chicago Press, 1973.

This is a collection of 1,400 book reviews previously published in the *Bulletin of the Center for Children's Books.* Most of the books were rated as "recommended" reading. The entries are listed alphabetically by the author's name and are categorized in several indexes. Its section on developmental values may aid book selection.

*Wilkin, Binnie Tate. *Survival Themes in Fiction for Children and Young People.* Metuchen, NJ: The Scarecrow Press, 1978.

This reference, which has comments and suggestions interspersed in the list of titles, divides entries into three main areas — The Individual, Pairings and Groupings, and Views of the World — which are then subdivided. The author believes "that a realistic presentation of human existence will help them [children] develop their own capabilities in problem solving." The books selected (some nonfiction is included) "are intended as samples that offer certain sensitivity to some of the individual and societal issues of the day." Bibliographic information is followed by a short summary of the book. Most titles included are from the 1970s.

Yonkers Public Library Children's Service. *A Guide to Subjects and Concepts in Picture Book Format.* New York: Oceana, 1974.

This extensive bibliography contains titles of picture books — ones with words and ones without words. No attempt is made to annotate books or to indicate which books are out of print, although many old editions are listed. The reference is divided into broad topic headings with some subheadings. Among the topics are: animals, babies, character traits, family relations, and growing problems.

*Yonkers Public Library Children's Service. *A Guide to Subjects and Concepts in Picture Book Format.* 2d ed. New York: Oceana, 1979.

This comprehensive bibliography indexes picture books — those with and without words. None of the books is annotated. It includes books printed before 1978, most of which were in print in 1977; a few out of print titles are included and are labeled "o.p." Some of the broad subject headings included are: animals, babies, character traits, emotions, family relations, and growing problems.

PROFESSIONAL READINGS

This bibliography includes professional books and articles that describe, analyze, and apply bibliotherapy. Titles preceded by an asterisk (*) are more recent, and thus did not appear in the *Bookfinder 1* Professional Readings bibliography.

Brown, Eleanor Frances. *Bibliotherapy and Its Widening Applications.* Metuchen, NJ: The Scarecrow Press, 1975.

Carner, Charles. "Reaching Troubled Minds Through Reading." *Today's Health* 44 (1966): 32-33, 75-77.

Cianciolo, Patricia Jean. "Children's Literature Can Effect Coping Behavior." *Personnel and Guidance Journal* 43 (1965): 897-903.

Cianciolo, Patricia Jean. "Interaction Between the Personality of the Reader and Literature." *School Libraries* 17 (1968): 13-17, 19-21.

Darling, R. L. "Mental Hygiene and Books." *Wilson Library* Bulletin 32 (1957): 293-296.

Edwards, Beverly Sigler. "The Therapeutic Value of Reading." *Elementary English* 49 (1972): 213-218.

Gray, Maxine. "Books — Another Use in Our Classroom." *Education* 79 (1959): 487-490.

Hartley, Helene W. "Developing Personality Through Books." *The English Journal* 40 (1951): 198-204.

*Heitzmann, Kathleen E. and William Ray Heitzmann. "Science of Bibliotherapy: A Critical Review of Research Findings." *Reading Improvement* 12 (1975): 120-124.

Hoagland, Joan. "Bibliotherapy: Aiding Children in Personality Development." *Elementary English* 49 (1972): 390-394.

Lejeune, Archie L. "Bibliocounseling as a Guidance Technique." *Catholic Library World* 41 (1969): 156-164.

*Lenkowsky, Barbara E. and Ronald S. Lenkowsky. "Bibliotherapy for the LD Adolescent." *Academic Therapy* 14 (1978): 179-185.

Lindahl, Hannah M., and Katharine Koch. "Bibliotherapy in the Middle Grades." *Elementary English* 29 (1952): 390-396.

Lunsteen, Sara W. "A Thinking Improvement Program Through Literature." *Elementary English* 49 (1972): 505-512.

Monroe, Margaret E. *Reading Guidance and Bibliotherapy in Public, Hospital, and Institutional Libraries.* Madison: Library School of the University of Wisconsin, 1971.

*Monroe, Margaret E., ed. *Seminar on Bibliotherapy.* Madison: Library School of the University of Wisconsin, 1978.

Moses, Harold A., and Joseph S. Zaccaria. "Bibliotherapy in an Educational Context: Rationale and Principles." *In Advances in Librarianship,* vol. 1, edited by Melvin J. Voigt. New York: Academic Press, 1970.

Newell, Ethel. "At the North End of Pooh: A Study of Bibliotherapy." *Elementary English* 34 (1957): 22-25.

*Nickerson, Eileen T. "Bibliotherapy: A Therapeutic Medium for Helping Children." *Psychotherapy: Theory, Research and Practice* 12 (1975): 258-261.

Olsen, Henry D. "Bibliotherapy to Help Children Solve Problems." *Elementary School Journal* 75 (1975): 423-429.

Rongione, Louis A. "Bibliotherapy: Its Nature and Uses." *Catholic Library World* 43 (1972): 495-500.

Rubin, Dorothy. "Bibliotherapy: Reading Towards Mental Health." *Children's House* 9 (1976): 6-9.

*Rubin, Rhea Joyce. *Bibliotherapy: A Guide to Theory and Practice.* Phoenix, AZ: The Oryx Press, 1978.

*Rubin, Rhea Joyce, ed. *Bibliotherapy Sourcebook.* Phoenix, AZ: The Oryx Press, 1978.

*Russell, Alma E. and William A. Russell. "Using Bibliotherapy with Emotionally Disturbed Children." *Teaching Exceptional Children* 11 (1979): 168-169.

Russell, David H. "Reading and the Healthy Personality." *Elementary English* 29 (1952): 195-200.

Russell, David H., and Caroline Shrodes. "Contributions of Research in Bibliotherapy to the Language Arts Program, I." *School Review* 58 (1950): 335-342.

Russell, David H., and Caroline Shrodes. "Contributions of Research in Bibliotherapy to the Language Arts Program, II." *School Review* 58 (1950): 411-420.

Sanders, Jacquelyn. "Psychological Significance of Children's Literature." *Library Trends* 37 (1967): 15-22.

Schwoebel, Barbara. "Bibliotherapy: A Guide to Materials." *Catholic Library World* 44 (1973): 586-592.

Sclabassi, Sharon Henderson. "Literature as a Therapeutic Tool: A Review of the Literature on Bibliotherapy." *American Journal of Psychotherapy* 27 (1973): 70-77.

Shepherd, Terry, and Lynn B. Iles. "What is Bibliotherapy?" *Language Arts* 53 (1976): 569-571.

Shrodes, Caroline. "Bibliotherapy." *The Reading Teacher* 9 (1955): 24-29.

Spache, George D. *Good Reading for Poor Readers.* 9th rev. ed. Champaign, Ill.: Garrard Publishing, 1974. Chapter 3, "Using Books to Help Solve Children's Problems."

Strunk, Orlo, Jr. "Bibliotherapy Revisited." *Journal of Religion and Health* 11 (1972): 218-228.

*Tartagni, Donna. "Using Bibliotherapy with Adolescents." *School Counselor* 24 (1976): 28-35.

Tews, Ruth M. "Progress in Bibliotherapy." *In Advances in Librarianship,* vol. 1, edited by Melvin J. Voigt. New York: Academic Press, 1970.

Tews, Ruth M., ed. "Bibliotherapy." *Library Trends* 11, No. 2 (October 1962). Entire issue.

Tiller, Karen. "Bibliotherapy and the Treatment of Emotional Disturbances." *Catholic Library World* 45 (1974): 428-431.

*Wass, Hannelore and Judith Shaak. "Helping Children Understand Death Through Literature." *Childhood Education* 53 (1976): 80-85.

Witty, Paul. "Promoting Growth and Development Through Reading." *Elementary English* 27 (1950): 493-500, 556.

Witty, Paul. "Reading to Meet Emotional Needs." *Elementary English* 29 (1952): 75-84.

Zaccaria, Joseph S., and Harold A. Moses. *Facilitating Human Development Through Reading: The Use of* *Bibliotherapy in Teaching and Counseling.* Champaign, Ill.: Stipes Publishing, 1968.

ANNOTATIONS

A GUIDE TO
CHILDREN'S LITERATURE
ABOUT THE NEEDS AND PROBLEMS
OF YOUTH AGED 2-15

1

Aaron, Chester

Spill

Atheneum Publishers, 1977.
(214 pages) o.p.

FAMILY: Unity
  Animals: responsibility for
  Death: of friend
  Maturation
  Nature: appreciation of

His mother works at a wildlife ranch, and Judy, his fourteen-year-old sister, keeps a menagerie of recuperating animals, while his father runs the family sheep ranch — but what interests Jeff Taylor, fifteen, is the gang at the Mother Earth cafe. His father worries about this interest, fearing that Jeff will drift into drug-taking and "hippy" life. Curtis Gallagher leads the gang, and it is the death of Curtis's brother Tony in a car accident, with Curtis driving, that has led Jeff to withdraw from his family and former friends: Tony had been Jeff's best friend. For her part, Jeff's mother wishes that he and Judy, formerly close, would be so again and that Jeff and his father would be reconciled. Since Tony's death, Jeff has lost interest in wildlife, too, even in King Kong, a giant anemone the two friends had discovered and watched over in the lagoon. One night Jeff gets to missing his family and goes to check on the anemone. There he muses, too, on how much he has missed his wildlife study. That same night an oil freighter crashes into another ship and spills oil into San Francisco Bay. The next day volunteers pour into the nearby wildlife ranch to clean up after the spill. While Judy helps direct the cleaning of the oil-soaked birds, Jeff works on a boom to block the oil from entering the lagoon. Recalling her brother's beloved King Kong, Judy ventures to the reef to see to its safety but falls, breaking a leg, and is later rescued by helicopter. Meanwhile Jeff helps revive a man felled by a heart attack. Throughout all this he is amazed and disgusted by the indifference of Curtis and the Mother Earth crowd. No matter, he has found his family again. As for the future: "Where he was going he wasn't sure; he might not know for some time; and he could only hope he'd be content when he got there."

The catastrophe in this book is based on a real California oil spill in 1971, but the story is of a family that finds itself through working together to meet the emergency. Though Jeff is the central figure, the author shifts viewpoints among the family members to allow each to comment on the three-day action. The resulting portrayal of a family, with its strengths and weaknesses, is compelling. The narrative includes much information on the ecology of northern California and the measures required to clean up an oil spill.

Ages 12-14

Also available in:
No other form known

A

2

Adler, David A.

A Little at a Time

Black/white illustrations by N. M. Bodecker.
Random House, Inc., 1976.
(30 pages counted)

AGE: Respect for
GRANDPARENT: Love for
  Curiosity

A little boy, full of questions, is taken by his grandfather to visit a museum. Afterwards, the two stop for ice cream. But the boy's questions never stop. How did the tree get so tall? Why is the street so dirty? Were buildings always so high? To each query, Grandpa gives the same answer: everything grows or changes just "a little at a time." When the child speaks admiringly of Grandpa's wisdom, Grandpa assures him that this too came "a little at a time."

The rhythmical give and take between a boy and his grandfather in this all-dialogue story conveys a gentle, loving relationship. Their conversation will help small children to understand and think about the gradual passage of time.

Ages 4-6

Also available in:
No other form known

3

Adoff, Arnold

Big Sister Tells Me That I'm Black

Black/white illustrations by Lorenzo Lynch.
Holt, Rinehart and Winston, Inc., 1976.
(21 pages counted)

AFRO-AMERICAN
  Self, attitude toward: respect

A small boy's big sister tells him to be proud of brown- and tan-colored people, all those who are called black. She reminds him of the hoped-for future, when boys will become young men and girls young women, strong in their joy, proud in their race. Get on the track, she tells him, read and write to become smart! And always remember that blacks are a family, that they are brothers and sisters.

In this story-poem, a young boy repeats in dialect verse his sister's advice to be proud of being black. While promoting black unity, the verse does not advocate

black separatism; it points out that young blacks must remember that their actions are part of the future of all blacks.

Ages 4-8

Also available in:
No other form known

4

Albert, Burton

Mine, Yours, Ours

Color illustrations by Lois Axeman.
Albert Whitman & Company, 1977.
(31 pages counted)

SHARING/NOT SHARING

Young children, shown in various situations, use things, parts of the body, and other people to demonstrate sharing and ownership. In one scene a boy and his mother are walking through the snow. He looks back at the footprints and says, "Mine, yours — ours." Another scene shows two children pulling on a rope, each saying "Mine." But in the next picture they are jumping rope together, illustrating *ours* and the idea of sharing. Friends, too, can be shared. A girl shares her friend with a boy and he, in turn, shares his friends with her, making all the friends "ours."

Yours, mine, and *ours* are difficult words for young children to understand. In this book, both words and pictures illustrate the concepts. The differences between individual and shared possessions are vague in some illustrations, and this might be confusing to young readers.

Ages 2-5

Also available in:
No other form known

5

Albert, Louise

But I'm Ready to Go

Bradbury Press, Inc., 1976.
(230 pages)

LEARNING DISABILITIES
  Communication: parent-child
  Friendship: lack of
  Friendship: making friends
  Peer relationships: avoiding others
  Rejection: peer
  Self, attitude toward: feeling different

Fifteen-year-old Judy Miller has trouble learning in school. Sometimes, while her teachers are talking, her mind wanders. When she gets nervous, her hands shake. She gets Ds in all her classes except English. Judy does not know why she has trouble paying attention, but she does know that she feels different from other people. Because her overweight boyfriend has similar troubles, he understands how Judy feels. One day Judy overhears her mother talking about her not being able "to figure out what to do at times — the way other people can." Her mother tells Judy's younger sister, Emily, that this is an "invisible handicap." Angry, Judy runs to her room. At school her learning ability is tested. The school psychologist recommends that the girl transfer to a school for children with learning problems. Judy does not want to go to what she thinks is a school for "weirdos" and "retards." She wants her family to be as proud of her as they are of Emily. Against her will, she is enrolled. One thing, however, Judy feels she does well: she can sing. And she lives near New York City. She makes it her "secret plan" to go to the city and audition for a record company. After practicing for months, she takes the bus into New York — but finds that she cannot audition because she has neither an appointment nor an accompanist, nor has she recorded before. Disillusioned, she goes home and retreats to her room. When Emily asks what is wrong, Judy shrinks from confiding in her, lest Emily think her stupid. But Emily insists, and Judy tells her the whole story. Emily says, "Oh Judy, don't feel so bad. I think it's a great idea." She even offers to be her guitar accompanist. In the days that follow, Judy begins to enjoy the special school, and Emily and she become closer.

This first-person account is written to an imaginary friend by an intelligent, sensitive girl with a learning disability. The reader learns much about the rejection and inadequacy felt by people with such handicaps. Convincing characterizations add vividness to this smoothly written narrative.

Ages 11-14

Also available in:
Braille — *But I'm Ready to Go*
Library of Congress

Paperbound — *But I'm Ready to Go*
Dell Publishing Company, Inc.

Talking Book — *But I'm Ready to Go*
Library of Congress

6

Alexander, Anne

Connie

Black/white illustrations by Gail Owens.
Atheneum Publishers, 1976.
(179 pages)

MATURATION
    Alcoholism: adult
    Boy-girl relationships
    Communication: parent-child
    Jealousy: peer
    Sibling: rivalry
    Suicide: attempted
    Values/Valuing: moral/ethical

Connie, an eighth-grade girl, has just moved to another, poorer part of town, her father having lost his job as vice-president of a small company following a merger. Her mother is a writer trying to make ends meet by writing for confession magazines. Connie has two brothers: Jeff, an exuberant eight-year-old whom she thinks terribly spoiled, and Dave, away at college. Almost worse, to Connie, than the humiliation of having her rich friends know that her father is unemployed is that Aunt Berta, an eighty-nine-year-old eccentric, is now living with the family and sharing Connie's room. When her dad finds a job as a janitor, Connie feels completely disgraced. But little Jeff loves the new house and its big backyard and busies himself building a fort and making a garden. It seems Aunt Berta is an expert on plants; soon the yard is full of friends and neighbors listening to her talk about plants and health foods. Two of the boys from Connie's school are regular visitors. One such regular is Joel Deerborn, a handsome boy of Indian ancestry, from Connie's school, a boy she has long been interested in. To Connie's amazement, Joel and Aunt Berta become great friends. Joel has been going steady with wealthy Leora Hyde, but they break up just before eighth-grade graduation. Suddenly Joel is suspended from school because drugs are found in his locker — and Connie is named as the informant. Her careful deduction says that Leora planted the drugs to frame Joel and Connie out of jealousy. Connie goes to the principal with her suspicions, then races to Leora's house to confront her. No one answers the door, but Connie, from going on errands for Leora, knows a house key is kept in the garage. Opening the garage door, she discovers Mr. Hyde sitting in the car with the motor running. He is dying of carbon monoxide poisoning. Connie screams, drags him out, and gives mouth-to-mouth resuscitation. Her screams alert the neighbors, who call an ambulance. As the ambulance drives away with Mr. Hyde, Connie is sure he is dead. A policeman takes her home, where she is violently ill and lets herself be babied by her mother and Aunt Berta. Then happy news arrives: Joel has been cleared of all charges. Leora had blackmailed a schoolmate whose stepfather is a doctor, planted the drugs, and called the principal, giving Connie's name. Moreover, Mr. Hyde is still alive. Joel comes over to see her, and it appears he will invite her to the graduation dance. He has always liked her and wanted to break up with Leora to date her.

In this intense, contemporary story, Connie has trouble adjusting to her family's newly reduced circumstances. In the beginning she wallows in self-pity and jealousy. But by the end, as she sits on her father's lap, she realizes that she is much more fortunate than the wealthy Leora whose parents are getting a divorce, whose alcoholic father has tried to commit suicide, and whose attempted frame-up will lead to social ostracism. Connie has a loving family, a great-aunt who has turned out to be an asset rather than a burden, and a boy friend. And she has saved a man's life.

Ages 10-13

Also available in:
No other form known

7

Alexander, Anne

To Live a Lie

Black/white illustrations by Velma Ilsley.
Atheneum Publishers, 1975.
(165 pages) o.p.

DIVORCE: of Parents
HONESTY/DISHONESTY
 Anger
 Change: resisting
 Friendship: making friends

When eleven-year-old Noel Jennifer Henning's parents are divorced, she and her younger brother and sister must move with their father to another city. Jennifer blames her mother for the divorce, and makes three decisions about her new life: from now on she will be called Jennifer, not Noel; she will never make friends again; and if asked about her mother, she will say she is dead. For Jennifer, life in the new home is difficult. She must help look after her brother and sister and do much of the housework. But at school a small group of girls befriends her, and however reluctantly, she does enjoy their friendship. Then her twelfth birthday is ruined, mainly because her birthday dinner is canceled by her sister's illness. There is a small birthday package from her mother; in anger, Jennifer sends it back unopened. Two days later Mrs. Henning arrives at the front door, furiously blaming Mr. Henning. Jennifer confesses to the snub and then pours out the hateful thoughts she has been holding inside — that her mother never wanted her and that her mother blames her for all that has gone wrong since the divorce. She confesses that she has told her friends her mother is dead. Later, mother and daughter have a quiet talk. Jennifer is told she was certainly wanted, and that the children share no blame for the divorce. Her mother again offers Jennifer the birthday gift — a locket that her own mother had given her on her twelfth birthday. Jennifer is consoled, even to the point of being able to tell her new friends the truth about her parents. Freed at last from hate and lies, Jennifer begins to look around her with new hope.

Jennifer's life aches with paradoxes. She is lonely, yet afraid to make new friends. She feels too young for the responsibilities thrust upon her, yet handles many of them well. Hatred of her mother drives her to lie, but the lies only entrap her. She finally learns there is freedom in truth — in believing what her mother tells her and in speaking truth herself.

Ages 9-12

Also available in:
No other form known

A

8

Alexander, Martha G.

I'll Be the Horse If You'll Play with Me

Color illustrations by the author.
The Dial Press, Inc., 1975.
(32 pages counted)

SIBLING: Relationships
 Sibling: younger

When young Bonnie wants to play with her older brother, she must do things his way. Thus, she is always the horse when they play horse and wagon, always the robber when they play cops and robbers. She even lets her brother use her new crayons, but when she complains that he has used all her paper, he quits, saying he won't play with a crybaby. Another older boy tells Bonnie she can play "52 pickup," and then drops a deck of cards on the floor for her to pick up. Bonnie tries to play with the cat, dressing it like a baby, but the cat just walks away. When her older brother tells her to go play with their baby brother, Bonnie echoes the older brother's feelings about her, saying, "Who wants to play with a baby brother?" But she notices the younger brother has learned how to pull the wagon. Now Bonnie plays horse and wagon with her baby brother and *he* is the horse!

This story shows the hurt feelings a younger child often suffers when trying to compete or play with an older brother or sister. Although the story ends humorously, it does not deny the difficulties of being a younger child. It provides good points for discussion. This is a sequel to *Nobody Asked Me If I Wanted a Baby Sister.*

Ages 3-6

Also available in:
No other form known

9

Allard, Harry

Miss Nelson Is Missing!

Color illustrations by James Marshall.
Houghton Mifflin Co., 1977.
(32 pages)

SCHOOL: Behavior
SCHOOL: Pupil-Teacher Relationships

The children in Miss Nelson's class behave badly, worse than any other children in the school. Even when Miss Nelson asks them nicely to settle down during story hour, they refuse. One day Miss Nelson is gone and a substitute teacher named Miss Viola Swamp takes her place. Dressed all in black, Miss Swamp reminds the children of a witch. She tolerates no foolishness and puts the children to work. As the days go by, the children begin to long for Miss Nelson. Some of them go to the police; others go to her home, but the sight of Miss Viola Swamp walking down the street frightens them away. Just when they think Miss Nelson will never return, she appears. Everyone listens to her instructions and sits quietly during story hour. When Miss Nelson asks them why they have changed, they are secretive. But Miss Nelson has her own secret — a black dress hanging in her closet at home — and she knows why the children have changed.

Young children learn to appreciate a good-natured teacher during her seeming absence. The story, with its bid for proper classroom behavior, avoids being obviously didactic through good-natured prose and illustrations. Classes may enjoy hearing it read aloud.

Ages 5-8

Also available in:
Film — *Miss Nelson Is Missing!*
Learning Corporation of America

Paperbound — *Miss Nelson Is Missing!*
Scholastic Book Services

10

Allen, Alex B., pseud.

The Tennis Menace

Black/white illustrations by Timothy Jones.
Albert Whitman & Co., 1975.
(64 pages)

SPORTS/SPORTSMANSHIP
Determination

For several years Andy has played tennis casually, but in this, his ninth year, he vows to take it seriously. Yet his intention to practice hard for an August tournament falters when he can find no partner except Sheila, a bossy girl, and no courts to play on. Soon, along his newspaper route, Andy spots a private court and arranges to tend the yard in exchange for using the court to train on. But a partner? Sheila barges in while he is practicing alone and proves a poor sport when playing. Naturally, Andy rejoices to discover that the owner's visiting granddaughter, Tracy, is a good player; even better, they are evenly matched. In the ensuing days they help correct each other's weakness. Unfortunately, Sheila reappears and demands to be included. But Andy feels almost ready for the tournament anyway, and encourages Tracy to enter. Alas, Tracy thinks she must return home before then and wishes him luck. Unknown to Andy, she postpones her leaving and enters the tournament, and both advance to the final round. In a closely fought match, Andy finally wins by taking advantage of Tracy's weak forehand stroke.

A boy determined to become a good tennis player surmounts a number of obstacles to attain his goal. Though winning is the thing, the story emphasizes good sportsmanship and even matching between players. Fast-moving and uncomplicated, this book should appeal to low-vocabulary readers.

Ages 8-10

Also available in:
No other form known

11
Alter, Judy

After Pa Was Shot

William Morrow & Company, Inc., 1978.
(189 pages)

DEATH: of Father
RESPONSIBILITY: Accepting
Crime/Criminals
Dependence/Independence
Loss: feelings of
Mourning, stages of
Trust/Distrust

A

Twelve-year-old Ellsbeth and her younger brother B.J. are outside playing when Uncle Charlie comes shouting the news that Pa has been shot. The year is 1904, the place, a small town in Texas where Ellsbeth's beloved Pa is an acting deputy sheriff. The night before, Pa had jailed a man for drunkenness, and after the man was released, he shot Pa. Two days later, Pa dies. Ma, who is pregnant, becomes listless, indecisive, leaving Ellsbeth in charge of all household chores and the care of her two younger brothers. After baby Maggie is born, Ma decides to move to a larger house and rent out the upstairs rooms to boarders. The income from the renters enables Ma to be home with the children, though Ellsbeth continues to do most of the cooking, cleaning, and child care. One of the boarders is a polite, well-dressed gentleman, Joseph Millard, a new clerk at the bank. Ellsbeth immediately dislikes and distrusts him, but her mother, infatuated with his charm, falls in love with him. In a short time, Ma marries Mr. Millard, and thereafter his smooth facade begins to crack. He is irritable with the children; he becomes increasingly rude to Ma; and he is outraged when Ma cannot give him the deed to the boarding house (she does not own it). Ellsbeth, who has seen Millard with a money box full of bills, confides her distrust of the man to her Uncle Charlie. One day her suspicions are confirmed when she comes home to discover that he has left, taking baby Maggie with him as a hostage. The sheriff appears minutes later to report that Millard has robbed the bank. In fact, the robbery is the climax of a well-planned scheme that Millard has executed in several other places. He establishes himself in a small town and becomes a trustworthy member of the local bank's staff. Then, when the timing is right, his partners rob the bank and later split the money with him. Before he can be linked to the robbery, he disappears from the town. Ma can hardly believe she has been part of such a plot. Ellsbeth, suspecting where Millard is hiding out, goes after him to rescue the baby. She finds him — but he holds her prisoner with Maggie. Later, when Millard tries to leave his hideout, the sheriff and Uncle Charlie are waiting outside to arrest him and rescue the girls. Ma regains her characteristic spunk and decides to divorce the crook and manage the boarding house by herself. Ellsbeth, for the first time since Pa's death, has some free time on her hands.

A young girl gives up childhood freedoms and takes on adult responsibilities when her mother becomes immobilized by grief. Reassured by a girl friend and by her Uncle Charlie, Ellsbeth tries to face the prospect of having her mother's oily boy friend around for years, but when he proves to be a worse villain than she thought, Ellsbeth is pleased to have him disposed of in an unexpected way. These characters seem to talk as they should, and their ventures and adventures never lag or seem unlikely. Only Ellsbeth's climactic tranquillity seems unlikely, what with brothers and boarders to care for.

Ages 10-13

Also available in:
No other form known

12

Ames, Mildred

What Are Friends For?

Charles Scribner's Sons, 1978.
(145 pages)

FRIENDSHIP: Best Friend
FRIENDSHIP: Meaning of
  Divorce: of parents
  School: classmate relationships
  Stealing

It is not friendship at first sight when eleven-year-old Amy, newly moved to California, meets Michelle, a fellow resident in an apartment building. But they find a common bond — both live with divorced mothers — and soon become best friends. But Amy finds drawbacks in their friendship: Michelle is indifferent, sometimes sarcastic about Amy's doll collection; and Michelle's unpopularity at school places Amy in a quandary. Other girls will play with her only if Michelle does not join in. Forced to choose, Amy is loyal to Michelle. But after Michelle damages one of her dolls and then snubs her, Amy drops Michelle to befriend other girls. When they later make up, the other girls drop Amy, and in a final twist, Amy is left alone. While the two are out shopping, Michelle steals a pair of earrings and, about to be caught, plants them on Amy. Unable to prove her innocence, Amy is let off with a lecture, but she tells Michelle they are through. Desperate to regain her friendship, Michelle then steals a valuable doll and gives it to Amy. The latter then discloses the dishonesty and compulsive stealing — the evidence being stolen goods in Michelle's closet. Michelle's father, a psychiatrist, takes the child to live with him.

The protagonist can never quite break with her demanding friend until a theft forces her hand. Besides this theme, the story deals with the effects of divorce on children and particularly the feelings the girls have toward their fathers. In Michelle's case, her father explains much of her willful, attention-seeking behavior.

Ages 9-11

Also available in:
No other form known

13

Ames, Mildred

Without Hats, Who Can Tell the Good Guys?

E. P. Dutton & Company, Inc., 1976.
(133 pages)

FOSTER HOME
Identity, search for
Rejection: parental

Eleven-year-old Tony Lang lived with the Sauter family for four years after his mother died and his father became an alcoholic. When the Sauters can no longer keep him, Tony is placed in a new home by a social agency. Mr. and Mrs. Diamond are happy to have him, but their eleven-year-old daughter, Hildy, is not so sure. Mr. Diamond has always wanted a son and has never been close to Hildy. Through Tony, he tries to relive his own childhood. First he decides to make Tony into a baseball player. The boy qualifies for Little League, but Mr. Diamond, angered at the coach, forces Tony to quit. At loose ends, Tony makes friends with Smitty, a classmate, who gives him a hobby plane in exchange for a stray cat. When Tony shows the plane to Mr. Diamond, the man exuberantly offers to fix the engine, takes Tony out to fly the plane, and later buys the boy two more. Beginning to feel at home with the Diamonds, Tony

even thinks Hildy an acceptable sister. Then one day his father appears unexpectedly. Assured that Tony is all right, he is clearly still too irresponsible to take the boy with him. When he leaves, Tony realizes he will never see him again. He tells Hildy he is staying for good — and she is delighted.

During Tony's talks with his social worker, he examines his feelings about his father, about the Diamonds, and about his past. At first he hates the Diamonds and cannot wait for his father to return. Gradually, however, he begins to understand and accept them as individuals. This touching story boasts believable characters and natural dialogue.

Ages 9-12

Also available in:
Cassette for the Blind — *Without Hats, Who Can Tell the Good Guys?*
Library of Congress

14

Anders, Rebecca

A Look at Aging

Black/white photographs by Maria S. Forrai.
Lerner Publications Co., 1976.
(36 pages counted)

AGE: Aging
AGE: Respect for

What is aging? Several generalities may describe it, but within each we find much variation. To some old people, aging brings illnesses; others enjoy good health. Though most have much free time, they use it variously; helping others, enjoying themselves, beginning new careers. Other old people are lonely. But all have valuable experiences to share with people of all ages. Close to death, they are also close to life.

A

Here is a description, in simple, clear language, of what aging means in American society. This book is one of the titles in the Lerner Awareness Series, intended to present complex subjects to very young children.

Ages 3-7

Also available in:
No other form known

15

Anders, Rebecca

A Look at Death

Black/white photographs by Maria S. Forrai.
Lerner Publications Co., 1978.
(36 pages counted)

DEATH: Attitude Toward

Death is difficult to understand and difficult to accept. People feel sadness and loss over the death of a loved one, but these natural emotions help them endure that person's death. Many old people prepare themselves and those they love for their deaths. Those who die suddenly or young cannot do this; their deaths seem especially unfair, difficult to accept. A period of mourning helps family and friends to express grief and to comfort each other. The sadness diminishes over time, leaving memories, often happy ones, behind.

The author does not avoid describing the painful aspects of death. She remarks that religious faith may comfort the bereaved and give them hope of life after death, but she promotes no particular view of death other than its naturalness. Parents and young children will find that the clear descriptions and photographs prompt discussion. This book is one of the titles in the Lerner Awareness Series, intended to present complex subjects to very young children.

Ages 3-7

Also available in:
No other form known

16

Anders, Rebecca

A Look at Mental Retardation

Black/white photographs by Maria S. Forrai.
Lerner Publications Co., 1976.
(36 pages counted)

MENTAL RETARDATION
Differences, human

The ability to learn — what we call intelligence — is not the same in all of us. Some of us are exceptionally intelligent, but some of us "have trouble learning even the simplest tasks." These people are called mentally retarded. The causes of retardation are many: a pregnant woman's accident or illness may cause her baby to be retarded; brain damage may occur during birth or may be caused by serious childhood illness. But mentally retarded people can and do learn, though more slowly than normal people. Many can learn trades; some can learn to read and write. By accepting and befriending retarded children, normal children can help them.

This short, simple book does not show the wide range of abilities among mentally retarded people, and the photographs do not always match the text. But the author does provide an introduction to mental retardation that, when discussed with an adult, will foster a young child's acceptance and understanding. This book is one of the titles in the Lerner Awareness Series, intended to present complex subjects to very young children.

Ages 3-7

Also available in:
No other form known

17

Anders, Rebecca

A Look at Prejudice and Understanding

Black/white photographs by Maria S. Forrai.
Lerner Publications Co., 1976.
(34 pages counted)

PREJUDICE
  Differences, human

To be prejudiced means to be inclined to judge people before knowing them firsthand. Many people can easily invent reasons to pre-judge others: they may dislike others' jobs, their religion, their color, or anything else that distinguishes them from the people judging. Prejudiced people fence themselves in; their world is narrow and cramped. People without prejudice try to "open gates," to enrich their lives by knowing and understanding a diversity of people. They see that every person has special talents and tastes, and a special background. In order to learn about these and perhaps to profit from them, one must not pre-judge anyone.

This book emphasizes what prejudice does to the judger, not to those subjected to it. The author encourages children to "open gates" not only to know people around them, but to be known. The text and the photographs are clear, inviting discussion. This book is one of the titles in the Lerner Awareness Series, intended to present complex subjects to very young children.

Ages 3-7

Also available in:
No other form known

18

Anderson, Mary Quirk

Step On a Crack

Atheneum Publishers, 1978.
(180 pages)

A

NIGHTMARES
  Child abuse
  Mental Illness: of adolescent
  Problem solving
  Stealing

Fifteen-year-old Sarah Carpenter has a recurring nightmare in which she kills her mother. She knows that, as surely as this dream terrifies her, it will be followed by her stealing some small object from a store; it always happens. When summer begins and Sarah's Aunt Kat — a moderately successful artist — arrives for a visit, Sarah begins sleepwalking and having new nightmares. Sensing that her condition may soon be out of control, Sarah is relieved when her school locker partner, Josie, draws a confession from her and offers to help her. Meanwhile, Aunt Kat postpones a planned departure after Sarah's mother is injured in a late-night fall, which Sarah fears she herself may have caused while sleepwalking. After consulting a clairvoyant and searching historical records, the girls discover information that triggers early childhood memories in Sarah, and she realizes, with upsetting clarity, that her mother once was given to abusing and abandoning her. Sure that Sarah cannot bear this recollection, Josie tells Mrs. Carpenter, while Sarah isolates herself in her room. Alone with her thoughts, Sarah also recalls that the mother who tormented her was Aunt Kat — who must be her biological mother. Dismayed by this revelation, Sarah seeks out Mrs. Carpenter to ask why Aunt Kat had acted as she did. From her, Sarah learns that young

Kat had suffered acutely from being a single parent and from lack of professional success, abusing her tiny daughter when the stress became too great. On professional word that Sarah would never remember her early suffering and that as matters stood the child was in mortal danger from her, Kat had allowed her older sister to adopt the three-year-old. Sarah, hurt and confused by what she has learned, cannot forgive Kat and views the woman's hasty departure with no regret. But as the summer passes and Sarah looks forward to professional counseling in the fall she is able to view Kat's actions with greater understanding and less bitterness.

This first-person narrative graphically portrays the main character's anguish over her dreams and subsequent behavior. The reader suspects, long before Sarah does, the cause of her troubles and longs to help her. Yet Sarah is not abandoned to her demons, remaining close to her parents, particularly to her mother. This book, for all its skillful pace and suspense (at some cost in glibness), is clear and firm on the dangers inherent in unskilled counseling and the emotional trauma that child abuse entails. Incidents of abuse include abandoning a small child in a fenced-in grave plot, and striking her brutally.

Ages 12 and up

Also available in:
No other form known

19

Angell, Judie

In Summertime It's Tuffy

Bradbury Press, Inc., 1977.
(230 pages)

CAMP EXPERIENCES
FRIENDSHIP: Meaning of
Loyalty

Eleven-year-old Elizabeth "Tuffy" Kandell is spending the summer at Camp Ma-Sha-Na. She likes the camp and her five cabin-mates, the two she already knows and the three she makes friends with at once. No two are alike. Verna likes things clean and orderly; Natalie cares mostly for clothes and boys; Iris is a loner, with her nose in her books. Uncle Otto (as he is called), the camp director, wants to "run a tight ship" and the girls soon find themselves in trouble. They are late for breakfast; their cabin is a mess. When Uncle Otto fires Sheila, the girls' cabin counselor, for returning to camp long after curfew, the girls, getting the idea from one of Iris's books on magic, make a voodoo doll of Otto. Into the doll's ankle they stick a pin, and later that day Otto sprains his ankle. Fearing their own magical powers, they completely dismantle the doll. But something new and interesting is always turning up. Iris is to play her guitar in the talent show. Uncle Otto seems mellower. Tuffy turns her attention to someone very interesting indeed — a boy named Alex.

Tuffy and her cabin-mates go through some typical summer-camp experiences: minor clashes with each other and the camp director, pranks, and the dawning of warm friendships. Tuffy grows up, too, over the summer, befriending and encouraging the quiet Iris, trying to understand the director's point of view, starting to take new notice of boys.

Ages 11-13

Also available in:
Braille — *In Summertime It's Tuffy*
Library of Congress

Paperbound — *In Summertime It's Tuffy*
Dell Publishing Company, Inc.

20

Angell, Judie

Ronnie and Rosey

Bradbury Press, Inc., 1977.
(283 pages)

BOY-GIRL RELATIONSHIPS
DEATH: of Father
MOURNING, Stages of
    Dependence/Independence
    Honesty/Dishonesty
    Parental: overprotection

On her first day at a new school, thirteen-year-old Ronnie Rachman is accidently knocked to the floor by Robert Rose. The two introduce themselves and find they have something in common: Ronnie, a girl, is by name only often thought a boy, and Robert, nicknamed Rosey, is teased about having a girlish nickname. That very same day Ronnie meets Evelyn, a friendly girl who has been Robert's best friend for years. The best friends plan a get-acquainted party for Ronnie, and there Ronnie learns that Robert is a gifted piano player, that Robert and Evelyn are rehearsing a pantomime for a local talent show, and that Robert and Evelyn want her to join them. The three begin to hang around together, and before long Robert asks Ronnie for a date. She hangs back, afraid Evelyn's feelings will be hurt, but Evelyn assures her that she and Robert are just pals. Then, on the second night of the talent show, tragedy strikes: Ronnie's parents have an automobile accident and her father is killed. Mrs. Rachman is transformed by grief. She insists that Ronnie stay home all the time; soon she puts restrictions on all phone calls. Ronnie is not to see Robert, but the two meet secretly at Ronnie's baby-sitting jobs. They are discovered, and Ronnie is again told to drop Robert. In desperation, Ronnie declares that she wishes she had died instead of her father — and in fact she is suffering from sleeplessness and fierce headaches. Sneaking out one night to see Robert, she returns to find her mother waiting. Unable to face another quarrel, Ronnie runs away, vowing never to go home again. To Miss Fisk, her gym teacher, she sobs out the whole story. Miss Fisk notifies Mrs. Rachman of Ronnie's whereabouts, and lets her spend the night. In the morning, Mrs. Rachman comes to get Ronnie, and seems much more herself. She apologizes to her daughter and vows that the future will be better. Ronnie spends the summer with a friend in Los Angeles, and when she returns in the fall, her mother is her old self. Ronnie and Robert look forward to a good school year together.

After her father's sudden death, Ronnie has no vent for her grief, and almost completely represses all thoughts of him. It is her mother's sudden, smothering possessiveness that brings her to despair, and finally leads her to deceive her mother outright. Only then does her mother get a grip on herself, so as not to destroy the love between mother and daughter. Ronnie and her friends are wholly recognizable teenagers who happen to be visited by a calamity and its baffling, frightening aftermath. The story ends hopefully but not patly.

Ages 11 and up

Also available in:
Braille — *Ronnie and Rosey*
Library of Congress

Paperbound — *Ronnie and Rosey*
Dell Publishing Company, Inc.

A

21

Angier, Bradford and Barbara Corcoran

Ask for Love and They Give You Rice Pudding

Houghton Mifflin Co., 1977.
(151 pages)

IDENTITY, SEARCH FOR
  Loneliness
  Love, meaning of
  Maturation
  Wealth/Wealthy

Wealthy but friendless Robbie Benson passes his seventeenth birthday alone. His hard-drinking mother is in a sanitarium in Italy; his father has been away for fifteen years. Since then, Robbie has lived with his Italian grandparents, the well-to-do Manellis, but now his only companion, his grandfather, has been left mentally impaired by a stroke. Robbie has recently discovered an old journal written by his father, and he reads a little of it nightly, hoping to learn something about the man and so perhaps about himself. In the meantime, several Ivy League colleges have turned the boy down for poor grades, and Vicki Parkinson has refused his fourteenth request for a date. One day, to his joy and amazement, she accepts. When Robbie visits Vicki's home, he finds himself infatuated with her mother, and with Vicki's whole close-knit, friendly family. Soon it becomes clear how little they care about his coming from wealth, how much they are interested in him personally. From Mrs. Parkinson, Robbie learns that his father is a writer. She gives him a copy of one of his father's books and encourages Robbie to find out where he is. The Parkinsons mean the world to the boy. But suddenly they are gone on a vacation in Norway, and his grandfather is dead. Loneliness overtakes him again. That summer

Robbie flies to San Diego to search for his father. He finds him, but conversation between the two is awkward, almost painful. When Mr. Benson disparages the Manelli family, Robbie finds himself leaping to their defense, finds himself feeling like a Manelli in no uncertain terms. His pride in this gives him a sense of being somebody, and he returns home determined to be that somebody even more fully.

Robbie's diary tells this story of a youth isolated from his parents and with too little sense of worth to find friends. Through the friendship of another family the boy is emboldened to present himself to his father, and from their conversation the youth discovers both what he does not want to be and what he does.

Ages 12-14

Also available in:
Braille — Ask for Love and They Give You Rice Pudding
Library of Congress

Paperbound — Ask for Love and They Give You Rice Pudding
Bantam Books, Inc.

Paperbound — Ask for Love and They Give You Rice Pudding
Scholastic Book Services

22

Anker, Charlotte

Last Night I Saw Andromeda

Black/white illustrations by Ingrid Fetz.
Henry Z. Walck, Inc., 1975.
(126 pages)

SECURITY/INSECURITY
  Friendship
  Parent/Parents: single

Eleven-year-old Jenny Berger and her divorced mother have recently moved into a new housing development, near which, while digging one day on vacant land,

Jenny is thrilled to unearth several fossils. As days go by, she digs more and finds more, hiding all she finds and reading up on her fossils in books. At first she plans to reveal her finds only to her scientist father, about whose Sunday visits she always feels unsure. But when a boy named Toby moves into the neighborhood, he and Jenny compare their two collections (he keeps snakes) and agree to collaborate on both. Jointly, they uncover several large stones containing clam fossils, but the old man on whose land they are trespassing, chases the children away. Still mindful of impressing her father, Jenny vows to have those stones, and tries, unsuccessfully, to bribe the landowner with cookies. They must go by night, Jenny decides. They do, only to find that the old man has destroyed all the rocks but one. Jenny breaks down in tears. Chastened, the old man finally understands why she wanted the rocks and gives her the last one. But before she can lay the whole collection before her visiting father, she must rescue it, in the hollow tree where it is hidden, from a bulldozer. She is slightly injured. When at last she displays her fossils to her father, he is pleased and impressed — and his solicitude for her injury pleases and impresses Jenny. He introduces her to a fossil expert at a local museum and accompanies her on fossil-hunts from then on.

Jenny's divorced father is a scientist, and in her anxiety to hold onto his love, Jenny is eager to impress his scientific mind. Her discovery of some fossils not only engages her own imagination but also provides father and daughter with a mutual interest. Children of divorced parents will understand Jenny's fear that her father will discontinue his visits and no longer care about her.

Ages 9-11

Also available in:
No other form known

23

Arkin, Alan

The Lemming Condition

Black/white illustrations by Joan Sandin.
Harper & Row Publishers, Inc., 1976.
(58 pages)

AUTONOMY
IDENTITY, SEARCH FOR

A

Bupper, a young lemming, wakes in his burrow, knowing the day is somehow important. His family is excitedly preparing for a journey. Outside, Bupper finds the normally bustling plain deserted. When his friend Crow asks, "What's up?" Bupper only repeats what he has heard: that the lemmings will soon head west. Knowing that only a half a mile west lies the ocean, Crow asks Bupper if he can swim. Bupper does not know. Uneasy at Crow's questions, the lemming seeks out his father for answers but receives only vague reassurances. Bupper turns to his Uncle Claude for answers but gets only cliches; Claude advises him to stop asking questions and adopt "a feeling of solidarity with his kind." Confused and frightened, Bupper has Crow fly him to a pond, where he finds he cannot even wade, let alone swim. Returning, he meets an old lemming — a stalwart, independent soul — who scoffs at this "going west" business. Lemmings, he says, cannot get together on anything. Bupper returns home and joins the migration anyway, and is swept up in a feeling of solidarity with all lemmings. But at the sea cliffs he is back to awareness and tries to retreat. The horde of lemmings carries him relentlessly along — until he falls into a crevice among the rocks. Bupper survives to walk "true east" the next morning. Asked for help by a few surviving lemmings, Bupper replies: "I'm not one of you. . . . I'm not a lemming anymore."

Contrary to the old canard, lemmings do not commit mass suicide by throwing themselves into the sea. But the author is not writing about lemmings, rather about people and how they can lose themselves in the impulses of a crowd. The lemmings Bupper meets on his search for truth are scathing portraits of certain human types. His search leads him to conclude that he cannot ever find out who he is and what he should do by following the crowd. With discussion, naive readers will get from this book what more thoughtful readers may apprehend on their own.

Ages 10 and up

Also available in:
Paperbound — *The Lemming Condition*
Bantam Books, Inc.

24

Arrick, Fran

Steffie Can't Come Out to Play

Bradbury Press, Inc., 1978.
(196 pages)

PROSTITUTION
RUNNING AWAY
  Dependence/Independence
  Fear: of physical harm

Fourteen-year-old Stephanie Rudd, beautiful and younger than she looks, has run away from Clairton, Pennsylvania, wanting more than the drudgery of housework while her mother takes in laundry. Steffie comes to New York City to be a model. Instead, she meets a man called Favor, who promises to protect her, showers her with expensive gifts, and encourages her to stay in his luxurious apartment. Soon Steffie has come to love the man — and proves her love, as Favor has

asked, by becoming a prostitute. When she begins working the street, Favor sends her to live with Brenda, another of his "wives-in-law," and here she is told that all she earns belongs to Favor and that she must do well or expect a beating. She goes along, both out of fear and to prove to Favor that she is better than his other girls and deserves his love. Arrested one evening, she makes the mistake of bragging about her pimp, and upon her release Favor makes her sorry. Another time, one of the "wives" arranges to have a customer slip Steffie a drug, to which the girl responds badly and has to be helped to Favor's car. Another "wife" picks a fight on the way and Favor, angered at the scene, slaps Steffie around. They are observed by a police officer, Cal Yarbro, who has been watching Steffie since her first day. Later, unknown to Steffie, he breaks Favor's leg and jaw, threatening more of the same if he keeps Steffie on in his stable. Favor decides that Steffie, though by now his top earner, is not worth the trouble she causes. Having nowhere to turn, Steffie takes Cal's advice and goes to a shelter for runaways. After talking with counselors there, she decides to return home.

The main character in this largely first-person narrative is a prostitute completely dependent on her pimp for love, security, and approval. He, in turn, thinks of her only as property, using her dependence to hold her. Because Steffie successfully escapes her situation, some readers may erroneously think it is easy to break away from a pimp at will. Also, early in the book, prostitution is glamorized — the new clothes, the pimp's gifts, the protection of a strong man — and this may deceptively beguile some young readers. As the story progresses, the danger and misery of prostitution become clear, without preaching. Although the book is frank, sexual encounters are not rendered explicitly. Far clearer are its treatments of the body as property, the danger from abnormal "tricks," the distrust and jealousy of other prostitutes, and the feelings of worthlessness and fear the main character suffers. Patrolman Yarbro and his partner are introduced in a third-person section in this otherwise first-person narration by Steffie.

Ages 12 and up

Also available in:
Paperbound — *Steffie Can't Come Out to Play*
Dell Publishing Company, Inc.

25

Ashley, Bernard

Terry on the Fence

Black/white illustrations by Charles Keeping.
S. G. Phillips, Inc., 1977.
(196 pages)

DELINQUENCY, JUVENILE
STEALING
VALUES/VALUING: Moral/Ethical
  Aggression: active
  Gangs: being bothered by

When Terry Harmer, just eleven, stalks out of his London home, furious at his mother's and sister's unfairness, he has no idea what the next forty-eight hours will bring. Seeking shelter from a storm, Terry is accosted by a gang of boys, runs, falls, is captured and threatened with a knife by the leader, Les, fifteen, who needs a guide through Terry's school to burglarize it. At the gang's hideout, Terry, exhausted and in pain from his fall, hopelessly consents. Once inside the school, the gang is interrupted by the caretaker and leaves with only two radios. From the caretaker's description, the headmaster links Terry to the gang and tells the boy's family. Terry turns one radio over to the police, finds Les, and goes with him to a "fence" to get the other back. Found there, the two are taken to juvenile court. Les admits his guilt, despite Terry's momentary attempt to protect him, and is sent to a community home. Aware

that Terry was forced into the burglary, the judge requires him to explain his protectiveness toward Les. Terry has seen the huge scar Les bears on his neck, evidence of his mother's furious temper, and sees Les himself as someone whose life has been too hard to handle properly. Though reluctant to disclose the details of Les's hardships in court, he finally explains to the judge that he had tried to protect the boy because, out of the arresting officer's sight Les had been "scratching his bad neck . . . till he made it bleed . . . he was just looking at me, asking me not to tell, and trying to smile." Hearing this, the judge discharges Terry unconditionally.

This is a frank, realistic portrayal of a boy caught in a situation he cannot cope with physically or morally. The descriptions of Les's gang terrorizing Terry and the appalling account of parental brutality and emotional aridity in Les's home are so clear they may upset some readers. Terry's family and home life are genial by comparison. Les's background is apparently responsible for his anti-social behavior, but the book does not settle this point. The British idiom and slang may make the book difficult reading here and there.

Ages 12 and up

Also available in:
No other form known

26

Babbitt, Natalie

The Eyes of the Amaryllis

Farrar, Straus & Giroux, Inc., 1977.
(128 pages)

GRANDPARENT: Respect for
  Imagination
  Superstition

B

Eleven-year-old Jenny Reade is going to the ocean for the first time in her life. The ocean: where years earlier her grandfather had drowned during a hurricane; where her father has ever since forbidden her to go; where her grandmother goes twice every day, at high tides, awaiting some sign from Grandfather's grave. Jenny loves the sea and her grandmother's tales about it, and now that Gran has broken an ankle, the two must go together. There Jenny meets Seward, an old man who walks the sand each day, claiming to guard the sea and its treasures. One morning, Jenny finds Grandmother's long-awaited message bobbing toward shore — the wooden female figurehead from the prow of Grandfather's ship, the Amaryllis. Grandmother, recognizing the figurehead, is ecstatic. But days later, Seward warns her to give the thing back to the sea or the sea will come after it. Gran stubbornly refuses. A hurricane begins building. As the storm increases in intensity, Jenny commands Gran to throw the figure into the sea lest they both be destroyed. At last Gran takes the figure and struggles toward the beach, intending to hurl herself into the sea with her treasure. At that moment, Jenny's father arrives. The figurehead is washed away, while Father carries Gran back to the house. The storm subsides. In the morning, Gran seems defeated. She agrees to return to the city to live with her son and his family. As the three drive down the beach, Jenny spots a bright red amaryllis floating ashore. She brings it to Grandmother, whose spirits revive at once — it is another sign from Grandfather.

In this well-written story of mystery and suspense, the reader must sort the fantasy from the real. Jenny herself, though unsure of how much to believe her grandmother's tales, remains loyal to the old woman and accepts the tasks she sets her.

Ages 11-14

Also available in:
Cassette for the Blind — *The Eyes of the Amaryllis*
Library of Congress

Paperbound — *The Eyes of the Amaryllis*
Bantam Books, Inc.

27

Bach, Alice

A Father Every Few Years

Harper & Row Publishers, Inc., 1977.
(130 pages)

MATURATION
SEPARATION, MARITAL
   Boy-girl relationships
   Guilt, feelings of
   Responsibility: accepting

Twelve-year-old Tim Cartwright is trying to sort out his feelings about his stepfather, Max, who had abandoned him and his mother, Margot, a year earlier. But Tim has a lot on his mind. He is still puzzled about his father, Ben, who left when Tim was five — and he wonders if he himself is the cause of both leave-takings. He also thinks Margot needs a husband, and so he tries to be the man of the house. But Margot, who is a real estate agent, worries him with her impulsive spending. As for friends, he is concerned about his good friend Joey, a hemophiliac, frequently bedridden and able to do very little. Melanie, Tim's best friend of many years, is in the ninth grade now, and has been acting strangely, accusing Tim of being too young to understand her. She wants to date boys, but annoyingly fails to recognize that he is a boy himself. And always there is the question of Max. Tim has an idea: during summer vacation, he and his friends will call every area code in the United States asking for a listing for Max's name. But

Margot has other plans, and wants Tim to vacation in California with her. Fearing this is another ruinous expenditure, he refuses to go and elects to stay with Melanie's family. While there, he suddenly makes extravagant advances to his old friend, and her mother sits down and helps the two young people sort out their feelings and reestablish their easy friendship. And still there is Max — but where? Tim comes to think that Margot will bring him back from California. With his friends' help he plans a welcome-home party for Max. But Margot returns alone, and Tim takes to his room for three days. When he finally permits her to talk to him, Margot tells him that they must give up hope of Max's return and learn to live happily without him. Together, they decide that two people can make up a family.

This is the story of a boy who badly wants a father for himself and a husband for his mother. After two fathers' departures, he takes upon himself some adult responsibilities, and feels guilty because he is not the man called for. He lives in fear that his mother will leave him too, though this fear lessens when she returns from a trip more determined than ever that she and her son will meet life together. The feelings of friend Joey and his parents about Joey's disease, Joey's feelings about possible death, his pain, and his friendship with Tim are handled in some depth.

Ages 11-13

Also available in:
Paperbound — *A Father Every Few Years*
Dell Publishing Company, Inc.

28

Bach, Alice

The Meat in the Sandwich

Harper & Row Publishers, Inc., 1975.
(182 pages)

COMPETITION
IDENTITY, SEARCH FOR
   Peer relationships
   Sports/Sportsmanship
   Values/Valuing: moral/ethical

B

Ten-year-old Mike Lefcourt dreams of becoming a famous athlete, but thinks himself a mediocre one. He also feels overlooked at home in favor of an older and a younger sister. All this changes when Kip Statler, an athletic boy Mike's age, moves in next door. Kip coaches Mike in soccer, driving him hard. He also coaches Mike's home life, telling Mike that the only boy in the family is like "the meat in the sandwich"; Mike should be exempt from the "woman's work" now shared by the whole family so that Mike's mother can pursue her painting. Soon Mike loses both his patience and old friendships because of Kip and soccer. When he takes the fifth-grade soccer team to victory over the sixth-grade, he is acclaimed a school hero. But his family, though happy for him, does not measure up in their praises. As hockey season approaches, Mike plans to repay Kip for all his help by coaching him in hockey — only to find Kip needs no coaching. Worse, the coach assigns the two to different teams. For Kip, a new team means new allegiances; he turns against Mike. When he trips Mike on purpose during hockey practice, Mike explodes, and an all-out fight ensues. Mike is badly beaten, his pride too crushed to allow him to go back to school. Finally, aided by his family and friends, he overcomes his feelings of failure.

In this first-person narrative, Mike desperately seeks to establish his self-worth. Misled, he equates winning with being liked and respected. His eventual understanding that people like him for what he is, not for what he does, is a major step. Some readers may find Mike's passion for success shallow and one-sided. At times the boys' competitive spirit, extensive training, and peer relationships seem more like young adolescents' than fifth graders'. But relations with family and friends are important here and described well.

Ages 10-13

Also available in:
Braille — *The Meat in the Sandwich*
Library of Congress

Paperbound — *The Meat in the Sandwich*
Dell Publishing Company, Inc.

29

Bailey, Pearl

Duey's Tale

Black/white photographs by Arnold Skolnick and Gary Azon.
Harcourt Brace Jovanovich, Inc., 1975.
(59 pages)

IDENTITY, SEARCH FOR
 Belonging
 Friendship
 Self, attitude toward: accepting

Young Duey is a maple seedling, who is blown free of the protective branches of his mother tree. The wind carries him to the river, where he settles onto a rough branch — a free floating, happy-go-lucky branch. In time, Duey floats free of Gabby, though not far, and is washed into a well-mannered, gentle, protective glass bottle, a lady bottle named "Slicker." With Gabby, they travel downstream to the ocean, where they eventually

separate. Duey misses his friends, but enjoys sightseeing as the elements bear him along. The next time he encounters his two friends, Gabby has been carved into an elephant walking stick owned by a gentleman, and Slicker is on display as a rare glass bottle in a shop window. Both friends have found important places for themselves, and Duey longs for a similar sense of belonging. Soon afterwards, he settles against the earth and begins to grow into a lovely maple tree. In time he is able to provide shade and protection for those who pass his way. When a young couple claims him as a symbol of their love, he feels content at last.

This odyssey of a maple seedling is an allegory of human friendships. Each character must search long without knowing what for. The conclusion implies a moral: that an individual's value lies in his being important to someone. There is much here for mature readers to discuss.

Ages 12 and up

Also available in:
No other form known

30

Baldwin, Anne Norris

A Little Time

The Viking Press, Inc., 1978.
(119 pages)

DOWN'S SYNDROME
PROBLEM SOLVING
 Communication: importance of
 Family: unity

Ten-year-old Sarah's four-year-old brother, Matt, has Down's Syndrome. Sarah loves him but knows that his presence often frightens those not used to him. All the same, she invites Ginny, a new girl in her class, over to play. Sure enough, Ginny recoils from Matt and from that day on avoids Sarah. It is only a matter of time before the aggrieved Sarah, in a moment of pique at her brother, hits him several times with a shoe. The outburst horrifies her parents, as does her angry avowal that Matt should be sent to a special boarding school with others of his sort, something Ginny had said. The father explains that such choices are not easily made, and for a time the subject is dropped. Sarah's mother cheers her up immensely by giving her a birthday party. But on the big day Matt almost ruins the festivities by getting lost. Thinking fast, Sarah's father turns the crisis into a game, offering a prize for finding Matt. The boy is found, and his father takes the opportunity to answer some questions about Matt and about Down's Syndrome. Both Sarah and her friends feel better once the subject has been openly discussed, and from then on, Sarah's life improves. Then her mother falls ill. For the first time the rest of the family sees what enormous work it is to care for Matt. Once out of the hospital, Sarah's mother herself sees that she cannot continue to do all that is necessary for Matt, and that he probably should have some special training. Soon the whole family agrees: Matt should go away to school for a while. At first the others are relieved not to be thinking and working for Matt day and night. But soon they find themselves remembering and talking of Matt's uniquely special brand of innocent laughter and joy. They miss him. He is brought back — but not before the family has arrived at definite plans to care for Matt without allowing his needs to become the center of family life.

This simply told first-person story dramatizes the love, anger, jealousy, and tenderness a retarded child's family can feel. It will arouse empathy in readers who have known people with Down's Syndrome and increase awareness and understanding in others.

Ages 9-11

Also available in:
No other form known

31

Barkin, Carol and Elizabeth James

Are We Still Best Friends?
Color photographs by Heinz Kluetmeier.
Raintree Publishers, Ltd., 1975.
(30 pages)

B

FRIENDSHIP: Best Friend
Arguing

Young Cindy and Ann are best friends. They walk to school together and play dress-up together. When Ann's cat has kittens, they play with them, and Ann promises to let Cindy take one home when it is old enough. Together they begin to build a bed for the kitten at school. But when it comes time to paint the bed, they start arguing. The teacher separates them, sending Cindy to work on a scrapbook and Ann to mold clay. While Ann works, she looks at Cindy and decides that Cindy is still angry. Ann tells her teacher it is no fun working without Cindy. At story time Cindy sits behind Ann, not beside her, and Ann is unhappy about this, too. Later, the teacher advises Ann to let Cindy know she isn't angry at her. Ann brings milk to Cindy and says, "Don't be mad anymore." Cindy says she is not but that she knows Ann is. Ann assures her that she is not angry either.

This delightfully simple story, narrated by Ann, shows the give and take necessary in any friendship. With the aid of their teacher the two girls resolve their feelings quickly, because they want to be friends working together. The expressive faces on the girls in the photographs dramatize the text.

Ages 4-7

Also available in:
No other form known

32

Barkin, Carol and Elizabeth James

Doing Things Together

Color photographs by Heinz Kluetmeier.
Raintree Publishers, Ltd., 1975.
(31 pages)

COOPERATION: in Work
SCHOOL: Classmate Relationships

Ms. Kimball's class is planning a party for Parents' Day, and Ms. Kimball reminds them that they must work together to make it a success. Eddie thinks up decorations; Peter suggests giving a dance performance; and Ann proposes singing. But Sarah interrupts to say that her parents both work and so cannot attend. Ms. Kimball suggests that Sarah invite her older sister instead. The children get to work: one group making bright paper flowers, another making paper chains, and still another painting birds on the welcome sign. The students also draw self-portraits, and choose three songs to perform. Then everybody takes home their invitations. Parents' Day arrives, and the children show their guests where to sit, proudly display the decorations, sing their songs, and dance. After refreshments, everyone goes home agreeing that the party has been a success.

Told mostly in dialogue, this account details the tasks and the working together that go into preparing a class party. Bright photographs (which show a very young, multi-racial class) add much to this simple text, which may be read aloud or read independently by second graders.

Ages 4-7

Also available in:
No other form known

33

Barkin, Carol and Elizabeth James

I'd Rather Stay Home

Color photographs by Heinz Kluetmeier.
Raintree Publishers, Ltd., 1975.
(31 pages)

FEAR: of School
School: classmate relationships

Young Jimmy fears going to his first day of school, even though his brother and sister say school is fun. "What if everyone else knows how to do things I can't do?" Jimmy frets. "What if no one wants to play with me?" At school the first day, his teacher urges him to play with Tom and Sarah, who are building a tunnel of large blocks. Jimmy refuses. Soon he thinks no one wants to play with him. He sees that Tom is struggling to make the top of the tunnel but cannot lift the necessary blocks. Finding that he can be of help, Jimmy thinks, "I'd like to crawl through that tunnel," and runs over to join Sarah and Tom. The three children finish the tunnel and have fun crawling through it. Later Jimmy gets the giggles with Tom when the teacher tells the class a funny story. By the time his mother arrives to take him home, Jimmy no longer fears school and asks her if he can invite Tom over after school the next day.

This picture story of a boy overcoming his fear of starting school is set in a class of children of diverse ethnic origins. Large color photographs and a simple text realistically but warmly capture mixed feelings of very young children playing, learning, and making friends at school.

Ages 4-6

Also available in:
No other form known

34

Barkin, Carol and Elizabeth James

Sometimes I Hate School

Color photographs by Heinz Kluetmeier.
Raintree Publishers, Ltd., 1975.
(31 pages)

SCHOOL: Pupil-Teacher Relationships
  Anger
  Communication: importance of
  Cooperation

The young narrator and his friend Peter view apprehensively the news that their teacher, Ms. Kimball, is going away briefly — and view with mistrust the substitute teacher, Mr. Coleman, who will, they feel certain, run the classroom differently. Sure enough, they are angered to find their fort of blocks dismantled and put away. And later, when Mr. Coleman assigns another student to help Peter put away the paints, a job Ms. Kimball had given the two friends, the narrator explodes. "It's not fair!" he yells, and spills a jar of paint. Mr. Coleman explains that he had not known of Ms. Kimball's arrangement; but he is pretty sure the narrator is angry at him. The boy admits he is. The next day is full of surprises. Mr. Coleman helps the class make cranberry sauce, and at recess he joins them jumping rope. Peter chooses him to be on his tag team, and later the class learns a circle dance. By the end of the day the boys have seen how much fun Mr. Coleman can be, and how understanding, for he remarks on how much they must miss Ms. Kimball. When the latter comes back, the children tell her all they did with Mr. Coleman, and the two boys realize that they are going to miss him as they did her.

When a substitute stands in for a well-loved teacher, two little boys experience a fear of changes, and anger at the stranger responsible. By showing them he understands and accepts their feelings, and by involving them in new projects they like, Mr. Coleman helps them overcome their fear and resentment. The color photographs illustrating this book show an ethnically diverse class, probably kindergarten or first grade.

Ages 5-7

Also available in:
No other form known

35

Barnett, Naomi

I Know a Dentist

Color illustrations by Linda Boehm.
G. P. Putnam's Sons, 1977.
(45 pages counted)

DENTIST, GOING TO

Six- or seven-year-old Sally, proud of her perfect teeth, visits a dentist for a check-up. A dental assistant shows her to a new, couch-like dental chair where Dr. Jenkins first inspects her teeth for dental plaque, an acidic coating that can cause cavities or infections of the gums. Then he explains how to brush teeth to reduce it. Next, he cleans her teeth and finds a shallow cavity. X-ray photographs reveal no others, so he fills the only one. Sally is sad that her perfect record is broken and asks how to prevent additional cavities. It is mostly up to her, Dr. Jenkins says. Eat well and avoid heavily sugared

B

foods and drinks; brush after eating; and either drink fluoride-treated water or ask the dentist for a fluoride treatment.

Sally gives a clear, first-person account of what happens in a dentist's office. The book should dispel a youngster's ignorance of procedures, though it may not quiet all fears. Already determined to have good teeth, Sally shows no fear and a great deal of curiosity. This book, designed for unassisted reading by first- and second-graders, is one in the publisher's Community Helpers series.

Ages 6-8

Also available in:
No other form known

36

Barrett, Judith

I Hate to Go to Bed

Color illustrations by Ray Cruz.
Four Winds Press, 1977.
(29 pages counted)

BEDTIME

A number of children give their reasons for disliking going to bed. One boy just resents his parents' saying that he must; another feels wide awake. Still others are unwilling to stop playing, or to take off their clothes, or to brush their teeth, with gooey toothpaste, or to crawl between cold sheets, or to enter a dark, monster-filled bedroom. "But if I have to go to bed," all look for the good side of bedtime. One little girl likes staying up for a few minutes longer to sip warm cocoa, while one little boy likes to wear his football pajamas. Still others cuddle with stuffed animals, or read under the covers, or talk to themselves about secret things, or shoot monsters

in the dark, or have adventures in their dreams. It is when they wake up that they realize getting out of a cozy, warm bed can be unpleasant. "What I hate most about going to bed at night is that I have to get up in the morning."

These first-person narratives set forth in simple language the pros and cons of going to bed. Young readers will be charmed by the candor of the reasoning and recognize its humor. No adult comments intrude.

Ages 4-6

Also available in:
No other form known

37

Barrett, Judith

I Hate to Take a Bath

Color illustrations by Charles B. Slackman.
Four Winds Press, 1975.
(30 pages counted)

BATHS, TAKING OF

Several youngsters are quick to state their reasons for disliking baths. One little boy feels that he is already clean, while one little girl with long hair dislikes getting it wet. Still another child feels a bath "washes off all the good dirt." Others do not want to remove favorite clothes, or have their hair and ears washed. "But if I have to take a bath," all agree, it means going to bed afterwards. Still, taking a bath can also be fun. They can create bubble islands, splash (but not too vigorously), sing loudly, play with boats or toys, and pretend to be turtles or submarines. Yet even these happy pastimes are ended when one must, eventually, leave the tub. "I think what I hate most about taking a bath is that I have to get out."

This set of first-person narratives charms its readers with one illustration per viewpoint per page, and a simple text written from each child's point of view. The very young should recognize the humor here and relish it. No adult comments intrude.

Ages 4-6

Also available in:
No other form known

38

Bartoli, Jennifer

Nonna

Color illustrations by Joan Drescher.
Harvey House, Inc., 1975.
(45 pages counted)

DEATH: of Grandparent
  Family: unity
  Grandparent: love for

A young boy narrates this story about the death of his grandmother, Nonna, and what came afterward. Following her death, the family is sad and quiet. Although the boy's mother cooks a favorite family dinner, no one eats it. Everyone is happy for a time when the older brother arrives on leave from the army, but soon they are quiet again. The following morning the boy and his younger sister, Amy, help their mother make cookies. Mother tells Amy that when she is older she can make Nonna's cookies, and the boy remarks that Nonna once told him the seven ingredients, which he wrote down. The day ends with the family going to the cemetery for the burial. The next day, Saturday, the relatives gather at Nonna's house to divide up her property. Remembering other Saturday mornings when he and Amy visited her, the boy feels that Nonna should be there. He cannot really believe she is dead. His mother reminds him

of all the good memories of Nonna they have. The passing seasons do bring back those memories, until it is Christmastime. Although this is the first Christmas without Nonna, nobody mentions it. But Amy has a surprise for Christmas dinner — she has baked some of Nonna's cookies. Sampling them, the boy says they are almost as good as Nonna's, and everyone laughs in appreciation.

This story shows how family life continues even after a loved one is gone. Everyone misses the grandmother and finds her death difficult to accept. But as time passes the family enjoys remembering her warmth and affection. The child's fixing Nonna's cookies during that first Christmas without her helps ease the sadness everyone feels.

Ages 4-9

Also available in:
No other form known

39

Bate, Lucy

Little Rabbit's Loose Tooth

Color illustrations by Diane de Groat.
Crown Publishers, Inc., 1975.
(30 pages counted)

TOOTH, LOSS OF

Little Rabbit has a loose tooth. That makes it difficult to chew hard foods, like carrots, and so she follows her mother's advice to chew hard foods with her other teeth. But while she is eating chocolate ice cream, Little Rabbit's tooth falls out. What to do with it? She could throw it away, put it in a necklace, or mount it. Instead, she puts it under her pillow for the tooth fairy, in whom she does not believe. She asks her mother to leave a present if the tooth fairy does not. In the morning, Little Rabbit wakes to find the tooth gone and a dime in its place.

Small children will recognize the inconvenience of chewing food with a loose tooth, as well as the value of the tooth — as part of the body — to the child who loses it. The existence of the tooth fairy is neither confirmed nor denied. Large, detailed pictures make this a good book to read aloud.

Ages 4-6

Also available in:
Paperbound — *Little Rabbit's Loose Tooth*
Scholastic Book Services

Talking Book — *Little Rabbit's Loose Tooth*
Library of Congress

40

Bates, Betty

Bugs in Your Ears

Holiday House, Inc., 1977.
(128 pages)

STEPPARENT: Father
STEPPARENT: Mother
    Adoption: feelings about
    Parent/Parents: remarriage of
    Stepbrother/Stepsister

Thirteen-year-old Carrie does not like Dominic, the man her mother is going to marry, nor does she like the idea of moving in with him and his three children. To complicate matters she is away visiting her grandmother when her mother gets married, and Carrie returns home to a new apartment. Her mother and Dominic lack time to prepare for Carrie, and so she spends her first night on the living-room couch. In the morning she tries uncomfortably to explain her presence to each of Dominic's children, but nobody listens. In exasperation she finally yells that she is their new sister and tells them they all have bugs in their ears. Soon Carrie gets acquainted with the members of her new family. Every day she and Newton ride the school bus together to the same eighth-grade class. After she helps him shed his unpopular know-it-all reputation, Carrie and Newton become friends. Fourteen-year-old Ginger and Carrie share a room. Ginger resents Carrie and purposely leaves her clothes scattered in Carrie's part of the room. Ginger is surprised to hear from her father that she must pick up the clothes and vacuum before she can eat dinner. After this, a more understanding relationship develops between Carrie and Ginger. Soon after that, Rick, Dominic's older son, gets the hiccups while playing in a high-school soccer game and cannot get rid of them. Using a trick her mother taught her, Carrie cures him just in time to play again. They agree that Rick will treat Carrie more respectfully and she will tell nobody about the hiccups. But Carrie still does not like Dominic or the idea of being legally adopted by him. Her mother will not listen to her. In court with her mother and Dominic, she tells the lawyer and judge that she does not want to be adopted, but the proceedings continue anyway. The following Saturday morning she is alone in the apartment with Dominic and feels uncomfortable. But he is not angry with her and tells her he is sorry she is not happy there. "Tell me if there is something I can do to make it better for you," he says. Suddenly she sees that he has been fixing her broken treasure box, though she had been sure he had forgotten his promise to do so. He has been working on it all this time — repairing it and replacing the old finish. Carrie is delighted and soon begins talking with Dominic about feelings she has never even told her mother. After this, Carrie and Dominic's children plan a surprise dinner for her mother and Dominic on their two-month anniversary — a jubilant affair where Carrie is introduced to Italian food and really feels part of the family.

This book, as told by Carrie, shows how difficult a parent's remarriage can be for children. Of course, not all new families would be brought together so abruptly. But the need for the four children in this family to work things out on their own shows the great capacity children have for making their own adjustments. Carrie's eventual acceptance of all the members of her new family and they of her is contrived, yet encouraging, and consistent with her character. This is an interesting story in limited vocabulary.

Ages 10-13

Also available in:
Braille — *Bugs in Your Ears*
Library of Congress

Paperbound — *Bugs in Your Ears*
Pocket Books, Inc.

41

Bates, Betty

The Ups and Downs of Jorie Jenkins

Holiday House, Inc., 1978.
(126 pages)

ILLNESSES: of Parent
MATURATION
  Loneliness
  Loss: feelings of

It is a pleasant summer for Jorie Jenkins, who will begin junior high school in the fall. Jorie's older sister, Marcie, is packed and ready to go visit their grandmother in Arizona, but just as the family is leaving for the airport, Jorie's father, a pediatrician, is called to the hospital to treat a patient. A short time later, a nurse from the

hospital calls to say that Dr. Jenkins has just had a heart attack. From then on Jorie's life is turned upside down. Her mother spends every day and most evenings at the hospital, leaving Jorie to fend for herself. Once the father is out of immediate danger, Marcie leaves on her trip. Even when Marcie returns, her time goes into making costumes for the school play, and she is not much company for Jorie. Jorie's best friend, Stephanie, is to play the piano for the same play, and spends all her afternoons rehearsing. In her loneliness, the usually friendly Jorie becomes touchy and depressed. On her first visit to her father in the hospital, she feels she is visiting a stranger. He is surrounded by machines, can say only a few words to her, and is not at all the strong, reliable, witty dad she had always known. She tries to avoid seeing him again, and occupies her time playing matchmaker for Marcie and a boy named Peter. Finally, she blurts out her feelings to her mother, who is sympathetic: "He is different, isn't he? It bothers me too, Jorie." On the opening night of the school play, both Marcie and Mrs. Jenkins are busy (Mrs. Jenkins has had to take over from Stephanie as accompanist), leaving Jorie to look in on her dad. At the hospital, she finds he has suffered a slight setback and needs company. She decides to miss the play to stay with him. In their bits of conversation when he is not dozing, Jorie and her father get to know each other again, and Jorie feels comfortable with him once more. When he comes home at Thanksgiving, still a little changed, she knows how dear he is to her still.

In this first-person narrative, an adolescent is shocked into realizing that life does not go on forever unchanged and according to plan. Aware that she cannot continue to depend on her father for everything, she begins to make some decisions for herself and to take some responsibility for helping her father accept his own changed life. Touches of wit keep this story from being unduly alarming or grim.

Ages 9-12

Also available in:
Paperbound — *The Ups and Downs of Jorie Jenkins*
Pocket Books, Inc.

42

Bauer, Marion Dane

Foster Child

The Seabury Press, Inc., 1977.
(155 pages)

FOSTER HOME
  Child abuse
  Fear: of physical harm

Twelve-year-old Renny has never seen her father and has lived with her great-grandmother since infancy, when her mother left her, never to return. When Gram has a stroke, Renny's Great-Aunt Florence turns the girl over to a foster agency, which places her with the Beck family. Four other foster children live with the Becks: a teenage girl, two young brothers, and Karen Rawls, a little girl whose father continually travels on business and whose mother is temporarily hospitalized for severe depression. The children all are frightened of Mr. Beck, a stern religious fanatic who believes the Lord sends him such children to be "saved." Renny distrusts him. One day when she is ill, Papa Beck comes to comfort her with talk of Jesus. His voice is soothing, and his hands begin to caress her back, then her breasts, then start to go under her pajama pants. Ralph, one of the boys, walks in and orders Beck to stop. From then on, Renny is terrified and longs to run away. When her friend Karen's father comes to visit, she tries to confide in him but cannot. Finally, she makes for Gram's house, taking Karen with her to keep the girl from Beck. But they discover the house empty, up for sale. They go to Aunt Florence's, where Karen's worried father eventually locates them. Some weeks later, new arrangements made, Mr. Rawls takes both girls home with him; Mrs. Rawls, home from the hospital, is waiting. Later the Rawls take Renny to see Gram, who has been placed in a nursing home and who is still unconscious. Renny, realizing that Gram will never be well, pours out the story of life with the Becks to the oblivious old lady. Mr. and Mrs. Rawls, overhearing, are deeply moved, and deeply grateful that, thanks to Renny, both girls are safe.

A series of shocks — the sudden illness and imminent death of a substitute parent, sexual advances by a frightening man, a realization of danger to herself and a friend — force a young adolescent girl to make some adult decisions. Not the least frightening of her discoveries is that her revulsion at the man's caresses is mixed with pleasure. The story's resolution — Renny's acceptance into the reunited Rawls family — though a relief, seems a little too good to be true. All that leads up to it is starkly realistic.

Ages 11-13

Also available in:
Paperbound — *Foster Child*
Dell Publishing Company, Inc.

43

Bauer, Marion Dane

Shelter from the Wind

The Seabury Press, Inc., 1976.
(108 pages)

RUNNING AWAY
  Maturation

Twelve-year-old Stacy is running away — from her father's remarriage and her unsympathetic stepmother — so suddenly that she has taken nothing with her.

Now, after hours in the Oklahoma sun and wind, she realizes how foolish her action has been, but is too stubborn to turn back. She wants her father to regret the remarriage and the baby that will soon be born to it. As night comes to the high panhandle country, Stacy — cold, hungry, and thirsty — crouches beneath a tree to sleep. When she awakens, she is befriended by a pair of white German shepherds. The dogs lead her to a small sandstone house, where Ella, a spunky old lady, gives Stacy food and water and listens to her story. Ella scolds her for being so foolish, but allows her to stay until she can make plans. During the next few days, Ella recounts to Stacy episodes from her own life. Stacy, in turn, confides in her all the anger and resentment she feels for her stepmother and the coming baby. As Stacy comes to know Ella, she begins to see her own life in the perspective of another's. When the female dog bears puppies, Stacy helps save a puppy's life, but later, to her horror, must drown it because it has a cleft palate. Meanwhile, Ella falls and badly twists her ankle, and Stacy walks to a neighbor for help. When Ella is taken to town to see a doctor, Stacy goes too, for she has decided, "I'd best go home." She will return to visit Ella, though, and pick out one of the puppies for her own.

This is a story about a girl who runs away and the wise old woman who helps her better understand herself and the "way it is." The story's ending implies that Stacy returns home with no easy answers, but that her time with Ella, both past and to come, will help her cope with the future.

Ages 10-13

Also available in:
Paperbound — *Shelter from the Wind*
Dell Publishing Company, Inc.

Talking Book — *Shelter from the Wind*
Library of Congress

44

Bawden, Nina Mary Kark

The Peppermint Pig

J. B. Lippincott Co., 1975.
(189 pages)

FAMILY: Unity
Maturation
Parental: absence
Pets: love for
Sibling: relationships

B

A thoroughly happy English family, Mr. and Mrs. James Greengrass and their four children, aged nine through fourteen, live comfortably in London. But when Father confesses to stealing money from the firm where he works in order to protect the guilty son of the owner, he is forced to leave his job. He decides to seek work in America while Mother and the children wait for him at the home of James's two sisters in rural Norfolk. The new life brings joys as well as difficulties. Mrs. Greengrass works as a seamstress to supplement the family income, and Lily and George, thirteen and fourteen respectively, take to country life with ease. But ten-year-old Theo, small for his age, must struggle to win the respect of the local children, particularly Noah. For nine-year-old Poll, who is mischievous and high-spirited, Norfolk is endlessly interesting. She is especially taken with a small pig Mother brings home. The family names it Johnnie, and throughout the first year in Norfolk it lives as a pet, growing large and plump. Father writes often from America, but he is not making as much money as he had hoped to. Just before his return, Poll one day comes home to find the pig missing. Without telling her, Mother has sold Johnnie to the butcher to help pay a bill, hoping that a birthday puppy she has given Poll will be pet enough. Poll, however, is grief-stricken for days. It is some time before she can accept the death of the pig and turn all her tenderness to the puppy. By the time Father reappears, she feels in command of her past.

In this story, family members mean a lot to each other. Though Father is seldom discussed during his absence, he is much thought of. Theo finally stops imagining him a sinister sort of thief and sees him as well-meaning and ordinary. For her part, Poll finds security when she realizes Father has not abandoned her. It is through Poll's experiences and her struggles to grow up that we primarily view events.

Ages 9-14

Also available in:
Paperbound — *The Peppermint Pig*
Penguin Books, Inc.

Talking Book — *The Peppermint Pig*
Library of Congress

45

Baylor, Byrd

Hawk, I'm Your Brother

Black/white illustrations by Peter Parnall.
Charles Scribner's Sons, 1976.
(45 pages counted)

ANIMALS: Love for
  Imagination
  Native American
  Nature: living in harmony with

Rudy is a young American Indian boy whose first words in his own tongue are those for "flying," "bird," and "up there," and whose constant and only wish is to fly. He would soar like a hawk, "smoother than anything else in the world." Unable to find someone to teach him to fly, Rudy concludes that perhaps only he of all the people on earth can learn how — is, in fact, a brother to the hawk. He steals a fledgling hawk from a nest on Santos Mountain, but instead of transmitting to Rudy the magic of flight, the hawk screams day after day as it battles to escape the cage. Rudy knows the hawk desires to fly free, but he keeps the bird until summer's end, hoping that somehow things will change. When they do not, Rudy takes the hawk high on Santos Mountain to freedom: "Bird, you can fly." The boy watches the hawk soar all that long afternoon. He calls to it and the great bird calls to him, and in his mind he and it are flying together. Rudy tells no one about his interlude with the hawk, but people see him change: his look is that of a hawk; and his eyes reflect the sky.

Drawing upon American Indian lore, this story shows a boy's gradual passage from desiring the power of flight and trying to extort it from nature to identifying with a hawk — and living harmoniously with nature. The boy sees he can no longer deny a hawk its natural powers but can, in a mystical way, participate in those powers. The lyrical free verse and the black line drawings evoke the wide, wild spaces of the American desert lands.

Ages 5-8

Also available in:
Paperbound — *Hawk, I'm Your Brother*
Charles Scribner's Sons

46

Beckman, Gunnel

Mia Alone

Translated from the Swedish by Joan Tate.
The Viking Press, Inc., 1975.
(124 pages) o.p.

ABORTION
UNWED MOTHER
 Anxiety
 Decision making
 Separation, marital
 Sex: premarital

Seventeen-year-old Mia Järeberg fears she is pregnant. She would like to confide in someone, seek advice, but from whom? Her parents are quarreling, and Mia doesn't want to worry her boy friend, Jan, until she knows for sure. She has tried to avoid Jan, but when he unexpectedly drops by one morning, she feels compelled to explain what is wrong. Jan is very kind and tells her he would like to marry her, but suggests they make no decision until after she knows the result of her pregnancy test. For Mia the next few days are turmoil. While she waits to know the results of the test, which has to be done twice, she tries to decide the best course if she is in fact pregnant: marriage? something else? She spends an evening with her father, and the two share their innermost concerns. He tells her that he and her mother are going to live apart for a while; Mia will stay with him, and her sister will go with her mother. Mia confesses her suspicion of pregnancy, and he tries to help her decide for herself what is morally and psychologically best if she is proved right. Later that night, Mia gets her period. She is relieved but too exhausted to be joyful. When she tells Jan, he seems glad to have gotten off so easily. She cannot understand her own confusion and loneliness, but her father reassures her that when one has been through so difficult an experience, such a reaction is normal.

Mental anguish over her supposed pregnancy is about as far as unmarried Mia gets in trying to make the best decision for herself, her boy friend, and the unborn child. She knows that her parents married because her mother was pregnant with *her*, and Mia does not want to marry before she is ready. Confiding in her father promises some clarity. In the end, not pregnant after all, she realizes that though she is relieved, "the relief seemed to have cost her so much." She will never again be naive. This serious, thought-provoking book is not for the reader who needs things lightened with humor; its central predicament, its characters, and its dialogue are always convincing. The author makes no judgment of Mia, and neither does her father.

Ages 12 and up

Also available in:
Cassette for the Blind — *Mia Alone*
Library of Congress

Paperbound — *Mia Alone*
Dell Publishing Company, Inc.

B

47

Beckman, Gunnel

That Early Spring

Translated from the Swedish by Joan Tate.
The Viking Press, Inc., 1977.
(121 pages)

GRANDPARENT: Love for
MATURATION
   Cardiac conditions
   Death: attitude toward
   Grandparent: living in child's home
   Separation, marital
   Sex: premarital

In the large Swedish city where she lives, eighteen-year-old Mia Järeberg has accepted her parents' separation and the fact that her mother and younger sister live elsewhere. But she is lonely, and so persuades her father to ask Gran, his mother, to leave the nursing home and come live with them. Although Gran has heart trouble, her doctor approves the move, and before long Mia and Gran are fast friends and confidantes. All the same, Mia sees much of her friends, and at a party she meets an attractive college student named Martin. She is flattered by his attention, but sure she will not hear from him again. But Martin is pushed from her thoughts when, back home from the party, she finds Gran having a heart attack. She helps her take her medication, and then — at Gran's request — the two sit talking of death and Gran's past life. The doctor arrives, pronounces this a mild attack, and departs. After midterm, Mia again dates Martin, but she declines to sleep with him and once again persuades herself that the relationship will go nowhere. But he calls, and they date again, and Mia does spend the night with him. Even after this, Mia sees no certain future for them, a view borne out by Martin's ensuing silence and absence. When he does happen by one evening while her father and Gran are out, Mia has a serious talk with him. She does not want a serious relationship, she says, but does want one that holds more than sexual attraction. She adds that she is sure Martin cannot give her what she seeks, or even understand what she is talking about. After Martin has left, Gran has a severe coronary. Mia's father is not at home, and Mia alone goes to the hospital with Gran, and is with her when she dies. Before leaving the hospital Mia notifies her father. Only then does she begin to try to comprehend all that has happened during this spring, "the spring when I understood *lots* of things I hadn't understood before."

In this sequel to *Mia Alone*, Mia finds a whole new relationship with her understanding, generous Gran. She also becomes a strong advocate of women's rights — a subject which comes up throughout the story. But several subjects treated here — acceptance of death, sexual freedom, women's rights, adjustment to parental separation — may well prompt discussion. As for sexual experience, the book's descriptions are candid without being clinical.

Ages 12 and up

Also available in:
Cassette for the Blind — *That Early Spring*
Library of Congress

Paperbound — *That Early Spring*
Dell Publishing Company, Inc.

48

Beckwith, Lillian

The Spuddy: A Novel

Delacorte Press, 1974.
(118 pages)

LONELINESS
MUTENESS
PETS: Love for
  Relatives: living in home of

Eight-year-old Andy lives with his mother in a small fishing village. His father, a fisherman, is away at sea for months at a time. Andy is lonely and has never spoken a word in his life. Nor does he speak when one day, without warning, his mother runs off. His father takes the boy to Aunt Sarah and Uncle Ben, who live in another village, and they seem delighted to look after him. But Andy's big day comes when he adopts an uncommonly intelligent stray dog, known in the village as "the Spuddy." The two become inseparable. But because Aunt Sarah will not keep a dog in the house, Andy must find a place for him to sleep. For a while, a cave on the moors does nicely, but when winter comes it is too cold and damp. Andy makes a bed for Spuddy in a workshop on the wharf where Uncle Ben works, but the shop's owner soon objects. Then Andy's friend Jake, the lonely owner of the fishing boat Silver Crest, offers to keep the dog on board and take him out on his weekly fishing trips. Andy is reluctant to be separated from Spuddy so much but decides Jake's idea is, after all, the best. And so Spuddy becomes a sea dog, coming home to spend weekends with Andy. In time, Andy too goes on short fishing trips with Jake, but it is almost two years before he is allowed to go on an expedition lasting several days. The first day, after the fishermen take in herring, they anchor in a bay off another village. The crew persuade Andy to go ashore for an hour or two, leaving Spuddy on board with Jake. But soon a severe blizzard is raking the coast. Unseen through the snow, the Silver Crest is dashed to bits on the rocks. The next day the bodies of Jake and Spuddy are found dead on the beach. Andy sees the gulls circling greedily over the body of his beloved dog — and speaks for the first time. Angrily he shouts, over and over, "No! No! No!"

In this artful and moving story, a boy and a stray dog share a mutual devotion — so strong that the dog's death transforms the boy. Lonely children and those who have loved a pet will share Andy's feelings. Life in a small fishing village is vividly described.

Ages 11 and up

Also available in:
Paperbound — *The Spuddy: A Novel*
Dell Publishing Company, Inc.

Talking Book — *The Spuddy: A Novel*
Library of Congress

49

Behrens, June York

Together

Color photographs by Vince Streano.
Childrens Press, Inc., 1975.
(39 pages)

FRIENDSHIP

One little girl is proud to say that Uncle Lin is her best friend. Another child likes a boy named Roger, who is nice to everyone. Another's best friend, Ed, enjoys the same games as he, and another little girl tells of her friendship with her dogs, who sleep in her room and whom she feeds and cares for. Other children claim a mother, a father, a grandmother, or a cousin as best friend. Still others have friends who climb trees, play

B

hide-and-seek, run and chase, share things, or like to pretend. One girl sums up all their feelings when she declares that "everyone needs a good friend."

This multiple first-person narrative explores the many kinds of friendship children form and some of the things children admire about their friends. The accompanying photographs clearly show that friendship knows no boundaries of age, race, or gender. The fact that all the situations and activities depicted are familiar ones enhances the likelihood that small children will want to discuss their own preferences in friends.

Ages 4-7

Also available in:
Large Print — *Together*
Childrens Press, Inc.

50

Berger, Terry

How Does It Feel When Your Parents Get Divorced?

Black/white photographs by Miriam Shapiro.
Julian Messner, Inc., 1977.
(62 pages)

DIVORCE: of Parents

A young girl is frightened by her parents' ceaseless arguing. Yet when a divorce is decided on, she feels responsible and tries to bring about a reconciliation. "I wanted to keep Mom and Dad together. . . . Why couldn't they love each other?" Her father moves into an apartment, and although she talks to him often and sees him on weekends, she misses him terribly. Even after the decree, she pretends he will return and remarry her mother. But that fantasy appears more and more unlikely — and for a time she takes to misbehaving. Only when she sees that her parents are in fact

happier than before does she calm down and try to be helpful. She still looks forward to visits with her father and fumes if he cancels them. But her fears about her own future subside when she sees how self-reliant her father has become, that he could even take care of her, if necessary. Ater two years, many things have changed. The girl and her mother live in an apartment; her mother works; the girl helps with dinner. The mother begins going out and, inevitably, the daughter wonders what life would be like if her mother remarried. She has mixed feelings about marriage for herself. While she is at camp, both parents come to visit, and she is deeply glad to see that their love for her is unchanged. She becomes more involved with new interests and friendships, and finds herself thinking less and less about her parents' divorce.

In this first-person account, a young girl describes the whole range of her feelings about her parents' divorce. This book reads easily but makes no attempt to gloss over hard times. It suggests, however, that in time the hurts will lessen. The use of photographs rather than illustrations gives the text extra immediacy. This girl's candid recollection could stimulate discussion among other children facing parental divorce.

Ages 6-11

Also available in:
No other form known

51

Berkey, Barry R. and Velma A. Berkey

Robbers, Bones & Mean Dogs

Black/white illustrations by Marylin Hafner.
Addison-Wesley Publishing Company, Inc., 1978.
(28 pages counted)

FEAR

Floods, elevators, slammed doors, robbers, bones, mean dogs, electric wires, dying — these might cause anyone, old or young, to be afraid. Sometimes a child's fear would seem to an adult entirely reasonable: one boy explains that he fears elevators, because once he was injured when one fell with him in it. Sometimes children control fear by their own actions: a boy tells us he fears slamming doors less than before, because he is now more careful opening and closing doors. Sometimes fears seem unreasonable: a boy fears being ten years old, because a book said ten is a "dangerous age." Sometimes parents are insensitive and make fears worse: the father of a boy afraid of water thinks it funny to pretend to tip over a rowboat. Often a child is afraid of one thing after another while growing up — and can look back and say, "But with most of my fears I get over them. Thank goodness!"

Children tell of their fears in their own words in this culling from over 1,500 children's essays. Readers of all ages will be amused by the text, the witty illustrations, and the sly asides in both. Groups of children may be prompted to discuss their own fears after having the book read to them. Everyone needs to be reminded of the authors' message: "it is okay to be afraid."

Ages 5-9

Also available in:
No other form known

52

Bernays, Anne

Growing Up Rich

Little, Brown and Co., 1975.
(343 pages)

Money, lots of it, has shaped fourteen-year-old Sally's life in ways she only becomes aware of when her mother and stepfather are killed in a plane crash and she must live with a middle-class family. Carefully schooled by her mother, Sally and her six-year-old half-brother, Roger, have effortlessly learned the difference between what is proper and what improper. Yet Sally, half-Jewish — her father, divorced from her late mother, is a rich gentile — is constantly bedeviled by the question of who she is: a Jew like her dead mother and stepfather, or a gentile like her father? Her father's open anti-Semitism further confuses her. Yet Sally wants to live with her father and his new young wife now. But she and Roger are compelled to live with Sam London, their guardian under her stepfather's will. Neither of the children fits in at London's home. Sam is grouchy, his wife, Judy, inelegant and sloppy, and their two sons are brats. Sally intends moving to her father's until he visits, and she sees him as he is — an alcoholic obsessed with appearances. Still, she feels she cannot abide the Londons. Then, in a series of encounters she begins to work herself clear of the priggishness of a sheltered past. And the Londons, accused by Sally of not wanting her and Roger, begin to shake loose from some of their habits. The odd guardianship works out and a mutual love develops and grows.

In this first-person narrative set in the mid-1940s, Sally looks back on a major change from growing up in the protected milieu of the rich to living in the hurly-burly of the commonplace world. There are no revelations as she makes the transition, but her shock and confusion are real enough as she learns that many of the standards by which she has been raised are not universal. These characters and their gropings in bewildered, fairly good will are easy to know and care about, and the telling of their story is wry and perceptive as Sally turns a cool eye on the world and on herself.

Ages 13 and up

Also available in:
Cassette for the Blind — *Growing Up Rich*
Library of Congress

53

Bernstein, Joanne E. and Stephen V. Gullo

When People Die

Black/white photographs by Rosmarie Hausherr.
E. P. Dutton & Company, Inc., 1977.
(39 pages counted)

DEATH: Attitude Toward
  Death: funeral issues

Death is a part of everyone's life. Doctors determine the moment of death by observing certain physiological signs. Some people, weighing the significance of death, ponder the nature of the soul. Moslem, Hindu, Jewish, and Christian views of the soul differ, and some people do not believe it exists at all. Similarly, funeral rites,

cremation, and burial are practiced variously, according to local custom. But virtually everywhere, after the death of a loved one, people grieve for a time and many feel weary, lonely, and angry. It is important to acknowledge these feelings.

This book deals straightforwardly and objectively with the subject of death. Each aspect the text discusses is illustrated with one or more clarifying photographs. The book may be helpful in preparing a child for the death of a loved one, or in consoling the child afterward. Children are encouraged to ask questions and to discuss their feelings about death as well as the ceremonies, customs, and beliefs surrounding it.

Ages 5-9

Also available in:
No other form known

54

Bethancourt, T. Ernesto, pseud.

The Dog Days of Arthur Cane

Holiday House, Inc., 1976.
(160 pages)

VALUES/VALUING
  Communication: parent-child
  Friendship: meaning of
  Maturation

After insulting an African exchange student by ridiculing the idea of Shamans or witch doctors (the student is one), sixteen-year-old Arthur Cane, a high school junior, wakes one morning to find that, still human of mind, he inhabits the body of a dog. He is chased from his suburban home and ends up in Greenwich Village, where he is adopted by Tyree, a former artist now almost blind. Arthur acts as a guide dog for Tyree, who earns a living as a street musician. From Tyree and his friends, Arthur begins to see that material things do not insure happiness, and that kindness, gentleness, and friendship are often more valuable. Arthur has just begun to accept his new life when he accidentally is separated from Tyree on the subway, is hit by a car, and is left in the street to die. He drags himself to a park, where he subsists on garbage and rests to regain his strength. Unwisely, he accepts meat from a man in a grease-stained raincoat and, when his stomach turns to "one huge knot of pain," realizes he has been poisoned. He saves himself by vomiting, but enough of the poison remains in his system to make him ill. Now he thinks only of returning home. By hiding on a crowded commuter train, Arthur returns to Manorsville and crawls to his house, where he collapses on the patio. His father reports the stray to the dog pound and a very sick Arthur is carted away. At the pound he is tenderly cared for by a veterinary student, but since no one claims him, he is slated for extermination. On the morning of his execution he awakes cold, naked — and human. He is reunited with his very angry parents, who demand to know why he ran away, but when Arthur truthfully explains his absence they promptly send him for psychoanalysis. On one visit to the analyst he drops in to see Tyree, who has had successful eye surgery. Alas, he cannot reclaim the friendship. He leaves thinking, "So long old buddy. Maybe some day, somehow, we'll be together and I'll be able to explain it all to you." As he begins his senior year, Arthur reflects on how those who cared for or hurt him during his "dog days" have reshaped his character.

In this first-person narrative, a bland, smug young suburbanite is shaken up for the better by a brief supernatural transformation. Friendship, affluence, and concern for people and animals all take on new meaning for him. Bizarre as Arthur's translation into a dog seems at first, it soon comes to seem just another way of being human. A secondary theme emerges: poor communication between parents and children.

Ages 11 and up

Also available in:
Braille — *The Dog Days of Arthur Cane*
Library of Congress

Paperbound — *The Dog Days of Arthur Cane*
Bantam Books, Inc.

55
Bethancourt, T. Ernesto, pseud.
New York City Too Far from Tampa Blues
Holiday House, Inc., 1975.
(190 pages)

B

RESOURCEFULNESS
TALENTS: Musical
  Change: new home
  Friendship: best friend
  Job

Tom is a twelve-year-old Hispanic-American who lives in Tampa, Florida — but not for long. One day his father, Pancho, announces that the family will be moving to New York City. Before they leave, Tom's uncle gives the boy a second-hand guitar, and Tom is beside himself with happiness. In New York, the family moves into the top floor of a shabby apartment building in a rundown neighborhood, where Tom quickly learns to fear a local street gang. They harass his younger sister, and when Tom steps in to defend her, they make trouble for him thereafter whenever he appears. Worse, they set off a fight which brings Tom trouble with the police and expulsion from school. This prompts the family's move to a safer neighborhood. Now Pancho decides that Tom should earn money shining shoes, and so he builds a shoeshine box and sends the boy out to work on Sundays, although Tom has to fight other boys to get and keep a place to work. The first day out, Tom meets Aurelio, an Italian-American boy his own age. As the two walk home together, they find that they both like music; in fact, they start singing. Soon after, Tom, with his guitar, and Aurelio, with his set of bongos, work up an act together. They try soliciting business for their shoeshining by singing in a bar but make such a hit as musicians that the owner gives them a job singing there every Sunday afternoon. Tom does not tell his parents how he is earning money, and since it is more than he would earn shining shoes, he gives his mother only what shoeshining would bring and hides the rest. Part of his savings he uses to buy Christmas gifts for the family. But Pancho accidentally discovers the hidden gifts before Christmas, and he accuses the boy of stealing. Tom discloses the job at the bar, and Pancho calms down. Through the school year, the boys play and sing for their clientele and bring home quite a bit of money. As school draws to a close, they ask to perform at the graduation exercises, are accepted, and Tom's mother agrees to make matching outfits for them. One day as they rehearse at Aurelio's house they meet a young man who owns a recording studio. Aurelio's brother's band is going to cut a record, and the young man wants to feature Tom and Aurelio with the group. The excitement of making the record and of performing at graduation brings the school year to a happy close. But the best comes last: both boys' applications are accepted by the New York City High School of Music and Art.

In his own witty way, Tom narrates the eventful, authentic-sounding, often funny story of his first year in New York City, where, along with another irrepressible boy, he finds his identity in the world of music. Readers interested in the recording business will find the detailed description of cutting a record appealing.

Ages 10-14

Also available in:
Braille — *New York City Too Far from Tampa Blues*
Library of Congress

Cassette for the Blind — *New York City Too Far from Tampa Blues*
Library of Congress

Paperbound — *New York City Too Far from Tampa Blues*
Bantam Books, Inc.

56

Blaine, Margery Kay

The Terrible Thing That Happened at Our House

Color illustrations by John C. Wallner.
Parents' Magazine Press, 1975.
(32 pages counted)

PARENT/PARENTS: Mother Working Outside Home
   Change: accepting
   Communication: parent-child
   Cooperation: in work
   Life style: change in

A young school-age girl and her little brother are happy with their mother, who is a "real" mother. She kisses them good-bye in the morning when they leave for school and fixes them toasted cheese sandwiches or tuna on a bun when they come home for lunch, and after school she listens to them talk about the day's happenings. Then she fixes them a snack and thinks up wonderful things to do. But all this changes when the mother returns to work as a science teacher. Now the children have to rush in the morning to get to school on time; they eat lunch at school; and after school their mother may be too busy with school work to talk to them. They also notice a change in their father. No longer a "real" father, now he fixes dinner and does household chores. He has no time anymore to sit and talk to the children. One night at dinner the little girl gets angry because no one is listening to her. She yells that nobody cares about anything or anyone and that since their mother has returned to work everything has changed. The whole family begins to talk about how things have changed and how to handle the changes. Soon parents and children are sharing the family work load, but are able to set aside some time every day to spend together.

The parents in this story fail to prepare their children for the changes that come about when the mother returns to work. It takes the anger and bewilderment of the young girl, who tells the story in the first person, to show the parents the difference between what they are doing and what the children have been used to. The advantages of full, frank discussion are shown. For all its humor, this book sets forth a thoroughly believable situation.

Ages 3-7

Also available in:
No other form known

57

Bloch, Marie Halun

Displaced Person

Lothrop, Lee & Shepard Co., 1978.
(191 pages)

REFUGEES
  Death: of father
  Dependence/Independence
  Fear
  Loneliness
  Responsibility: accepting
  War

In hopes of escaping Russian rule, fourteen-year-old Stefan Wasylenko and his father have fled the Ukraine during the final days of World War II. Staying in camps for displaced persons, Stefan is alarmed at how easily the people speak their minds — seeming not to fear reprisals from anyone. He is also dismayed that his father, a renowned botanist, insists on hauling along a battered valise containing a botanical treatise he has written on the Ukraine. His father wants the manuscript published after the war. When he, his father, and a friend stop at a farm near the western edge of Thuringia, they find a barn to sleep in and two meals a day in exchange for work. But on their way to the fields, the three are caught near a military convoy under strafing, and Stefan's father is critically wounded. He is taken to a hospital in a nearby town, while Stefan gathers their belongings, but in the nightmare of events the boy leaves his father's manuscript behind. When his father dies, Stefan blames himself for having abandoned the manuscript. Living now in a refugee camp, Stefan becomes ever more depressed, and it is only at war's end that he begins once more to take notice of things around him. With many other refugees he leaves Thuringia ahead of its oncoming Soviet rulers and moves to the American zone of occupation. There he becomes friendly with some Soviet troops stationed in the American barracks, playing an accordion they have given him. He enjoys their attention until they force him to play as they load unwilling refugees on a truck for return to the Ukraine. When Stefan sees some friends in the group, he stops playing and attacks a soldier. This is all the crowd needs to set upon the other soldiers, driving them away, and all Stefan needs to give him the determination to steal into the Soviet sector and retrieve his father's manuscript. As he looks at it, he realizes that to compile it was an act of freedom on his father's part: only a free man, not a slave, could have produced such a loving legacy.

The main character of this story has difficulty accepting the self-reliance thrust upon him and the integrity and courage of others. The author has used "diaries and firsthand accounts of Ukrainian refugees in World War II" for the background of this suspenseful book, whose lost, lonely refugees are all too convincing.

Also available in:
No other form known

58

Blue, Rose

The Preacher's Kid

Black/white illustrations by Ted Lewin.
Franklin Watts, Inc., 1975.
(52 pages) o.p.

PREJUDICE: Ethnic/Racial
SCHOOL: Classmate Relationships
  Integration: school busing
  Rejection: peer
  Values/Valuing: moral/ethical

Linda, a fifth grader, expects no real trouble when thirty-two black students are to be bused to her school from a nearby community. But some parents oppose the busing and organize a school boycott that her father, Reverend Maynard, refuses to support, thus incurring a good deal of anger himself. On the first day of the busing, Linda and her friend Barbara find the school doors barricaded by protesting parents. The bus filled with black students pulls away, but not before Linda hears herself called "the preacher's kid" by classmates. That afternoon Linda is surprised to learn that, because she tried to attend school, she may not be invited to her friend Cheryl's Halloween party. Even so, when school reopens a few days later, she goes again. This time the black students get off the bus but are turned back by eggs and tomatoes. Once again the school is closed, and fewer and fewer of her friends will play with Linda. At home, her father receives harassing phone calls; Linda wishes he would stop opposing the protesters so that the two of them could regain their old standing. Like her friend Barbara, she is allowed by her parents to choose whether or not to return to school. When school reopens yet again, Linda goes, so as not to make her father unhappy. This time the attending students enter under police escort. Sure enough, Linda is not invited to the Halloween party. "I could still have Cheryl as my friend," she explains to her aunt and uncle, "if I say my parents made me go to school and if I don't go to school on Monday." But she decides to go anyway, because it is the "right place to be." Once again there are demonstrations — this time by friends and parents who are black. Returning home, Linda finds Cheryl and Barbara waiting for her and describes her decision: "The only right thing to do was to go to school." Soon Linda's father is dismissed from his church and finds another only after some difficulty. Visiting the new church, Linda is proud when a girl asks her if she is "the preacher's kid."

A youngster makes an unpopular stand and risks losing her friends in doing so. Although guided by her parents' example, she is left to make up her own mind. Linda's father is depicted as a tolerant man who, even while disagreeing with the boycotters, shows compassion for their fears and confusion. Linda's story is believable if at times heavily moralistic.

Ages 9-12

Also available in:
No other form known

59

Blue, Rose

Seven Years from Home

Black/white illustrations by Barbara Ericksen.
Raintree Publishers, Ltd., 1976.
(58 pages)

ADOPTION: Identity Questions
  Arguing
  Jealousy: sibling

Mark Cranston is adopted. Today, his eleventh birthday, the only thought that gives him joy is that in seven more years he can begin to search for his "real" parents. Not that the Cranstons do not treat him like a son: many times they have told him they love him and chose him specially. But Mark accuses them of loving their nine-year-old son by birth, Peter, better. Peter retaliates by charging that Mark is better treated just because he is adopted. For two weeks the boys battle over the question. One day at the supermarket, Mark sees a woman who resembles his image of his mother and in his excitement, drops the groceries. Sensing what is going on in his mind, Mrs. Cranston loses her temper. She accuses him of ingratitude and says she hopes he finds his biological parents and they turn out to be "bums." Knowing how much he has upset her, but not knowing how to apologize, Mark goes off alone for the rest of the day. That night another quarrel with Peter turns into a fist fight. Angered, Mr. and Mrs. Cranston firmly explain that both boys are their sons and loved equally. As punishment for their quarreling, the boys are restricted in their activities for a week. Instead of feeling resentful, Mark and Peter are proud of their parents for finally settling the issue.

A young boy struggles to accept the love of his adoptive parents and to let go of what is here shown as an empty hope. Although the book ends predictably, its simply told story features natural dialogue with a ring of truth.

Ages 8-12

Also available in:
Talking Book — *Seven Years from Home*
Library of Congress

60

Blue, Rose

The Thirteenth Year: A Bar Mitzvah Story

Black/white illustrations by Ted Lewin.
Franklin Watts, Inc., 1977.
(85 pages)

JEWISH
RESPONSIBILITY: Accepting
  Death: of grandparent
  Family: unity
  Grandparent: love for
  Illnesses: terminal
  Maturation
  Values/Valuing: moral/ethical

Twelve-year-old Barry Fried is studying for his bar mitzvah — a Jewish religious ceremony in which he will gain the privileges accorded adult male members of the congregation. Each afternoon he studies with Cantor Michaelson, learning the Torah, which is the body of the Jewish scriptures, and the haftarah, selections from the books of the Prophets. But the fact that his parents seem unusually edgy disturbs Barry, until he decides they are worried about the bar mitzvah party plans. Barry asks his grandfather to help him practice his Torah and haftarah readings, and it is during one of these study sessions that the boy learns his grandfather has terminal cancer. Shaken by this discovery, he calls his cousin to tell her. She adds a confidence of her own — she has heard that Barry's father is suffering serious business reverses. After this revelation, Barry calls his parents and asks them to come to Grandpa's. There he chides them for their secrecy, reminding them that his bar mitzvah means he is ready to face and share in family crises. Barry and his parents decide to change the bar mitzvah plans. They will hold a kiddush for the congregation instead, and on the next day, have a bar mitzvah party at their home for close friends and relatives. The day following the party, Grandpa enters the hospital and soon dies. Barry finds the death hard to believe until he joins in the kaddish, a prayer for the dead, as an adult member of the Jewish faith, wearing the prayer shawl worn by his father and grandfather before him.

This story contains a wealth of information about Jewish religious traditions. It particularly delves into the meaning of the bar mitzvah, the study it entails, and the sense of growing up that a young man feels preparing for it. The closeness of Barry's family is impressive, as is the deep love and respect the boy feels for his paternal grandfather.

Ages 10-12

Also available in:
No other form known

61

Bornstein, Ruth

Little Gorilla

Color illustrations by the author.
The Seabury Press, Inc., 1976.
(30 pages counted)

LOVE, MEANING OF
 Self, attitude toward: accepting

From the day of his birth, everyone in the jungle loves Little Gorilla. He makes friends with a butterfly, a parrot, a giraffe, and even a lion, all in the course of his first year. But at the end of that year, Little Gorilla is no longer little but huge. His great size, however, makes absolutely no difference in how much his family and friends love him.

Colorful illustrations tell nearly the whole story of Little Gorilla and his jungle family. Small children will especially like this story, which teaches that being loved has nothing to do with one's size or appearance.

Ages 2-5

Also available in:
Paperbound — *Little Gorilla*
Scholastic Book Services

62

Bottner, Barbara

Jungle Day or, How I Learned to Love My Nosey Little Brother

Color illustrations by the author.
Delacorte Press, 1978.
(29 pages counted)

SIBLING: Relationships
 Cooperation: in play

Today is Jungle Day at school, and seven-year-old Jackie, unable to sketch a recognizable animal to take to class, is fast approaching a state of panic. When her little brother, five-year-old Wayne, offers to help, Jackie snubs him as too young to be of use. Wayne is still watching his sister work when her classmate, Margaret Hooper, gifted in art but vain, drops by to show off her splendid jungle creation and mocks Jackie's efforts. As Margaret smugly strolls away, Jackie retorts that she and Wayne together are creating a spectacular beast.

Happy to be suddenly included in his sister's plan, Wayne unleashes a torrent of ideas — all of which Jackie scorns. In desperation, Wayne challenges Jackie to paste the best parts of all her pictures together, creating a new animal altogether. Jackie, realizing that Wayne's is a splendid idea, urges him to help. In the end, brother and sister are as delighted with each other as they are with their joint achievement.

In this witty first-person narrative, a little girl discovers that her brother can be a help rather than a hindrance. Both text and illustrations show the two awakening to a new respect for each other. The illustrations make use of the comic-strip device of overhead balloons to record some of Jackie's thoughts.

Ages 4-7

Also available in:
No other form known

63

Bova, Benjamin William

City of Darkness: A Novel

Charles Scribner's Sons, 1976.
(150 pages)

GANGS: Being Bothered by
GANGS: Membership in
Rebellion
Responsibility: accepting
Running away

Ron Morgan, sixteen, lives in a "Tract," a U.S. city of the future. The Tracts are vast pollution-free, domed areas, where all houses look the same, the weather is controlled, and the people live programmed lives. A few "traditional" cities still stand, and tourists from the Tracts are permitted to visit them for several weeks each summer. Ron yearns to visit New York City on his own, and when an argument with his father provokes him to run away, he goes there. He is picked up in the city by an attractive girl named Sylvia, who offers to share her quarters with him. In her shabby apartment in a run-down neighborhood, Ron awakens in the night to find that Sylvia has disappeared — and taken all his money. When he goes out to find her, he is beaten and his identification — his only warrant to leave the city — is stolen. Sylvia later returns, and Ron learns that, like others in the city, she belongs to one of several gangs forced to live there all year round, who, to survive, make money off the tourists in the summer, so as to endure the winter, when the city is closed and trade impossible. Sylvia stole to survive. Now the city has closed and Ron too is trapped for the winter. When Sylvia's gang leader learns Ron is a skilled mechanic, he offers him protection in exchange for work. Already the gangs have begun to fight each other for food, fuel, and housing. Several members of Ron's gang are killed and Ron is forced into hiding. Again he is offered protection, this time by the Muslims, a powerful black gang, and accepts, living with them until spring, when the city is reopened. Sylvia comes to him. She has gotten back his identification. He can return to the Tract. But he cannot convince her to join him, and leaves alone with a new perspective on life, power, and the future.

A young man struggles to survive in an environment wholly unlike but no better than the sterile, regimented world of his upbringing. Shocked by the enforced poverty and crime in this alien society, he tries to remain honest and true to others in a place where such values are unknown. While this fiction is futuristic, it is peopled with characters rounded, recognizable, and even touching.

Ages 12 and up

Also available in:
No other form known

B

64

Bradbury, Bianca

Boy on the Run

The Seabury Press, Inc., 1975.
(126 pages)

IDENTITY, SEARCH FOR
RUNNING AWAY
  Dependence/Independence
  Divorce: of parents
  Parental: overprotection

Twelve-year-old Nick Fournier, Jr., lives in a New York City apartment with his mother, a rich divorcee whom he calls by her first name. Nick feels trapped at home in a life run by others, and decides to test his self-sufficiency by running off. The perfect opportunity arrives with an invitation to his grandmother's home on Finnycut Island. To talk his mother into letting him go alone, he must also discuss the trip with his father and the psychiatrist his mother has been making him see. Nick secretly sells some belongings to buy a knapsack and other gear and once gone, makes a detour to another island instead. Sure that someone will call the police when he fails to arrive at Finnycut, he sends notes to his parents and grandmother explaining his "test" and reassuring them that he will arrive in a few days. Meanwhile, he dyes his hair to avoid recognition and buys a sleeping bag and an old bike. The long, lonely nights on the beach go by without recourse to the tranquilizers his psychiatrist had prescribed, and an abandoned puppy affords him a chance to look out for another living being. Nick also meets a boy his own age, and at first Nick conceals the fact that he is a runaway; but as their friendship develops, Nick tells the boy the truth and is accepted no less than before. When Nick finally arrives several days late at his grandmother's house, he has learned new things about himself, his parents, responsibility, and life in general.

Testing himself on his own, Nick finds self-confidence, friendship, and a sense of humor, all that was beyond him under the thumb of an extremely protective mother and at arm's length from his remarried father. Indeed, he has learned to be more forthright with them too, and proved himself worthy of trust and respect.

Ages 11-13

Also available in:
No other form known

65

Bradbury, Bianca

"I'm Vinny, I'm Me"

Black/white illustrations by Richard Cuffari.
Houghton Mifflin Co., 1977.
(200 pages)

ORPHAN
SELF, ATTITUDE TOWARD: Respect
  Cooperation: in work
  Family: unity
  Resourcefulness
  Responsibility: accepting
  Sibling: love for

Vinny Waters is almost seventeen, lives with her brother in an oceanside town, and dreads the summer tourist season. Orphans after the recent death of their mother, she and twelve-year-old Tim must work like demons, running their aging motel while the summer children frolic on the beach. The town council has allowed her and Tim to live without guardians at the motel, under the watchful eyes of the concerned townspeople. As the drudging summer wears on, Vinny sometimes thinks of the foster homes she and Tim might each have gone to — had they not so fiercely wanted to remain together. Then the State Welfare Department investigates their situation with a view to placing them in foster homes after all. Vinny's uncle and guardian (a local judge) and other townspeople vouch for their well-being, but the State is not persuaded. Characteristically, Vinny goes right on doing what she thinks right, whether or not it endangers her position: she befriends a youth in legal trouble for possession of illicit drugs, and she agrees to Tim's taking a full-time job on a boat, despite the Department's objection. A Department hearing on their status goes badly, and Vinny is downcast. Although she considers herself a nobody, she cannot shake the conviction that she and Tim belong not in foster homes, but in town. At last, the Welfare Department buckles under the Town's opposition to their plans and allows the two to go on as they have been, provided Tim quits his job. Vinny cannot see how she can force him — and then Tim quits as a birthday present to her, saying he will help with the motel.

Oppressed by the combined burdens of self-support and official interference, a teenage girl during one trying summer comes to appreciate the worth of what she is doing, as well as her own good instincts. Contrasted with her eventual success is the failure of a friend to kick a drug habit. Although the sympathetic townspeople sometimes seem too good to be true, and some characters — for instance, the "hippy" couple who operate the local laundromat — are stereotyped, the main characters are warm, affectionate people whose struggles and determination are believable.

Ages 12 and up

Also available in:
Braille — *"I'm Vinny, I'm Me."*
Library of Congress

Cassette for the Blind — *"I'm Vinny, I'm Me."*
Library of Congress

66

Bradbury, Bianca

In Her Father's Footsteps

Black/white illustrations by Richard Cuffari.
Houghton Mifflin Co., 1976.
(172 pages)

MATURATION
  Animals: love for
  Boy-girl relationships: dating
  Parent/Parents: single

B

Since her mother's death from cancer two years earlier, eleventh-grader Jenny Wren has lived with her father, a veterinarian. She longs to become a vet like him, and indeed to become his partner. One night the two awaken to discover that the animal hospital, only yards from their house, is on fire. It burns to the ground. Underinsured, Dr. Wren cannot rebuild until, at Jenny's urging, he dips into her college savings fund. Construction begins, but while Jenny is worrying about how to pay the bills, her father begins dating a teacher, Eve Simmons. Jenny resents this woman perhaps taking the place of her mother and diluting her own relationship with her father. But Hokie Jones, the boy next door, begins asking Jenny for dates, and soon she has a romance of her own to think about. One afternoon she and her father are called upon to rescue a dozen or more dogs and cats left stranded in a filthy, deserted trailer. Eve comes too, and as she and Jenny work side by side to capture the animals, Jenny develops new respect for her father's friend. Her father later tells her that he has asked Eve to marry him, and that Eve will go on teaching to help Jenny through college and vet school. Jenny likes it all.

Working with her father's new woman friend to save some animals and feeling her own blossoming romance with Hokie both help Jenny to like and respect this woman who in fact will be her stepmother. The characterizations are believable; the plot and relationships develop naturally.

Ages 11 and up

Also available in:
Paperbound — *In Her Father's Footsteps*
Scholastic Book Services

67

Bradbury, Bianca

Where's Jim Now?

Houghton Mifflin Co., 1978.
(174 pages)

CRIME/CRIMINALS
SIBLING: Half Brother/Half Sister
  Ambivalence, feelings of
  Death: of father
  Parent/Parents: single

Since his father's death, fourteen-year-old Dave Harrison has been the man of the family, helping his mother, Beth, fulfill his father's dream of reopening an old fishing lodge. They work hard preparing the lodge for winter when another complication arises. They learn that Jim, Mr. Harrison's son from a previous, unhappy marriage, and long kept from the Harrisons' sight by his mother, has been convicted of stealing a car. Knowing how Jim's mother neglects him, they decide to take the nineteen-year-old in when he is released. Things go well at first — Jim provides much-needed help around the lodge — but Dave, feeling Jim wants to take over, begins to resent him. And he fears Jim's fascination with Mr. Harrison's pistol his father normally locked in a drawer. At times Dave admires Jim's humor and generosity, but the resentment and fear stay with him. Both Dave and his mother are dumbfounded when Jim steals another car that spring purposely to be sent back to the rehabilitation institute, where he maintains he "belongs." Sent to prison instead, Jim returns a changed person — a man, hardened and restless. Wary of him, worried when he takes up again with a friend from prison, Beth and Dave eventually send him away after he shoots animals with the pistol. Toward the end of summer, Jim shows up with his prison friend and asks to stay the night. His friend, despite Jim's feeble protests, robs the lodge. The police cannot find the two until Jim calls in, giving their location. Before they reach him, Jim is shot dead by his prison mate for telling.

Here is a realistic story of the close ties between a boy and his mother and their inability to reach the boy's half brother, however much they and he try. In the end Dave realizes that regardless of Jim's thievery and the ease with which he was led into crime, he "was my brother." Dave resolves never to draw back from such a needy person again.

Ages 11-13

Also available in:
Braille — *Where's Jim Now?*
Library of Congress

68

Brady, Mari

Please Remember Me: A Young Woman's Story of Her Friendship with an Unforgettable Fifteen-year-old Boy

Doubleday & Company, Inc., 1977.
(104 pages)

CANCER
COURAGE, MEANING OF
  Illnesses: terminal

Mari Brady, a recreation worker in the New York Memorial Sloan Kettering Cancer Center, feels drawn to a new patient, fifteen-year-old Graham Banks, newly admitted for a few days of tests. In fact Graham's friendliness and energetic personality attract most people. He is discharged but soon returns, this time to undergo chemotherapy for cancer of the lymph glands. Even so, his wit and horseplay brighten life for everyone near him. Meantime, Graham and Mari's friendship deepens, and he confides to her his feelings about having cancer. Impressed by his courage and fortitude, Mari also finds herself growing closer to Graham's parents. The boy undergoes surgery, makes a quick recovery, and is released. But he returns a third time, the cancer having spread to his lungs. After further therapy, he again returns home — until severe headaches bring him back to the hospital. This time he accepts death as the near and inevitable outcome. He asks his classmates and neighborhood friends to stop visiting him and tries to spend more time with his parents. His fortitude does not desert him, although he sometimes questions the purpose of his suffering. When he begins to fail rapidly, he asks Mari to write a letter to his wayward cousin, urging the boy to live his life to the fullest and not waste his youth and health on drugs. Graham and Mari say good-bye, and Graham goes home for Christmas. In a few days he is dead.

This is a true story of the author's friendship with a courageous young cancer patient and his family. But it also provides an inside view of life in a cancer ward, the author's own thoughts about the disease, her admiration for the many courageous patients and for the dedication of most nurses and doctors. This book is memorable for its compassion, and is a little sentimental.

Ages 12 and up

Also available in:
Paperbound — *Please Remember Me: A Young Woman's Story of Her Friendship with an Unforgettable Fifteen-year-old Boy*
Pocket Books, Inc.

69
Bram, Elizabeth
I Don't Want to Go to School
Greenwillow Books, 1977.
(32 pages counted)

SCHOOL: Entering

B

Little Jennifer does not want to go for her first day at kindergarten. She says her doll is sick. She seems unable to decide which dress to wear. She apparently cannot decide which bowl to eat her cereal out of, and so decides not to eat at all. Then she cannot find her shoes until she looks under her bed. At last, standing at the window, she sees all the children on the block hurrying to school, laughing and talking as they go. She summons her mother to take her to school. When her mother picks her up at lunch time, Jennifer tells her how much she likes kindergarten now that she has learned a new game and met many new friends.

Jennifer's reluctance to start kindergarten is overcome thanks to her understanding and patient mother. The little girl's stalling tactics will be familiar to many children, and some funny touches — Jennifer's checking the refrigerator for her shoes — together with the happy, though pat, ending, may reassure some youngsters equally uneasy about starting school.

Ages 3-5

Also available in:
No other form known

70

Brancato, Robin Fidler

Blinded by the Light

Alfred A. Knopf, Inc., 1978.
(215 pages)

CULTS
   Boy-girl relationships
   Communication: parent-child
   Sex: premarital
   Sibling: love for

Gail Brower, a sophomore at Munroe University, wants to locate her older brother, Jim, who has gone off with the Light of the World Church (L.O.W.) and writes evangelical letters home with no return address. Determined to find him, Gail and her boy friend, Jim's old friend Doug, attend a cult meeting but learn nothing. Then Gail, under an assumed name, attends a weekend retreat on the L.O.W. farm. There she learns that Jim is in Philadelphia — and begins to suspect the L.O.W.'s of lying about their activities and purpose and trying to control her mind. Frightened, she flees the place, calling Doug from a nearby town. Driving her back to school, Doug cautions her to be extremely careful in future dealings with the cult, and when Gail learns that the members know her identity, she sees his point. A few days later, Gail's parents introduce her to Mat Ferrar, a deprogrammer hired to rescue Jim, and she agrees to assist in the rescue, which will be aided by Mat's informant within the cult. But when a cult member brings her a note from Jim asking that she join him at the cult-owned hotel in Philadelphia, she drops everything and goes, telling no one, hoping to persuade Jim to leave the cult voluntarily. Instead, Gail ends up bargaining with Jim: she will spend two days with the cult and he in turn will spend a weekend at home. Her two days end — after much hard work, little sleep, and even less food — with an evening meeting where Father Adam, the cult leader, is present. Gail watches the proceedings with bewilderment, but joins an eager crowd in pressing forward to meet the leader. Suddenly, she is pulled from the crowd and hurried from the hotel by Doug. He tells her the informant will try to lead Jim out on the pretext of following her. But a freak accident kills the informant; the rescue fails; and Gail coaxes Doug into taking her back to the hotel to talk with Jim. There Gail helps Jim admit he has some doubts about L.O.W. and extracts a promise that he will meet Doug and herself away from the cult for a day.

This engrossing contemporary look at a religious cult introduces the subject of mind control through environmental conditioning and diet, but it makes no attempt to explain the psychology thoroughly. Gail's being swept emotionally and physically into the adulating crowd about to commit themselves to the leader and his work is a bit too sudden to be believable. It is implied that, if not rescued by Doug, Gail might be the insidious group's next follower. The sexual relationship between Gail and Doug is handled matter-of-factly by the author but concealed by Gail from her parents.

Ages 11-14

Also available in:
Paperbound — *Blinded by the Light*
Bantam Books, Inc.

71

Brancato, Robin Fidler

Something Left to Lose

Alfred A. Knopf, Inc., 1976.
(179 pages)

LOYALTY
  Alcoholism: adult
  Friendship: best friend
  Friendship: meaning of
  Peer relationships: peer pressures

Jane Ann, almost fifteen, longs to know if she has landed the leading role in the school play, and her friend Rebbie Hellerman, a believer in astrology, assures her that the stars are favorable. Jane Ann's other close friend, the accomplished, intelligent Lydia, is less sure. Rebbie is an impetuous, daring girl, who is in constant trouble — skipping school and playing practical jokes — and Jane Ann's parents have warned their daughter about Rebbie's influence. But Jane Ann knows that Rebbie's father is often gone away and her mother is alcoholic, and she is determined to be loyal. When Rebbie's prediction about the play comes true, Jane Ann is even more inclined toward Rebbie and astrology. Sure enough, Rebbie soon takes advantage of her loyalty. One day she talks Jane Ann into skipping school and gives her so much beer to drink that she misses a rehearsal. Then Rebbie's mother is hospitalized, and shortly after, Rebbie "sees" in a horoscope that her mother is in grave danger. She steals her father's car, persuades Jane Ann to skip school again, and tries to drive to the hospital in a heavy fog. When the car stalls on the highway, the girls are forced to call home for help. They learn that Rebbie's father has died of a heart attack that morning. The family doctor takes charge and eventually persuades Rebbie that she is responsible for her own life. Jane Ann comes to see that loyalty does not mean merely going along with unreasonable demands.

Having indulged in the caprices of a woolly-minded friend, Jane Ann learns that she must defend her own convictions though she disappoints others. She and Rebbie both find that common sense is more reliable than superstition. These discoveries, coming to characters who seem closer to twelve than to fifteen, and somewhat flat, too, are yet impressive and are driven home with authentic dialogue and neat plotting.

Ages 12-14

Also available in:
Paperbound — *Something Left to Lose*
Bantam Books, Inc.

72

Brancato, Robin Fidler

Winning

Alfred A. Knopf, Inc., 1977.
(211 pages)

QUADRIPLEGIA
  Boy-girl relationships
  Courage, meaning of
  Determination
  Suicide: consideration of

Gary Madden, a high school senior and star football player, is strapped into a Stryker frame in his hometown hospital, unable to move. Two weeks earlier, he had fractured a vertebra during a football game and been left paralyzed. Courageously he awaits the doctor's prediction of the extent of the permanent damage. Meanwhile, friends visit; his parents spend every possible moment with him; and his girl friend, Diane, remains loyal. The high school principal sends three of Gary's

B

teachers to help him keep up with his lessons, one of them Ann Treer, a young woman widowed a year earlier in a car accident, who tutors him in English. Understanding of Gary's grief and shock, Ann Treer becomes his confidante. When she learns from the doctor that Gary's legs will be permanently paralyzed, she insists Gary be told. He again shows great inner strength, and spiritedly begins rehabilitation. He soon recovers limited use of his arms, and learns to use a wheelchair — but then he falls seriously ill with a bladder infection. A high fever brings delirium, and the boy becomes despondent. He thinks first that he will be a burden to others all his life, then that he is going to die, should in fact commit suicide before he causes any more trouble. As Gary's fever breaks, he finds Ann there, and the two talk freely. Ann tells him that he is needed — by his family, by Diane, by Ann herself. She explains how he has helped her to find her own emotions again, to permit herself to feel despite her husband's death. Her encouragement helps Gary renew his own confidence.

This is the story of a young man's struggle to accept great and sudden physical limitations, and a changed appearance — diminished weight and muscle — yet new respectable self-image. In the midst of self-doubt, he vacillates between needing and driving off friends. Ann Treer, who helps Gary believe in his capabilities, finds that her friendship with him is just the therapy she herself has needed. This honest, memorable story lingers longer than its characters. It does not shrink from clinical detail, such as Gary's embarrassment at unwanted erections and his need for urinary catheters.

Ages 12 and up

Also available in:
Paperbound — *Winning*
Bantam Books, Inc.

73

Brandenberg, Franz

I Wish I Was Sick, Too!

Color illustrations by Aliki.
Greenwillow Books, 1976.
(32 pages counted)

ILLNESSES: Being Ill
JEALOUSY: Sibling
  Attention seeking

Every member of the family helps care for young Edward when he is sick, and his sister, Elizabeth, envies Edward all that attention. Besides, while he is being pampered, she must do the household chores. Elizabeth wishes she were sick, too. A few days later, she is. Now it is her turn to get all the attention, and Edward does the household tasks good-naturedly. Elizabeth wishes she were well. When she is, she and Edward do something special for each member of the family. They decide that the best part of being sick is getting well.

Elizabeth envies the attention Edward receives while he is ill, but finds little to enjoy when she falls ill herself. The illustrations in this humorous story show not a human family, but a family of kittens.

Ages 3-7

Also available in:
Paperbound — *I Wish I Was Sick, Too!*
Penguin Books, Inc.

Paperbound — *I Wish I Was Sick, Too!*
Random House, Inc.

74

Brandenberg, Franz

Nice New Neighbors

Greenwillow Books, 1977.
(56 pages)

FRIENDSHIP: Making Friends
  Change: new home

The six Fieldmouse children, Annette, Bertrand, Colette, Daniel, Esther, and Ferdinand, have just moved into a new neighborhood and want to make new friends. Father Fieldmouse points out the child next door jumping rope. The Fieldmouse children run next door to play with her. But she wants to play by herself. The children return home, and Father Fieldmouse points out the children across the street playing tag. The Fieldmouse children run across the street to play tag, too, but the Lizard children want to play by themselves. The children return, and Father tells them that the children up the street are playing ring-around-the-rosy. The Fieldmouse children run up the street to play ring-around-the-rosy with the Grasshopper children, but they too want to play by themselves. Once again the Fieldmouse children return home. This time Father Fieldmouse tells them that the children around the corner are playing hide-and-go-seek, and the Fieldmouse children run around the corner to join in the neighborhood children's game. But the Snail children want to play by themselves. The Fieldmouse children return home and announce that no one will let them join in their games. Mother says that the neighbor children will play with them once they get to know them better. Father suggests that they play on their own, and the children decide to perform "Three Blind Mice." Suddenly all the children in the neighborhood want parts in the Fieldmouse children's play. Parts are given to each,

and the children rehearse all day; in the evening they perform for the neighborhood, to great acclaim. The next day, the Fieldmouse children jump rope and play tag, ring-around-the-rosy, and hide-and-go-seek with all the other children, who are happy to have made such nice new friends.

In this beginning reader, the Fieldmouse children want to make friends in their new neighborhood, but the other children are not very cordial. Newcomers often must rely on their own resources for a while. Youngsters who have encountered a new neighborhood will sympathize, and may use the Fieldmouse technique to advantage.

Ages 6-8

Also available in:
Paperbound — *Nice New Neighbors*
Scholastic Book Services

Record — *Nice New Neighbors*
Scholastic Book Services

B

75

Brandenberg, Franz

A Secret for Grandmother's Birthday

Color illustrations by Aliki Brandenberg.
Greenwillow Books, 1975.
(32 pages counted)

GIVING, MEANING OF
SECRET, KEEPING
  Grandparent: Love for

On a visit to their grandmother, two young cats — Elizabeth and her brother, Edward — want to prepare gifts for Grandma's approaching birthday, but have no idea what to give. Whenever Elizabeth remarks that she loves to visit Grandma, or loves the smells of her house or loves her apple cookies or blueberry jam, Edward asks what she is making for a gift. A lavender sachet? A potholder? A basket? To all these Elizabeth replies, "It's a secret." And when she asks what Edward is making for a gift, he answers the same. And it is a secret, for secretly they have given each other ideas for gifts: Elizabeth gives Grandma everything that Edward has suggested; and Edward gives Grandma a poem that repeats all that Elizabeth has said she loves at Grandma's.

These animal characters seem very human in their unintentionally cooperative exchange of gift ideas, and in their awakening to the joy of giving. Beginning readers may be able to read much of this book independently. The illustrations, which give the cats all the furnishings of humans, should tempt youngsters to identify their intricate details.

Ages 3-7

Also available in:
No other form known

76

Brandenberg, Franz

Six New Students

Color illustrations by Aliki Brandenberg.
Greenwillow Books, 1978.
(56 pages)

SCHOOL: Entering
SCHOOL: Pupil-Teacher Relationships

Ferdinand Fieldmouse has decided he will hate his first day of school. After all, his older brothers and sisters have stated plainly enough how much they dislike this or that subject; surely Ferdinand will too. Once at school, however, Ferdinand is pleasantly surprised. When he tells his teacher that he dislikes arithmetic, she suggests he draw a picture. He draws a castle and adds up the number of its towers. He dislikes botany, but she

tells him to draw a flower and name its various parts. He hates physical education, but discovers that he likes to play ball. That evening at home his family asks how he liked school. It was fine, he tells them, because he did not have to work on the subjects he disliked. His family pointed out that he did in fact work on those subjects — and Ferdinand sees that he likes school after all.

A clever teacher helps a first grader enjoy his first day of school. The illustrations in this beginning reader depict the Fieldmouse family as mice, the other school children as other kinds of small animals.

Ages 5-7

Also available in:
Talking Book — *Six New Students*
Library of Congress

77

Branscum, Robbie

Johnny May

Black/white illustrations by Charles Robinson.
Doubleday & Company, Inc., 1975.
(135 pages)

BOY-GIRL RELATIONSHIPS
  Jealousy: peer
  Menstruation
  Poverty
  Puberty

Nine-year-old Johnny May, a plainspoken tomboy, lives with her grandparents in the isolated hills of Arkansas in the late 1940s, her father dead, her mother forced to live and work in the city to support her. The girl's two aunts are considered "old maids" at nineteen and twenty-two, and perhaps because she can beat up all the boys in her school, Johnny May herself has no friends at all. But she meets her match one day at the funeral of a neighbor, Mrs. Berry, when she picks a fight with twelve-year-old Aron, who is new to the neighborhood. The two call a truce and become friends — fishing, sharing secrets, and swimming naked in the creek together. When the widower, Mr. Berry, begins courting her Aunt Irene, Johnny May confides in Aron her suspicion that Mr. Berry has murdered his four previous wives and that Irene will be next. No sooner has Aron agreed to help Johnny May look into this further, then Sue Ella, Johnny May's cousin from the city, arrives on a visit, charming Aron with her feminine airs and graces. Jealous Johnny May forsakes for a day her year-round, practical jeans for one of Sue Ella's frilliest frocks, and sets off to show herself to Aron. But the dress is too small, and is ripped and buttonless by the time Johnny May abandons her purpose. Ashamed, afraid of punishment, the girl hides in the woods. There is a sudden storm, a flash flood, and just in time there is Mr. Berry to rescue her. But Johnny May is only more deeply certain that the scoundrel hides his true nature behind heroism and kindness. Johnny May turns again to the question of a dress, and is momentarily defeated in this as well: despite the onset of her first menstrual period, she picks more than enough strawberries to pay for a new dress all her own — when the death of their cow forces the whole family to pool their cash to replace the animal. Luckily, Johnny May's mother sends her money enough to buy a dress, and presents for her aunts, grandparents, and Aron, too. That leaves the question of Mr. Berry's former wives, and Johnny May confronts him forthrightly with her suspicions. He readily explains the innocent fate of each — and Johnny is so embarrassed at her melodramatic speculations that she can imagine Aron scorning her forever as a fool. On the contrary, Aron surprises her with a gift of new hair ribbons, and asks her to be his girl friend.

This first-person narrative takes its spunky heroine well into puberty in a remote setting and a less complicated time than our own. The dialogue is colorful and the humor earthy. But sophisticated readers may find Johnny May too naive for her age. Her questions and qualms about her changing body seem real enough, but her ignorance of the physical differences between boys and girls seems unlikely. Swimming naked with Aron, she observes: "Aron had something growing on him, low down in front. Leastways I figured it must be growing there or he would have pulled it off. . . . I reckoned it must of been something that happened to him when he was real young to be so used to it by now."

Ages 9-12

Also available in:
Cassette for the Blind — *Johnny May*
Library of Congress

Paperbound — *Johnny May*
Avon Books

78

Branscum, Robbie

The Saving of P.S.

Black/white illustrations by Glen Rounds.
Doubleday & Company, Inc., 1977.
(127 pages)

LOVE, MEANING OF
  Chores
  Identity, search for
  Parent/Parents: remarriage of
  Religion: questioning
  Running away

Unlike her older brothers and sisters, unlike most people in her Arkansas hill neighborhood, twelve-year-old Priscilla Sue — P.S. — has not, in the church where her father preaches, come forward to be saved. She wants to, but she considers herself a confirmed black sinner. Then, too, she must work endlessly at chores: her mother has been dead since P.S. was born and somehow the girl has taken all responsibility for the farm and the house. No one thanks her or helps her. Nonetheless, she loves her father dearly — and when he starts courting Cora Lee, a widow from town, P.S. feels aggrieved and threatened. But all her efforts to save Pa from this widow with her two daughters succeed only in making Pa more resolute to marry. Worse, he marries the widow and P.S.'s favorite brother becomes engaged to the older daughter. Convinced that no one loves her, P.S. runs away. But in time, the experiences and adventures of her flight cause the girl to reflect on her life and consider what she has done. Found by one of her brothers and taken home, she recognizes that she must not again run away, because others, including her stepmother, do in fact love her. Nevertheless, P.S. remains emotionally numb until at church she suddenly realizes that she has liked being a martyr and has held God away in order to be different from others. With that self-understanding, she comes forward for saving.

A tough, stubborn girl who cannot bear to see her father remarry pits all her energies against it. Failing, she runs away and in her flight discovers, bit by bit, how twisted her ideas and actions have been. This first-person narrative shows how easy it is to regard others as threatening when one already feels insecure. The rural Arkansas setting proves both informative and lively.

Ages 9-12

Also available in:
Cassette for the Blind — *The Saving of P.S.*
Library of Congress

Paperbound — *The Saving of P.S.*
Dell Publishing Company, Inc.

79
Branscum, Robbie

The Three Wars of Billy Joe Treat

McGraw-Hill Book Co., 1975.
(90 pages)

PARENT/PARENTS: Power Struggle with
SCHOOL: Pupil-Teacher Relationships
  Autonomy
  School: classmate relationships

Thirteen-year-old Billy Joe, who first understands what "war" means when the United States enters World War II, soon applies the term to his relations with his bullying teacher, Mr. Marshall. A third war breaks out between Billy and his mother when he refuses to eat at her table until she treats him like the man he is. She treats him like a child and gives him the chicken neck, for instance, instead of a man's portion. Soon the war between them is a test of will. Three brothers have gone to the Army and Pa has stopped working since one died in battle. Billy must work the farm alone. He eats on his own by stealing food from the pantry and foraging outdoors. That spring his brother Gene, on crutches from a war injury, arrives home but is not able to help with the farm. In a confrontation that summer, Billy vents his resentment at being treated like a child — when, after all, he works like a man. Ma, finally admitting after months that she has tried to keep him young, then formally asks him to the table. That war is settled, but the war with the teacher Marshall breaks out that fall. Marshall beats Billy's sister. The boy attacks him, but he beats off them all. Someone then shoots Marshall dead, and later Billy and his friends are shot at, too. Billy can make no sense of this until Gene explains that he — a spy-hunter, not a recuperating soldier — has killed Marshall, a Nazi spy, in self-defense. It is Marshall's partner who is shooting at the boys. Gene thinks Marshall had hidden something at the schoolhouse. Billy searches there and finds a shortwave radio and a map. Marshall's partner then traps Billy, but Gene arrives to capture him.

A stubborn youth tells in the first-person about his struggle to compel his mother to acknowledge his manhood. Though she tries to reassert authority at the end, Billy is now secure in his sense of self — is, in fact, half-owner of the farm. The spy episode lacks the detail and emotional logic of Billy's war with his mother, but the latter keeps the book from seeming a period piece.

Ages 9-11

Also available in:
No other form known

80

Breinburg, Petronella

Shawn's Red Bike

Color illustrations by Errol Floyd.
Thomas Y. Crowell Company, Inc., 1976.
(25 pages counted)

DETERMINATION

Young Shawn sees a red bicycle in a shop window and announces, "I want that red bike." It is both expensive and too large, and Shawn's mother offers another instead. But Shawn has his heart set on the red bike. Every week he goes to the store with his pocket money, making payments on the bike. He helps a friend's father wash his car and helps his Aunt Hillary take care of her baby for two days. At last, the bike is his. The older boys say it is too big for him to be able to ride. Shawn tries but

soon falls off. He remounts and manages to ride to the corner but falls off again. He turns to his friends and says, "I'll go around the corner tomorrow." "Proudly" he wheels his new red bike in through the front door of his home.

A little boy's determination to achieve his goal pays off in this short story with bold, colorful illustrations. Children with goals of their own will be encouraged to persevere.

Ages 3-6

Also available in:
No other form known

81

Bridgers, Sue Ellen

Home Before Dark

Alfred A. Knopf, Inc., 1976.
(176 pages)

FAMILY: Unity
IDENTITY, SEARCH FOR
LIFE STYLE: Change in
  Boy-girl relationships
  Death: of mother
  Maturation
  Migrant workers
  Parent/Parents: remarriage of

James Earl Willis, his wife, and their four children have never had a place to call home. The Willises have traveled around Florida as migrant farm workers for as long as fourteen-year-old Stella can remember. But today the family is going home — to the tobacco farm in North Carolina where James Earl grew up, the farm his brother Newton now owns and operates. Stella rejoices — she longs for a home — but her mother, Mae, a faded, anxious woman, does not; Mae prefers the rootless, anonymous life of a migrant, in which she is not required to be anybody. Out of love for his brother, Newton gives the new arrivals a tenant house and furniture and provides work for James Earl. Stella works hard to make the house homey, and swears never to leave it: "what counted for her was here, inside walls that didn't move in the dark or carry her somewhere as strange and unwelcoming as the last place she'd been." Then she meets Toby Brown, a neighbor boy her age, and he falls in love with her. Stella also meets Rodney Brown, a boy from town, who has money to spend and drives a car. Stella is impressed by Rodney — he can take her places she has never been — and he, in whom no girl has ever shown an interest, is bowled over by her. Meanwhile, James Earl is beginning to feel at home on the farm, though Mae longs to be traveling again. Then one day during a thunderstorm, Mae is struck by lightning and killed instantly. Toby tries to comfort Stella, coming to see her the night of the funeral; for a long time, he holds and kisses her. Rodney sees them together, and hires two high school boys to beat up Toby. The boy is so badly hurt he must be hospitalized. He recovers, but thereafter is more cautious with his feelings for Stella. Knowing Rodney ordered Toby's beating, Stella tells him she will never see him again, and turns all her attentions to Toby. Meanwhile James Earl, struggling with his grief and loneliness, is attracted to Maggie Grover, a single woman who owns a small department store in town. Maggie, despite her money and lovely old home, is lonely too. The two begin dating and soon are married. Stella is happy for her father, but she will not leave the tenant house to live with the rest of the family at Maggie's. She stays on in the only place that has ever been home to her. Then, little by little, she comes to realize that Maggie's can be home too. Three months later, at the start of the new year, she moves in.

This novel weaves into the lives of the Willis family the stories of many friends and relations who touch them and help shape their lives. The populous narrative is handled deftly, and characterizations remain vivid. Still, Newton's matter-of-fact description to James Earl of their terminally ill mother's violent suicide and the violence inflicted upon Toby may distress some readers.

Ages 12 and up

Also available in:
Paperbound — *Home Before Dark*
Bantam Books, Inc.

82

Brightman, Alan

Like Me

Color photographs by the author.
Little, Brown and Co., 1976.
(47 pages counted)

MENTAL RETARDATION
  Differences, human

The little boy who tells this story wonders whether other children are like him or different from him. He explains that he is retarded, but that the word only means he is "slow to learn how to do things and act in some places." Basically, he concludes, all people have likenesses and differences. The way one views a retarded child is up to each individual; "what's really important is how hard we all try."

The book is not only a useful explanation of the meanings of "retarded," but also a small boy's plea for understanding and acceptance. It is written in verse and illustrated with color photographs of young children at play in the park and at the beach.

Ages 3-8

Also available in:
Paperbound — *Like Me*
Little, Brown and Co.

83

Bronin, Andrew

Gus and Buster Work Things Out

Color illustrations by Cyndy Szekeres.
Coward, McCann & Geoghegan, Inc., 1975.
(63 pages)

SIBLING: Rivalry
  Problem solving
  Sharing/Not sharing

Two young brothers, Gus and Buster, often fight over things, with sly Gus most often the winner. When both boys want to sleep in the bottom bunk bed, Gus wins by manipulating a coin-flip. On a rainy day, he takes all the indoor toys for himself, leaving Buster with only a baseball glove, a bat, and a bicycle. That selfishness backfires, however, when the rain stops and Gus has no outdoor toys to play with. At mealtime, Gus is annoyed by his brother's dreadful table manners, and nags him about chewing with his mouth open. Gus has to stop, though, when Buster starts to cry. Then there is the question of which television show to watch: Gus wants to watch football, Buster, a checker game. In the ensuing quarrel, they break the television set but settle their differences. They play football themselves, then play checkers, and each in turn is a winner.

Two little brothers, pictured in this easy reader as raccoons, contend for the same things, as brothers will. Young readers may feel sorry for Buster, and be glad to see Gus lose sometimes. But they will recognize the humor in the outcomes of their bickering as well as the affection these furry siblings feel underneath.

Ages 4-7

Also available in:
Braille — *Gus and Buster Work Things Out*
Library of Congress

Paperbound — *Gus and Buster Work Things Out*
Dell Publishing Company, Inc.

84

Brooks, Jerome

The Testing of Charlie Hammelman

E. P. Dutton & Company, Inc., 1977.
(129 pages)

BOY-GIRL RELATIONSHIPS: Dating
DETERMINATION
SELF, ATTITUDE TOWARD: Body Concept
SHYNESS
WEIGHT CONTROL: Overweight
  Communication: importance of

Sixteen-year-old Charlie Hammelman, an only child, self-conscious, overweight, has just lost his best friend: his high school teacher, Charlotte Kaplan, the only person on earth Charlie ever confided in, has died. Charlie's parents can offer no comfort, for the family seldom talks about anything. Besides, his father, a philandering, handsome, successful businessman, has nothing but complaints about his son. For several days, Charlie grieves alone. Then, deciding that something must be done to honor Miss Kaplan, he goes to the cemetery to tell her he is going to make her proud of him. He resolves to confront his father with some complaints of his own. He vows to learn to swim, despite his terror of water and his dread of undressing in front of other boys. (Swimming is a graduation requirement at his high school.) He has already asked Shirl Darner to go steady, and she has accepted. He goes home full of determination, but wilts when his father, as usual, can find no time to talk to him. As the school year ends, Shirl invites Charlie for a weekend at the summer camp where she works, and full of timidity, accepts. Once there, trusting Shirl's kindness, he lets himself be persuaded to don shorts and play Frisbee with strangers. And when school reconvenes, he registers for a swimming class at the YMCA. What a relief to learn he does not have to swim naked. And the water feels fine!

In this first-person account, a shy young man describes how he realizes the courage to carry out promises he has made to a dead teacher. By his own determination, and with the help of a girl who encourages him much as the teacher had, he becomes a success to himself. Charlie's closeness to Shirl is realistic and affecting, but other dialogue, in striving for contemporaneity, seems merely flippant and coarse. Still, Charlie's story could reach and help adolescent boys who are too used to suffering themselves in silence.

Ages 10-13

Also available in:
Cassette for the Blind — *The Testing of Charlie Hammelman*
Library of Congress

Paperbound — *The Testing of Charlie Hammelman*
Pocket Books, Inc.

85

Brown, Fern G.

Hard Luck Horse

Black/white illustrations by Darrell Wiskur.
Albert Whitman & Co., 1975.
(128 pages)

ANIMALS: Love for
 Determination
 Friendship: making friends

It is instant love when eighth-grader Cristi sees a new sorrel horse unloaded at the stable where she works, but she cannot afford to buy him. Cristi suspects another rider, Allison, of coveting the sorrel as a birthday present, one which her parents could afford. Cristi pays for surgery when the horse is found to have eye cancer, but she becomes no more sure to get him when he recovers, and she bitterly accuses Allison of deceit. When Allison protests, saying she wants only the horse she already has, Cristi refuses to listen. But when the sorrel is sold to someone else, Cristi is heartbroken and tries to make amends with Allison, even alerting her to a serious fault in her riding technique that could prevent her from winning the barrel race on rodeo day. As a result of Cristi's advice, Allison wins, with Cristi running a close second. Though Allison shares the prize with her, a greater prize awaits Cristi: the earlier buyer returns the sorrel and, with a loan from her parents, Cristi buys him.

A girl's love for a horse overcomes a series of obstacles to owning him; but the same intensity of feelings causes her to resent another girl unjustly. For those interested in horses, there is much about horse training and equine medicine here, but those who look for character development will find that the story moves too quickly. The characters are nevertheless fresh as far as they go, and the book should appeal to slow or reluctant readers — especially if they like horses.

Ages 9-11

Also available in:
No other form known

86

Brown, Fern G.

Jockey — or Else!

Black/white illustrations by Darrell Wisker.
Albert Whitman & Co., 1978.
(128 pages)

ANIMALS: Love for
CAREERS: Planning
  Determination
  Identity, search for
  Problem solving

Thirteen-year-old Benjy arrives at the Spearses' horse farm to work for the summer and learn to be a jockey. The Spearses' son, Paul, derides Benjy's dream, and Benjy himself begins to question it on account of his awkwardness. Yet he gets along with horses and can teach others. He is teaching Mara Salamon to ride — secretly, because her horse-hating mother is a quarrelsome neighbor to the Spearses. As weeks go by, Benjy comes to love working around the Spearses' horses, and his pet talking crow, Arcaro, befriends a horse named Trouble Seeker, who lives up to his name in every way, and often on the Salamons' property. But an outing at the racetrack shatters Benjy's dream: he sees, hopelessly, just how gifted and able jockeys must be. The Spearses, including Paul, console him, pointing out that a good horseman does not necessarily have to be a good

jockey. At first, Benjy cannot quite accept this. Meanwhile, Trouble Seeker gets loose and damages the Salamons' lawn. Mrs. Salamon threatens to sue — but subsides when the Spearses' entry, with Mara riding Trouble Seeker, wins first prize in a parade. Benjy vows to become a veterinarian or a teacher of horsemanship.

A boy wanting desperately to be a jockey realizes he is not a natural rider and turns his sights on other ways of working with horses. Benjy's story unfolds briskly and pleasantly, in simple language.

Ages 9-12

Also available in:
No other form known

87

Brown, Fern G.

You're Somebody Special on a Horse

Black/white illustrations by Frank G. Murphy.
Albert Whitman & Co., 1977.
(128 pages)

ANIMALS: Love for
HANDICAPS
HELPING
  Maturation
  Perseverance
  Sports/Sportsmanship

Eighth-grader Marni has spent so much time working with her horse, Koke, to win first prize in a horse show that her grades have suffered. By June, she looks forward to a summer of riding, but her parents have decided Koke must be sold and Marni must work on her reading and writing. She is heartbroken. One day the head of her riding school asks Marni to help with a riding class he is starting for handicapped children. She convinces her parents to let her work with the class and keep her horse until the end of summer on condition that she study her English every morning. On the first day, while the handicapped students are getting acquainted with the horses, she meets Kevin, the boy she is to teach. Kevin must wear a special safety helmet and body harness to help him sit steady and erect. But even with people leading the horse and supporting the rider, Kevin loses his balance often. As Marni and Kevin become friends, she tells him she must sell her horse soon but first hopes to win a blue ribbon at the next horse show. It is announced that in the upcoming show the handicapped riders can perform whatever feat they choose. He confides his hope of riding alone across the arena. Marni doubts this is possible. Six days before the show Marni finds Kevin near Koke's stall crying because he is the only one in his class who still cannot ride alone. Marni decides to help him instead of practicing for her own event. He improves considerably but still is not always able to get across the arena upright. The day of the show Marni does poorly in her first two events out of concern for Kevin. As his turn approaches, Kevin is scared. Still, he just manages to get across. Marni is elated. In her own last event she can now concentrate fully on her jumps and wins the blue ribbon — but the ecstasy she expected is missing. And after the show she must choose between selling Koke to the head of the stables or to Kevin's parents. Kevin and his family are moving out of town, and so if she sells Koke to them she will probably never see the horse again. Still, she realizes that Kevin needs Koke to build up his self-confidence, just as she once needed the horse to build up hers. Once she decides to sell Koke to Kevin, she experiences the joy she expected from the blue ribbon.

Marni's desire to help others is further explored in a sub-plot involving an adopted four-year-old boy who has not spoken since the death of his biological parents a year before. As his baby-sitter, Marni tries to draw him out of his shell. She succeeds when she takes the boy riding on Koke. This book relies on plot at the expense of solid characterization. Marni's parents seem dim, and the author relies on role-reversals to develop them. But the story does show that helping others succeed can be at least as rewarding as succeeding oneself. A good selection for readers seeking an eventful story told in limited vocabulary.

Ages 10-13

Also available in:
No other form known

88

Brown, Marc Tolon

Arthur's Nose

Little, Brown and Co., 1976.
(32 pages counted)

SELF, ATTITUDE TOWARD: Accepting
 Self, attitude toward: body concept

School-age Arthur is an aardvark, with an aardvark's nose like the rest of his family. One day Arthur no longer likes his nose: it gets stuffed up and red when he has a cold; it gives him away in hide-and-seek; his friends seem to think it funny; and it is quite unlike any other nose in his class. Arthur feels freakish and unhappy. But his decision to have it changed takes his friends by surprise. They accompany Arthur to the rhinologist, or nose doctor, and wait outside. Inside with the doctor, Arthur models pictures of all types of noses but nothing looks right — excepting Arthur's own nose. When he emerges from the office with his nose intact, his friends are relieved, and he is content: Arthur likes his looks.

His unusual appearance distresses Arthur, for he wants to look like his friends. He thinks they would like him better if he did. But he finds that his nose is part of what makes him special, an individual, and he decides to keep the nose he has.

Ages 3-7

Also available in:
No other form known

89
Bruna, Dick

I Can Dress Myself
Color illustrations by the author.
Methuen Publishers, 1977.
(25 pages counted)

DEPENDENCE/INDEPENDENCE

A very young brother and sister are going to a party, to which they will wear matching outfits. As the girl describes each garment to be worn, both children dress themselves, from their underwear to their boots, coats, and hats.

Very simple and colorful illustrations add one garment per page to this first-person story for the youngest reader. Children can identify each article of clothing and name its color.

Ages 2-4

Also available in:
No other form known

90
Bruna, Dick

Miffy in the Hospital
Color illustrations by the author.
Methuen Publishers, 1975.
(25 pages counted)

HOSPITAL, GOING TO
  Surgery: tonsillectomy

B

Miffy, a little rabbit, has a sore throat, and the doctor says she must go to the hospital. Even though she cries at the thought, Mother takes her. Once there, she is still frightened — until a nurse takes her by the hand, helps her undress and get into bed, and gives her an injection that "only hurt a little." Soon, Miffy falls asleep. When she awakens feeling rather strange, the nurse tells her that her throat will no longer hurt and she will soon feel better. As if to prove this, Miffy's parents appear with a present — a nurse doll — and Miffy decides that she no longer minds being in the hospital.

Some routine hospital experiences that might frighten a little child are ignored or treated superficially in this book. But this same light treatment makes it suitable as an introduction to hospitalization for just such a child. Simple line and color illustrations maintain the light tone.

Ages 2-5

Also available in:
No other form known

91

Budbill, David

Bones on Black Spruce Mountain

The Dial Press, Inc., 1978.
(126 pages)

ADOPTION: Feelings about
LONELINESS
    Identity, search for
    Orphan

Seth and Daniel, thirteen and good friends, have grown up in the shadow of Black Spruce Mountain — Seth since birth and Daniel, an orphan, since his adoption five years earlier. Now they are spending five days on their own in the mountain wilderness. What has specially drawn them is the mountain's legend: seventy-five years earlier an orphan boy had run away from a foster home; some say his bones lie in a cave on the mountain and his ghost haunts the wilderness. The boys will try to solve the mystery. Neither quite believes the legend, but Daniel, far more than Seth, wants to. And it is Daniel who stumbles on an old hillside house whose contents convince both that the legend is true. Eagerly they press on to the mountain, where Daniel finds more evidence, a cave with a human skeleton in it. Later that night, after a hazardous return to camp during a storm, Daniel explains his moodiness, how he feels at one with the lost boy and knows how unbearably lonely he was, lonely as only an orphan can be. Only after a dream the next day in which he realizes that everyone is lonely does Daniel recognize that loneliness is not unique to orphans; it is part of all lives. His life-long depression lifts, and Daniel returns home, free from his deepest fears.

An adopted orphan cannot shed the feeling that he is not wanted. A journey to resolve the legend of a lost orphan, with whom he intensely identifies, frees him from this fear. The story is neither a straight suspense story nor a character study, but something like a parable, and the real action is psychological, as the boys close in not only on the mystery of the mountain, but on Daniel's pent-up emotions, too. Accounts of the boys' wilderness camping techniques will add appeal for those who enjoy the outdoors. This book is a sequel to *Snowshoe Trek to Otter River.*

Ages 10-13

Also available in:
Paperbound — *Bones on Black Spruce Mountain*
Scholastic Book Services

92

Bulla, Clyde Robert

Keep Running, Allen!

Color illustrations by Santomi Ichikawa.
Thomas Y. Crowell Company, Inc., 1978.
(30 pages counted)

SIBLING: Youngest
    Resourcefulness

Allen's mother has told him that when he is playing outdoors he must stay with his older sister and two older brothers. But Jenny, Mike, and Howard run everywhere they go and, because he is small, Allen has difficulty keeping up with them. One day, while trying to keep up in the park, Allen falls on the grass. He notices how cool and soft it is. In fact, lying on the grass and watching the clouds drift by proves so comfortable that Allen decides to ignore his brothers and sisters when they beg him to keep running. They cannot leave him behind, so they join him — and discover the pleasures of lying on the grass doing quiet things.

A little boy cannot do what older children can, but thinks he must. By inventing his own activities, the boy is satisfied. The illustrations enhance the text by conveying Allen's feelings and the peaceful pleasures he and his siblings discover.

Ages 4-6

Also available in:
No other form known

93

Bulla, Clyde Robert

Shoeshine Girl

Thomas Y. Crowell Company, Inc., 1975.
(84 pages)

VALUES/VALUING: Materialistic
Dependence/Independence
Friendship: meaning of
Job
Relatives: living in home of
Responsibility: accepting

Ten-year-old Sarah Ida Becker is a handful to her parents, and so is sent to spend the summer with her Aunt Claudia when her mother falls ill. But Sarah Ida does not want to spend her summer with Aunt Claudia. Her aunt makes her help with the household chores but — on the mother's instructions — gives Sarah no allowance. Sarah Ida sees money as a means toward independence. She talks a neighbor girl into lending her money, but Aunt Claudia makes her return it. Determined to have money in her pocket, and despite her age, Sarah Ida looks for a job. She is finally hired by Al Winkler at his shoeshine stand. To Sarah Ida's surprise, Aunt Claudia does not object. Winkler teaches Sarah Ida to make shoes shine like glass and to thank a customer whether he gives a tip or not. He also tells her

stories about his life. The work is hard, but Sarah Ida comes to like it and to like Al, too. One day, on an errand, Al is hit by a car. Before he is taken to the hospital, he gives Sarah Ida the key to the shoeshine stand and instructs her to lock up. Instead, Sarah Ida keeps the stand open until Al can come back. A few days after Al's recovery, Aunt Claudia receives a letter from the girl's father; his wife is going to the hospital for several months, and he badly needs his daughter at home. Although Sarah Ida does not want to leave Al and her job, she sees that her place is with her father and goes home.

This story shows how a young, unruly girl comes to respect other people and their needs through the responsibilities of a job. It also shows how her own need for independence is tempered by a friendship.

Ages 8-10

Also available in:
Braille — *Shoeshine Girl*
Library of Congress

Paperbound — *Shoeshine Girl*
Scholastic Book Services

94

Bunin, Catherine and Sherry Bunin

Is That Your Sister? A True Story of Adoption

Black/white photographs by the authors.
Pantheon Books, 1976.
(35 pages)

ADOPTION: Explaining
ADOPTION: Interracial

Six-year-old Catherine Bunin is adopted. She is questioned a lot by other children about her family and about adoption, more than other adopted children she knows — because, as she says, "my mother and I don't look anything alike. We don't have the same kind of skin or face or hair." Although the questions sometimes annoy her, she patiently answers them all. Citing the experience of her much darker-skinned four-year-old sister, Carla, she explains that children are adopted through agencies. They do not live at the agencies, but with foster parents, people who take care of them until they have permanent homes, "forever families." Catherine describes how the social worker comes and talks to all members of a family before bringing a child into their home to live. After Carla had lived with the Bunins for six months, Mr. and Mrs. Bunin had gone to court to adopt her, which simply meant they had sworn before a judge to take care of Carla. When the people ask Carla who her "real" parents are, she explains that her real parents "are the mom and dad who take care of me and love me."

Written in the first person, in Catherine's language, this book describes the feelings of an adopted child and the process of adoption. Catherine's mother, Sherry, says, "The fact that we are an interracial family presents some special situations, but it does not keep our story from being a typical account of adoption."

Ages 4-8

Also available in:
No other form known

95

Bunting, Anne Evelyn

High Tide for Labrador

Black/white illustrations by Bernard Garbutt.
Childrens Press, Inc., 1975.
(77 pages) o.p.

JUDGMENT, EFFECT OF EMOTIONS ON
  Change: resisting
  Courage, meaning of
  Parent/Parents: single

Though his father has been dead seven years, thirteen-year-old Jimmy Donovan measures everyone against him — his mother, her suitor Big Simon, and himself — and finds all wanting. His resentment of Big Simon, who he feels is trying to replace his father, is not softened when the man lands for Jimmy a much-coveted training job on a fishing voyage to Labrador. At sea, Jimmy's resentment turns to hatred when Big Simon defends him from a crewman who has called the lad a "Mama's Boy." Jimmy's chance to prove himself comes after the boat dodges dangerous pack ice entering a harbor near the fishing grounds. Waiting with two other boats for the pack to recede, Captain Will says in Jimmy's hearing that he wants to be first on the banks in order to ensure a good catch, but that their one chance to beat the others — sending a lone man ahead to set nets — is too risky. That night Jimmy sets out with the nets in a dory, but is trapped in the ice and swept out to sea. Trying to save the dory and its precious nets from being crushed, Jimmy gets his ankle painfully pinned between the boat and the ice. Hours pass — and then Big Simon arrives, rescuing Jimmy from certain death. Jimmy sees how petty he has acted in the past, and wants to apologize. Yet all he can say is, "Thanks. Thanks, Big Simon." Safe in the motor-driven dory Big

Simon has brought, the boy asks if they can still reach the fishing grounds and set the nets before the other boats. They can — and do, together.

The memory of a dead parent can embitter a youngster toward anyone who seems ready to usurp that place. But in the end, Jimmy sees that he must let his father go, and that to do so is no betrayal. The fishing background here is both instructive and exciting, and may well draw a reluctant reader on.

Ages 9-11

Also available in:
No other form known

96

Bunting, Anne Evelyn

Magic and the Night River

Color illustrations by Allen Say.
Harper & Row Publishers, Inc., 1978.
(45 pages)

GRANDPARENT: Love for
   Age: respect for
   Animals: responsibility for
   Japan
   Pride/False pride

Once again, Yoshi, a young Japanese boy, is helping his grandfather load the cormorants into baskets onto the fishing boat. The boy is acutely aware that this may be the last night he and Grandfather, a master fisherman who has worked with as many as twelve birds, will fish with the fleet. Kano, the gruff and burly owner of Grandfather's boat, has said that Grandfather's catch is lately too small to cover his rent; he may have to replace the old man. But Grandfather is revered among fishermen for his forty years' experience; Yoshi cannot understand Kano's disrespect. Nor can he fathom the man's cruelty to his own cormorants, which a wise man treats with kindness. But now the boats are positioned, and he and Grandfather carefully take the cormorants from their baskets, releasing them to the end of their cords. As each bird swims back to the boat, its throat bulging with fish, Grandfather and Yoshi gently stroke its neck and murmur thanks, as the fish are disgorged into the catch baskets. Will Kano notice how large their catch is? Suddenly all that is clear is that the boats have collided and the cormorants' cords have tangled. The struggling birds may be injured or killed. Yoshi and Grandfather unleash theirs — knowing they may never return. But soon the cormorants fly back to the boat, their throats bulging. As often as the youth and the old man release them into the night, they return — until the catch baskets are overflowing. Kano, too, has released his birds, but they, having known little kindness, escape into the blackness. As the fishermen return to shore, Kano proclaims Grandfather a man of magic. But Yoshi knows what Kano will never know: Grandfather's magic is kindness.

In this warm and gentle tale of the Japanese fishermen who fish with birds, an admiring boy learns that it is his grandfather's kindness to his birds, and patience with an ill-tempered colleague, that preserve his preeminence with his fellows and set a shining example to be followed.

Ages 5-9

Also available in:
No other form known

97

Bunting, Anne Evelyn

One More Flight

Black/white illustrations by Diane de Groat.
Frederick Warne & Company, Inc., 1976.
(92 pages)

FREEDOM, MEANING OF
IDENTITY, SEARCH FOR
RUNNING AWAY
  Orphan

Dobby, age eleven, has once again run away from the residential treatment center he has lived at most of his life. Now, hiding in the mountains outside the city, Dobby has frightened second thoughts. Then, into the clearing walks a young man carrying a hawk, one he is obviously trying to teach food-gathering in the wild. As the man leaves, Dobby boldly steps forward and asks to go with him. The man, Timmer, consents, and goes on to explain that he lives at a nearby bird sanctuary where he cares for and trains to return to their natural habitats large birds now unfitted by injury or domestication. Timmer stops to buy groceries, and unknown to Dobby, calls the treatment center to confirm his suspicion that Dobby is a runaway. He is given permission for Dobby to stay through the next day. At the sanctuary, Dobby is enthralled by Timmer's gentle way with the birds. He begs to stay indefinitely, and Timmer must confess that he has reported him. But they will go to the mountains the next day to release two birds. In the morning, Dobby tries to flee in Timmer's jeep, but the man stops him. The two drive to the mountains, and while Dobby watches Timmer caring for the birds, he begins to see the importance of readiness to freedom. That night, someone tries to break into the sanctuary. Dobby successfully defends the birds from the intruder. He is a hero, and when Timmer returns him to the treatment center, he promises the boy continued friendship and, if arrangements can be made, a future job at the sanctuary.

In the few hours Dobby spends with Timmer and the birds, the boy learns how foolish he has been to keep running away from the treatment center before being ready for freedom. Looking forward to working at the bird sanctuary gives him new purpose. This pastoral, understated story makes its point without heavy-handed moralizing.

Ages 10-13

Also available in:
Paperbound — *One More Flight*
Dell Publishing Company, Inc.

98

Bunting, Anne Evelyn

Skateboard Four

Black/white illustrations by Phil Kantz.
Albert Whitman & Co., 1976.
(63 pages)

LEADER/LEADERSHIP
  Clubs
  Jealousy: peer
  Responsibility: accepting

Nobody rides the park trails on skateboards more skillfully than the members of the Skateboard Four: Morgan, Big John, Tim, and Paco — until Albert moves into the neighborhood. When he attempts to join the group, the Four ignore him. He begins doing stunts by himself, and soon the Four are only part of his audience. Realizing that Albert is more skilled than he, Morgan, the club leader, agrees with Tim that Albert should be allowed to join. But just as the other members had to pass a test of

Ages 12 and up

Also available in:
No other form known

101

Burningham, John Mackintosh

The Baby

Color illustrations by the author.
Thomas Y. Crowell Company, Inc., 1975.
(19 pages counted)

SIBLING: New Baby

A little boy remarks that the baby in his family makes a mess of its food. Still, he helps his mother bathe the baby and take it for carriage rides. But, the boy confides, there are times when he dislikes the baby because it cannot play with him yet; he hopes that it will soon grow up.

Colorful, simple crayon illustrations are a perfect accompaniment to the extremely simple text of this first-person narrative. These same illustrations might be used to encourage discussion. The whole could prepare a very young child for the arrival of a new sibling.

Ages 2-5

Also available in:
No other form known

102

Burningham, John Mackintosh

The Blanket

Color illustrations by the author.
Thomas Y. Crowell Company, Inc., 1975.
(19 pages counted)

TRANSITIONAL OBJECTS: Security Blanket

A young boy, who always takes a special blanket to bed, is distressed when he cannot find it. He asks his parents to help, and they search where adults would: in the bathroom, in the closet, in the car. But the boy finds it under his pillow and at once contentedly goes to sleep.

This first-person narrative makes a very small book whose size alone will attract very young children.

Ages 2-5

Also available in:
Paperbound — *The Blanket*
Hanes

103

Burningham, John Mackintosh

Come Away from the Water, Shirley

Color illustrations by the author.
Thomas Y. Crowell Company, Inc., 1977.
(24 pages counted)

IMAGINATION
Parental: overprotection
Play

Young Shirley and her parents, quite ordinary people, visit an ordinary ocean beach on a routine outing. While Shirley's parents hector her about what to do and what

B

to watch out for, the girl wanders to the oceanside, sees a stray dog, and imagines that she and it are rowing out to a pirate sailing ship. Mother warns her not to pet the dog, who might have turned up from anywhere — while the dog attacks a pirate forcing Shirley to walk the plank. Then the girl and the dog are busy fighting off nine pirates — and Mother is reminding her, "That's the third and last time I'm asking you whether you want a drink." Having escaped with a treasure map, Shirley and the dog set sail — while Mother interjects that Father, after his rest, might have a game with Shirley. Just as Shirley holds up a bejeweled crown from a treasure chest, Mother, exclaiming at the late hour, wakes Father. Shirley and the dog sail back under ominous night clouds — and the family leaves the beach.

A young girl disregards her parents' prosaic observations and admonitions to imagine a richly detailed adventure story starring herself and a stray dog. Essential to the contrast of parental ordinariness and the girl's wild adventures are the illustrations, which show the parents in drab colors and, on the facing page, vividly colored narrative scenes of Shirley's imagined adventure. Though children may not catch all the story's droll humor, they should delight in Shirley's use of ordinary happenings to set off one vivid imagining after another.

Ages 4-7

Also available in:
No other form known

104

Burningham, John Mackintosh

The Friend

Color illustrations by the author.
Thomas Y. Crowell Company, Inc., 1975.
(19 pages counted)

FRIENDSHIP: Best Friend
Arguing

A little boy tells about his best friend, Arthur. They play in a sandbox and on a tricycle and, when it rains, play inside with toys or else watch TV. They quarrel over a teddy bear, and Arthur leaves. Dejected, the little boy admits he has other friends but says Arthur is different: he is his *best friend.*

The brief text is simple to read and ends on a happy note: the last picture shows Arthur and the boy together and smiling. The small size of this book and its amusing illustrations will appeal to very young children.

Ages 2-5

Also available in:
Paperbound — *The Friend*
Hanes

105

Burningham, John Mackintosh

The School

Color illustrations by the author.
Thomas Y. Crowell Company, Inc., 1975.
(19 pages counted)

SCHOOL: Entering

A little boy tells us that in school he learns to read, write, and sing. He also says that at school he eats lunch, paints pictures, plays games, and makes friends. Then, after a full day, he returns home.

Colorful, simple crayon illustrations go well with this extremely simple first-person narrative. These same illustrations might be used to encourage discussion. The whole could be used to help prepare a very young child for beginning school.

Ages 3-5

Also available in:
No other form known

106

Butler, Beverly Kathleen

A Girl Called Wendy

Dodd, Mead & Co., 1976.
(211 pages)

IDENTITY, SEARCH FOR
NATIVE AMERICAN
  Divorce: of parents
  Illnesses: of sibling
  Life style: change in
  Prejudice: ethnic/racial
  Relatives: living in home of
  Running away
  Sibling: love for

Wendy Gerard, a fifteen-year-old Native American living at a mission boarding school on the Menominee reservation with her seven-year-old sister, Jill, is stunned at the news that her parents have divorced. She is further demoralized when Mrs. Gerard, having no means of support, allows Aunt Brenda to take the girls to her home in Milwaukee for the summer. There,

Wendy is startled to see the close resemblance she bears to Mae, her late cousin, and resists Aunt Brenda's efforts to enhance the resemblance. Struggling both to maintain her own identity yet accept city life, Wendy is only further confused by Russell, a militant Native American college student boarding with Brenda. She weighs his bitter condemnation of white America against Aunt Brenda's efforts to obscure their heritage. Unable to sort out her feelings about any of it, Wendy tearfully admits to herself that she does not know who she is or what she wants to be. She is certain of only one thing: she and Jill must rejoin their mother — living on the Menominee reservation with their great-grandmother — in order to be happy. Leaving a note for Aunt Brenda, the girls, with Russell and his friends, travel to the reservation, where they settle down in Granny's plain log cabin. It is only when Jill becomes critically ill and Wendy is invited once again to live with Aunt Brenda that the older girl faces the confusions she earlier ran away from. Considering now the local school, the local prejudice, and the way they live, and setting it next to what she knows of city life, she realizes that no matter what she chooses to do, she must be true to herself.

A Native American adolescent learns to accept herself by accepting her heritage and talents. Meanwhile, the bond of love between the girl and her sister sustains each during crises. It is with Wendy that the reader is able to share a resurgence of pride in a rich ethnic history and an awareness of the wounds of prejudice. By setting forth both militant and conservative views on Native Americans, the book allows its readers to draw their own conclusions, as must the main character.

Ages 12 and up

Also available in:
No other form known

107

Byars, Betsy Cromer

The Cartoonist

Black/white illustrations by Richard Cuffari.
The Viking Press, Inc., 1978.
(119 pages)

INFERIORITY, FEELINGS OF
  Creativity
  Deprivation, emotional
  Jealousy: sibling
  Loneliness
  Privacy, need for

The single thing that lonely, pigeon-toed twelve-year-old Alfie likes about his dreary, untidy home is the attic, where he retreats to draw cartoons. He hopes to become a famous cartoonist some day, but right now he cannot even interest his family in what he draws. His mother is addicted to TV and garrulous reminiscences of no-good Bubba, the older son she idolizes; his grandfather endlessly complains about government; and his older sister, Alma, resenting her mother, is aloof toward them all. At school, Alfie's fascination with cartooning receives no more encouragement than at home. His best friend, Tree, thinks drawing pictures a huge waste of time, and the mathematics teacher, not amused at all when she finds him drawing instead of figuring, tells Alfie he is flunking math. Hurrying home from school to the seclusion of the attic, Alfie meets Alma and unwelcome news: Bubba has lost his job, and he and his wife are coming to live in the attic. Unwilling to lose his refuge, Alfie locks himself in. Neither the family nor Tree can coax him down, and Alfie, silent and numb, listening to the talk below, remains overnight in the attic with his cartoons. Next day, Bubba's plan changes: they will go to live with his wife's parents. Weary, aware that he has won nothing by his stand, Alfie rolls up his cartoons and carries them downstairs, knowing that for better or for worse, that is where he belongs.

Here is the spare, haunting story of a boy whose talent goes unrecognized however much he seeks the approval of others, and who then retreats to a private place of his own. What he fails to recognize is how much he relies for inspiration on his sometimes comic, always lively family. The ending suggests (but does not insist) that he will henceforth pursue his ambition, neither dodging nor deferring to the unheeding life around him.

Ages 8-12

Also available in:
Cassette for the Blind — *The Cartoonist*
Library of Congress

Paperbound — *The Cartoonist*
Dell Publishing Company, Inc.

108

Byars, Betsy Cromer

The Pinballs

Harper & Row Publishers, Inc., 1977.
(136 pages)

FOSTER HOME
FRIENDSHIP: Meaning of
  Security/Insecurity

One summer three unrelated foster children come to live with the Masons. Thirteen-year-old Harvey's legs have been accidently run over by his drunken father. Thomas J. has been a foundling in the home of elderly twin sisters since he was two. Now, six years later, both sisters are hospitalized. Carlie, in her early teens, does not get along with her second stepfather, and when he knocks her unconscious during a fight, she is taken to the Masons. Each child reacts differently in the new household. Harvey, his legs in casts, is quiet and discouraged; he tells the others he broke his legs playing football. Thomas J. is lonesome for the elderly sisters; any reminder of them makes him sad. Carlie is bossy, stubborn, and insulting, but also fiercely loyal to anyone she likes. She grows to like Harvey and Thomas J. Mr. and Mrs. Mason offer encouragement to each child, and little by little this uneasy grouping becomes a family. Mr. Mason takes Thomas J. to the hospital to see the sisters, and by reminiscing about his own feelings as a boy, helps the boy express himself. Mrs. Mason teaches Carlie to sew, and explains that it is because she cannot bear children of her own that she and her husband have opened their home to foster children. One day Harvey's father comes to visit him. Harvey accuses him of confiscating all the letters his mother ever sent him, but his father insists that the mother — who had left home years earlier — has never written to him. When his father leaves, Harvey feels hollow. Withdrawn, he refuses to eat or talk. Worse, a serious infection develops in one of his legs and he must be hospitalized. Carlie is determined to "save" him. She plans a celebration for his birthday, and she and Thomas J. get him a puppy for a gift. The puppy brings Harvey tears of joy, and from then on his health improves steadily. Meanwhile, the elderly twin sisters have died, and little Thomas J. attends their funerals. By now a real bond has developed among the three children. Carlie sums up one result of this solidarity in announcing that she wants to live a purposeful life.

Life at the Masons' contrasts sharply with the pathetic home life each child has left. Carlie's enthusiasm, backed up by the loving guidance of the Masons, cheers all three children. Carlie herself, who has felt like a "pinball" — an object having no control over itself — learns that she can, with effort, lead a life that makes things better. Humor keeps this satisfying story from becoming sugary.

Ages 10-13

Also available in:
Cassette for the Blind — *The Pinballs*
Library of Congress

Film — *The Pinballs*
Walt Disney Production

109

Byars, Betsy Cromer

The TV Kid

Black/white illustrations by Richard Cuffari.
The Viking Press, Inc., 1976.
(123 pages)

B

REALITY, ESCAPING
  Imagination
  Parent/Parents: single
  School: achievement/underachievement

Lennie, about eleven, not only watches TV constantly, he also turns his experiences and daydreams into TV characters and plots. Apart from TV, Lennie is friendless, for he and his mother have picked up and moved far too often to have put down roots in a community. Now they have a home, a motel inherited by his mother, but TV still dominates Lennie's life. His mother has to forbid his watching it until his grades improve. Even so, he fails a test but persuades his mother that it was far from a total loss. Thinking TV, though not watching it, he wanders off to a nearby lake, where he enjoys entering and playing in vacant summer homes. A police car on patrol sends him underneath a house to hide, and, after the car has passed, as he is crawling out, Lennie is bitten by a rattlesnake. His desperate attempts to seek help starting to be overtaken by the effects of the venom, Lennie treats the wound as he has seen it done on TV — cutting into it, sucking out the blood and venom, and applying a tourniquet — and hopes some-one comes. The policemen return, (they have heard of a "prowler" there) and rush Lennie to a hospital. His friendship with the policeman who found him helps lighten his hospital stay, but Lennie's real joy comes when his mother rents a TV set for his hospital room. Yet with the first commercial Lennie realizes TV is not life. "It was close enough to fool you . . . if you weren't careful, and yet those TV characters were as different as a wax figure is from a real person." Equally sudden is his determination to work on a report for school about rattlesnakes, to make up for his failing grades.

For Lennie, watching TV is more than a simple diver-sion; it is an alternative to a life the boy has not done well at. But his "coming up against life hard" discredits TV and its pat formulas in Lennie's eyes. The boy chooses real life, and his eagerness to write about some-thing that concerns him illustrates the change. Although Lennie's mother is obviously struggling alone to run the motel and raise her son, no explanation is given for his father's absence.

Ages 9-12

Also available in:
Cassette for the Blind — *The TV Kid*
Library of Congress

Cassette/Book Set — *The TV Kid*
The Viking Press, Inc.

Paperbound — *The TV Kid*
Scholastic Book Services

Record — *The TV Kid*
The Viking Press, Inc.

110
Caines, Jeannette Franklin

Daddy

Black/white illustrations by Ronald Himler.
Harper & Row Publishers, Inc., 1977.
(32 pages)

DIVORCE: of Parents

Every Saturday, Windy's father takes her to spend the day with him and Paula. Young Windy loves these Sat-urdays, when Daddy plays hide-and-seek with her, takes her to the supermarket, and they make chocolate pudding together. Paula makes dinner, and dresses Windy in old curtains to play bride. When they are apart, Windy worries about her daddy. When they are together, she is joyful.

A little girl enjoys spending Saturdays with her father, who always makes their day a special occasion. Although it is never stated, the reader is led to believe that Windy's parents are divorced. Whether Daddy is now married to Paula is not clear. But being with an absent father regularly is shown to be sheer happiness. This could distress children whose parents don't visit regularly.

Ages 4-8

Also available in:
No other form known

111

Cameron, Eleanor Butler

To the Green Mountains

E. P. Dutton & Company, Inc., 1976.
(180 pages)

MATURATION
  Daydreaming
  Separation, marital

Kath Rule and her mother, Elizabeth, live in South Angelo, Ohio, where Elizabeth manages the local hotel. Kath's father — a gruff, solemn man ridden by failure — owns a small, unproductive farm in the country. He comes to town once a month to see his wife and ask for money. Kath hates him for being such a burden to her mother; he in turn resents Kath, blaming her for the breakdown of his marriage. Kath, now in her early teens, has been visited by a recurring dream in which she and her mother are moving back to Vermont to be with Kath's maternal grandmother. Before the summer ends, Kath longs to see the dream realized. For when Elizabeth buys a set of law books for Grant, the black headwaiter of the hotel, Cornelia Sill, the town busybody, starts a rumor that Grant and Elizabeth are lovers. When Grant's wife, Tiss, Elizabeth's long-time friend, feels neglected by her husband in favor of his law books, she begins going out with a man named Cade. Meanwhile, Kath's devoted friend Herb tells Kath he loves her, his unsettling seriousness making her fear for their friendship. Brooding about her mother, Kath one evening confronts her: "Why do you stay married to a man whom you do not love, and who cares nothing for me?" After their ensuing talk, Elizabeth finally decides to divorce her husband, leave their small town and its gossip, and go back to Vermont as Kath had dreamed. Before they leave, Kath has discovered that Tiss and Cade are lovers (Tiss, shortly thereafter, is struck and killed by a passing train). And Elizabeth, encouraging Grant one last time to keep studying law, has reassured herself that theirs has been only a friendship on both sides. Herb tells Kath that he is going to England to live with his uncle. Kath leaves South Angelo with mixed emotions.

A colorful, realistic assortment of characters peoples Kath's life that summer: the gossipy, sharp-tongued Mrs. Sill; the albino Herb, serious, devoted, and mature beyond his years; Grant, solemn and dignified; Mrs. Rule, gracious, hard-working, determined. Kath herself, naive but with her mother's spunk, grows into a young woman, but not without seeing the sordid, painful side of life. This story is set during World War I, but its characters and events are universal.

Ages 11 and up

Also available in:
No other form known

C

112

Campbell, R. Wright

Where Pigeons Go to Die

Rawson Publishers, Inc., 1978.
(157 pages)

GRANDPARENT: Love for
PETS: Responsibility for
  Age: aging
  Death: attitude toward
  Illnesses: of grandparent
  Love, meaning of

Hugh Baudoum, now fifty, revisits his grandfather's house before selling it, and as he wanders about the rundown yard, he recalls vividly events forty years past. Back then, his grandfather, whom he calls Da, kept pigeons for racing and gives one to Hugh. Four years after this, when Hugh is ten, they enter Dickens and two other birds in a 600-mile race. Eating lunch the same day the birds are being trucked to Illinois for release, Da is felled by a stroke and taken to a hospital, while the boy looks on and remembers the warmth of their companionship and the many things Da has taught him. Meanwhile, the race begins, and Dickens leads — until he is attacked and wounded by a falcon, then driven far south by a storm, and there grazed by shotgun fire. Back in the hospital, Da, after a brief improvement, is fading. Hugh longs for him to live but then realizes how Da would hate to linger on in a useless body. He remembers also how Da once struck a covenant with him, that he would see to it that Da died in his own bed. Yet after Da suffers a second stroke, the doctor decides to send him to a nursing home. Determined to keep his promise, Hugh sneaks into the hospital early the next morning, smuggles his almost helpless grandfather out, and pulls Da home on a wagon. That same day Dickens, though badly injured, flies in, almost a full day after the winner. Soon after, Da dies, and in a few months, Dickens too is dead.

Here is a subtle, almost poetic story of how a grandfather introduces a boy to his passion, racing pigeons, and through this introduces him to life and to death, and thereby helps the lad grow up. The story dramatizes the loving companionship grandparents can offer a child that parents cannot. The constant shifting between time periods and an allusive, metaphorical style make this book most suitable for mature readers.

Ages 12 and up

Also available in:
Paperbound — *Where Pigeons Go to Die*
Warner Books, Inc.

113

Carle, Eric

The Grouchy Ladybug

Color illustrations by the author.
Thomas Y. Crowell Company, Inc., 1977.
(40 pages counted)

AGGRESSION
SHARING/NOT SHARING

At five o'clock one morning, two ladybugs, one friendly and one grouchy, land on the same leaf, both eager to breakfast upon the juicy aphids they find there. The friendly ladybug offers to share them, but the grouchy one offers to fight, winner take all. Then, when the challenge is accepted, the grouchy one backs down, saying, "Oh, you're not big enough for me to fight," and flies off. Hour by hour thereafter, the grouchy ladybug challenges ever-larger creatures: at six o'clock, a yellow jacket, at seven a beetle, at ten a lobster, at noon a snake, and at four an elephant — all of whom, although reluctant to fight, accept the challenge. But to even the puzzled elephant, the ladybug replies, "Oh, you're not big enough," and flies off. At five o'clock, the bug encounters a whale. It hurls its challenge but gets no answer. It challenges just the whale's fin: no reply. Finally it challenges the whale's tail — and is slapped clear across the sea, back to the land and the very leaf it had left at five o'clock that morning. The friendly ladybug, still feasting on aphids aplenty, offers to share some of its dinner. The grouchy ladybug says, "Thank you." The friendly ladybug says, "You're welcome."

This story of a disgruntled bug who learns the advantages of getting along with others is told on pages that become wider as the creatures whom the bug challenges get bigger. The page showing the yellow jacket is less than two inches wide; the lobster's page is four inches; the whale's (and binding of the book) is eight and a half. A clock pictured at the top of each page shows the hour of each encounter. The illustrations are large and brightly colored; they and the format will appeal to very young readers.

Ages 3-7

Also available in:
Paperbound — *The Grouchy Ladybug*
Scholastic Book Services

114

Carle, Eric

The Mixed-Up Chameleon

Color illustrations by the author.
Thomas Y. Crowell Company, Inc., 1975.
(31 pages counted)

SELF, ATTITUDE TOWARD: Accepting

A small chameleon is quite content with its uneventful life of color changes and fly-catching — until it views the splendid animals in a zoo. It is only then that it thinks itself little and weak, and wishes it were more like the animals it sees. As the chameleon speaks its wish, it begins to imagine itself growing parts of the animals it admires. This is lovely — until the chameleon discovers that it is so confused by its new appendages that it cannot catch a fly when it is hungry. Its heartfelt wish to return to its former state is granted, and that state is the loveliest of all.

In this colorfully illustrated story of self-acceptance, the chameleon's desire to be more impressive is one any small child can share. Though the text is brief, the lesson is clear. Vivid illustrations show all the imagined changes the chameleon undergoes.

Ages 4-8

Also available in:
No other form known

115

Carlson, Dale Bick

Triple Boy

Atheneum Publishers, 1977.
(172 pages) o.p.

C

GUILT, FEELINGS OF
MENTAL ILLNESS: of Adolescent
  Alcoholism: of mother
  Boy-girl relationships
  Communication: parent-child
  Friendship: meaning of
  Suicide: attempted

Paul Austin, now sixteen, first "lost time" — brief memory loss — years earlier, when his father blamed him for not saving his three-year-old brother, Stevie, from being run over by a train. Paul next lost time a year later when his mother, a successful painter, divorced his father, an unsuccessful writer. Through the years he has continued to lose time — an hour, a week — but cannot understand why, and desperately longs to learn if he is "crazy." His mother, lost in alcoholism, and his father, bitter and defeated, cannot help. Paul's best friend, Frank, and Frank's girl friend, Claire, just do not know enough. The first to understand Paul's state is a beginning psychiatrist, John Marsh, a casual acquaintance from the nearby beach. John discovers that two dissociated personalities take Paul over at different times. Both first arose from Paul's guilt feelings: the one called Mike, brilliant and interested, himself, in psychiatry, first came after Stevie's death; George, affectionate and steady and good at sports, came after the divorce. Both take over when Paul is threatened by strong emotions.

Afraid that explaining his condition might be psychologically damaging to Paul, John works toward integrating Mike and George with Paul's "real" personality. But the two continue to struggle to take over Paul, and as the summer begins, Paul loses time more frequently. Seeing Paul's deterioration, John takes him to Dr. Jason, an experienced psychiatrist, who after therapy tells Paul what the trouble is — not psychotic but psycho-neurotic — and that it can be corrected. Unable to believe this, Paul tries to kill himself by lying, like Stevie, in front of a train. But he is seen, blacks out, and comes to in the hospital, where John again attempts to integrate the three personalities. Mike consents and disappears forever, becoming a full functioning part of Paul's personality. George resists, but as the school year goes by and Paul finally understands that he has his own life to live, that his parents' unhappiness was not his fault, and that love is no longer dangerous for him, Paul becomes just himself. George, too, disappears.

This is a realistic, sometimes funny account of a teenager's mental illness — *grande hysterie,* "disassociative behavior, the process in which a group of mental activities break away from the main stream of consciousness and functions as a separate unit." In this case, two separate childhood traumas produce two distinct personalities. The characterizations of all three of Paul's selves are rounded and believable. Frank and Claire seem too sweet to be true, whereas Paul's parents behave believably. The description of Paul's brother's death is harrowing.

Ages 13 and up

Also available in:
No other form known

116

Carlson, Natalie Savage

Marie Louise's Heyday

Color illustrations by Jose Aruego and Ariane Dewey.
Charles Scribner's Sons, 1975.
(32 pages counted)

BABY-SITTING: Involuntary

Marie Louise, a little mongoose, finds a sweet, fat banana: today must be her heyday. All the same, her mother insists she baby-sit with a possum's five children. The tots finally exhaust Marie Louise with their games — and then refuse the nutritious meal she offers. Instead they run off to play, eat poison berries, and are saved only when Marie fetches the Witch Toad with her loathsome, though magic, brew. Recovered, the five young possums defend their eating of the berries with five silly reasons, including "because." Furthermore, they assure their mother that they behaved very well in her absence; Marie bids good-bye, saying to the mother, "I'm glad I'm me and not you." But at home, her own mother reminds Marie Louise how she herself once refused lunch only to chew a poison vine later on. The child wonders why on earth she would have done such a thing — and no better excuses occur to her than those the possums had given. Next day, the possums come over bringing flowers — another heyday.

Pressed into baby-sitting, Marie Louise cannot understand the contrary behavior of her charges. Reminded of her own behavior as a child, she cannot understand that either. The moral: children do things first and think up reasons later. Young children will understand these delightful possums perfectly, and, like Marie Louise, learn something about themselves. This story is one in a series about Marie Louise.

Also available in:
Talking Book — *Marie Louise's Heyday*
Library of Congress

117

Carlson, Natalie Savage

Runaway Marie Louise

Color illustrations by Jose Aruego and Ariane Dewey.
Charles Scribner's Sons, 1977.
(32 pages counted)

LOVE, MEANING OF
RUNNING AWAY

One day the good little mongoose Marie Louise is naughty, and her mother spanks her. Marie Louise gets mad, packs her sack, and says to her mother, "You don't love me anymore. I am going to find a new mama." Her mother gives her a sandwich in case she gets hungry. But when approached, the mother snake does not want Marie Louise because one more naughty child would give her the "tail tizzies." Neither does the mother duck, the mother turtle, the mother armadillo, nor the Witch Toad want her. But the toad sends her down the path to catch a lady who has just come along asking for a child. Marie Louise wonders who that could be — and now hopes it is none of the animals she has already asked. Then she sees her mother and calls to her. Mama hugs Marie Louise and tells her that she, too, is running away. "It would be lonely at home with no one to love and care for," she says. "You are really the best mama," Marie Louise says. "Let's run away home."

Few young children will fail to recognize this little mongoose's hurt feelings and sudden desire to run away. Her mother wisely lets the child go, knowing she will return on her own. This perceptive book assumes that young children need to express their feelings and make their own mistakes. Its delightful, childlike illustrations make it a good book to read aloud.

Ages 3-6

Also available in:
No other form known

118

Carpelan, Bo Gustaf Bertelsson

Dolphins in the City

Translated from the Swedish by Sheila La Farge.
Delacorte Press/Seymour Lawrence, 1976.
(145 pages)

MENTAL RETARDATION
Change: new home
Friendship: meaning of
Maturation

Gerda Lundren and her retarded son, Marvin, about twenty, have lived on Bow Island all their lives. When the property is sold, the two are forced to move into the city, where they live in a dark one-room apartment, and where Gerda takes a job cleaning in a factory. Fourteen-year-old Johan Bergman, a boy who knows and understands Marvin and Gerda from summers spent on the island, aids them in the city. But Gerda's work is long and tedious; she misses the beauty and freedom of the island. The change is even more difficult for Marvin; he is given a job sorting papers in a warehouse, but like his mother, he feels stifled by the city. During their first city winter they rejoice in a visit to Bow Island, where Marvin and his mother and Johan and his parents spend Christmas with old Otto Söder and his daughter Nora, long-time friends of both families. One day in the spring, Marvin is falsely accused of attacking one of the girls who lives in the Lundrens' apartment building. He is devastated by the accusation and runs away, intending to drown himself. He is rescued, but for several days will not respond to anyone. Gerda quits her hated job to take care of him, and after his recovery, he is enrolled in a trade school for handicapped people, where he excels in carpentry. In June, Nora, whose father has died, comes from the island with an exciting idea. She wants Gerda and Marvin to come live with her: Gerda will keep house, and Marvin will work as a carpenter for a local boatbuilder. Johan and his family will even spend their vacation there. Nora's idea brings joy to them all.

Johan, the storyteller, paints a vivid, perceptive portrait of Marvin, who suffered brain damage at birth. Like normal people, Marvin loves freedom and beauty and hates cruelty, pain, and tiresome tasks that wear out the soul as well as the body. When difficulties press in on him, he thinks of dolphins, who represent peace and freedom to him. "They carry me away when I'm scared and drowning." Johan understands Marvin's trapped feelings especially well, because he feels similarly about the city and his strict, demanding school. This sequel to *Bow Island: The Story of a Summer That Was Different* is not an exciting, fast-paced book, but a description of people and their ability to cope with life and change.

Ages 12-14

Also available in:
No other form known

119

Carrick, Carol

The Accident

Color illustrations by Donald Carrick.
The Seabury Press, Inc., 1976.
(30 pages counted)

DEATH: of Pet

Young Christopher and his parents are vacationing at their summer cottage. One evening Mother and Father go canoeing, leaving Chris at the cottage watching television with his dog, Bodger. Soon Chris decides to walk to the lake with Bodger to meet his parents on their return. Traffic on the road is heavy, and when a pickup truck suddenly rounds a bend, Christopher calls Bodger a split-second too late from the other side of the road. Bodger runs right in front of the truck and is killed. The driver stops, examines the dog, and sadly explains to the stunned little boy that the dog is dead. Just then Christopher's parents appear, and the boy is sure they can make everything all right. They cannot, and his father just nods while the driver explains what happened. Christopher is angry and hurt. That night all he can think about is how he could have avoided the accident, and how much the dog's death was his fault. Next morning, his father tells him he has buried Bodger by the brook, and Christopher runs angrily into the woods. But he returns, and his father suggests they take the canoe and hunt for a stone to mark Bodger's grave. Christopher becomes absorbed in finding the perfect stone and finally chooses one with markings that remind him of the birch tree by the brook. As they put the stone on the grave, his father recalls how the dog used to try without success to catch trout in the brook. Christopher starts to laugh, then cries, and feels better when his father comforts him.

This quiet story with its subdued illustrations sensitively and honestly expresses a young boy's feelings of anger, guilt, and grief at the death of his pet. With his parents' support and understanding, Christopher is able to accept the death.

Ages 4-8

Also available in:
Talking Book — *The Accident*
Library of Congress

120

Carrick, Carol

The Foundling

Color illustrations by Donald Carrick.
The Seabury Press, Inc., 1977.
(30 pages counted)

PETS: Love for
Decision making

Weeks afterward, young Christopher still mourns the loss of his dog, who was run over by a truck. Though he plays with a puppy from next door, he cannot imagine any dog taking the place of Bodger. His father, thinking the boy needs a dog of his own, takes him to an animal shelter. Shown several dogs, one of which he likes a lot, Chris maintains he wants no pet. He does not know why, he just feels that way. On the return drive, he tells his father that taking another dog would be unfaithful to Bodger. Without pressing the point, his father explains that rescuing an abandoned dog would in fact show love for Bodger. Confused, Chris wanders to the docks — and finds the puppy from next door. But when he brings it back to its owner, she disclaims it, grumbling that the summer tourists must have left it. Chris names the puppy Ben and tells his parents that Ben is now his.

Children often think that acquiring a new pet means disloyalty to a lost or dead one. Chris never actively decides to take the puppy he has found: it is there; no one claims it; and he finally understands that caring for a needy pet is no betrayal of a dead one. This warm story is a sequel to *The Accident,* and is one in a series of books featuring Chris.

Ages 5-8

Also available in:
Talking Book — *The Foundling*
Library of Congress

121

Carrick, Carol

The Highest Balloon on the Common

Color illustrations by Donald Carrick.
Greenwillow Books, 1977.
(32 pages counted)

LOST, BEING

In the village where little Paul lives, all the houses are built around an open public park, a common. Today, Old Home Day, the villagers have set up on the common an old-fashioned county fair, with food stands, display booths, and games. Everyone from the village has come, including Paul and his parents. The boy takes a ride on a fire engine, then eats a hot dog. His father buys him a big, yellow balloon and ties it to Paul's wrist with a long string. After Paul watches a contest of competing ponies, he wanders off by himself. When he cannot find his parents, he is frightened, realizing he has lost his way. The common looks so unfamiliar that he fails to recognize his own house. At last his father finds him, having sighted the large balloon still tied to Paul's wrist and floating high above the heads of the crowd.

Paul's familiar playground, the common, becomes a threatening place when he gets lost. The illustrations will help readers visualize the excitement and activity of a small-town celebration.

Ages 4-7

Also available in:
No other form known

122

Carrick, Malcolm

Tramp

Color illustrations by the author.
Harper & Row Publishers, Inc., 1977.
(48 pages)

FRIENDSHIP: Making Friends
LONELINESS
SHYNESS
  Rejection: peer

A young London boy finds a secret place in town to play by himself, without other children to pick on him but with the company of venturesome imaginary friends. One day when he comes to play he finds an intruder — a tramp who has collapsed from illness and hunger. The boy is angry and a little afraid of the stranger. But he daily brings food, then plays nearby, sharing his imaginary friends with the slowly recovering man. After several days, Tramp (as he has come to think of him) disappears. The boy grieves for and resents his lost — and only — friend, and comes back daily to see if Tramp has returned. Gradually the boy accepts the loss. Then one day he speaks to a neighbor girl, Sally James, whom he has long admired. When she responds kindly, he goes home happy. Perhaps he will make a new friend.

A boy tells us how, shy and lonely, he had hidden away where he could pretend to be a hero and a winner. Tramp is the one real person allowed in his secret place, and the boy is saddened to lose that one friend. His experience, however, gives him the courage to try to befriend someone else.

Ages 7-9

Also available in:
No other form known

123

Castle, Sue

Face Talk, Hand Talk, Body Talk

Black/white photographs by Frances McLaughlin-Gill.
Doubleday & Company, Inc., 1977.
(63 pages counted)

COMMUNICATION: Importance of
  Emotions: accepting

Even a newborn baby talks in body talk — saying, I am angry, I am hungry. As the child grows, so does the body's vocabulary. Though facial expressions convey many feelings — anger, sadness, and joy among them — they say much more when combined with hand and arm gestures. The entire body can express moods, hard and tight in excitement or anger, limp and floppy in fatigue or relaxation. True, children's postures and gestures may differ while expressing the same feelings, but they leave no doubt about what those feelings are.

This is one book in which photographs speak louder than the text. In a foreword, the author suggests that teachers or parents invite children to play the Body Talk game presented later in the book: look at the photographs and guess what the pictured children are saying. Not only can youngsters reading this book learn to "read" body talk, they may also more readily accept emotions as the pictures and text affirm them: "Sometimes you feel lonely . . . or shy . . . or afraid!"

Ages 4-7

Also available in:
No other form known

124

Cate, Dick

Flying Free

Black/white illustrations by Trevor Stubley.
Thomas Nelson, Inc., 1975.
(94 pages)

FAMILY: Relationships
MATURATION
  Accidents
  Freedom, meaning of

Every evening when his father returns from the mine, Billy accompanies him to their Town Council plot, where the family raises hens and pigeons. If Billy is bored by his father's beloved pigeons, his older sister, Sandra, and her boy friend, Steven, are almost scornful of so unproductive an investment. Self-assured and often sarcastic, Steven sometimes rubs Billy the wrong way, and Billy's father deplores the way the young engaged couple spend their money on unnecessary furnishings like a color television set. One evening Sandra asks her father if he would mind giving up a little of his plot — just where the pigeons are — so she and Steven can keep a few pigs. Billy's father walks out of the house in a fury. Some days later an accident at the mine traps Steven and five other men, and Billy's father goes to help with the rescue. Fortunately, Steven is brought up with nothing worse than a broken leg. As he recovers, Billy visits him nearly every evening and finds a Steven

both more patient and more modest since the accident. In fact, winning 250 pounds in a football pool, Steven uses the money as a down payment for a house instead of a color television. One evening, Billy's father ailing, Steven goes with Billy to tend the pigeons. Watching them fly about, he remarks that he has been assigned a Council plot and thinks he will raise pigeons too. Steven says that when he had been trapped in the mine, "I suppose I just thought it would be nice to just see them like that, flying free."

This quiet, straightforward story, set in the North of England, shows how an accident draws a family closer together and sobers a young man's plans for the future. Like Billy's father before him, Steven lives through a potentially fatal accident and comes to share the older man's love of pigeons and the freedom they represent. Through Steven, Billy learns more about the mine and miners. This book's limited vocabulary would appeal to older readers needing easy material.

Ages 8-10

Also available in:
No other form known

C

125

Cate, Dick

Never Is a Long, Long Time

Black/white illustrations by Trevor Stubley.
Thomas Nelson, Inc., 1976.
(92 pages)

FAMILY: Unity
MATURATION
  Death: of pet
  Grandparent: love for
  Illnesses: of grandparent

Billy is nearly twelve when the family dog dies of old age. His father refuses to get another: "We'd never get . . . one as good as her." Billy's spirited, seventy-five-year-old grandmother thinks differently. "Never is a long, long time," she tells Billy. Close to Christmas, and close to completion of the crib the boy and the grandmother are refinishing for the soon-due first great-grandchild, the grandmother falls ill. Much against her will, she is hospitalized, the crib turned over to a friend to finish. Christmas preparations at Billy's house are minimal. "It doesn't seem right somehow," says Billy's mother. "Not with my mother being so poorly." But two days before Christmas the grandmother is sent home to the family, and celebration begins in earnest. Sitting at Christmas dinner, claiming the wishbone as always, and energetically cracking nuts, the grandmother seems herself again. In February Billy's sister has her baby, a girl as the grandmother predicted. Billy is not nearly as taken with the baby as everyone else seems to be. But as he watches her in the crib, he feels grown up for the first time. Some days later, Billy and his father hear the cries of a newborn lamb. On the walk back to the house the father says he has been thinking about getting another dog, a puppy. "Everybody else seems to be having babies, so I don't see why we can't."

With the turning of the year and intimations of both birth and death, a boy thinks of himself as an adult for the first time. Relationships change, as between Billy's sister and her husband as the birth of the baby nears; minds are changed, as the father's is about getting a new dog. Steadily pleasant, but weak in character development, this story may not hold every reader's interest. Although the locale is never specified, certain mining customs and turns of phrase suggest this story takes place in England. It is a sequel to *Flying Free*.

Ages 9-11

Also available in:
No other form known

126
Chandler, Edna Walker

Indian Paintbrush

Black/white illustrations by Lee Fitzgerrell-Smith.
Albert Whitman & Co., 1975.
(128 pages)

CHANGE: Resisting
LIFE STYLE: Change in
NATIVE AMERICAN
  Belonging
  Change: new home
  School: pupil-teacher relationships
  Self, attitude toward: feeling different

Maria Lopez's mother had been born on the Sioux Indian Reservation where the family now lives, but Maria, about ten, is teased so much about speaking Spanish and looking different — her father, now dead, was a Mexican-American — that she wants to return to Arizona, which is home to her. Maria feels so much the outsider that she refuses to attend school, where the local children shun her when they do not outright fight her. That the locals also dislike her older brother, Pedro, an activist trying to change the conditions of Indian life, intensifies her loathing of the Reservation. The only Sioux with any sympathy for her, Maria thinks, is Billy Lone Deer, and even he teases her most of the time. The only enthusiasm in Maria's life is provided by her bumptious young brother, Juanito, who gets into everything. He accompanies her to school when Maria, curious about the new teacher, Miss Jean Brave, attends just to see what she is like. Miss Brave's refreshing way of teaching holds her. Even the community, so often suspicious and opposed to change, recognizes Miss Brave's worth and wants her to return the following year. When she remains undecided, Maria places Paintbrush flowers in her luggage to insure her return — at least Sioux folklore says it will. Maria is not a bit surprised when Miss Brave announces at her going-away party that she will come back in the fall.

A girl removed from the easy-going, gracious Mexican-American society of Arizona mistakes the different ways of the Sioux for hostility toward her. Aided by a teacher, Maria begins to understand and accept the Sioux community and to feel she belongs.

Ages 9-11

Also available in:
No other form known

127

Charlip, Remy and Lilian Moore

Hooray For Me!
Color illustrations by Vera B. Williams.
Parents' Magazine Press, 1975.
(32 pages counted)

AUTONOMY
Identity, search for

A young child discovers that we think of ourselves in a variety of ways — as a wife, sister, second cousin, or stepfather; as the niece's or nephew's uncle or aunt or as a cousin's cousin. People even view themselves as being their cat's pillow, their shadow's body, the family's dishwasher, a wriggler, and their "best friend's friend (sometimes)." But whatever we see ourselves as at a given moment, we should be proud of ourselves.

This first-person narrative explores the many ways in which we take identity through work, and so forth. Each self-description appears as a caption beside the self-describer; the graphic layouts may confuse some readers.

Ages 3-6

Also available in:
No other form known

128

Chetin, Helen

How Far Is Berkeley?
Harcourt Brace Jovanovich, Inc., 1977.
(122 pages)

LIFE STYLE: Change in
PARENT/PARENTS: Single
  Change: new home
  Friendship: making friends
  Maturation

Michael Blythe has lived all her twelve years with her mother and maternal grandparents. She has never met her father, though she knows that he is Mexican, that his parents forbade the marriage to her mother before Michael was born, and that she is named after him. Now mother and daughter are moving from Los Angeles to Berkeley, California, where Michael's mother will be attending graduate school. They will live in an old mansion with three other young women (all staunch feminists), some cats, and a man named Al who is writing a book and making a living by selling orange juice and cookies from a pushcart. Michael meets a boy her own age who helps her get acquainted with the new neighborhood, and is on the whole enjoying her new life and friends until one day it occurs to her that her mother and Al may be falling in love. The more she thinks about that, the more distressed she becomes, until, in anger, she sprays water all over Al's orange-juice cart and runs away. That night she calls her mother to come and get her. They talk, and her mother explains that though she and Al do care for one another, they will never do anything that is not right for both

C

herself and Michael. Michael confesses that she has always hoped she would find her father. Her mother says that she will do all she can to that end, but adds that it is not always wise to "open closed doors." Soon after, by the time her grandparents come for a visit, Michael has decided that Al is not so bad after all.

An adolescent girl describes to us her realistic and natural feelings toward her absent father, her ways of adjusting to new surroundings and meeting some "unusual" people. But the thought of her mother marrying is more than she can bear — until her mother convinces her that no decisions will be made without the girl's consent. Sex is discussed freely and frankly several times in this story. Both mother and daughter can, in fact, speak freely to each other about anything.

Ages 11-13

Also available in:
No other form known

129

Child Study Association of America

Families Are Like That! Stories to Read to Yourself

Black/white illustrations by Richard Cuffari.
Thomas Y. Crowell Company, Inc., 1975.
(143 pages)

FAMILY: Relationships
FAMILY: Unity
LOVE, MEANING OF

Starting off this collection, little Pedro is worried because Papa, who always comes home from his week-long job on Friday nights, has not arrived yet. Then Rosina, the young daughter of a fisherman, proves to her father that a woman on a fishing boat brings no bad luck — and can even bring good. Six-year-old Penny is

reassured by his adoptive mother that her love for him makes him truly her own little boy. Rafer's birthday is made happy and memorable when his divorced father comes to spend the day with him. Matthew, who has grown up in a "children's shelter," has never known a mother or father, and has lived in two previous foster homes, comes to live with the Walterses, in whom at last he finds love and a feeling of safety.

This collection of ten short stories, or excerpts from books by various authors, describes children and parents experiencing disappointment, love, sorrow, contentment, joy — a wide variety of family feelings. The drawings depict many of the characters as members of minority groups. The texts are of a length and nature to encourage reading aloud.

Ages 6-9

Also available in:
Cassette for the Blind — *Families Are Like That! Stories to Read to Yourself*
Library of Congress

130

Choate, Judith Newkirk

Awful Alexander

Color illustrations by Steven Kellogg.
Doubleday & Company, Inc., 1976.
(31 pages)

RESPONSIBILITY: Accepting
  Imaginary friend

Young Alexander always seems to be "stuffed with silly tricks." He hides in a pillowcase to surprise his mother, scares his father and sister, looms up like a clothes-wrapped ghost from Grandma's laundry basket, and serves Grandpa a mud-pie lunch. Each time, family members chuckle and tell him, "That was awful, Alexander!" Thus, one day, when he is caught feeding his sandwich to the dog, he blames the mythical Awful Alexander. From then on, he blames Awful for unfinished vegetables, late bedtimes, and stolen cookies. It is only when he is hurt in a fall from a ladder that he discovers there is only one Alexander who gets hurt — himself.

The main character puts blame on an alter-ego for things he himself should not have done. Young children will readily understand this boy's use of an imaginary counterpart — pictured as a larger, horned version of himself — and see the disadvantage of this protective device as well.

Ages 4-7

Also available in:
No other form known

131

Chorao, Kay

Molly's Moe

Black/white illustrations by the author.
The Seabury Press, Inc., 1976.
(30 pages counted)

LOSS: of Possessions
Determination

Little Molly habitually loses toys and items of clothing. Today her mother makes a deal with her: if the child will see to it she does not lose anything while the two are out shopping, Mother will buy her a treat. Molly begs to take along her favorite toy, a stuffed animal named Moe, and Mother consents. After each stop along the way, Molly checks to see that she still has all her belongings, and at the last stop, the bakery, Molly chooses her treat: a cake with pink roses. Mother and

daughter arrive home, both feeling proud that Molly's clothes are still intact — until Molly realizes with horror that Moe is missing. Mother calls each store: no Moe. Molly cries herself to sleep. Suddenly she awakens, for a dream has reminded her where Moe is — at the bottom of the shopping bag. She celebrates her find with a piece of cake topped by the biggest pink rose.

This delightfully familiar story will appeal to any young child who has lost something — and more particularly to "chronic losers," who will see that the habit of losing can be overcome.

Ages 4-7

Also available in:
No other form known

132

Christman, Elizabeth

A Nice Italian Girl

Dodd, Mead & Co., 1976.
(139 pages)

COURAGE, MEANING OF
JUSTICE/INJUSTICE
PREGNANCY
SEX: Premarital
   Guilt, feelings of
   Judgment, effect of emotions on
   Roman Catholic
   Unwed mother

During her junior year in college, Anne Macarino, a motherless, shy, serious girl whose conservative Italian father is a small town's mayor, begins dating Stephen Albright, a boy she thinks her superior in looks and popularity. Although she tries to keep their friendship casual, sure it has no future, she falls in love with Steve and gives in to his sexual advances. In February she

C

tells him she is pregnant. Steve seems helpless, says he needs all his money for law school, and she will not tell her family because of the shame it will cause them. Her upbringing rules out abortion. That leaves adoption. Steve just happens to know of a lawyer in St. Louis who handles private adoptions; an Italian couple named Biondo would pay Anne's medical, hospital, and living expenses in return for her baby. Anne is wary, particularly about registering with the doctor as Mrs. Biondo, but Steve persuades her, telling her bluntly that the well-to-do Mr. Biondo is her only backing. After finishing out the school term and giving her family an excuse for her summer's absence, Anne goes to wait out her pregnancy in St. Louis, fully intending on returning to school in the fall. But, suddenly she discovers she is the victim of an adoption plot — Steve coldly planned her pregnancy in return for three thousand dollars. "This was a special order, right? They wanted an Italian girl, right?" she overhears him say to the lawyer. Grief and shame give way to hardened determination, and Anne decides she will keep her baby. She refuses any further help from the Biondos, who tell her they, too, were tricked and beg her forgiveness, beg to help her. Anne soon finds she cannot make it on her own and does agree to stay with the Biondos for the remainder of her pregnancy provided that she can keep her baby. She finds their kindness stifling and their subtle campaign for the child difficult to fight. Soon she is convinced that they would not be suitable parents for her child. Though everyone around her argues to the contrary — the Biondo's family priest and Steve and even Anne's two older brothers, who have found out and threaten to withhold all money unless she gives up her baby — Anne sticks by her decision. In the hospital, recovering from her delivery, she ignores her brother and has the nurse bring her son.

In this intriguing story, a college girl's first experience with love and sex brings harsh consequences. Despite Anne's high principles, her innocence and naivete induce situations she is not prepared to deal with. Only when she finally decides to trust herself, to stand up for her judgment, does she appear strong and mature. She makes realistic plans for herself and her baby, but the reader is left with the feeling that there are difficult times ahead for this girl who cannot go home because she cannot bring herself to tell her father of her circumstances. Readers sympathize with her newfound determination, though they may not agree with her decision. The book provides excellent discussion opportunities, and readers will be drawn to speculate on the exact extent of the Biondos' involvement. While not an indictment of premarital sex, this book dramatically demonstrates its effects on one girl's life.

Ages 12 and up

Also available in:
No other form known

133

Christopher, Matthew F.

The Fox Steals Home

Black/white illustrations by Larry Johnson.
Little, Brown and Co., 1978.
(178 pages)

DIVORCE: of Parents
SPORTS/SPORTSMANSHIP

Twelve-year-old Bobby Canfield, third baseman for the Sunbirds baseball team, is increasingly distracted from baseball by his parents' recent divorce and the fact that his father, who shares his devotion to sports, may see Bobby only on weekends. Saturdays become his favorite day; under his father's coaching, Bobby begins to excel, especially at stealing bases, for which he is nicknamed "the Fox." One day Mr. Canfield brings a woman to a game, introducing her as Mrs. Wilson, mother of Walter Wilson, who pitches for another team. A short time later, Walter tells Bobby that Mr. Canfield has given permission for the two boys to use his boat, and while Bobby is skeptical, he agrees to give Walter a ride. Out on the water, Walter lights a cigarette. When Bobby tells him to put it out, Walter accidentally tosses it against a leaky gas line. The explosion throws both boys into the water. Neither is injured, but the boat is demolished. Mr. Canfield is furious, especially when Walter tells him Bobby is the one who had smoked. Bobby denies this, and his father believes him. Later, when his father tells him that he has taken a job on a freighter and will be gone at least a year, Bobby is so distressed by the news that he can hardly concentrate during the next game — the game against Walter's team. Seeing his father and grandfather in the blcachers, he rallies — and heroically steals second, third, and home to win the game for his team.

A young boy struggles to accept his parents' recent divorce. His mother, preoccupied with her own interests, has little time for Bobby; but his father, whom Bobby idolizes, gives the boy support and encouragement, at least until he decides to leave the country on a venture of his own. By that time, Bobby seems to have enough self-confidence to get along without him. There is more baseball here than characterization.

Ages 8-10

Also available in:
No other form known

134

Christopher, Matthew F.

Glue Fingers

Color illustrations by Jim Venable.
Little, Brown and Co., 1975.
(46 pages counted)

SPEECH PROBLEMS: Stuttering
SPORTS/SPORTSMANSHIP
  Embarrassment
  Self-esteem

C

Billy Joe, in about seventh grade, can catch a football as though he had "glue fingers." But when a football coach, who has watched Billy Joe playing for fun, comes to the family farm to invite the boy to play on his team, Billy Joe says no, he will not play on anyone's team. What he does not say is that his stammer makes him too afraid the other players will laugh at him. His brothers plead with him to accept, and so Billy Joe grimly reviews his decision. Before he goes to sleep that night he decides he will play after all. Why would he have to talk on the football field? Mr. Davis is pleased at his change of mind, and after several practices with the team, the boy is ready for his first game. But he misses a pass during a crucial play, and that unnerves him. Then, during the third quarter, he catches a long pass and runs for his team's first touchdown of the game. In the final seconds of play, he repeats the performance and scores the winning points for the team. Coach Davis congratulates Billy Joe — who is proud of himself — for playing well and for having the courage to join the team in the first place.

A self-conscious stammerer sees that his speech trouble need not keep him from playing a sport in which he excels. His courage pays off when he becomes a hero in his first game. While Billy Joe's anxiety over possible ridicule is made real enough, this slight plot ends patly. But the book could encourage other youngsters who stammer, and inform others about them.

Ages 7-9

Also available in:
No other form known

135

Chukovsky, Kornei Ivanovich

The Silver Crest: My Russian Boyhood

Translated from the Russian by Beatrice Stillman.
Holt, Rinehart and Winston, Inc., 1976.
(182 pages)

MATURATION
Determination
Education: value of
Prejudice: social class
Russia
Self-discipline

During his fifth year at the Russian gymnasium, or school, eleven-year-old Kornei is expelled. His mother is told by letter that he has failed to progress in his studies and is a bad influence on his classmates. Kornei is devastated; he is innocent of the charges, and afraid of the effect of his dismissal on his mother, who places tremendous value on Kornei's getting ahead. He tries everything to get himself reinstated — then finds out that he (along with several others) is the victim of a plot: the authorities have denied him a formal education because his mother is unwed, owns no property, and is a member of the working class. Though Kornei is stunned by this information, he is relieved to know that Tsarist politics are to blame, not his shortcomings. He determines to educate himself and begins studies with his friend Timosha. But his self-discipline wears thin,

and he drifts away from friends as well as studies. Kornei leaves home and becomes a loafer; despising himself, he seems unable to reform. Time passes, and one day he visits Timosha. Encouraged by his friend, he resumes his studies. Years later he is graduated, and ultimately he achieves his boyhood dream — becoming a writer.

Kornei Chukovsky relates this account of his own growing-up in Russia at the turn of the century. His perceptive portrayals of his family and classmates, the neighbors, and the school officials are filled with wit and tenderness. Although he also presents a candid picture of Tsarist Russia and its politics, the story is universal in appeal.

Ages 12 and up

Also available in:
No other form known

136

Clark, Mavis Thorpe

If the Earth Falls In

The Seabury Press, Inc., 1975.
(165 pages)

PARENT/PARENTS: Substitute
Love, meaning of
Maturation

Louise has grown up in a small mining town in Australia, knowing neither father nor mother. For some fifteen years, Aunt Eva has raised her, even refusing marriage out of devotion to the child. Now Louise is secretly planning to run away to the city. She will steal her aunt's treasured Chinese glass painting and sell it for the money she needs. One night, taking the painting out to examine it, she breaks it, and hides the pieces under the house. Her carelessness has ruined all hope of getting to the city. But her new friend, Jonathan, promises to lend her money. Two things puzzle her about Jonathan, however: his mysterious hikes into the mining country and the fights he has been having with Bruce Burton. One Sunday, Louise goes to the hills herself — and meets Bruce Burton, also looking for Jonathan. The two trace Jonathan to an old mine shaft, which Bruce believes may contain valuable antique bottles and jars. Louise now understands why the two young men have been fighting: Bruce wants these treasures for himself. Louise strikes out at him, and the two fall into the shaft, narrowly missing being buried alive. They discover Jonathan in an adjacent tunnel. After many hours the three of them find a way out. Among the townspeople digging at the main entrance to find them, Louise sees Aunt Eva. The look on her aunt's face shows her how much Eva loves her. Louise will not run away after all.

This story of an adolescent who wakes up to parental love uses some Australian English. The slow pace of the first half may discourage some readers from following through to the exciting ending. As the young people struggle to find a way out of the mine, they begin to understand what honor and respect are.

Ages 11-14

Also available in:
Cassette for the Blind — *If the Earth Falls In*
Library of Congress

137

Cleary, Beverly Bunn

Ramona and Her Father

Black/white illustrations by Alan Tiegreen.
William Morrow & Company, Inc., 1975.
(187 pages)

FAMILY: Relationships
    Parent/Parents: mother working outside home
    Smoking

C

Seven-year-old Ramona is alarmed to learn that her father has lost his job. Hoping to make money herself, she starts acting out television commercials in private, but when one day a homemade crown for a margarine ad gets so entangled in her hair that her father has to cut it out, her show-business career is nipped in the bud. Home life turns grim. Mom is working full time, and her father becomes bored with housekeeping. Ramona and her sister, Beezus, launch a campaign to get him to quit smoking — but when he tries, he becomes even more irritable. Soon enough, both parents are down on Ramona for having volunteered to play a sheep in the approaching church Christmas pageant on the understanding that her hard-pressed mother will make her costume. Home life improves when her father gets a job, but when the night of the pageant arrives and Mom has only managed to convert a pair of pajamas into a "sheep suit," Ramona balks at wearing it. Then some older girls call her "cute" and blacken her nose with mascara. She thinks herself a fine sheep after all. Seeing her parents in the audience, she feels proud of them. Seeing her father wink at her, she knows they are proud of her, too.

A period of family ups and downs teaches Ramona new things about her family, and her father's anxious irritability ends by only drawing her closer to him. Both text and illustrations are brisk and delightful. This is one in a series of books about Ramona and her family and friends.

Ages 7-10

Also available in:
Cassette for the Blind — *Ramona and Her Father*
Library of Congress

Filmstrip — *Ramona and Her Father*
Miller-Brody Productions

Paperbound — *Ramona and Her Father*
Dell Publishing Company, Inc.

138

Cleary, Beverly Bunn

Ramona the Brave

Black/white illustrations by Alan Tiegreen.
William Morrow & Company, Inc., 1975.
(190 pages)

FAMILY: Relationships
SCHOOL: Pupil-Teacher Relationships
SIBLING: Relationships
  Fear: of darkness

Six-year-old Ramona Quimby is bursting with anticipation: in September she will begin first grade, and soon after she will have a bedroom all to herself. She and her older sister, Beezus, have been sharing a room, but now, thanks to her mother's new part-time job, the family can afford to have a new room built on to the house. But Ramona's first-grade teacher turns out to be stiff, strict, and unresponsive, and Ramona decides Mrs. Griggs dislikes her. Moved into the new bedroom, Ramona finds she is afraid of the dark and misses talking and giggling with Beezus. Trying to be brave, she tells none of this to her parents, and her life becomes routinely miserable day and night. When Mrs. Griggs includes in the girl's favorable school progress report two complaints, Ramona is furious. Worse, she thinks her parents side with the teacher; she bursts into tears, crying that everyone is against her. At last, she and her parents talk everything over, and she begins to feel better. "Show us your spunk," says her father, and Ramona finds the courage to start over both with Mrs. Griggs and the new bedroom.

This is an amusing and touching story of a little girl who tries to keep all her woes to herself. When, inevitably, the adults in her life come to seem insensitive, she learns the value of opening up. The illustrations are also amusing. This book is one in a series about Ramona and her family and friends.

Ages 7-10

Also available in:
Paperbound — *Ramona the Brave*
Scholastic Book Services

Talking Book — *Ramona the Brave*
Library of Congress

139

Cleaver, Vera and Bill Cleaver

Dust of the Earth

J. B. Lippincott Co., 1975.
(159 pages)

FAMILY: Unity
  Animals: responsibility for
  Change: new home
  Communication: lack of
  Cooperation: in work

Fourteen-year-old Fern Drawn and her family are moving to a sheep ranch near Chokecherry, South Dakota, inherited from Fern's maternal grandfather. The Drawns have always been poor, but Fern feels that something more important than money is also missing from her family — affection. Each of the six family members seems isolated in private concerns, insensitive to the thoughts and feelings of the others. Fern worries that this mutual indifference will make it difficult for the family to organize a new way of life. Because her father must take a bank job in Chokecherry and her older brother, Hobson, refuses to interrupt his schooling, Fern alone must tend the sheep. She readily interrupts her own education to stay at home, but quickly learns that caring for sheep is not easy. Just when things begin to seem hopeless, Hobson quits school to help his sister, much to her surprise. Then, after the expensive arrival of a new baby, Fern's father loses his job. Yet Fern senses that the family is drawing together, its members becoming more cooperative. During the period of furious activity in the spring, when lambs are born, the family acts as a unit to care for the young sheep. Fern decides that "the old feelings of desertion and aloneness have weakened between us."

Fern's first-person account is candid and sensitive about the other family members and their strengths and weaknesses encountering the challenges of ranch life. Her colorful descriptions of the rugged South Dakota land and its early pioneers give an idea of what the Drawns must measure up to. And her humor, together with several funny plot incidents, enlivens what might otherwise be a grim tale.

Ages 12 and up

Also available in:
Cassette for the Blind — *Dust of the Earth*
Library of Congress

Paperbound — *Dust of the Earth*
New American Library

140

Cleaver, Vera and Bill Cleaver

Queen of Hearts

J. B. Lippincott Co., 1978.
(158 pages)

C

GRANDPARENT: *Living in Home of*
RESPONSIBILITY: *Accepting*
  Age: respect for
  Dependence/Independence
  Sibling: older

Twelve-year-old Wilma, who is "not a great thinker or a great anything," has many friends, all imaginary. But they suddenly desert her when she moves in to care for her seventy-nine-year-old grandmother, Josie, who has suffered a mild stroke. Granny seems bent on regaining her independence by driving out Wilma and her six-year-old brother, humiliating the girl and accusing the boy of stealing. But Wilma stays, knowing "Granny was afraid. Of someone who might come in the night to rob and harm her, of people in the street, of living, of dying, of herself, of having now to depend on others to tell her what to do, of trying to make some sense out of a world she could not flee until that too was decided for her, Granny was afraid." As the girl watches Granny and a neighboring old widower struggle, sometimes foolishly, to maintain their independence, Wilma begins to see that the way people treat old people makes growing old an awful business. Yet her sympathies for old people do not change the dreary reality of caring for Granny, and the girl leaves happily when a couple move in to take over. Still, she cannot regain her imaginary friends — and soon enough is unwillingly back with Granny, who has driven out the too-watchful couple. Seeing that Granny needs to be needed, Wilma talks her into baking bread for sale. The scheme works well, but again

Wilma welcomes release when an aunt comes to take charge. Soon enough the aunt is sent packing, and this time Wilma comes back willingly — though not eagerly — aware that she, not Granny, calls the tune.

Although there is no love lost here between grandmother and granddaughter, either in the beginning or the end, along the way the two come to respect each other as the girl cajoles, lures, and sometimes physically maneuvers her grandmother to a practical point between dependence and independence. Wilma's candid views of adults, her parents included, as well as the horrors inflicted on old people, cut through personal and social appearances without being cynical. The ending offers no happy resolution; rather, the reader is left feeling that the girl and her grandmother will go on together indefinitely.

Ages 10-13

Also available in:
Cassette for the Blind — *Queen of Hearts*
Library of Congress

Paperbound — *Queen of Hearts*
Bantam Books

141

Cleaver, Vera and Bill Cleaver

Trial Valley

J. B. Lippincott Co., 1977.
(158 pages)

RESPONSIBILITY: Accepting
  Appalachia
  Boy-girl relationships
  Family: unity
  Orphan

Sixteen-year-old Mary Call Luther, her parents dead, lives with her younger brother and sister in a small house in the Blue Ridge country of North Carolina. An older sister, Devola, and her husband, Kiser Pease, are their legal guardians and want to take them in. But Mary Call resists, wanting to raise the two children herself. And while they complain she is a hard taskmaster, the children do love her dearly. One day they find a five-year-old boy in a wooden cage nailed to a tree. He tells them his name is Jack Parsons, that he was left in the cage by the "Widder Man," and knows nothing about his mother or where he came from. Kiser and Devola wish to adopt the child, but Jack wants to stay with Mary Call. Despite her reluctance to take on another child, she is drawn to the boy and takes him home. Meanwhile, Mary Call muses on two young men who want to marry her: an honest, hard-working neighbor; and a well-to-do social worker from Virginia. But she has her hands full. The authorities, unable to find out anything about the boy, place him with the Peases as a ward. During his first night with them, Jack runs away. Both the family and the townspeople search the mountains but cannot find him. Mary Call then remembers the wooden cage. The searchers find the boy there, but as he rushes to meet them, he falls into a rain-swollen creek. Mary Call dives in to save him. Both her suitors are there: the neighbor rescues the boy; the social worker rescues Mary Call. The episode enables her to make two decisions: that raising Jack is a responsibility she wants; and that, though she doesn't yet plan to marry, she favors the neighbor over the social worker, because he saved Jack.

Mary Call is an avid reader; she pursues knowledge and wants her younger brother and sister to do the same. She also impresses upon them the importance of self-respect, honesty, loyalty, and kindness. She herself tells the story, a sequel to *Where the Lilies Bloom*, told in the same vivid way.

Ages 12 and up

Also available in:
Cassette for the Blind — *Trial Valley*
Library of Congress

Paperbound — *Trial Valley*
Bantam Books, Inc.

142

Clifford, Ethel Rosenberg

The Rocking Chair Rebellion

Houghton Mifflin Co., 1978.
(147 pages)

AGE: Aging
NURSING HOME, LIVING IN
  Careers: planning
  Helping
  Problem solving

Fourteen-year-old Penelope "Opie" Cross does not foresee that when she promises to visit her elderly neighbor and friend, Mr. Pepper, at the Maple Ridge Home for the Aged, she will soon be working there as a volunteer. By summer, Opie is working at Maple Ridge four days a week. One of the residents Opie likes best is Mrs. Sherman, who has purchased a headstone for her cemetery plot, finds that the company has gone out of business, and cannot afford to buy another stone. Opie enlists her father's aid, and the two of them hit on a solution to which Mrs. Sherman agrees: she crochets a bedspread, raffles it off to women in the neighborhood, and thereby earns enough to buy another headstone. Meanwhile another Maple Ridge resident, Mrs. Longwood, confides to Opie that she is having trouble getting spending money from her guardian. Opie again turns to her father, a lawyer, asking him to advise Mrs. Longwood. She also persuades the Maple Ridge Home's administration to change the site of its annual Family Fair to the public street, so that the neighbors and residents can mingle. Both clearly enjoy the event, and it is because of the party that old Mr. Pepper and some of the home's active residents see and purchase a house for sale on the same street. There they plan to live, share chores, and be far more independent than they have been in Maple Ridge. But some neighbors who want no communal living on the block try to prevent the move by taking Mr. Pepper to court. Mr. Cross defends him and wins the case. Soon, the newly self-sufficient senior citizens are settled and valued in the neighborhood.

Opie's first-person narrative illuminates some of the troubles that can beset elderly people living in nursing homes. Throughout her story, two views of the elderly are expressed: first, that they "are in the way, especially if they're any kind of physical or financial problem" to their relatives: second, that the elderly may be capable people preferring to lead independent and productive lives. A second theme finds Opie's career plans at odds with those her parents have for her, although all the arguing that arises on the subject seems premature in the life of a fourteen-year-old.

Ages 11-13

Also available in:
Braille — *The Rocking Chair Rebellion*
Library of Congress

Film — *The Rocking Chair Rebellion*
NBC Special Treat: Daniel Wilson Productions, Inc.

C

143

Clifton, Lucille

Amifika

Black/white illustrations by Thomas DiGrazia.
E. P. Dutton & Company, Inc., 1977.
(29 pages counted)

FEAR
PARENTAL: Absence
  Afro-American

Little Amifika wonders why his mother has been laughing and singing all day, until, from bed, he hears her tell his Cousin Katy that his father is coming home from the Army. His mother goes on to say their two small rooms are so cluttered with old things that she plans to get rid of whatever her husband will not remember or miss. The thought strikes Amifika that he could be one of the things to be thrown away; if he cannot remember his father — and he cannot — then why should his father remember or miss him? The boy spends the next day in hiding so as not to be thrown away. When his cousin comes to help his mother get rid of things, Amifika, determined to take care of himself if his mother will not, darts out the door and hides behind a tree. There he falls asleep. He awakens to find a man is holding him. And he does remember his father after all.

Children often worry needlessly about inventions of their own imagination. They will rejoice with Amifika when he finds out his fear is unnecessary. This story of a black family is written in Afro-American dialect.

Ages 4-7

Also available in:
No other form known

144

Clifton, Lucille

Everett Anderson's Friend

Black/white illustrations by Ann Grifalconi.
Holt, Rinehart and Winston, Inc., 1976.
(23 pages counted)

FRIENDSHIP: Meaning of
  Gender role identity: female
  Prejudice: sexual

Young Everett Anderson lives with his mother in apartment 14A. He is disappointed to find that his new neighbors in 13A are all girls. Of Maria, the one his age, he thinks, "Girls named Maria who/win at ball/are not a bit of fun/at all." One day, Everett loses the key to his apartment. Maria invites him in to wait for his mother to come home. At Maria's, Everett has a "nice surprise." He finds that Maria's mother makes *tacos* and calls him *muchacho,* and that he enjoys himself there. He decides that even though Maria is a girl, she is fun after all: "And the friends we find/are full of surprises/Everett Anderson realizes."

A small boy who has avoided playing with girls is pleasantly surprised to find that they can be as much fun as boys. This short, simply told story about sexual prejudice is easily understood by small children.

Ages 4-7

Also available in:
No other form known

145

Clifton, Lucille

Everett Anderson's Nine Month Long

Black/white illustrations by Ann Grifalconi.
Holt, Rinehart and Winston, Inc., 1978.
(31 pages counted)

SIBLING: New Baby
STEPPARENT: Father
  Afro-American
  Family: unity
  Love, meaning of

Everett Anderson, a young black boy, decides that even though his mother has become Mrs. Tom Perry, he will keep the name he has. Nobody minds. Mr. Perry says that whatever their names are, the three of them have a lot of love — enough, Everett decides, when he learns his mother is pregnant, to share with the new arrival. But Mama seems tired and does not play with him as much as she did before. To Everett, it seems as if this is Mr. Perry's fault. He and his stepfather have a serious conversation, and Mr. Perry explains that, though Mama may seem different, she is still the same person who has always loved her firstborn. Thus Everett Anderson soon announces with great pleasure indeed the arrival of little Evelyn Perry.

It is sometimes difficult for a child to share a parent with a new stepparent or new sibling. This story, with its warm illustrations and gentle verse text, reassures the reader that a child can be loved as much after a parent's remarriage or the arrival of a new sibling as he or she was before. There are a number of other stories about Everett Anderson.

Ages 4-7

Also available in:
No other form known

146

Clifton, Lucille

Everett Anderson's 1-2-3

Color illustrations by Ann Grifalconi.
Holt, Rinehart and Winston, Inc., 1977.
(30 pages counted)

PARENT/PARENTS: Remarriage of
  Stepparent: father

Everett Anderson, a young black boy, wants to know why his mother has been so much happier since a man named Tom Perry has been calling on her. Mama explains to Everett that, even though she misses his father, life goes on — and that is why she is seeing Mr. Perry. Then Everett wonders whether, if his mother remarries, three in their apartment — 14A — might not be one too many. But he and Mr. Perry have a talk, and the latter says simply that he knows he cannot take Everett's father's place. He will be himself, if given the chance. Everett decides that even if things don't always go smoothly, he can get used to three people living in 14A after all.

Gently, thoughtfully, a little boy explores his misgivings about getting a stepfather; after candid talks with his mother and her suitor, he comes to accept the idea. This book precedes one in which Everett faces the prospect of a new baby to the family: *Everett Anderson's Nine Month Long.* They are two of numerous books about Everett and his family and friends.

Ages 4-6

Also available in:
No other form known

C

147

Clifton, Lucille

My Brother Fine with Me

Black/white illustrations by Moneta Barnett.
Holt, Rinehart and Winston, Inc., 1975.
(25 pages counted) o.p.

SIBLING: Love for
SIBLING: Older
*   Afro-American*
*   Running away*

Eight-year-old Jonetta — Johnny for short — is helping her five-year-old brother, Baggy, run away from home. Baggy wants to leave, because "he say he tired of Mama and Daddy always telling him what to do. He say he a Black man, a warrior. And he can make it by hisself." Johnny helps because she wants things as they were when she was an only child. Off Baggy goes with his baseball bat and his treasures in a shopping bag, before his parents get home from work. Johnny rejoices in the way life will be now that she does not have to take care of her brother: "I feel just like Dr. King say, free at last." She decides to clean up their room, an easy job now that Baggy's minibike pictures are not cluttering up the floor. Nor will he be bothering her at night. But will it be so quiet that she will be scared? She decides to go play with her friend — then remembers that her friend has to watch a younger sister, and with Baggy gone, who will play with the younger girl? Johnny even wonders what will happen to all the peanut butter and jelly Baggy usually has for lunch. With nothing else to do, she decides to wait for her parents on the front steps. There she finds Baggy. He has decided to stay home and take care of his family. Johnny says, "I'm real glad. I don got used to him, you know. My brother fine with me."

This story makes clear that mixed feelings may be a part of a healthy, affectionate relationship between an older sister and her younger brother. The first-person narrative is written in imaginative Black English that lends itself to reading aloud. Jaunty pencil sketches go well with the text.

Ages 5-8

Also available in:
No other form known

148

Clifton, Lucille

Three Wishes

Color illustrations by Stephanie Douglas.
The Viking Press, Inc., 1976.
(29 pages counted)

FRIENDSHIP: Meaning of
WISHES
*   Afro-American*

Nobie, about twelve, believes that if she finds a penny on New Year's Day with her birthday year on it, she can make three wishes and they will come true. On New Year's Day, she finds just such a penny. Casually she remarks to her friend Victor, "I wish it weren't so cold." Instantly the sun comes out. Later, following an argument with Victor, she says to him, "I wish you would get out of here." Victor leaves. But sadness overtakes the lucky girl, because she has wasted two wishes. She asks her mama what would be a good final wish, and Mama says, "Good friends." Nobie wishes for a good friend, and immediately Victor reappears.

A young girl, uncertain whether she believes in a superstition, coincidentally sees three wishes come true.

Nobie's story is written in Black English. Bold illustrations will show up well to a read-aloud audience, and discussion of Nobie's wishes and the meaning of friendship may well follow the reading.

Ages 6-8

Also available in:
No other form known

149

Clyne, Patricia Edwards

Tunnels of Terror

Black/white illustrations by Frank Aloise.
Dodd, Mead & Co., 1975.
(157 pages)

FRIENDSHIP: Meaning of
RESOURCEFULNESS
RISK, TAKING OF
    Courage, meaning of
    Fear: of death
    Fear: of the unknown
    Leader/Leadership

Drawn by tales of hidden treasure and rare fossils, five junior high friends set off to explore an underground cave. Roy, the leader, is the first to test his makeshift ladder descending the twenty-foot entrance shaft. Though concerned about overcast skies and a possible flooding rain, the others follow; they are Roy's friend Andy, Andy's ten-year-old sister, Roy's girl friend, and a scientifically inclined classmate named Chad. They investigate the east tunnel, then head back to their starting point for lunch. Along the way Roy notices an old barrel but is disappointed to find it contains no treasure. Too large to fit through the narrow entrance, Chad reasons. After lunch they decide to take the heavier backpacks up to the surface before investigating further. But Andy and Chad accidentally meet midway up

the ladder and under their combined weight it breaks. With no other means of getting out and no one knowing their whereabouts, they are trapped. Despair turns to panic when rain starts falling outside and the cave begins filling with water. Roy and Chad argue over what to do next. Roy wants to use Chad's inflatable raft to float them on the rising waters to the top of the entrance shaft. Remembering the barrel, Chad wants to look for another cave-opening down the west tunnel. Roy agrees to this when Chad points out that the water might not lift the raft all the way to the entrance. Heartened to find the west tunnel sloping upward, taking them away from the deepening water, they cannot escape the water rushing through the cave's roof with increasing force. Progress up the tunnel is slow, and the group is near exhaustion when Chad spots a crudely etched arrow on one wall pointing to another chamber at least thirteen feet above them. With only two flashlights left alight, time is running out. Roy makes it to the chamber and helps the others up. Sure enough, they find an opening, and twelve hours after they had entered the cave, they are at last safely out.

This engrossing adventure story records the five explorers' new understanding and appreciation of one another as they seek to escape their entrapment. Most conspicuously, Roy, athletic and self-assured, and Chad, intellectual and preoccupied, overcome their earlier impatience with each other and come to respect each other's welcome talents. Roy's girl friend finds, in her parents' relief at her return, much more parental love than she had been aware of. Shadowy illustrations heighten the suspense here, but characterization is thin and the dialogue sometimes stiff and contrived.

Ages 10-12

Also available in:
No other form known

150

Coatsworth, Elizabeth Jane

Marra's World

Black/white illustrations by Krystyna Turska.
Greenwillow Books, 1975.
(83 pages)

BELONGING
FRIENDSHIP: Best Friend
    Grandparent: living in child's home

Young Marra lives with her father and grandmother in a small cottage on an island. Marra is a lonely, quiet child, seldom spoken to by her father and disliked by her stern, temperamental grandmother, whom she fears. Her mother, Nerea, had disappeared soon after Marra's birth. The girl's only friend is a storekeeper until a new girl, Alison Dunbar, moves to the island. Alison likes Marra, who is before long showing her her favorite island haunts. Alison's mother, too, is drawn to Marra, and teaches her to do simple household tasks and dress more fashionably. One day the two girls take a picnic lunch to the east end of the island, a place Marra's father has always forbidden her to go. As the girls rest atop a cliff, they are startled to hear a mysterious sweet singing. Marra is moved to tears, and feels a new surge of life and hope within her. From that day, her life changes, for she feels differently about herself. Her classmates include her in their schoolyard games. Her teacher takes more interest in her. Even her grandmother sometimes speaks kindly to her. One night Marra wakes up feeling that she must run to the east cliffs. There she hears the enchanted music again and sees ghost-like dancing on the beach. She imagines that she speaks with her mother, whom she identifies with one of the seals — and feels instinctively that her mother loves her. The next morning she cannot be sure whether her journey was a dream or real. What is clear is that the shy, awkward girl is becoming a lovely young woman. With Alison, she sets off one summer day to row to a neighboring island. Engulfed by a heavy fog, the girls turn and aim for home, but cannot see their landing place. Suddenly out of the sea appears a gray seal, who guides the rowboat to the pier. Marra calls the seal Nerea, but it disappears, and they cannot recall who rescued them. Marra's grandmother scolds the girls for being on the sea in such weather, then invites them in for hot chocolate and cookies.

The illustrations add to the vividness of this enchanting, mystical story. Marra is transformed from a plain, dull child into an attractive young woman by making friends and by feeling that she is loved and valued.

Ages 8-11

Also available in:
No other form known

151

Coerr, Eleanor

Sadako and the Thousand Paper Cranes

Black/white illustrations by Ronald Himler.
G. P. Putnam's Sons, 1977.
(64 pages)

ILLNESSES: Terminal
    Courage, meaning of
    Death: attitude toward
    Japan
    Leukemia

Eleven-year-old Sadako is a runner, and dreams of being the best runner in her school in Hiroshima, Japan. One day, following a race, a strange dizziness comes over her. After that, and not only when she runs, the dizzy spells recur, and she decides not to tell anyone.

But one day in the schoolyard, the dizziness consumes her and she collapses. At the hospital, her illness is diagnosed as leukemia — the result of radiation poisoning from the atomic bomb dropped on her city some years before. The family is grief-stricken, but Sadako vows to get well. In the hospital, her best friend brings her a gift, a crane made of folded gold paper. The friend teaches Sadako how to fold paper cranes and tells her a legend: if she folds a thousand paper cranes, the gods will make her healthy. Sadako begins, and each day her brother hangs from the ceiling the day's new cranes. For a time her health seems to improve, but when the sickness drains her energy and causes her great pain, she knows she will not recover. Yet she continues to make paper cranes. One night she makes number 644. It is her last. She dies, a heroine to her family and friends. Her classmates continue making cranes until all one thousand are folded; they are buried with her.

According to the prologue, the story of Sadako is "based on the life of a real little girl who lived in Japan from 1943 to 1955. She was in Hiroshima when the United States Air Force dropped an atom bomb on that city. . . . Ten years later she died as a result of radiation from the bomb. Her courage made Sadako a heroine to children in Japan." A monument has been erected in the Hiroshima Peace Park in Sadako's memory. This book is a memorable, poignant but not sentimental account, carefully researched.

Ages 11 and up

Also available in:
Paperbound — *Sadako and the Thousand Paper Cranes*
Dell Publishing Company, Inc.

152
Cohen, Barbara Nash

Benny
Lothrop, Lee & Shepard Co., 1977.
(154 pages)

INFERIORITY, FEELINGS OF
  Empathy
  Family: unity
  Jewish
  Sibling: rivalry
  Sports/Sportsmanship

C

Twelve-year-old Benny Rifkind's family may be closely knit in the traditional Jewish way, but Benny feels there are only three people on his side — his sister, Evie, his Aunt Goldie, and his buddy Henry — and everybody else is against him; especially his older brother, Sheldon. Most people want him to be what he is not, smart like Sheldon. It is 1939, and his father, keenly aware of anti-Semitism overseas in Hitler's Germany, urges Benny to befriend a German Jewish refugee boy. Although far from being friends, Benny and Arnulf are mutually sympathetic — but Benny is wrapped up in baseball to the virtual exclusion of everything else. Only Henry feels as urgently about baseball, practicing batting with Benny in every spare moment. Once Benny shows Mac, the team captain, he can play well, his way is clear to being on the class team — until Mr. Rifkind refuses to let him off work at the family grocery store to play games. On the day of the big game, Mac makes it clear that Benny either leaves the store to play or is off the team forever. Benny leaves and helps win the game. But after skipping work he is punished by his father: he cannot attend the World's Fair the following Sunday with the family. Yet Benny does leave home that Sunday — when Aunt Goldie calls to report that Arnulf has run off, no one knows where. Benny knows where, for he has seen underneath Arnulf's haughty ways how homesick he is. He takes the searchers to the pier where a ship is sailing for Germany, and there they find Arnulf. It is a different situation and a different Benny the Rifkinds find on their return, for Benny is a hero of sorts and, more important, has gained confidence in himself. Over Sheldon's protests, Mr. Rifkind agrees to make arrangements to let Benny off to play baseball.

Ability at baseball and an intuitive understanding of a refugee's character are the touchstones by which this boy gains self-confidence. Benny's first-person narrative shows how the expectations of a family, especially when an older child has made a mark, can handicap a child from realizing his own worth.

Ages 9-11

Also available in:
No other form known

153

Cohen, Barbara Nash

Bitter Herbs and Honey

Lothrop, Lee & Shepard Co., 1976.
(159 pages)

EXPECTATIONS
IDENTITY, SEARCH FOR
JEWISH
PREJUDICE: Ethnic/Racial
  Boy-girl relationships

As Becky Levitsky begins her senior year in high school in 1916, she finds herself questioning some of the beliefs and traditions of her Jewish family. Her father owns a dry goods store and both parents expect Becky to work there after graduation until she is married. But Becky is a scholar, and longs to further her formal education, although she knows that in 1916 few Jewish girls attend college. When the Levitskys observe Yom Kippur, Becky's parents invite Henry Braude, a distant relative, to be Becky's dinner partner, and she at once dislikes the young man, whom she considers pompous and self-centered, and resents her parents' clear belief that he would be a good husband for her. Meanwhile, at school, Becky has come to feel very close to Peter van Ruysdaal, a gentile. Knowing that neither family would approve of their dating, the two meet secretly, both of them preferring a "secret love" to none at all. But after several months, Peter grows impatient with their deception and demands to meet Becky's parents. When she explains that this would betray her defiance of them, something she cannot risk, Peter accuses her of being "clannish, anti-social, and narrow," and leaves. Becky, knowing the romance has come to an end, would like to remain a friend to Peter. After arguing for her parents' permission, she invites him with two other gentile friends to a Passover dinner and they accept. As Becky explains the meaning of a ritual to the guests, even she better appreciates her faith and culture. But before the dinner is over, Peter's irate father arrives to demand Peter leave with him. The boy had told his parents he was spending the evening at a friend's house. This incident tells Becky: "Like Peter, I had learned something this Seder night. I had learned I was a Jew and I could never be anything else. I would never want to be anything else." Later, Henry Braude asks Becky to marry him, but she explains that she cannot, because she does not love him. But she is accepted for Barnard College, and her parents consent to her going.

Two young people with different cultural backgrounds learn more about their own identities while briefly in love. Becky finds that she is proud of her Jewishness, and Peter realizes that prejudice can breed suspicion on both sides. This story provides interesting descriptions of Jewish beliefs and customs, while portraying a close-knit, loving family. Though set early in our century, this story's depiction of religious tension is all too timely still.

Ages 11-13

Also available in:
Talking Book — *Bitter Herbs and Honey*
Library of Congress

154

Cohen, Barbara Nash

Where's Florrie?

Black/white illustrations by Joan Halpern.
Lothrop, Lee & Shepard Co., 1976.
(44 pages)

LOVE, MEANING OF
RUNNING AWAY
   Discipline, meaning of

Florrie, a little girl in turn-of-the-century New York City, is afraid of her stern father. Though he has never spanked her, she thinks him mean and unloving. That is why when, at a friend's prodding, she builds a fire in her miniature iron stove against all Papa's warnings and is discovered, she flees down an alley and hides until her father passes by. Florrie then follows streets she does not recognize and comes upon a carousel, which she watches until sunset. When the carousel leaves, Florrie, realizing she is lost, sits on the curb and cries. And that is where Papa finds her and gently urges her to come home. She agrees, and Papa sweeps Florrie into his arms. That is when she notices Papa's moist cheeks and knows that, though she might think him mean, he does love her.

This charming, first-person narrative describes a young girl afraid of a father who does not know how to show affection. Because of this inability, Florrie assumes her father feels none. Only when his worry over her safety brings him to tears does little Florrie understand.

Ages 6-8

Also available in:
No other form known

155

Cohen, Miriam

"Bee My Valentine!"

Color illustrations by Lillian Aberman Hoban.
Greenwillow Books, 1978.
(32 pages counted)

SCHOOL: Classmate Relationships
   Consideration, meaning of

Jim, in first grade, excitedly awaits Valentine's Day. Louie, who is new to the class, asks, "What is Valentine's?" Anna Marie and Willy explain that it is a holiday on which everyone tries "to get the most cards." But the teacher emphasizes that "everybody must send a card to everybody else in first grade. Then nobody will be sad." But the children ignore their teacher's admonition, and when valentines are distributed at the class party, George, having received the fewest, hides in the coatroom. Worried that George may even be crying, the students play musical instruments and dance to entice him back. When George reappears, Willy places a paper crown on his head and Sammy gives George a favorite instrument. Soon George is playing along with the others and enjoying the party.

In this engaging story of a richly mixed grade-school class, the students see their responsibility for heedlessly causing one boy's feelings to be hurt. The feelings expressed by the children, and the hubbub created by a class party, are effectively portrayed. The book is one in a series about Jim and his classmates.

Ages 5-7

Also available in:
Paperbound — *"Bee My Valentine!"*
Dell Publishing Company, Inc.

156

Cohen, Miriam

When Will I Read?

Color illustrations by Lillian Aberman Hoban.
Greenwillow Books, 1977.
(32 pages counted)

EDUCATION: Value of
* Goals*
* School: classmate relationships*

Jim wants terribly to be able to read. It is not enough that he recognizes signs and his own name, for "that's not really reading." Jim's friend George claims to be reading when he recites the words of his favorite story — but another student insists that George is reciting from memory. Even when Jim and the other students have dictated an experience to the teacher and Jim is "reading" his aloud, he feels thwarted. It is just after he has decided to stop "worrying about reading" that he notices that the sign on the hamster cage reads, "Do let the hamsters out," instead of "Don't let the hamsters out." He hurriedly informs his teacher. She congratulates him: he has "really read the sign." Jim is thrilled because, as he says, "I waited all my life" to read.

In this honest picture of classroom life, the reader meets a boy with a yearning to be able to read. The illustrations no less than the text catch both his impatience and his delight amid the bustle of the classroom. This book is one in a series about Jim and his classmates.

Ages 4-6

Also available in:
Cassette for the Blind — *When Will I Read?*
Library of Congress

Filmstrip — *When Will I Read?*
Educational Enrichment Corporation

Paperbound — *When Will I Read?*
Dell Publishing Company, Inc.

157

Cohen, Peter Zachary

Bee

Black/white illustrations by Richard Cuffari.
Atheneum Publishers, 1975.
(187 pages)

COURAGE, MEANING OF
RESPONSIBILITY: Accepting
* Fear: of physical harm*
* Perseverance*

Herb's father fixes cars and moves often, and at their latest home in Wyoming his fourteen-year-old son realizes a dream — he lands a summer job helping an old rancher named Rudy Kemp. "Follow directions" is Rudy's constant advice, and Herb follows them. The next spring Rudy gives him an excitable horse named Bee to ride. Bee throws Herb several times, once dangerously, until the boy is frightened to ride him. Nevertheless, when Rudy asks him along to search for a few stray cattle, Herb and Bee set off. But Herb fails to "follow directions," tries to round up the strays alone, and Bee bolts. Rudy, who has ridden up, turns the run-away horse to safer ground but is then thrown when a cow charges his own horse. Rudy aches, but Herb is burning with embarrassment and remorse. After Rudy is taken off to the hospital, the boy tries to redeem himself by riding that "stupid horse" a second time to recover the strays himself, and again Bee throws him. Resolutely ready to try yet again, Herb checks himself when several men suddenly drive up, intending to rustle a herd grazing nearby. Determined to stop them, Herb damages the truck's engine and gallops off on Bee. The latter's natural inclination to run keeps Herb narrowly ahead of the rustlers, and he is able to phone the sheriff, who arrives in time to capture them. When the rancher whose cattle they had rustled offers him a horse, Herb declines in favor of Bee: "If you've got nine or ten straight miles you sometimes want to do in a kind of a hurry, you can like him a little."

A boy learns to control his fear of a dangerous horse, among other things, and to follow directions, but not always. The author achieves suspense with no loss of realism by insisting on close attention to Herb's thoughts as he tries to outwit Bee, round up the stray cattle, and stop the rustlers. Readers will enjoy this fast-paced story with characters who talk plainly and make their mistakes in the open.

Ages 10-13

Also available in:
Braille — *Bee*
Library of Congress

158

Coleman, William Laurence

Orphan Jim: A Novel

Doubleday & Company, Inc., 1975.
(204 pages)

RUNNING AWAY
SIBLING: Relationships
   Abandonment
   Dependence/Independence
   Prejudice: ethnic/racial
   Relatives: living in home of

C

Thirteen-year-old Trudy — abandoned by her father in 1952 after her mother's death — runs away with her seven-year-old brother, Jim, rather than be sent to an orphans' home. Not liking Jim, she plans to leave him with Uncle Earl in Montgomery, Alabama, before moving on. After an adventurous journey the two arrive in Montgomery only to find that Uncle Earl's wife and two children vehemently oppose taking Jim in and will do everything possible to make them miserable. Trudy, learning of their plan to place them in an institution, runs away with Jim once more. But before they leave the city, a tramp rapes Trudy and beats Jim. Numb and hungry, Trudy begs for food in the black part of town and ends up at the house of Hazel Fay, a black woman known locally as a prostitute. Taking the two white children in, Hazel convinces George Harris, her white lover and provider, to let them remain. Trudy quickly recovers and finds a job. A complex ruse by Hazel to circumvent segregation laws enables Jim to enroll in a white school. Tipped off by a co-worker of Trudy's, the school authorities and Uncle Earl threaten the whole arrangement; but Hazel turns the authorities aside and Trudy convinces Uncle Earl to forget about Jim and herself. Mr. Harris dies that summer, and Hazel, in grief, moves away. But first she establishes Trudy and Jim in their own apartment. And Trudy — older, independent as ever, and now with money — supports Jim through adolescence to manhood.

Written as a first-person reminiscence, Trudy's absorbing narrative follows two white children as they seek help from white relatives but only find it with a black woman and her white lover. The characters here are willful and strongly drawn, and swearing occurs where it would in life. The rape scene, though conveying the brutality of the act, does not go into sexual detail. Readers interested to follow this story are certainly mature enough not to be thrown off by its darker moments.

Ages 13 and up

Also available in:
Braille — *Orphan Jim: A Novel*
Library of Congress

Paperbound — *Orphan Jim: A Novel*
Dell Publishing Company, Inc.

159

Collier, James Lincoln

Give Dad My Best

Four Winds Press, 1976.
(219 pages)

PARENTAL: Unreliability
RESPONSIBILITY: Accepting
 Job
 Stealing

It is 1938, and the Great Depression still rules. Fourteen-year-old Jack Lundquist's father sings "Happy Days Are Here Again" but cannot produce them. Warren Lundquist is a trombonist who has had no steady job in seven years, during which time his wife has been committed to a mental hospital. Now Jack and his younger brother and sister may be separated because their father cannot support them. Desperate to keep the family together, Jack begs Dad to take a steady job of some kind. But Warren Lundquist, dreaming of success in music, refuses to consider other work. Jack finds a job at a boat club, and there, among the rich, he thinks about stealing. Opportunities arise but Jack resists temptation — even when he learns that the club steward takes kickbacks on liquor sales. Not even when the family receives an eviction notice does Jack give in, determined as he is not to steal until he has no choice. That time soon comes. Dad tells everyone not to worry, but does nothing. When Jack protests, his father hits him; the boy runs to the club. Going straight to its hiding place, he steals the kickback money and uses part of it to pay back-rent. Only then does he see that the theft has solved nothing: Dad does not care about keeping them together, but thinks only of himself. Jack returns the rest of the stolen money, secure only in the knowledge that the steward must keep quiet. The children leave for separate homes. Warren Lundquist leaves for New York, pursuing success.

A young adolescent tries to force his father to act like a father. Failing, the boy assumes his father's family responsibility, only to realize that the effort, like his father's dream of happy days, is inadequate: his father can no more change his ways than he himself can discharge a father's duties.

Ages 10-14

Also available in:
Cassette for the Blind — *Give Dad My Best*
Library of Congress

160

Colman, Hila Crayder

After the Wedding

William Morrow & Company, Inc., 1975.
(189 pages)

LIFE STYLE
MARRIAGE: Teenage
 Values/Valuing: materialistic

In love, eighteen-year-old Katherine Holbrook and twenty-year-old Peter Lundgren swear that nothing will destroy that love. Although Katherine has always lived in New York City, she loves the country and longs to live apart from the competitive, commercial concerns of the city. Peter, who had come from Iowa to New York two years before to train for radio and television, has tired of the pressures of the city. The two rent a small farmhouse in northern New York and are married, pledged to living "independently together," each sharing the other's life without interfering with it. Katherine loves the farmhouse and the simple life they lead, but soon Peter is bored and restless. He quits his job at the local radio station because of differences with his boss. He even changes his mind about New York City, deciding he wants to try for the big-city success in television. Katherine cannot understand the change in Peter and refuses to return to the city. Peter then spends his weeks in the city and weekends at the farmhouse, often bringing home friends from his new social circle, more and more disparaging the "country lifestyle." Money and success obsess him. Finally he insists that Katherine move back to the city, arguing that the farmhouse is too primitive to live in through the winter. She gives in — but in their tiny apartment at the top of a high-rise, she is miserable. Her only hope is that the baby they by now expect will mend the marriage. But little Laura cannot unite such mismatched minds. When spring comes, Katherine decides to move with her to the farmhouse. Peter announces that he wants a divorce, and Katherine is devastated, then relieved. She returns to the farmhouse to make a new life for herself and her daughter.

Two young people discover that being "independently together" cannot work for them. When one of them changes in what he wants, the other is forced to make a choice. Katherine decides her own way of living means more to her than a "lopsided" marriage. This candid picture of a doomed marriage is largely hers.

Ages 12 and up

Also available in:
Talking Book — *After the Wedding*
Library of Congress

161

Colman, Hila Crayder

The Amazing Miss Laura

William Morrow & Company, Inc., 1976.
(192 pages)

AGE: Respect for
 Grandparent: living in home of
 Maturation
 Talents: artistic
 Values/Valuing: moral/ethical

Seventeen-year-old Josie Smyrski lives on a large farm in Connecticut with her parents and her eighty-year-old grandfather. Having just won a local prize for one of her paintings, Josie yearns to go to a good art school. But her grandfather will not sell even a few acres of land to help pay for her schooling — a cantankerous, stubborn, selfish, senile old man, she thinks, just like everyone over sixty. Desperate for money, Josie hears that Laura Van Dyk, the eccentric widow of a celebrated local painter,

C

needs someone through the summer to run errands and to be a companion. She jumps at the chance. She has always admired the Van Dyk Mansion, and would rather spend the summer there than in her grandfather's "dump." She also thinks Laura Van Dyk's connections in the art world could aid her own ambitions. At first Laura seems hard to bear, lucid one minute, befuddled the next, and always demanding something. Nor will she sell any of her husband's paintings to pay bills, to Josie an annoying reminder of her grandfather's attachment to his land. But with time Laura proves sharp-witted, for the most part, with a sly sense of humor. It is Henry, Laura's brother-in-law, who appalls Josie, with his disrespect and insensitivity to Laura. Henry is bent on hoarding his brother's paintings within the family for money reasons alone. By now devoted to Laura, Josie and Laura's loyal nephew, Michael, persuade the widow to hold an exhibition where some paintings will be sold and all will be properly appreciated. The show goes well and Laura enjoys herself tremendously. The following night, however, Laura has a heart attack. Henry uses her illness as an excuse to put her in a nursing home. Josie feels she has lost a friend. But at summer's end, Josie's grandfather offers to sell some land so she can go to art school. Josie will not let him; she has come to understand how paintings or land can represent a lifetime of work and achievement.

In this realistic story, the upsetting aspects of aging — physical deterioration, mental confusion, approaching death — are discussed frankly. The joyful aspects of caring about others are made no less clear. Josie finds that aging can have its rewards if one lives among loving, respectful people.

Ages 11-14

Also available in:
Paperbound — *The Amazing Miss Laura*
Scholastic Book Services

162

Colman, Hila Crayder

The Case of the Stolen Bagels

Black/white illustrations by Pat Grant Porter.
Crown Publishers, Inc., 1977.
(32 pages counted)

REPUTATION
SCHOOL: Negative Experiences
  Justice/Injustice
  Problem solving
  Responsibility: accepting
  School: behavior
  School: pupil-teacher relationships

Around the middle of his grade school career, Paul has acquired a reputation for being quick-tempered and overly fond of bagels. Having been warned by his parents and teacher to control his temper, he hits a classmate for taking his sweater. The teacher blames Paul alone, which he feels is unfair. Then, a week later, when Paul's clay pot gets broken, he blames the same boy and punches him again. In the scuffle, the boy damages some posters, causing their classmates to resent Paul. Heaped with unjust blame, Paul does not want to return to school the following week. But he does go, and finds his teacher has brought bagels for the class to decorate. Paul at once takes a bite, and his teacher asks him to stop. Later, when she sees him standing near the bagels, she accuses him of planning to take one. When, the next day, nearly half the bagels are discovered missing, there is no question who is responsible. Paul protests his innocence, but neither his teacher, his classmates, nor the principal will listen. His parents do believe him, but tell him that their belief in him is the only help they can give, and that he must somehow clear himself. Paul decides his only chance is to catch the real thief returning for the remaining bagels, and he watches the school from his bedroom window that night. He sees not one but three culprits, runs over, and captures one of them — a baby raccoon. Paul goes to school the next day, presents his evidence, and proves his innocence. The teacher apologizes and, at his friend's suggestion, Paul decides to bring in his polished rock collection to add to a planned school sale.

Paul is bewildered and angry because no one at school listens to his side of difficulties and conflicts that arise. Although the story line and ending of this book lack depth, its value lies in its presentation of a spot many children get into: finding themselves being judged with bias or wanting to change a bad reputation once it has been established. Paul's parents encourage his confidence by trusting him and allowing him to find his own way out. When he proves his innocence, he feels differently about school and himself as well, and chooses to give something of himself in return. Its illustrations, brevity, and large print should increase this book's appeal to younger or less able readers. Read aloud to younger children, it may well stimulate discussion.

Ages 7-10

Also available in:
No other form known

163

Colman, Hila Crayder

Ethan's Favorite Teacher

Color illustrations by John Wallner.
Crown Publishers, Inc., 1975.
(31 pages counted)

PERSEVERANCE
SCHOOL: Achievement/Underachievement
SCHOOL: Classmate Relationships
School: pupil-teacher relationships

Young Ethan hates school. He thinks study is boring and repetitious, especially arithmetic. He wants to know things like why the sky is blue, but his classmates laugh at the question and his teacher scolds him for inattention. Ethan does like the zoo, which he visits often. The zookeeper is his friend and answers all his questions. One day Ethan goes to see Sadie and Bill, the orangutans, but is told they are at school learning how to play tic-tac-toe. The zookeeper assures Ethan that many animals can learn by working hard and doing the same thing over and over. After Sadie returns, the zookeeper invites Ethan to play tic-tac-toe on the electronic board attached to her cage. Ethan does but loses repeatedly. Encouraged by the zookeeper, he keeps at it and finally wins. When his teacher offers the class a field trip, Ethan suggests the zoo and tells his classmates they can play tic-tac-toe with Sadie. During the trip, Ethan surprises everyone with his knowledge of the animals, but at the orangutan's cage he urges the smartest girl in the class to play tic-tac-toe first. She plays five games and loses every one. Then Ethan tries. The first game is a draw, and the girl laughs at him. He plays another game, concentrating hard, and wins. Ethan's teacher pronounces Sadie a good teacher and hopes Ethan will work as hard in school as at the zoo.

In this story a young boy discovers the satisfaction of achievement through practice and hard work. Scientific information about the learning capacity of orangutans is presented in a simple manner. The message — hard work yields success — is enlivened by animal lore and a touch of humor in the text and the illustrations.

Ages 7-9

Also available in:
No other form known

164

Colman, Hila Crayder

Nobody Has to Be a Kid Forever

Crown Publishers, Inc., 1976.
(117 pages)

MATURATION
SEPARATION, MARITAL
   Dependence/Independence
   Parent/Parents: fighting between
   Reconciliation, parental
   Women's rights

Thirteen-year-old Sarah Grinnell is aware that her mother feels bored and wasted as a housewife. She also sees how unsympathetic her father is to this unhappiness, insisting on dinner and all the comforts, as usual. The standoff worsens daily in bitter arguments until Mrs. Grinnell, true to a longstanding threat, leaves home shortly after Christmas. Now Sarah is angry, hurt personally by what seems her mother's willful indifference to her. Yet, she finds herself defending her when the eldest daughter, Didi, accuses Mother of acting like an irresponsible teenager. To further complicate matters, Didi leaves home in February to live with her boyfriend. One evening, shortly after Didi's departure, Mr. Grinnell gets drunk, starts weeping, and confesses to Sarah that he thinks himself a failure. Knowing that he wanted to be an artist, Sarah urges him to begin painting again. But he refuses, saying he has established a way of life he cannot escape. During the weeks that follow, Sarah visits her mother and notices that, like her father, she seems dissatisfied and would like to end the separation. Thus, when Mr. Grinnell loses his job, Sarah takes matters into her own hands. She tells her mother that Father resigned and is going to live at their summer home and paint. Mrs. Grinnell is delighted and starts making plans to join him. But Sarah's attempt to reconcile her parents fails when Mr. Grinnell discovers it and makes her telephone and confess the ruse to Mother. He then leaves and Sarah awaits his return. He does return, and tells Sarah that he has talked to her mother and begun working things out between them. By the end of June, the Grinnells have moved to their summer home, where they live simply, while Mr. Grinnell paints and hopes to sell his work and Mrs. Grinnell works at a job.

In this first-person narrative in diary form, a sequel to *Diary of a Frantic Kid Sister,* Sarah learns to live — uncomfortably — with her parents' separation. But she never gives up hope of a reconciliation nor her search for ways to accomplish it. Because she manages finally to bring it off, readers whose parents are separated may be tempted to try to do likewise. Young adolescents will find this an easy and appealing story.

Ages 10-13

Also available in:
Paperbound — *Nobody Has to Be a Kid Forever*
Pocket Books, Inc.

165

Colman, Hila Crayder

The Secret Life of Harold the Bird Watcher

Black/white illustrations by Charles Robinson.
Thomas Y. Crowell Company, Inc., 1978.
(71 pages)

FANTASY FORMATION
   Friendship: making friends
   Peer relationships: avoiding others
   Self, attitude toward: feeling different

At nine, Harold does not mind that his parents work long hours or that he is friendless; alone, he can invent fantastic daydreams. His parents are always urging him to bring classmates home, but at school the taunts of "loner" only worsen when it is discovered that one of Harold's favorite daydreaming spots is a secluded lake cove where birds and ducks nest. The other children, especially a boy named Frank Rugby, think it funny to call him "the nutty birdwatcher." But Harold considers the duck family his friends and the cove his own. Thus it comes as a great shock when a couple named Adams purchase the land adjacent to the cove. Mr. and Mrs. Adams tell Harold he may continue to play there, but ask him to tell people who might use and litter the beach that it is now privately owned. Yet when Harold asks one such, a burly, harsh man named Spike, to leave the beach, the man threatens him. Harold tells the Adamses. They warn him to leave Spike alone, and Mr. Adams says he will talk to the police. Harold follows their advice — until he discovers that Spike has killed and eaten two of the ducklings. Distraught and determined to prevent further "murders" of his friends, the boy hides in the underbrush. When the man returns, Harold tackles him, grabs his shotgun, and runs to Mr. Adams, who holds Spike at gunpoint. The police are summoned, and it is learned that Spike is a known felon. Because of his bravery, Harold becomes a hero and is deluged with calls and invitations from classmates. He refuses them all until, at his mother's insistence, he agrees to see Frank Rugby. Amazingly, it turns out that Frank enjoys games of pretending as much as Harold does, and the two become friends.

Alone much of the time, a child turns to fantasy for adventure. Fearing ridicule of his fantasies, he prefers to remain friendless. It is an impulsive act of bravery that brings Harold sudden wide popularity, an act and a consequence not all readers will find entirely credible.

Harold himself is easy for readers to get to know, not least when he realizes that other children, too, like to imagine things.

Ages 8-10

Also available in:
No other form known

166

Colman, Hila Crayder

Sometimes I Don't Love My Mother

William Morrow & Company, Inc., 1977.
(190 pages)

C

DEATH: of Father
Boy-girl relationships
Communication: parent-child
Dependence/Independence

Seventeen-year-old Dallas Davis and her mother, Ellen, are stunned when Henry Davis, a lively, energetic, outgoing man, dies of a heart attack at forty-one. Dallas is grief-stricken at losing her father, but Ellen, a quiet, introverted woman wholly dependent on her husband, is rendered helpless. Unable to make the simplest decisions, she now relies on Dallas in everything. Just out of high school, Dallas is planning to attend Dartmouth College in the fall. Her grandparents urge her to postpone college a year to stay with her mother. Dallas resents her mother's dependence but, persuaded Ellen cannot be left alone, agrees. Ellen lives in despondency. Afraid of her thoughts and afraid of being alone, she nevertheless refuses to see her own friends and begins tagging along with her daughter's. Meanwhile, Dallas's long-time friendship with Vic Waters is blossoming into romance. Vic encourages Dallas in her efforts to become freer of her mother, to have a life of her own, but Ellen spends more and more time with

Dallas's crowd, enjoying especially the attention of the boys. Dallas tells her mother she must find her own friends, but Ellen refuses to listen, saying it is only Dallas who resents her presence. Dallas cannot go on a ski trip unless her mother is chaperon. The daughter decides to make a break, and gets a part-time job at the library. Her mother only withdraws further. The young people plan another trip, and another tug of war ensues. In the meantime, Dallas and Vic's mother have been planning a surprise birthday party for Ellen. Dallas invites her parents' old friends, and Ellen's mother, whom Ellen herself dislikes, comes from Florida. At the party, Ellen's mother fastens onto one person after another, too aggressive, trying to fit where she cannot. As Ellen watches, she realizes how foolish she herself has been. After the party Dallas confronts Ellen, announcing they must both lead their own lives. Quietly, sadly, her mother agrees. She seems to understand, and Dallas can hope that Ellen will make it on her own.

Interweaving Dallas's viewpoint with her mother's, the author candidly presents both mother's and daughter's reaction to Mr. Davis's death. The story illustrates the complex and differing reactions that people experience after the death of a loved one.

Ages 12 and up

Also available in:
Paperbound — *Sometimes I Don't Love My Mother*
Scholastic Book Services

167

Colman, Hila Crayder

Tell Me No Lies

Crown Publishers, Inc., 1978.
(74 pages)

IDENTITY, SEARCH FOR
UNWED MOTHER: Child of
  Honesty/Dishonesty

Twelve-year-old Angela's mother is going to be married, to Larry, and while Angela likes Larry, she does not want him to adopt her. She secretly yearns to find her father, who abandoned them, according to her mother, when Angela was a baby. Larry's pressing the adoption matter only leads to a quarrel in which the girl forces her mother to admit that Angela was conceived during a "summer affair," and that José, the girl's father, left without knowing of the pregnancy and later married. He lives in nearby Provincetown with his wife and three sons. Angela accuses her mother of deceiving her and wrests her consent that Angela go to Provincetown, where she can stay with her mother's friend Margaret, who is acquainted with José and his family. In Provincetown, Margaret introduces Angela and José, saying only that Angela is the daughter of the girl he dated many years earlier. And so Angela spends a day with José's family. Out on their fishing boat, she longs for José to acknowledge her as his daughter but begins to see that neither might gain from that. In the evening, José tells her that though he has wished for a daughter, life does not always give us everything we want. He makes it plain that the matter of their relationship must be closed. Angela confides her sorrow and disappointment to Margaret, who shows her that her mother lied not to hurt her but to save her later pain. Content, Angela goes home to her mother and Larry.

A girl obsessed with learning the identity of her father, sure that she cannot know herself until she meets him, learns that her identity depends on herself, not on who her parents are. This story ends both satisfyingly and realistically, without moralizing about unwed mothers or their children.

Ages 10-12

Also available in:
No other form known

168

Colman, Hila Crayder

That's the Way It Is, Amigo

Black/white illustrations by Glo Coalson.
Thomas Y. Crowell Company, Inc., 1975.
(90 pages)

FRIENDSHIP: Meaning of
MATURATION
RUNNING AWAY
   Change: resisting
   Death: of father
   Gender role identity: male

Fifteen-year-old David, on probation for breaking into a house, has run away from his home in New York. Since his father's death, everything at home has changed. His mother expects him to take responsibility and "be a man" — yet she treats him with little respect and will not let him make his own decisions. Now he finds himself wandering around Oaxaca, Mexico, purposeless. Sitting in a cafe wondering what to do next, he observes a Mexican boy about his own age selling what he says are bark paintings done by his old uncle. David is amazed at the boy's poise and determination. Despite poor Spanish, David translates the boy's sales pitch for two women tourists who later hire David to drive their old car on sightseeing expeditions. On one trip the car breaks down. When the women give the broken-down vehicle to Pedro, who says he can fix it when parts arrive, David is jealous. The boys end up taking turns driving it while Pedro sells more paintings. But all is not harmonious. David does not believe Pedro's uncle paints such pictures on the bark of the amata tree, and Pedro thinks David a typical spoiled American who believes all Mexicans are lazy cheats. Mutual irritation finally leads them to decide to split up. But while waiting in a bus station to go nowhere, David hears a radio announcement that an earthquake has struck Pedro's village — and he realizes he cares about Pedro. He finds him and they set off for the village, driving all night. Fortunately, they find no one hurt. David meets Pedro's uncle and sees for himself how the bark paintings are made. And to his shame, the boy learns that though a year younger than himself, Pedro, whose father has also died, supports with the sale of the paintings not only his whole family, but some other villagers as well. Now Pedro must stay and help build a new house. David is at sea again. At Pedro's prompting, he elects to go home, knowing that whatever he must face up to there, it will be less than an earthquake.

Seeing a contemporary more disadvantaged than he, yet more purposeful and responsible to others, jars David from a course of aimless flight. He finds the maturity his mother has denied him — enough, in fact, to decide to get on a new footing with her. Although this story clearly intends to point a "moral," and thus the characterizations are not richly conceived, the book could be thought-provoking to readers having trouble facing change and accepting responsibility.

Ages 11-13

Also available in:
No other form known

C

169

Conaway, Judith

I Dare You!

Color photographs by Katie Maloney.
Raintree Publishers, Ltd., 1977.
(30 pages)

RISK, TAKING OF
   Peer relationships: peer pressures

Young Davy and Carol decide to form a club whose members will dare each other to do things. Davy's most challenging dare is to climb the roof of an old house, and he is delighted at accomplishing it. Carol then triple-dares him to skateboard down the sidewalk with his hands over his eyes. Davy knows it is dangerous, but pretends he is not afraid. Skating blind, he collides with his mother and she falls and sprains her wrist. Carol says, "Maybe we shouldn't play 'I Dare You' anymore. One of us could really get hurt next time." Davy replies, "I think you're right."

This brief depiction of young children and the dangerous demands they frequently make upon each other could stimulate group discussion. Full-page photographs expand the text and clearly illustrate consequences.

Ages 5-7

Also available in:
No other form known

170

Conaway, Judith

I'll Get Even

Color photographs by Mark Gubin.
Raintree Publishers, Ltd., 1977.
(30 pages)

ANGER
   Rejection: sibling
   Sibling: relationships

Young John wants to help his older brother and some friends put together a new kite. But his brother tells him, "You'll only be in the way." John goes off and broods on ways to get even with his brother, including throwing a bucket of water on the kite so that it cannot fly. John cannot understand why his brother is "so mean" to him. "What have I done?" he asks himself. "Why doesn't he like me?" Soon the boys are finished putting the kite together, and John's brother waves to him and says, "Hey, John, do you want to help us fly this thing?" "Do I?" John replies, "Sure I do!" and he joins the other boys happily.

Although the young narrator is hurt by his brother's curt dismissal, and longs for revenge, when his brother invites him to return and play his anger is short-lived. Younger siblings will empathize with John and his desire to be included. This story is enhanced by beautiful photographs.

Ages 4-7

Also available in:
No other form known

171

Conaway, Judith

Sometimes It Scares Me

Color photographs by Katie Maloney.
Raintree Publishers, Ltd., 1977.
(30 pages)

FEAR

Young Ben is six years old. He talks about things that scare him: his swimming lessons, ghosts, and what people think of him. "Sometimes," he says, "I'm just a little afraid of other people." But Ben understands that everyone is afraid of different things. His brother, Tim, was afraid when he was lost in a department store. Tim is also afraid of groups of people, because he is shy. Tim and Ben take turns trying to frighten each other with plastic spiders and snakes. At the end of the story, Ben is trying to scare Tim with a fake monster's hand.

Young Ben is an honest, understanding six-year-old. He admits his fears without shame or embarrassment. He understands that everyone is afraid of something. He shows sympathy and understanding for Tim's fears when he says, "Boy, it must be hard to be shy." The intended humor in the photograph of the monster's hand on the final page may detract from the reassuring tone of the story.

Ages 3-7

Also available in:
No other form known

172

Conaway, Judith

Was My Face Red!

Color photographs by Katie Maloney.
Raintree Publishers, Ltd., 1977.
(30 pages)

EMBARRASSMENT
  Empathy
  Peer relationships

C

The young girl telling the story goes to a party wearing a long party dress. Her friends, Aaron, Neil, Cathy, and Mitchell, are dressed casually, and they laugh at her. She is embarrassed. But Aaron tells her about the time he went to a wedding with a terrible haircut. "Boy, was my face red that time!" he admits. Neil tells about the time he fell into a garbage can and his friends laughed at him. Mitchell and Cathy tell their own stories of embarrassment. The narrator sees that "everyone does silly things once in a while" and has a good time at the party. Later she sees Aaron walking around with his hands over his mouth. He tells her that he does not want anyone to see how funny he looks since losing one of his front teeth. She smiles and tells him not to worry: she has lost both front teeth.

The young narrator learns through the reassurances of her friends that "everyone feels embarrassed sometimes." Knowing this, she is able to reassure one of them when *he* feels embarrassed. Full-page photographs alternate with pages of text to supplement the story.

Ages 4-7

Also available in:
No other form known

173

Conaway, Judith

Will I Ever Be Good Enough?

Color photographs by Bruce Witty.
Raintree Publishers, Ltd., 1977.
(30 pages)

INFERIORITY, FEELINGS OF
Self, attitude toward: confidence

A young girl looking ahead to growing up has high hopes. She thinks about becoming a famous scientist or an admired explorer. But the books she must study in the here and now are hard for her. She considers being a model, but fears she is not pretty enough. Is she, she wonders, good enough for any career? "Sometimes it seems as if everything is too hard." She envies her friend Meg, whom she thinks pretty, smart, and able to do everything well, especially gymnastics. When Meg teaches the narrator some of that gymnastic skill, she in turn teaches Meg how to crochet. By the end of the story, the narrator is saying, "I wonder if I could ever be good enough to fly a plane? You know, if I really wanted to, I think I could."

Although this first-person account is very short, the solution over-simplified, it could offer reassurance to readers not up to longer, more complicated material. Full-color photographs add interest and meaning.

Ages 6-9

Also available in:
No other form known

174

Cone, Molly Lamken

Call Me Moose

Black/white illustrations by Bernice Lowenstein.
Houghton Mifflin Co., 1978.
(166 pages)

EXPECTATIONS
IDENTIFICATION WITH OTHERS: Story Characters
Camp experiences
Friendship: best friend
Loneliness
Parental: interference

Although Martha's two sisters have left home, their reputations for athletic prowess continue to haunt Martha, who is about ten and clumsy. Martha identifies strongly with story characters and would rather read than play games, but her parents press her to practice athletics. Her determination to resist is bolstered by a newfound friend, Harriet, whose informal, irreverent ways Martha delights in. Then Martha is sent to a summer camp, and hates it. During her three weeks there, she refuses to take part in anything. Instead she treasures an empty box Harriet has given her as a token of their friendship — and reads books. Her only other interest derives from seeing a moose — and then imagining herself a moose, advising others to "call me moose." Finding on her return that Harriet has a new friend, Martha tears up the carton and resolves to stay a moose. She makes and wears antlers; she speaks only moose calls ("aw-aw-aarh"); and she gallops headlong through the neighborhood. Only when she meets Michael, another "reading freak," does she temporarily resume human behavior. One day Harriet's younger sister — prompted by Harriet — teases her about Michael, and Martha, in a rage, dashes from the house. Harriet and her new friend pursue her, forcing her to swim across a stream to escape. After drying out at Michael's, Martha doffs her antlers for good. Calm and composed, she returns home to advise her parents to "call me Diana" — the huntress of Greek myth.

A girl escapes from relentless parental pressures by identifying with characters in fiction. When she loses a friend she has wholly committed herself to, she assumes the identity of a solitary moose. Though the author suggests that Martha's parents' nagging lessens, she does not develop this towards a resolution. Martha's loneliness and unease before the expectations of others will be keenly felt by readers, not so the Moose sequence, which seems ridiculous at points.

Ages 9-11

Also available in:
Braille — *Call Me Moose*
Library of Congress

175

Conford, Ellen

Eugene the Brave

Color illustrations by John Larrecq.
Little, Brown and Co., 1978.
(32 pages)

FEAR: of Darkness
  Sibling: relationships

Eugene, a young possum hitherto unafraid of the dark, one day trembles before the oncoming night. His parents reason with him; his older brother, Randolph, reminds him that the moon and stars provide light to see by — unless, adds his sister, Geraldine, it is rainy or cloudy or. . . . As their parents go off to forage for food, Randolph assures Eugene that nothing can get him — "except," Geraldine says, "maybe a vampire bat." Eugene's shriek brings his parents running. His is no

braver the next night, and thereafter sleeps during the scary night and stays awake during the day. Determined to cure his fear, Geraldine tries to accustom Eugene to scares by frightening him again and again. But Eugene laughs her off. Finally, by pretending to be a ghost, Geraldine lures him into the forest. Intent on giving chase, Eugene does not notice that night has fallen. Geraldine falls into a deep hole, and Eugene — though fearful and on guard against snakes and poisonous spiders — rescues her. Back home, Geraldine proclaims him a hero; his parents and brother agree — and Eugene says wonderingly, "I had no idea I was that brave."

Immune to his family's insistence on the way nocturnal animals normally live, a young possum finally overcomes his fear of the dark when going to the rescue of someone else. Eugene's discovery of his own bravery is set down as whimsically as are the illustrations of this funny tale. The story is one in a series about the possum family.

Ages 5-7

Also available in:
Paperbound — *Eugene the Brave*
Little, Brown and Co.

176

Conklin, Paul

Choctaw Boy

Black/white photographs by the author.
Dodd, Mead & Co., 1975.
(64 pages)

NATIVE AMERICAN
  Change: accepting
  Loyalty

C

The ranch-style home where eleven-year-old Clifton Henry lives in Mississippi could fit in a suburb — except for the pigpen in back and Uncle Bob within, telling a story about Kashe-ho-ta-pa-la, the deer with a human head. *"Chahta siah Hoke"* — "I am a Choctaw" — is the message that Clifton's older sister, DeLaura, tries to instill as she narrates a pageant of the tribe's history at a local fair. Nearby, Clifton is enjoying the traditional stickball tournament. He also enjoys dancing the old, elaborate tribal dances at school. But his passion is trading baseball cards. One winter day he and his cousin Travis accompany Clifton's father on errands, and Mr. Henry talks about his youth, when life was closer to the old ways. Now these ways are dying because the tribal elders who remember them are themselves dying. DeLaura and others can try to preserve and teach the traditional lore, but the Choctaw are powerfully attracted to modern ways. Three of the Henry's own children have moved away from the small Mississippi reservation. Even visiting an ancient mound, the heart of the old Choctaw nation, Clifton lets his thoughts drift to baseball. Later, listening to one now-distant brother who visits them, Clifton dreams of a future life in a big city.

This factual narrative of the history, circumstances, and pride of the Choctaw people also dramatizes the present divided loyalties of a Choctaw youth, held by the Choctaw past, drawn by the American present. Though Clifton's parents fear for the youngsters caught between old and new ways, Clifton himself does not sense the difficulties. This book, which describes the situation without passing judgment on it, provides excellent material for discussion of divided allegiance.

Ages 9-12

Also available in:
No other form known

177

Cook, Marjorie

To Walk on Two Feet

The Westminster Press, 1978.
(93 pages)

AMPUTEE
   Accidents: automobile
   Limbs, abnormal or missing
   Prosthesis
   Self, attitude toward: feeling different
   Self, attitude toward: pity
   Wheelchair, dependence on

A victim of an automobile accident in which a friend had been killed, fifteen-year-old Carrie Karns has had both legs amputated below the knee. Fearing pity and scorning to "stump around on wooden legs," Carrie apparently refuses to see friends, use her wheelchair, or be fitted with prostheses. Yet she does use her wheelchair — to eavesdrop on a conversation between her mother and the doctor. Despite finding the chair easy to use, Carrie keeps her accomplishment to herself. While practicing one evening after her family is asleep, Carrie spies a break-in at a nearby school and, telephoning the police, prevents a burglary. The next day, when a reporter appears at the house, Carrie confesses that it was by using the chair that she was able to see the burglary. Soon after this, Carrie is studying, visiting with friends, and even attending a basketball game. When her younger brother suggests that her prostheses will "look better than nothing," Carrie reluctantly tries them on. Finding them easy to work, and not unattractive, Carrie begins physiotherapy. She wears the legs on a date, and though she cannot walk as yet, stands proudly when she wants to. But the burglary is not behind her. When one of the burglars, who evaded capture but fears Carrie can identify him, abducts her and a wild car chase ensues, Carrie relives her accident. Rescued, she is finally able to discuss the accident and all she has felt about her injury.

The disablement, anger, self-pity, and depression a teenage amputee feels are vividly dramatized in this engrossing but somewhat contrived story. Because she wants only to forget the accident that caused her injuries, Carrie fights shy of everything and everyone connected with it — and experiences recurring nightmares. When she sees that her anguish, usually taken out on her family, causes them anguish in turn, she begins to sort things out. The encouragement of family and friends helps her in facing, and sometimes overcoming, the limitations she encounters. Also touched upon are phantom pains in missing limbs, mobility without artificial aids, and the possible effects of medication upon one's emotions.

Ages 11-14

Also available in:
No other form known

178

Corcoran, Barbara

Axe-Time, Sword-Time

Atheneum Publishers, 1976.
(201 pages)

LEARNING DISABILITIES
MATURATION
  Boy-girl relationships
  Expectations
  Separation, marital
  War

Seventeen-year-old Elinor Golden has completed four years of high school, but now, in September of 1941,

instead of going off to college with her friends, she is beginning another year of high school courses, with little confidence that she will ever qualify for college, as her mother insists she do. In elementary school, while golfing with her father, Elinor had been struck in the head by a golf ball, and lay in a coma for 24 hours. Apparently fully recovered, she has had difficulty reading and spelling ever since. This autumn it seems inevitable that the United States will enter the war against the Axis powers, and Elinor longs for patriotic work to do. Meanwhile, her parents are moving toward divorce, and her father moves to an apartment, leaving Mrs. Golden to her highly social life and dreams of the same for her daughter. Then Elinor's English teacher asks the girl to join her as a volunteer airplane-spotter for the U.S. Army. A poor reader, Elinor proves an excellent spotter. When her boy friend, Jed, comes home from college to announce he has enlisted, and her brother joins the Ski Patrol, Elinor feels she can no longer remain in school. Ignoring her mother's disapproval, she applies to an employment agency and is given a job inspecting miniature radios for the U.S. Navy, and in a short time is given a promotion. Before Jed leaves for active duty, he tells her that he wants to marry her someday.

Growing up is rarely easy, and young Elinor must buck a reading disability and the fears, shocks, and distractions of her country's entrance into World War II. We follow her gradually dawning independence in a time when fear of losing a loved one in battle — and the shock of actual casualty — are part of daily life.

Ages 11 and up

Also available in:
Talking Book — *Axe-Time, Sword-Time*
Library of Congress

C

179

Corcoran, Barbara

The Faraway Island

Atheneum Publishers, 1977.
(158 pages)

GRANDPARENT: Living in home of
SHYNESS
    Anxiety
    Fear: of school
    Security/Insecurity

Fourteen-year-old Lynn Grenville is spending a year with her grandmother on Nantucket Island. Lynn has always been shy, and when her father, just appointed a Fulbright lecturer in geography, had announced a move to Belgium for a year, she had been terrified of going to a new home, a new life, and new language. Her father had sympathetically suggested she spend the year with her grandmother instead. Lynn is relieved, but still bothered by the thought of going to a new school. Soon Lynn meets some girls on Nantucket, but they are not very friendly. That settles it: she takes advantage of her grandmother's forgetfulness, does not enroll in school, and does not attend. She passes the days outside, reading and caring for her pet lamb, Cyrano, carefully avoiding places where she may be seen. The plan works for almost two months, until an irascible old neighbor, Abner Mitchell, gives away her secret — and does so in front of some other islanders, the Smalls, who already think Lynn's grandmother senile and incapable of looking after herself or Lynn. Apart from feeling guilty for deceiving her grandmother, Lynn is frightened that the Smalls have enough authority and evidence to put her grandmother in a nursing home, as they have threatened. It is Grandma's doctor, ministering to a cold Grandma has caught while clamming with Lynn, who assures the two that the Smalls can do nothing. Hurt by Lynn's deception, Grandma nevertheless understands why Lynn had been afraid of school, for, as she explains, she too had been shy when she was young. Lynn enrolls the next day and finds school not as bad as she had expected.

Lynn realizes that her fears are irrational, but that does not help her overcome them. She seems always to have been shy, but now, with dental braces and being unusually tall for her age, she feels harried and driven by conditions beyond her control. Her grandmother's uncritical acceptance makes her less afraid of her own awkwardness; and one boy who befriends her at school makes her feel less isolated among strangers.

Ages 10-13

Also available in:
No other form known

180

Corcoran, Barbara

Hey, That's My Soul You're Stomping On

Atheneum Publishers, 1978.
(122 pages)

MATURATION
    Age: respect for
    Change: accepting
    Divorce: of parents
    Grandparent: living in home of

Rachel, sixteen, is staying with her grandparents while her parents decide whether or not to divorce. Her grandparents are warm, understanding people and she enjoys them, but at the motel in Palm Springs, California, where they are staying, most of the other guests are over sixty, too. Rachel likes most of them but yearns for the company of someone her own age. Out walking one day, she meets young Ariadne Appleby, distant but reachable, and they talk. She learns that Ariadne's mother has been an actress; that Ariadne hates her stepfather; that she is anti-Semitic; and that she has a brother, Alan, who is fourteen and very intelligent. Despite Ariadne's eccentricities and prejudices, Rachel becomes a friend of both Appleby youngsters. She especially values Ariadne and Alan when she learns that her parents will indeed be divorced. Why, she wonders angrily, can they not stay together, when so many couples at the motel seem still in love after many decades of marriage? Rachel chooses to stay with her grandparents until she finishes school. Why go home to a mother she considers both overprotective and melodramatic? One day the Applebys invite Rachel to take the aerial tramway to see the view from eight-and-a-half thousand feet above sea level. On the way up Ariadne feels sick, but Mrs. Appleby ignores her, seeming embarrassed to be seen with her. Suddenly Alan takes over, speaking calmly to his sister, comforting her. Rachel is appalled by Mrs. Appleby's behavior — and thinks herself probably better off being smothered than ignored. Struck by Alan's loyalty, his genuine concern for his sister, Rachel decides to go back home and help her mother get used to being single again.

When she discovers that Alan had been beaten by his father, and that Ariadne is suicidal, Rachel considers herself lucky to have parents who at least love her, though not each other. Alan's noble actions and her grandparents' love help her aspire to qualities her parents lack: concern for others, stamina, generosity, perspective. Her feelings for her mother are reawakened. Rachel's state of mind is described at times in letters to her brother at school in England.

Ages 11-14

Also available in:
No other form known

181
Corcoran, Barbara

Make No Sound
Atheneum Publishers, 1977.
(148 pages)

DEPRIVATION, EMOTIONAL
MAGICAL THINKING
PARENTAL: Negligence
PARENTAL: Unreliability
SECURITY/INSECURITY
   Change: new home
   Sibling: half-brother/half-sister

Melody Baxter, about thirteen, and her two older half-brothers, George and Brian, have come to expect the unexpected from their oft-divorced, alcoholic mother. This time Mrs. Baxter's quest for a good life has brought them to Hawaii, where she finds a job managing an apartment building in a small town. Deciding that the one-bedroom apartment she is allotted is too small for all of them, she rents an old fishing hut for the three children. Lonely and frightened her first night in the hut, Melody turns to her radio for comfort, and discovers a late-night performer called Kahuna the Enchanterer, whose soothing music and legends about the Islands she listens to from then on. Hearing elsewhere so much frightening talk of earthquakes, tidal waves, and volcanic eruptions in the Islands, she is drawn more and more to the sorcery and the supernatural in Kahuna's tales. They quiet her fears. She writes to Kahuna, signing herself Hiika, sister of Pele — the goddess of the volcano — and takes a stick she has found on the beach to one of the ancient temples to have it sanctified. On an overnight trip to the city with her mother, Melody leaves their hotel room in the early morning to catch a glimpse of Kahuna leaving the radio station. While she waits, an earthquake hits, but she is taken to safety by a Civil Patrol driver. Meanwhile, George and Brian are around very little. George has moved in with Mr. Poha, a kindly minister, and Brian, quite beyond his mother's control, is running wild. One night he returns to the hut with friends, barges into Melody's room and breaks her radio. She grabs her magic stick and puts a death curse upon him. Later that night, he is hospitalized with a skull fracture after a fight. Melody thinks her curse is responsible and concludes that only the goddess Pele can undo it. Early next morning, she travels to the crater the goddess is said to inhabit. While making her sacrifices, Melody loses her footing and awakes in the hospital with a broken wrist. A letter has been found in her pocket addressed to Kahuna, and he has been called to identify her. Melody is surprised to find him an ordinary person, not even Hawaiian, and he is surprised to find his correspondent so young. And Melody finds food for thought in the news that Brian's condition had improved even before she got to the crater. Mrs. Baxter takes Brian to a specialist on the mainland, leaving Melody and George in care of Mr. Poha. He and Kahuna help Melody to see the bogusness of her magic.

In this book an anxious girl in strange, sometimes dangerous new surroundings allows her fears to lead her to uncritical belief in local superstitions. Her feckless mother and equally neglected brothers are no help. Only when two other sympathetic adults listen to her fears and honestly try to answer them does Melody begin to abandon her fantasies. Melody's story is melodramatic, but her predicament seems all too real. The Hawaiian setting and lore cannot help but be interesting.

Ages 10-13

Also available in:
No other form known

182

Corey, Dorothy

Tomorrow You Can

Color Illustrations by Lois Axeman.
Albert Whitman & Co., 1977.
(32 pages counted)

MATURATION
SIBLING: Youngest

Small children often want to do what their older brothers and sisters do — catch a ball, swing by themselves, get dressed without help, go to school, paint a picture, share a toy, tie a shoe, read. When they grow bigger, stronger, and older they will be able to accomplish all these things and more.

Through words and pictures this book shows many such activities, offering encouragement to small children who feel left out or discouraged watching older siblings or friends. Time is a difficult concept for young children to grasp, but this book makes "tomorrow" concrete and within reach.

Ages 2-5

Also available in:
No other form known

183

Corey, Dorothy

You Go Away

Color illustrations by Lois Axeman.
Albert Whitman & Co., 1976.
(31 pages counted)

SEPARATION ANXIETY

Parents go away and come back, and so do children. There are brief separations: a mother hides behind a blanket for a moment and then reappears; a child runs across the room and back; a child disappears under a bed and pops back out again. Some separations last longer: two children lose sight of their mother in a supermarket; a group of children stay with a baby-sitter while their mothers shop; a little girl goes to kindergarten. Sometimes parents go on a trip, with suitcases, leaving the children with Grandmother. When the parents return, everyone is delighted.

This simple picture book with a brief text is not intended to overcome a child's deep-seated fear of being separated from parents. But it provides an opportunity to talk with very young children about separation, and about being with people besides one's parents.

Ages 2-5

Also available in:
No other form known

184

Crawford, Charles P.

Letter Perfect

E. P. Dutton & Company, Inc., 1977.
(167 pages)

MATURATION
PEER RELATIONSHIPS: Peer Pressures
   Guilt, feelings of
   Practical jokes/pranks
   Values/Valuing: moral/ethical

Chad, B.J., and Toad are inseparable in their junior high school and out of it — all for one and one for all. After Mr. Patterson, their English teacher, fails B.J. for cheating and Chad for allowing him to copy, the three meet, agree they hate school in general and Patterson in particular, and decide to plan a perfect crime. In training to elude detection, each plans and executes a prank and produces proof of having gotten away with it. Chad follows the unwitting Mr. Patterson home and steals a letter as evidence that he was undiscovered. Reading the letter, the three find that Mr. Patterson once had a mental breakdown in the Navy. B.J., concluding he is thus a "psycho," wants to blackmail him. Chad protests but then goes along after the two convince him the scheme is all hypothetical. Suddenly it no longer is. The other two ask $60 to keep quiet, and Mr. Patterson appears near another breakdown. Chad takes the letter from B.J.'s locker and returns it to Mr. Patterson, apologizing for taking it in the first place. B.J. and Toad consider Chad a traitor and to get back at him, B.J. plants three marijuana joints in front of Chad's locker, where the assistant principal finds Chad standing over them. He accuses the boy of using grass, but Mr. Patterson comes to Chad's defense, saying the joints are his own. Mr. Patterson never returns to the school again, and Chad later discovers that he is teaching at a small private school in another city. Chad has matured enough to consider his former friends no friends at all.

Chad, the first-person narrator, worries about a joke but goes along until it turns into outright crime, his need for friendship overriding his moral sense. This story unfolds logically and believably as an idle idea gets out of hand, finally endangering its perpetrators as well as its victim. Discussion of Milton's *Paradise Lost* in the English class provides a philosophical commentary on evil and the easy path to it. The dialogue contains a good deal of profanity.

Ages 12 and up

Also available in:
Cassette for the Blind — *Letter Perfect*
Library of Congress

Paperbound — *Letter Perfect*
Pocket Books, Inc.

C

185

Crayder, Dorothy

Ishkabibble!

Black/white illustrations by Susan Vaeth.
Atheneum Publishers, 1976.
(101 pages) o.p.

NAME-CALLING
Problem solving
School: classmate relationships

Eleven-year-old Lucy is dismayed at being the butt of her classmates' ridicule. Ever since popular Terry started calling her "Luce the Goose," the other children make honking sounds at her approach. Today, Valentine's Day, she feels miserably certain she will receive no cards at all. On the street, a comical-looking fat lady with a wart on her nose prods her into telling why she looks so sad. The woman, named Annie, professes to be a *guru* and says that Lucy can be her first "client." She suggests that Lucy try "ishkabibble" on her tormentors: the next time she is teased she should just say "ishkabibble" and ignore them. Ignored, they will probably stop. That day at school, when Terry starts her chanting, Lucy, despite her preparedness, gets so nervous that she cannot even pronounce "ishkabibble." She returns downcast to Annie, who lends her an old banner with the word printed large across it. At school the next day, Lucy brandishes her banner, and all teasing subsides. When Terry sees she cannot upset Lucy anymore, she starts in on Maureen. But Lucy just brings Maureen to Annie, who takes her on as her next "client."

In a zany story about real pain, a kindly eccentric shows a girl the way to find out what teasing is all about. The girl does, averts it, and turns to help a friend along the same way.

Ages 9-12

Also available in:
No other form known

186

Crowe, Robert L.

Clyde Monster

Color illustrations by Kay Chorao.
E. P. Dutton & Company, Inc., 1976.
(29 pages counted)

FEAR: of Darkness
Bedtime

Clyde is a young monster who lives in the forest with his monster parents. He is growing up well for a monster: he lives in a cave, is becoming uglier every day, and knows how to breathe fire on the lake to make steam rise. Clyde also loves to play and turn somersaults. But Clyde is afraid of the dark and refuses to sleep in his cave. When his parents ask him what he is afraid of, he responds, "People. I'm afraid there are people in there who will get me." Even though Clyde's father breathes fire into the cave to light it up and show him there are no people hiding there, Clyde fears that some will jump out from under rocks and get him once he is asleep. His mother asks him, "Would you ever hide in the dark under a bed or in a closet to scare a human boy or girl?" Clyde answers, "Of course not!" Then his father explains that people would not do that either since a long time ago people and monsters made a pact not to scare each other. Clyde is somewhat reassured and goes into his cave to sleep, asking only that they "leave the rock open just a little."

Although Clyde is reassured enough by his parents to try sleeping in his cave, his fears do not disappear all at once. Talking about a child's fear of darkness from a monster's point of view can be an amusing and reassuring experience for a child. The color illustrations of engaging, not frightening, monsters enhance the story.

Ages 3-6

Also available in:
No other form known

187

Cunningham, Julia Woolfolk

Come to the Edge

Pantheon Books, 1977.
(79 pages)

IDENTITY, SEARCH FOR
ORPHAN
  Depression
  Loneliness
  Running away

At ten, Gravel Winter is left by his drunken father at a foster farm on the excuse that his father must go off and make a new start alone. What sustains Gravel for the next four years is his friendship with a sympathetic boy nicknamed Skin. With Skin's sudden, forced departure to another home, Gravel goes out of control, attacks the principal, and is locked up. When summoned, his father declares, "I don't want him," and Gravel sinks into despair. He escapes by night, and three highways and five towns later is taken in and fed by a kindly signpainter named Paynter. Though reluctant at first, Gravel accepts Mr. Paynter's offer of a permanent home. In domestic warmth and security, the boy learns the household chores and helps Mr. Paynter in his work — but continuing bouts of depression, made worse by his host's coming home drunk one night, persuade Gravel that he must leave. Mr. Paynter, who loves him like a son, says he will always be welcomed back. In another town, Gravel meets three people: Mr. Gant, a blind, wealthy miser who gives him a room in exchange for Gravel's being his "eyes"; Mrs. Prior, a lame woman who gives him his meals in exchange for the use of his legs; and Ethel Ransome, a nearly deaf woman who wants conversation. Each uses Gravel for a selfish purpose, and Mr. Gant is especially demanding. He has for years been blackmailing a servant named Williston into near-slavery with knowledge of a murder Williston committed. When Williston plots to murder Gant and steal his money, the loyal Gravel warns Gant — but too late. Gant has murdered the servant and threatens to accuse Gravel of the crime if the boy does not take Williston's place in captivity. Gravel senses he is bluffing. But he sees, too, that he has been used by them all without finding what he himself wants. He must "fill up the hollows of himself creating a new person." Saying good-bye to the three, he returns to say good-bye to Mr. Paynter as well. But the bond of trust between them is too strong. He stays with Paynter.

This is a moving, if sometimes depressing story of a boy's journey to discover himself and his worth. Before he can establish a deep relationship with anyone, Gravel must surmount early, crippling betrayals of his affection. Mature readers will respond to these characters' intense emotions and to the allegorical nature of Gravel's journey.

Ages 9-13

Also available in:
Paperbound — *Come to the Edge*
Avon Books

C

188

Cusack, Isabel Langis

Ivan the Great

Black/white illustrations by Carol Nicklaus.
Thomas Y. Crowell Company, Inc., 1978.
(45 pages)

HONESTY/DISHONESTY
Communication: parent-child
Trust/Distrust

Nine-year-old Robby Morrison has always "behaved and never told a lie." But when he receives a parrot from his parents, trouble starts. Robby insists that the parrot has asked to be called Ivan; his parents have not heard the bird say anything and doubt Robby's word. In the days that follow, his parents again question his honesty: did a girl named Australia, wearing purple lipstick and pearl earrings, really demand his new lunch box; did some big boys really push Robby into a puddle, as he says? Time goes on, and Robby gets in deeper by again mentioning the girl with purple lipstick and by speaking of being in a fight at school. When one lie — about the fight — is discovered, his parents accuse him of being a compulsive liar. He is redeemed only when his mystery girl shows up at the front door one afternoon; his mother realizes her son has been truthful almost all the time.

Parents too quick to mistrust their son feel vindicated when they do find him lying. Because the right and wrong of different kinds of lying are discussed — the white lie to prevent hurt feelings, the self-serving lie — this book could be used to spur discussion. It could also be used to explore ways the main character could have shown his parents he was telling the truth.

Ages 7-10

Also available in:
No other form known

189

Dahl, Roald

Danny: The Champion of the World

Black/white illustrations by Jill Bennett.
Alfred A. Knopf, Inc., 1975.
(198 pages)

PARENT/PARENTS: Single
Nature: appreciation of
Problem solving
Stealing

Danny, who is nine, lives alone with his father, William, in an old gypsy wagon in southern England. William owns a small gas station in the country, and Danny helps him pump gas and fix cars. Danny's mother has been dead for years, and he and William do everything together. But one night the boy awakens to find his father gone. Later William explains that he had been poaching pheasants in Hazell's Wood, an old skill he has not indulged since his wife's death. The landowner, Victor Hazell, is a bad-tempered brewer who richly deserves being robbed of his game. Like his father before him, William teaches Danny to poach: raisins are much the best bait for pheasants. But the next attempt comes to grief: William falls into a pit trap for poachers and breaks an ankle. Danny rescues him before the gamekeepers can get to him. Together they plot revenge: the ruin of Hazell's shooting party by their poaching all the pheasants. But how? Danny invents a way and thus becomes a most distinguished poacher: they put sleeping powder into the raisins, and then scatter these in the Wood. It works. They haul 120 sleeping pheasants to the vicar's; his wife will deliver them to the gas station in a specially outfitted baby carriage the next day. But the birds wake up as they are being wheeled to the station and, still sleepy, flop about. Hazell then drives up in his shiny Rolls Royce to demand that they be returned. They are, much to his car's damage. Finally they fly off, all but six, who have eaten too much sleeping powder. Danny and his father take two, the vicar two more — and the local policeman two as well. Eager for more sport, Danny and his father next plan to poach trout from a nearby stream.

Danny's first-person narrative shows why poaching is so storied a pastime in England. Almost everyone conspires against the local landowner and his gamekeepers. But what raises this book above a humorous poaching yarn is the deep love portrayed between father and son. What is "suitable" for children or adults does not interest them; all they do they do together, sharing their lives, including the risks.

Ages 10 and up

Also available in:
Paperbound — *Danny: The Champion of the World*
Bantam Books, Inc.

Talking Book — *Danny: The Champion of the World*
Library of Congress

190

Danziger, Paula

The Pistachio Prescription: A Novel

Delacorte Press, 1978.
(154 pages)

INFERIORITY, FEELINGS OF
　Appearance: concern about
　Asthma
　Boy-girl relationships
　Parent/Parents: fighting between
　Sibling: rivalry

D

Unlike her Greek namesake, thirteen-year-old Cassandra Stephens does not make dire predictions; her life is bad enough as it is. Every time her parents quarrel — and they often do — Cassie suffers an asthma attack. Teasing by her older sister, Stephanie, or by her mother — almost anything at all — can likewise plunge Cassie into such attacks, or into an array of imagined illnesses for which her accustomed "cure" is pistachio nuts. Only Andrew, her younger brother, and Vicki, her best friend, can be depended on not to distress her. Such is Vicki's faith in her that she urges Cassie to lead a slate of candidates at school against a clique running for "freshperson" (ninth-grade) offices. Through real fears and imagined illnesses, Cassie campaigns well until she suffers a self-inflicted disaster: trying to look better for Bernie, a boy she has met and is attracted to while campaigning, Cassie tweezes out her eyebrows and must resort to sunglasses. In the dark himself about the glasses, Bernie sticks by her anyway. She fears others will laugh at her "plucked chicken" appearance if she doffs the glasses before the eyebrows have grown back. In fact, it is after she stands up to a strict, often unjust, and unpopular teacher, who orders her to remove the glasses, that she gains enough recognition and popularity to win a narrow victory as class president. But instead of celebrating, Cassie has a severe asthma attack that night — when her parents announce their plans to divorce. But that is when Stephanie and Cassie, seeing that their age-old rivalry stems from uneasiness in the family, come together and make plans to try to reconcile their parents. Soon, though, both girls know and accept that their parents never will live together again.

The girl narrating this story in the first person starts out vacillating between love and hate for her family, and ends by understanding and accepting them. Of particular note in Cassie's progress to wisdom is her friendship with Bernie, for it is here that she discards a morbid concentration on her appearance and her health, to be considerate of Bernie's needs and vulnerabilities. These contemporary teenagers are portrayed with humor, understanding, and some playful exaggeration, the last quality to ease young readers into a little self-appraisal themselves.

Ages 11-13

Also available in:
Paperbound — *The Pistachio Prescription: A Novel*
Dell Publishing Company, Inc.

191

Dauer, Rosamond

Bullfrog Builds a House

Color illustrations by Byron Barton.
Greenwillow Books, 1977.
(56 pages)

FRIENDSHIP: Meaning of
  Cooperation: in work

Bullfrog knows exactly what he wants to do — build a house — but details, such as where to begin, stymie him. At the lakeside site he has chosen, he meets Gertrude, a female bullfrog, and asks if she can advise him how to build a house. "Start with what you like best," she says. Bullfrog builds a diving board on the front porch. With Gertrude's help he goes on to build and furnish the house, but something seems to be missing. He asks Gertrude about it, and she suggests a roof might be nice. Later, it is she who asks him if something is missing. After some thought, Bullfrog says no, and she leaves. Alone now, he considers diving from the board — but does not feel like it. He does not feel like doing anything, in fact, and decides he is coming down with a cold. What is wrong, after all? He has a house, a diving board. . . . Suddenly he jumps up, shouting "GERTRUDE!" Dashing off, he finds her, but unable to say what is wrong, he stammers, "I just wondered if you would care to . . . play cards." They return, play checkers; and then Bullfrog asks her to stay forever.

More than furniture, walls, and a roof is needed to make a house a home. An absent-minded bullfrog in this read-alone story stumbles on this truth only after he has built a house and finds it empty without a companion. This book is a sequel to *Bullfrog Grows Up*.

Ages 4-7

Also available in:
No other form known

192

Dauer, Rosamond

My Friend, Jasper Jones

Color illustrations by Jerry Joyner.
Parents' Magazine Press, 1977.
(31 pages counted) o.p.

IMAGINARY FRIEND
  Responsibility: avoiding

Young Teddy has a very useful imaginary friend named Jasper Jones. One day while Teddy is in his room, his bed breaks. When his mother comes to see what happened, Teddy blames his friend and tells his mother she cannot speak to Jasper Jones because he has gone for a walk. She gives Teddy a message for him: *"No more broken beds."* Then Teddy's parents fix the bed. The next afternoon Father comes into Teddy's room while he is taking a nap and discovers Teddy's clothes all over the floor and his dresser drawers full of leaves. When his father asks what happened, Teddy blames it on Jasper Jones. Father cannot speak to Jasper since he has gone for a walk, but he tells Teddy to give Jasper a message: *"No more leaves in your bureau!"* Teddy and his parents put the clothes back into the drawers. That evening when Teddy's parents come to his room, they find the walls painted with peanut butter. They tell the boy that since Jasper Jones is his friend and has probably gone for a walk, he will have to clean up after Jasper. Teddy scrubs the walls, but he does not like it. At bedtime Teddy tells his parents that Jasper Jones is going to visit another little boy tomorrow.

Clever illustrations make this story of a young boy and his mischievous imaginary friend a delight to read. Each page illustrates Teddy's two worlds: in the top two-thirds, in color, we see Teddy up to no good; in the bottom third, in black and white, we see him with his parents, surrounded by the results of his mischief.

Ages 3-6

Also available in:
No other form known

193

Degens, T.

The Game on Thatcher Island

The Viking Press, Inc., 1977.
(148 pages)

IDENTIFICATION WITH OTHERS: Peers
  Bully: being bothered by
  Cruelty
  Honesty/Dishonesty
  Judgment, effect of emotions on
  Violence
  Visiting

Several risks stand between eleven-year-old Harry Chase and a game of war on Thatcher Island, and Harry usually avoids risks. But his admiration for the older boys who asked him along overrides his inhibitions and judgment. He asks permission from his parents to go on a "picnic" outing, and to ensure that they grant it he asks Sarah, his eight-year-old sister, and John, a Fresh Air Program summer visitor, to accompany him. But he fails to tell Doug, the organizer of the game, out of fear he will refuse to let two more people come. Harry's week is haunted by the risk of being found out at home, the risk of bringing along Sarah and John unasked, and brooding about an earlier near-death by drowning. John, always touchy about being a "charity case," already suspects Harry of being up to something. Nonetheless, John and Sarah happily wade ashore to the Island that Saturday — and are immediately captured by Doug's team. Harry, still in the boat, tracks them down but watches from the brush, feeling helpless, while the team tortures the two, and throws them, bound and gagged, into a sand pit, where they are showered with burning matches. Furious at the boys' cruelty and furious also at having been blind to their real characters, Harry captures Doug after the others leave and, joined by Sarah and John, tortures him as he had tortured the girl and boy. Only after he accidentally almost kills Doug can John and Sarah persuade Harry to leave. On the way back by boat, John almost drowns; Harry rescues him. Now Harry feels calm and free. He confesses his lies and guilt — and John, recognizing the change in Harry, admits to doing some lying himself.

His idolizing of older boys leads a youth into a savage game where he recognizes their true characters and his own as well. The author's use of two viewpoints, Harry's and John's, lets us know why John lies to the Chases to conceal his poverty but not how Harry resolves his deceitfulness, fury, and shame. The strong emotions and violence in the last third of this book will be weathered more easily by mature readers. Overall, this suspenseful, fast-moving story shows how violence begets violence and the risks invited in manipulating adults. Readers are likely to want to discuss this book.

D

194

DeLage, Ida

Am I a Bunny?

Color illustrations by Ellen Sloan.
Garrard Publishing Co., 1978.
(32 pages)

IDENTITY, SEARCH FOR
  Teasing

A little brown bunny becomes uncertain of his identity when several other creatures tease him. A rooster says that his being brown suggests he is a rat; a pig, noting his whiskers, calls him a cat; a cow says that such a sitting-up posture affirms he is a squirrel; a duck says that his hopping indicates a frog. At each tease, Bunny's mother reassures him he is a bunny — even though he is brown like a rat, has whiskers like a cat, sits like a squirrel, and hops like a frog. But it is when a lot of other little brown bunnies invite him to play that he recognizes with delight how, most of all, he is like other little brown bunnies.

Enchanting, colorful illustrations tell most of the young bunny's story in this beginning reader. Young readers will enjoy the witty teasing and be touched by little Bunny's concern over who he really is.

Ages 3-6

Also available in:
No other form known

195

Delaney, Ned

Rufus the Doofus

Color illustrations by the author.
Houghton Mifflin Co., 1978.
(32 pages)

ATTENTION SEEKING
  Belonging
  School: classmate relationships

Rufus has no friends. At his elementary school, no one pays any attention to him. He just likes the goldfish and thinks they like him. But one day Rufus accidentally spills worm chowder all over Zelda, and the entire class laughs. Delirious over the first attention he has ever received, Rufus runs wild all day. He puts glue on the slide, puts spiders in other children's clothes, and growls. When a new girl, Maybelline, appears, the children are all eager to impress her. Mortimer shows off by doing a headstand and accidentally upsets the fishbowl over his own head. Rufus rescues the fish, then rescues Mortimer by pulling the fishbowl off. He becomes the class hero and the immediate favorite of Maybelline.

A little child tries to get the attention of his peers and teacher by acting silly, in this exuberantly exaggerated story. Witty, colorful illustrations depict the children as small funny animals.

Ages 4-6

Also available in:
No other form known

196

Delaney, Ned

Two Strikes, Four Eyes

Color illustrations by the author.
Houghton Mifflin Co., 1976.
(32 pages)

GLASSES, WEARING OF
Peer relationships: peer pressures

Toby Mouse loves everything about baseball, including the noise of the crowd and the smack of the bat. But on the field without his glasses, Toby cannot hit, misses catches, and even runs by first base. No amount of advice, weightlifting, calisthenics, or jogging aids his playing — but neither will he risk his teammates' ridicule by playing with his glasses on. Only after he is sent off the field after another missed catch does he put them on — whereupon, the game apparently lost, he is given a chance at bat. Glasses firmly in place, Toby hits a home run and brings in two other runners. His now victorious teammates vote him best player — and ask why he had not worn his glasses before.

Toby has reason to fear being looked down on; his teammates heckle him badly for his poor playing. Small wonder, too, that he tries through exercise to make up for poor eyesight. But when circumstances compel him to correct his real defect, he learns that his teammates care about performance, not appearance. The author's cartoon illustrations are both colorful and witty.

Ages 5-8

Also available in:
No other form known

197

Delton, Judy

It Happened on Thursday

Color illustrations by June Goldsborough.
Albert Whitman & Co., 1978.
(30 pages counted)

SUPERSTITION
Illnesses: of parent

Jamie believes that Thursday is his lucky day. His Cub Scout den meets then; he once had a perfect spelling paper on that day; his birthday once fell on a Thursday; and on a Thursday he once received a baseball autographed by Hank Aaron. That is why, when Jamie's mother falls ill and is hospitalized, he counts on things to improve on Thursday. But by Thursday his mother is in the hospital and her condition appears to have grown worse. Not until Friday, when the family receives word that tests have come out favorably and Mother will be home Sunday, do things brighten. And by Sunday, Jamie realizes that, though one can look for good things to happen on Thursdays, they may happen all week long.

Children reading this story may begin to see that good fortune does not necessarily obey the calendar or any other automatic summons. Secondarily, they may be interested in how a family feels and acts about the illness of one of its members.

Ages 5-8

Also available in:
No other form known

D

198

Delton, Judy

My Mom Hates Me in January

Color illustrations by John Faulkner.
Albert Whitman & Co., 1977.
(32 pages counted)

COMMUNICATION: Parent-Child
PATIENCE/IMPATIENCE

Because young Lee Henry's mother is sick and tired of winter — it is January — she finds nearly everything he does or wants to do too messy, too noisy, or taking too much of her time. Finally, in exasperation, she sends him outside with instructions to keep dry, have a good time, not slide into a tree or lose his mittens, and not to get snow in his boots. Outside, Lee Henry slides on his saucer and just misses a tree, makes angels in the snow and gets all wet, and loses a mitten. When he returns, his mom is unhappy to see him back so soon. He sneezes and she sends him to take a warm bath, then complains because he splashes on the floor. At dinner she tells him not to tip his chair. By now, Lee Henry wants winter to go away, too. Next morning his mom sees a robin outside, and her mood brightens at the prospect of spring. Now she feels like doing the things Lee Henry wants to do. They make popcorn balls and make monsters out of clay, and she reads him his favorite book. They talk about how much fun he will have when it gets warm, and then they go into the kitchen to share a popcorn ball and a milkshake. Lee Henry says, "My mom hates me in January (unless she just hates *January*). But she'll love me again in May."

Parents are human, and their feelings about outside events often influence the way they treat their children. The mother in this first-person narrative is impatient with her son because she dislikes the weather, but he shows how children can both understand mood changes in their parents and see that bad moods are only temporary.

Ages 3-6

Also available in:
Filmstrip — *My Mom Hates Me in January*
Westport Communications

199

Delton, Judy

Two Is Company

Color illustrations by Giulio Maestro.
Crown Publishers, Inc., 1976.
(47 pages)

JEALOUSY: Peer
  Friendship: best friend

Bear and Duck are best friends. But Duck is being very attentive to their new neighbor, Chipmunk, and this annoys Bear. It is not so bad when Duck gives a party to welcome Chipmunk, but when he invites her to go blackberry-picking with them, Bear is far from pleased. Not eager to share his and Duck's secret berry patch with anyone else, Bear reluctantly agrees to the plan. Then, on the way home from berry-picking, Duck reveals that he has asked Chipmunk to join them at the fair. Angrily Bear informs him that it will be an inconvenience for three to attend the fair together: the rides are made for two and "someone will have to sit alone." But when Bear discovers that Chipmunk has considerately been weeding his garden, he has a change of heart. He tells Duck that after all it would be just fine if the three of them went to the fair together.

Bear's terse comments resemble the straightforward talk of children and clearly express his fear of being eased out. This is a story especially suited for beginning readers.

Ages 4-7

Also available in:
Paperbound — *Two Is Company*
Xerox Publishing Company

200

Dexter, Pat Egan

Arrow in the Wind

Thomas Nelson, Inc., 1978.
(160 pages)

DIVORCE: of Parents
FAMILY: Unity
    Animals: responsibility for
    Parent/Parents: single
    Stealing: shoplifting

After his parents' divorce, eleven-year-old Ben Arrow takes out his anger and disappointments on his mother, his sister Kara (a year younger than he), and sometimes on himself. Abandoned by Dad, as he sees it, Ben feels misunderstood by Mom, who is cross and touchy whatever he does. One day Mom announces that they must move — the house is too big to take care of — but the children promise to help out so that they can stay put. Ben takes a newspaper route, and in doing so comes to know better a neighborhood bully named Joe Tepper. Behind Joe's brusque front, Ben recognizes fear and insecurity and sees how Joe's home life, with no father and a mother who makes him shift for himself, affects his character. At first apprehensive about Ben's new friend, Kara and Mrs. Arrow warm to Joe after he rescues Ben's bicycle from thieves. Ben helps Joe with work, and Mom and Kara help him to improve his appearance, hygiene, and manners. But their "rehabilitation" does not curb Joe's stealing, which Joe himself does not regard as wrong. One day Joe slips a shoplifted camera into Ben's bag to avoid detection. Ben is caught, but refuses to name the real thief and accepts the consequences of his silence — a court appearance. Joe promises not to steal again, and a judge dismisses the case, noting that Ben has satisfactorily resolved the matter. The friends are reconciled, but Ben remains troubled about the future, his family, himself. He sees in his father's coming visit the answer to everything — only to find his father a virtual stranger, who arrives and departs, changing nothing. For her part, Mrs. Arrow is seeing another man. Will she remarry, even abandon Ben and Kara for this man? The children sabotage a dinner Mom invites him for, and at last she understands. Trust, she tells them, is what they need: she will never leave them even if she remarries. Still, the family has fallen behind; the house is too much for them. A spring flood forces the issue: they must evacuate, and Mrs. Arrow will sell the house later. But Ben's dog has just had pups, who cannot be evacuated. Ben vows to stay. Joe, his own home swept away, joins him, and finally Kara and Mrs. Arrow agree to stay too. Though Mom worries and the waters are rising, Ben knows they will manage.

A divorce initially disrupts the Arrow family, yet they recover to become a stronger unit than before. In a subplot we watch the reformation of a neighborhood tough as the family befriends him (a story begun in the author's *The Emancipation of Joe Tepper*). The use of a dog and her pups as a multiple symbol — of renewal, of a fatherless family, of a mother's devotion — makes for a preachy but plausible ending.

Ages 10-13

Also available in:
No other form known

D

201

Distad, Audree

The Dream Runner

Harper & Row Publishers, Inc., 1977.
(151 pages)

IDENTITY, SEARCH FOR
MATURATION
    Courage, meaning of
    Death: of friend
    Goals
    Loneliness
    Perseverance

Sam McKee, almost thirteen, likes to run, alone and just for the joy of running. "He didn't run for prizes.... That was for other people, people he only heard about." During the summer Sam works hard cleaning out cattle pens, for he and his mother need the money, having been abandoned by his father years before. The unpleasant work is lightened by the yarns of Clete, Sam's co-worker, whose grandfather was a Native American. Among other things, Clete tells Sam about the vision quest that Indian boys undertook in their passage to manhood. One day Sam's mother gets word that her husband has died, and deciding "to do the decent thing," she sets off on a journey of several days to the funeral. Next day, Clete does not arrive at work, and Sam finds him ill at home. Rushing off for the doctor, Sam returns to find Clete dead, apparently from a stroke. Having lost a father and a best friend within days, Sam feels the need of some word, some guidance. Alone he sets off for the mountains and on the way meets Mrs. Em, a retired schoolteacher, who knows the mountains and their wild horses well. She tells him how to find the vision site, where the young braves sat, waiting for power, waiting for selfhood. Sam makes the rugged climb to the site, but injures his ankle on the way. Thinking it only sprained, he spends the night at the site, then heads back down. But now the pain in his ankle is so great that he passes out again and again, dreaming of horses and his mother. Then, in a vision, a runner leads him to the road, where Mrs. Em, worried by his long absence, finds him and gets him to a hospital. The ankle is broken but will mend, and he will run again. As they talk, Mrs. Em helps Sam see that his vision "was mostly like yourself. As if you were looking for yourself." Sam agrees, "It's like having something to live up to ... finally ... something to live up to."

This is a powerful, thought-provoking story of a lonely, grieving boy's passage to manhood. Sam's endurance and need for self-knowledge are revelations to him, and his climb down the mountain, setting successive short goals — reach the clump of trees, then the fence post, then the cottonwood — is a paradigm of growing up, which no one can do all at once. The author's description of rugged landscape is of a high order, and her use of Native American culture is both sure and respectful.

Ages 10-13

Also available in:
Paperbound — *The Dream Runner*
Harper & Row Publishers, Inc.

202

Dixon, Paige, pseud.

May I Cross Your Golden River?

Atheneum Publishers, 1975.
(262 pages)

DEATH: Attitude toward
    Amyotrophic lateral sclerosis
    Courage, meaning of
    Family: unity
    Sibling: relationships

Eighteen-year-old Jordan's life has been happy and commonplace. He is part of a close-knit, if fatherless, family, where mother and youngster are mutually respectful. He plays tennis, has a girl friend, and thinks he may one day become a lawyer. The sudden weakness in his knees is at first dismissed as "tennis knee." Later, when he loses the use of one leg and cannot raise his arm, he decides to see his family doctor, who recommends tests at the Mayo Clinic. The finding is amyotrophic lateral sclerosis, Lou Gehrig's disease, progressive, incurable, and fatal. At first he is furious at the doctor for being unable to cure him. Then he fastens his hopes on the chance of a wrong diagnosis, or, failing that, the possibility that the disease will arrest itself. But his brother warns: "Be ready. Don't tell yourself fancy stories and have to be jolted out of them later on." Coming home, Jordan looks around the house with aching nostalgia. His emotions surprise him: the sudden fighting of tears at being given a puppy, nearly unbearable gratitude for the kindness and concern of his family, and his anger that the family doctor cannot stop the disease either. Slowly Jordan admits to himself the truth of the disease and his own limits. "Discipline" and "Carpe Diem" — seize the day — become his words. He considers suicide once, but decides against it. Illness or not, life goes on, as his family prepares for a wedding and a birth. As the disease progresses, Jordan makes known his preferences for a memorial service and arranges to donate his body to science. Two goals he must achieve before he is bedridden: to be best man at his brother's wedding and to take part in the christening of his sister's baby. A few weeks after the christening, Jordan collapses and is carried to bed. As the book ends, he is still alive but too weak now to talk.

Though Jordan's death is finally imminent, the reader is left not with the grievousness of his dying, but with the value of his life. Throughout his illness, he, his family, and his friends clear-sightedly struggle to transform their fear and grief into words and deeds that allow Jordan the dignity of dying in his own way. His mother resists over-protecting her son; his brother listens steadily through all of Jordan's changing moods; and his best friend simply treats the boy with respect. Jordan's realistic struggle is not melodrama but a moving affirmation of life.

Ages 12 and up

Also available in:
Cassette for the Blind — *May I Cross Your Golden River?*
Library of Congress

D

203

Dobrin, Arnold

Gilly Gilhooley: A Tale of Ireland
Color illustrations by the author.
Crown Publishers, Inc., 1976.
(32 pages counted)

PROBLEM SOLVING
  Anger
  Dependence/Independence

Gilly Gilhooley is clever, Irish, quick-tempered, and old enough to seek work — a volatile mixture, as we shall see. Warned by his father not to lose his temper but to "remember the laughter that is in you," Gilly sets off on his quest. At the first farm he comes to, he lands a job, hard work that he does diligently until one day he arrives a bit late and his boss bawls him out. Quick to anger, Gilly tells his boss to "go to the Devil" and quits. His second job at a larger farm ends similarly when he is shown to a hayloft to sleep in after a hard day's work. His third job is at a small, poor farm. His first supper there is several fish heads and tails on a platter and two small potatoes aswim in watery soup. About to explode once more, Gilly instead tears off his shirt and makes as if to swim after the potatoes. The farm family laughs —

and laughs again when Gilly returns the next day with only the heads and tails of fish he has caught, saying he thought they never ate the "in-betweens." Not only does the family then feed their worker better, but Gilly himself, recognizing the worth of laughter, seldom loses his temper again.

A boy has reasonable grievances about how he is treated, but he expresses them unreasonably — the upshot being that everyone's temper rises. Once he learns to couch his complaints in jokes, he finds that his employer not only laughs but sets things right.

Ages 5-8

Also available in:
No other form known

204

Dodd, Wayne

A Time of Hunting

The Seabury Press, Inc., 1975.
(128 pages)

MATURATION
VALUING/VALUING: Moral/Ethical
Ambivalence, feelings of
Boy-girl relationships
Decision making
Nature: respect for

During the Great Depression, hunting is a way of life to fourteen-year-old Jess, his dad, and their dog, Queenie. After Queenie loses some of her sense of smell, Jess's dad pays $50, a large sum in those days, to buy a purebred hound. He and Jess have high hopes for the new dog, but it proves to be, as Dad puts it, "a purebred back-of-the-sedan coon hound." The dog is returned, but Jess vows to buy it back with money he will earn from selling animal skins. Yet after killing an opossum, the first large animal he has killed, Jess vomits. His feelings about hunting seem to be changing, and when he finally overcomes his shyness towards Imogene, a local girl, he tells her about them; she can only say she is glad he told her. Jess's dad offers advice, but this is no help either. The boy's distaste for guns and violence mounts after a tense confrontation with another boy who wants to make a game of their shooting at each other. Then Jess witnesses a fight in which a man is fatally injured, and he is called on to identify the assailant. Still determined to earn money to buy the dog, Jess again goes hunting. Queenie trees a raccoon, and during the ensuing melee Jess must club it on the head to kill it. The next day, rather than skinning the raccoon, Jess sits wondering what the creature is really worth. He concludes that the dog costs too much; he is not worth killing for. The raccoon Jess buries in the woods; hunting, he decides, is not something he will do much.

The boy in this first-person narrative tries to sort through his conflicting feelings about hunting and then to explain them to a girl. He loves the hunt itself but dislikes the hunt's object, killing an animal. Parallel to his resolving this issue is the change in his relations with Imogene, from a boyish showing off to a sharing of feelings with her. The story is neither pro- nor anti-hunting but rather a natural unfolding of events toward a believable resolution.

Ages 11-14

Also available in:
No other form known

205

Dolan, Edward Francis and Richard B. Lyttle

Bobby Clarke

Black/white photographs (collection).
Doubleday & Company, Inc., 1977.
(94 pages)

SPORTS/SPORTSMANSHIP
  Diabetes
  Leader/Leadership

We see Bobby Clarke, a real-life professional hockey player, first strap on skates when he is four, a late starter in the hockey-crazy town of Flin Flon, Manitoba. Thereafter his consuming ambition is to be a hockey player. But his talent seems confined to team play, and coaches in youth leagues consider him average. And after learning that Bobby, at fifteen, has diabetes, they advise him to quit. Still, the boy insists on playing. A medical specialist, pointing to other athletes who have diabetes, says there is no reason he cannot continue, provided he takes insulin daily and sticks to a special diet. Bobby's entrance to junior hockey at seventeen is unspectacular, but in three years he rises to become one of the premier players in the league. Yet his diabetes keeps professional scouts at a distance. Finally chosen in the second round of the draft by the Philadelphia Flyers, Bobby proceeds to spark the team and in his third year is named captain — an acknowledgment of his leadership and aggressive play. Bobby then leads the Flyers to two consecutive championships in the mid-70s and is voted Most Valuable Player in three out of four years.

Here is a standard biography of a professional athlete that, for the most part, confines itself to events, giving them little background. Clarke's diabetes and his aggressive, sometimes violent play are superficially dealt with as facts, not as keys to understanding who Clarke is. Still, children having diabetes should benefit from seeing how Clarke has successfully met the exacting requirements of professional hockey.

Ages 10-12

Also available in:
No other form known

206

D

Dragonwagon, Crescent

When Light Turns Into Night

Color illustrations by Robert Andrew Parker.
Harper & Row Publishers, Inc., 1975.
(32 pages)

NATURE: Appreciation of
  Privacy, need for

Ellen is a friendly young girl with a compulsion to be by herself "when light turns into night." As evening comes, she must "go away and be alone and hear no noises." Her parents understand, and remind Ellen only to be back for supper. Leaving the farmhouse, Ellen races up a hill through tall grass standing like water, and there lies down watching and listening and smelling for "the night about to happen." And as she savors the day's passage to evening, she feels both here and now and far away. As "that time between night and light" gives way to the dark, Ellen leaves for a "people place." Yet she knows she will be back again for that magic moment.

This relaxing, introspective story, told in the first-person, is written in free verse whose sensuous images and repeated phrases mark a child's contentment and delight at evening. Direct, unadorned illustrations make clear the naturalness of solitary communion with nature.

Also available in:
No other form known

207

Dragonwagon, Crescent

Will It Be Okay?

Color illustrations by Ben Shecter.
Harper & Row Publishers, Inc., 1977.
(32 pages)

FEAR
Communication: parent/child
Security/Insecurity

The little girl in this book worries about many things: big dogs, snakes, thunderstorms, being disliked, and forgetting her lines in the Thanksgiving play. Her mother discusses each fear with her, suggesting ways to overcome it. Fear of a dog: "You stand perfectly still and unafraid and it stops barking, and comes to you, and sits quietly beside you." Fear of snakes: "You keep a flute by your bed and play a song, and the snakes hear, and are quiet, and happy, and love you." Forgetting lines in a play: "You make up new ones then and there." In short, even if all of her fears come true, everything will "be okay." When the little girl asks what would happen if her mother died, the mother says that the love between them would not die, and so life would go on.

Told in dialogue, this story shows how a close and responsive relationship between parent and child could help a child confront fears and perhaps overcome them. Some of the mother's reassurance is realistic, some is farfetched. Throughout their talk, the love between parent and child is evident.

Also available in:
No other form known

208

Dragonwagon, Crescent

Wind Rose

Black/white illustrations by Ronald Himler.
Harper & Row Publishers, Inc., 1976.
(31 pages)

CHILDBIRTH
Love, meaning of

The child Wind Rose is conceived in love. Her mother writes, "Your father was inside me and we were wrapped so tight and close and loving...." While she is in the womb, both parents think of her, wonder what she will be like. Mother explains how her body changed: "I got round as a pear, I got round as a peach, I got round as the moon!" Wind Rose is born at home with only a midwife attending. For mother, the birth is both joyful and difficult: "I had to work and work and breathe and breathe.... The hole you came out of me through was a stretching, burning circle." Wind Rose is named after the summer wind blowing on that day.

In jubilant, poetic language, a mother writes a testimony of love to her daughter. The text and illustrations are frank; some parents may object to this for young children.

Ages 4-8

Also available in:
No other form known

209

Duczman, Linda

The Baby-Sitter

Color photographs by Brent Jones.
Raintree Publishers, Ltd., 1977.
(30 pages)

BABY-SITTER
Separation anxiety

A young boy's parents are going out for the evening, and although his grandparents usually stay with him, tonight he will have a baby-sitter. He is afraid his parents may never come home. He would then be left with the baby-sitter forever. He explains to his mother that he needs no sitter, but she is not convinced. He wonders if the baby-sitter will be mean to him, and he thinks of ways to get even. The baby-sitter arrives, and her name is Holly. She asks him if he wants to pop some popcorn. They like the same television programs. Holly has even brought a book to read aloud — a book he likes. "Holly is nice," the boy muses. "Maybe I'm going to like having a baby-sitter."

Young children with similar fears about baby-sitters may be encouraged to discuss their worries after hearing this story. Full-page photographs enhance the narrative, which is good for reading aloud.

Ages 4-7

Also available in:
No other form known

210

Dunnahoo, Terry

Who Cares About Espie Sanchez?

E. P. Dutton & Company, Inc., 1975.
(152 pages)

FOSTER HOME
IDENTITY, SEARCH FOR
REJECTION: Parental
Crime/Criminals
Death: of sibling
Friendship: making friends
Life style: change in
Running away
Self, attitude toward: respect

Fifteen-year-old Espie Sanchez runs away from home when her mother's boy friend tries to molest her. But it is Espie the police arrest, because it is the third time she has run away. She is threatened with being sentenced to juvenile detention, but a neighborhood foster mother, Mrs. Garcia, agrees to have Espie live with her instead, if necessary. Sure enough, when Espie's mother tells a judge she never again wants to see her, the girl is placed with Mrs. Garcia. Espie's roommate, Denise, another of Mrs. Garcia's foster daughters, is a member of the Law Enforcement Explorer Group (L.E.E.G.), an organization which trains young people as police assistants. Espie is drawn to the idea, and when the police academy accepts her, she begins a tough training course in eight all-day Saturday sessions. Though she can hardly endure the strict discipline, the physical fitness courses, and the difficult classroom instruction, she perseveres and passes the mid-term exam. Meanwhile her twelve-year-old brother, Julian, has come to see her a few times at Mrs. Garcia's, often enough for Espie to see that Julian has been "popping pills." But before she has a chance to try to persuade him to quit, he dies of an overdose. Grief-stricken, Espie tries to run away again, but Denise and her friend Carlos follow and persuade her to come back. Espie wants revenge for her brother's death. Thus she discloses to the narcotics bureau the name of Julian's supplier, and buys drugs from him twice herself, as evidence against him. With adequate evidence, the police arrest him. By now, Espie's training at the academy has ended. Mrs. Garcia sews her a uniform, and when graduation day arrives, there are her new friends — Mrs. Garcia, Denise, Carlos, and several people from the police force — on hand to honor her.

The kindness and loyalty of a foster mother and a roommate and the encouragement of several police officers influence a high-spirited girl to set her sights and focus her energies. Espie's stubbornness and will help her gain self-respect and pride for the first time in her life.

Ages 10-12

Also available in:
Talking Book — *Who Cares About Espie Sanchez?*
Library of Congress

211

Duvoisin, Roger Antoine

Periwinkle

Color illustrations by the author.
Alfred A. Knopf, Inc., 1976.
(29 pages counted)

COMMUNICATION: Misunderstandings
  Friendship: making friends

Periwinkle is a lonely giraffe, the only creature she knows who speaks English. Lamenting to herself the lack of anyone to talk to, she is astonished when a frog announces that she speaks English, too. It turns out that Lotus, the frog, has also longed for someone to talk to, and the two begin talking six to the dozen. But with each

unable to force the other to listen, the two part in disgust. Later, Periwinkle reasons that she should have listened, and Lotus reproaches herself similarly. Each absolutely insists that the other talk. Their insistence leads to an argument, and the argument to dangerous inattention. A jackal pounces on the frog — but drops her when Periwinkle gives chase. Again Lotus departs, and again the giraffe is lonely. She now realizes that they must talk *with* each other. Fortunately, Lotus sees the same, and they begin swapping childhood memories. They are soon inseparable friends.

Here is a nicely turned lesson in how a common language divides as well as unites; the trick is to use language generously. Both giraffe and frog only see their mistakes after making them and figuring out what went wrong. Young readers can enjoy the story for itself, and learn that no one should do all the listening or all the talking.

Ages 4-7

Also available in:
No other form known

212

Duvoisin, Roger Antoine

Petunia's Treasure

Color illustrations by the author.
Alfred A. Knopf, Inc., 1975.
(30 pages counted)

GREED
  Boasting

Petunia the goose discovers a closed trunk on the bottom of the river, and decides it must be full of treasure. She returns to the barnyard and gaily informs her friends that she is now rich. The other barnyard animals discuss this turn of events among themselves and decide that Petunia can well afford to buy all of them gifts. In the days that follow, they besiege her with outlandish suggestions and demands — even arguing among themselves as to who is most deserving among them. Petunia, distressed by this discord, returns to the river to check her treasure — and to her relief discovers the trunk open and empty. She breaks the news to the barnyard animals as gaily as before, and they realize, with embarrassment, that they have been foolish and greedy.

This amusing tale illustrates the perils of bragging and greed. Though Petunia herself is not greedy, she gives into arrogance and inflated pride over wealth that is purely imaginary. This is one of several stories about Petunia.

Ages 5-8

Also available in:
Talking Book — *Petunia's Treasure*
Library of Congress

213

Dygard, Thomas J.

Winning Kicker

William Morrow & Company, Inc., 1978.
(190 pages)

WOMEN'S RIGHTS
  Leader/Leadership
  Prejudice: sexual
  Sports/Sportsmanship

In his thirty-seventh and final year coaching football at Higgins High School, tough, blunt, decisive John Earlingham looks forward to a great season — until seventeen-year-old Kathy Denver, a senior, tries out for place-kicker. Nothing he can do will dissuade her from trying out. As for his hopes she will fail, Kathy proves to be his best place-kicker. And as for his fear her presence will disrupt the team, it soon comes true. During practice the players watch the crowds and reporters out to watch Kathy. Opposed by a weak team in its opening game, Higgins plays so badly that Earlingham blames his team for making a circus of practice. Though Kathy kicks the crucial point that wins the game, 7-6, she later quits because she feels that her presence is a detriment to the team's performance. By now, Earlingham knows the team can solve its problems only if she remains, but he does not try to change her mind; he just silently approves when she gives in to the players' persuasion and rejoins the team. This time, the players concentrate on football. Then the coach of the team Higgins is to face that week questions Kathy's eligibility and calls her very presence on the field unfair because no player will be rough with a girl. These questions go unresolved and Higgins, aided by Kathy's field goal, wins again. Before the next game, against the powerhouse of the conference, the State High School Athletic Association urges the coach to withhold her from play "in the interests of fairness to all concerned," but Earlingham refuses. Kathy is ruled eligible. But early in the game, a player is blocked into her and she falls, breaking an ankle. Nonetheless, Higgins sweeps to a 47-0 victory. The next day Coach Earlingham, who has given special athletic letters to only two players, gives a special letter to Kathy for leadership.

Told from a coach's viewpoint, this story is only secondarily about a girl who plays on a football team and primarily about a coach who sees his job as making men out of boys — and his perplexity when one of the boys is a girl. His solution to the different courses of action urged on him by feminists and traditionalists is to treat Kathy as he would any male player — on her merits.

Ages 11-14

Also available in:
No other form known

214

Eisenberg, Phyllis Rose

A Mitzvah Is Something Special

Black/white illustrations by Susan Jeschke.
Harper & Row Publishers, Inc., 1978.
(31 pages)

GRANDPARENT: Love for
  Jewish

Little Lisa's two grandmothers could hardly be nicer, or
less alike. Grandma Esther tells stories, makes quilts,
and teaches Lisa to make strudel. She also explains the
meaning of "mitzvah": "A mitzvah, Lisa, is like a good
deed, only much more.... A mitzvah is a very big
blessing." Grandma Dorrie is a "swinger." She owns
two wigs, serves gumdrop wine, and plays the flute.
One weekend Lisa plans a mitzvah for both grandmothers: she invites them to sleep over at her house. Esther
makes strudel, which Dorrie finds delicious. Dorrie
plays the flute, and Esther and Lisa dance. All three
agree it is the best mitzvah ever.

The little girl who narrates this story adores her unalike
grandmothers equally — for different reasons. Lively
illustrations make the characters more vivid.

Ages 5-8

Also available in:
No other form known

215

Elfman, Blossom

A House for Jonnie O.

Houghton Mifflin Co., 1976.
(175 pages)

UNWED MOTHER
  Communication: parent-child
  Dependence/Independence
  Parental: absence
  Pregnancy
  School: pupil-teacher relationships
  Suicide: consideration of

Sixteen-year-old Joanne "Jonnie" Olson is pregnant
and unmarried. Ceaseless arguments with her divorced
mother, special school classes with other pregnant teenagers which teach her nothing she wants to know —
everything drives Jonnie to yearn for a home of her
own. There she could raise her child and have her boy
friend, Billy, visit, all without interference from her
mother and teachers. Jonnie's mother's intention to
marry her own boy friend, Abel, increases the girl's
longing to move out; she wants no part of a household
that has dispensed with her father. As for him, surely
the lure of a home and a new baby will bring him, like
Billy, rushing to her side. Three pregnant teenage classmates join Jonnie in renting the house, the four pooling
their welfare checks for what none could afford alone.
But two move elsewhere, and Jonnie realizes that her
dreamed-of independence may be short-lived. Turning
to Billy for help, she finds he wants her to sell her infant
for a "stake" with which they can begin a new life.
Revolted, Jonnie returns to her mother's home to keep
an appointment with her father. Instead of his comforting presence, she finds only an impersonal letter and
money. Reeling under disappointment, Jonnie rushes
back to her own house, her mood suicidal. But she

decides she wants her own life and that of her child more than the peace of death. After her baby is born, a confused, desperate Jonnie turns to Abel for comfort and advice, and chooses to keep the child, though it means she will lose Billy. She wants also to try to understand her mother, who seems both loving and loyal.

Unhappiness at home and at school drives an unwed, pregnant teenage girl to seek independence and love elsewhere. All of her anger at her lot is directed at her mother, to whom she has never been close. The advice of several teachers, who thought they had no influence on their pregnant students, helps the girl to recognize the value of her life and reject the thought of suicide. Jonnie's often half-baked reason is clearly not helped by her frequent resort to superstition and movie magazines. If, with the birth of her baby, she appears to mature with almost magical rapidity, this does not detract from the persuasive realism, especially in the dialogue, of her story up to then.

Ages 12 and up

Also available in:
Braille — *A House for Jonnie O.*
Library of Congress

Paperbound — *A House for Jonnie O.*
Bantam Books, Inc.

216

Erickson, Russell E.

Warton and Morton

Lothrop, Lee & Shepard Co., 1976.
(64 pages)

SEPARATION FROM LOVED ONES
  Communication: misunderstandings
  Sibling: relationships

E

Warton and Morton are brother toads living comfortably under an old tree stump. At home Warton likes to clean and Morton enjoys cooking. After finishing the spring cleaning, Warton persuades his brother to go on a camping trip with him, and the two pack their gear and set out the next morning. That night, Warton and Morton decide to camp by a little stream. While Warton sets up the tent, Morton prepares a delicious meal, and both conclude that the trip is off to a fine start. But during the night there is a flash flood, and Warton and Morton are separated. Warton searches for his brother downstream, where the water runs into a swamp. There, a frog and a loon join Warton in searching, but to no avail. The next day Warton builds a raft to explore the swamp further. Soon he meets two muskrat brothers, Orville and Hiram, who promise to help him. But first the three of them attend the Muskrat Spring Dance and Festival — which is interrupted with the news that the muskrat town has been flooded by the beavers' dam upstream. The muskrats decide to confront the beavers, but Warton, instead of joining them, continues searching for his brother. Taking his raft upstream he encounters the muskrats and beavers, anyway — and finds Morton. Just as the muskrats have helped Warton, the beavers have helped Morton. The beavers tell how they tried to discuss the dam-building with the muskrats, but the muskrats wouldn't listen and threw stones at them. The toad brothers help the muskrats and beavers settle their differences, each pointing out how wonderfully kind the animals have been to them. Then the two toad brothers sail on the raft for home.

The toad brothers provide an example of satisfying sibling relationships and concern for others. Their encounters with two quarreling groups of animals illustrate the importance of communication between neighbors, as well as between friends. This is a sequel to *A Toad for Tuesday.*

Ages 4-7

Also available in:
Cassette for the Blind — *Warton and Morton*
Library of Congress

Paperbound — *Warton and Morton*
Dell Publishing Company, Inc.

217

Ernst, Kathryn

Charlie's Pets

Color illustrations by Arthur Cumings.
Crown Publishers, Inc., 1978.
(32 pages counted)

PETS
  Pets: responsibility for

Charlie has never been allowed to have pets, and so when he discovers three roaches under the kitchen sink, he puts them in a jar and hides it in his room. He cares for the roaches, studies roaches in insect books, and is aghast when his mother, who has discovered he has them — and discovered more around the house, and called an exterminator — adamantly insists he get rid of them. Charlie argues to keep them, but his mother's edict stands, and he takes the roaches to school, where they become the subject of a class science project. The first evening his pets are gone, Charlie spends chiefly in his room, drawing pictures of them and of all the other pets he wishes he had. The next morning, when Charlie's mother knocks on his door, he does not want to let her in. But lo, she has brought him a present — two fluffy rabbits to be his very own pets.

Children who long for a pet will understand Charlie's passion and resentment, though not all children will end up as fortunate as he. He does, however, provide an example in assuming responsibility for pets.

Ages 5-8

Also available in:
No other form known

218

Ernst, Kathryn

Mr. Tamarin's Trees

Color illustrations by Diane de Groat.
Crown Publishers, Inc., 1976.
(30 pages counted)

NATURE: Respect for
  Nature: appreciation of

Mr. Herbert Tamarin so dislikes raking leaves that he loses sleep brooding about it. He broods so long that, despite his wife's warning, he cuts down all the trees in his yard. That winter, he notices that the snow — formerly screened by trees — drifts high against the house. In spring, the ground becomes wet and spongy, for there are no tree roots to soak up rain. And in summer, the house — which had been shaded and cool — becomes an oven. The Tamarins decide to sell the house — but no one wants a treeless property. The Tamarins then plant some young trees, and after many years, when their house is again shaded, they are content. And Herbert no longer bristles at falling autumn leaves.

With gentle wit, the reader is shown the unexpected cost of mindlessly maiming the natural environment. Moreover, one can infer a lesson here about disproportionate fussing over the commonplace.

Ages 5-8

Also available in:
No other form known

219

Erskine, Jim

The Snowman

Color illustrations by the author.
Crown Publishers, Inc., 1978.
(32 pages counted)

ARGUING
COOPERATION: in Play
  Problem solving

Berkley, a young bear, likes to play in the snow. Meeting his friend Calvin, he suggests that the two of them build a large snowman. And so they do — but once finished, they begin arguing over who owns it, and they get into such a snow fight that the snowman is ruined and they themselves are cold, tired, and wet. Later, after warming up and drying off, the two return to the snowy outdoors to resume their fight; instead, they contemplate their ruined snowman. Chastened, they set about building some little snowmen and go sledding together.

In this simple story, two little friends work together until a selfish disagreement arises. In the ensuing fight, they settle nothing and unwittingly destroy the fruits of their cooperation. They — and young readers — see that fighting is unproductive but cooperating gets results.

Ages 3-6

Also available in:
No other form known

220

Etter, Les

Get Those Rebounds!

Black/white illustrations by James Calvin.
Hastings House Publishers, Inc., 1978.
(119 pages)

SPORTS/SPORTSMANSHIP
  Expectations
  Identity, search for
  Reputation
  Self, attitude toward: confidence
  Sibling: rivalry

Despairing of ever making his tall lanky body perform as well as his Los Angeles Laker brother's, Rick Hanley, a fifteen-year-old black youth, has quit the high school basketball team before his clumsiness and hot temper get him cut. But soon afterward Rick joins a city team coached by the Reverend Jerry Caswell, a former college All-American. Jerry never compares him with his brother, only pushes him to do his best with what he has got. Soon Rick is making shots he thought he never could. As the season progresses, Rick makes friends with Russ Williams, a teammate who has dropped out of school to help his widowed mother support their family. Following a loss to the Panthers, current league champions, Rick meets Russ's older brother, Frank — an undependable sort who does nothing at all to help the family. It is then that Rick realizes Russ also lives under the reputation of an older brother. But Russ tries to lead his own life. One day Russ misses an important practice before a championship rematch with the Panthers. Concerned, Rick goes looking and finds Russ with Frank, who insists on driving the boys home. Soon the police are following; a high speed chase ensues, and when caught the three are arrested. The car they are in is stolen. Luckily, Rick and Russ are immediately released to Jerry's custody, and Jerry explains the situation to parents and authorities so that Russ and Rick are cleared before the game. (Frank faces a hearing.) At the game, both play so outstandingly that they are offered positions on next year's high school varsity. Russ declines — he cannot go back to school. But Jerry surprises him with the news that Frank, as a condition of his probation in Jerry's custody, will take Russ's place as bread-winner. Now both boys decline the offer; they want to go on playing for Jerry.

This fast-moving story, easy to read, is filled with basketball action. It explores many aspects of sportsmanship, and details as well the hard work an athlete must go through to be in top form. Within its basketball frame, the book shows the struggle of two young men to move away from their older brothers' differing reputations and to build their own identities. Rick, for instance, learns a slower playing tempo that allows him tighter coordination. From this, other self-discipline follows.

Ages 10-13

Also available in:
No other form known

221

Ewing, Kathryn

A Private Matter

Black/white illustrations by Joan Sandin.
Harcourt Brace Jovanovich, Inc., 1975.
(88 pages)

PARENT/PARENTS: Single
  Friendship: meaning of
  Imagination

Nine-year-old Marcy lives with her divorced mother, who sells real estate. In fact, the mother has just sold the house next door, and Marcy hopes that Mr. and Mrs. Endicott, the buyers, will bring with them children her age. But her elderly neighbors have no children at all. Still, Marcy likes Mr. Endicott's smile and easy warmth and begins visiting him. She helps him hang pictures, repair an old martin house, and even shops with both of the Endicotts on Saturdays. For school, Marcy writes a composition about repairing the martin house, beginning, "Today my father and I . . . ." The paper is returned with her first "Very Good." She shows it to Mr. Endicott, who says he can see why her teacher would think so highly of it — but Marcy's mother is worried by the girl's reference to Mr. Endicott as her father and reminds her daughter that this is only make-believe. Marcy is not, however, making believe how apprehensive she is about spending a weekend with her real father, whom she has not seen in years. When she discusses her fears with Mr. Endicott, he suggests that her father may feel just as frightened. Going further, he adds that she just might have a good time, but Marcy becomes angry at this and yells, "He's never come to see me all these years . . . I don't want him to be my father at all!" Some time later, Marcy returns to the Endicotts' but finds the door locked. When Mr. Endicott finally appears, he tells the girl that Mrs. Endicott has died. He himself will move back to the town where his friends are. Marcy resents the decision, and regards his moving away as a rejection of her. A few days later, Marcy and Mr. Endicott are working in his garden, and he remarks that Marcy will be moving away too, because her mother is remarrying. Marcy protests: "I wouldn't have!" When Mr. Endicott finally does move away, the girl writes a composition about him called "Going Away." She ends by writing: "Now I see my father everywhere . . . it hurts so hard . . . it is better to go away. Soon I am going away with my mother and Mr. William Compton. P.S. It is a very private matter."

Marcy's friendship with Mr. Endicott is of a kind new to her, and it stirs her imagination. She gets on well with her mother, but her mother corrects her a good deal, which can hurt. Mr. Endicott takes her as she is. Marcy's writing about him as her father is never made much of by her mother or by Mr. Endicott. The reader is left feeling that Marcy's perceptiveness and sensitivity will enable her to build a satisfying relationship with her new father. The book at one point explains that custody of children is as a rule given to the mother, a dated generality.

Ages 8-10

Also available in:
Braille — *A Private Matter*
Library of Congress

222

Fanshawe, Elizabeth

Rachel

Color illustrations by Michael Charlton.
Bradbury Press, Inc., 1975.
(27 pages counted)

WHEELCHAIR, DEPENDENCE ON
    Handicaps

Young Rachel needs a wheelchair to get around, but she does most of the things other children her age do. She goes to school with her sister, takes her turn feeding the school gerbil, and helps clean up when class is over. Rachel's friends like to push her, but she can push herself and not always slowly. Because she cannot board the bus, her mother picks her up at school. At home, when her grandmother comes for tea, Rachel helps get things ready. Then her father sits next to her. She plays games with her Brownie troop, swims almost unaided, and plans to learn to ride a horse soon. She and her family have vacationed in the mountains, where Rachel

took some funny pictures. She often talks with her father about the many things she could be when she grows up.

This very simple, straightforward story shows that a child restricted to a wheelchair need not necessarily be restricted in her activities, abilities, or fun. Bright, crisp illustrations point up the similarities between all children, handicapped or not.

Ages 4-6

Also available in:
No other form known

223

Farley, Carol J.

The Garden Is Doing Fine

Black/white illustrations by Lynn Sweat.
Atheneum Publishers, 1975.
(185 pages)

DEATH: Attitude Toward
    Guilt, feelings of
    Illnesses: of parent
    Illnesses: terminal

Corrie Sheldon, a high school freshman in Michigan, cannot accept the fact that her father is dying of cancer. Every night Corrie and her mother visit her father at the hospital, and if he is awake he always asks Corrie about his garden. Mrs. Sheldon wants Corrie to tell him that the garden is doing fine even though winter has begun and the garden is dead. But Corrie cannot bring herself to lie, feeling not only that that would be cheating her father but also accepting the idea that he will never come home and see for himself. Corrie thinks a great deal about this warm, vibrant man who cares so much more about people and nature than about money and possessions. And throughout Mr. Sheldon's illness, strangers show her with kind words and attempts at repayment just how great her father's generosity has been. At first Corrie foregoes many high school activities — plays, athletic events — because she feels guilty if not at the hospital with her father or at home taking care of her younger brothers. Gradually she realizes that while her father will eventually die, she will never completely lose him. As with his garden, he has put much of himself into caring for her.

Corrie's refusal to believe that her father is dying leads her into much confusion about herself and him. Only after she realizes that her father will live on in memory is she able to accept his eventual death. The story takes place in late 1945, and imagining that earlier time enhances the book's theme of reminiscence. Corrie's memories of her father are touching and beautifully handled, not depressing. Nor does this book describe Mr. Sheldon's death.

Ages 11 and up

Also available in:
Braille — *The Garden Is Doing Fine*
Library of Congress

224

Fassler, Joan

Howie Helps Himself

Color illustrations by Joe Lasker.
Albert Whitman & Co., 1975.
(32 pages counted)

CEREBRAL PALSY
Perseverance
Wheelchair, dependence on

Howie is a happy little boy who likes things other boys like: eating chocolate ice cream, watching the snow fall,

riding in his father's car. But because Howie has cerebral palsy and needs a wheelchair, there are some things he cannot do — run, jump, hold a pencil, play with blocks. His parents help him do things he cannot do himself. Sometimes his sister finds time to play ball with him or draw him funny pictures. When his grandmother visits, she takes him to the park. Howie likes his family, and school too. He goes every day in a special bus to a special class. The bus has an elevator that lifts him and his wheelchair aboard. At school Howie learns the alphabet, learns to pronounce words, learns to count. He also does exercises to strengthen his arms and legs. But what he wants to learn more than anything else is to move his wheelchair all by himself as his classmates do. His teachers show him the way, but Howie cannot do it. He works at it but sometimes gives up in tears. One day as Howie's father arrives to take him home, Howie looks at him standing in the doorway across the room, takes a deep breath, and turns the wheelchair around by himself. Then he pushes the wheels as far and as hard as he can. When he looks up, he is right in front of his father. He and his father hug and drive home.

Handicapped children may have to acquire special skills and strengths in using special equipment. This same specialness in the way they do things can cause embarrassment or fear in other children, feelings this book seeks to allay. Handicapped children will identify with Howie, but almost any child will recognize Howie's will to get about on his own steam.

Ages 5-8

Also available in:
Cassette — *Howie Helps Himself*
Instruction/Communications Technology, Inc.

Cassette for the Blind — *Howie Helps Himself*
Library of Congress

Filmstrip — *Howie Helps Himself*
Westport Communications

225

Feagles, Anita Macrae

The Year the Dreams Came Back

Atheneum Publishers, 1976.
(146 pages)

MATURATION
SUICIDE: of Parent
  Boy-girl relationships
  Guilt, feelings of
  Parent/Parents: remarriage of

Although a year has passed since teenage Nell's mother committed suicide, Nell has not accepted the loss. Never close to her mother, she mourns her death anyway, hiding an inner dread that she had caused it. Then Nell meets Amy Traynor, older than herself and just moved to town to open a bookstore. Nell introduces Amy to her father, and soon all three have become friends. Father, enjoying Amy's companionship, seems less gloomy, more open. Soon Nell begins to date Gordon Greene, a boy from her neighborhood. Life is changing for the better. In the summer, Amy invites Nell and her father on a week's vacation with her at a friend's summer home. After their return, Nell's father tells her that he and Amy plan to be married. Nell is stunned. She insists that his marrying Amy would ruin everything — and then she runs away. Intercepting her on her way out of town, Gordon insists on going with her. They talk about her violent reaction to her father's decision, and Gordon helps her to see her inner fear that if Amy becomes her stepmother, she will lose Amy too. Calmed by this insight, Nell agrees to go home, able to accept her father and Amy's plans.

For a year after her mother's death, Nell tries to suppress her grief and worry over her mother's suicide. During that time, she does not even permit herself the luxury of daydreams. But with Amy's joining the family, and her own new friendship with Gordon, Nell takes a fresh look at life. The daydreams return.

Ages 11-14

Also available in:
Paperbound — *The Year the Dreams Came Back*
Pocket Books, Inc.

226

Ferry, Charles

Up in Sister Bay

Black/white illustrations by Ted Lewin.
Houghton Mifflin Co., 1975.
(228 pages)

F

BOY-GIRL RELATIONSHIPS
FRIENDSHIP: Meaning of
MATURATION
  Change: accepting
  Nature: appreciation of
  Prejudice: ethnic/racial
  Prejudice: toward handicapped persons

Since childhood, seventeen-year-old Robbie Van Epp has shared a dream with his three best friends, Jim, who is a Chippewa Indian, lively and pretty Livvie, and Charlie, whose apparently worsening physical disorder (which brings on seizures) has not dampened his spirit. For years the four have planned — and saved — to homestead at Loon Lodge, an unspoiled site north of their hometown, Sister Bay, Wisconsin. In the summer of 1939, Robbie is troubled by a series of events that happen in Sister Bay. The town's largest industry, a tannery, is partially destroyed by fire, and Charlie is arrested for arson. On the same night, Alvia Ivors, the tannery owner, dies of heart failure. Grieved by Alvia's death, certain of Charlie's innocence, Robbie concludes that both are victims of a conspiracy led by Herr Doktor, a prominent citizen of Sister Bay. Herr Doktor has long wanted to buy the tannery from Alvia, but she had refused to sell. Was the fire one last move to force her out, and was her timely death more than Herr Doktor had banked on? She was, it seems, in debt to Herr Doktor and he steps in immediately to take over the business. But Robbie, Jim, and Livvie find a new will written by Alvia, specifying that her property is to be otherwise disposed of, and they also find evidence of Herr Doktor's guilt for the fire. To top things off, the will deeds to the four youngsters four horses and whatever tools of Alvia's may help to build their homestead. Charlie is released from jail — soon to be twenty-one, old enough to sign the homestead papers. The dream seems at hand. But Robbie's father has just taken a job in Chicago and wants the family to move there. Robbie, who has just pledged his love to Livvie, is devastated. Then Charlie has a fatal seizure. Suddenly the dream is in ashes. Yet just before Robbie leaves for Chicago, Livvie's father decides to sign the papers for the youngsters. Robbie leaves, already looking forward to his return to Sister Bay.

A summer of setbacks and disasters almost convinces Robbie to put aside a lifelong hope and accept the philosophy that realism means settling for second best. But his girl friend's love and the kindness of older friends, together with his own tenacity, redeem his present and secure his future. These believable characters are sometimes given stiff dialogue, but the mistrust of handicapped people and the anti-Indian prejudice they must combat are all too realistic, especially for the period. Their unwavering love for the land is moving, the mystery they tackle, enticing.

Ages 12 and up

Also available in:
No other form known

227
Fife, Dale

North of Danger
Black/white illustrations by Haakon Saether.
E. P. Dutton & Company, Inc., 1978.
(72 pages)

COURAGE, MEANING OF
TRUST/DISTRUST
   Ambivalence, feelings of
   Risk, taking of
   Secret, keeping

Longyearbyen is the administrative center of the Spitsbergen Islands north of Norway, and for a few days in 1940 its population is one. England, expecting a German invasion, evacuates the people, but twelve-year-old Arne Kristiansen remains behind. Only Arne, trusting no one else, can warn his father, a refugee Norwegian Underground leader wanted by the Nazis and now absent on a scientific expedition 200 miles away. The father must be told not to return, and there is no other way to reach him than by foot. Thus, at the beginning of the dark polar winter, Arne sets off, making slow progress and worried that he will not arrive in time. He takes a short cut across a newly frozen fjord, but near the far shore the ice breaks up; he loses his gear and barely reaches land. But a reclusive trapper, Hans Braun, finds Arne and gives him shelter and new gear. At first glad that Braun offers to accompany him, Arne soon suspects he is a German spy and takes flight on skis. But when Arne comes to a shelter the following day, Braun is there. Fleeing again, Arne plunges into a crevasse. Braun rescues him and takes him back to the hut. Then Braun is stricken with a malaria attack. Looking for medicine, Arne finds a photograph of Hans in a German Army uniform. Confirmed in his suspicions, the boy once again sets off alone, but soon he is overtaken by the conviction that he must trust the man who twice saved his life, and he returns to care for Hans. Recovered after a few days, Hans explains away Arne's suspicions. A chaplain in the German Army during World War I, he had come home a confirmed pacifist. Seeing another war coming, he had left for Spitsbergen and an isolated life. After a rapid journey north, the two reach Arne's father. Though Hans chooses to remain, the Kristiansens escape by a fishing boat.

Needing companionship on a dangerous journey, a boy yet fears that any companion will endanger his father's safety. Readers can readily understand Arne's distrust of Braun, but they may be puzzled over his sudden decision to trust him after all. The terse, exciting narrative is based on a true incident.

Ages 10-12

Also available in:
No other form known

228

Fife, Dale

Who Goes There, Lincoln?

Black/white illustrations by Paul Galdone.
Coward, McCann & Geoghegan, Inc., 1975.
(63 pages)

AFRO-AMERICAN
PROBLEM SOLVING
  Clubs

The membership of the Plum Street Athletic Club (Lincoln, a black youth, presiding; Wilbur and Bunky listening) are astounded that Hands and his Stickballers want to join them. They fail to see that their clubhouse is the attraction — until they are turned out of their enjoyable meeting place. What to do? Lincoln sees his way clear after showing Wilbur and Bunky around the boarded-up firehouse, once an opera house, now soon to be destroyed, on Plum Street. Not only does Lincoln plan to stage an initiation ceremony there, he hopes to save the building for a community center. But how? One way is to prove the building's historical importance. But is a former opera house important enough? Lincoln's investigations turn up nothing except an old woman's mutterings that the building was once a "railroad station." He does find an old notebook, in still older opera costumes, but can make nothing of its references to "bales of cotton." Whatever its past use, the firehouse is fine for the Club initiation, until a policeman comes. Hiding in a cabinet, Lincoln discovers a moving panel that gives onto an underground tunnel. But after exploring it with Wilbur and Bunky, Lincoln is caught by the policeman. Next morning he walks downstairs to face the music, but ends up saving the firehouse. The "railroad station," the tunnel, and the "bales of cotton" suddenly make sense: the opera house was a station on the pre-Civil War underground railroad by which slaves escaped north.

The author deftly weaves a mystery story out of a youngster's search for a new clubhouse and his attempts to preserve a building. By telling enough to whet curiosity about the underground railroad but not enough to satisfy it, the story proves an excellent introduction to this episode in Afro-American history. This is one in a series of books about Lincoln and his family and friends.

Ages 8-10

Also available in:
Paperbound — *Who Goes There, Lincoln?*
Scholastic Book Services

F

229

Fife, Dale

Who'll Vote for Lincoln?

Black/white illustrations by Paul Galdone.
Coward, McCann & Geoghegan, Inc., 1977.
(63 pages)

LEADER/LEADERSHIP
  Creativity
  Honesty/Dishonesty
  School: classmate relationships
  Values/Valuing: moral/ethical

Young Lincoln Farnum has decided to run for the office of class president, basing his campaign on a simple promise to do what is right. Among other things he hopes to get permission from the owner of an empty lot beside the school to use it for a class garden — but he doesn't promise this. Lincoln begins to doubt his strategy when he discovers that his opponent — the class bully, Bill, called "Mooch" — is promising to change cafeteria food, extend recesses, reduce homework, and lengthen vacation time. As the election draws closer, Lincoln still runs his campaign honestly, until Mooch, with the help of his uncle, hands out free peanuts to all the students. Feeling he is sure to lose now, Lincoln promises everyone in his class a chocolate shake if he wins. It is this promise that he thoroughly regrets, knowing he cannot make it good. That is why, on election day, he stands before the class and confesses to trying fraudulently to buy their votes; he is therefore withdrawing his name from the ballot. Lincoln bolts from the room. It is not until he returns that he learns he has been overwhelmingly elected. Later, when he is instrumental in exposing a bookie joint near the school, it appears that with some intercession by a policeman, the class will get its garden.

The point is made that election promises which cannot be kept should not be made; even a candidate for school office has a moral obligation to the voters. Interwoven in this cautionary story, one of several about Lincoln, is a mystery concerning a store-front church which is a cover for a gambling den. Lincoln's part in exposing its real function is almost too good to be true, but it saves the main story from sinking of its own didactic weight.

Ages 8-10

Also available in:
No other form known

230

First, Julia

Amy

Prentice-Hall, Inc., 1975.
(84 pages)

SCHOOL: Achievement/Underachievement
SCHOOL: Classmate Relationships
  Prejudice: ethnic/racial

Amy Hadley, in the sixth grade, finds she cannot stand two things — math and Donald Randall. Not liking to do what she cannot do well, Amy neglects her math assignments and refuses to attend after-school help sessions. Her classmate Donald she thinks will be able to "give lessons in stuffed-shirtedness by the time he's fourteen"; she is continually annoyed by his intolerance of others. Thus, when her mother informs her that no one in her class — including Donald — can be left out of her Halloween party, Amy is highly distressed. Just as she has feared, the party falls apart when Donald's slighting remark to a black classmate starts a fight. The next day, when Amy receives a failure notice in math, she discards it. Soon she is running for class vice-president against Donald — and wins, only to be told that in failing math she has disqualified herself for the office. Having boasted at home of her victory, Amy sees that she must tell her parents about the failure notice and her disqualification. That confession persuades her parents that the punishment she has made for herself is worse than any they could devise. Her parents also decide she will attend the tutoring sessions in math, for she is intelligent and able to succeed when necessary. Of her own accord, Amy becomes more tolerant of Donald, who has apologized to her for being bossy and closed-minded; she thinks he may be able to change, just as she has.

This amusing first-person narrative candidly shows how and why one might combat an inability to work toward success in a school subject one dislikes. Similarly, it shows how an unquestioned dislike for someone with opinions contrary to one's own may display the same prejudice one so heartily disapproves of. Understanding parents and teachers aid Amy in recognizing her own intolerance. Children who have reading difficulties may find this book easy to read and interesting.

Ages 8-11

Also available in:
No other form known

231

First, Julia

Move Over, Beethoven

Franklin Watts, Inc., 1978.
(121 pages)

F

TALENTS: Musical
    Ambivalence, feelings of
    Communication: parent-child
    Decision making
    Expectations
    Freedom, meaning of
    Parental: control
    Problem solving
    School: classmate relationships

Being talented can have its drawbacks. For twelve-year-old Gina it means sacrificing free time after school to practice the piano. Her piano teacher and her mother (her father is dead) both expect her to have a career as a concert pianist and agree that four hours of practice each day is necessary for her advancement. For her part, Gina loves to play the piano ("I could practice ten hours and feel it was ten minutes"), but she is also powerfully drawn to the extra-curricular activities junior high offers, and envies her friends who are free to choose and take part. Sam, her grandfather, understands her feelings, but since he no longer lives with Gina and her mother, she cannot count on his daily support. After a lecture publicizing the orchestra, Gina impulsively decides to audition, even though the rehearsals are two afternoons a week. She passes the audition but does not tell her mother, fearful of her disapproval and feeling guilty of seeming ingratitude and frivolousness just when her mother has resolved to buy her a very expensive baby grand piano. In the orchestra, Gina meets Joshua, a boy involved in several school activities who sings at the Metropolitan Opera as well. He seems to have none of Gina's problems of choice. As her friendship with Joshua and her enjoyment of the orchestra deepen, so does the conflict of loyalty within her, and she seeks out Sam's advice. He agrees that she deserves other interests and talks with her mother, but her mother does not see that she is living Gina's life for her. Soon after, her mother announces that she has heard of a school in New York for musically talented children and is determined to send Gina there. The idea of leaving her own school and friends is unthinkable to Gina. Now she goes to Joshua for help, but he asks *her* advice instead. What with his duties at the Met and his other activities, his parents disapprove of his own busy schedule. Astonished to see the similarity of their difficulties, and disappointed to see that Joshua cannot help her, Gina absently repeats her mother's advice instead of talking with Joshua as a friend and fellow sufferer; he leaves abruptly, hurt and angry. At home, Gina finds her mother filling out the New York school application but dismayed by the tuition cost for out-of-towners. Gina seizes the opportunity to express herself honestly, and her mother understands. Together they work out a compromise between piano-practice and time for other things — right in town.

Gina's thirteenth year brings conflict. Now in junior high, she wants the freedom to explore chances open to her, and less pressure to perfect the particular talent she has always shown. Gina's mother is the last to know her daughter's thoughts, both because Gina withholds them from her and because she believes so strongly that "a woman has to have a career," a view that may have assumed great importance in her own life with the death of Gina's father five years earlier. Gina is fortunate in having friends and another adult, her grandfather, with whom she can talk, although ultimately she finds she must resolve her conflict by initiating a talk with her mother. Taking that responsibility, Gina finds her mother willing to compromise: music can remain an important part of her life, but that life can accommodate other activities as well. This sensitive first-person account may well stimulate discussion between parents and children of offspring's rights.

Ages 10-13

Also available in:
Cassette for the Blind — *Move Over, Beethoven*
Library of Congress

232

Flory, Jane Trescott

The Unexpected Grandchildren
Color illustrations by Carolyn Croll.
Houghton Mifflin Co., 1977.
(30 pages)

LONELINESS
SHARING/NOT SHARING
　Life style: change in

A child daring to set foot on the Newtons' perfect lawn is summarily ordered off; and in the Newton house, "not so much as a shoe [is] out of place." That children never come to their house, even on Halloween, does not trouble the Newtons — for children make messes. Consequently, a letter promising a visit and signed "Your Unexpected Grandchildren" jolts the couple, especially since they have no children. Mr. Newton dismisses the letter as a bad joke, but his wife, looking less lonely than before, bakes cookies — "just in case." Days pass and they wait — first anxiously, then frantically — until they notice the letter is addressed to someone else. Seeing his wife grow paler than before, Mr. Newton places an advertisement announcing a party on Saturday: "Wanted: Grandchildren to borrow." But no one comes; they feel terrible. Determined to hold a party, Mr. Newton persuades a little boy to invite other children, and eventually twenty-three show up. The Newton home becomes a madhouse — and they love it. Scarcely are the children out the door before the Newtons begin preparing for next Saturday's visit, sure they now have enough of everything: "toys and treats and LOVE."

That an older couple arrange their lives rigidly means they seal themselves from the world, especially from children. Once they welcome children — and confusion — into their lives, they happily discover that every day need not be the same as the one before. Though this story provides an extreme case of seclusion and a near-ideal resolution to it, children may be helped to understand why some adults avoid them, and how sharing can make one happy.

Ages 4-7

Also available in:
No other form known

233

Fowler, Carol

Daisy Hooee Nampeyo
Black/white photographs (collection).
Dillon Press, Inc., 1977.
(74 pages)

NATIVE AMERICAN
TALENTS: Artistic
  Pride/False pride

The Hopi Indian life in the Arizona desert lands into which Daisy Hooee Nampeyo is born in 1910 has changed little over the centuries. She is often cared for by her grandmother, Nampeyo, who sees that the little girl is well-versed in the legends and rituals of the Hopi way. Herself a famous potter, Nampeyo teaches the art

to Daisy, who takes readily to it. But the girl develops cataracts, and by the time she is ten, Daisy is nearly blind. A wealthy white woman, a patron of the arts interested in Indian affairs, takes Daisy to Los Angeles for surgery, and her sight restored, the girl remains there with her benefactor throughout high school. Already remote from life on the Reservation, she becomes more so during her study of art in France. On returning to the Reservation, Daisy recognizes she must choose between worlds. She chooses the Hopi. She marries and bears three children (but later divorces her husband) and during this time she helps Nampeyo revive an earlier tradition of pottery. Moving then to Zuni Pueblo, Daisy strives to restore that tribe's earlier artistic traditions and introduces new techniques and motifs into silversmithing. By the end of the 1940s, she returns to her own potting and encourages Zunis to revive their earlier potting skills. Throughout the following years, Daisy's fame spreads, and by the 1970s she travels widely to demonstrate her art. But she finds her most important teaching at the Pueblo, where she, like her grandmother before her, schools another generation in artistic traditions.

This book, one of a series of biographies of Native Americans, tells of an Indian potter, deeply proud of her tribe, who has, while retaining and sometimes restoring the artistic traditions of that tribe, added to them. Though the author includes much historical and cultural information about the sources of Hopi art and tradition, she does not analyze the sociological or physiological sources of Daisy Hooee Nampeyo's art. This book need be no less inspiring to talented children for that.

Ages 11 and up

Also available in:
No other form known

234

Francis, Dorothy Brenner

The Flint Hills Foal

Black/white illustrations by Taylor Oughton.
Abingdon Press, 1976.
(124 pages)

STEPBROTHER/STEPSISTER
STEPPARENT: Mother
  Animals: love for
  Responsibility: accepting

Ten-year-old Kathy thoroughly dislikes her new step-mother, Flo, and Flo's son, Jay, and is pretty sure that they return the feeling. She tries to get along with them to please Dad, but Jay's bragging and Flo's scolding are hard to take. Kathy's chief solace is her work at a nearby ranch where Hank, an old, wise horseman, teaches her horsemanship. When Kathy rescues Flash, a nearly dead foal, and is nursing her back to health, she is more and more away from home. But she must prepare the formula at home, and as usual Flo scolds her. At times Jay helps her out, but at other times he teases Kathy about the stupidity of horses or brags about his exploits. Meanwhile, Kathy fears the foal will be sold or that she will not be allowed to work with her. Her fears seem confirmed when Flash bites her. Terrified of getting tetanus, Kathy is afraid to tell her dad about the incident outright but makes a scene that alerts him all the same. It is this experience that helps Kathy recognize Jay's behavior as stemming from his fear of horses. And this insight leads to another: Jay and Flo do not want to exclude her from the family. Her other worries are laid to rest when the ranch owner returns and says he will not sell Flash. Instead, he appoints Kathy as the foal's custodian and Jay as the buyer of her food.

A girl who misinterprets the actions and words of her stepbrother and stepmother realizes later that they have not been against her at all. This book, though thin in substance, makes a useful point about confusing actions with motives. The story does not explore the children's feelings about their parents' divorces.

Ages 8-11

Also available in:
Paperbound — *The Flint Hills Foal*
Scholastic Book Services

235

Freeman, Lucy

The Eleven Steps

Color illustrations by Julie Brinckloe.
Doubleday & Company, Inc., 1975.
(43 pages counted)

SIBLING: Love for

Eight-year-old Jimmy adores his older sister, Mary, who usually includes him in whatever she is doing that is fun. One afternoon Mary brings her friend Horace home, and ignoring Jimmy completely, takes Horace to her room to show him her stamp collection. Jimmy climbs the eleven steps to her room, but she yells, "Get out!" Jimmy cannot understand her behavior. That night he dreams that he destroys her stamp collection, and the dream seems so real that he wakes up afraid and remorseful. The next morning Mary, having forgotten her rudeness, invites Jimmy along to a stamp collectors' meeting. When she cannot find her stamp album, Jimmy again fears that he did what he thought he dreamed. Then he spies the book, where Horace had put it away. He is so relieved to be back on good terms with Mary that he thinks he may start a stamp collection of his own.

A young boy who idolizes his sister is hurt by her momentary bad temper, and relieved when it blows over. This book makes clear that such lapses can occur in a close, loving sibling relationship.

Ages 8-10

Also available in:
No other form known

236

Freschet, Berniece

Little Black Bear Goes for a Walk

Black/white illustrations by Glen Rounds.
Charles Scribner's Sons, 1977.
(32 pages)

CURIOSITY
Dependence/Independence

Little Black Bear's small world is bounded by his mother's watchful eye. But one day, unwatched while his mother sleeps, and thinking himself finally big enough for a walk, he ambles down a path to sample the big world. Sniffing at an old log, he smells perfectly delicious bugs. Then a porcupine trundles from out of the log, and the cub, puzzled by its quills, recognizes the warning in the creature's grunt and decides the quills look dangerous. After several more encounters, he follows a buzzing bee to a tree hollow and pokes his nose inside. Stung at once, he scrambles down the tree crying. His mother runs up to comfort him but, hearing the bees, knows honey is nearby. Protected against stings by thick fur, she sticks her paw in the same hole and brings out honey, which Little Black Bear finds of all food, the "*best* of all."

A young animal exploring unfamiliar territory sometimes guesses how nature works and sometimes finds out the hard way. Here is a pleasant beginning reader

showing the difference between acting solely according to senses — as when the cub follows a bee — and combining forethought with sensation — as when the mother bear follows her nose and finds honey and uses her protective hide to get some. The cub also learns the risk of independence and other lessons of experience.

Ages 4-6

Also available in:
No other form known

237

Friskey, Margaret Richards

Rackety, That Very Special Rabbit

Color illustrations by Margrit Fiddle Quinn.
Childrens Press, Inc., 1975.
(29 pages)

PRIDE/FALSE PRIDE
Differences, human
Self-esteem

Rackety Rabbit thinks himself "special" because he has a soft, furry coat — and that his two rabbit friends must be special, too, and squirrel and chipmunk as well, since all of them have fur too. When Rackety meets the crow, and tells him that he and his friends are feeling special, the crow says it must be because they think they have feathers. Later, when Rackety chats with the snake, the snake opines that they feel special because they think they have scales. When Rackety and his friends go to the water and ask the frog if he thinks fur is special, the frog says, "No. I am in skin." Rackety goes home to ponder all this. Finally he has a happy thought and goes to tell his friends: "Fur or feathers,/Scales or skin./It doesn't matter/What you're in./You're SPECIAL!"

Rackety thinks that their fur makes his friends and himself special. When he meets animals that do not have fur and finds that they too think they are special, Rackety must re-define "special." While the question of what makes each of us unique and admirable is worth examining, this book goes about exploring it in a contrived (though perfectly clear) manner. Its playful repetitions of phrasing and colorful illustrations add zest. Oddly, all animals referred to by gender in this book are male.

Ages 3-5

Also available in:
Cassette — *Rackety, That Very Special Rabbit*
Childrens Press, Inc.

Large Print — *Rackety, That Very Special Rabbit*
Childrens Press, Inc.

238

Gackenbach, Dick

Do You Love Me?

Color illustrations by the author.
The Seabury Press, Inc., 1975.
(46 pages counted)

FREEDOM, MEANING OF
  Loneliness
  Nature: respect for
  Pets: love for

Lonely Walter Becker, about six, lives on a farm with no playmates, only his parents and his older sister, Boots. One summer day, Walter spies a strange little bird darting back and forth by the mailbox and making a humming sound. Walter is so interested that he wants to catch the bird and keep it for a pet. When it darts into the mailbox, Walter slams the door — and accidentally kills the bird. Frightened and sad, the boy carries the limp body to his sister. Boots gently explains that she cannot make the bird well, and furthermore that some animals are not meant to be handled or held captive. Walter buries the bird. Pondering this idea of a need to be free, Walter frees his bug collection and the turtle he has kept in a shoe box. "Do you love me," he wonders as they depart. That afternoon Boots surprises Walter with a puppy. The boy is apprehensive at first, thinking he may hurt the puppy by fondling it. But the puppy snuggles up to him and licks his face. The two play together all afternoon and Walter is no longer lonesome.

The accidental death of a bird helps a young boy to understand that different creatures have different needs. The puppy's warm response to Walter is the perfect antidote for his sorrow over killing the bird. This gentle little story is one that children may want to discuss.

Ages 5-8

Also available in:
Cassette for the Blind — *Do You Love Me?*
Library of Congress

Paperbound — *Do You Love Me?*
Dell Publishing Company, Inc.

239

Gackenbach, Dick

Harry and the Terrible Whatzit

Color illustrations by the author.
The Seabury Press, Inc., 1977.
(32 pages counted)

FEAR: of the Unknown
  Self, attitude toward: confidence

Young Harry knows there is something terrible in the cellar. How does he know? He just knows; the cellar is dark and damp and smelly. But despite his warning,

Mother goes down into the cellar. Poor woman, she never believes him. For an interminable time Harry waits by the door until, seizing a broom to ward off . . . whatever it is, he enters the cellar and commands whatever it is to explain what has happened to Mom. "A double-headed, three-clawed, six-toed, long-horned Whatzit" then rounds the furnace and says he last saw Harry's Mom near the pickle jars. Sure that this is a lie, Harry swats the Whatzit with the broom. As he presses the attack, the Whatzit grows smaller and smaller. Curious, Harry asks why. "Because you aren't afraid of me anymore," the Whatzit explains. Harry then advises him to try his friend Sheldon's cellar next door. Thanking him, the Whatzit disappears. After a further search, Harry finds his mother in the garden. Though she at first does not believe his story about the Whatzit, later on she vows that as long as he is around, she will never worry about the Whatzit. Still later, Harry, hearing a scream from next door, bets that Sheldon has looked in the cellar.

In this whimsical tale of grace under pressure, a little boy tells in the first person how he met and conquered his fear. Fear may be of the dark or of a Whatzit, but children can take from this story Harry's solution to any nameless fear: give it a name and a shape and a few healthy swats, and it will shrink and eventually go elsewhere.

Ages 4-7

Also available in:
Paperbound — *Harry and the Terrible Whatzit*
Scholastic Book Services

240

Gackenbach, Dick

Hound and Bear

Color illustrations by the author.
The Seabury Press, Inc., 1976.
(32 pages counted)

FRIENDSHIP: Best Friend
PRACTICAL JOKES/PRANKS

G

Hound is silly, Bear sensible, but the two are nonetheless best friends. In the first story, Hound paints the window on Bear's home black so that Bear, waking the next morning, goes back to sleep, thinking it still nighttime. On the following morning, Bear is waiting for sunrise so that he can eat, when Hound comes to tell him of the trick. Bear has missed a whole day. Too bad, Bear says, because he had planned a surprise party yesterday for Hound's birthday. In the second story, Hound persuades Bear to play a game of pretending each to be the other. Bear, as Hound, thoroughly cleans Hound's house, and Hound, as Bear, eats snacks while waiting for an important package. When the package arrives, Hound sends it back — a fine joke. Too bad, Bear says, for the package contained a sweater, a present for Hound. In the last story, Hound presents Bear with another package. Wary of tricks, Bear opens the package and finds another package inside. If this is another trick, he warns, Hound loses a friend. Hound tells Bear to trust him, and Bear opens the next box — to find a nice hat. A better present than the hat is Hound's promise never to trick him again.

Hound's penchant for practical jokes endangers his friendship with Bear. As the last story shows, Bear's annoyance is not at being tricked but at the malicious nature of the tricks: tricks are all right if they do not harm someone. That Hound ends up the victim of his first two tricks underlines the moral.

Ages 4-6

Also available in:
No other form known

241

Galbraith, Kathryn Osebold

Spots Are Special!

Black/white illustrations by Diane Dawson.
Atheneum Publishers, 1976.
(30 pages counted)

IMAGINATION
  Communicable diseases: chicken pox
  Sibling: relationships

When young Sandy comes down with chicken pox, her brother, Eric, is quick to tease her. But as he soon discovers, Sandy makes chicken pox almost a privilege. That evening Eric finds Sandy perched on the table in her room, snarling and hissing. "I'm a great fierce leopard in her tree," she tells him. Eric wants to play too, but Sandy explains, "Only people with real spots can be leopards." The next afternoon he finds Sandy crouched on the rug, croaking and leaping, pretending to be a green spotted frog hunting for her dinner. Eric cannot play because he does not have real spots. As the days go by, he begins to feel left out. On Saturday, though, Eric bursts into Sandy's room, chewing on his bedroom slippers, growling, and snarling. Sandy begins to chide him — but now Eric has chicken pox, too, and the special spots that entitle him to play.

The book illustrates how imagination can make even the most exasperating situations into adventures. The bright drawings nearly tell the story themselves. The children appear to be between the ages of four and six.

Ages 4-7

Also available in:
No other form known

242

Gantos, Jack

Fair-Weather Friends

Color illustrations by Nicole Rubel.
Houghton Mifflin Co., 1977.
(32 pages counted)

PROBLEM SOLVING
  Friendship: best friend

Maggie and Chester, the closest of friends, live in the "freezing North," where the ground is always covered with snow and ice. Chester, who hates the North, plans a vacation in the South and invites Maggie to join him. Once in the South, Chester is positive he has reached paradise, and decides to live there. Maggie, on the other hand, is so miserably uncomfortable that she feels like biting Chester. The two friends face the fact that they must part to be happy, and Maggie goes back to the North. They do keep in touch though, writing each other and visiting "just as often as they can."

This story points out that two friends, even these two fanciful creatures, can remain close despite differences in taste and a separation of many miles. Child-like illustrations will appeal to the younger reader.

Ages 4-7

Also available in:
No other form known

243

Garrigue, Sheila

Between Friends

Bradbury Press, Inc., 1978.
(160 pages)

DOWN'S SYNDROME
  Change: new home
  Friendship: meaning of
  Prejudice: toward handicapped persons
  Sibling: new baby

Jill Harvey, a sixth grader who has recently moved from California to Massachusetts, discovers that all the girls who might be her friends are away on vacation. As one way to occupy her time, she takes a job walking Mrs. Lacey's dog. On these strolls, Jill often passes the home of Dede Atkins, an eighteen-year-old girl with Down's Syndrome. They talk, and a friendship develops. When the other neighborhood girls return, Jill finds that they want nothing to do with Dede. When Dede comes over, Jill's own mother avoids her. Jill is puzzled. She knows Dede to be a sensitive friend and an excellent listener. Still, when school begins, Jill sees less of her friend, who attends a special school. But when she invites Dede to a party, one mystery is cleared up: Mrs. Harvey confesses beforehand to having once borne a severely deformed baby who lived only a few hours, and to finding Dede a constant reminder that the baby she now expects may also be born handicapped. Having faced her fear, Jill's mother now tries to be nice to Dede. It is at Christmastime that Jill's friendship is sorely tested. Dede invites the younger girl to her school Christmas party. Unsure how she will feel about the students who attend Dede's school, Jill hedges. But a discussion of her fears with her father and Dede's mother leads her to accept. Then she is offered a weekend in Boston with school friends and

cancels the acceptance. Plagued by guilt, she can hardly plan the Boston trip. Finally she cancels that, even in the face of hurt feelings, and goes to Dede's party instead. She enjoys herself, finding no reason to fear the special people she meets. A few months later, Dede moves to Arizona. Jill realizes that she will miss this girl who, of all the people she knows, "knows more about being a friend than anyone else."

This sensitive story explores the fears and prejudice that often surround mentally handicapped people. It demonstrates that retarded people can possess special talents, unseen because of their handicap. But Jill's life is touched by more than Dede. The sudden death of Mrs. Lacey, and the girl's feelings about that; adjustments to a new home; other new friends — all these, too, are important to Jill. Although this book is written for the intermediate reader, its appeal extends to the adolescent and would encourage discussion in groups.

Ages 9-12

Also available in:
Braille — *Between Friends*
Library of Congress

G

244

Gelman, Rita Golden and Warner Friedman

Uncle Hugh: A Fishing Story

Black/white illustrations by Eros Keith.
Harcourt Brace Jovanovich, Inc., 1978.
(46 pages counted)

NATURE: Appreciation of
  Death: attitude toward

Young Tom McCallister lives near a stream inhabited by a large and canny fish he has named Uncle Hugh, after an uncle living in Scotland. Tom considers the fish a friend and is glad that no one has caught it. When the real Uncle Hugh visits, he and Tom go fishing, and the man teaches his nephew the proper way to cast. He then tells Tom that he talks to fish and often feels "the flow and pull of the stream" when he is alone in the woods. Tom attaches no importance to the words — until early one September morning he hooks Uncle Hugh, and without a struggle, the fish lies dead on the water. Tears running down his cheeks, Tom gently picks up his beloved fish, and his uncle's words come back to him. Now he has a meaning for "the flow and pull of the stream."

Quietly, without mystification, a child is introduced to the dignity and power of nature by a kindly relative. But he fully understands it only when he participates in the death of a creature he has loved.

Ages 5-8

Also available in:
Paperbound — *Uncle Hugh: A Fishing Story*
Xerox Publishing Company

245

Gerson, Corinne

Passing Through

The Dial Press, Inc., 1978.
(193 pages)

COMMUNICATION: Importance of
SUICIDE: of Sibling
   Cerebral palsy
   Communication: parent-child
   Homosexuality: male
   Hostility
   Prejudice: ethnic/racial
   Prejudice: toward handicapped persons
   Values/Valuing: materialistic

In an attempt to fill the void left by her older brother's suicide, fifteen-year-old Liz Jordan has become a tutor. Liz likes her pupil — Sam Benedict, a wheelchair-bound victim of cerebral palsy — and tells him of her close relationship with her dead brother, Paul. She does not tell Sam of her hatred of her parents' bigotry and materialistic values. Nor does Sam know that Liz has told her parents nothing of him or of her visits to his home. Only during an argument about Thanksgiving plans does Liz finally tell them about Sam and the invitation she has from his family to join them for Thanksgiving dinner. When Mr. Jordan hears this, he belittles Sam for being "spastic" and less than bright. The Jordans call the Benedicts "dirty Polacks," telling Liz that they themselves have "worked long and hard to get away from people like that." A shocked, disgusted Liz angrily retorts that it is they who are "dirty-minded and grubbing to be something you're not and never will be." She promptly leaves to spend the weekend with the Carsons, a couple she baby-sits for, admires, and visits often. After the weekend, Liz tries to follow the advice the Carsons have given her. She talks frankly with her parents, but finds that they continue to disparage the Benedicts. Liz goes right ahead and has Thanksgiving dinner with Sam's family while her parents celebrate with friends. After dinner, Liz and Sam go over to the Jordan home, and there, Liz shows Sam her brother's last letter — one she has shown to no one, since, in it, Paul proclaims his homosexuality. Later, the Jordans return and find Liz and Sam fallen asleep. They seem to suspect an earlier sexual episode, and since nothing Liz can say satisfies them, she telephones the Carsons the next afternoon asking to spend the weekend. At the Carsons' Liz tells Mrs. Carson she wants to live with them. But before Liz receives a clear answer, the Jordans appear — Paul's letter in hand. After a long discussion, it is decided that Liz will remain at home, and, in the days that follow, relations with her parents seem to improve. Sam and Liz drift apart, realizing that the time they needed each other is past.

In this tense, sometimes painful story, Liz struggles with and finally accepts both her brother's suicide and his homosexuality. Through her friendship with Sam and the Carsons, she also begins to understand — but not approve of — her parents' values and their clumsiness with her. Also explored in detail is the close bond between Liz and Paul, the Jordans' prejudices, and Sam's adjustment to his handicap. The bitter arguments erupting in this book often go unresolved, adding to the tension throughout. What comes through clearly is the importance of having someone to share one's thoughts with calmly and trustingly.

Ages 12 and up

Also available in:
Paperbound — *Passing Through*
Dell Publishing Company, Inc.

246

Gessner, Lynne

Malcolm Yucca Seed

Black/white illustrations by William Sauts Bock.
Harvey House, Inc., 1977.
(63 pages)

NAME, DISSATISFACTION WITH
NATIVE AMERICAN
   Honesty/Dishonesty

Malcolm, a Navajo boy about ten, is not known on the reservation by that name. It is a "white man's name," given him at an off-reservation school. The boy badly wants an Indian name like his oldest brother's "Wolf Fighter" or his other brother's "Water Bearer." But to acquire a special name he must perform a notable deed. He thinks the time may be at hand after he drives a coyote away from a flock of sheep — and embellishes the tale by saying he has killed the coyote. But he is given no name. He makes up a story about driving a mountain lion away from sheep, though all he has seen is a lion cub. Still no name. When a chance does come to show bravery — a sudden rainstorm endangers the sheep he watches over — Malcolm tries to run away, staying with the flock only because flooding bars his escape. At home the same storm washes away the garden. Afraid his family will go hungry, Malcolm gathers yucca seed to make flour and to plant. (The shoots are eaten like potatoes, the fruit is like squash, and the roots make soap.) Graciously accepting his offering, his father reminds him his main contribution was to protect the sheep, for they can always sell sheep for food. His father brushes aside Malcolm's confession that his tales of bravery were a sham and that he tried to run away during the storm. Everyone, his father says, feels fear. For gathering the food, he gives Malcolm the name, Yucca Seed. The yucca "will remind us of our son, Yucca Seed, who loves his family very much and who brought them this wonderful gift."

An Indian boy's desire for a special name leads him to twist the truth and even lie outright. Eventually he earns an Indian name, not by showing bravery, but by showing concern for those he loves. Underlying this book's main themes are the tensions in Malcolm's life between living Navajo and living "white." His father, who has moved back to the reservation after going away to school, wants his son to learn both ways before choosing. Malcolm Yucca Seed has not made the choice yet, but the question colors much of his thought.

Ages 8-10

Also available in:
No other form known

Gill, Derek Lewis Theodore

Tom Sullivan's Adventures in Darkness

Black/white photographs (collection).
David McKay Company, Inc., 1976.
(106 pages)

BLINDNESS
DEPENDENCE/INDEPENDENCE
DETERMINATION
  Education: special
  Pets: guide dog
  Talents: musical

Like too many other premature babies born during the 1940s, Tom Sullivan is placed in an incubator where an excess of oxygen blinds him for life. From then on his family's desire to protect him only makes Tom more determined to meet and compete with sighted people. Soon, about the only thing he cannot do with his friends is participate in sports. At Perkins School for the Blind, where he masters Braille and learns to use a white cane, Tom finally finds a sport he can compete in on an equal basis with sighted people — wrestling. He goes on to win the U.S. National Title and an invitation to participate in the Olympic trials. Continually seeking new challenges, he also learns to play golf, swim, ride horses, and skydive — his favorite sport. Absent without leave from Perkins School, Tom meets a traveling musician, who inspires him to study music. Soon a member of the school's famous choir, Tom meets President Johnson at a White House concert. Upon graduation, he receives scholarships to both Harvard and Yale, but attends a smaller college first, where a newfound friend helps him master many unforeseen difficulties. At Harvard, Tom continues his study of psychology and music, begins composing his own songs, and gets a summer job singing in a Cape Cod club. While there he meets his future wife, Patty, and is invited to appear on the "Tonight" show. This leads to several recording contracts and concert invitations. Though busy with this and school, he is lonely for Patty and one day decides to clear his mind by going skydiving. He jumps and waits for instructions — but realizes too late that the transceiver in his helmet is not working. With no one to tell him when to prepare for landing, he could be killed. He decides then and there that if he survives, he will ask Patty to marry him. He survives, and she agrees, but her father needs some persuading. Finally, seeing that Tom's blindness is not hereditary, seeing how self-sufficient he is, and learning that Tom has been offered a job as an entertainer at a salary of $1,000 a week, Patty's father changes his mind. Today, Tom is the father of two children, the owner of a "most intelligent" seeing-eye dog who has once saved his master's life, and a nationally recognized entertainer.

Tom Sullivan's inspiring story shows how far a self-requirement of excellence and a determination to live life fully can take a blind person: farther than most sighted people. To Tom Sullivan, blindness is a challenge, not a handicap. Even so, mature readers may find the unmixed optimism of this narrative surprising and the protagonist's unfailing good humor implausible. Tom's privileged childhood — which takes nothing away from his drive and ability — is an advantage not all blind children share. This book includes much general information on blindness, such as the ways in which blind people develop their other senses to tell them what their eyes cannot.

Ages 10-14

Also available in:
Cassette for the Blind — *Tom Sullivan's Adventures in Darkness*
Library of Congress

Paperbound — *Tom Sullivan's Adventures in Darkness*
New American Library

Ginsburg, Mirra

Two Greedy Bears

Color illustrations by Jose Aruego and Ariane Dewey.
Macmillan Publishing Company, Inc., 1976.
(32 pages counted)

GREED

Two bear cubs set out to explore the world — two very competitive bear cubs. If one is thirsty, the other is thirstier. If one drinks his fill, the other drinks more. If one has a stomachache, the other's is worse. And when they come across a big, round cheese, of course they fall to quarreling over how to divide it. And while they argue, a sly fox approaches and offers to settle the matter. She breaks the cheese in two, making sure one piece is bigger than the other. Of course the bears object, and so the fox takes a bite from the bigger piece. Again the bears complain that the pieces are unequal. Begging their patience, the fox continues to reduce the two pieces by turns until only two scraps remain. Having eaten her fill, the fox flicks her tail and walks off — leaving two tiny crumbs of cheese, exactly equal.

This story, adapted from a Hungarian folk tale, wittily shows how greed can turn gain into loss.

Ages 3-8

Also available in:
No other form known

249

Girion, Barbara

The Boy with the Special Face

Color illustrations by Heidi Palmer.
Abingdon Press, 1978.
(30 pages counted)

APPEARANCE: Concern About
  Freckles
  Hair style, importance of

Young Perry James Larner has bright red hair impossible to keep in place; his freckles, which he has tried to erase, are countless; his eyes, of no particular color, have been called the color of ginger ale. His parents call his face "interesting." But Perry does not like what he sees in the mirror while dressing for school, and at school he compares his hair unfavorably to his classmates'. He finds also that the teacher keeps catching him out — there is no way to hide with an interesting face. When his teacher announces that a television producer will come Monday to hold auditions for a commercial, Perry no sooner hears than he forgets the prospect. When he arrives at school Monday wearing old clothes while the other children are in their finest, he does remember. But so what: he has no chance of being chosen. Yet after everyone tries out, the producer chooses him: "We want *this* boy with the interesting face."

A boy disdains the face and unruly hair which others call "interesting" and wants instead to be conventionally good-looking. Older readers may be dubious about television as the arbiter of appearance or anything else, but youngsters — like Perry — may be impressed.

G

Ages 5-8

Also available in:
No other form known

250

Glass, Frankcina

Marvin & Tige

St. Martin's Press, Inc., 1977.
(232 pages)

FRIENDSHIP: Making Friends
  Adoption: feelings about
  Afro-American
  Alcoholism: adult
  Inferiority, feelings of
  Loneliness
  Love, meaning of
  Unwed mother: child of

Tige, an eleven-year-old black boy in Atlanta, Georgia, likes neither stealing nor finding customers for his unwed prostitute mother, but he must do both if the two are to survive. But Tige's mother suddenly dies, and the boy — despairing of the future — wanders into a park to commit suicide. There Marvin Stewart, a middle-aged white man scavenging for bottles, stops him and invites him to stay overnight at his apartment. The next morning Tige leaves, but he later meets Marvin begging. Again the boy returns to the apartment, resolving that he will leave when he finds something better. Marvin wants the boy to stay but does not try to persuade him; he does set down rules for him: no cursing and no stealing. Tige accepts, but warily. After some cross purposes, the two become such fast friends that Marvin — before his wife died, a successful advertising man — considers starting over again. But before he can act on his resolve Tige falls seriously ill, and Marvin is forced to ask help from Tige's father, whom he has earlier traced. Richard Davis, the father, eventually agrees to pay the hospital expenses and to take Tige home to his own family. (He had wanted to adopt the boy years earlier, but Tige's mother would have none of that.) Marvin reluctantly agrees and takes the boy to the Davises once he recovers. For the next few months, he hears nothing from Tige, and he is miserable. But toward autumn, his spirits are transformed, when Tige comes to invite him to his birthday party and promises to visit him often thereafter.

A man and a boy, separated by age, race, and culture, nonetheless come to respect and finally to love each other. This is not a story in which everything comes out all right: Marvin does not start over again and remains, as Tige says, "sked" of the world; and Tige is dissatisfied that his father does not spend more time with him. The author has a fine ear for dialogue, and Tige's dialect, though marked, does not seem affected.

Ages 12 and up

Also available in:
Paperbound — *Marvin & Tige*
Fawcett World Library

Talking Book — *Marvin & Tige*
Library of Congress

251

Glovach, Linda

Let's Make a Deal

Color illustrations by the author.
Prentice-Hall, Inc., 1975.
(48 pages)

FRIENDSHIP: Best Friend
PETS: Love for
  Problem solving

Tom and Dewey go to elementary school and are best friends. Together they build a tree house just for themselves. Together they find a stray puppy, name her Lucy, and give her a doghouse at the bottom of the tree (though sometimes she visits at their homes). But one day it develops that Tom and his family will soon move to a nearby city to live with Tom's grandfather. The boys feel terrible; they will miss each other. Because they certainly cannot decide who should keep Lucy, they decide to walk in differing directions and see which boy Lucy follows. Lucy chooses Tom. So depressed is Dewey that he stays away from the tree house the rest of the week. But the morning before Tom is to leave, Lucy is sitting on Dewey's stoop. So badly does Dewey want the dog that he keeps her and does not even go to say good-bye to Tom until too late. But the next day he is ashamed, and decides he must return the dog to Tom. Boy and dog take a bus to the city, find Tom's new home, and find Tom overjoyed to see them. But he tells Dewey to keep Lucy: Grandfather has a bird and a cat, and besides, Lucy would be unhappy in the city.

A close friendship is put to the test by distance and by the two boys' wanting the same pet. Fortunately, both can be content with the outcome. Children who have been parted from friends by a move, or who have had to give up a pet, will sympathize with Tom and Dewey.

Ages 8-11

Also available in:
Cassette for the Blind — *Let's Make a Deal*
Library of Congress

252

Godden, Rumer

Mr. McFadden's Hallowe'en

The Viking Press, Inc., 1975.
(127 pages)

FRIENDSHIP
  Animals: love for
  Helping

G

Each member of the Russell family of Scotland has inherited one hundred pounds at the death of Great Aunt Emily. Eight-year-old Selina and her older sister, Muffet, buy ponies, Selina's pony displaying a temperament just like her own — quick-tempered, stubborn, mischievous. Every time Selina goes riding in the Scottish highlands, her pony marches right onto land belonging to a Mr. McFadden, infuriating the cantankerous old hermit, who permits no trespassing. In the meantime, the townspeople learn that Great Aunt Emily has left twenty thousand pounds to build a new town park. The only plot of land suitable is owned by the same Mr. McFadden, who refuses to sell. One day, while McFadden is tending his sheep, a boulder falls and crushes his leg. Selina finds him, helps him home, and brings the doctor. During his recovery, she brings him food daily, and she and her parents tend his crops and animals. This outrages the neighbors, who want no part of the old man after his refusal to sell land for the park. One day Selina brings with her a young orphan boy she has befriended, Tim Scobie. Cross old McFadden takes a liking to the boy. By fall, McFadden's neighbors are harassing him, but Selina is planning a nice Halloween for him. Halloween night, a gang of boys put turf on top of his chimney, causing the smoke to back up. Tim Scobie manages to get it down before any damage is done. The same boys tie Selina to a tree, but

McFadden rescues her. It is a turning point for the old man. Touched by the loyalty of these two children, he donates the park land to the town, and when Tim's aunt abandons him, McFadden offers to adopt the boy. McFadden attends the park dedication. One little girl has taught him how to have friends and to be one.

This simple, well-told story shows friendship without being preachy about it. An ending that might have seemed contrived is instead natural and appropriate.

Ages 9-11

Also available in:
No other form known

253

Gold, Phyllis

Please Don't Say Hello

Black/white photographs by Carl Baker.
Human Sciences Press, 1975.
(47 pages)

AUTISM
  Education: special
  Friendship: meaning of

When Paul Mason and his family move into their new home, Billy, Alan, Jimmy, and Charlie — all neighborhood boys — introduce themselves to Paul. They also meet his younger brother, nine-year-old Eddie, and ask why he seems to ignore them. Paul explains that Eddie is afraid — of the new house and all the new neighbors, and "sometimes Eddie is just afraid." Dropping over to Paul's during the summer, they find that Eddie avoids them, does not talk the way most boys do, and often runs away when they talk to him. Finally Billy's parents forbid him to associate with Paul, and Mrs. Mason and

Paul's older sister, Lizbeth, sit down to explain Eddie's handicap to the boys. Eddie, and children like him, are autistic — "have trouble getting outside of themselves enough to get along with other people in what would be considered the normal way." The boys point out that while Eddie has trouble doing some simple things, he can do other very difficult things easily; Lizbeth explains, "I think for all of us some things are easier and some things are harder to do. For Eddie it's even more that way." Mrs. Mason adds that, though no cure is known for autism, Eddie attends a special boarding school where "they understand his special problems and know ways to help him." When school begins, the boys lose track of Eddie, but in the spring, Mrs. Mason asks them to join the family when they pick him up for summer vacation. At the school, the boys observe the special help being given to autistic students. And later, at home, they notice that Eddie has changed in some ways. He now seems more interested in watching children and calls himself "I" instead of "you."

This simple portrayal of autism describes some of its symptoms and tries to show the reader that understanding and acceptance can do much to help the autistic child get along in the world. In addition, the book explains the educational instruction available to autistic children and touches briefly on some of the behavior modification that helps counter the autistic child's isolation. The author, herself the mother of an autistic child, explores the mystifying condition with compassion and intelligence. Here is a well-presented message for children and adults too, about a complicated, misunderstood, and still not wholly explained phenomenon.

Ages 7 and up

Also available in:
No other form known

254

Goldman, Susan

Cousins Are Special

Color illustrations by the author.
Albert Whitman & Co., 1978.
(32 pages counted)

RELATIVES

Young Sarah is taken by her mother to visit her cousin, Carol Sue, for the first time. Right away the two girls, who are the same age, play together like best friends, exploring the house, playing ghosts, and finger-painting. Yet when Carol Sue points to a photograph of Sarah's grandmother and says, "She's *my* grandma," they argue; neither understands how her "grandma" can be the other's. Their mothers settle the quarrel by explaining that they themselves are sisters, daughters of the woman the two girls call their "grandma," and so the girls are members of the same family. Sarah now realizes why she loves Carol Sue. "She's more than my friend. She's my cousin."

This simple first-person narrative clearly explains the kinship of cousins to young children. The illustrations complement and expand the text.

Ages 3-5

Also available in:
No other form known

Goldman, Susan

Grandma Is Somebody Special

Color illustrations by the author.
Albert Whitman & Co., 1976.
(32 pages counted)

GRANDPARENT: Love for
  Visiting

When a little girl visits her grandmother in the city, they make up the cot, look at photo albums, and watch fire engines and buses from the balcony of the tall apartment building where the grandmother lives. They fix the dinner that the girl likes best; then she draws her grandmother a picture, which "she hangs right up on the kitchen door." They play cards, read stories, look at Grandma's jewelry, and thoroughly enjoy each other.

A little girl tells this story of her visits to Grandma, visits she enjoys because her grandmother lives an exciting life, working and going to school in the big city. The visits matter greatly to the girl because her grandmother pays so much attention to her: listening to her read, helping her bathe, brushing her hair. This is a loving account of the special love a grandparent can give a child, a love especially welcome when a new baby has arrived in the family.

Ages 4-7

Also available in:
Cassette — *Grandma Is Somebody Special*
Instructional/Communications Technology, Inc.

G

Goldreich, Gloria

Season of Discovery

Thomas Nelson, Inc., 1976.
(156 pages)

BRAIN INJURY
PREJUDICE: Ethnic/Racial
TWINS: Fraternal
 Death: of friend
 Jewish
 Mental retardation
 Sibling: relationships

Twelve-year-old Lisa Robinow wishes that her twin brother, Donny, were not severely brain-injured and living at boarding school, wishes that he could attend Hebrew school, work on school projects, and attend youth-group meetings with her instead. But it bothers her more to know that, when she has her bat mitzvah, Donny should be celebrating his bar mitzvah, but he will not, because he cannot memorize. Soon Lisa is absorbed in Hebrew school and the instruction given by Dr. Rothenberg concerning the Holocaust. Her youth-group volunteer work has her reading to Mrs. Rothenberg, a survivor of a concentration camp, who now suffers from a disabling brain tumor. It is from these two people that Lisa learns a revulsion for the swastika that a neighbor named Andrews has painted on his house. But when she and her parents visit Donny, her brother is uppermost in all minds. In fact, Lisa finds that, though she loves and takes pride in Donny, she a little envies the constant attention her mother showers on him. But

Lisa herself is no less concerned when, back home, Mrs. Rothenberg is hospitalized. When Lisa visits Donny in December during Hanukkah, she has only one thing on her mind, asking Donny's counselor, Lennie, to teach her brother the Hebrew prayer she brought. Then in March, Mrs. Rothenberg is readmitted to the hospital and dies, and Lisa realizes just how much her friend's experiences and reflections on life have influenced her. That is why Lisa goes to the Andrewses' house one night and obliterates the swastika with paint. Andrews sees her retreating figure but is restrained by his stepson, who loathes Andrews's bigotry. In the days that follow, Lisa is glad to see that the swastika does not reappear. Then, as April approaches, she is caught up in the preparations for her bat mitzvah. For on that special day, she and Donny, home for the celebration, will — and do — read together the prayer she had asked that Donny be taught.

During the year she prepares for her bat mitzvah, Lisa comes to realize that the people around her can enrich her life and guide her in making decisions. Her close and loving relationship with her brain-injured brother, Donny, is no less rewarding than her close friendship with the more worldly wise Mrs. Rothenberg. Lisa also seems to find strength beyond her years to cope with her mother's remorseful behavior about Donny. If Lisa in fact seems too good to be true in this slightly slow story, Donny's place in his family's feelings is well drawn. One notices that the father is only a minor character.

Ages 11-13

Also available in:
No other form known

257

Gonzalez, Gloria

Gaucho

Alfred A. Knopf, Inc., 1977.
(144 pages)

IDENTITY, SEARCH FOR
Change: resisting
Puerto Rican-American

After six years of living in upper Manhattan, eleven-year-old Gaucho dreams of returning with his mother to their native Puerto Rico. Gaucho's father has been dead for some time, and he and his older brother live with their mother, who is on welfare. Gaucho gets a job in a local grocery, but not for the amount of money he wants. Then he is hired by Blanco, a man powerful on the street, to deliver some packages of unknown content. Mama feels so proud of her enterprising son that she tells Gaucho he may have a Halloween party. He is overjoyed, and in the following days, they plan it. But the night of the party, Blanco asks Gaucho to make a delivery. Reluctantly, but afraid of Blanco, Gaucho goes with him to another part of town to deliver a shopping bag to an old woman. The police, who have been watching Blanco, spot the boy and chase him, where-upon he falls and injures his knee badly. Losing the police and finding Blanco, he accepts a ride home in time for his party. Still frightened and in pain, Gaucho has a fine time anyway. Next evening, Gaucho hears Blanco has been shot to death evading arrest as a counterfeiter. Sure of his own innocence, Gaucho neverthe-less fears arrest himself. In time his knee heals and his fear ebbs. He will just keep quiet about working for Blanco. And he has made so many friends in the neigh-borhood, he will forget his dream of going back to Puerto Rico.

A boy, lonely and uncomfortable in a rundown neigh-borhood in New York City, longs to return to the people and place he scarcely remembers, the Puerto Rico of his imagination. Even while being drawn into shady employment, he is making friends, finding his way, learning how to handle himself. Soon the city is home after all. Gaucho's story is told with understanding and insight.

Ages 10-13

Also available in:
Film, ABC Afterschool Special — *Gaucho*
Martin Tahse Productions

Paperbound — *Gaucho*
Dell Publishing Company, Inc.

258

Gordon, Shirley

Crystal Is My Friend

Color illustrations by Edward Frascino.
Harper & Row Publishers, Inc., 1978.
(32 pages)

FRIENDSHIP: BEST FRIEND
FRIENDSHIP: MEANING OF
Etiquette

When young Susan invites her best friend, Crystal, to spend the night, Susan's mother firmly instructs her to treat Crystal as a guest. This means Crystal must have first choice in everything. By the time Crystal has cho-sen Susan's bed, the games they play, and the television programs they watch, Susan says of her guest, "I wish Crystal was still just my friend." All the same, she does not protest when Crystal adds raisins — which Susan hates — to the brownies, and takes the best clothes for dress-up. But by evening she is so angry that she cannot sleep. She punches her pillow so loud that she wakes

Crystal. They talk about the evening and decide to go back to their old way of choosing — "first dibs." Susan gets her bed back, and the girls are restored to good spirits. The next morning they get dressed, eat breakfast, and play Susan's favorite game, Monopoly. After Crystal leaves, Susan's first thought is about when her friend can spend the night again.

Susan describes how an evening's fun between two girl friends is nearly spoiled when they must act as hostess and guest. This book teaches that friendship is sharing, not one-sided giving. The illustrations catch the two girls' easy playfulness.

Ages 6-9

Also available in:
No other form known

259

Gordon, Shirley

Crystal Is the New Girl

Color illustrations by Edward Frascino.
Harper & Row Publishers, Inc., 1976.
(32 pages)

FRIENDSHIP: Making Friends
  Discipline, meaning of
  Friendship: best friend

Crystal is the new girl in the third grade, but Susan does not want to be her friend. When the teacher seats Crystal next to her, Susan ignores Crystal's efforts to get acquainted. This does not stop Crystal, who comes to school the next day wearing a remarkable pair of sunglasses with plastic ducks on the frames. The following day she brings Susan a present, an old Alka Seltzer tablet. Unable to ignore Crystal's antics any longer, Susan makes friends with her after all. But they begin to distract each other, and after several warnings the teacher punishes the girls for talking in class. On another occasion they are sent to the principal's office. When Susan's mother hears of this, she scolds Susan. The teacher assigns the girls to seats across the room from each other, but they continue to have fun together, sharing their lunches and playing catch at the playground. At home, Susan announces that she and Crystal will be friends forever. When Crystal goes away with her family for summer vacation, Susan looks forward to seeing her friend again in the fall.

Though the two girls do not let the teacher's disciplinary actions end their friendship, they understand they have misbehaved and dislike their punishment, as the cartoon illustrations make clear. The pictures likewise depict Susan's activities at home with her mother and show the fun the two girls have as friends.

Ages 4-7

Also available in:
No other form known

260

Graber, Richard

A Little Breathing Room

Harper & Row Publishers, Inc., 1978.
(121 pages)

PARENT/PARENTS: Punitive
  Communication: lack of
  Illnesses: of sibling
  Parent/Parents: respect for/lack of respect for
  Sibling: love for

Ray Decker, thirteen in 1935, finds it extremely difficult to please his father. Mr. Decker continually interrupts his son, unjustly accuses him of being thoughtless, and holds him accountable for things he has had no part in. When Ray's eight-year-old brother, Bud, becomes ill at a church supper, Ray takes him upstairs where the air is cooler. Ray's girl friend joins them, and Mr. Decker bursts in. He accuses Ray of being "absolutely disgraceful" and, refusing to listen to explanations, denounces the boys for their "sinful behavior." Ray privately asks his mother to intercede, but she confides that her husband cannot manage the family business without her help — and that he drinks, has affairs, and "takes after" his sons in an effort to "prove he's a big man, a proper father, and a breadwinner." But she assures Ray that when the time comes, he, not she, will be the one to bring his father "to his knees." Shortly before summer vacation begins, Bud breaks his leg. Despite explanations to the contrary, Mr. Decker blames Ray and confines him to the house to care for his brother and "meditate" on the evil of his ways. On the day Bud is to have his cast removed, Mr. Decker demands that it remain another week. With his mother's private permission, Ray takes Bud to the doctor, where the cast is removed. That evening, discovering what has happened, Mr. Decker strikes Ray, knocking him to the floor. Shaken and dazed, Ray rises and butts his father in the stomach. At this point, Mrs. Decker intervenes. She places a long-distance telephone call to Ray's grandparents and arranges a month-long visit for the boy for "a little breathing room." The next afternoon Ray boards a bus, wishing his father would "let up on a guy once in a while."

The reader all too fully shares young Ray's bewilderment and anger under his father's hail of humiliating abuse. At the conclusion of this first-person narrative, we are left with the impression that further nastiness will occur but that the boy will stand up to it. If he will always be estranged from his father, the bond of love between the two brothers can leaven the anger and tension Ray feels. The mother, though seeming ineffectual, when necessary sets limits for both her sons and husband.

Ages 10-14

Also available in:
No other form known

261

Graham, John

I Love You, Mouse

Black/white illustrations by Tomie de Paola.
Harcourt Brace Jovanovich, Inc., 1976.
(30 pages counted)

G

LOVE, MEANING OF

A little boy is daydreaming how he would shelter and care for the house pets and the farm animals he loves. He also imagines himself soothing and assuring the animals in the forest that they too will be protected while they play together. When evening nears, and the boy's dreaming is interrupted by his father, he notices that he himself is cared for as he would care for those he loves. He is told that he is loved, has a home, and has a "bed with warm quilts, a kiss on the nose, and a quiet good-night" always at hand.

The illustrations deepen the tone of serenity and security in this simply worded text, the whole expressing the idea that love may be shown in many ways. Though the boy only imagines the manner in which he would demonstrate his love, the father can prove with tangible evidence his love for his son.

Ages 4-7

Also available in:
Paperbound — *I Love You, Mouse*
Harcourt Brace Jovanovich, Inc.

262

Green, Phyllis

Ice River

Black/white illustrations by Jim Crowell.
Addison-Wesley Publishing Company, Inc., 1975.
(48 pages counted)

CHANGE: Accepting
  Pets: love for
  Stepparent: father

Dell Carling, whose parents are divorced, lives with his
pregnant mother and his stepfather, John Gray. Though
Dell's father has promised to visit, he does not appear,
and this, coupled with his mother's pregnancy, makes
Dell feel wholly alone, but for his dog, Mutt. One afternoon, while Dell's mother and stepfather are seeing the
doctor, Dell and his best friend, Izzy, take Mutt with
them ice skating on the river. Before they realize it, they
are floating downriver on an ice floe. Luckily, the boys
alert a man on shore, and soon a helicopter and a boat
are speeding to their rescue. As the helicopter
approaches with its ladder lowered, a frightened Mutt
leaps into the icy water. Izzy jumps in to save him, but
unable to find him in the deepening darkness, returns to
the floe. As Dell reaches out to help Izzy, Izzy begins to
sink. Dell quickly lies down on the ice, extends his arm
to his endangered friend and, with the help of a man
who has descended the helicopter's ladder, pulls Izzy to
safety. Once on shore, Dell is warmly welcomed by his
stepfather, who explains that Dell's mother is in the
hospital because she has lost the baby. This double loss
is too much for Dell, and he sobs in John's arms. At
home, after a call from his father, Dell confides to John
that, no matter what his father says, he will probably
never visit. Dell also confesses his anger and sadness
over the changes in his life and is reassured when his

stepfather seems to understand. Late that night, when a
whining Mutt appears at the back door, John and Dell
welcome him to a warm kitchen and dinner. At last,
settled in bed with his dog, Dell begins to think affec-
tionately of his stepfather.

Though seeming shallow at times, this book voices the
unsaid thoughts of many children who must cope with
divorce and a new stepparent. It implies, too, that the
main character is able to accept the changes in his life
only with the help of an understanding adult. While
relations between the boy and his father and the boy
and his stepfather are not explored much in the book,
they could be speculated upon in follow-up discussion.

Ages 8-10

Also available in:
No other form known

263

Green, Phyllis

Mildred Murphy, How Does Your Garden Grow?

Black/white illustrations by Jerry Pinkney.
Addison-Wesley Publishing Company, Inc., 1977.
(89 pages)

AGE: Respect for
FRIENDSHIP: Making Friends
LONELINESS
  Change: new home
  Curiosity
  Neighbors/Neighborhood

Her family's move from New Jersey to California lands
ten-year-old Mildred Murphy in an older neighborhood with few children her own age. Bored and lonely,
she watches the neighbors through her father's tele-
scope, and one day sees an old woman sneaking into the

garage apartment of the Calloways' house across the street. Next day, when the Calloways leave for work, Mildred goes over to confront the intruder and finds her to be a lonely, destitute woman named Gertie Wilson, too frightened to be dangerous. In fact, Gertie is a widow who has spent the last of her savings to come live in the apartment at the invitation of her friend, Mrs. Calloway's mother, who had then died suddenly without telling of this arrangement to her daughter. When Gertie had approached the Calloways herself, they had implied the apartment was unlivable. Desperate, Gertie had secretly stayed on. Mildred decides to keep Gertie's secret and to help her. But one afternoon Mr. Calloway sees Mildred coming away from the garage and warns her not to come around, because the garage is dangerously infested with termites; it will have to be torn down soon. Mildred tells Gertie, who decides to call her daughter in Detroit, much as she hates being dependent on anyone. Her daughter will pay her fare back and then likely put her in a retirement home. Mildred promises to see her off at the bus station, but at the last moment falls ill, and Gertie postpones her departure until Mildred is well. Meanwhile, Mildred's mother finds her daughter's diary, and the secret is out. Mildred's parents escort her over to tell the Calloways, and while Mr. Calloway and Mr. Murphy wait for Gertie to come out, the latter escapes — just before the garage roof collapses. Unharmed, Gertie reappears and apologizes to the Calloways. She goes to stay with a sympathetic neighbor until she can decide what to do next. Mildred, too, ponders Gertie's future and tries to think of ways for her to make money. She decides on babysitting and baking, and passes out leaflets advertising Gertie's skills. "I have lots of plans for you," she assures her friend.

In this first-person narrative, written as a diary, a lonely girl learns that most people suffer from loneliness. By helping a poor and elderly woman, Mildred forgets her own unhappiness and determines to find ways to help others forget theirs. The characters in this book are well-drawn, particularly Mildred's mother, who in fact relishes solitude. She responds thoughtfully to Mildred's questions about old age, explaining that circumstances often compel families to put an elderly family member into a retirement home. This book ends uncertainly and so may inspire discussion.

Ages 9-11

Also available in:
Paperbound — *Mildred Murphy, How Does Your Garden Grow?*
Dell Publishing Company, Inc.

264

Green, Phyllis

Walkie-Talkie

Addison-Wesley Publishing Company, Inc., 1978.
(96 pages)

HYPERACTIVITY
  Friendship: meaning of
  Rejection: parental
  Wheelchair, dependence on

In this, his fourteenth year, Richie graduates from sixth grade. He is hyperactive, friendless, breaks things, and causes trouble at home and in school. Most of the time he knows what he does but cannot stop himself. During thunderstorms, he goes completely out of control. "My teeth start to chatter, then all of me shakes. And when the thunder comes, I can't sit anymore. I'm up and whirling in circles. I feel like I'm out of my mind.... My mother grabs me and holds me down.... I bite her shoulder, not on purpose. I can't stop my teeth moving and her shoulder is there." His father humors Richie and predicts he will outgrow all this, but his mother complains and finally says, "I'm through." Given a pair of walkie-talkies for his birthday, Richie overhears a

G

speech lesson and later meets the speaker, Norman, probably a victim of cerebral palsy, anyway confined to a wheelchair. Norman's tutor, Patty, cares for him while his parents are away. Richie finds that Norman and Patty value his presence, and Patty praises him for getting Norman outdoors, taking him to sandlot baseball games, where Norman does some coaching. Richie comes to feel this is his best summer and is able to control himself somewhat. But his control falls apart suddenly. He is alone with Norman when a storm strikes, and Norman laughs at his crazed behavior. Once the storm is over, Richie retaliates by cutting off the lights and, pretending to be a burglar, terrorizes Norman until the latter is sick and nearly injured seriously. Richie later tries to make up with Norman, but Norman will have none of it, nor will Patty. Richie broods about the future, frightened now for himself.

A hyperactive boy tells honestly of a summer in which he begins to control his impulse-ridden life, only to see the control swept away. First-person narration allows the reader to see both Richie's pleasure in making trouble and his first inquiries into his own actions and motives. It is his new awareness that lends hope to an otherwise open ending: Richie has glimpsed a better side of himself, but no one knows if he will ever recapture it. The characterizations and situations here are believable, but neither boy's affliction is defined, and neither boy appears to be receiving any professional help, an unlikely omission.

Ages 10-13

Also available in:
No other form known

265

Greenberg, Barbara

The Bravest Babysitter

Color illustrations by Diane Paterson.
The Dial Press, Inc., 1977.
(29 pages counted)

BABY-SITTING
COURAGE, MEANING OF
FEAR: of Storms

Little Lisa loves Heather, her favorite baby-sitter. One evening when Heather is taking care of her, a thunderstorm erupts, and it turns out that Heather is afraid of thunder. Little Lisa assures her that thunder cannot hurt anyone. Throughout the evening, while the two make a collage, cook supper, read, and play dress-up, Heather is nervous. Lisa keeps suggesting things to do to keep Heather's mind off the storm. When it finally subsides, the two agree that Lisa has been the bravest baby-sitter — she has taken care of Heather and looks forward to doing it again.

Children may be amused by the twist in this story: the child who proves to be more courageous than her babysitter. The accompanying illustrations add a light, sometimes funny touch.

Ages 4-8

Also available in:
Cassette for the Blind — *The Bravest Babysitter*
Library of Congress

266

Greene, Constance Clarke

Beat the Turtle Drum

Black/white illustrations by Donna Diamond.
The Viking Press, Inc., 1976.
(119 pages)

DEATH: of Sibling
SIBLING: Love for
  Mourning, stages of

Kate tells how her younger sister, Joss, almost eleven, is saving money to rent a riding horse. She loves horses, and would own one if she could. Mr. Essig rents horses for thirty dollars a week, and Joss is sure she will have that much when she gets her birthday money. Kate, at twelve, is Joss's best friend, and though she does not share Joss's fervent love for horses, she does help her clean the garage for the horse to sleep in. On her birthday, as anticipated, Joss receives money in the mail from Grandma, and so is able to take the required thirty dollars to Mr. Essig. When the horse is delivered later that day, Joss is ecstatic, pampers him thoroughly, and gives rides to the neighborhood children. Some days later, the sisters take Prince and go for a picnic. They climb an apple tree to eat their lunch, and Joss climbs higher to look down at Prince. Suddenly the branch breaks, and Joss is hurled to the ground. Kate, terrified by Joss's silence, runs for help. But Joss is dead. Kate's world is turned upside down, and in the days and weeks that follow she tries to understand what has happened. Only after time does she see that someday the pain of her loss will be lessened. Right now, the hurt remains.

Kate narrates the story of her last, and special, summer with her sister. The days immediately following Joss's death — the funeral and the parents' grief — are handled sensitively but without sentimentality.

Ages 10-13

Also available in:
Cassette for the Blind — *Beat the Turtle Drum*
Library of Congress

Paperbound — *Beat the Turtle Drum*
Dell Publishing Company, Inc.

267

Greene, Constance Clarke

I and Sproggy

Black/white illustrations by Emily McCully.
The Viking Press, Inc., 1978.
(155 pages)

JEALOUSY
STEPBROTHER/STEPSISTER
  Change: resisting
  Parent/Parents: remarriage of

Ten-year-old Adam lives in a New York City apartment with his mother, but his divorced father, who has remarried in England, is coming with his new wife and daughter to live in Adam's neighborhood. The boy is overjoyed at having his father so near, but he loathes the idea of sharing him with an English stepsister. Sproggy (as for some reason she is called), also ten, seems "taller, stronger, smarter, able to handle herself better than he." Adam behaves rudely to her from the very start. When his best friends, Kenny and Steve, make her a member of their hitherto all-male club, he is furious. Adam's good friend Charlie, the apartment handyman, tells him not to be so nasty; Sproggy needs friends in her new country. For their part, Charlie and his wife, having

G

enrolled in night classes at a city university, are honored by the governor during Continuing Education Week with an invitation to a lawn party at his mansion. Adam has always longed to get inside the nearby mansion and is overjoyed for Charlie. But more surprises await Adam. The day before the party, he comes across a group of neighborhood girls teasing Sproggy. She slips and falls in the street, and he helps her up and treats her to a Coke. Sproggy is all gratitude and Adam quite puffed with pride. The next day, Charlie wheels his invalid wife to the mansion, with numerous neighborhood children tagging along. Adam and Sproggy peer through the fence and then Sproggy spies her uncle among the other party guests. Uncle Dick invites the two to come in, and Adam feels his kindness to Sproggy more than rewarded.

A boy who often daydreams of being a hero is surprised first by his own surliness toward his stepsister, then by her regarding him as a hero and how good that makes him feel — about both of them. An invitation to the governor's party suggests that it even pays to be her friend. This is a perceptive, often amusing book, peopled with vivid, lively characters whose dialogue seems exactly right.

Ages 9-11

Also available in:
Paperbound — *I and Sproggy*
Dell Publishing Company, Inc.

268

Greene, Constance Clarke

I Know You, Al

Black/white illustrations by Byron Barton.
The Viking Press, Inc., 1975.
(126 pages)

FRIENDSHIP: Best Friend
PARENTAL: Absence
  Maturation
  Menstruation
  Parent/Parents: remarriage of
  Parent/Parents: single
  Puberty

At twelve-and-a-half, the narrator is a year younger than her best friend, Al, short for Alexandra. Al is the only girl in her own class who has not had her menstrual period, but she takes this casually, saying that she may never have it. Al's more immediate concern is her divorced mother's boy friend. She hopes her mother will not remarry; Al already has a father — one she has not seen in six years. Soon the long-absent father comes to town, calls her up, and asks her out to dinner. Al is angry that he can suddenly appear after such a long absence and smugly expect to see her. But her friend, the narrator, says, "I know you, Al.... You'll go — anything for a free meal." The next day Al, very excited, says her father wants her to attend his wedding. Al is unsure about going, and again her friend tries to calm her: "Al, I know you. You will do the right thing and go." By now, Al's feelings have put a strain on both girls, but during preparations for the trip, the two make up. After the wedding, Al calls her friend long-distance and tells her all went well: she likes her father's new family and they like her; she has had her first period; and she has met an interesting boy. Back at home, Al tells her friend she understands her father better and will try to forgive his earlier neglect. "The older I get, the more I know that not only is almost nothing perfect, but almost nobody, no person, is either."

In this story the narrator's level-headedness and common sense help her friend Al through some trying events. The author shows a keen ear for adolescent dialogue. With all its humor and informality, the story rings true. This book will appeal more to girls than boys, and is a sequel to *A Girl Called Al* but stands on its own.

Ages 11 and up

Also available in:
Paperbound — *I Know You, Al*
Dell Publishing Company, Inc.

269

Greenfield, Eloise

Africa Dream

Black/white illustrations by Carole Byard.
The John Day Company, Inc., 1977.
(29 pages counted)

AFRICA
AFRO-AMERICAN

A girl dreams one night that she journeys to the Africa of long ago, the Africa of her ancestors. And there, in that time, she wanders through its markets, and reads and understands its ancient books. Then she dreams herself in the village of her "long-ago granddaddy with my daddy's face"; joyously welcomed there, she dances and sings a song of greeting. Tired after wandering all over Africa, she dreams that her long-ago grandma rocks her to sleep.

In this first-person narrative, a young black girl tells of the long-ago Africa of her dreams. Simple verse and attractive illustrations convey the pride, warmth, and familiarity of the Africa she imagines.

Ages 3-6

Also available in:
No other form known

270

Greenfield, Eloise

First Pink Light

Color illustrations by Moneta Barnett.
Thomas Y. Crowell Company, Inc., 1976.
(39 pages counted)

SEPARATION FROM LOVED ONES
Determination
Love, meaning of

His father has been gone for almost a month, and young Tyree wants to welcome him home in a special way. He builds a hideout, using a chair and cardboard, from which he plans to leap out and surprise Daddy when he arrives early in the morning. But his mother wants him to go to bed: Daddy will wake him. Tyree becomes angry; he wants to be already awake when Daddy comes. His mother relents. He can wait up in a big chair, and at morning's "first pink light" he can hide and surprise Daddy. Tyree settles in with a pillow and a blanket — and soon falls asleep. He does not wake up completely even when his father arrives, lovingly picks him up, and carries him to bed.

A little boy who does not know his limits is overjoyed when he thinks he has gotten his own way about staying up all night; as he drops off to sleep he realizes his mother has won after all. Still, he does loyally greet his father just by being there when he arrives. Both text and illustrations have a gentleness and warmth that invite reading this book aloud.

Ages 3-6

Also available in:
Paperbound — *First Pink Light*
Scholastic Book Services

Talking Book — *First Pink Light*
Library of Congress

271

Greenfield, Eloise

Good News

Color illustrations by Pat Cummings.
Coward, McCann & Geoghegan, Inc., 1977.
(32 pages)

PRIDE/FALSE PRIDE
 Baby-sitting: involuntary
 Communication: lack of

Little James Edward is running home from school to tell his mother the good news: he has learned to read! The three words he recognizes are printed on the piece of paper he carries in his pocket. As he runs he thinks about all the other words he will soon know. He passes by his friends and his two younger brothers, but he will not stop to tell them. Mama must be told first. When he arrives at home, Mama is making supper, and he proudly announces, "Mama, I can read!" But she barely acknowledges him, tells him he must look after his baby sister, and when he begs twice more to be heard, he is scolded for his persistence. Finally he shares his news with the baby, who giggles ecstatically. Soon both children begin to laugh and James Edward is cheered. After playing with the baby for a while, he again wants to approach his mother, but he knows she is still busy.

Maybe tomorrow, he thinks, his mother will have time to listen to him — and by then he may even know more words.

A little boy, exuberant about his new skill, is discouraged when his mother has no time to listen to him. Desperate to share his excitement, he tells a baby sister, whose giggles of happiness console him.

Ages 5-6

Also available in:
No other form known

272

Greenfield, Eloise

Me and Neesie

Color illustrations by Moneta Barnett.
Thomas Y. Crowell Company, Inc., 1975.
(36 pages counted)

IMAGINARY FRIEND
 School: entering

Young Janell enjoys playing with her imaginary friend, Neesie, though Janell's mother does not quite understand it. Getting ready for a visit from Aunt Bea, the mother says: "I guess I can stand you making up a friend, but Aunt Bea's old and nervous, and I don't want you upsetting her." Later, when Aunt Bea starts to sit down on the couch, Janell cries out, "Don't sit on Neesie!" — and Aunt Bea beats on the sofa with her cane to get rid of "the ghost." The next day is Janell's first day of school. Neesie is sad and stays in bed, but the excited Janell goes off to school and has a wonderful time. When she returns, she cannot find Neesie — her best friend, her only playmate until now. Then Janell thinks about school and her new friends there. She decides not to tell them about Neesie because she is "just mine." Then Janell puts her head in her mother's lap and listens to her read.

This first-person narrative describes a young girl with no playmates who fills her need for them with an imaginary friend. Although her parents don't encourage this friendship, they are tolerant and understanding. The abrupt disappearance of the imaginary friend after the child's first day at school may seem contrived.

Ages 4-7

Also available in:
No other form known

273

Greenfield, Eloise

Talk About a Family

Black/white illustrations by James Calvin.
J. B. Lippincott Co., 1978.
(60 pages)

FAMILY: Relationships
SEPARATION, MARITAL
SIBLING: Relationships

Genny, about eleven, eagerly awaits the arrival of her oldest brother, Larry, who is coming home from the Army. Her friend Mr. Parker agrees to let Genny's family and friends hold a homecoming party in his backyard, and Genny's happiness is complete — except when her parents argue, which is often. When Larry does arrive, all disputes are temporarily set aside, and the family enjoys an evening at home together. But in the morning, while Larry is out seeing friends, the parents fight again. Genny's younger sister, Kim, is so distressed that she locks herself in her room. Genny and her parents pull themselves together and go to Mr. Parker's to prepare the party for Larry. When they return, they find that Kim has posted signs all over the house, saying, "UGLY." Larry comes home and demands an explanation. Getting it, he characteristically talks everyone into high good humor, and they go to the party and stay that way. Next morning at breakfast, however, Father announces that he is moving out of the house. Kim, thinking she is at fault, begins to cry. Genny gets angry — at her parents first, then at Larry, because for the first time she can ever remember, he cannot set things right. She seeks out Mr. Parker for comfort, and he explains that people and families are always changing. When she joins her brothers and sister at the park, she knows they will talk and face the situation together. The family will be different, but they will get used to it.

Young Genny is angry and confused, because her parents cannot work out their differences and keep the family together. Disappointed in her adored older brother, who has always been able to "fix things," she must finally accept the fact that he cannot glue together a broken marriage. There is no pat resolution here. The pain of a sundering family is not denied, but neither is the strength of enduring love.

Ages 8-10

Also available in:
Paperbound — Talk About a Family
Scholastic Book Services

G

274

Greenwald, Sheila

The Secret in Miranda's Closet

Black/white illustrations by the author.
Houghton Mifflin Co., 1977.
(138 pages)

AUTONOMY
IDENTITY, SEARCH FOR
  Communication: parent-child
  Courage, meaning of
  Creativity
  Gender role identity: female
  Self, attitude toward: accepting

Being the bland daughter of a busy, professionally ambitious, staunchly feminist mother is not fun. When Miranda's presence at home would conflict with Olivia's work or social life, the girl is sent to a baby-sitter or play group. One day, at the home of a sitter, Mrs. Nesbit, Miranda discovers an antique doll in the attic — the most beautiful doll she has ever seen. The fact is, Miranda has been given dolls only once in her life, and disdained that particular set as being primitive and ugly; she had much preferred her trucks and trains, thereby pleasing her mother. Now Miranda endows Dinah — for that is the doll's name, according to Mrs. Nesbit — with all the qualities she herself longs for: Dinah is at ease in conversation, poised, witty, and graceful. Best of all she is now Miranda's; Mrs. Nesbit's kindness even comes up with the doll's trunk of clothes. Miranda decides that Dinah will be a secret. Thus, when Olivia forgets to enroll Miranda in some group activities over Christmas vacation, the girl insists that she prefers "an unscheduled time to rest and dream" on her own. She does ask her mother whether she mentions dolls in her feminist lectures. "Are there any girls *left* who play with dolls?" is the reply. Undaunted, Miranda goes on preparing a house for Dinah in the back of her closet. She goes shopping for just the right wallpaper and rugs, and so meets many new people and situations, describes exactly what she wants, makes independent decisions — and even makes a friend of her own. In further talk about dolls, she learns that her mother had been given nothing but dolls as a child and had to struggle to express her real interests. But Dinah remains a secret. Then, at a party Olivia gives, her boy friend's daughter discovers Dinah, calls Miranda a "doll freak," and shows Dinah all around. Miranda is mortified, and her mother is hurt, but several guests admire the doll and Miranda's work on its home. A worse surprise awaits. The next day Olivia loses her job at the university. Suddenly Miranda sees her mother shaken, her energy gone, her mind bent upon how to get by. Miranda decides to help by selling Dinah, but when an antique dealer tries to cheat her, she refuses to be fooled, drops a well-chosen expletive, and leaves. When she tells her mother what happened, Olivia says they must always keep Dinah as a symbol of independent choice. She is proud of Miranda's spirit and says so.

Miranda and her mother see each other incompletely. The girl sees her mother as strong and successful, and Olivia sees her daughter as the perfect non-sexist child. Miranda's struggle to discover who she is, apart from her mother's image of her, balances feminist and traditional values. She is a most likeable character. With Dinah as her alter ego, she ventures into new situations, and in so doing internalizes the qualities she at first attributed to the doll. Large print and illustrations make this book even more accessible to middle-grade readers.

Ages 8-11

Also available in:
Paperbound — *The Secret in Miranda's Closet*
Scholastic Book Services

275

Griese, Arnold Alfred

The Way of Our People

Black/white illustrations by Haru Wells.
Thomas Y. Crowell Company, Inc., 1975.
(82 pages)

COURAGE, MEANING OF
FEAR
Expectations
Native American
Shame

In 1838, thirteen-year-old Kano, an Indian youth living in Alaska, is honored for killing unaided his first large game animal. But what Kano fears is to hunt alone, lest the spirit of the forest, Nakani, capture him; once already, after getting lost in the forest, he has given way to panic. His fear makes him deeply ashamed. Having confided the secret to his older sister, Maya (his mother is dead), Kano has to disclose it to his father, a noted hunter, to save Maya from being punished for accompanying him on a hunt. If Kano cannot hunt alone, he will bring immense shame to his family and exile to himself. That summer, he seeks help from an old forest recluse and gradually loses his fear of Nakani. The Old One also teaches him how to avoid getting lost. But in that fall's hunt, Kano, forgetting to spot landmarks, becomes lost again, panics, and runs mindlessly through the forest. Later his father finds him and decries that Kano will be sent in the spring to work for Russian fur traders. As the long winter begins, Kano meets a Russian doctor, and trusting him, allows himself to be vaccinated against smallpox even though the other villagers, fearing the vaccine causes the white man's disease, refuse to be treated. Told by the doctor, Ivan, to come find him if smallpox breaks out, Kano sets off with a dog team shortly after a villager falls sick. Losing the trail, he remains calm, discovers a new way to determine direction, and continues on to find Ivan. Too busy to return himself, Ivan entrusts vaccine to Kano, telling him how to administer it. After Kano successfully treats the villagers, he resolves to try hunting again and to learn from the white men how else to help his people.

The author explains in a prologue his intention to show what it was like for a young Indian to fail, through fear, to live up to the tribal code. The ending, which shows the boy thinking his way out of trouble rather than panicking, leaves no doubt that Kano can now control his fear. But without some awareness of the cultures of hunting tribes, readers may find it difficult to assess the gravity of Kano's failure. Some anthropological background would be an excellent complement to this otherwise compelling story of a youngster suffering under others' expectations.

Ages 9-12

Also available in:
Cassette for the Blind — *The Way of Our People*
Library of Congress

276

Griese, Arnold Alfred

The Wind Is Not a River

Black/white illustrations by Glo Coalson.
Thomas Y. Crowell Company, Inc., 1978.
(108 pages)

COURAGE, MEANING OF
Eskimo
Resourcefulness
Values/Valuing: moral/ethical
War

In the Aleutian Islands early in World War II, Sasan, thirteen, and her brother, Sidak, who is ten, live among some fifty other Aleuts on Attu Island. Their mother is dead, and their grandmother, who had cared for them during their father's continuing absence, has recently died, leaving the two alone. But not unprepared, for their grandmother had instructed them in the Old Ways of the Aleuts. That knowledge sees them through a sudden storm when they take a kayak around the island to a fishing camp. Returning to the village on foot the next day, they must hide from invading Japanese troops. That night, Sidak impulsively enters the village to try to free the village people, who are imprisoned in their own homes, and Sasan must go after him. Finding the village well guarded, they decide to paddle the kayak to the United States Navy base at Kiska Island some distance away. But before they set out, they discover an unconscious Japanese soldier. Sidak wants to leave him, but Sasan's conscience demands she revive him. "Both our church and the Old Ways tell us to love our enemies," she says. When a search party comes for him, the soldier does not give the children away. Rid of the soldier, Sasan and Sidak set out for Kiska and are picked up by an American submarine.

A preface gives the historical background to this story of how two courageous children try to foil the Japanese capture of Attu Island. But there is another struggle here, between the girl's espousal of the Old Ways and the boy's conviction that the Old Ways are no longer good. The suspense in this simply told tale is fun without being alarming.

Ages 9-12

Also available in:
No other form known

277

Grimes, Nikki

Growin'

Black/white illustrations by Charles Lilly.
The Dial Press, Inc., 1977.
(107 pages)

FRIENDSHIP: Best Friend
  Afro-American
  Communication: parent-child
  Death: of father
  Talents

Yolanda's world is shattered when her father is killed in an automobile accident. Pump (as she is called, short for "Pumpkin") has never been close to her mother and could always show her poems to her father. Her mother once called her poems "mumbo jumbo." Now her mother wants to move to another (though, again, black) neighborhood, forcing Pump to leave her closest girl friend and attend a new school. Pump is determined to hate everyone she meets. On the first day in her new class, she takes a particular dislike to Jim Jim, the class bully, who unfortunately sits next to her. On her way home from school, Jim Jim teasingly blocks her path. But when he finds she will not back off, he respects her and to her surprise, they become friends. Jim Jim confesses that he has become a bully on the advice of his friend Big Lil, a woman regarded as loose by the community. His bullying hides his shyness and protects him from other bullies, a secret he has never told anyone but Lil. Soon Yolanda discovers that Jim Jim is quite an artist, and the two begin to collaborate on books. Time flies by when they work together, and one night, Yolanda stays too late at Jim's house. For her punishment, she must clean the house. It is while cleaning that she finds some poetry her mother wrote in high school. When she asks about it, her mother explains she has discouraged Pump from writing to spare her the disappointment of trying to sell her work. From here on, though still determined to write, the girl feels a bond with her mother, and happier at home. School, however, bores her — so much so that one day she and Jim Jim hide in the music room to avoid standing around outdoors during a fire drill. But they discover there really is a fire, and they are trapped. It is Big Lil, the neighborhood outcast, who, disregarding all warnings, enters the building and saves them. Yolanda and Jim Jim, who have always liked Big Lil, are happy to see their self-righteous neighbors treating Lil decently for once.

In this first-person narrative, a lonely girl grows close to people she has initially disliked, and discovers that a person's most visible traits are not always the real or most important ones. The characters in this all-black story (with some black dialect) are vivid but a bit thin emotionally; Pump's feelings about the death of her father are disposed of in a few paragraphs. But as an anecdotal account of a compelling friendship, the book is at all times believable.

Ages 9-11

Also available in:
No other form known

In short stanzas of free verse, children examine their feelings. Some black children wish they could move to a country where there is no prejudice. A little girl on her way to church with her mother wonders why they could not invite the Lord over to their house. Another little girl hopes soon to be playing with some children on the other side of a gate, and yet another tells of feeling happy and safe when she is with her older sister. While one child longs for school to begin, another ponders what to write for school composition. Other children voice bewilderment over a mother who refuses to communicate, speculate about how school can change the way people live, and muse on the death of a grandparent.

Each verse in this short anthology expresses an emotion or thought common to children, sometimes in language common to black people. The children in the illustrations are black; the thoughts expressed are universal to children. This book can stimulate group discussions of children's feelings.

Ages 5-9

Also available in:
No other form known

G

278

Grimes, Nikki

Something on My Mind

Black/white illustrations by Tom Feelings.
The Dial Press, Inc., 1978.
(31 pages counted)

EMOTIONS: Identifying
    Afro-American

279

Gripe, Maria Kristina

The Green Coat

Translated from the Swedish by Sheila La Farge.
Delacorte Press, 1977.
(170 pages)

IDENTITY, SEARCH FOR
Death: of father
Determination
Identification with others: adults
Separation, marital
Values/Valuing: moral/ethical
Women's rights

On Saturday, May 13, 1972, outside Kopmann's Department Store, thirteen-year-old Frederika decides to change into "Her Self." And lo, this quiet, withdrawn loner, badgered by Irma, her strong, outspoken feminist mother, to become a truly modern woman, to be more like Florence, her older sister, or like Philip, her younger brother, now seemingly becomes strong, invulnerable, and outspoken herself. She does not know for sure what has sparked the change — perhaps her mother forcing her to buy a green coat rather than a jacket. And yet, when Mother had asked the children to treat her as an equal and call her Irma, Frederika had ceased to regard her as a mother. The girl has continued to love Dad, even though Irma had deplored his ineffectual, escapist ways and finally driven him from the house. A year later, he was to be killed in an auto accident. During that year, by imitating Irma's bluff style and cutting sarcasm, Frederika becomes the leader of her class. But ironically, she is drawn against her will into friendship with the class nonentity, a wealthy but deeply unsure girl named Britt, who idolizes her, buys a coat like hers, follows her around. When classmates tease Britt, Frederika defends her — then feels obliged not to desert her. Wishing to withdraw, she finally accepts it as her duty to bring out the "true" Britt. This she does by encouraging her to take up athletics, at which she excels, and instilling her with confidence in general. When Britt no longer needs her as a model and protector, Frederika, acknowledging this, wonders whether there are yet talents and resources within herself that have nothing to do with imitating her mother, nothing to do with being what Britt wanted her to be. She resolves to find out. First, she gets rid of the green coat.

In this story the author draws sharp portraits of a bumbling and loving father, an efficient and willful mother, and a girl attached to both. Frederika at first renounces her father's gentleness to imitate her mother. Her ensuing friendship with Britt helps Britt to grow up, but leaves Frederika with the suspicion that she herself is still covering up unexamined hopes and fears. She will no longer be her mother — let her mother be that. Frederika will be herself. It may take an experienced reader to understand the allusions and symbols the author has used to portray a girl trying to find her true feelings and real character. It is character that guides this book, not plot.

Ages 13 and up

Also available in:
No other form known

280

Grohskopf, Bernice

Children in the Wind

Atheneum Publishers, 1977.
(190 pages)

FRIENDSHIP: Meaning of
  Communication: parent-child
  Cults
  Inferiority, feelings of
  School: classmate relationships

Lenore Pickel is immediately attracted to her new ninth-grade classmate, Chris Rivers, a girl who is everything she is not: lovely, sophisticated, aloof. Though the girls become friends, Chris evades questions about personal matters to the point of lying. She says her father is dead; later, that her mother, whom she intensely dislikes, has driven him away. Lenore cannot help but distrust her new friend. Lenore is befriended by a bright schoolmate named Marah, who questions her about her friendship with Chris but will not say why she is interested. Lenore has her own troubles: her mother wants to move out of the city, to follow the company she works for; her father wants to stay. Lenore wants to stay too, but neither parent asks her opinion. To spite them both, she attends a meeting of a religious cult with Chris and is attracted by the love and sense of community she feels there. Chris, after her boy friend runs off to join the cult, considers following his lead. Instead, she goes off with her father. Later, Marah reveals that she knows from her father's notes — he is a psychiatrist treating Mrs. Rivers — that Mr. Rivers is a former Nazi officer. It follows, Marah says, that Chris would have been a bad influence. Lenore, understanding now why Chris had hidden her past, upbraids Marah for tarring the daughter and the father with the same brush. Lenore vows never again to be deceived by appearances. She even makes up her mind to agree to her family's moving away — unnecessarily, because her parents have decided to stay put while her mother tries commuting to her job.

This detailed story of friends, parents, and offspring is narrated by Lenore in a wry, deprecating tone. With experience, Lenore comes to see things as they are: the idealism of a religious cult being as likely to mislead as the idealism of Mr. Rivers as a young Nazi; someone's air of distinction — Chris's sophistication — concealing what is in fact deep loneliness. All three girls — Lenore, Chris, and Marah — are struggling to establish their own identities in the welter of their parents' complicated lives.

Ages 11-13

Also available in:
No other form known

281

Grohskopf, Bernice

Shadow in the Sun

Atheneum Publishers, 1975.
(182 pages)

WHEELCHAIR, DEPENDENCE ON
  Anger
  Communication: importance of
  Jealousy
  Rejection

Thirteen-year-old Frances thinks her month's stay with her Aunt Louise on Cape Cod will be boring, but then she becomes the paid companion to a fourteen-year-old girl confined to a wheelchair. Wilma Byher spends her summers with her father, her winters with her divorced mother, but she much prefers her father. Wilma is sarcastic, outspoken, and demanding, and Fran soon finds herself angered and confused at Wilma's mood swings. Pleasant one moment, Wilma turns cruel the next, but soon Fran begins to catch on: Wilma hates the pity others show her and deeply resents her father's overprotectiveness. Worse, Wilma fears that the upcoming birth of a child to Mr. Byher's second wife, Gretchen, will displace her. Fran herself offends Wilma deeply by making friends with Jack, a hard-working local youth to whom Wilma is attracted. Then Gretchen's baby is born and Wilma's father remains at the hospital hours longer than Wilma thinks is necessary. She turns nasty again and lashes out at Fran by claiming that Fran's Aunt Louise is a lesbian. Fran walks out, furious and dismayed. Later, not finding Wilma at home, Mr. Byher seeks Fran out and blames her for allowing Wilma to go off alone. Stung by his unfairness, Fran retorts: "Wilma thinks you don't like her because she's crippled.... You didn't come home from the hospital — you stayed with the baby.... She thinks you hate her. That's why she says such terrible things." Mr. Byher is speechless, stricken. The phone rings: Wilma is in the hospital after falling into a nearby marsh. Later that day, at the hospital, Mr. Byher assures Wilma of his love and asks her to come live with him and Gretchen and the new baby — something he has always wanted but never asked, thinking Wilma happier with her mother.

Here is a story of how a fairly ordinary girl learns to befriend a handicapped girl by being as honest and at ease with her as with anyone else, avoiding the pity and condescension so often shown handicapped people. This is a strong, realistic exploration of the fear, bitterness, anger, and frustration felt by a handicapped person who just wants "to be ordinary with legs."

Ages 10 and up

Also available in:
No other form known

282
Grollman, Earl A.

Talking About Death: A Dialogue Between Parent and Child

Black/white illustrations by Gisela Héau.
Beacon Press, 1976.
(98 pages paperbound)

DEATH: Attitude Toward

The narrator is explaining death to a child whose grandfather has died. Gently, simply we learn that Grandfather will not be coming back, because his body no longer has life. Those who loved him will long to have him back, and in grief they may cry, or feel somehow responsible, even feel resentful. These emotions are perfectly all right, and, if felt, should be expressed or talked about. No one fully understands death, but all people will eventually die. The child can still talk about Grandfather and will always have him in memory.

This simple, honest explanation of death is accompanied by a Parents' Guide which suggests various ways to use the book. A section entitled "For Further Help" lists and describes people and agencies that may also help. "For Further Listening, Reading, and Viewing" lists books for children and adults, as well as cassettes and films, all providing more information.

Ages 6-10

Also available in:
No other form known

283

Grollman, Earl A.

Talking About Divorce: A Dialogue Between Parent and Child

Black/white illustrations by Alison Cann.
Beacon Press, 1975.
(87 pages)

DIVORCE: of Parents

A young child's parents are no longer getting along with each other. Sometimes Mommy cries; Daddy is not home as much as he used to be. The narrator explains as a parent might that Mommy and Daddy are not going to live together anymore, that they are going to get a divorce. But the child is not at fault — is, rather, the happy, wonderful part of their lives. The child may be sad or angry or frightened about the divorce, and should go ahead and show it. The parents want to know about such feelings. Mommy and Daddy still love the child and will always take the very best care they can of one so well loved.

The illustrations here should help parent or child understand the feelings that accompany divorce. The text approximates a wise parent's voice. The purpose over all is to assist adults in helping children through a divorce. Two lists are appended: "For Further Help" is a directory of agencies and associations able to provide support and information, and "For Further Reading" is an annotated bibliography of pertinent books for children and adult publications dealing with aspects of divorce.

Ages 7-10

Also available in:
Paperbound — *Talking About Divorce: A Dialogue Between Parent and Child*
Beacon Press

284

Grollman, Sharon Hya

More Time to Grow. Explaining Mental Retardation to Children: A Story

Black/white illustrations by Arthur Polonsky.
Beacon Press, 1977.
(98 pages)

MENTAL RETARDATION
    Sibling: relationships

Nine-year-old Carla is puzzled by her five-year-old brother, Arthur. He seems different from other children: he cannot tie his shoelaces, or color, or play kickball. Sometimes it angers Carla to have such a brother. And what is making her parents so sad lately? One day they take Carla for a walk and her father explains to her that Arthur is retarded. The boy has less capacity to learn than other children and will require extra help. Carla is bewildered, frightened, angry, resenting Arthur even more; he seems stranger than ever to her, and she stops playing with him. One day in the drugstore, Sam, the man behind the counter, gives her a candy bar, and tells her about his daughter, a little girl who is retarded. Carla goes home and starts acting friendlier to Arthur, whereupon he teaches her a song he has made up. The whole family is happy at Carla's change of heart.

The story of Carla and Arthur is followed by a series of thought-provoking questions and activities designed to help children understand what retardation is. An

G

appended "Parents' and Teachers' Guide" by Robert Perske suggests ways adults can use this book. Also included is an annotated list of organizations, books, and films dealing with mental retardation.

Ages 6-10

Also available in:
No other form known

285

Guest, Judith

Ordinary People

The Viking Press, Inc., 1976.
(263 pages)

DEPRESSION
GUILT, FEELINGS OF
Communication: parent-child
Mental illness: of adolescent

Seventeen-year-old Conrad Jarrett has recently returned home after eight months in a mental hospital. He had almost managed to commit suicide by cutting his wrists with a razor blade. Now he is back at school, trying to adjust to life on the "outside." Twice a week he visits Dr. Berger, a psychiatrist, who tries to help him understand the events of the last year and a half. The trouble had begun with the death of Conrad's adored roistering older brother, Buck, who had drowned two summers earlier in a sailing accident. After that, Con had become more and more remote. His good grades had dropped, and he had lapsed into severe depressions. Then he had cut himself, and confinement had followed. Now he must learn again to care about school assignments, to get along with his parents (who he

thinks mistrust his sanity), and to get close to his friends. Dr. Berger does help him to see how all this can be done, and life looks brighter. Con begins dating Jeannine; his school work goes well. One day, talking to Dr. Berger, he is struck by a sudden new thought: ever since the accident, he has felt his mother blames him for Buck's accident — and he has blamed himself, for hanging on to the overturned boat while Buck had let go and drowned. Meanwhile, Con's parents are gripped by the death and its aftermath in deeper and deeper ways. Cal Jarrett accuses his wife of being uncaring, too involved with herself. Beth Jarrett finds Cal unduly anxious and over-protective of Con. Both parents have changed in their grief. The two drift apart, and finally, at Beth's request, separate. Con, however, has understood a good deal. He has forgiven his mother for what he had thought was her blame of him. And he has stopped blaming himself. He has accepted his father's wisdom: there are some things in life that cannot be explained — only endured.

We meet Con on his return to school; all prior events are revealed through dialogue and flashbacks. Alternating chapters are told from Con's point of view and his father's. This intensely dramatic story presents three distinctive personalities, each attempting to surmount inadequacy in the grip of grief and self-doubt.

Ages 13 and up

Also available in:
Cassette for the Blind — *Ordinary People*
Library of Congress

Paperbound — *Ordinary People*
Ballantine Books, Inc.

Film — *Ordinary People*
Paramount Pictures Corporation
Wildwood Enterprises Production

286

Gunther, Louise

A Tooth for the Tooth Fairy

Color illustrations by James Cummins.
Garrard Publishing Co., 1978.
(48 pages)

TOOTH, LOSS OF
  Problem solving

While playing at a playground, Rose, about six, loses a
front tooth. She puts the tooth into her pants pocket, but
while she is hanging upside down on the climbing bars
it falls out and is lost. Her friends Anna and Oscar help
her hunt, but it cannot be found. Rose is afraid that if
she has no tooth for evidence the tooth fairy will not
leave money under her pillow. Oscar suggests she use
an old set of false teeth of his grandfather's; Rose and
Anna try to make a tooth of papier maché; they examine
a shark's tooth to see if it might pass as a substitute.
Nothing seems right. Then Anna takes a photograph of
Rose showing the space where the missing front tooth
was. Rose shows the picture to her parents and puts it
under her pillow that night. In the morning she finds the
picture gone and money under the pillow. She treats
Anna and herself to ice-cream cones.

A little girl and her best friend, with successive
attempts, finally find the right evidence to bolster a true
but otherwise questionable report. The falling out of the
girl's tooth occurs matter-of-factly, without pain or
apprehensiveness.

Ages 5-8

Also available in:
No other form known

287

Haar, Jaap ter

The World of Ben Lighthart

Translated from the Dutch by Martha Mearns.
Delacorte Press, 1977.
(123 pages)

BLINDNESS
  Accidents
  Family: unity

Ben Lighthart, a high school boy, awakens one day in a
hospital bed with an agonizing headache and heavy
bandages on his eyes. It is explained to him: several
days earlier he had been struck by a motorcycle; a head
injury has left him completely blind. For days, as Ben
drifts in and out of consciousness, he is flooded with
terror and self-pity. Only as he regains strength and
awareness is he able to think more clearly; at times he
even accepts his blindness. Through his brief period of
training in new ways of doing things, his roommates
encourage him — "Keep on loving life . . . make something of it," says a college boy with a terminal illness —
and Ben learns that others have equally hard lots to get
used to. When at last Ben is well enough to go home,
everyone at home insists on treating him the same as
always. But Ben soon knows that his blindness changed
almost everything. His parents and a classmate try to
teach him to type and to read Braille, and encourage
him to catch up on his studies. But the work is overwhelming. Reluctantly, Ben and his parents admit that
he will be best equipped for a lifetime of blindness by
taking his formal education at a boarding school for
blind people. Though saddened to leave his family, Ben
does not doubt the decision he and they have made.

A young man suddenly blind for life is pitched into
despair at first. Before very long, however, he begins to

H

view his situation with rational care and arrives at sensible decisions for himself. Knowledgeable older readers may be puzzled at the meager counseling and training afforded Ben and note the corresponding largesse of family encouragement and brisk progress toward compensatory skills and independence. But the characters are no less liable to despair, anger, and fear of the future — are, in short, recognizably human.

Ages 10-13

Also available in:
Paperbound — *The World of Ben Lighthart*
Dell Publishing Company, Inc.

288

Hall, Lynn

Flowers of Anger

Black/white illustrations by Joseph Cellini.
Follett Publishing Company, 1976.
(127 pages)

FRIENDSHIP: Best Friend
REVENGE
  Death: of pet
  Loss: feelings of
  Love, meaning of

Carey and Ann, both sixteen, both crazy about horses, have been inseparable best friends for five years. Carey owns a horse, Sarge, passed on from an older cousin who has gone away to college. Ann, however, had saved for two years to buy Nipper, and has raised and trained her singlehanded, to the great admiration of the local riding club. Ann and Carey enter their horses in a show. The night before the big day, Carey is to stay at Ann's house, and Ann brings Nipper from the stable outside of town and ties her in the backyard. As the two girls are about to go to sleep, they hear a gunshot. Rushing to the window, they see that Nipper is gone. Did she break her halter at the sound of the shot and run off? They begin to search — and are horrified to find Nipper dead in the next yard, their neighbor, George Greenawalt, standing near with a rifle in his hand. The horse had been damaging his exquisite and acclaimed rose garden, George insists. He was defending his property. Heartbroken, Ann begins a mourning that will go on for weeks. Her father settles out of court with George, and George writes Ann a check for the value of the horse. But she tells Carey that money cannot replace Nipper; she only wants to hurt George as badly as he has hurt her. If the only thing precious to George is his garden, a showplace of beautiful roses and shrubs, then the garden it will be. Carey is appalled at the thought of such destruction and tries everything in her power to change Ann's mind. Just buy a new horse, she begs, and forget about revenge. But Ann grows more bitter each day, leaving Carey to wonder whether she must find a new friend. Ann watches George's house for two weeks to determine when he is usually out. When she is sure she will not be caught, she sneaks into George's garden and methodically drenches each rose bush and shrub with gasoline. Carey watches from a distance, unable to stop her. Gradually Carey realizes that she is still Ann's friend, even after this. But what consequences lie ahead for Ann?

Vengefulness wreaks a great change in Ann and greatly endangers her friendship with Carey. For her part, Carey sees how deep is that friendship when she finds herself ready to continue it. Carey tells this thought-provoking story, discussing in the course of it both same-sex friendship and her feelings about dating. The ending, which leaves the future to the reader's imagination, provides subjects for discussion.

Ages 10-12

Also available in:
Paperbound — *Flowers of Anger*
Avon Books

289

Hallman, Ruth

I Gotta Be Free

The Westminster Press, 1977.
(92 pages)

RUNNING AWAY
  Communication: parent-child
  Crime/Criminals
  Dependence/Independence

Jay, seventeen years old, is fed up with his father's overbearing interference. Pushed too far one day about always eating, he runs away, hitching a ride south with a young man named Lee Johnson and his fifteen-year-old sister, Linda. Heading for Florida, Lee acts so suspiciously that Jay wants out, but he is attracted to the shy, fearful girl and stays with them even when they reach home. Lee takes him night fishing that night and by the time Jay realizes that "fishing" means robbing, Lee tells him he cannot back out. He is in too deep. A detective follows the escaping pair. Seeing him, Lee ducks out of his car, instructing Jay to drive home. There, Jay and Linda are arrested. After the two separately tell Detective Mason how Lee managed things, Lee is arrested and the charges against the two are dismissed. Linda, whose parents are dead, departs to an aunt's. Undecided where to go, Jay tells the understanding Mason about his father. Without telling him what to do, the policeman suggests that he regard his father not simply as a father but as a person. Jay returns home to find that Mason has called ahead. Father and son begin to talk, and this time Jay knows very well what he wants, and it is not what his father wants. But his father is going to listen.

By returning to confront his father, Jay shows he has learned that running away is no answer to parental bullying; freedom is not found but won. This story, with its sketchy plot and characters, moves so quickly that its awkward moments — especially Jay's failure to understand what is so obviously happening during the night-fishing expedition — slip smoothly by. This is a good selection for readers with limited vocabularies.

Ages 10-13

Also available in:
Braille — *I Gotta Be Free*
Library of Congress

290

Hamilton, Gail, pseud.

Titania's Lodestone

Atheneum Publishers, 1975.
(200 pages)

IDENTITY, SEARCH FOR
  Family: unity
  Life style
  Prejudice: social class
  Self, attitude toward: feeling different

Fifteen-year-old Priscilla Parkins is elated. She and her older brother, Peter, and their unconventional parents have returned to the United States to live in Priscilla's late grandfather's house, after many years of wandering in Europe. Paul, the father, wears his hair in a pony-tail, and the self-styled Titania, their mother, wears motley European clothes and carries a lodestone for family luck. Still, Pris dreams of living as a "normal" American teenager, in a real home. But the family van breaks down in a small Massachusetts town. Paul takes work as a mechanic, and the family camps nearby — until they come upon the shell of a castle modeled after Hampton Court which they forthwith heat and insulate and move into. With a sinking heart, Pris realizes that they are there for the winter, never mind the grandfather's house. But she is consoled by a lost or abandoned Afghan hound she finds and immediately adopts, naming him Prince Hassan. When school begins, Priscilla is both evasive about her parents and the family's past life and, unlike Peter, easily offended. She is also amazed that two newfound friends, Jimmy and Kath, envy her past. Uneasy when her mother addresses a school assembly on transcendental meditation, Priscilla only relaxes after it is clear that her mother is well received. Just before Christmas, everything goes wrong: the grandfather's house is destroyed in a storm and Prince Hassan is reclaimed by his owner. Her dream house is gone, and Priscilla despairs of ever seeing her beloved dog again. But when her parents and friends present Hassan to her as a Christmas gift, Pris realizes that her real dream house is where one feels loved and at ease with oneself, one's family, and one's proven friends. As for Titania's lodestone, it stands for the good luck the Parkins family makes for itself.

A teenage girl desperately desires a conventional, stable family life, but comes to see that loving family life is the greater prize. For all her parents' bohemian outlook, Priscilla's family is rich in natural feeling, and her growing perception of this is skillfully portrayed. Her story is made even more sympathetic by the entries from her journal scattered through it. A secondary theme of social prejudice culminates in an unsuccessful attempt by some of the townspeople to evict the Parkins family.

Ages 11-13

Also available in:
Braille — *Titania's Lodestone*
Library of Congress

291
Hamilton, Virginia

Arilla Sun Down
Greenwillow Books, 1976.
(248 pages)

IDENTITY, SEARCH FOR
MATURATION
Jealousy: sibling
Native American
Pride/False pride
Sibling: younger

Arilla Adams, twelve, has no close friends at school and feels like a stranger even in her own family. Arilla's mother, who is black, runs a dance studio, but the daughter refuses to enroll and calls the girls who do "snobs." Arilla's father, a restaurant supervisor, is part black and part Indian, and his wife calls him "erratic" for his habit of disappearing from time to time — to where, Arilla does not know, though her mother seems to. It is her older brother, Jack Sun Run Adams, who has Arilla nearly sick with envy and resentment, at least sometimes. Above all, Jack Sun Run is *proud* that he and his father are Indians or, as he says, "Amerinds." Both the boy and his father have the word "sun" in their names, and Jack Sun Run, a good horseman, wields a lasso with amazing accuracy and projects such extraordinary presence that girls flock to him. Arilla's parents think the world of him. Saddled with such a brother, Arilla wonders what and who she is. She knows she likes rollerskating, but her mother forbids her to go to the rink. (It is one of the nice things that Jack Sun Run sometimes does for her that he sneaks off with Arilla to the rink after their parents are asleep.) Arilla likes to write, too, but who pays attention to that? Jack Sun Run seems always to steal the show, even at her twelfth birthday party. Jack and her father make matters worse by giving her a horse on that occasion, when she hates horses. But she becomes a good horsewoman in spite of herself, and rides a lot with her brother, wondering sometimes whether he might want her dead. One day they are out riding a good distance from home when an ice storm is suddenly upon them and Sun's horse falls on him, hurting him badly. Knowing she has no one else to depend on, Arilla goes for help. Sun spends a week in the hospital. Meanwhile their father has disappeared again, and since Sun cannot fetch him this time, Arilla goes. It seems that Mr. Adams at intervals feels impelled to return to his hometown, to renew old ties and restore his sense of himself. He tells her that Jack had once saved her life. He says he thinks Jack sometimes goes too far with his Indian "act." Arilla for the first time feels that someone is on her side. She confesses her secret passion for rollerskating, and her father promises to go with her sometime. She begins to feel that she belongs.

Saving her older brother's life at long last gives Arilla the confidence to assert herself, the way Jack always has. Her struggle to find her own identity makes a memorable if slow-moving book. Because she tells her story both in the present and in flashbacks, with some passages of dialect, this book will appeal most to advanced readers.

Ages 12 and up

Also available in:
Cassette for the Blind — *Arilla Sun Down*
Library of Congress

Paperbound — *Arilla Sun Down*
Dell Publishing Company, Inc.

292
Hanlon, Emily

It's Too Late for Sorry
Bradbury Press, Inc., 1978.
(222 pages)

BOY-GIRL RELATIONSHIPS
MENTAL RETARDATION
 Marijuana
 Peer relationships
 Prejudice: toward handicapped persons

Kenny's favorite sport is football and Phil's is making people uncomfortable. By their sophomore year in high school the two, formerly best friends, have grown apart, the end of their friendship following on Phil's mocking of a mentally retarded youth named Harold. Kenny apologizes for Phil to Harold's older brother and is drawn into playing with Harold. This casual acquaintance expands to a full-scale project when Rachel, the girl Kenny likes, enlists him to help her teach Harold to get on with others. More interested in Rachel than in Harold, Kenny pitches in, but as his feelings for her deepen, he increasingly resents the time Rachel spends with Harold and helping at a school for mentally retarded people. Just before summer, the two break up over this point. When next he sees Rachel and Harold, Kenny is stoned on marijuana pressed on him by Phil, and he abuses them. Bewildered by Kenny's behavior, Harold runs away and is not found until several days later. Kenny's attempts to apologize are rebuffed by Rachel and Harold's brother, and only his job teaching children to swim saves Kenny from a wholly miserable summer. But by fall he begins to accept what has happened and what it means. Rachel softens to him after a time, and although she can never feel about him as she once did, she lets him know that one ugly incident cannot negate all the help he once gave Harold.

In this first-person narrative, Kenny involves himself in the serious business of aiding a mentally retarded youth out of a purely selfish motive. Hence, he comes to see his eventual cruelty to Harold as compounded of jealousy and resentment as well as plain prejudice. Of note here is how Harold, having spent years being ignored in an institution, improves rapidly when given affectionate personal attention. Less persuasive is the extremity of misbehavior Kenny is brought to supposedly by smoking marijuana.

Ages 11-14

Also available in:
No other form known

293

Hapgood, Miranda

Martha's Mad Day

Black/white illustrations by Emily McCully.
Crown Publishers, Inc., 1977.
(32 pages counted)

ANGER

Martha, about four, wakes up Saturday morning feeling "big and fierce and mean." She jumps out of bed and throws her favorite stuffed toy, Pig, across the room. After leaving the water running in the bathroom, and turning the volume up on the television, and misbehaving at breakfast, she goes outdoors. There she pretends she is queen and must be obeyed by everyone. Back at home for dinner, she announces that she is not sorry for the way she has been acting, and that she is staying up until midnight. Her parents, making no response, go to their room. But at 9:30, as if nothing has happened, Martha's mother sends her to bed. From her bed, Martha's room seems so large, dark, and quiet that Martha retrieves Pig and apologizes to him.

This brief text follows a little girl through a day-long mood of aggression, which alters when she finds she needs comforting. Because the source of the child's aggressive mood is not mentioned, this text could be used in many situations. Reading and discussing it could help small children to accept occasional moods of unfocused anger.

Ages 3-6

Also available in:
No other form known

294

Harris, Dorothy Joan

The School Mouse

Color illustrations by Chris Conover.
Frederick Warne & Company, Inc., 1977.
(33 pages counted)

ANXIETY
FEAR: of School
  Friendship: making friends

Six-year-old Jonathan does not like school: there is a barking dog he must pass on the way, and a third grader who likes to take his hat; and sometimes his teacher is cross. Then too, there are so many things to remember: his lunch, his notebook, his raincoat when it rains, and how to print. But Jonathan takes both mouse and jeep to school and shows the class how the mouse rides. It is decided that the mouse will stay and be a school mouse. That afternoon, Toby, a classmate, walks home with Jonathan. And that night, as Jonathan snuggles into bed, he looks forward to going to school the next day.

A little boy is so preoccupied with what he dislikes about school that he can see nothing good in it. But both his dislike and his feeling of helplessness abate when he shares a surprising pet with the class and makes a friend. Whether or not his mouse really talks to Jonathan is something readers or listeners could discuss. This long narrative reads aloud well and is a sequel to *The House Mouse*.

Ages 6-8

Also available in:
No other form known

295

Harris, Robie H.

Don't Forget to Come Back

Color illustrations by Tony De Luna.
Alfred A. Knopf, Inc., 1978.
(37 pages counted)

BABY-SITTER
  Separation anxiety
  Tantrums
  Transitional objects: security blanket

Little Annie is fit to be tied, because her parents are going out for the evening. First she offers to go with them, promising to be no trouble, but Mother turns her down. At dinner, Annie refuses to eat, complaining of a serious stomachache which can only be cured if her parents stay home. Then she insists on packing her most precious possessions — including her blanket — in her knapsack so that she can go along. But when Bob, the baby-sitter, arrives, she hides, then throws a tantrum, demanding that her parents remain until she finds her blanket. Bob soon discovers the blanket in the knapsack, and her parents leave. Annie is outwitted and

resigns herself to the situation. As they go out the door, they promise to come home that same night. Annie admonishes them not to "forget to come back."

Annie tries intrusion, minor blackmail, plain insistence, and then a tantrum — anything to keep her parents from going out for the evening. Her fear of abandonment is genuine, but can only be proved groundless by their going and returning. Her parents' calm in the face of her alarm is reassuring to the reader as well as — eventually — to Annie. Parents may wish to read this book aloud, then start a family discussion of it to allay small children's fears.

Ages 3-7

Also available in:
No other form known

296

Härtling, Peter

Oma

Translated from the German by Anthea Bell.
Black/white illustrations by Jutta Ash.
Harper & Row Publishers, Inc., 1977.
(95 pages)

GRANDPARENT: Living in Home of
GRANDPARENT: Love for
  Maturation
  Orphan
  Parent/Parents: substitute

Kalle, five, is orphaned by a car accident and goes to live with Oma, his 65-year-old grandmother in Munich. The first few months he stays home from school, getting to know Oma, making his rounds with her — to market, to visit friends, to the Welfare Office, where she demands the support money due her. The boy often winces at her brusque, sometimes insulting manner, but he likes her keen humor and the fact that she takes him seriously. It is mutual. Once in school, where he makes friends quickly, he must rebuke her interference in a fight, and Oma learns to let him choose both his friends and his fights. Kalle, in turn, learns to listen patiently to her oft-repeated stories, one of her favorites deriving from their vacation honoring Kalle's eighth birthday. Out walking with him, Oma had fallen into a turnip pit. Sputtering mad, she had dragged herself out, but afterward, retelling the story, she makes her escape sound more colorful than it had been, and Kalle rebukes her for lying. Oma only laughs: "When you've had a dull life as I have, you have to invent some excitement...." During Kalle's third year in school he gets into trouble for unfinished homework, but when the volatile Oma comes to talk with his teacher, Kalle offers deep thanks for her unexpected tact. Still, the trouble at school brings the social worker. Her questions about Oma's health and provision for the boy frighten him — and anger the grandmother. "I won't be sick!" she vows. But shortly before Kalle's tenth birthday she does fall ill and must stay in the hospital for two weeks. For her return, Kalle puts out a "Welcome" sign and hugs her for the first time, as she has always hugged him. Kalle is deeply relieved and feels his life is back to normal — but Oma reminds him, "You must learn to do without me, you know." After his birthday party, she talks frankly with him about his future and how long she expects and hopes to be a part of it. "I've made up my mind to live as long as I can," she says. "But making up your mind isn't enough, though it helps."

Orphaned at the age of five, a boy begins a new life with his loving, outspoken grandmother. She knows she does much that seems strange to the boy, but she does not attempt to stand in for his parents; instead, she makes time for them to get used to each other. They learn from each other, and grow to love and need each other. As the boy grows older and more independent they can at last discuss her inevitable death and his future. The short, diary-like comments by the grandmother following each chapter offer frank, sometimes poignant, insights into an older woman who is coping with increasing age and her grandson's strengthening youth.

Ages 8-11

Also available in:
No other form known

297

Hassler, Jon

Four Miles to Pinecone

Frederick Warne & Company, Inc., 1977.
(117 pages)

CRIME/CRIMINALS
VALUES/VALUING: Moral/Ethical
   Guilt, feelings of
   Loyalty
   Peer relationships

Tom Barry, a high school boy from St. Paul, begins his story with the words "Summer is over"; this book is the story of that astonishing summer. Tom first recalls the end of the school year, when his report card reported an F for English. He goes to see the English teacher to request a change of grade, pointing out that he has gotten all As and Bs on the tests. Mr. Singleton points out the forty-seven Fs earned on the assignments Tom has never turned in. The teacher offers one avenue to a passing grade: Tom must write a story forty-seven pages long. The drama of that summer commences the very next day, when the grocery store where Tom is working is held up, and the owner badly beaten. Tom has recognized one of the robbers as his school friend Mouse Brown. But he cannot bring himself to tell Mr. Afton, the police detective — out of loyalty to his friend and the knowledge, too, that Mouse is supporting an unemployed, suicidal father, a neurotic mother, and two little brothers. For the rest of the summer, Tom struggles with the guilt of thus protecting Mouse. He is still struggling when, over the Labor Day weekend, he journeys to the wilds near Pinecone, Minnesota, to watch his aunt and uncle's resort while they are away. Someone has been stealing boat motors from residents in the area. At the resort, Tom goes out fishing with an elderly recluse named Lester Flett, and they talk about loyalty in friendship. That night Tom sees a motor being stolen from his uncle's boat, and when he runs to get Lester he finds him storing the stolen motor in a shed full of motors. Suddenly a van drives out of nowhere and nearly runs Tom down. Hiding, he hears Lester and the driver of the van, Bruno Rock, making plans to drive all the stolen motors to Canada and sell them. Bruno wants to find Tom and kill him, but Lester says no. Heading for town to get the sheriff, Tom is overtaken by the van, and Lester and Bruno leap out. Eluding them and circling back, Tom is himself just pulling away in the van when Bruno leaps onto its roof. With Bruno stuck there, Tom drives the four miles to Pinecone and turns the case over to the sheriff. Convinced now that crime cannot be looked away from, Tom returns to St. Paul and tells Mr. Afton everything he knows about Mouse Brown. At the library, he writes the whole story for Mr. Singleton, not in forty-seven pages but in the 117 we have just finished reading.

This exciting novel captures urban life in St. Paul and life in the wilds of northern Minnesota in the words of a high school junior. But the English teacher, the grocer, Mouse Brown, Lester Flett, and Tom's father are portrayed no less warmly and memorably for that. The story stresses the working-class values of working hard, telling the truth, and getting through school. Crime — and laziness — do not pay. When, at the end, Tom

explains to Mouse why he has turned him in, and Mouse spits in his face, Tom knows both that he has betrayed a friend and that he was right to do so.

Ages 10-14

Also available in:
No other form known

298

Hautzig, Deborah

Hey, Dollface

William Morrow & Company, Inc., 1978.
(151 pages)

VALUES/VALUING: Moral/Ethical
  Friendship: best friend
  Homosexuality: female
  Love, meaning of

New students at a private school for girls, Valerie and Chloe, both fifteen, quickly become close friends. What especially binds them is their disagreement with opinions and concerns of their classmates. Though they often talk of sex and occasionally date, neither girl is particularly attracted to boys. Valerie senses a special current of attraction between Chloe and herself. Worried that this might be perverse, she asks her mother and then a teacher about homosexuality. Upset that neither can say it is right or wrong, unnatural or not, she considers asking Chloe but fears being rebuffed or called weird. Indeed, her fears seem confirmed when Chloe, after the sudden death of her father, avoids her. Later Chloe explains she was not avoiding her, only attending her mother, and Valerie agrees to come over shortly after the school term ends. Going to bed in the same bed, the girls caress each other. Confused, unable to discuss what this means, Valerie flees home the next morning before Chloe awakens. Only when the two return from their summer jobs do they meet and discuss their feelings. Chloe is sure she is not a lesbian but Valerie is less sure about herself. They do agree that what they feel is not wrong. "How do you separate loving as a friend and sexual love — or do they cross over sometimes?" They decide to go on as before.

Two adolescent girls, especially the narrator, are confused and afraid of their feelings for each other; they wonder if such feelings are pathological or wrong. They try to get answers from adults, to no avail — no one has pat answers here. The girls agree that they will always be best friends, but they both know that a sexual attraction did, and still does, exist between them. This book candidly discusses sex — intercourse, orgasm — as well as homosexuality.

Ages 12 and up

Also available in:
Cassette for the Blind — *Hey, Dollface*
Library of Congress

Paperbound — *Hey, Dollface*
Bantam Books, Inc.

299

Hayes, Geoffrey

Bear by Himself

Color illustrations by the author.
Harper & Row Publishers, Inc., 1976.
(32 pages)

PRIVACY, NEED FOR

Sometimes Bear likes to be by himself: to think, to talk to the river, to fly his kite — alone and free. When he feels like it, he window-shops or explores his own backyard. Sometimes he does nothing at all. After a day all to himself, he comes home to his warm house, goes to bed, and dreams.

This simple story shows that spending some time alone is necessary and valuable. The illustrations convey tranquillity and effortless enjoyment of living.

Ages 4-6

Also available in:
Paperbound — *Bear by Himself*
Xerox Publishing Company

300

Hayes, Sheila

The Carousel Horse

Thomas Nelson, Inc., 1978.
(127 pages)

PREJUDICE: Social Class
  Friendship: making friends
  Self, attitude toward: respect
  Values/Valuing: materialistic

Eleven-year-old Fran Davies, her teacher father temporarily out of work, is ashamed of her mother's job cooking that summer for the wealthy Fairchild family in Connecticut. No one should be a servant, she thinks, nor certainly a servant's child. Fran stays with her mother at the Fairchild summer place (her father and brother take summer jobs elsewhere), but for "the principal of the thing" spurns the friendly overtures of Andrea, the Fairchild's own eleven-year-old. To Fran, Andrea lives a life closed to her, as fantastic as the beautiful carousel horse decorating Andrea's bedroom. Fran's cousin Brenda, who lives in the same town, says Andrea is in fact a snob; Fran much prefers the company of Brenda and her friends. But when they seem to snub her, Fran's complaints are overheard by Andrea, who admits to being lonely also. Recognizing Andrea's doubts and loneliness, Fran befriends her after all. Yet the friendship is fragile, trembling at any suggestion that Fran is a "servant" — until at a private sleepover Andrea talks about her mother's divorce, and Fran recognizes that the girl has lost the family life Fran takes for granted. No amount of money can make up for that loss. At summer's end, Andrea promises to give Fran the carousel horse for her birthday, but Fran declines it. No longer a symbol of luxury to her, it now looks menacing; a symbol of all Andrea has lost. Fran wants Andrea to visit for a weekend instead. Fran also asks Brenda to convince her friends that Andrea is no snob.

A child from a middle-class family, ashamed of her mother's work as a servant, practices a snobbery of her own in this first-person narrative. Her attitude changes when she recognizes that no amount of money can help the troubles of a wealthy girl. All of this occurs logically enough, but without much emotional clarity or power.

Ages 10-12

Also available in:
No other form known

301

Hazen, Barbara Shook

Gorilla Wants to Be the Baby

Color illustrations by Jacqueline Bardner Smith.
Atheneum Publishers, 1978.
(30 pages counted)

IMAGINARY FRIEND
SIBLING: New Baby
  Jealousy: sibling

Fortunately, the little child (about three) telling this story has her imaginary friend, Gorilla, around when she wants to air her complaints about the new baby. No one else will listen to her. First, the baby is "either sleeping or yelling its head off," and all this in the child's own room. Then the baby commands the whole

family's attention. Here Mother interrupts the complaints by saying she will take the child shopping while Grandma baby-sits, provided the child does not bother the baby. The child then decides to play baby with Gorilla and ends by demonstrating how real babies scream. Immediately Mother and Grandmother rush upstairs: "WHAT'S WRONG WITH BABY?" The child claims innocence; nobody bothered the baby. Mother then drives a bargain: if the child does not wake the baby, and puts on a clean shirt, and if Gorilla stays home, she will take the child shopping.

In this first-person narrative, a little child summons up an imaginary character sympathetic to the child's complaints about being displaced by a baby. The mother recognizes the child's use of Gorilla by including him in the bargain she strikes, and the child shows similar awareness with a tentative plan to give Gorilla to the baby for a playmate once school starts. As pictured in the drawings here, the child could be of either sex, and so could appeal to boys and girls alike.

Ages 3-5

Also available in:
No other form known

302

Hazen, Barbara Shook

Two Homes to Live In: A Child's-Eye View of Divorce

Color illustrations by Peggy Luks.
Human Sciences Press, 1978.
(40 pages counted)

DIVORCE: of Parents

Before Niki's parents' divorce, the boy had overheard their quarrels, which had frightened him. After one particularly bitter one, Niki's father had left home, but not before assuring him that the divorce would not be Niki's fault, that "grown-up problems" were the cause of his departure, that he loved Niki very much and would always be his father. Niki's mother had also assured her son that, though parents may "fall out of love," they never stop loving their children. In Niki's words, "They are divorced from each other. But not from me." Despite his anger over the divorce, Niki endeavors to accept both his homes. But he confesses to wishing that his parents would remarry. Both tell him firmly that his wish is impossible. It is then that Niki begins to dwell less on the divorce and more on the good things he does with each parent. In fact, he recognizes that he is happy and loved in both homes.

In this first-person narrative about his parents' divorce, a child struggles against taking sides, feeling walked out on, grief, and anger. The child's own language is persuasive, as is the continuing love his parents show for him and his growing sense that they are three different but connected people. Though written for young children, this book could prove useful to the older children of divorcing parents. The illustrations show an appealing, tousled child in jeans who could be a boy or girl, thus allowing easier identification by all children.

Ages 5-8

Also available in:
No other form known

303

Hazen, Barbara Shook

Why Couldn't I Be an Only Kid Like You, Wigger

Black/white illustrations by Leigh Grant.
Atheneum Publishers, 1975.
(31 pages)

ONLY CHILD
SIBLING: Relationships

Wigger is an only child. His friend, who has many brothers and sisters, thinks Wigger is in all ways better off. Wigger gets to go out to eat with his parents and has his Christmas presents all to himself. He doesn't have to share his room or wear hand-me-downs or look after babies. His friend cannot understand why Wigger wants to come to his house all the time, until Wigger explains that sometimes it "gets lonely being an only kid."

Each boy sees only the best of the other's situation. The black and white drawings illustrate clearly and humorously the disorder that can arise in the life of a large family. Wigger's life is contrasted as staid, quiet, and uninteresting.

Ages 4-7

Also available in:
Paperbound — *Why Couldn't I Be an Only Kid Like You, Wigger*
Atheneum Publishers

304

Hegwood, Mamie

My Friend Fish

Black/white illustrations by Diane de Groat.
Holt, Rinehart and Winston, Inc., 1975.
(29 pages counted)

DEATH: of Pet

While waiting for the bus that will take him to summer day camp, a boy called Moose daydreams of fishing. He likes fishing more than anything else; so much, in fact, that when the bus reaches camp in the heat of the day and the other children race to the swimming pool, Moose sets off with his camp counselor, pole in hand. They spend nearly all day on the dock without a nibble. Only when they are ready to leave does Moose get a bite — but the long-awaited fish is so small that the counselor recommends he throw it back. To Moose, however, the fingerling is as good as a whale. He names it Fish and carries it carefully home on the bus in a bucket of water. His sisters, as expected, are revolted by his new friend. But Moose installs Fish in his bedroom and keeps him company all evening until bedtime. The boy sleeps soundly and wakes eagerly — only to find that during the night his pet has died. Moose's father tries to comfort him, saying that Fish had probably been homesick. Hearing this, Moose decides to return Fish to the stream near the camp. Tucking him lovingly into a cigar box beside a few favorite toys, Moose and the family ride to the stream to say farewell. Moose cries a little, says a prayer, and feels better. Reminding the others that he is a big boy and a great fisherman, he vows that he will not cry anymore.

This touching story told by Moose recounts his grief over the death of his pet. His vow not to cry again, though probable for a boy this age, may seem commendable to some children, less so to parents or teachers. Moose's family sympathizes wholly with his grief.

Ages 4-8

Also available in:
No other form known

305

Heide, Florence Parry

Growing Anyway Up

J. B. Lippincott Co., 1976.
(127 pages)

FEAR
REALITY, ESCAPING
  Communication: lack of
  Guilt, feelings of
  Maturation

When Florence Stirkel's mother tells her they are moving from Florida to Lattmore, Pennsylvania, Florence is sure she cannot handle the change. Florence's Aunt Nina, who travels a lot, has found a job in Lattmore for Florence's mother, and has arranged for Florence to attend a private high school for girls there. Florence's mother can hardly tear herself away from the television set to tell her anything about the place they are going to. All in all, the panicky Florence feels as if she is "being taken somewhere like a sack of potatoes." Heading for a strange school in a strange town, how can she "make it all safe?" She makes her room "safe" every night by looking at each of the corners a certain number of times; the number of times increases with her anxiety. She acts out similarly safe-making rituals over people and objects. But some people she can never make safe, among them her mother's new boy friend, George, the first man her mother has gone out with since her husband's death when Florence was little. Aunt Nina agrees with Florence that George is a dreadful bore. But Florence feels alive when the bright and charming Nina is around. Her aunt talks constantly, unlike Florence's mother, and often tells stories about Florence's father, whom the girl remembers only sketchily. Thus when Nina goes off to England on a visit just as Florence finds out that her mother and George are planning to marry, Florence feels ignored, abandoned. Soon she decides to run away. Going out the door, suitcase in hand, she meets Nina coming back. Her aunt asks what is wrong — and at that moment the girl remembers something; she had been angry at her father once for going away on a business trip, and she had not put her usual good-luck kiss on his suitcase. He had been killed on that trip. Florence has felt ever since that his death had been her fault. With Nina's encouragement, Florence talks about the past and sees that his death had been no one's fault. Suddenly relaxed and calm for the first time she can remember, she falls asleep in Nina's arms. Later, in boarding school, her mother and George married, Florence thinks, "I've grown up more or less. . . . But I couldn't have done it without Aunt Nina." And Aunt Nina thinks about her, remembering how Florence had needed a friend.

A young adolescent, troubled by forgotten feelings of guilt and isolated from friends by her fears and compulsions ("nervous habits"), comes to see herself in a different perspective when a wise aunt patiently talks things over with her. Nina points out that there were probably people around Florence who could have helped her, if she had let them. Although happy to have Nina's help, Florence sees that she must continue to grow up on her own, find her own friends, make her own life, and allow her mother to do the same. Although the self-understanding seems abrupt and contrived, Florence's fears, loneliness, and eventual insight will speak to

quite a few girls who have felt similarly fearful and alone. Wry humor prevents this book from being depressing.

Ages 12-14

Also available in:
Paperbound — *Growing Anyway Up*
Bantam Books, Inc.

306

Heide, Florence Parry

Secret Dreamer, Secret Dreams

J. B. Lippincott Co., 1978.
(95 pages)

MENTAL ILLNESS: of Child
   Communication: lack of
   Education: special
   Muteness

A word for Caroline is "alone." At thirteen, she neither reads nor writes, and only occasionally does she utter a word. No one knows whether she understands what is said. Sometimes she "spins a web" to escape hearing others, and sometimes she strives to decipher a message from her surroundings. Encountering a stray dog one day, she senses an understanding between them and brings it home. Her dad says she can keep the dog, but her mother disagrees. While they argue, Caroline spins a web, until Dad smiles, showing it is safe. Dad asks her the name of the dog, and she answers "Brumm," a sound that comes easily. Her sister, Amy, complains about Brumm and the favoritism shown Caroline, and again Caroline chooses not to listen. But attention to others in her special-education class is acute. Though aware that they do not share a language, Caroline tries to make connection with the other students. Nightly Dad reads to her, and Caroline wonders if here in the strange marks on paper is the message she awaits. In an aquarium the family visits, Caroline suddenly pounds on the glass to attract the attention of a giant sea turtle. The turtle, she is certain, knows the secret. Though taken from the aquarium, she still feels the secret close at hand. In a dream that night, she sees the connection. Unable to tell the family about it, Caroline races up and down the stairs with the message "forever undelivered," while Brumm barks helplessly.

This is an "as if" story: the first-person narrator is not the disturbed girl but her special-education teacher, writing what she thinks Caroline feels; this is "my story, not hers," she writes. The narration is less a story than episodes showing moods, and they can be read in several ways and so should prompt much discussion. The general meaning is clear enough: Caroline needs a "language" to connect her to others. Though the ending sees her find a message — the story does not say what it is — she still possesses no means to tell it. Yet we come away with some idea of how an emotionally disturbed child feels and how her family feels as well.

Ages 13 and up

Also available in:
Paperbound — *Secret Dreamer, Secret Dreams*
Pocket Books, Inc.

307

Heide, Florence Parry

When the Sad One Comes to Stay

J. B. Lippincott Co., 1975.
(74 pages)

FRIENDSHIP: Meaning of
LONELINESS
    Separation, marital
    Values/Valuing: materialistic

Young Sara has moved to a new city with her mother, Sally, who explains that they left the little girl's father because he lacked ambition and would never be successful. Sally is an outgoing social climber bent on an entirely new life for herself and her daughter. Although Sara is impressed by their new home, she misses her father, who was happy and lively and always thought of interesting things to do. Sally encourages Sara to make friends with other girls in the neighborhood, but Sara is shy and makes only one new friend, an old woman named Maisie, who invites her inside her deteriorating brownstone for hot chocolate and cookies. Soon Sara's visits become a daily routine. Maisie teaches her how to knit. She also teaches her how to avoid the "Sad One," an imaginary character who always knows when someone is lonely and will "move in" and make the sadness permanent. One day Sally announces she will be leaving town for a few days. Sara wants to stay with Maisie and Maisie wants to have her — but Sally prefers that she stay with the socially influential Carters, who have children Sara's age. But lacking the Carter's invitation, Sally agrees to let her daughter stay with Maisie. The next day Sara brings home a dress Maisie has bought for Sally. The mother laughs at the dress and calls it "deliciously horrible." When the Carters do invite Sara over, and Sara must go, the little girl finds herself too shy to know how to make friends with the three Carter girls — until she shows them the dress that Maisie sent. Now Sara laughs at it and refers to Maisie as "the funniest old lady." Seeing that the girls are interested, Sara describes her visits to the old woman, playing up all Maisie's peculiarities, much to the delight of the girls and to her own pleasure at making friends.

The story draws contrasting portraits of Sally, the ambitious and social-climbing mother, and Maisie, the eccentric but gracious old lady, and places Sara between the women and the values they hold. By her mockery of Maisie, Sara chooses the way of material possessions and social position over friendship and caring.

Ages 8-11

Also available in:
Paperbound — *When the Sad One Comes to Stay*
Bantam Books, Inc.

308

Helena, Ann

I'm Running Away

Color photographs by J. P. Atterberry.
Raintree Publishers, Ltd., 1978.
(31 pages)

RUNNING AWAY
  Communication: parent-child

Young John is angry — again. His mother has forbidden him to play in the park until he cleans up his room. Instead of doing that, John broods about all the times his parents have forbidden him to do things, and he decides to run away. Having packed his "best stuff," John announces his intention to his mother. She acknowledges that she and his father will miss the boy, whereupon the father comes in and asks John his reasons for leaving. John recalls to him all the things they refused to allow, and his father tries to explain: he loves his son and wants nothing to happen to him. His father also admits that sometimes they have neglected to explain their reasons. But he wishes John would not run away; the boy would miss a trip to the circus and a visit to Grandma's to see the new kittens. John decides to stay — at least until after the circus.

In this first-person narrative, a little boy decides to leave home to punish his parents for strictness. But when they talk it over with him we begin to sense how much they care about him and want to be fair. Photographs add expressiveness to the text.

Ages 5-8

Also available in:
No other form known

309

Helena, Ann

The Lie

Color photographs by Ellen Pizer.
Raintree Publishers, Ltd., 1977.
(30 pages)

HONESTY/DISHONESTY

The young girl telling this story looks forward to "show and tell" time at school, because her friend Nancy says she has something very special to present. Sure enough, Nancy shows the class a necklace, which her mother has made, on which hangs a white heart with a pink flower painted on it. The whole class thinks it beautiful. At recess, the narrator goes back into the classroom to get her jump rope. She stops to get another look at the necklace, and as she is examining it the necklace drops and breaks. She looks around to see if anyone has noticed, but no one has. She decides to say nothing. Later, the broken necklace is discovered. When asked if she broke it, the girl says no. Ms. Smith, the teacher, says that she thinks someone in the class did it, but the narrator is afraid to say that she did. What, she wonders, would happen if she told Nancy? Would Nancy not be her friend anymore? But she feels ashamed at not telling the truth. In the end, she decides that she must tell Nancy and face the consequences, whatever they may be.

The young girl describes the guilt and fear of discovery she feels, as well as her fear of the consequences. This brief story is enhanced by full-page photographs. The open ending invites group discussion.

Ages 5-8

Also available in:
No other form known

310

Helmering, Doris Wild and John William Helmering

We're Going to Have a Baby

Color illustrations by Robert H. Cassell.
Abingdon Press, 1978.
(32 pages counted)

SIBLING: New Baby

When his mother is going to have a baby, four-year-old Jimmy excitedly tells his friend Joe, who already has a baby sister. Joe warns Jimmy that babies "scream and cry a lot," can't go to the bathroom properly, need feeding, and keep parents busy. After listening to Joe, Jimmy wonders anxiously whether their baby will be that bad. In fact, he begins to cry. A neighbor, Mr. Bond, discovers why the boy is crying, and explains that to feel angry, afraid, and happy when he thinks about the baby is perfectly all right. But there is something else to look forward to: Jimmy will be the baby's big brother and "a baby loves its big brother." After their talk, Jimmy stops worrying and feels good again about the coming baby.

With the advice from a neighbor, a little boy accepts his mixed feelings toward the arrival of a new baby. In this beautifully illustrated, first-person narrative, joy, anger, and sadness are all discussed as natural responses to such an event. One of the authors is a sixth-grade boy, who has drawn on his own remembrances.

Ages 3-7

Also available in:
No other form known

311

Hentoff, Nat

This School Is Driving Me Crazy

Delacorte Press, 1976.
(154 pages)

COMMUNICATION: Parent-Child
  Discipline, meaning of
  Promise, keeping
  School: negative experiences
  Schools, private: boys'

Twelve-year-old Sam Davidson goes to Bronson Alcott School, where his father is headmaster. Sam wants his father to treat him like a son, but Mr. Davidson, busy and professional, treats Sam like any other student. The boy wants to transfer to another school, where he could be just that, but his father won't let him. At Alcott, Sam's pranks and jokes earn him a reputation as a troublemaker. His mother thinks he is trying to attract his father's attention, but Mr. Davidson thinks Sam likes to make trouble. That reputation makes Sam a suspect when thefts break out at school. Tim Rawlins, a classmate, confesses to Sam that he is forced to steal by three bullying tenth graders. Fearing he will be beaten up if this gets out, Tim makes Sam promise not to tell. When Tim is then caught stealing, the tenth graders force him to tell Mr. Davidson that Sam is behind the thefts. His father confronts Sam with the accusation, but he denies it and refuses to explain: "I made a promise not to tell *anybody*." They argue and Sam runs from the office. He convinces Tim to come with him the following morning to tell the headmaster the truth. While the boys are talking to Mr. Davidson, two of Sam's friends find another student who was forced to steal and bring him to the meeting. The older boys are expelled. Later, Mr. Davidson assures Sam that he has faith in him and never believed the accusation.

Sam is a bright, energetic, and rebellious boy. He yearns to be closer to his father, but Mr. Davidson gives little time to him outside of school and little attention inside. After the run of thefts, Mr. Davidson begins to treat Sam as a son, not simply another student. The dialogue includes profanity.

Ages 11-15

Also available in:
Paperbound — *This School Is Driving Me Crazy*
Dell Publishing Company, Inc.

312

Herman, Charlotte

The Difference of Ari Stein

Black/white illustrations by Ben Shecter.
Harper & Row Publishers, Inc., 1976.
(150 pages)

JEWISH
SELF, ATTITUDE TOWARD: Accepting
  Ambivalence, feelings of
  Differences, human
  Maturation
  Peer relationships: peer pressures
  Self, attitude toward: feeling different

Eleven-year-old Ari Stein is Jewish, and during World War II he and his parents have just moved to Brooklyn from the Lower East Side of New York City. Always before, Ari's friends had been very much like him. In this new neighborhood, the boys are different. His new friends, Maxie, Lippy, and Brownie, are Jewish, but they do not go to "shul" on "Shabbos," and they do not go to Hebrew classes after school. They think such old customs keep them from being "all-American." Ari always wears a "yarmulke," but the boys persuade him to give it up. Although they do like Ari, he doubts he is one of the gang. Thus when Maxie, always full of mischievous ideas, wants to buy equipment to shine shoes for spending money, Ari allows himself to be talked into borrowing money from his mother's savings box. But shining shoes turns out to be less lucrative than expected, and Ari's conscience bothers him so much that he will not go to shul until he has replaced the money. Fortunately, another one of Maxie's schemes does pay off, and Ari puts the money back. But he decides he cannot go along with any more of Maxie's whims. Remembering a saying of Hillel's, "If I am not for myself, who will be for me?" Ari decides he can be friends with Maxie only if he is faithful to his own conscience first. Meeting Sheldon Greenspan, whose background, interests, and ideals are like Ari's own, makes the decision easier to live with: Ari now has a new friend.

Most readers will find Ari's tangle with mixed feelings familiar. Learning to stand up for one's own beliefs is an important part of growing up. Though they know he is ill at ease in his new neighborhood, Ari's parents trust him to make decisions according to his moral training. Jewish customs, the period, and the city are well described, and the boy's antics are amusing. But Ari's dilemma is shown with quiet seriousness and told in his own voice.

Ages 9-12

Also available in:
Braille — *The Difference of Ari Stein*
Library of Congress

313

Herman, Charlotte

Our Snowman Had Olive Eyes

E. P. Dutton & Company, Inc., 1977.
(103 pages)

AGE: Aging
GRANDPARENT: Living in Child's Home
GRANDPARENT: Love for
    Maturation

Ten-year-old Sheila has misgivings about her elderly grandmother, Bubbie, moving into their apartment. She likes Bubbie and has enjoyed many overnight visits at Bubbie's apartment — but giving up half of her room, even for someone she loves, is another matter. Besides, her best friend, Rita, warns that even the most loving grandmothers, once moved in, turn into witches. Happily, Bubbie proves a pleasure to have around: she bakes wonderful cookies and shows Sheila how to take cuttings from plants. She likes Bach, Sheila's favorite composer, and they share secrets — including Sheila's peeking at her sister's private journal. No, it is the grandmother who is dissatisfied — bored with only sleeping, eating, and being scolded by her daughter for overdoing. One night Sheila hears her crying. She tells her mother, who then invites Rita's grandmother, Mrs. Plumb, for lunch — company Bubbie's own age. Bubbie dislikes Mrs. Plumb but takes to pretending to go to lunch with her every day just to get out of the house. She really visits an elderly antique-shop owner for long talks and the exquisite lunches he cooks. When Sheila follows Bubbie one day and discovers her secret, it becomes one more the two can share. Sheila's mother, in her turn, finds out, and is so delighted at Bubbie's new friendship that she invites Julius to dinner. But her nerves over cooking for a gourmet prompt Sheila to call

on him and ask what he likes. For good measure, she assures Julius that, married to Bubbie, he need not worry about money: their family will gladly help out. That evening the eagerly awaited Julius never comes. Bubbie goes to see what has happened and returns, shocked at his believing that she wants to get married. Sheila is crushed. But Bubbie says Julius was no great friend if he would not even bother to ask if what Sheila had said was true. Deprived of her daily outing and hopelessly bored, Bubbie decides to go live with her son. Sheila considers running off too, but realizes that Bubbie has to live her own life. To expect her to stay forever would be selfish. Before Bubbie leaves, she gives Sheila a new diary for her very own — and shows her a hiding place for it.

Sheila and her grandmother understand each other. Unlike her mother, the girl has no preconceptions about aging and thinks of Bubbie as a friend, not an old person who must be coddled. But as a friend herself, Sheila has to understand that what is fine for her is not necessarily adequate for Bubbie. Sheila tells this story.

Ages 9-11

Also available in:
No other form known

314

Hickman, Janet

The Stones

Black/white illustrations by Richard Cuffari.
Macmillan Publishing Company, Inc., 1976.
(115 pages)

PATRIOTISM
    Harassment
    Parental: absence
    Peer relationships: peer pressures
    Prejudice: ethnic/racial

During World War II, Garrett McKay, eleven, misses his father, a soldier in France who is eventually reported missing in action. From the first, Garrett blames the Nazis for his father's absence and assumes that all Germans are Nazis. He and his friends regularly play war, and while Garrett has the honor to be the intelligence officer, he is also the youngest in the group and continually tries to prove himself. The site for their play is the property of an irascible and eccentric old man, known as Jack Tramp, whose windows they like to break with green apples and mud balls. Jack chases the boys off with his shotgun. When Garrett discovers that Jack Tramp's real name is Adolf Schilling, he decides that Jack must be a Nazi, and eagerly reports this "intelligence" to the other boys. A "real" enemy to fight! But Garrett's new pride of discovery is soon capsized, when his mother invites Jack to dinner. The other boys find out and demand that Garrett prove his loyalty by stealing something from Jack's garage. Jack catches them, chases them, and in firing his shotgun kills a favorite neighborhood dog. A fire at his house on Halloween night only convinces the neighbors further that Jack is deranged; Linnie, Garrett's little sister, convinces an inquiring Welfare worker when she reports having seen a jack-o-lantern carved with a swastika sitting by Jack's house. To protect the real perpetrator, Garrett tells the Welfare man that Linnie makes up stories. In her anger, Linnie then runs off to a picnic area called The Stones. By the time Garrett finds her, a storm and flash flood have marooned her beyond reach. Luckily Jack Tramp, fleeing the neighborhood to avoid being put away, sees Linnie too. He saves her, but collapses from overexertion. He is hospitalized, treated for several long-neglected illnesses, and eventually put in the county home. The next time a friend of Garrett's calls Jack "the old Nazi," Garrett rallies to Jack's defense.

This is a thought-provoking story of how misguided patriotism can have tragic results. Garrett ends up to

have harassed someone just because his name has an unpopular ethnic origin. The boy learns the importance of knowing all that one can before passing a judgment.

Ages 9-12

Also available in:
No other form known

315

Hinton, Nigel

Collision Course

Thomas Nelson, Inc., 1976.
(159 pages)

GUILT, FEELINGS OF
RESPONSIBILITY: Avoiding
  Accidents: hit and run
  Honesty/Dishonesty
  Judgment, effect of emotions on
  Stealing

Fifteen-year-old Ray realizes he is no longer the naive boy he was or that his parents still think him, but is he a man? One night he "borrows" a motorbike for a joyride and ends up crashing into a woman getting out of her car, killing her. Running terrified from the scene, he jumps into a bus, only to run afoul the conductor, for he lacks the fare. Giving the conductor a false name and address, he promises to send it. From then on he is torn between two selves, the one calculating how to escape detection, the other bitterly accusing himself for the hit-and-run. At times Ray feels he must tell someone but then glimpses the gulf now separating him from his parents and friends. At other times he prides himself on his surprising skill at lying; he plans to send the police an anonymous letter to throw them off his track. Meanwhile, troubled by Grandma's illness and their younger son, Derek, Ray's parents scarcely notice his anxiety.

And so it continues throughout the week: Ray endures school, helps his soccer team tie a crucial game, goes to a party and gets drunk, and meets a girl he particularly likes. The following day he prepares the letter for the police but leaves it at home on his desk to go and visit Grandma at the hospital. Without any idea of what Ray has done, she talks philosophically about death and inevitability. Yet Ray still tries to run from the consequences of the accident: taking a bus home, he dashes away when the same conductor recognizes him. His mind is racing with a new alibi for the night of the accident. He telephones his house — but learns that the police have identified him, have searched his room and found the letter. He goes home, to find them waiting.

Ray's decision to stop running away from his crime does not mean he accepts his guilt, rather that he begins to find a position for judgment external to his strongly divided emotions. This realistic psychological study is both intense and thoughtful, and perhaps a little slow for some readers.

Ages 11 and up

Also available in:
Paperbound — *Collision Course*
Dell Publishing Company, Inc.

316

Hinton, Susan Eloise

Rumble Fish

Delacorte Press, 1975.
(122 pages)

IMITATION
  Alcoholism: of father
  Deprivation, emotional
  Gangs: membership in
  Loneliness
  Sibling: younger

Rusty-James, a young adolescent, wants to be exactly like his older brother, Motorcycle Boy, leader of a street gang before the gangs were wiped out by narcotics. The toughest "cat" in the neighborhood, Motorcycle Boy is a combination of "Robin Hood, Jesse James, and the Pied Piper," feared or admired by everyone. But the younger brother never uses his head, and is always in trouble for stealing or drinking or fighting. True, he resembles his brother physically, but there is something more than thinking things through that sets the older boy apart. "People looked at him," Rusty-James tells us, "and stopped and looked again. He looked like a panther or something. Me, I just looked like a tough kid, too big for my age." The boys' alcoholic father, a one-time lawyer, talks to the older boy in sober moments — long discussions that Rusty-James cannot follow. He wishes they would "talk normal." About the gang days which Rusty-James yearns for, Motorcycle Boy says things like: "Apparently it is essential to some people to belong — anywhere." He understands that people will follow him. What bothers him is that he cannot think of anywhere to go. Rusty-James knows what *he* wants, but it does him no good. When a sly former friend steals Rusty-James's girl friend, it looks as if the younger boy has lost what little respect he has ever had. He can think of nothing to do but continue to follow Motorcycle Boy around, hoping the secret of his success will rub off. One night the two break into a pet shop, but to Rusty-James's amazement, instead of rifling the cash register, his brother turns all the animals loose. Motorcycle Boy is trying to reach the river to liberate a bowl full of Siamese fighting fish when he is shot dead by a police officer. Rusty-James spends five years in a reformatory.

This story is told in flashback in Rusty-James's first person, after the boy has left the reformatory. It is a realistic but depressing story of two young losers, whose lives, if stark, bleak, and often violent, are memorable, and provide many openings for discussion.

Ages 12 and up

Also available in:
Braille — *Rumble Fish*
Library of Congress

Paperbound — *Rumble Fish*
Dell Publishing Company, Inc.

Talking Book — *Rumble Fish*
Library of Congress

317

Hintz, Sandy and Martin Hintz

We Can't Afford It

Color photographs by Brent Jones.
Raintree Publishers, Ltd., 1977.
(30 pages)

EXPECTATIONS
MONEY: Management

Too big for her small tricycle, the girl who narrates this story wants a new shiny green bike, one with a horn and streamers. Her father says they will shop for a new bicycle on Saturday, but warns her not to set her hopes too high; a new bicycle may be more than he can afford. When Saturday comes, she and her parents find a new, shiny, yellow bike with a basket, and a new green one just her size. But her father says they can't afford a new bike after all. They find a used one for sale. "I want a new bike," the girl insists. "Not one that some other kid rode." The paint on the used one is scratched, and one fender is dented. Her father suggests they paint it, and describes how they can shine it up. He says they can even fix the dent. The girl begins to think about buying a horn and streamers. By the end of the story she is saying, "Dad and I are going to make this the best bike in the whole world."

The girl in this first-person narrative is disappointed and somewhat angry that her family cannot afford a new bicycle. However, once reassured that the used bike can be fixed up to look new and shiny, she looks forward both to working with her father and the end result. Beautiful full-page photographs alternate with the pages of the text.

Ages 4-7

Also available in:
No other form known

318

Hirsch, Karen

My Sister

Black/white illustrations by Nancy Inderieden.
Carolrhoda Books, Inc., 1977.
(29 pages counted)

MENTAL RETARDATION

For a little boy, having a mentally retarded sister can sometimes be trying. He does not mind that she cannot speak clearly — he can understand her — or that she always plays with the same toys and takes a long time to learn new things. But it sometimes does bother him that she seems to get all the attention, and that she has a bigger bedroom than his. When he tells his parents this is not fair, they reply, "No, it isn't really fair," and then they explain that she has the bigger bedroom because it is nearest to them and to the bathroom. To cheer him up, they build him a bookshelf out of orange crates and paint his room. He does feel better — but cannot escape the feeling that his sister makes the family different from others and gives rise to trouble on family outings. There was the time at the beach when a woman had chased his sister away, and some children had laughed at her. His father explains that some people are a little afraid of retarded children, or misunderstand them. Then the boy feels hurt for his sister, and wishes, for her sake, she could be like other children. One thing sure, *he* loves her dearly.

This first-person narrative honestly recounts a child's feelings about a retarded sibling. Understanding parents help him cope with his resentment, and help him, too, to appreciate his sister as a special person with a notable capacity for gentleness and love.

Ages 6-8

Also available in:
No other form known

319

Hirsch, Linda

The Sick Story

Black/white illustrations by John Wallner.
Hastings House Publishers, Inc., 1977.
(38 pages counted)

ILLNESSES: Being Ill
  Decision making

Finding herself with a cold and a slight fever, young Miranda decides to stay home from school for a few days. During her first day at home, she relishes her parents' extra attentiveness and the fact that she has no chores or homework to do. During the second day, she finds herself bored and her mother's patience wearing thin. And Miranda welcomes the after-school visit of a friend who brings homework and news that the class is to put on a play of *Alice in Wonderland*. Miranda's friend also confides that the part of the Queen has yet to be cast. It is then that Miranda weighs staying at home in pampered comfort against returning to school and responsibilities, the risk of a relapse, but a chance at local fame — and chooses the latter.

Children will share this main character's enjoyment of a brief, pampered vacation from everyday activities, and agonize with her when she must choose between continued luxury and the public limelight.

Ages 6-9

Also available in:
No other form known

320

Ho, Minfong

Sing to the Dawn

Black/white illustrations by Kwoncjan Ho.
Lothrop, Lee & Shepard Co., 1975.
(160 pages)

EDUCATION: Value of
GENDER ROLE IDENTITY: Female
  Decision making
  Jealousy: sibling
  Poverty
  Prejudice: sexual
  Sibling: love for
  Sibling: rivalry
  Women's rights

Dawan, fourteen, is the daughter of long-suffering, stoical Thai peasants, whose landlord has always taken most of their rice crop as rent, leaving them barely surviving but accepting of their traditional lot in life. Dawan and her brother, Kwai, who is a year younger, are in the same grade in the village school; indeed, Dawan would not be there at all but for having begged her father, who thinks it pointless for girls to be educated. Not so, the children's untraditional teacher, who impresses upon the children the importance of learning to think and applying that skill to bettering the lives of their people. With their teacher's encouragement Kwai and Dawan vow to one day do just that. But the two need further education. Once a year, a scholarship to study at the City School is given to the best village student. Dawan, receiving the highest mark on the examination, wins it, Kwai coming in second. But, against her grandmother's solitary encouragement, her father forbids her to accept the scholarship. Her grandmother is the only family member who encourages her. Dawan tries to enlist the support of the head abbot at the temple, but he is unsympathetic and dour. Angry and leaving the temple, Dawan meets her friend Bao, a girl who sells caged birds in the market place, and is just in time to see Bao's brother hit her for not making enough money. Kwai, provoked by a remark of Bao's also tries to hit her and in the scuffle hurts his sister. Dawan is frightened and shocked, and Kwai is startled by his own behavior, realizing that by pushing people around he is not living up to his own ideals. He decides not to tell his father he came in second, and argues for Dawan when she confronts their father to demand her rights. The day Dawan leaves for the city, Kwai has second thoughts about having helped her and tries to avoid saying goodbye. But at the last minute, he does, and shows her that he accepts the new way that things have turned out.

Though Dawan sometimes doubts the practicality of her decision to seek better schooling and become a social activist, she has courage and a finally unshakable belief in her mission to better her tradition-bound people. It saddens her to see her brother jealous and miserable at running second in a test, but she does not give up what is rightfully hers for the sake of tradition. Dawan's story is full of interest but leisurely in pace.

Ages 10-13

Also available in:
No other form known

321

Hoban, Lillian Aberman

Arthur's Pen Pal

Color illustrations by the author.
Harper & Row Publishers, Inc., 1976.
(64 pages)

SIBLING: Older
  Prejudice: sexual

Instead of having the younger sister he has, Arthur, a chimpanzee, would prefer a younger brother — in particular, Sandy, his pen pal. Arthur does not like his sister Violet's complaining and the fact that she is able to best him at jumping rope. He is sure that Sandy, who is learning karate and plays the drums, would be much more chipper and fun. But when Sandy sends him a photograph showing that she is a girl, Arthur decides that Violet is a more suitable sister. After all, Violet cannot beat Arthur at wrestling as Sandy can her brother.

This book, written for the beginning reader, makes no bones about the dissatisfaction a brother can feel with a younger sister. Though it is not emphasized, sexual prejudice is evident in Arthur's assuming that only boys learn karate and play drums.

Ages 4-7

Also available in:
Braille — *Arthur's Pen Pal*
Library of Congress

322

Hoban, Lillian Aberman

I Met a Traveller

Harper & Row Publishers, Inc., 1977.
(182 pages)

HOMESICKNESS
LONELINESS
  Friendship: meaning of
  Israel
  Jewish
  Parent/Parents: single
  Security/Insecurity

Eleven-year-old Josie Hayden and her mother have come from Connecticut to Israel to be with "their own people." Since separating from her husand years earlier, Mrs. Hayden has had several affairs, and it is because her current lover, Boris, lives there that she and Josie have come to live in Jerusalem. Josie hates Jerusalem, where she attends a mission school, has no friends, and is antagonized by a troublemaking classmate named Matthias. Her mother is frequently away with Boris, sometimes overnight, leaving Josie alone. The girl longs to return to Connecticut, but Mrs. Hayden will not hear of it. Josie makes friends with Mira, an older woman who has recently emigrated from Russia, and conceives the idea of deserting her mother and persuading Mira to come back with her to Connecticut. Then Grishna, an old friend of Mira's moves to Jerusalem. Grishna is a puppeteer, and before long the three friends make a puppet show ready for public performance. Thus Josie hopes to make money for her travel fund. But her dream of Connecticut is dashed when she learns that Mira will marry Grishna. Finally she and her mother have a long talk. Realizing finally how miserable Josie has been in Jerusalem — and having broken with Boris — Mrs. Hayden agrees to return to the United States at the end of the school term, but not to settle down. She wants to travel, perhaps to Canada.

Josie's memories of her childhood in Connecticut are nothing like her present life in Jerusalem, where everything is strange to her. She longs for the security of a home in one place — and in the United States. Her mother, for her own reasons more than Josie's, agrees to go back but not to settle down. Josie is resigned to take what she can get. This book has much to tell of present-day Jerusalem and the lives of those relocating there.

Ages 10-12

Also available in:
No other form known

323

Hoban, Russell Conwell

Dinner at Alberta's

Black/white illustrations by James Marshall.
Thomas Y. Crowell Company, Inc., 1976.
(39 pages counted)

ETIQUETTE

Arthur Crocodile has terrible table manners. His mother says he eats "like a regular little beast." Faced with family complaints, Arthur goes to his room and plays his electric guitar loudly. One day his sister, Emma, brings home her friend Alberta Saurian; Arthur, impressed by Alberta's beauty, plays for her as never before. Alberta stays for dinner, but Arthur can hardly eat for trying to imitate her perfect manners. After Alberta goes home, Arthur makes up a song in her honor. When Alberta invites Emma and Arthur to dinner at her house, Arthur practices good table manners for a week, learning to chew with his mouth closed, hold his fork properly, and use his napkin. The evening at the Saurians is a success; Arthur's manners are flawless. Resentful of the attention Arthur is getting, Alberta's brother, Sidney, watches him all evening, trying to copy his good manners. Arthur's after-dinner guitar-playing delights everyone but Sidney, who coaxes Arthur outside to see his treehouse. When the two return, Sidney's clothes are dirty and he has a puffed-up lip. Arthur has momentarily set aside his new manners to try to teach Sidney to improve his own. Arthur and Emma return home in a good mood.

Arthur, pictured as a thoroughgoing crocodile, declines to improve his table manners until he sees a good reason for doing so — his infatuation for Alberta. Witty illustrations assist this humorous, painless lesson for the very young.

Ages 5-7

Also available in:
Paperbound — *Dinner at Alberta's*
Dell Publishing Company, Inc.

Talking Book — *Dinner at Alberta's*
Library of Congress

324

Hocken, Sheila

Emma and I

E. P. Dutton & Company, Inc., 1977.
(211 pages)

BLINDNESS
PETS: Guide Dog
   Dependence/Independence
   Prejudice: toward handicapped persons
   Resourcefulness

It is the early 1950s, in England, and Sheila, partly blind from congenital cataracts, does not know she differs from other children until she enters school. Her parents, partly blind themselves, want Sheila and her brother, Graham, also partly blind, to live among sighted people as much as possible. They succeed in keeping Sheila in public schools, even though her sight steadily deteriorates. After graduating, Sheila finds a job as a switchboard operator, but her impaired vision makes commuting difficult. That is when she acquires Emma, a guide dog. Intelligent and attentive when working, affectionate and joyous when not, Emma captivates Sheila and makes her so independent that she leaves home and moves with a sighted woman friend to an apartment. Later, again by way of Emma, Sheila meets her future husband, Don Hocken (but must wait several years to marry him, for he hesitates to divorce until his daughter is fourteen). Other benefits follow from the confidence Emma gives her owner: Sheila finds a better job; she takes an apartment by herself; and she gives speeches to raise funds for guide dogs. Once Don has divorced, the two marry. But one more big decision awaits Sheila. She has had surgery on her eyes before, but her brother is urging her to try again. She agrees, and the operation is a success. All of the difficulties of learning to judge distance and move by sight prove wonderful nuisances compared to "the infinite black pit" she has escaped.

The theme of this autobiography is a blind woman's struggle for independence and how a guide dog provides it. The relationship between Sheila and her dog is warmly portrayed, and the information given on guide-dog training is instructive. There are many ways to be blind, the author tells us, explaining how her family shaped her particular way by insisting that she rely upon herself. Sighted readers of her story can learn much about how to act toward blind people, and may well ponder anew what the author calls "the wonder of sight."

Ages 12 and up

Also available in:
Cassette for the Blind — *Emma and I*
Library of Congress

Paperbound — *Emma and I*
New American Library

Talking Book — *Emma and I*
Library of Congress

325

Hoff, Sydney

The Littlest Leaguer

Black/white illustrations by the author.
Windmill Books and E. P. Dutton & Company, Inc., 1976.
(48 pages)

HEIGHT: Short
  Little League
  Perseverance

"Of all the players in the Little League, Harold was the littlest." Despite advice that he wait until next year, Harold doggedly continues his quest for a starting position. But failure follows him: infield grounders bounce over his head and outfield flies outdistance him. For all the boy's determination, the coach is forced to bench him. Just to remain with the team, Harold cares for equipment, and supplies his teammates with cold drinks. And his coach's reminder that many great ball players were short keeps the bench-warming Harold coming back game after game. Comes the championship game, Harold's team — up to bat in the last of the ninth — has three men on base and two outs. With Big Leon, the hard-hitting first baseman, coming to bat, the team feels confident of victory. But Leon twists his ankle and is unable to bat. In desperation, the coach calls on a stunned Harold, who stands as tall as he can in the batter's box. Two quick strikes go by — after

which Harold uses his size to advantage: he crouches at the plate to make the strike zone as small as possible. The confused pitcher lofts three successive balls over the plate, then tosses his change-of-pace pitch — which Harold belts over the fence for a game-winning home run. As he touches home plate, Harold's teammates hail him as the "biggest leaguer of them all."

Encouragement from his coach, quick thinking, and persistence help a short boy to shine in the sport he enjoys. This simple book requires only a rudimentary knowledge of baseball for Harold's big moment to be understood, and short readers may feel especially gratified. Illustrations show one female team member, though she is not mentioned in the text.

Ages 5-8

Also available in:
No other form known

326

Holl, Adelaide Hinkle

Small Bear Builds a Playhouse

Color illustrations by Cyndy Szekeres.
Garrard Publishing Co., 1978.
(48 pages)

AUTONOMY
  Creativity
  Friendship: meaning of
  Play

After eating a picnic lunch with his mother, Small Bear finds he has nothing to do. His mother encourages him to build a playhouse to which he might invite his friends. Small Bear accepts the suggestion and starts looking for a suitable place to build. Suddenly all sorts of his animal friends are offering advice on how and where to build houses. Small Bear discards all their ideas in favor of his own, but then fears he has slighted his friends and cannot ask them to the finished play-house. Even so, he sets about building and is very proud of the results. But being alone in the playhouse is no fun, and he tentatively asks his friends over. They all come and find the playhouse wonderful — even if it is not what they would have built themselves.

With encouragement from a parent, the main character tries out his own ideas for making something he wants. He also finds that, despite differing opinions and tastes, friends may still enjoy one another's company. This book is for beginning readers.

Ages 5-7

Also available in:
No other form known

327

Holland, Isabelle

Alan and the Animal Kingdom

J. B. Lippincott Co., 1977.
(190 pages)

PETS: Love for
RESPONSIBILITY: Accepting
  Alcoholism: adult
  Orphan
  Pets: substitute for human relationship
  Problem solving
  Speech problems: stuttering
  Trust/Distrust

Alan MacGowan has been an orphan since three, shunted from one relative to another. He mistrusts adults, especially officials: when his Uncle Ian died, and Alan had to move again, the authorities killed three of Alan's pets, even though at his next home his great-aunt could care for them. Now, at nine, Alan is a silent boy, who stutters when nervous; he prefers his animal friends. Living now with Great-aunt Jessie, he has col-lected six strangely assorted pets, which she tolerates, supplies with food, and calls "the animal kingdom." Then Aunt Jessie has a heart attack alone on the street, and at the hospital, with no identification, is only able to give her phone number before she dies. Reached at home, Alan rushes to the hospital. Finding his aunt dead, he also finds the slip of paper with the phone number, destroys it, and leaves. Great-aunt Jessie is buried as an anonymous pauper, and Alan can at last live alone with his pets. To neighbors' inquiries about Jessie, he answers that she is away caring for a sick friend. But Mr. Laurence, headmaster of Alan's school, and his wife become suspicious when they are repeat-edly unable to reach Jessie about some volunteer work. Meanwhile, Alan must take his sick kitten to a veteri-narian, and over the next few weeks Alan and Dr. Har-ris become friends. Soon Alan confesses the lie he is living, and Harris admits he is an alcoholic. Still, Alan admires Harris and secretly hopes Harris will provide a home for him. One night Alan's dog is struck by a car. Alan, unable to reach Dr. Harris, takes the dog to another vet. Then he goes to Harris to get money to pay the bill, finds him in a drunken stupor, and realizes the man cannot be depended on. He then steals money from school to pay the bill. He goes home, and, no longer able to control his pent-up grief and hatred for Dr. Harris and his unreliability, begins to scream and cry and break everything in sight. Meanwhile, Mr. Lau-rence, having discovered the theft, and suspecting Alan, goes to the apartment. When the boy refuses him admit-tance, he breaks down the door. Laurence calms the boy and forces him to tell his story. He takes the boy home, promising that the animals will be safe. The Laurences keep Alan with them, but because Mrs. Laurence has asthma, they cannot keep the animals. When the Laurences bring home an orphaned poodle, often non-allergenic, for him, he does not want it. Finally he agrees to accept the new puppy. When the puppy becomes ill Alan takes it to Dr. Harris, who has now joined a group to combat alcoholism. He hopes for complete rehabilitation and that later he will prove an acceptable foster parent for Alan.

Though Alan prefers his animal kingdom to people, he sees that he is not able to handle adult responsibilities all by himself. Finally he discovers that several adults in his neighborhood are genuinely interested in his well-being. Alan's experiences being shunted from one relative to another have caused him to distrust adults so thoroughly that his decision to hide his great-aunt's death and subsequent efforts to cover up her absence seem realistic and logical. His need to share his overwhelming burden with others follows logically and results in a poignant, unusual, yet highly believable first-person narrative.

Ages 10-13

Also available in:
Cassette for the Blind — *Alan and the Animal Kingdom*
Library of Congress

Paperbound — *Alan and the Animal Kingdom*
Dell Publishing Co., Inc.

328

Holland, Isabelle

Dinah and the Green Fat Kingdom

J. B. Lippincott Co., 1978.
(189 pages)

FAMILY: Unity
WEIGHT CONTROL: Overweight
    Harassment
    Imagination
    Pets: substitute for human relationship
    Security/Insecurity
    Self-Improvement

Dinah Randall, twelve, often retreats to her Green Kingdom, a great oak tree, to daydream and write about a world where fat people are liked. At home, Mother nags her to lose weight, and Dad agrees with Mother; Dinah's teenage brother, Tony, teases her; and her ten-year-old cousin, Brenda, who shares her room, is an unfailing model of neatness and thin perfection. Brother Jack, nine, is sympathetic to Dinah, and an ungainly puppy she buys for 23¢ loves her outright. Dinah also meets acceptance at the Van Hocht house, where three nicely fat adult sisters live in contentment. One of the sisters has a son about Dinah's age, Sebastian, who stammers and limps from cerebral palsy. Dinah feels uncomfortable talking to him. As for the puppy, to keep him Dinah agrees to meet conditions her mother sets down: eat no snacks, return directly home after school, and attend a nutrition class. Wary of the class, Dinah relaxes when her teacher points out that no one can or will bully her into losing weight; she can only do it for something she wants. In a week, she loses five pounds. Expecting to be praised, she is only teased again by Tony (her dress is too tight, still) and criticized by Mother. A quarrel ensues, and Dinah cries out that they are "a rotten family" and runs into the rainy night. With her puppy she comes to the oak tree. Unable to recapture the Green Fat Kingdom, Dinah writes stories about other things; then, fearing she has forfeited the puppy, she takes it to Sebastian for safekeeping. For the first time she can talk to the boy about his handicap. The Van Hochts call the Randalls to tell them she is there. On the way home, Dad comforts her and says that she and her mother must come to terms; he cannot mediate between them. Mother then admits she has mistreated Dinah, and promises to stop it. She even has praise for Dinah's stories and encourages her to keep on writing.

In this first-person narrative, we get the viewpoint of a girl who feels that other people make her fatness a problem: a perfectionist mother, a teasing brother. In the end she comes to distinguish what her father calls the "mechanics" of losing weight from her reactions to unflattering comments. The discussions here of the psychology and physiology of fatness in America, though preachy at times, provide sound information and portray a variety of attitudes toward it.

Ages 10-13

Also available in:
Paperbound — *Dinah and the Green Fat Kingdom*
Dell Publishing Co., Inc.

329

Holland, Isabelle

Of Love and Death and Other Journeys

J. B. Lippincott Co., 1975.
(159 pages)

COMMUNICATION: Parent-Child
DEATH: of Mother
   Illnesses: of parent
   Life style: change in
   Mourning, stages of
   Parent/Parents: respect for/lack of respect for

Fifteen-year-old Meg, whose parents have been divorced since before she was born, has never met her father. All her life she and her free-spirited mother have lived and traveled in Europe. During the summer, Meg lives in Italy with the people her mother calls "The Pride" — the mother herself, a stepfather named Peter, and an artist friend named Andrew — in a cottage outside Perugia, where her mother runs a tour guide service and Peter writes borderline pornography. One day on a tour, Meg's mother becomes ill. She sends Meg to stay with a friend, an American who rents a castle called Civitella every summer, while she herself goes for a diagnosis. Once at the castle, Meg learns that her father, too, is coming soon to Civitella. Meg rejoins her mother — only to learn that the latter is seriously ill and

will undergo surgery to remove a cancerous growth. Her mother's post-operative recovery is rapid, though the doctor warns that the disease may have spread. Together again, mother and daughter discuss Meg's father. The girl is angry and hurt: it seems that the reason her father has never visited her is that he does not know she exists. Her mother had been unsure who had fathered Meg, and so concealed the birth from him. With time, family resemblance has settled the point. Next day Meg rides with someone from Civitella to meet her father at the train station. She is prepared to hate him for neglect of her mother but will comply with her mother's request to stay at Civitella for a week to get to know him. In the ensuing days, however, she finds he is a kindly, gentle man. Everything about him surprises her: he is an Anglican priest; he is married; his wife is a doctor; their little boy has died; the man feels guilty and partly responsible for the divorce from her mother. One night Meg has a terrifying nightmare that persuades her that her mother is going to die, and she runs to her father for comfort. The next day, he takes her back to her mother's and returns to New York. The illness advances rapidly, and the mother dies at home. Meg does not cry. She cannot believe that that emaciated dead body belonged to her mother. Even at the cremation Meg's only feeling is relief at getting rid of that awful body. It is only when, living now with her father, she receives a painting from Andrew of her mother as she remembers her — full of laughter and mischief and love, wearing her usual floppy hat and yellow dress — that Meg is finally able to grieve.

Within a very few months, an adolescent learns family secrets, meets an unknown parent, and loses a parent to death. Although Meg has been treated as an adult by her mother, her stepfather, and her father, she cannot always feel like one in the crises that beset her. The death of her mother signals also the death of Meg's childhood and way of life. Her ability finally to grieve allows her to accept the future, however changed. The mother's unconventional mind and way of life may be difficult for some readers to comprehend or accept.

Ages 11 and up

Also available in:
Paperbound — *Of Love and Death and Other Journeys*
Dell Publishing Company, Inc.

Talking Book — *Of Love and Death and Other Journeys*
Library of Congress

330

Holmes, Efner Tudor

Amy's Goose

Color illustrations by Tasha Tudor.
Thomas Y. Crowell Company, Inc., 1977.
(27 pages counted)

LONELINESS
ONLY CHILD
  Animals: responsibility for
  Nature: respect for

Young Amy lives on a farm with her mother and father. One day while they are hard at the harvest, preparing for winter, Amy hears the sound she has been waiting for all fall: the cry of the wild geese who stop at the nearby lake every year on their journey south. Their work done and supper eaten, Amy and her father head down to the lake with a sack of corn. But a marauding fox gets there first and injures one goose. Amy and her father carry the goose back to the barn and nurse it back to health. Amy longs to keep it for a pet, but the flock remains at the lake, unwilling to leave without their companion. One gander circles over the barn every night, calling to his mate. Then one day the flock rises up into the sky, its unison farewell cry filling the air. Amy knows that her cherished goose is well enough to

join them. A lone bird drops out of the immense V-formation and circles back, as if searching — and Amy rushes to the barn, embraces the goose, then sets her freely soaring. Amy is left alone, thinking of spring, when the flock will come again.

In this moving story a lonely only child on a farm longs for a close friend to care for and love. She thinks she has found this friend in a wild goose, but in the end recognizes the need for it to join its mate. The deep respect for nature and wild creatures, out of which this story rises, is beautifully conveyed in full-color illustrations depicting the loneliness of the child no less vividly than the exaltation of the flight of the geese.

Ages 8-11

Also available in:
No other form known

331

Honig, Donald

Hurry Home

Color illustrations by Fred Irvin.
Addison-Wesley Publishing Co., 1976.
(32 pages counted)

ILLNESSES: of Parent
  Decision making
  Guilt, feelings of

Tommy Graham, who is about nine, is not sure he should go off to play in a championship baseball game, because his father is ill. When the family doctor arrives, Tommy makes up his mind to forgo the game. Going to the park to tell the coach, he cannot get his attention and is hustled onto the playing field. Worried about his father, Tommy does not play well. It is only when he realizes that ending the tie game is up to him that his play improves. He hits a double and gets to third base on a teammate's single. When another teammate hits a pop-up, Tommy tags third base and scores at home plate. He does not stop to be congratulated but runs for home, where he discovers that his father's illness is not serious.

A young boy feels torn between playing in an important game and being with an ill parent. Winning the game seems the only way out; his mind no longer divided, he wins. Tommy's dilemma is clearly and feelingly told.

Ages 7-9

Also available in:
Paperbound — *Hurry Home*
Xerox Publishing Company

332

Hooks, William Harris

Doug Meets the Nutcracker

Black/white illustrations by Jim Spanfeller.
Frederick Warne & Company, Inc., 1977.
(80 pages)

SELF, ATTITUDE TOWARD: Feeling Different
  Gender role identity: male
  Ostracism
  Perseverance
  Values/Valuing: aesthetic

To nine-year-old Doug, ballet is "rotten, silly girl stuff!" and he is livid when he has to go to a performance of "The Nutcracker" because his sister, Julie, is playing one of the mice. He is humiliated to ride to the auditorium on a public bus, accompanied by a girl with a long, gray tail. At curtain time, resigned to being utterly bored, Doug settles back in his seat and tries to ignore his surroundings. But soon he is paying attention. The scenery is wonderful. He becomes caught up in the story, enthralled by the dancers. By intermission he is exhilarated, and by the end of the ballet, to his mother's surprise, he is shouting "Bravo!" During the next few days, Doug decides he wants to take ballet lessons. He is delighted to find that, because so few boys study ballet, a scholarship is available to him. His mother expects him to be discouraged when, while he is trying on tights at Capezio's, Doug's dressing room curtain falls down, and all the girls in the shop collapse into giggles. But Doug is undeterred. Although he expects to be teased about his dancing, a week goes by and no one at school says a word. But when he tries to join the weekly Saturday stickball game, the boys turn on him with vicious teasing and a beating that knocks him unconscious. He wakes up in the hospital, resolved that he will never speak to his friends again — and never give up ballet. On Monday one of the boys from the stickball game promises Doug that no one will "bug" him anymore. Doug suspects they will stop calling him a sissy but never stop thinking he is one. Even with all the teasing he knows he still faces, he vows to continue. His father, remarried and living in Texas, tells him encouragingly over the phone that if Doug dances the role of the Nutcracker the following Christmas, he will come to see the performance.

Doug's mother wisely does not press Doug either to continue or to give up dancing. She tells him frankly the kind of scorn he can expect to meet sometimes because of his choice, and supports him once he has clear-sightedly made up his mind. The boy's parents, though divorced, are on friendly terms, and his father is kept informed about what the children are doing. His father's approval as a male not involved in dancing reassures Doug, even though his own commitment is already firm.

Ages 8-11

Also available in:
No other form known

333

Hopkins, Lee Bennett

I Loved Rose Ann

Black/white illustrations by Ingrid Fetz.
Alfred A. Knopf, Inc., 1976.
(39 pages counted)

COMMUNICATION: Misunderstandings
   Boy-Girl relationships
   Friendship: keeping friends

Harry Hooper loves Rose Ann enough to send her two valentines. But in return, he receives one he does not like — a letdown. Then Rose Ann goes to a Little League baseball game with Larry Lyon and insults Harry's ability after he has asked to walk home with her — betrayal! But Harry chooses to forgive Rose Ann and offers her one more chance to respond to his affection by printing "Harry Loves Rose Ann" on the sidewalk. Next day, he finds his name changed to Larry's and accuses Rose Ann of making the change — clearly this girl is no longer worth serious attention! Poor Harry, little does he know that Rose Ann had given him what she thought was her best valentine. He would also be surprised to learn that she went to the baseball game with Larry and his sister and his mother, just because Rose Ann's mother arranged it. And she regrets her remark about Harry's baseball prowess. Most of all, Harry would be surprised to learn that Rose Ann, having never liked Larry, was not the one who changed Harry's inscription on the sidewalk. Too bad, Rose Ann now prefers to spend time with her best friend, Vera. "Having one friend like Vera is better than loving Harry or Larry, who both act stupid!"

This two-part first-person narrative enacts a pre-adolescent crush in two stories, the same incidents being told from Harry's and Rose Ann's points of view. What is shown is that neither knows or tells the whole story, and neither asks the other what happened. Here is amusing and thought-provoking material for discussion.

Ages 6-9

Also available in:
No other form known

334

Houston, James A.

Frozen Fire: A Tale of Courage

Black/white illustrations by the author.
Atheneum Publishers, 1977.
(149 pages)

COURAGE, MEANING OF
FRIENDSHIP: Meaning of
   Eskimo
   Parent/Parents: single
   Resourcefulness
   Values/Valuing: moral/ethical

During his thirteen years, Matt Morgan has lived many places. After his mother dies, Matt accompanies his father, a geologist, to Frobisher Bay in the Canadian Arctic, where Mr. Morgan hopes to find copper. But he must find it before other prospectors do and busies himself planning a helicopter search while Matt attends school and makes friends with an Eskimo boy his age named Kayak. When Mr. Morgan's helicopter goes down in a storm and an ice fog grounds air searchers, Matt and Kayak set off on a snowmobile to search. (Matt is the only person to whom his father confided his true flight plan.) But the boys are forced to abandon the snowmobile and a blizzard sweeps down on them, forcing them to rely on survival techniques taught Kayak by his grandfather. Lost and with slim chances to survive, they stumble on the dwelling of a wild man, a former

Frobisher Bay resident, who gives them a night's lodging before telling them to leave. On the journey out, Matt finds gold nuggets, which he stuffs into his pack. Later, just as Kayak had foreseen, Matt discards the gold as too heavy to carry. The next day they set out across the frozen Frobisher Bay for home, only to be swept out to sea as the ice begins to break up. They face certain death — until Matt signals a plane with a mirror, and the ring of seal's blood Kayak has spread attracts a rescue helicopter. Hospitalized back at the settlement, Matt is reunited with his father, who has walked away from the crash, and has decided to take a job as teacher at the local school.

This fine adventure story tells of two youths, one an Eskimo, combining talents in order to survive. At times their disparate values work against them — Matt's acquisitiveness and Kayak's moments of fatalism, for example. But the boys prevail, and Matt comes to recognize the wisdom of Eskimo customs, however odd they seem to him. The Eskimos themselves, and the Arctic locale, are vividly described.

Ages 10-13

Also available in:
No other form known

335

Hughes, Shirley

David and Dog

Color illustrations by the author.
Prentice-Hall, Inc., 1978.
(32 pages counted)

TRANSITIONAL OBJECTS: Toys
  Giving, meaning of
  Loss: of possessions
  Sibling: love for

His older sister, Bella, has seven teddy bears, all of which she takes to bed, and his baby brother likes hard, biteable toys; but David, about three, has only one soft toy, named Dog, which he takes everywhere. Thus Dog comes along to school when David goes with his mother to pick up Bella. Waiting, David holds Dog up to view preparations for the school fair, and then Bella comes amid a flurry and bustle, and David forgets about Dog. At bedtime, after being unnaturally quiet, David says, "I want Dog." But a search turns up nothing, and David spends a restless night missing Dog sorely. At the fair the next day, Bella asks David if he wants to race. No, he does not feel like racing. And he becomes, if anything, sadder when Bella wins a huge teddy bear. Wandering off to look at the goods for sale, David spots Dog in a used-toy stall. Not having enough money to buy him back, he races to find his parents but only finds Bella. Together they rush back — only to meet a little girl carrying Dog away. She refuses Bella's offer to buy him. But Bella, seeing the girl admire the newly won teddy bear, arranges a trade: bear for Dog. David first hugs Dog, then Bella.

A boy's complete attachment to a toy changes to complete misery when he loses it. Pleasant illustrations vividly convey a range of emotions — including Bella's mixed feelings about the trade. All the same, Bella comforts David by saying she did not much like the teddy bear; besides, there would be no room in her bed for it.

Ages 4-7

Also available in:
Braille — *David and Dog*
Library of Congress

Paperbound — *David and Dog*
Prentice-Hall, Inc.

336

Hughes, Shirley

George, the Babysitter

Color illustrations by the author.
Prentice-Hall, Inc., 1975.
(30 pages counted)

BABY-SITTER

Teenage George baby-sits for Mike, Jenny, and Baby Sue every day while their mother is at her job. Aided by Mike and Jenny, George tries to do some housework, too. Together they do the dishes, straighten up the bedroom, and rearrange the toy chest. Then, while Sue naps, the three pick some flowers and make lunch. After lunch, Jenny and Mike amuse themselves, but when their roughhousing proves too rough, George takes them out to buy candy and play in the park. Later in the afternoon, George and the children watch television, wash the lunch dishes, and bathe Baby Sue. When Mother comes home, George collapses in a chair, amazed he has made it through the day, while Mother praises the children: "How could George have managed without them?"

In this thoroughly contemporary picture book, a young man is a baby-sitter while a mother works at a job. The delightful illustrations capture both home life and neighborhood life as they are lived right now.

Ages 4-7

Also available in:
No other form known

337

Hunt, Irene

The Lottery Rose

Charles Scribner's Sons, 1976.
(185 pages)

CHILD ABUSE
FEAR: of Physical Harm
HATRED
LOVE, MEANING OF
  Children's home, living in
  Death: of friend
  Deprivation, emotional
  Giving, meaning of
  Mental retardation
  Trust/Distrust

Frequent physical abuse at the hands of his mother and her boy friend, Steve, has left seven-and-a-half-year-old Georgie fearful and sullen. His only interest and delight is a school library book about flowers and gardens. Suddenly, in a neighborhood lottery, he wins "best prize in the world" — his very own rosebush. But where to plant it? Then Georgie is hospitalized after a brutal beating by Steve and later sent to a boy's school in the country, still brooding on the welfare of his rosebush. When Georgie meets the school director, Sister Mary Angela, she kindly suggests several locations on the school grounds for his rosebush, but Georgie has seen a beautiful garden: the perfect setting. But no, the woman who lives there, with her five-year-old mentally retarded son, Robin, and his grandfather, allows no one to tamper with her garden, a memorial to her husband, recently killed in a car accident along with her older son. Georgie plants his rosebush in Molly Harper's garden anyway, only to find it lying on the school grounds next morning. He immediately goes to replant it, but Molly appears and threatens to burn it. Overcome by fear, anger, and illness, Georgie collapses at her feet and his shirt slips off his back, revealing the scars of many beatings. Molly dissolves at the signs of such suffering and carries the unconscious boy back to school. While recuperating, Georgie learns that his rosebush flourishes in Molly's garden. Now he refuses to believe in her change of heart; someone must have forced her to do what she has done. That summer, Georgie makes good friendships with Robin (whom he plays with patiently for hours) and with Robin's grandfather (who teaches him to read). But his hatred for Molly remains unchanged, though many try to change it. Still he is curious about her, curious about her dead son. He declines to study dramatics because Molly, a former actress, will be teaching the class, but he does watch the rehearsals, learning everybody's lines. Then a player has to be let go — and Georgie is delighted to step in and perform his part. Afterwards, he retreats to his rosebush. One morning, little Robin, left unattended, slips out of the yard and drowns in the nearby lake. The death of his young friend is almost more than Georgie can bear. After the funeral, he digs up his rosebush and placing it in a wheelbarrow, walks the three miles in the dark to the cemetery. Molly drives up just as Georgie starts to dig a hole by Robin's grave. Together they plant Georgie's gift to Robin. When they are finished, Georgie is finally able to ask Molly the question that has been on his mind for so long: "Did you born me a long time ago and I forgot?" She replies, "I didn't 'born' you, but you're mine — no matter where I go or what I do — you're mine.... "

When a young boy who has been physically and emotionally abused is rebuffed by a stranger, he withdraws. When he receives love and affection he slowly learns how to love in return. Fear, distrust, and hatred are emotions Georgie has known for so long that they seem safe and right. Fortunately, he is not pressed to change, but rather given plenty of time to test the people in his new surroundings and develop a feeling of safety.

Readers will strongly sympathize with Georgie and applaud his strong will. Though the passages on physical abuse are short and not too graphic, this melodramatic story is painful to read. Children who have been abused may also find Georgie's eventual good treatment too good to be true.

Ages 11 and up

Also available in:
Paperbound — *The Lottery Rose*
Grosset & Dunlap, Inc.

338

Hunt, Irene

William: A Novel

Charles Scribner's Sons, 1977.
(188 pages)

FAMILY: Unity
  Change: accepting
  Cooperation: in work
  Death: of mother
  Determination
  Responsibility: accepting

Their father is dead, their mother dying, and the Saunders children — Amy, thirteen; William, eight; and nearly-blind Carla, four — fear being separated. Seeking help to ensure that they remain together, Mrs. Saunders turns to Sarah West, a pregnant, unwed sixteen-year-old girl who has moved onto their Florida street. Sarah turns out to be resourceful and just as determined as Mama Saunders to keep the family together. She even increases it, being quite as determined to keep her own baby, Elisabeth, after the child is born during a hurricane. Their home destroyed by the storm, the Saunders move in with Sarah. Three years after Mama has died, the family, aided by friends and neighbors, remains intact. William works at gardening and Sarah, besides working in town, sells her paintings and manages the household. But increasingly, Amy bridles at family responsibilities. William worries that the constant quarrels between Sarah and Amy will break the household. They do. Amy, brought home drunk from a wild party, bitterly accuses Sarah of trying to run her life and goes to live with a neighbor. Only after Carla undergoes surgery that gives her sight are Amy and Sarah reconciled. Amy settles down and marries. But a new threat arises: friends urge Sarah to attend art school. Promising to return, she reluctantly accepts a scholarship to a school far away, while her cousin moves in to take her place at home. But William knows that things will never again be the same.

This chronicle of how a family of three black children and a white girl and her baby stays together for four years is told from William's viewpoint. Readers will sympathize with his desire to keep a young, loving family together, but they will also see the impossibility of his hopes. "Nothing abides," Sarah tells him consolingly as they part; he must face things as they are, not see them as he wants them to be.

Ages 12 and up

Also available in:
Cassette for the Blind — *William: A Novel*
Library of Congress

Paperbound — *William: A Novel*
Grosset & Dunlap, Inc.

339

Hunter, Evan

Me and Mr. Stenner

J. B. Lippincott Co., 1976.
(157 pages)

DIVORCE: of Parents
STEPPARENT: Father
 Parent/Parents: remarriage of

Eleven-year-old Abby O'Neill does not want her mother to divorce her father. Neither does she want Mr. Stenner to divorce his wife and marry her mother. Loyal to her father, Abby refuses to like Mr. Stenner at all. She likes the new house she and her mother have moved to, but resents Mr. Stenner's moving in and playing father to her before either divorce is settled. Yet little by little, likable traits in Mr. Stenner impress her. Still, she is embarrassed that he and her mother cannot yet marry. Eventually, both divorces are final, and Mr. Stenner and her mother are married. They plan a leisurely honeymoon in Italy — and they take Abby with them. Happy to be included, enchanted with the trip, she comes to feel a genuine warmth toward her stepfather. Yet no matter how many good times they enjoy, loving two fathers continues to seem wrong. All the same, just before the three are to go home, Abby does admit to herself that she loves Mr. Stenner and tells him so. He says he loves her, too.

This frank, first-person narrative dramatizes some of the dilemmas divorce can cause. Abby will no longer live with her father, yet feels uneasy accepting a stepfather. She does not finally settle on one or the other, but sees that her love and respect for her stepfather in no way diminishes what she has always felt for her father. Touches of humor throughout the book prevent it from becoming depressing or discouraging.

Ages 10-13

Also available in:
Paperbound — *Me and Mr. Stenner*
Dell Publishing Company, Inc.

340

Hunter, Kristin Eggleston

The Survivors

Charles Scribner's Sons, 1975.
(308 pages)

LOVE, MEANING OF
VALUES/VALUING: Moral/Ethical
   Afro-American
   Crime/Criminals
   Ghetto
   Illnesses
   Loneliness
   Trust/Distrust

Lena Ricks, a middle-aged black woman who owns a dress shop in a slum, believes she has survived so far by trusting no one and working hard. When a thirteen-year-old boy called B. J. turns up to help at the shop, she wonders what he is after and keeps on wondering even though B. J. has become a favorite with her customers and with Lena herself. She suspects that he, like her former husband, dreams of becoming a big-time thief. Determined to improve him, Lena takes B. J. to his former school so that she can find out why he was expelled. But he runs off and soon meets Bobo, a teenage thief whom he idolizes. Told by B. J. how to rob Lena's shop, Bobo ransacks the place. Lena is convinced B. J. has set her up, and she turns him out. For the next week she lives aimlessly, until she decides to look for B. J. — and finds him lying ill in a squalid tenement. Complaining about his father, who lies asleep in the same room, B. J. asks to be taken away. Though sympathetic, Lena refuses to help him. She also refuses his father — whom she is shocked to see is her former husband — when he asks Lena to take him back. Returning to her apartment, Lena suffers a stroke. She is taken to a hospital but insists the hospital also bring in B. J. for treatment as her son. After Lena recovers, Mamie, a black nurse, and B. J. cajole her into resuming a normal life. Yet Lena, while allowing B. J. to live at the shop and to act as a virtual business partner, still fears he will scheme against her. When, at Christmas, he gives her a diamond ring he has bought from a "fence," her suspicions drive him off to stay with the Boggses, a family of thieves in league with his father. Involved in a robbery with Bobo, B. J. is caught. His father is killed in an "accident" staged by the Boggses, and B. J. himself faces a jail sentence — until Lena assumes custody, renames him Bruce James Ricks, and gives him a home at her apartment. B. J. tells her that he has a sister, Brenda, only twelve years old, now living in a foster home: "She can cook and clean real good, and she loves to sew. I'll bring her here tomorrow."

This is a story about two people of differing moral codes who yet come to rely on each other. Just as the conditions of a black slum have formed their moralities — Lena's virtuous and often righteous, B. J.'s sly and opportunistic — so the circumstances of their friendship and dependence modify them. Lena accepts her need for trust and companionship, and B. J. recognizes the fantasies implicit in his ambitions. Strong language and vivid scenes set forth the circumstances and propel a lively narrative.

Ages 12 and up

Also available in:
Talking Book — *The Survivors*
Library of Congress

341

Hurwitz, Johanna

The Law of Gravity

Black/white illustrations by Ingrid Fetz.
William Morrow & Company, Inc., 1978.
(192 pages)

DIFFERENCES, HUMAN
  Communication: parent-child
  Friendship: making friends
  Weight control: overweight

Margot Green is stumped. Her teacher tells the graduating fifth graders to undertake projects over the summer. But what, Margot asks herself, can she learn during the long, hot summer in New York City? Her father, a concert musician, will be on tour; her mother is no help; and the few friends Margot has are leaving town. Suddenly she hits on the ideal project: getting her mother to come down from their apartment. Not once in nine years has she descended to the street, her only explanation: "What is there to go downstairs for?" Margot searches the library for clues to her mother's behavior, and Bernie, a sixth grader from her school, offers to help. Soon Bernie is helping her on the project and taking Margot to places she has never heard of. One day he suggests that Mrs. Green is embarrassed to come down because she is so fat; Margot tries to interest her mother in a diet. But nothing works. Finally Bernie asks why bringing her downstairs is so important to her. Margot ignores the question and decides to frighten her mother into going out by hiding overnight in the public library. It works. When Bernie takes her home, they meet Mrs. Green on the street talking to a policeman. Rather than rejoice, Margot goes upstairs and cries. Her mother, crying herself, confesses that however much she tries to go downstairs, she cannot force herself to.

Margot drops the project, calling it "rotten." Less harsh, her father reminds her that we can only change ourselves; no one should try to manipulate someone else.

In this first-person narrative a girl comes to appreciate the attractions of the city where she lives and the importance of accepting people as they are, not as she would have them to be. Her father's advice to love and accept her mother helps her to answer Bernie's question about why changing her mother is so important to her: she had wished her mother to be like other mothers.

Ages 10-13

Also available in:
Paperbound — *The Law of Gravity*
Scholastic Book Services

342

Hutchins, Patricia

The Best Train Set Ever

Color illustrations by the author.
Greenwillow Books, 1978.
(56 pages)

FAMILY: Unity
  Cooperation
  Giving, meaning of
  Sharing/Not sharing

Each morning young Peter lingers so long admiring a train set in a store window that his brothers and sisters have to hurry him on to school. But it is entirely clear what Peter would like for his birthday. His parents (secretly, because no one in the family keeps a secret) try to buy the train set but cannot afford it. They settle for buying the engine. The four other children each buy another piece of the set. On his birthday Peter is downcast to see the train gone from the window — until he receives five gifts that add up to "the best train set ever." In the second story all the children make costumes for a Halloween party except for Maria. Her sister and brothers donate parts of their costumes to her — a pair of swimming flippers; straw from a hula skirt; a small, conical wizard's hat; feathers from an Indian headdress — from which Maria makes an ostrich costume that wins first prize. In the third story the family plans a Christmas party for visiting relatives. With four days to go, they are eagerly preparing it; with one day to go, they come down with measles and are quarantined. The relatives will not visit again until the summer, and the wait seems endless. But eventually they gather at a picnic for "the best Fourth of July Christmas Party ever."

Here are three stories showing how a family works — by cooperation, by encouragement, and by generating good cheer whenever they are able to. If the stories are somewhat idealized, the illustrations show a family down to earth and lifelike. This book is for beginning readers to read to themselves.

Ages 5-8

Also available in:
No other form known

343

Hutchins, Patricia

Happy Birthday, Sam

Color illustrations by the author.
Greenwillow Books, 1978.
(30 pages counted)

DEPENDENCE/INDEPENDENCE
Height: short
Resourcefulness

Young Sam wakes on his birthday, delighted to be "a whole year older." He stretches to reach the light switch in his room, but still cannot; it is the same for the hanger for his clothes and the faucets on the sink. Unable to reach the doorknob, he must wait for his mother to let in the postman, who brings a birthday package. The gift, from Sam's grandfather, is a small chair. Standing on it, Sam switches on the light, takes his clothes from the hanger, and does everything he has always been too short to do.

A child finds that a birthday, though marking an advance in years, by itself brings no sudden increase in physical capacity. But the intelligent use of a birthday gift does help him to do things he could not do before. Children will readily identify with the importance Sam gives to doing things "all by himself."

Ages 5-7

Also available in:
No other form known

344

Ichikawa, Satomi

Friends

Color illustrations by the author.
Parents' Magazine Press, 1976.
(32 pages counted) o.p.

FRIENDSHIP

Everyone needs friends. Children need them to play with, to study with, to make believe with, to share secrets with, and sometimes to share the blame with. "Grandpas can be best friends too." With friends, one can get dirty, go exploring, and make music. Life would be empty without friends.

The bright illustrations in this book capture the happy — and sometimes less than happy — moments in friendship for even the youngest reader. Read aloud, this book could encourage listeners to talk about their friends and about friendship.

Ages 3-7

Also available in:
No other form known

345

Irion, Ruth Hershey

The Christmas Cookie Tree

Color illustrations by the author.
The Westminster Press, 1976.
(54 pages counted)

CHANGE: New Home
GERMAN-AMERICAN
   Friendship: making friends

Young Eva, about seven, does not rejoice with her parents in their recent move from Philadelphia to Pennsylvania Dutch country. Having grown up there, her parents are familiar with the country area and its customs, but Eva has left everything she knows for a strange place where the people talk differently. The mailman, for example, asks her if she is an *Auslander* (outlander) and if she *"kannscht die Dietsch schwertz"* (can speak the local dialect of German). Yet Eva enjoys talking to him in English, even when he cracks local jokes she cannot appreciate. But a rehearsal at church for a Christmas program leaves her downcast: none of the children speak to her, and she is certain they laugh at her. With nothing to do the next day, Eva discovers a set of Great Granny's cookie cutters. Like Great Granny and Grandmother before them, Eva and her mother make cookies for a Christmas cookie tree, a venerable local custom. Then it is Christmas Eve, time for the church program, and Eva suddenly recalls that she has

no present to leave at the nativity crib, as is customary. So she brings the cookie tree, "the gift of her heart," and finds the children now smile at her. So her wish, made on the first cookie she had eaten, comes true: she makes friends with the local children.

The contrast here between mainstream American culture and the Pennsylvania Dutch variant underlines the distance between them. A child comes to appreciate local customs and fit in. The story and characters, of slight importance in themselves, are vehicles for presenting Pennsylvania Dutch culture. The illustrations, done in the *Fraktur* style of early Pennsylvania Dutch art, are charming, and together with an appendix on making cookies for a Christmas cookie tree and a brief history of the Pennsylvania Dutch (really Germans), introduce readers to a little-known ethnic community in the United States.

Ages 8-10

Also available in:
No other form known

346

Isadora, Rachel

Max

Color illustrations by the author.
Macmillan Publishing Company, Inc., 1976.
(30 pages counted)

GENDER ROLE IDENTITY: Male
   Play

Young Max plays a good game of baseball. On Saturdays, he walks with his sister Lisa to her dancing school, then on to the park for his weekly baseball game. One Saturday, with lots of time before his game, he goes into Lisa's class and watches. Soon he is stretching at the *barre,* trying to do splits, joining in at the *pas de chat,*

I

and trying leaps with the other students. Max has fun in ballet class. Later, when he is up to bat, he hits a home run. Max has discovered a new way to warm up for baseball: Lisa's dancing class.

Young Max is portrayed as an energetic youngster, who discovers that ballet is not only fun, but an excellent way to warm up for baseball. He includes it in his regular baseball training. The all-girl dancing class accepts Max; no sex discrimination is shown by Max or the class.

Ages 4-7

Also available in:
No other form known

347

Isadora, Rachel

The Potters' Kitchen

Color illustrations by the author.
Greenwillow Books, 1977.
(30 pages counted)

CHANGE: New Home
  Family: unity
  Moving

The Potters, a happy family who live in the country, love their kitchen more than any other room. Always abustle with family, friends, and food, it is a warm, noisy place. But when Mr. Potter changes jobs and the family moves to a city apartment, they find their shiny, new kitchen all but alien. Even so, Mrs. Potter encourages the children to make new friends — and soon the new kitchen is as full of friendship, family life, and good smells as the old one was.

The illustrations add emotion to this simple text. Hesitation, sadness, anxiety, and family warmth are vividly

depicted. Indeed the pictures alone might encourage children to express their own trepidations about moving, or trepidations overcome.

Ages 4-8

Also available in:
No other form known

348

Iwasaki, Chihiro

What's Fun Without a Friend?

Color illustrations by the author.
McGraw-Hill Book Co., 1975.
(26 pages)

PETS: Love for
  Loneliness
  Pets: substitute for human relationship

Little Allison and her mother will be going to visit Grandma at the seashore, but Allison must leave her little brown dog, Tippy, with a neighbor. She tells Tippy that she will have no fun without him. When she arrives at Grandma's she puts on her bright red bathing suit, turns to ask Tippy how she looks, then remembers he is at home. Sure enough, she is not having fun. That night with Mother's help, Allison writes Tippy a letter. She tells him recent news, but she also confides that she misses him and wants Father to bring him along when he joins the family. The very next afternoon he does just that and an overjoyed Allison changes into her bathing suit and, with Tippy at her heels, races to the beach. There the two friends play each day of vacation — until Allison is almost as brown as Tippy and can dog-paddle almost as well too.

Any child who owns a companionable pet will recognize the main character's intense loneliness when she must leave her dog temporarily. Though Allison is reunited with Tippy, young readers should be cautioned that not all vacations can accommodate pets.

Ages 4-7

Also available in:
No other form known

349

Jacobson, Jane

City, Sing for Me: A Country Child Moves to the City

Color illustrations by Amy Rowen.
Human Sciences Press, 1978.
(35 pages counted)

CHANGE: New Home
  Friendship: making friends
  Moving

Having just moved from a house in the country to an apartment in the city, young Jenny finds city life and its sights and sounds grim, even frightening. From the window in her room she cannot see the sky; in the halls of her building she imagines lurking terrors; city noises she finds deafening. A short walk with her brother, Greg, is not reassuring, and on a longer walk to the park next day Jenny becomes separated from Greg, and is left standing on a corner, afraid to cross the busy street. She tries to find her way home, but does not recognize her building, and sits down on some steps to rest, hoping that Greg will return. But Rosa appears. Just Jenny's age, she had watched her move in, and she points out Jenny's building — right across the street. Rosa offers to show Jenny the neighborhood, and together the girls savor the delicious smells of a bakery, the pungent aromas of a delicatessen, a world of scents and tastes Jenny has never dreamed of. Toward afternoon's end, Rosa

shows Jenny the striking view of the city from the top of her building, remarking that in so large a city there are plenty of people like themselves. Pondering that and her new friend and their experiences together, Jenny returns home. She is beginning to like the city.

The main character, bewildered and distressed after moving from a familiar rural home to a vast, bustling city, discovers that friendship can alter perceptions and lessen fears. Once she is shown what the city can offer, she begins to accept her new home. The fears and loneliness experienced by old and young alike at being moved to alien surroundings are well caught. Jenny's parents are never mentioned, which may seem a glaring omission.

Ages 6-10

Also available in:
No other form known

350

Jensen, Virginia Allen

Sara and the Door

Color illustrations by Ann Strugnell.
Addison-Wesley Publishing Company, Inc., 1977.
(29 pages counted)

PROBLEM SOLVING
  Dependence/Independence

After little Sara closes the door, she finds that her coat is stuck fast in it, and the knob is out of her reach. She tries to slide out of the undislodgable coat, but discovers she is trapped in it. Calling out for help and receiving no reply, and with visions of being held prisoner until bedtime, Sara begins to cry. When her tears fall on her coat buttons, she begins to pull and tug on them — fruitlessly

— until she discovers some holes through which to push the buttons. She unbuttons her coat, slips out of it, and walks away feeling very good indeed.

This story, told in simple rhyme, demonstrates that necessity is the mother of invention. Sara learns that she must depend on herself when no one is around to help her. Detailed and appealing illustrations vividly express her feelings as she reasons out the solution to her difficulty.

Ages 2-5

Also available in:
No other form known

351

Jeschke, Susan

Sidney

Black/white illustrations by the author.
Holt, Rinehart and Winston, Inc., 1975.
(30 pages counted) o.p.

SELF, ATTITUDE TOWARD: Accepting

Sidney, a young chicken, disguises himself as a fox to fool other chickens. But even after a fairy chicken gives him a fine fox mask, the others still know he is just Sidney and goad him to go out and fool a fox. Sidney ventures forth to try. Max Fox first tackles him around the legs but then apologizes handsomely for having mistaken him for a chicken. Needing a companion, Max invites Sidney along and, somewhat uneasily, Sidney goes home with Max. There he meets Henrietta, Max's sister, and is soon playing with her: she imitates other animals and he guesses which ones; then the two fall to imitating ducks. All this while, Sidney magically becomes more and more like a fox in appearance though in thinking and tastes he remains a chicken. That evening, tired of being a fox, he sneaks back to the chicken cage, only to be stoned and driven off — as a fox. While Sidney laments his fate, the chicken fairy appears and tells him the fox mask will come off only if he convinces someone he is a chicken. This seems impossible, but then Sidney has an idea; he rushes to Henrietta, wakes her and, imitating a chicken, asks what he is. A chicken, she says sleepily, and at once Sidney is fully transformed back into a chicken.

Here an animal fulfills all too well a wish to be taken for another animal, his natural enemy, and then finds he is mistaken for the predator. Unlike the classical fairy tales, this story illustrates no single moral point: Sidney is foolish, but not morally culpable, for his predicament.

Ages 4-7

Also available in:
Paperbound — *Sidney*
Holt, Rinehart and Winston, Inc.

352

Jewell, Nancy

Bus Ride

Black/white illustrations by Ronald Himler.
Harper & Row Publishers, Inc., 1978.
(32 pages)

FRIENDSHIP: Making Friends
SEPARATION ANXIETY

Young Janie's stomach flutters as she boards a cross-country bus alone for a night trip to see Grandpa. Her parents ask an old woman, Mrs. Rivers, to look after Janie, but the girl misses her parents at once. Oddly, it is when Mrs. Rivers remarks that Janie probably does miss her folks that missing them ceases to hurt so. And as they trade comments on the passing scene, the girl warms to the old woman and begins to take an interest in the bus, including its tiny bathroom — though her companion allows that she likes bathrooms in buildings better, because they "don't move around." While Mrs. Rivers naps, the girl sits listening to bus noises until, lulled by motion, she also falls asleep. Later, Mrs. Rivers wakes the girl and helps her get ready to meet Grandpa. As Janie says good-bye, she promises Mrs. Rivers to sit with her the very next time they meet on a bus. And though part of her wants to run to Grandpa, another part wants to ride on and on with her newfound friend.

Besides being a story of how a grandmotherly woman aids an excited little girl on a bus trip, this book is a pleasant primer for youngsters on what a long-distance bus trip is like, with accurate descriptions down to the way to flush the toilet. There is a picture of Janie seated on the toilet, where "she had to hold onto the doorknob to keep from falling off the toilet seat." The depiction of Mrs. Rivers, with her matter-of-fact comments laced with homespun wit, should make readers hope they will have a seat-mate like her on a bus.

Ages 4-8

Also available in:
No other form known

353

Jewell, Nancy

Cheer Up, Pig!

Color illustrations by Ben Shecter.
Harper & Row Publishers, Inc., 1975.
(32 pages)

LONELINESS
RESOURCEFULNESS

Pig is in a good mood and, wanting to share it with friends, is disappointed to find the barnyard deserted. Feeling suddenly lonely, he rolls in the mud to cheer himself up. When this is unsuccessful, he decides to have a snack at his trough, but the food seems tasteless. In a final attempt to rid himself of the blues, Pig tries to sleep, but wakes himself by rolling over into a puddle. He begins to cry but is distracted by a bird overhead who is chirping loudly. Looking up, he sees three young robins receiving their first flying lesson. Pig is struck by the thought that he would have missed this event had he been with friends. Now well pleased, he returns to his pen, where he enjoys a hearty meal and a relaxing dip in the mud. When a friend finally does stop by, Pig, who is enjoying his solitude, excuses himself.

One learns to cope with loneliness by finding advantage in solitude. Text and pictures follow the recognizable cycle of Pig's feelings from euphoria to melancholy to contentment.

Ages 4-8

Also available in:
No other form known

354

Johnston, Norma

If You Love Me, Let Me Go

Atheneum Publishers, 1978.
(162 pages)

AGE: Senility
GRANDPARENT: Living in Child's Home
MATURATION
    Change: accepting
    Death: of grandparent
    Friendship: best friend
    Love, meaning of
    Self, attitude toward: confidence

It is 1920, and sixteen-year-old Allison Standish, having become more self-confident through her summer friendship with Lisa Farraday, is looking forward to the new school year. But Allison's grandmother worries her. Gran, who lives with the Standishes, has become senile, sometimes violent, often disoriented. Someone must always be with her. This drain on Allison's time is balanced by the good news that Lisa (whose parents are going through a scandalous divorce) will be going to Allison's school. Soon both girls are busy and happy with school activities, and Allison finds not only self-confidence but perfect mutual trust in the friendship. But Gran grows worse; one day she tries to strike Allison, falls, and breaks her hip. She is rushed to the hospital and while recuperating, develops pneumonia. Allison, unable any longer to recognize this decrepit old woman as her Gran, confides her grief to Mario Rienzi, a hospital orderly working his way through medical school. Mario helps her to understand and accept Gran as she is. Soon Gran can be taken home, but she will be bed-ridden and need even more care. With this added burden, Allison has also noticed a sudden coolness in Lisa. She questions her, and is grievously unprepared for the answer: Lisa wants an identity apart from "Allisonandlisa." Feeling betrayed and bewildered on every side, Allison enrolls in a volunteer project at the hospital to keep her mind off Lisa and Gran. At the hospital she again confides in Mario, pouring out her troubles. He listens attentively and offers advice. Soon the two find they are in love, and Allison, too, discovers that individuality is at least as valuable as friendship. This sense of self and her love for Mario sustain Allison when Gran dies. For Allison now knows that love between family members or close friends allows for letting go, accepting change, and continuing with life.

This moving first-person narrative portrays a family straining to care for a senile grandparent. Things are made no easier by the failure of the family business and the inability of Allison's older brother to face new challenges. Also dealt within this sequel to *The Swallow's Song* are the need for bosom friends to adapt and grow, alcohol abuse, and an awakening of love between a young man and woman. Indeed, some readers will find the book plot-heavy, although each plotline is logical and the characters are always credible.

Ages 12 and up

Also available in:
No other form known

355

Johnston, Norma

A Mustard Seed of Magic

Atheneum Publishers, 1977.
(184 pages)

FRIENDSHIP: Meaning of
MATURATION
  Boy-girl relationships
  School: classmate relationships
  School: pupil-teacher relationships
  Unwed mother

Tish Sterling, fifteen, views the approaching new year, 1902, with apprehension. Her boy friend, Ken Lapham, has moved away. Mary Lou Hodges, who has had a baby "out of wedlock" the previous summer, has returned to school, causing a minor scandal. Tish has a talent for writing and longs to write something on her own, but she feels "dried up" in "Sourpuss" Albright's English class. She asks Mrs. Owens, another English teacher and a friend, to criticize her writing, and Mrs. Owens obliges, suggesting in general that Tish focus on structure. Tish continues to submit essays to Mrs. Owens, who proves herself a strict editor — so strict that Tish's pride is hurt. Angry, she avoids Mrs. Owens, though she continues to write her class assignments. Meanwhile, Mary Lou wants to be accepted by Tish's social crowd but is making a fool of herself: she acts loud and flirtatious, and dresses flashily. Tish, already her friend, tries to advise her, but Mary Lou only resents her efforts. One night, Mary Lou tries to run away, but is stopped by Tish's brother, who brings Mary Lou to the Sterling home. The three young people talk together, and Mary Lou starts over in winning friends. Tish, also, has a friendship to mend. Her discovery that Mrs. Owens writes cheap romances to supplement her income has made her resent her rigorous mentor all the more. When Tish finally talks to her, learning among other things that Mrs. Owens has been supporting a terminally ill husband, their friendship deepens. By now, school has let out for summer vacation, and with two renewed friendships and Ken coming to spend the summer, Tish feels she has everything to look forward to.

The spring of 1902 is a difficult time for Tish, but proves to be a maturing time as well. She learns that, for a writer, no amount of care and beautiful thoughts can make up for a disorderly, hard-to-follow form. Similarly, she learns that for all her impulsive and skillful ability to help out others, she must reserve some care and energy for herself. And she must beware of judging another person on inadequate information. This book, with its many characters and sub-plots, is a sequel to *The Sanctuary Tree*. Although set in the distant past, its characters and moral issues seem not at all dated.

Ages 12 and up

Also available in:
No other form known

356

Johnston, Norma

The Sanctuary Tree

Atheneum Publishers, 1977.
(219 pages)

J

CHANGE: Resisting
FAMILY: Relationships
  Belonging
  Boy-girl relationships
  Illnesses: of parent
  Maturation

For Tish Sterling, trouble begins in the summer of 1901 when she turns fifteen. Gramps dies, and practical, headstrong Mama decides to sell his comfortable old farm in Pennsylvania. Tish, living in the Bronx, New York, has spent many summers on that farm, and cannot bear to say good-bye to it. But the family — Mama and the six children — go there to prepare for the sale. Tish is further saddened that she will be separated for the length of her stay from her boy friend, Ken, back home. Ken promises to visit his uncle's farm, also in Pennsylvania, but the season passes, and he does not come. Grandpa's farm is sold, its furnishings are auctioned, and the family returns to the Bronx. There Tish is shocked to learn that Ken and his parents are moving. Ken's brother, having gotten a neighborhood girl pregnant, ran away. His family now feel like social outcasts and are leaving. Tish feels terribly alone. Worse difficulty arises when Father, who directs a secretarial school, must undergo surgery and lengthy hospitalization. Mama decides to run the school, but the children are left to do the housework. Busy at home, Tish falls behind in her schoolwork, cannot take part in school projects and longs to be with Ken and her friends. With Father home at Thanksgiving, life improves. The

December issue of the school magazine contains an essay by Tish secretly submitted by a friend. Best of all, Mama suggests she invite Ken for Christmas. On Christmas morning the two young people at last have time to talk alone about all they have learned during their time apart. Neither feels bound to the relationship nor ruined by the separation, but with their special feelings for each other, both look forward to a long-time friendship.

Tish's sixteenth year takes her through several anxious months of feeling alienated from family and friends and suffocated by pressures. She looks for sanctuary in the tree at Grandpa's, in Ken, in "the way things used to be." Finally she discovers peace and sanctuary within herself. This first-person narrative is the third in a series about Tish and her family. It is preceded by *The Keeping Days* and *Glory in the Flower*. Although set in the early 1900s, it presents hard times that can befall any teenager in any period.

Ages 12 and up

Also available in:
Cassette for the Blind — *The Sanctuary Tree*
Library of Congress

357
Johnston, Norma

The Swallow's Song
Atheneum Publishers, 1978.
(192 pages)

COMMUNICATION: Lack of
COMMUNICATION: Parent-Child
  Age: senility
  Boy-girl relationships: dating
  Emotions: identifying
  Friendship: meaning of
  Grandparent: living in home of
  Values/Valuing: moral/ethical

Allison Standish, a teenager in the 1920s, looks to her sixteenth birthday to mark the starting point of a new and exciting life. Instead, it seems at first to mark just the opposite. Her parents have decided to spend the summer in Ocean Grove, New Jersey, to look after Allison's maternal grandmother, who lives there and who has taken to wandering the streets at off hours in her nightgown. They discover upon their arrival that Grandma has become absent-minded, but also suspicious and hostile as well. The house is filled with gloom and unease. Worse, Allison's father, who owns a store in New York, can only be in Ocean Grove on weekends; he is unaware of the troubles brewing. Formerly fond of the little town, Allison, like her restless older brother, Jerry, finds that this year she wants more than a summer home and a nice time with her family. Strolling down the beach one day in search of something to do, she meets Lisa Farraday, and later, Lisa's wealthy family, including Lisa's brother, Dirk, a most attractive college man. Allison and Lisa become close friends, as do Jerry and Dirk; soon Allison is going to fancy parties and dances with the Farradays and dating Dirk. She is completely taken with the Farraday glamor: Lisa's attractive, sophisticated parents know all the latest steps; Dirk is suave and drives a fancy new car. In such company Allison has more than escaped the mounting tensions at home: she has "arrived." But her view of the Farradays is badly shaken when she sees Mr. and Mrs. Farraday fighting, and shattered when, not finding his wife at home, Farraday staggers drunk (Prohibition is in force) into the Standish house looking for her. At the same time, Allision is beginning to see Dirk's darker side: his irresponsibility, his serious sexual advances, his illegal liquor supply. Her feelings toward him are changing. It is not until Jerry and Dirk are arrested for possession of cocaine and liquor, and Dirk tries to pin the blame on Jerry to protect his inheritance, that Allison realizes what kind of company she has been keeping. Jerry's arrest decisively brings Allison's family together and makes them see how little they have been communicating with one another. As things turn out, Allison and Lisa's friendship survives.

In this first-person narrative, a teenage girl finds hitherto placid family life disrupted, first by her grandmother's mental deterioration, then by friendship with a family whose values challenge those her own family has always taken for granted. She is startled by changes in her own behavior but has no one with whom to discuss her conflicting emotions about her boy friend, the habit of emotional restraint being so firmly established in her own family. It takes a crisis to bring her feelings and the others' into the open. This story rests on sound characterizations and loses no timely application by being set many years ago. It is continued in the sequel *If You Love Me, Let Me Go.*

Ages 12 and up

Also available in:
No other form known

358

Johnston, Tony

Night Noises: And Other Mole and Troll Stories

Color illustrations by Cyndy Szerkeres.
G. P. Putnam's Sons, 1977.
(63 pages)

J

FRIENDSHIP: Meaning of
  Fear: of darkness
  Tooth, loss of
  Wishes

In the first story, Troll finds Mole contemplating a four-leaf clover he can wish on. Troll protests, "You have *me*, Mole. I am your rain-or-shine friend." Every wish Mole makes, Troll promises to carry out, and Mole sees he needs no four-leaf clover; he has a friend. In the second story, Troll, about to leave Mole's place for home, decides to stay because of the rain, which will frizz his hair. Mole, intent on napping, pushes him out the door. But soon he runs after Troll to ask him back. Troll refuses, and Mole warns him he will catch cold. Finally Mole prevails, and Troll comes inside. Later, Mole catches cold. In the third story, Troll complains that a tooth of his is falling out. Mole ties one end of a string to a doorknob, the other to the tooth, and tells Troll to say when. Troll remains silent, and then sneezes. The tooth falls out. Troll thanks Mole all the same for sitting with him. In the last story, Mole is snugly abed when he hears frightening noises. Several times he calls Troll, and Troll reassures him that the noises are "friendly night noises." Mole prepares to fall asleep when Troll rushes in, frightened himself by night noises. They stay together through the night, feeling good "listening to the night noises with each other."

This collection of stories shows the qualities of friendship by measuring it against wishing, annoyance, pain, and fright. The stories show that although friendship may not conquer all, it can comfort the two friends. This is a beginning reader.

Ages 4-7

Also available in:
Paperbound — *Night Noises: And Other Mole and Troll Stories*
Xerox Publishing Company

359

Jones, Penelope

I Didn't Want to Be Nice

Color illustrations by Rosalie Orlando.
Bradbury Press, Inc., 1977.
(32 pages counted)

CONSIDERATION, MEANING OF
 Greed
 Jealousy: peer

Nettie the squirrel is going to Andrea's birthday party, but she does not want to "be nice," as her mother instructs her to be. Nor does she want to give Andrea the beautifully wrapped present she carries. Arriving at Andrea's house, she bridles when the birthday girl grabs the present and opens it. She also broods over her unsuccess at the peanut hunt. It is only after Andrea gives Nettie a large piece of chocolate cake, a red balloon, and a little basket full of gumdrops, that Nettie realizes she has enjoyed herself, and remembers to thank Andrea and wish her a happy birthday.

In this authentically childlike first-person narrative, children should quickly sense the feeling behind the main character's rudeness — jealousy. This could lead to a discussion of such feelings in oneself or in others.

Ages 4-7

Also available in:
No other form known

360

Jones, Ron

The Acorn People

Black/white illustrations by Tom Parker.
Abingdon Press, 1976.
(76 pages)

COURAGE, MEANING OF
HANDICAPS
 Camp experiences

At first the sheer unanimity of disease and disfigurement at the summer camp for severely handicapped children stuns the new counselor. He has signed on for what he supposed was a comfortable summer job helping children, not for being a round-the-clock nurse. Yet every movement of the five children he and his co-counselor Dominic care for requires the young men's assistance. Convinced the job is hopeless, the narrator strings together a nut necklace from acorns — a nutty symbol for the craziness he feels. Soon everyone in the cabin makes necklaces. They become known as the Acorn People: Benny B., the wheelchair rocket; Spider, the limbless talker; Thomas, victim of muscular sclerosis who nonetheless endures; Martin, wise in his blindness; and Aaron, confined to a wheelchair and unable to eliminate his wastes normally. But their building solidarity and venturesomeness is bound to collide with the strict schedule set down by the camp director. So they ignore it. They swim when the girls do; they climb a mountain, discovering as much about themselves as about the land. Catching the mood, the camp nurse, Mrs. Nelson, teaches the girls to apply makeup. But the director, alarmed by these departures, orders a return to the schedule. Led by Mrs. Nelson, the camp resists and on the final day stages a Water Extravaganza that caps an unruly and joyous stay.

The author of this true, first-person narrative cannot initially see beyond these children's obvious pain, afflictions, and limitations, and his zeal to help them cannot stay the distance. But as his charges reveal themselves to him, he finds he can back up their own spirit and confirm their own insights. They cannot conquer their handicaps — an epilogue notes that the five boys were dead by the time of publication. But they temporarily conquer the social pressures that would confine them with labels — "blind child," "cripple," and so on. Readers of this memorable book may well forget the handicaps but not the courage of these children.

Ages 10 and up

Also available in:
Cassette for the Blind — *The Acorn People*
Library of Congress

Paperbound — *The Acorn People*
Bantam Books, Inc.

361

Jordan, June

New Life: New Room

Color illustrations by Ray Cruz.
Thomas Y. Crowell Company, Inc., 1975.
(52 pages)

SIBLING: Relationships
  Change: accepting
  Cooperation
  Problem solving

Ten-year-old Rudy Robinson, his nine-year-old brother, Tyrone, and his six-year-old sister, Linda, seem on their way to becoming a crowd. Their mother is going to have a baby, and there will not be enough room for it in their two-bedroom apartment under present arrangements, with the boys sharing one small bedroom, the parents the other larger room, and Linda sleeping in the living room. Mr. and Mrs. Robinson decide to move the boys into the larger bedroom, take the boys' room themselves, and move Linda in with Rudy and Tyrone. The children see difficulties in this arrangement, but feel that things can be worked out. While Mrs. Robinson is in the hospital having the baby, Mr. Robinson and a friend move the furniture to its new places. At first the children feel shy and a little afraid because their new room seems so big and strange. In order to help them feel more at ease, Mr. Robinson gives Rudy, Tyrone, and Linda poster paints and tells them to paint the room as they see fit. Soon the children have covered the windows and walls with bright colors. Then they sort through their toys, deciding what to keep and what to throw out. Their first night in the new room is scary, but the children move their cots closer together, and wake up the next morning feeling that the room is their own. When Mrs. Robinson comes home from the hospital with the new baby, everyone is happily in place.

Because parents and children discuss the room changes, the latter are able to adapt to them quickly. The children feel less crowded when they learn to cooperate with one another. Working together and the willingness to accept change are stressed without moralizing in this short, sometimes humorous book.

Ages 4-8

Also available in:
Talking Book — *New Life: New Room*
Library of Congress

362

Kantrowitz, Mildred

Willy Bear

Color illustrations by Nancy Winslow Parker.
Parents' Magazine Press, 1976.
(31 pages counted)

FEAR: of School
TRANSITIONAL OBJECTS: Toys
  School: entering

The night before his first day at school, a little boy is talking to his toy bear, Willy, about what the next day will bring. The boy is nervous and cannot sleep. Pretending that it is Willy who is sleepless, the boy turns on a light, gets the bear a glass of water, and finally takes him into bed to snuggle. When morning comes, the boy rushes around, brushing his teeth, washing his face, getting dressed, and eating breakfast. Willy remains in the bedroom and is not ready. The little boy leaves without him, promising to tell him all about school when he returns.

This funny monologue, a boy's talk with his toy bear, expresses many children's nighttime worries, in particular those that arise the night before the first day of school. The boy's nervousness is alleviated by caring for his "friend" the bear. Preschool and kindergarten children may well enjoy it read aloud.

Ages 4-6

Also available in:
Paperbound — *Willy Bear*
Parents' Magazine Press

363

Kaplan, Bess

The Empty Chair

Harper & Row Publishers, Inc., 1978.
(243 pages)

DEATH: of Mother
MATURATION
STEPPARENT: Mother
  Communication: parent-child
  Guilt, feelings of
  Jewish
  Parent/Parents: remarriage of

Nine-year-old Rebecca Devine is the daughter of Russian-Jewish immigrants to Canada. It is the time of the Great Depression, and her father is wholly preoccupied with the grocery store he owns adjacent to the family home. Money is tight, and Mama helps in the store, though she has not been feeling well lately. One day she tells Becky and Becky's younger brother, Saul, that she is expecting a baby. Becky is ecstatic, and is sure the baby will be a girl. But the night of Becky's tenth birthday, her mother is taken to the hospital, where both Mama and baby die in the night. Becky is grief-stricken. Unable to bear Mama's absence, she soon believes Mama is visiting her at night. Meanwhile, well-intentioned relatives have begun to search for a suitable new wife for Papa. The children resent this interference, and Papa seems merely indifferent, though he does tell Becky he had promised Mama he would remarry for the children's sake. One prospective wife is Sylvia, a gentle, attractive woman both children like. But Becky feels she would betray Mama by approving a marriage, so she tries to remain aloof. In time Papa and Sylvia do marry, and Becky warms toward Sylvia in spite of herself. But Mama still haunts her in the night, and now Becky believes Mama walks through the house, looking for ways to get even with the family. The child acts so strangely that Sylvia finally insists Becky explain herself. The girl admits her fear that Mama will punish her for loving a stepmother. To convince Becky that Mama is gone, Papa takes her to the cemetery to see the grave. Becky's nightmares cease, and she begins to remember Mama once again as loving and kind. When Sylvia announces her own pregnancy, Becky begins to call her "Mummy."

This first-person narrative deftly dramatizes the customs, beliefs, and feelings of an Orthodox Jewish family. Becky is a naive child whose mother has not yet told her the facts of life, has instead told her she is too young for them. Hence, Becky believes that kissing makes babies, which come out of the mother's navel. The book's main theme is a child's grief and guilt at the death of a parent, modulating into her acceptance of and ability to love her stepmother.

Ages 10-14

Also available in:
Cassette for the Blind — *The Empty Chair*
Library of Congress

364

Katz, Bobbi

Volleyball Jinx

Black/white illustrations by Michael Norman.
Albert Whitman & Co., 1977.
(64 pages)

INFERIORITY, FEELINGS OF
  Competition
  Sports/Sportsmanship
  Superstition

Ann and Lori, best friends in the sixth grade, both like sports. Ann is the better athlete but is superstitious.

When their teacher announces tryouts for a girls' volleyball team, Ann gets so excited she blurts out her "lucky" phrase: "Rabbit, rabbit!" Later, their teacher agrees to give extra practice to an unconfident Lori on the condition that if she makes the team, Lori will tell him what "Rabbit, rabbit" means. On the evening before tryouts, Ann brings her pet mouse over to Lori's house for luck. Both girls make the team. In fact, Ann is elected team captain, and contrives to bring her pet mouse to school and to their first game, again for luck. She also explains to her teacher: "If you say 'Rabbit, rabbit' the first thing on Monday morning, the whole week will go well." He agrees to say it to help the team — and when they win their first match he suggests that she make the mouse the team mascot. Ann's team wins the next three matches. But in their first home match, they lose the first two games and must win the third to stay in first place. Before that game their coach, Mrs. Jansen, hands out jelly beans from her husband. Ann has never cared for Mr. Jansen, whom she calls "the Shadow" because he is so attentive to his wife. Ann decides he is a jinx. During the game a ball hits her mouse's cage, the mouse runs off, and they lose the game. The team agrees that "the Shadow" is a jinx — but Mrs. Jansen, when Ann tells her her hunch, emphatically does not. She works the girls even harder to prepare for the next home match. Ann tells her teacher that with the jinx on hand, her mouse gone, and two injured players, her team does not stand a chance. At the home match, the team wins the first game, and Ann hurries into the second, hoping to win it before "the Shadow" arrives. He enters, but so does her teacher, who has found the mouse. Ann is overjoyed, and the team goes on to win. Later, Ann thanks the teacher for winning the game for them, but he tells her the team did it with all their hours of practice. Mrs. Jansen's husband takes the whole team out for pizza, and Ann decides that "sometimes a jinx is not so bad."

Ann allows her superstitions not only to control her feelings about herself and others, but also to affect her teammates as well. Expecting failure, they lose; expecting victory, they win. Without lecturing, this book shows the value of self-confidence and the pervasive effect of one's expectations of good or ill.

Ages 9-11

Also available in:
No other form known

365

Kaye, Geraldine

Tim and the Red Indian Headdress

Color illustrations by Carolyn Dinan.
Childrens Press, Inc., 1976.
(24 pages)

GIVING, MEANING OF
Sharing/Not sharing
Sibling: older

When Tim is given an Indian headdress of brightly colored feathers, his little sister, Betsy, starts clamoring: "Me too, Betsy want hat." Tim's mother explains that the "hat" belongs to Tim and sets about trying to interest Betsy in something else. Meanwhile, Tim slips away to Mr. Brown's farm, where he gathers some feathers; he takes them home, paints them, and attaches them to a piece of tape. He then presents Betsy with a headdress of her own and the two play in a wigwam their mother has made.

The little sister in this story is not the first younger sibling to want to imitate an older sibling in just about everything. Her big brother avoids the anger and jealousy which might follow this "me too" demand by using

his imagination, time, and effort to make Betsy happy instead — an example to older siblings that avoids the preachy.

Ages 5-7

Also available in:
No other form known

366

Kaye, Geraldine

The Yellow Pom-Pom Hat

Color illustrations by Margaret Palmer.
Childrens Press, Inc., 1976.
(24 pages)

CONSIDERATION, MEANING OF
Grandparent: love for

Gran, who has been ill and needs peace and quiet, has come to visit Jane's family. Otherwise Jane would not dream of wearing the ridiculously large yellow hat Gran knits for her. When her friends make fun of the hat, Jane gives up, and tries to make it disappear. She throws it in a tree, but a misguidedly thoughtful boy brings it down. She tries to bury it in the garden, but her dog digs it up. Finally, in desperation, Jane cuts three holes in it. When Gran sees the ruined hat, she is neither peaceful nor quiet — but Dad slips it over the teapot, as a tea-cozy. Noting that Jane no longer has a hat, Gran promises to knit her a red one for Christmas. But Jane is not worried — Christmas is a long way off.

Though it remains unspoken, in this otherwise broadly told narrative, readers will recognize a little girl's disgust at an unwanted, unattractive gift, and the sheepishness she feels for not liking it.

Ages 5-7

Also available in:
No other form known

367

Keats, Ezra Jack

Louie

Color illustrations by the author.
Greenwillow Books, 1975.
(34 pages counted)

LONELINESS
  Ghetto
  Inferiority, feelings of

A puppet show given by Susie and Roberto for the children in their rundown neighborhood attracts Louie, who is about seven. Neither Susie nor Roberto has ever heard Louie say a word, but when Gussie, a puppet clown is brought on, Louie stands up and calls out, "Hello!" So entranced is Louie that he continues calling to Gussie, holding up the show, and blocking people's view. Only when Gussie starts answering, welcoming Louie, asking him to sit down because "there's lots more to come," does the little boy subside. After the show, Susie brings Gussie to Louie to say good-bye, and the boy grasps the puppet and holds on until Roberto tells him Gussie is tired and must sleep. Back at home, Louie dreams of feeding Gussie from a giant ice-cream cone — until the cone suddenly disappears, leaving Louie floating among children who make fun of him. Louie wakes, saddened by the dream, to be told by his mother that someone has left a note telling him to follow a green string outside the door. At the end of the string, Louie finds Gussie — a gift — and a sign saying, "HELLO."

Touched and excited by a puppet, a little boy briefly forgets the poverty and solitude he lives in, only to be cast down again when the puppet is taken away. In the otherwise bright, sharp illustrations here, Louie's nebulous features convey his vague sense of self at first, but the final sequence of illustrations shows the transformation of his emptiness into joy when the puppeteers surprise him with the puppet as a gift. This book is one in a series by this author.

Ages 3-7

Also available in:
Paperbound — *Louie*
Scholastic Book Services

368

Keats, Ezra Jack

The Trip

Color illustrations by the author.
Greenwillow Books, 1978.
(33 pages counted)

CHANGE: New Home
  Imagination
  Loneliness

Louie's family has just moved in, and Louie knows no one, not even a cat or a dog. Having no one to play with, longing for the old neighborhood, he simulates it in miniature in a shoe box. In his imagination, Louie walks down the old street but sees no one. Suddenly — still imagining — he is confronted by costumed figures, his old friends out trick-or-treating. At that moment, Louie's mother calls him; she helps him into his Halloween costume, and sends him outside to trick-or-treat with neighborhood children.

Having recently moved, a young boy longs for his friends and the familiar surroundings of his old neighborhood. A powerful imaginer, he nevertheless finds that however deeply he yearns for things to be as they were, nothing really happens except in the present. Bold, almost garish, illustrations help convey the atmosphere of Louie's fantastic Halloween daydream.

Ages 4-7

Also available in:
Paperbound — *The Trip*
Scholastic Book Services

369

Keller, Beverly Lou

The Beetle Bush

Color illustrations by Marc Simont.
Coward, McCann & Geoghegan, Inc., 1976.
(64 pages)

INFERIORITY, FEELINGS OF
  Resourcefulness

Disappointed in her efforts at painting, at baking, at writing poetry, Arabelle Mott posts a sign on her bedroom door: "Arabelle Mott, Failure." Hoping to boost her confidence, her parents encourage her to plant a garden. Once again she works diligently — but grows more weeds than flowers, has snails on her tomatoes, finds a mole eating her carrots, and gets black beetles on her bush bean plant. The landlord declares the garden a mess, but Arabelle has had enough of failure. She puts on display her beetle bush — with over one hundred healthy beetles — her mole hole, her snail trail, and her weed seeds. After all, some people cannot grow anything! The landlord, seeing things in a new light, brings his son to see the snails and beetles. Poking among the weeds, the boy finds one more tribute to

Arabelle's industry — a watermelon. That evening, saying goodnight to her garden, Arabelle goes to her room and takes down the sign.

After too many failures, one little girl wrestles out from under her feelings of being able to do nothing right. Working in her garden, she can vent anger through strenuous physical activity, but it is her wit that finally saves her from despair.

Ages 5-8

Also available in:
Braille — *The Beetle Bush*
Library of Congress

Paperbound — *The Beetle Bush*
Dell Publishing Company, Inc.

370

Keller, Beverly Lou

Don't Throw Another One, Dover!

Color illustrations by Jacqueline Chwast.
Coward, McCann & Geoghegan, Inc., 1976.
(63 pages)

TANTRUMS
  Sibling: new baby

Dover Beech rebels when told he must stay with Grandmother while his mother is in the hospital having a baby. In fact, he throws a tantrum, but it does no good. Once at Grandmother's, Dover throws another tantrum, but Grandmother ignores him and goes outdoors. Dover hears a hair-raising yowl and rushes to the door in time to see Grandmother baring her teeth and shaking her fists at a tree. Now a little afraid of Grandmother, Dover follows her through her chores and sees her smack the floor with a hammer and repeatedly kick the cellar door. Is she, he hesitantly asks, having tantrums? She explains that she was chasing a cat from a bird's nest, fixing a loose floor board, and loosening a sticky door. How much good are tantrums, reflects Dover, when Grandmother can be so alarming without even being angry? Father arrives, to take Dover home to meet his new baby sister — and the boy is just about to try one more outburst in hopes of staying with Grandmother, but she stops him: "You've thrown one tantrum in my house . . . . If you're going to throw another, you have to throw it where you won't bother me or my animals." Dover feeds the animals, plays with the dog, packs his suitcase, and goes home to see the baby. Helping to bathe her, he decides he wants to take her along next time he goes to see Grandmother.

Young children will recognize the temptation to raise the roof when new and mysterious changes occur in one's family. Dover wants things to stay as they were. This beginning reader dramatizes his attempts to stop change — and where they get him — but his reconciling himself to a baby sister proves a pat ending rather than an interesting experience in itself.

Ages 4-7

Also available in:
No other form known

371

Keller, Beverly Lou

Fiona's Bee

Color illustrations by Diane Paterson.
Coward, McCann & Geoghegan, Inc., 1975.
(47 pages)

FRIENDSHIP: Making Friends
   Shyness

Little Fiona has no friends. She buys a dog's feeding dish, fills it with water, and sets it on the porch, hoping a thirsty dog will come along and bring its young owner with it. Instead, a bee falls into the water. Fiona cannot bear to see the poor creature drown, so she lifts it out with a twig. The bee slowly drags itself onto her finger, up her arm, and onto her shoulder. Fiona, afraid that if she brushes him off he will get angry and sting her, decides to walk to the flower bed in the park, thinking the flowers will attract the bee. On her way to the park, she meets several children, and each one, seeing the bee, is awed by Fiona's bravery. They follow her to the park and by the time she reaches the flower garden, quite a group has gathered. Fiona sits by the flowers while all her followers stand back. The bee flies to the flowers, and Fiona says good-bye and walks away. All the other children walk her home, and promise to return to play the next day. Fiona's bee has brought her new friends.

A little girl's courage and kindness to a drowning bee are indirectly responsible for her making friends. This witty, simple account demonstrates how concern for something or someone else can overshadow concern for oneself, and often lead to pleasant results. The book is written for the young independent reader, who will be delighted by its satisfying ending. It should also read well aloud.

Ages 5-8

Also available in:
Braille — *Fiona's Bee*
Library of Congress

Paperbound — *Fiona's Bee*
Dell Publishing Company, Inc.

372

Keller, Beverly Lou

The Genuine, Ingenious, Thrift Shop Genie, Clarissa Mae Bean & Me

Black/white illustrations by Raymond Davidson.
Coward, McCann & Geoghegan, Inc., 1977.
(62 pages)

FRIENDSHIP: Best Friend
  School: classmate relationships
  Self, attitude toward: feeling different

Marcie Wills, eleven, has been picked by Clarissa Mae Bean, the most outrageous girl in school, to be her very best friend — a dreadful distinction. Clarissa is untidy, unwashed, and gets all her clothes at thrift shops. Marcie tries to avoid her, but Clarissa follows her everywhere. Soon her old friends are treating Marcie the way they treat Clarissa: like an outcast. Yet she grudgingly accepts Clarissa's companionship, though not her friendship. Still, she wonders why she feels badly when Clarissa misses the bus for a school picnic. With Marcie, Clarissa lets her imagination run wild. She spots unheard-of spies at City Hall, and preposterous smugglers in the streets. She gives Marcie odd presents: a decrepit briefcase full of comic books and a thrift-shop Persian rug. Yet, that summer, Clarissa announces she has won a scholarship to study at The School of American Ballet in New York. Marcie has never paid much attention to Clarissa's ballet talk, and is not much impressed. Meanwhile, summer camp with Clarissa is a disaster, as expected; everyone avoids them. Upon their return, Marcie and her family move to another neighborhood, and Clarissa goes off to New York to study. Marcie notices that she feels shaken and lost seeing Clarissa off at the airport. But they correspond — and Marcie finds they are becoming good friends through their letters. Soon she misses Clarissa mightily and cannot wait for her visit at Christmas. She also hates her new neighborhood, where she cannot avoid seeing her snobbish cousin every day. Nor can she avoid attending a Christmas performance of "The Nutcracker," in which her cousin is a sugarplum fairy. Nor, alas, can she avoid her cousin's smarting condescension at the cast party afterwards; she begins to know how it must have felt to be Clarissa Mae Bean. But how it feels now becomes clear when all balletomanes' eyes in the room turn toward her old friend Clarissa Mae, by now the talk of the dance world for her promise. Being a friend of Clarissa, Marcie is invited out during the holidays by every one of her cousin's insufferable friends. Her mother is pleased that she is finally meeting some nice, sensible girls. But Marcie turns them all down. She wants to spend all of her vacation with Clarissa.

Marcie expresses all her changing feelings about Clarissa with breezy humor and off-hand honesty. She is not the only youngster to find it easier to be serious when she writes than when she talks, and it takes long correspondence before she sees she has a friend. Clarissa, on the other hand, knows from the beginning. By the end of the story, Marcie has not come to resemble her eccentric friend, but she does have a good idea how it feels to be different.

Ages 10 and up

Also available in:
No other form known

373

Kelley, Sally

Trouble with Explosives

Bradbury Press, Inc., 1976.
(117 pages)

FRIENDSHIP
SCHOOL: Pupil-Teacher Relationships
SPEECH PROBLEMS: Stuttering

Polly Banks is eleven years old when she moves "for the umpteenth time in six years" to Atlanta, Georgia. To Polly, each move means that another teacher and another class of students will discover that she stutters. The new teacher, Miss Patterson, is a bird-like, militaristic woman whose chief aim in the classroom is to keep order. But in class Polly makes friends with Sis Hawkins, a confident, easy-going girl who refuses to let Miss Patterson intimidate her. Then there is Polly's new "shrink," Dr. Maxie, whom she also likes. (Because of her stuttering, Polly has been seeing psychiatrists for several years.) Dr. Maxie discovers that Polly stutters most when keeping some hurt or worry bottled up and when talking about herself. She encourages Polly to speak up about what is on her mind, especially to her parents. Meanwhile, Miss Patterson one day asks Polly to lead the class in the Pledge of Allegiance. Polly stutters badly and starts to cry, causing some classmates to laugh at her. Sis leaps to her defense. Miss Patterson, angered because Sis has spoken out of turn, orders her to write the Pledge seven hundred times. Stoically, Sis begins. But two weeks — and two hundred Pledges — later, Miss Patterson finds that the girl has been writing during class time, and tears up all she has done. Sis runs home in tears, locks herself in her room, and refuses to return to school. Incensed, Polly organizes her classmates to fight back. All agree to write Pledges through a whole school day, no matter what Miss Patterson says or does. By noon of the first day, Miss Patterson is in a rage, and Sis and Polly go to the principal for help. The teacher is taken home, and a substitute replaces her for the remainder of the term. Meanwhile, Polly has made several friends. By the time her father is appointed vice-president of his company, and the family buys a home to settle down in, Polly has stopped seeing Dr. Maxie — and stopped stuttering.

A wise psychiatrist and a loyal friend help a girl to overcome a lifelong handicap. Encouraged by Dr. Maxie, Polly learns to say and do what she believes in. Coincidentally, her family moves at last into a permanent home, ending the necessity for Polly to keep starting over making friends. Among so many credible characters, Polly's tyrannical teacher seems overdrawn.

Ages 10-13

Also available in:
Braille — *Trouble with Explosives*
Library of Congress

Paperbound — *Trouble with Explosives*
Scholastic Book Services

374

Kellogg, Steven

Much Bigger Than Martin

Color illustrations by the author.
The Dial Press, Inc., 1976.
(30 pages counted)

SIBLING: Youngest
  Resourcefulness

Sometimes Henry finds it fun being Martin's little brother. But lately Henry is tired of being the smallest. When he and Martin play together, Martin always runs things. He also gets the biggest piece of cake and is

K

allowed to swim out to the raft. Henry wishes he could grow even taller than Martin. He tries stretching himself, watering himself, and eating lots of apples — but he does not grow an inch. He only gets a stomachache from eating too many apples. Henry imagines growing big as a giant, but soon realizes he would be too big to fit in the house or play with the other children. When Henry finally finds out that Martin was little once too, he is much happier. Martin himself tries to make Henry feel better about being the littlest. And Henry tries to help himself by making a pair of stilts.

This good-humored first-person narrative faces squarely the annoyance of being littler than others. Henry finds that his imagined ways of becoming bigger than Martin are simply impractical — while the stilts he makes are a temporary help. The detailed, cleverly drawn illustrations will interest young children.

Ages 4-7

Also available in:
Paperbound — *Much Bigger Than Martin*
The Dial Press, Inc.

375

Kent, Deborah

Belonging: A Novel

The Dial Press, Inc., 1978.
(200 pages)

BLINDNESS
  Belonging
  Friendship: making friends
  Identity, search for
  Maturation
  School: pupil-teacher relationships

Wanting to feel just like everyone else her age, Meg chooses to attend public high school instead of the Institute for the Blind. On the first day, the crush of students nearly overwhelms her, but she is no less happy to be one of the crowd at last. She finds her classes easily, and though annoyed by well-meaning but over-solicitous fellow students, maintains her composure. What troubles her more is the welter of school regulations. Happily, her English teacher, Frances Kellogg, turns out to be not one to go by the book; when Ms. Kellogg mentions that she needs students to work on the school literary magazine, Meg jumps at the chance to work with congenial people. At magazine staff meetings she meets Lindy and Keith, two outright misfits who prefer their individuality to being popular. Lindy does a lot of unpopular things: among them riding a bicycle to school, running a paper route, and hiking to picturesque spots. Meg likes Lindy, but this new friend's delight in doing only what she likes — when Meg wants so desperately to be just like everyone else — makes Meg hold back. Keith, on the other hand, is apt to burst into Wagnerian arias at the top of his voice at inopportune times. Uneasy over this, Meg prefers not to be seen with him. In the way of "normal" friends, Meg gets to know Jeff, a football player, and his girl friend, Karen. Soon she has a crush on him and is jealous of Karen — not only because of Jeff but also because Karen has so many friends and gives so many parties. Though Meg has nothing in common with Karen, she feels complimented when Karen asks her to help with English homework. In return for that help, Karen invites her to a party. Meg is so transported by the prospect of an evening with the "right" crowd that she forgets she had promised to go with Ms. Kellogg, Keith, and Lindy to see "La Traviata" the same night. She lies to get out of that. But the party, to her dismay, is a disaster. It is all drinking, smoking pot, and playing kissing games. When Jeff makes deprecating remarks about Ms. Kellogg, the last of Meg's desire to belong to Karen's circle disappears.

Afraid her defection may have cost her a real friendship, she apologizes to Lindy and explains her feelings. Having herself had the feelings once, Lindy understands. More pressing is the suddenly looming possibility that Ms. Kellogg will be fired because she is thought to be emotionally unstable. Meg herself has noticed oddities in her teacher's behavior, but nothing serious enough to be fired for, as Lindy and Keith agree. All the same, Ms. Kellogg is forced to resign — and the three friends publish an editorial in her defense. The principal is appalled, accuses them of not knowing all the facts, and considers suspending Keith and Lindy. Although the editorial had been her idea, he offers to excuse Meg because of her blindness. The girl flatly insists on equal treatment. Fortunately for the three, their parents understand, and Meg, Keith, and Lindy spend part of their three-day suspension attending a Broadway musical. Meg knows now what is worth "belonging" to.

In this sensitive first-person narrative, Meg discovers that it is not her blindness that sets her apart from her contemporaries but her individualism. She realizes she belongs with those who appreciate her talents and share her interests. Blind students may be inspired by this story and sighted students instructed how the blind feel.

Ages 11-14

Also available in:
Cassette for the Blind — *Belonging: A Novel*
Library of Congress

Paperbound — *Belonging: A Novel*
Grossett & Dunlap, Inc.

376

Kerr, Judith

The Other Way Round

Coward, McCann & Geoghegan, Inc., 1975.
(256 pages)

MATURATION
REFUGEES
RESPONSIBILITY: Accepting
  Careers: planning
  Dependence/Independence
  Family: unity
  Fear: of physical harm
  Internment
  Jewish
  Prejudice: ethnic/racial
  War

Fifteen-year-old Anna, her parents, and her older brother, Max, have settled in London after fleeing Nazi Germany in 1933. Anna's father, a celebrated writer in pre-Nazi Germany, has found little work in London, and with the approach of war the family is living on Mother's income as a social secretary and estate archivist. As war accelerates in Europe, Anna begins secretarial school under the sponsorship of the Relief Organization for German Jewish Refugees. At the same time, Max, on a scholarship to Cambridge, is arrested as an enemy alien and sent to an internment camp. After Continental Europe is lost to Hitler, Anna spends the summer worrying about invasion and watching aircraft dogfights over London. It is during the worst of the London Blitz that Max — released from detention but unable to join the armed forces — gets a job teaching at his old prep school. In late autumn, Anna too looks for work but, because of her German citizenship, finds only a low-paying job as an aide to a wealthy Mrs. Hammond in a Red Cross office. Summer again nears, and

Anna mentions to Mrs. Hammond Max's desire to join the Air Force. Having many friends in the military, Mrs. Hammond is able to speak on Max's behalf and he is soon in pilot training. Anna herself feels restless, rudderless, and enrolls in an evening class at a local art school. Soon, besides her job, she is absorbed in her studies, in making new friends at school, and in her dawning love for her art teacher, John Cotmore. All these things make the war years pass swiftly; but none is of comfort when Anna discovers that John is living with another student, whom he loves. Time slows, and Anna ignores her drawings. She even — out of spite — rejects an offer of an art scholarship. But in time she recovers from this first, lost love, begins to draw again, and applies for the same scholarship. When the war ends, she has reasons of her own to celebrate: Max is safe; she and her family can become naturalized citizens; and she can pursue a career in art.

This sequel to the fictionalized autobiography *When Hitler Stole Pink Rabbit* concerns a teenage girl's maturing in wartime London. Unity and mutual aid help this refugee family through poverty, anti-German prejudice, fear, loneliness, and the London Blitz. But family unity in the interest of survival does not prevent Anna from disagreeing with her mother on the way to her own independence.

Ages 12 and up

Also available in:
Paperbound — *The Other Way Round*
Dell Publishing Company, Inc.

Talking Book — *The Other Way Round*
Library of Congress

377
Kerr, M. E., pseud.

Gentlehands

Harper & Row Publishers, Inc., 1978.
(183 pages)

MATURATION
VALUES/VALUING: Moral/Ethical
  Boy-girl relationships: dating
  Grandparent: respect for
  Peer relationships: peer pressures
Wealth/Wealthy

Buddy Boyle is sixteen and thinks he is in love with eighteen-year-old Skye Pennington. Buddy's parents disapprove, both because Skye is older and because her parents are very wealthy. Mr. Boyle, a policeman, thinks Buddy is snobbishly impressed with the Pennington wealth, and when the boy lies twice to conceal that he has gone swimming at Skye's house, Boyle is so angered that he knocks Buddy down. Unable to produce any monied family members for Skye to meet near at hand, Buddy seeks out his wealthy, estranged grandfather, Frank Trenker, whom he has met only twice; Mrs. Boyle hates her father for having remained in Nazi Germany during World War II — and having remained indifferent to their welfare when she and her mother emigrated to the United States. But Skye and Buddy like the man. Skye finds him cultured, and Buddy hopes to learn worldliness from him to use with Skye's friends. Over his parents' objections, Buddy moves in with his grandfather, and continues seeing Skye over a happy summer. But this happy interlude is shattered when one of the Penningtons' summer guests, a journalist, reveals in the local newspaper that Frank Trenker is "Gentlehands," an infamous Nazi war criminal, who, along with another named Renner, has found this locale a refuge from persecution. In stunned disbelief, Buddy defends his grandfather at every opportunity, but subsequent articles support the accusations so stoutly that the boy has to believe them. When Trenker leaves town to escape punishment, Buddy remembers a message the man had asked him to convey, and although Trenker escapes, Buddy's information leads the authorities to Renner, who is arrested. Buddy feels betrayed; his grandfather is gone, and Skye breaks up with him and goes away to school. He vows to forget everything that has happened this treacherous summer.

In this first-person narrative, Buddy finds that smooth manners and elegant appearances can hide a lot. His disillusionments leave him sorely disappointed but may stand him in good stead when he judges people in the future. This thought-provoking book can promote discussion about values, love, and loyalty.

Ages 11-14

Also available in:
Paperbound — *Gentlehands*
Bantam Books, Inc.

378

Kerr, M. E., pseud.

I'll Love You When You're More Like Me

Harper & Row Publishers, Inc., 1977.
(183 pages)

BOY-GIRL RELATIONSHIPS
IDENTITY, SEARCH FOR
  Expectations

Wally Witherspoon, almost a high school senior, is the son of a funeral director in a New York City suburb. Wally's father, a conservative, stuffy man, expects him to enter the family business after graduating and to marry Harriet Hren, a willful, prudish girl who tells Wally what to do. One day at the beach, Wally meets Sabra St. Amour, teenage star of a popular daytime television serial. He meets her again later that week when he, Harriet, and his friend Charlie, who claims to be a homosexual, are spending an evening at the local dance club. The two boys invite Sabra to join them after the dance, and jealous Harriet walks out. Wally, Charlie, and Sabra go for a stroll on the beach anyway, and find they like one another. The three continue to see each other and finally Harriet writes Wally that he and she are finished. More relieved than sorry, he continues seeing Sabra. One day, talking with his father yet again about the family business, Wally announces that he will not become a mortician but he is going to college to pursue a career in linguistics. Meanwhile, Sabra has been trying to decide whether or not to stay with her television show or go to college herself. One night, Wally takes her to a party. Sabra, never at ease with people her own age, can only play out her television personality. Embarrassed and unhappy, she gladly leaves with Wally, and the two drive into New York City, where she tells Wally she cannot leave show business after all. She also says good-bye. Back at home, Wally does not see her again. But he does look forward to his senior year, while Charlie takes a job at the funeral home.

Wally talks about his father's business wittily, but the prospect of being forced to become a funeral director is finally too much for him to take. Like Wally's father, Sabra's mother has tried to keep her locked into a pre-arranged future, and for Sabra independence may prove more difficult. This story is told alternately by Sabra and Wally, and its characterizations, dialogue, and relationships are convincing.

Ages 12 and up

Also available in:
Paperbound — *I'll Love You When You're More Like Me*
Dell Publishing Company, Inc.

379

Kerr, M. E., pseud.

Is That You, Miss Blue?

Harper & Row Publishers, Inc., 1975.
(170 pages)

SCHOOLS, PRIVATE: Girls'
    Abandonment
    School: classmate relationships
    School: pupil-teacher relationships
    Separation from loved ones
    Values/Valuing

When her mother leaves the family to seek an independent life, fourteen-year-old Flanders Brown is enrolled by her father in an Episcopal boarding school. She does not quite fit in. She rooms alone in an almost-empty dormitory that is supervised by Miss Ernestine Blue, an unmarried science teacher. Miss Blue is thought strange by the students and faculty alike, because she is so intensely, even fanatically, religious. Flanders, however, respects Miss Blue and on occasion comes to her defense. When Flanders, who wants to believe in God, refuses to join Carolyn Dardmaker's atheist club, she is snubbed by her only friends. Then Miss Blue is fired for chanting strange prayers in public and talking about visits from Jesus. The girls now reunite in a common cause — to present Miss Blue with a farewell gift from the school. Knowing how she has admired a portrait of Mary, Queen of Scots, belonging to the school, the girls steal the painting and present it to her with a note bearing the name of the headmistress. When school authorities discover the theft, they fine the girls and notify their parents. Out of this complicated experience of personal loyalty Flanders is moved to seek her mother out. She does not return to the school, and in time remembrance of the school and her classmates fades. But she does not forget Miss Blue.

Flanders's strength lies in her ability to remain true to her own beliefs and values despite upheaval at home. This book satirizes boarding-school life, is both witty and subtle, and requires a mature reader.

Ages 11-14

Also available in:
Cassette for the Blind — Is That You, Miss Blue?
Library of Congress

Paperbound — Is That You, Miss Blue?
Dell Publishing Company, Inc.

380

Kerr, M. E., pseud.

Love Is a Missing Person

Harper & Row Publishers, Inc., 1975.
(164 pages)

MATURATION
    Boy-girl relationships: dating
    Jealousy: sibling
    Parent/Parents: remarriage of
    Prejudice: ethnic/racial
    Values/Valuing: materialistic

Suzy Slade, fifteen years old and with wealthy, divorced parents, is in ninth grade at a high school in a fashionable Long Island community. She says of herself, "I am . . . the Slade daughter the father chose not to take to New York to live with him." Suzy works as a volunteer at the local public library and feels close to two people on the staff: Nan Richmond, a junior in high school and the first black ever employed at the library; and Gwendolyn Spring, middle-aged and still missing a lover of thirty-five years before. Suzy spares little thought for her family and resents her older sister, a radical named Chicago, who is the Slade daughter who does live in New York City with their father. Suddenly, Chicago returns, announcing that she is disillusioned with her father and his wealth. When Mr. Slade invites Suzy to New York, hoping that she will now live with him, she finds that he has married a nineteen-year-old working girl who memorizes famous quotations to impress her. Feeling sorry for her father, Suzy departs, only to find worse disarray on Long Island: Chicago has fallen in love with Nan Richmond's boy friend, Roger Cole III, an all-star black athlete and valedictorian of the class. Gwendolyn Spring's wartime lover has returned, not to marry her, as she hoped (he has married someone else), but to borrow money from her. And a valuable painting is missing from the library's erotica collection, one which Nan had taken to show Roger, not knowing of his new love, and which Chicago and Roger now plan to keep until the library agrees to certain demands: abolition of fees for library cards, acquiring a bookmobile, enlarging the collection of black literature, and opening the erotica collection to the public. Suzy discovers the painting in Chicago's knapsack and tells Miss Spring, who calls the police. Chicago and Roger are arrested but released on bail put up by Mr. Slade. They jump bail and disappear.

Suzy Slade tells this story of her family and friends, of loving and losing. She is perceptive about people's strengths and weaknesses and no less so about the contradictions in society, seeing the irony of her sister's becoming a revolutionary who daydreams on her silk monogrammed sheets of "leveling" social differences, and treats her black lover to a ride in her new motorboat. Yet this book takes economic inequality and racism seriously, along with divorce and remarriage and interracial dating. Suzy ponders the power of love to create missing persons out of old friends. This is a richly plotted story whose dialogue crackles.

Ages 12 and up

Also available in:
Paperbound — *Love Is a Missing Person*
Dell Publishing Company, Inc.

Talking Book — *Love Is a Missing Person*
Library of Congress

381

King, Cynthia

The Year of Mr. Nobody

Black/white illustrations by Malcom Carrick.
Harper & Row Publishers, Inc., 1978.
(60 pages)

K

IMAGINARY FRIEND
  Maturation
  Sibling: middle

For Abbot Dodge, a four-year-old boy, the year of Mr. Nobody begins on his birthday, when he is at last taken to the amusement park. He has a wonderful time until he is told he cannot join his older brother, Evan, on the roller coaster ride because he doesn't "measure up": there is a red line at the entrance to the ride, and no one whose head does not reach it can go in. That night Abbot invents Mr. Nobody, an invisible friend who can do anything and go anywhere. Mr. Nobody helps him get through the crises of this year: brother Evan leaving for school, for which Abbot is too young; baby brother Sandy playing with Abbot's toys; Abbot's being too young to be out after dark on Halloween and getting sick at Thanksgiving. Evan is sick for Easter, and receives a yearned-for knife from Father for his birthday. Mr. Nobody gets Abbot treats on Halloween, cures Evan, and shows Abbot how to whittle with an imaginary knife. Summer comes, and the family goes to a farm in Vermont. There, Abbot spends more time with Evan and the two get to sleep in the converted chicken house instead of having to sleep in the bedroom with baby Sandy. One night a bull gets loose and charges at Father. Abbot slips out of the chicken house, runs to the barn, grabs a pail of salt, and brings it back to Evan, who lures the bull back to the pen. When the summer is over, Abbot and Evan head for school, together.

This is a funny, touching, and finally gratifying story of a middle child who is too young to go to school with his older brother and too old to cry and eat with his fingers like his younger brother. An imaginary friend helps him through a difficult year. But at a climactic moment of danger, when a bull is loose, Abbot knows that "Mr. Nobody [can't] help him now. That bull [is] real." Abbot gains confidence and pride in himself and is finally looked on by his parents as being more like his older brother than his baby brother. He learns that tomorrow does come and that everyone does finally get bigger and older.

Ages 6-8

Also available in:
No other form known

382

Kingman, Lee

Break a Leg, Betsy Maybe!
Houghton Mifflin Co., 1976.
(245 pages)

BOY-GIRL RELATIONSHIPS
IDENTITY, SEARCH FOR
  Loneliness
  Maturation
  Peer relationships
  Talents: artistic

Seventeen-year-old Elizabeth Cythera Wilkersen Maybe bears a weight in life more substantial than her name. Her parents and her stepfather, too, are dead. Therapy undergone earlier has defined her condition— a double identity crisis and shock over three deaths— without improving it. Now Betsy lives with her aunt and uncle and attends a public high school. Both withdrawn and bored, her chief interest is in Nick Gretschkin, a classmate, but he is virtually engaged to Francena "Stackie" Delahey. An acquaintance urges her to try out for the school's drama club, and since Nick is a member, she does, and wins a role in a play. Stackie and Nick, as usual, earn leading roles. But Betsy finds in theater the direction and involvement she needs. At the cast party, Betsy and Nick are suddenly alone together, talk companionably and, just as Nick kisses Betsy, Stackie walks in. That ends that: Nick remains with Stackie, and Stackie ignores Betsy. As winter passes, everyone except Betsy makes plans for college. She, on the other hand, inquires about a drama school in England. That spring all her efforts are directed at winning the leading female role in *Our Town* — but it goes to Stackie. Suddenly Nick quits the play and he and Stackie are no longer together. Betsy learns from Stackie that Nick may have cancer. Betsy talks to Nick — and finds him relieved: tests have confirmed he has Hodgkins Disease, but his chances of recovery are excellent. When she is accepted by the English drama school, Betsy almost declines to go so as to remain with Nick, for they have grown closer and closer. But he persuades her to go after all. By now, Betsy knows she is reconciled to life: "Who wants to run away from any of it, anywhere? No matter what comes next, I'm ready for it."

This first-person narrative, written partly in the style of a play and partly as a diary, discovers Betsy's pleasure in acting and her difficulty in winning a boy from a talented, popular, pretty girl. Through both she comes to find herself. Their story also involves many subplots about members of the drama club. Over all, the pace is leisurely but plot and characters are realistic. Readers interested in theater will find pleasure in the theater lore and practice woven through this book.

Ages 12 and up

Also available in:
Paperbound — *Break a Leg, Betsy Maybe!*
Dell Publishing Company, Inc.

383

Kingman, Lee

Head Over Wheels

Houghton Mifflin Co., 1978.
(186 pages)

QUADRIPLEGIA
TWINS: Identical
   Accidents: automobile
   Anger
   Family: unity
   Guilt, feelings of
   Nightmares
   Self, attitude toward: feeling different
   Wheelchair, dependence on

Kerry and Terry Tredinnick are identical seventeen-year-old twins — until an automobile accident leaves Terry with a shattered jaw, a broken leg and ankle, and a broken neck. Kerry escapes the same accident (which kills the driver) with only slight injuries. During his first weeks in the hospital, Terry is placed in a Stryker frame, which holds him immobile until surgery fuses his crushed vertebrae. The family is told by the doctors that, though Terry's arms can move a little, he is considered quadriplegic, having no feeling from the shoulders down, and will never walk again. This news and Terry's helplessness make Kerry feel guilty: he is walking and Terry never will. To lighten his burden of guilt and to support his twin however he can, Kerry visits Terry as much as possible. But other thoughts plague Kerry during these visits: why is Terry so withdrawn? And does he, against the doctors' firm diagnosis, really believe he will walk again? Terry's girl friend is far more troubled, refusing at first to see him; then, when she does, recoiling physically and emotionally, although Terry does not at first notice. She finds herself powerfully drawn to Kerry instead. Kerry's girl friend is far steadier, more natural, and more encouraging with Terry, while remaining loyal to his brother. As Terry's condition improves, he is taken off the Stryker frame and moved to the rehabilitation center. While he is there, he and Kerry both go through periods of depression, withdrawal, and anger. Meanwhile, their parents and younger brother and sister adjust to Terry's condition and try to meet the mounting hospital bills. Terry also endures therapy sessions which will help him utilize those muscles he can control. The sessions are no less demoralizing than helpful. As a quadriplegic, Terry cannot sense his body; he becomes nauseated when he sits up, cannot cough, sneeze, or belch, and must haul his useless legs wherever he goes. At long last, he is able to go home, to live in the basement apartment that has been adapted to his needs. There he takes care of his personal needs and begins to see friends. But he has so little to do with his family that Kerry senses he is building a wall between them and himself. And it is not until Terry suddenly wants to share a confidence with Kerry, and torturously hoists and drags himself up most of the two flights of stairs, that the twins come to see that, although they will never be identical again and must lead their own lives, they will always be close.

In this tense, candid story the reader is taken through the accident, injury, and slow rehabilitation of an adolescent boy. Events are viewed from both Terry's and Kerry's perspectives — giving the reader an understanding of both the victim and one who escaped. The abilities and limitations of quadriplegics, depending upon the degree and location of spinal damage, are

K

explained in detail. So too the monetary hardship the extended hospital stay places on the family, how each family member adjusts to the situation, how the quadriplegic views himself and the way others view him. Withal, this is a serious story without being depressing or melodramatic.

Ages 12 and up

Also available in:
Braille — *Head Over Wheels*
Library of Congress

Paperbound — *Head Over Wheels*
Dell Publishing Company, Inc.

384

Klein, Norma

Blue Trees, Red Sky

Black/white illustrations by Pat Grant Porter.
Pantheon Books, 1975.
(57 pages)

PARENT/PARENTS: Mother Working Outside Home
PARENT/PARENTS: Single
  Baby-sitter
  Sibling: older
  Work, attitude toward

Eight-year-old Valerie wishes that her widowed mother did not work and that her baby-sitter, Mrs. Weiss, did not treat her like a baby. She also dislikes the way Mrs. Weiss favors her younger brother, Marco. One evening when Marco falls asleep before dinner, Valerie has her mother all to herself, and as they eat and read together, Valerie feels as if her mother were sharing a secret with her. All the same, during a weekly tennis outing with her mother and her mother's boy friend, Valerie feels left out; even Marco is more coordinated than she. And

when, one day, her mother rebukes her for skipping baseball at day camp, Valerie cries and Marco protests. "If she doesn't try," the mother explains, "she'll never know if she likes it or not." Valerie does know that she eventually wants to be either an astronaut or an artist like her mother; her friend wants to be a concert violinist, and together they talk about their ambitions. Soon after this, Valerie's mother leaves on a trip with her boy friend, and during her absence, Valerie and Mrs. Weiss spend a long afternoon searching the neighborhood for Marco. After finding him, Valerie is in no doubt of Mrs. Weiss's goodness and how much she would hate to lose her. Her mother back, Valerie asks her if she is now going to get married and quit working, but her mother says that even if she married, she would continue to work. Of her work she says, "It's like a special place you can go where everything is the way you want. Trees can be blue and skies can be red. It's hard sometimes, not all of it is good, but if you didn't have it, it would be a hole in your life."

In eight episodes the author asserts that both men and women should be free to choose what they want to do, and that women no less than men need satisfying careers. Marco's wish to become a ballet dancer is politely passed over by Mrs. Weiss but defended by Valerie. Yet the author skillfully captures the vacillating and mixed feelings between brother and sister; also the way that opinion can be tied to age. The book contains some silly sex banter — "I'm going to China to see your vagina.... I'm going to Venus to see your penis" — silly because it seems contrived and extraneous to any point being made.

Ages 7-10

Also available in:
Paperbound — *Blue Trees, Red Sky*
Dell Publishing Company, Inc.

385

Knotts, Howard

Great-grandfather, the Baby and Me

Black/white illustrations by the author.
Atheneum Publishers, 1978.
(30 pages)

GREAT-GRANDPARENT
SIBLING: New Baby
   Loneliness

A little boy is bewildered by the unknown identity of a baby sister he has not yet seen. After his father leaves for the hospital to bring Mom and the baby home, the boy tries to calm himself, as he often has, by gazing into a nearby stream. Unable to figure out who his baby sister could possibly be, he cries. Feeling lonely, he runs to his great-grandfather but can say nothing about his distress. His great-grandfather continues reading — yet at some time (the boy is not sure when) begins telling a story of wheat fields he helped harvest as a young man in the vast lands of western Canada. The two things he remembers most: the lonesomeness of the country, and the bitterness of the alkaline water. One Sunday he and a friend rode to see a new baby at a distant homestead. He recalls vividly the sweet water he drank there before seeing the baby. The boy then interrupts to ask what the baby did. "Absolutely nothing," the old man says. "The baby just slept." He explains they did not ride all that way so the baby could see them; because of their own lonesomeness, they had to see the baby. Finished with his tale, the old man accompanies the boy to the house to drink a glass of "sweet water." And then they go out to "meet the new baby."

Within this first-person narrative, a little boy relates a story told by his great-grandfather. The boy never shows his awareness of the story's relation to his own concerns, but his willingness to greet his new baby sister afterwards shows that his anxiety over her has been dispelled. The allusive style, although appropriate to the story, may escape some young readers; adults using this book might plan on discussing the connections between the old man's reminiscence and the young boy's situation.

Ages 5-8

Also available in:
No other form known

Knudson, R. Rozanne

Fox Running: A Novel

Black/white illustrations by Ilse Koehn.
Harper & Row Publishers, Inc., 1975.
(182 pages)

FRIENDSHIP: Meaning of
SPORTS/SPORTSMANSHIP
   Identity, search for
   Native American
   Perseverance
   Talents: athletic

"I am Fox Running," the young Indian woman tells Kathy "Sudden" Hart and MacDonald "Champ" Davis, who have just caught up with her after having seen from their car "a desert runner . . . a flash," as they drove home from a track meet with Coach Guy Calvin. The coach, always on the lookout for runners, wants to offer Fox an athletic scholarship at Uinta University. Fox wants to accept it but must first win a test race. Everything seems set until Fox shies from the starting gun and is unable to run the race. Even then Calvin wants to offer her a scholarship but Fox has meanwhile heard about his brutal treatment of Sudden after she dropped a baton in an Olympics relay race: Fox spurns the offer. She tells Sudden she is no stranger to bad luck: her grandfather, Old Legging, with whom she had lived, is dead; she has never attended any school, let alone a university. Sudden, troubled by her own bad luck, agrees to teach Fox to read and write English. In return, Fox will teach Sudden to run like an Indian. Delighting in their outdoor runs, Sudden decides to compete in the Olympic Trials that summer. And she urges Fox to run the mile and try for the Olympics too. Champ, won over after Fox runs a sub-four minute mile in practice, persuades Coach Calvin to let Fox and Sudden train their own way. While they do, Sudden learns why Fox shies from the gun — her grandfather, crushed under a horse, had made Fox hand him the pistol with which he shot himself. Fox helps Sudden overcome her fear of dropping a baton, and the two friends advance through the Trials to the Olympics. After leading the American relay team to victory, Fox breezes through the 1500-meter race in record time, hearing neither gun nor crowd but only Old Legging urging her on in every lap.

Two young women, hampered in their running by events in their past, aid each other to realize their running talents. Friendship and perseverance pay handsomely. But the author's elliptic style, so effective in conveying the sensations of running, makes the story line, implausible to begin with, at some points unclear. The secondary characters tend to be stereotyped, and their sudden conversion to Fox's philosophy of running is unconvincing. But readers interested in the sport of running may forgive such defects.

Ages 11 and up

Also available in:
Paperbound — *Fox Running: A Novel*
Avon Books

387

Knudson, R. Rozanne

Zanbanger

Harper & Row Publishers, Inc., 1977.
(162 pages)

GENDER ROLE IDENTITY: Female
PREJUDICE: Sexual
SPORTS/SPORTSMANSHIP
  Competition
  Cooperation: in play
  Justice/Injustice
  Problem solving

With the new gym floor installed, Suzanne "Zan" Hagen can hardly wait to begin girls' basketball practice. Her best friend and private coach, Arthur Rinehart, has helped Zan greatly with her shooting, and she is optimistic about her team's chances for the coming season. But she has not reckoned on her coach's zeal for femininity. Mrs. Butor disapproves of Zan's aggressive play, preferring instead decorum at all times. Zan feels helpless. As usual, Arthur comes up with a plan; he flatters Mrs. Butor outrageously and gains her assent. He coaches Zan and E. J., the two best players on the girls' team, for eight days, then matches them against the rest of Mrs. Butor's girls. Zan and E. J. easily outscore the others, after which the boys' team — the Generals — takes over the gym, and Coach O'Hara invites Zan to scrimmage with them. All but one of the boys give her a hard time, but Zan holds her own, as Arthur takes notes from the sidelines. But that Monday Zan finds she has been cut from the girls' team. Faithful Arthur then goes to Coach O'Hara and asks that Zan be allowed to play on his team; but O'Hara says the principal and school board would never allow it. Arthur decides to take her case to court, where he himself pleads for her right to play with the Generals. On the second day of the hearing Coach O'Hara surprises everyone by testifying for Zan himself. "I want her on my team . . . because she plays well," he says, adding, "Hagen's a winner, make no mistake." The judge rules in Zan's favor and orders immediate tryouts with the Generals for all eligible girls. Zan makes it as a substitute, and E. J. is added later in the season to replace an injured player. But now Zan is resented by both her own teammates and opposing teams, some of which simply refuse to play against a girl, and forfeit their games. But as the season progresses, the Generals are playing team ball more and winning more. The Generals — all but the team captain and his friend — are accepting Zan, realizing she is not just a determined player but a good one. Then, near the end of the season, a crucial loss shows the team's problem. The two holdouts begin to cooperate and the Generals win their final game, the league championship, and the tournament. "We had won," says Zan. "We had won each other."

In this timely story of sexual discrimination in school athletics, a teenage girl wins the legal right to play on the team of her choice, then earns the right with her playing skill. Interestingly, it is her male friend who comes to her rescue time and again, and he is the one who brings her case to court. Away from the basketball court, Zan seems helpless, unable to defend herself. Basketball lingo abounds in this book and will itself attract some readers. Although a first-person narrative, the story quotes other viewpoints to summarize some events. *Zanballer* precedes this book and *Zanboomer* follows it, both of them dealing with Suzanne Hagen and sports.

Ages 10-13

Also available in:
Paperbound — *Zanbanger*
Dell Publishing Company, Inc.

Knudson, R. Rozanne

Zanboomer

Harper & Row Publishers, Inc., 1978.
(183 pages)

DETERMINATION
SPORTS/SPORTSMANSHIP
  Friendship: meaning of
  Loyalty

K

Suzanne "Zan" Hagen, an ardent high school athlete, has been playing baseball since she was a child. This is an exciting spring for her: she has qualified to play shortstop for the high school baseball team. Her best friend, Arthur Rinehart, acts as Zan's personal coach, filming her, analyzing her strengths and weaknesses, showing her how to improve. Zan becomes the team's power hitter and earns the nickname "Zanboomer," taking the team through the exhibition season undefeated. But the first conference game, however, brings disaster. In the seventh inning, Zan whacks the ball into outfield, but as she slides into home plate, she collides with both pitcher and catcher. She goes to the hospital with a concussion and torn shoulder ligaments. Her baseball season is over. To keep her spirits up while her shoulder is healing, Rinehart persuades her to run every day and helps her improve her stride and speed. He reads books on running and turns his basement into a training room. Zan herself hopes to get back to baseball for the championship round of the state tournament, but her team is eliminated in the playoffs. School closes for the summer, and Zan is overwhelmed with the feeling that she failed her team by not rejoining them soon enough. She refuses to get out of bed. Rinehart is not heard from for several days, and when he reappears it is with yet another scheme: Zan will begin training now for cross-country running in the fall. At first she refuses, seeing no point in playing a non-team sport, but Rinehart brings her around. Zan cooperates enthusiastically. After rigorous training all summer Zan competes in her first race and wins the trophy.

This first-person narrative, told by Zan but interrupted briefly by Rinehart, is the story of two powerhouses: Zan, who loves to compete and achieve, and Rinehart, a brilliant coach and organizer. Rinehart's loyalty is extraordinary and his tact is no less so; he helps Zan without using her. But his scientific mind does meditate on possible reasons for her competitiveness. The long, detailed descriptions of training and competition here will appeal to girls who love sports. Hardly a model of graceful prose, this book could encourage girls to overcome obstacles on the way to all sorts of goals. It is preceded by two other books about Suzanne Hagen and sports, *Zanballer* and *Zanbanger.*

Ages 10-13

Also available in:
No other form known

389

Kroll, Steven

That Makes Me Mad!

Color illustrations by Hilary Knight.
Pantheon Books, 1976.
(32 pages)

ANGER
  Emotions: accepting

Almost everything makes Nina angry at some time, for she is at a touchy age, three or four years old. Nina gets angry when her parents tell her she will like something they must know she does not — like eating fish — or when they send her to bed even though she wants to watch TV, or blame her for a mess her younger brother has made. Nina is angry when her parents ignore her or fail to come when she calls them. Balky objects also annoy the little girl — a toy bear that refuses to be found or clothes that refuse to fit. And sometimes she becomes angry at herself. Hers is a world full of things to anger her but, as she tells her mother, "it makes me feel better when you let me tell you how angry I am."

In this first-person narrative, a little girl addresses her parents, first telling them what angers her in general, then giving examples. The cartoon-like illustrations lend force to a clear exposition and sometimes add to the text — as when Nina, having stayed up late to watch TV, is shown fallen asleep. The emphasis throughout is on a youngster's viewpoint, not an adult's, and there is no attempt to gauge the reasonableness of what makes Nina mad. In discussion, children may want to confide what makes them mad, or consider what Nina might have done differently. This book might also act as a primer for parents who need to see that children have feelings altogether their own.

Ages 4-7

Also available in:
No other form known

Lagercrantz, Rose

Tulla's Summer

Translated from the Swedish by George Blecher and Lone
Thygesen-Blecher.
Black/white illustrations by Lady McCrady.
Harcourt Brace Jovanovich, Inc., 1977.
(121 pages)

PARENT/PARENTS: Fighting Between
  Communication: parent-child
  Friendship: best friend
  Honesty/Dishonesty

The summer before Tulla enters fourth grade, her parents rent a cottage by the seashore. Tulla's father, a fisherman, is usually away at sea, and so this is one of the few times the family is together. It could seem just as well they are not together more often, because when they are, Tulla's parents fight continually and her baby brother seems to cry all the time. The girl's only friend is Bella, a neighbor, to whom she frequently goes for consolation, often telling Bella grand, untrue accounts of her background and home life. One day Tulla's father tells her that he and her mother may get divorced. Tulla is relieved that the fighting may end. More, she romanticizes the idea of being the "child of a broken home," thinking she would finally receive some love and attention from both parents. Later, her parents tell her they are staying together after all, and have resolved their differences. Tulla is heartbroken, certain that the fights will resume and her parents' neglect of her continue. Only at this do her mother and father begin to ask and to understand what is troubling her. They offer comfort and a surprise: her best friend, Susanna, can come for a visit. But during Susanna's stay, Tulla notices that they too have disagreements and sometimes even dislike each other. Now Tulla understands even better her parents' arguments. Just as disagreements with her friend do not end their friendship, her parents' disagreements need not end their marriage.

The cut and dried conventional solution is not always the best way out of difficulty, as Tulla learns. Nor do dashing untruths earn one lasting respect. And for better or worse, friendships seldom remain static: change is an inevitable part of life. Tulla's summer brings her a mature understanding of human relationships.

Ages 8-11

Also available in:
No other form known

391

Lampman, Evelyn Sibley

The Potlatch Family

Atheneum Publishers, 1976.
(135 pages)

SELF, ATTITUDE TOWARD: Accepting
  Alcoholism: of father
  Identity, search for
  Native American
  Pride/False pride

Plum Lanoor, a high school freshman, is ashamed of her family, members of the Pacific Coast Chinook tribe, and particularly of her father, a drunkard, often deposited unconscious at their doorstep. Plum rarely smiles, and is ostracized by her classmates. Friendless, she always shares a seat on the school bus with much overweight Mildred, a fellow outcast. Mildred considers Plum her best friend, which further embarrasses Plum, for not even Mildred has her apparent disadvantages. Once Simon, Plum's gregarious twenty-five-year-old half brother, had won respect for himself and for the family as a high school athlete. But Simon has been to fight in

L

Vietnam and is recovering from his wounds in a veteran's hospital too far away to visit. Thus, when he appears unexpectedly the family is ecstatic. Plum's father even vows to stop drinking. Simon tires easily and takes a lot of medicine but shrugs off questions. He also seems to have something on his mind, pressing his brother Milo to find out all he can about Chinook ancestral customs. It turns out that Simon wants to hold a potlatch, a Chinook feast with elaborate, traditional exchanges of gifts. Simon invites everyone they had known on their former reservation and even hikes through the woods to find his great-grandparents, who still live by the old ways he wants to discover. On the great day, the family, skeptical at first, joins in the proceedings and is soon caught up. But when Simon proposes to make the potlatch a weekly event, a tourist attraction, many of his Indian friends protest that reviving old ways will make them more conspicuous and despised by the whites than ever. Plum is especially afraid of this. But Simon explains how important it is for Indians as well as whites to know the Indian has a proud culture of his own. As Simon has predicted, the weekly potlatch is a great success among tourists and Indians alike. But before the third weekend, Simon goes to the hospital for a checkup and dies there. In a note sent back with a friend, he tells the family that he had known his condition was terminal, but they must not grieve for him: he has been happy with them these last months. More, they are to continue the potlatch in pride — and they do, using the profits to establish a scholarship fund for the Native Americans. The popularity of the feast grows, and television coverage of it makes Plum a celebrity at school. But even as she acknowledges the attention she has yearned for, she realizes that her only true friend all along has been Mildred.

Telling her own story, Plum finds that she has been scaring off possible friends with her glum, defeated air, not with her race or social standing. The traditions with which Simon seeks to make her proud of her race are an engrossing part of a well-told story.

Ages 11-13

Also available in:
Talking Book — *The Potlatch Family*
Library of Congress

392

Lapp, Eleanor J.

In the Morning Mist

Color illustrations by David Cunningham.
Albert Whitman & Co., 1978.
(32 pages counted)

GRANDPARENT: Love for
  Nature: appreciation of

The sun is still hidden by the mist when a little boy is awakened by his grandfather to go fishing for trout. As the two walk hand in hand to the stream, the lad picks out through the mist some apple trees, some grazing sheep, and a black cat. When the boy notices that the big, dead elm looks as if it were hung with lace, Grandfather tells him it is really spiderwebs "beaded with mist." Grandfather and the boy follow the old logging trail through the woods, and Grandfather points out the doe and fawn watching them as they pass. At last they arrive at the trout pool and settle down to fish. As the morning mist rises, the two carry home a full creel for breakfast.

The simple text and soft, expressive illustrations of this first-person narrative convey the beauty and peacefulness of early morning in the country. The author captures beautifully the closeness felt by grandfather and grandson as the only people moving through this landscape.

Ages 4-8

393

Larsen, Hanne

Don't Forget Tom

Translated from the Danish by Peggy Blakely.
Color photographs by Creative Circle.
Thomas Y. Crowell Company, Inc., 1978.
(25 pages counted)

MENTAL RETARDATION

Handicapped people cannot fully use some part of the body, and for six-year-old Tom this part is the brain. He is mentally handicapped, "can't understand as quickly as you or I. He needs more time to learn to do things." Tom needs help to eat and to dress; his mother helps him and prepares meals she knows Tom can handle. Then too, Tom's "brain can't tell him fast enough when he needs to use the toilet, which is a real nuisance. So he has some special protective padding, and this is a great help." But it is important that he accomplish things on his own. Though he enjoys being with his family, he sometimes becomes sad or angry when he sees his friends or his younger brother doing so easily what he cannot do well or at all. He takes special medication to help his "body behave," and rests a part of each day; overtired, he becomes cross. A special teacher visits him, for he cannot yet attend school, and with some help he paints pictures, molds clay, and solves picture puzzles.

Mental retardation is among the least visible of handicaps, and the photographs here, besides showing Tom in his daily routine, also show this to be true. The boy appears to be a normal, impish youngster doing normal things. It is when he does abnormal things and becomes cross or jealous that an understanding of retardation is so important to those who know Tom or someone like him. The author asks children to remember Tom when they meet a mentally retarded person. This very frank pictorial account should help young children understand retardation.

Ages 5-8

L

394

Lasky, Kathryn

I Have Four Names for My Grandfather

Black/white photographs by Christopher G. Knight.
Little, Brown and Co., 1976.
(46 pages)

GRANDPARENT: Love for

Young Tom has four names for his grandfather: "Poppy," "Pop," "Grandpa," and "Gramps." The elderly man is the boy's best friend. They share hats, runs, an interest in old trains, fishing, hammering, planting, and games. When Tom feels low or angry he can call up his grandfather and talk to him. Then he feels better and much loved.

This attractive book, with its black and white photographs, sets forth a special, loving relationship between a boy and his grandfather. Their joyous companionship is shown to thrive on exploring, learning, even teasing. Although the boy mentions death and asks when the grandfather will die — Grandfather replies, "How do I know?" The sunny disposition of the book includes no shadows.

Ages 3-6

Also available in:
No other form known

395

Lattimore, Eleanor Frances

Adam's Key

Black/white illustrations by Alan Tiegreen.
William Morrow & Company, Inc., 1976.
(128 pages)

SELF, ATTITUDE TOWARD: Confidence
SIBLING: Relationships
   Resourcefulness
   Sibling: youngest

Adam, who is six, chafes at being "the bottom step" of the five Ritchie children. He always receives hand-me-downs, for instance, never anything new. One day he finds a key that his sister Meg, who is eight, thinks magical. After opening several different locks with it, Adam tends to agree and wears the key everywhere, hung on a cord around his neck. He comes to believe that the key does bring him good fortune. For instance, his mother buys him an Indian suit, at a thrift shop, and a saleslady adds a bow and arrow set to overcome his misgivings about its being secondhand. He needs only a playmate, and he finds another "Indian" in Wesley, a new boy at school. With his key, Adam can, moreover, help his family. He lets Sabrina, his thirteen-year-old sister, into a house where she is locked out while baby-sitting. Similarly, when a family friend locks herself out, Adam lets her in, and his parents reward him. Gilbert, his ten-year-old brother, complains that the key is responsible — so why praise Adam? To distract Adam from Gilbert's taunts, his mother takes him to examine a house for sale. When the others leave, Adam is accidently locked in. His key is no help, for the doors are padlocked from the outside. Unable to alert others, he begins to climb down a rickety ladder; Gilbert arrives to steady it. Proud that he got out himself, Adam decides not to wear the key in the days that follow. On the evening of his birthday, he intends giving the key to Gilbert. But he drops it, and no one can find it. "But now he — and Gilbert, too — could get along without it."

The youngest child in a large family, finding a key that apparently opens any lock and brings good luck as well, gains confidence, at first in the powers of the key and then in himself. Children from sizable families will readily understand both Adam's pride in aiding his brothers and sisters and his sensitivity to their criticism.

Ages 7-9

Also available in:
No other form known

396

Lee, H. Alton

Seven Feet Four and Growing

The Westminster Press, 1978.
(95 pages)

HEIGHT: Tall
SELF, ATTITUDE TOWARD: Accepting
   Animals: love for
   Decision making
   Peer relationships
   Shyness
   Sports/Sportsmanship
   Teasing

At fifteen, Bill Saunders stands tall, a bit over seven feet four inches. But height is not what bothers him. It is what people say about it, his painful self-consciousness, and the nuisance of his special needs — an oversize bed, custom-made clothes and shoes, etc. Bill must soon decide whether to attend summer basketball camp to be eligible for the local team in the fall. His father's ambition for him, his friends, and the coach all press him to sign up, but, aware of his clumsiness and poor coordination, he would prefer to spend the time reading and caring for his many pets. Worse, he remembers the bad moments and games, not the good ones. Still undecided, Bill wakens from a nap one day to find his cat injured. The veterinarian he takes the cat to, Corrine Morgan, befriends him, recognizes his love for animals, encourages his self-confidence, and offers him a part-time job. While he is there, a girl he has been too shy to speak to comes for her dog and they naturally fall to talking about being tall — at six feet she towers over other girls. She encourages him to make his size an asset and to ignore wisecracks. Feeling more confident in basketball and in much else, Bill decides to attend camp — but now knows that he wants to be a veterinarian, not a professional basketball player.

Despite the basketball theme, this book describes little actual play; both the situation and its resolution are mainly presented in lengthy conversations. These make clear Bill's view of things, the drawbacks of tallness. But readers small or tall may find it difficult to feel entirely sorry for a boy so tall, so bright, so handsome, and so thoughtful.

Ages 9-12

Also available in:
Braille — *Seven Feet Four and Growing*
Library of Congress

Cassette for the Blind — *Seven Feet Four and Growing*
Library of Congress

Le Guin, Ursula Kroeber

Very Far Away from Anywhere Else

Atheneum Publishers, 1976.
(89 pages)

L

BOY-GIRL RELATIONSHIPS
IDENTITY, SEARCH FOR
   Loneliness
   Self, attitude toward: feeling different

Seventeen-year-old Owen Griffiths is a loner, a reader, a thinker, and a social misfit. He wants to go to MIT and become a scientist, but his parents plan to send him to a local college. His efforts to imitate the other boys' preoccupations with sports, cars, and girls have been futile. One rainy day he meets Natalie Field, and for the first time, another person makes a difference in his life. Natalie is a musician, and like Owen, a loner and a thinker. The two spend hours discussing how the mind works, how music and thinking are alike, and how strong are social pressures to conform. Each feels the other is a true companion. Then Owen decides he is in love with Natalie, and begins to act toward her the way he thinks a person in love ought to act. One day at the beach he grabs her and kisses her. Natalie is angry. She says she does not want a romantic relationship with him, and embarrassed and confused, Owen takes her home. Afterwards, out driving, he has an accident that wrecks the car his father had given him for his birthday. When he wakes up in the hospital three days later, he remembers nothing. For several weeks he lives in a fog, refusing to see Natalie, or even do homework. One day he learns that some music composed by Natalie will be played at a concert. Owen attends and her music moves him to tears. Later they talk. Natalie confesses that she had been wrong to discipline her life so thoroughly as to shut out love. Their relationship resumes, stronger than before. Owen also takes a stand with his parents: helped by a scholarship and the insurance money from the car, he will go to the school of his choice.

Owen and Natalie's romance is unusual. The author shows the unique communication between these two people, and allows Owen to tell the story wittily. Through the discussing and sharing of dreams, plans, and limitations, the young people come to a better understanding of themselves and make realistic decisions for the future.

Ages 12 and up

Also available in:
Cassette for the Blind — *Very Far Away from Anywhere Else*
Library of Congress

Paperbound — *Very Far Away from Anywhere Else*
Bantam Books, Inc.

398

Leigh, Bill

The Far Side of Fear

The Viking Press, Inc., 1977.
(154 pages)

COURAGE, MEANING OF
FEAR
   Bully: fear of
   Leader/Leadership
   Lost, being

Thirteen-year-old Kenny Birkett is frankly afraid of Patrick O'Brien, the local bully. One wintry day Patrick, violently restless at home with his shrewish mother, sneaks off to look for trouble and finds Kenny and his friend Peter sledding near Haggott's abandoned quarry. Maliciously, he pushes their sleds into the quarry,

where one falls into the Sink, a steep hole in the quarry floor, so dangerous it is the cause of the quarry's closing. All three clamber down after the sled, and there Petra and Paula, Patrick's sisters, find them when they come looking for their brother. Nearby blasting for highway construction has opened a new cave, and Petra follows the boys into it — but another blast suddenly causes a rockfall, trapping the four in the cave. Frightened and aware they have no chance where they are, Pete leads them deeper into the cave, searching for another outlet. Eventually they discover a hole leading to the surface and attract attention by yelling. But their would-be rescuers are unable to drill down and instead lower explosives to them, calling down instructions for setting them off. But the explosions touch off a cave-in, and Pete's ankle is badly sprained. They are on their own again. Alternately led and goaded by Kenny, the other three trudge deeper into the cave system, looking for still another way out. Their chances steadily dim as time passes, and they undergo a series of further mishaps. Hungry, bone-weary after narrowly escaping from a flooding chamber, they stumble onto a series of caves used by prehistoric people. Hopeful that the surface is near, they despair the more when they cannot find an opening. It is only by chance that they find themselves beneath a tree and Patrick chops their way to the surface.

This harrowing adventure reduces Kenny to his most elemental quality, a dogged will to survive that enables him to lead others, who are similarly altered, if more dimly. Indeed, there is more of adventure than character in this story, even though the action is viewed from multiple viewpoints.

Ages 10-14

Also available in:
No other form known

399

Leigh, Frances

The Lost Boy

E. P. Dutton & Company, Inc., 1976.
(112 pages) o.p.

SIBLING: Relationships
 Differences, human
 Embarrassment
 Judgment, effect of emotions on

Kate Forrester, seventeen, comes home to Malaysia from a boarding school in England — hoping to meet her lost brother. Seven years earlier, a hospital fire in Indonesia had killed her mother and Brian, or so it had been thought. But now an eight-year-old boy has been found, rescued from the hospital fire by a Chinese woman, who has raised him. He is either Brian or a Dutch boy who was also in the hospital at the time. Neither Kate nor her father can identify the boy. It is the same for both ten-year-old Cessy and Donald, about fourteen, the other Forrester children, who soon arrive from England too. Cessy thinks she would know if the boy remembered a marble game, but she cannot find the "special" marbles she needs for it. Their father reminds them the boy cannot be identified by any English manners, having "had to fight tooth and nail . . . to keep himself alive" among the persecuted Chinese minority in Indonesia. Still, his conduct embarrasses them all and Cessy considers him "uncivilized."

Though Kate and Donald lean toward keeping him, regardless of his identity, Mr. Forrester, citing the financial burden, intends sending him to Holland if he turns out to be Dutch. Sure enough on a vacation the boy is heard to say a Dutch word, and that seems to settle it, for he speaks no English. No longer worried that his conduct reflects on them as a family, the Forresters begin to appreciate the boy for what he is, and he, growing accustomed to them, shows them his resourcefulness and generosity. Even Cessy now wants to keep him. His having used what seemed to be a Dutch word is explained away — the word sounds much like one in Chinese. Before Kate can tell her father this, Cessy begins idly playing with some "special" marbles she has bought. The boy, calling out "SPECIAL!" snatches one, just as in the game Cessy and Brian had played years before.

A family expecting to find traces of an English upbringing in a boy who may be their brother is instead shocked by his tough wiliness. This dramatic rendition of the old puzzler pitting heredity against environment should provoke discussion. Then too, the experience of fitting a foreign child into a strange new family and place will be recognized by any family who has brought a foster or adopted child into their home. An important subtheme here is Kate's attempt to avoid attending a university, as her father wishes, so as to begin teaching.

Ages 10-13

Also available in:
Talking Book — *The Lost Boy*
Library of Congress

LeRoy, Gen

Emma's Dilemma

Harper & Row Publishers, Inc., 1975.
(123 pages)

FRIENDSHIP: Best Friend
GRANDPARENT: Living in Child's Home
   Allergies
   Change: accepting
   Emotions: accepting
   Loss: feelings of
   Maturation
   Only child
   Pets: love for

Thirteen-year-old Emma dotes on her sheepdog, Pearl. One night while Emma is baby-sitting for Herbie, the six-year-old pest in the apartment down the hall, Herbie asks if Emma has a best friend. Emma says Lucy is her best girl friend, but her "really best friend" is Pearl. Indeed, even best friend Lucy notices how much time Emma spends with the dog. Nor does Lucy neglect to tell Emma how sensitive and "uptight" Emma has become. They cannot be honest with each other anymore, because Emma is always "approving or disapproving." Emma, however, thinks she takes things more seriously than Lucy does, and that she is just acting more maturely. She believes her "maturity" causes the frequent knots in her stomach when she is upset. Lucy points out that being "uptight" has nothing to do with being mature. Offended, Emma feels more distant from Lucy than ever — and continues to worry. She is especially ruffled by the coming change in her living arrangements. Her grandmother, whom she has never met, is moving in permanently. After Grandmom arrives and spends a few hours telling stories of her youth, Emma begins to like her. Then comes Grandmom's violent allergic reaction to Pearl. Emma's parents and grandmother are as appalled as Emma that Grandmom should be allergic to Pearl. But arrangements are made for Pearl to live with Emma's Aunt Edith in the country. Emma is fit to be tied about giving up her beloved pet, and she cannot hide her feelings. After she tries unsuccessfully to give Pearl to Herbie's mother, affectionate Herbie, most upset, takes Pearl and runs away, thinking he and the dog can live in the basement where Emma can see Pearl anytime. His absence causes an uproar. Later, when Emma finds him, Herbie confesses that he only ran away to help her. To get him out of the basement, Emma explains to Herbie why Pearl must go, and in doing so, comes to understand it herself. She asks him to help by accompanying her and her mother when they take Pearl to the country. She imagines her grandmother must feel terrible about causing such commotion. The next day at Aunt Edith's, Herbie gives Emma the moral support she needs to say good-bye to Pearl. Emma realizes that even a six-year-old can be a best friend.

Throughout this story Emma believes she is grown up and responsible because she worries. She really grows up when she accepts a friendship and learns to recognize and understand the feelings of others, even in adversity. The dialogue here is especially well done, and the ending is both happy and clear-sighted.

Ages 9-12

Also available in:
Paperbound — *Emma's Dilemma*
Harper & Row Publishers, Inc.

401

LeShan, Eda J.

Learning to Say Good-By: When a Parent Dies

Black/white illustrations by Paul Giovanopoulos.
Macmillan Publishing Company, Inc., 1976.
(82 pages)

DEATH: Attitude Toward
DEATH: of Father
DEATH: of Mother
  Mourning, stages of

The several stages of grief that children go through when a parent dies embody a range of feelings and questions that should be aired honestly and made part of the whole family's grief. Shielding or deceiving children or admonishing them to be brave can show more good intention than awareness of a child's best interests. In immediate decisions about the funeral, viewing the body, and burial, everyone present should express honest feeling and opinion. A child's fears, left unspoken, may only intensify — and one of the commonest of these is of what will happen to the dead person after burial. Sources of answers to this and other questions are listed. But a child's first response to a death may be flat disbelief: he or she may remember perfectly the parent's face, voice, actions. Only after weeks or months does the child begin to understand that the parent will never return. There will be renewed and more intense weeping, yet the intervening growth and learning will, themselves, make the accepted fact somewhat easier to bear. The child's visual and aural memory of the parent may recede now, to be replaced in part, eventually, by remembered feelings. But recovery from death is in general eased if memories are not supressed: the "work of mourning" must be done, the sadness be fully felt

until it recurs after longer and longer intervals. In the present, the child may feel several things: what will become of me now? will I die too? was it my love and need that caused this death? will my other parent die too? Children may also feel angry at the desertion, relief that the dead parent can no longer do hurtful things, anger at the living parent. The comfort and companionship of other adults, especially those with whom the person lost can be talked about, can ease the burden. Other children may help too, though older ones will know better than younger ones how to support and cheer a grieving companion. To be sure, parent or child may find a death in the family overwhelming and need professional counseling to come to terms with their feelings. Especially for children, other large changes coming even in the last stages of recovery — moving, a marriage, a new school — may prove more difficult than they otherwise would; these events too must be faced with full, candid talking over. Death, when faced honestly and with surrounding love, can teach a child about life: since no one else proves quite like the dead parent, each of us must be unique; and since so much connected with the dead parent remains behind, no one is ever fully lost. It is when children can at last express joy in their own living that they have said the best kind of good-bye to a parent who has died.

Honesty is finally the greatest comfort in extreme grief, for children no less than adults. The author wants young people to see clearly the range of responses they may feel to a parent's death, responses they need neither fear nor regret. Written for children, this book may well assist whole families in facing a death. LeShan is a noted educator and family counselor. The illustrator has matched the sympathetic warmth of the text.

Ages 12 and up

Also available in:
Paperbound — *Learning to Say Good-By: When a Parent Dies*
Avon Books

402

LeShan, Eda J.

What's Going to Happen to Me? When Parents Separate or Divorce

Black/white illustrations by Richard Cuffari.
Four Winds Press, 1978.
(134 pages)

DIVORCE: of Parents
SEPARATION, MARITAL
 Abandonment
 Ambivalence, feelings of
 Communication: parent-child
 Emotions: accepting
 Parent/Parents: remarriage of
 Parent/Parents: single
 Sibling: relationships
 Stepbrother/Stepsister
 Stepparent: father
 Stepparent: mother

In the first section of this book the author discusses and disposes of the worry common among children of separated or divorced parents that the child is in fact to blame for the breakup. She then offers real reasons why a divorce may occur. She encourages the child to identify and understand his or her feelings — guilt, sadness, fear, loss, anger — about marital separation and explores the "fear of abandonment." We learn that the child may in fact have conflicting feelings about his or her parents' splitting up, how children may get help from trained counselors, and the value of children talking frankly with their parents about feelings. Actual divorce brings still more feelings, and we are told how these are likely to change with time. The author explains forms of custody and visitation rights, and points out that during a necessary period of adjustment the parents, too, are suffering — and may use children for their own ends — encouraging them to become go-betweens or to take sides. The author cautions children to avoid this and to make clear to parents that they find it distasteful. She then discusses the possible effects of divorce on an only child and on the relationships between siblings. The daydream that parents will remarry is gone into, as are delayed emotional reactions to divorce and how to cope with a parent's new companion. In a fourth section, the author explores common difficulties children encounter with a new stepparent and the feelings which must be recognized and understood if a child is to accept the remarriage of a parent. Similarly discussed is the adjustment required for living with stepbrothers or stepsisters. It is pointed out in closing that children can and should use the experience of divorce to help them in other experiences later in life.

In direct, honest language, and with no less warmth and understanding, the author, a noted family counselor, answers many of the questions that assail children about divorce. We are told that the examples and anecdotes used here are from real life. Throughout the text, emphasis is placed on recognizing and accepting the diverse emotions which divorce, separation, or parental remarriage can give rise to. This book could be read as an accompaniment to counseling, could be read by parents and children together, and could prove valuable to friends of children whose parents are divorcing. It includes a list of additional readings for children and adults.

Ages 8 and up

Also available in:
No other form known

403

Lesikin, Joan

Down the Road

Color illustrations by the author.
Prentice-Hall, Inc., 1978.
(32 pages)

PROBLEM SOLVING

Two companions, a Garter Snake and a Box Turtle, travel along a road looking for a home, but find none that suits them both. Long, thin Garter Snake fits a hollow log perfectly, but stubby Box Turtle finds it too narrow. And so it goes for a hole in the ground, for a tree limb, for a boot, and for a toadstool, one creature always finding fault with the other's choice. Eventually they stop to rest by a broken-down stone wall. For once they agree: its cracks and crannies are too small for either of them. But lo — various animals, some larger than they, live there. Soon both friends have found satisfactory homes there too.

Two friends looking for a house find that friendship does not mean that needs are identical. Finally, other animals show them a stone wall fit for both. Young readers or listeners may enjoy second-guessing the friends' choices of homestead and which will fit which.

Ages 4-6

Also available in:
No other form known

404

Levoy, Myron

Alan and Naomi

Harper & Row Publishers, Inc., 1977.
(192 pages)

MENTAL ILLNESS: of Adolescent
REALITY, ESCAPING
REFUGEES
VALUES/VALUING: Moral/Ethical
  Friendship: meaning of
  Jewish
  Peer relationships: peer pressures
  Prejudice: ethnic/racial
  Trust/Distrust

L

It is 1944 in New York City, and twelve-year-old Alan Silverman is reluctantly trying to befriend a Jewish refugee about his own age, a girl from France named Naomi. But Alan's overtures endanger his hard-won standing with the neighborhood boys. Being Jewish, an avid student, and a book reader, he is already suspect, avoiding the epithet "sissy" only by playing stickball well and being a friend of Shaun, a tough Irish Catholic. Naomi is deeply withdrawn, for she has seen Nazi police brutally beat her father to death; Alan almost despairs of breaking through to her. Soon, though, by various shifts and stunts — talking through a dummy, playing the fool — he gently coaxes her into the real world, and as they in fact become friends, he finds he no longer cares if their secret friendship becomes known, nor does he care what the boys call him. Naomi begins attending school, and all goes well except that Shaun, accusing Alan of not trusting him enough to tell him about Naomi, has broken with him. Then one day as Naomi and Alan are going home from school, the local bully calls them "dirty Jews." Alan fights him and is beaten badly. Nonetheless he has won a victory of sorts by proving he is not a sissy. He and Shaun make up. But the fight has reminded Naomi of Nazi violence and her father's death, and she regresses into a terrified, unreachable withdrawal. She is sent to a mental hospital. On the day her father was killed, he and Naomi had been tearing up maps which could have tipped off the Nazis as to the whereabouts of French and Jewish resistance fighters. When Alan visits Naomi in the hospital, she sits miming the tearing of paper, over and over, unseeing.

A sensitive Jewish boy gently befriends and encourages the tenuous trust of a deeply disturbed Jewish refugee girl, at the risk of inciting the latent anti-Semitism around him. As she emerges from her emotional isolation, he finds new self-assurance too. His joy at her seeming recovery is movingly conveyed, as is his stunned grief at her eventual lapse into psychosis. Readers will find the starkly dramatic ending of this story impressive, though some will recoil from Naomi's unsparing account of her father's death.

Ages 11-14

Also available in:
Paperbound — *Alan and Naomi*
Dell Publishing Company, Inc.

405

Levy, Elizabeth

Lizzie Lies a Lot

Black/white illustrations by John Wallner.
Delacorte Press, 1976.
(102 pages)

HONESTY/DISHONESTY
   Grandparent: living in child's home

Nine-year-old Lizzie often tells little lies to her Nana in self-defense against the old lady's carping criticism — and not only to Nana. She lies to her parents too, as when she says she is to star in a dance assembly at school, when no such assembly is planned. One day Lizzie and her best friend, Sara, find a stray cat in a vacant house. Lizzie longs to keep the cat and tells lies to Sara about her mother and about cats. When her parents refuse to let her keep the cat, Lizzie lies to Sara about letting the cat go — but Sara is beginning to sense her friend's dishonesty. The following Saturday, playing at Lizzie's home (Nana lives there too), the girls get into trouble with Nana, and when Lizzie lies to Nana, Sara is so upset she no longer wants to play. The next Monday is supposedly the day of the dance assembly at school. When Lizzie's parents question her about it, she confesses she made the whole thing up. In fact, she finally admits that she lies frequently. Her parents reprimand her but then talk to her about how she might stop lying. Lizzie admits she is more comfortable with the truth, and says she will try. She even confides some of her "whoppers" to Sara, and the two become best friends again.

A little girl becomes a compulsive liar — to impress people, to get out of trouble, but usually for no reason at all. Not until her best friend accuses her of lying does she see the trouble she is making for herself and decide to try telling the truth. Children who often lie will understand Lizzie, and may come to understand children around them who tell tales.

Ages 9-11

Also available in:
Paperbound — *Lizzie Lies a Lot*
Dell Publishing Company, Inc.

406

Lexau, Joan M.

I'll Tell On You

Black/white illustrations by Gail Owens.
E. P. Dutton & Company, Inc., 1976.
(25 pages)

FRIENDSHIP: Meaning of
HONESTY/DISHONESTY
LITTLE LEAGUE
RESPONSIBILITY: Avoiding
  Guilt, feelings of
  Pets: love for
  Pets: responsibility for
Sports/Sportsmanship

Rose and Mark, friends and neighbors, have been practicing for Little League tryouts; both acknowledge that
Rose's weak spot is fielding. On the way to the park
Mark's dog, Spud, bites a little girl who kicked him —
the coach's daughter. Frightened, Mark insists they
leave at once and later learns that the girl must have
rabies shots if the dog is not found. Rose asks Mark to
confess, but he refuses. That evening, after hearing a
television announcement about the little girl and talking with her parents about rabies shots, Rose calls
Mark. "If you don't tell, I'll have to," she says. "No you
won't," Mark says. "You wouldn't tell on a friend." The
next day, tryout day, Rose assures Mark that she will not
say anything until tryouts are over, but by now, Mark is
more worried about his dog (is it sick, will it die?) than
he is about not making the team. Tryout time arrives;
they go separately to the field. Mark brings Spud and
confesses to the coach. Angry, worried about his daughter, the coach postpones tryouts and rushes off with the
dog. At home, Rose mopes about, worrying that she may
have lost a friend. Her mother explains that Mark's dog
is in no danger, because he has had anti-rabies shots.
Before the postponed tryouts the next afternoon, the
coach and Mark exchange apologies. Rose does well in
running and batting. When it comes time for her to
field, Mark shouts encouragement and throws her his
old glove to use. Later, the coach begins picking the
team: his own son first, then Mark, but when he finally
comes to Rose, Mark interrupts. "If you don't pick her
for the team," he says, "I don't want to be on it." The
coach continues looking at Rose. "We need a good runner in the outfield. So I'll try you out there if you really
work on the catching."

In this well-written story of a friendship, a boy and girl
help each other to be their best. Mark helps Rose
become a Little Leaguer by practicing with her daily,
and Rose helps Mark accept responsibility for his dog
by vowing to tell the truth if he does not. Although by
his confession Mark stands to lose both his dog and his
chance at the team, Rose stands to lose even more —
Mark's friendship. Some readers may resent the coach's
favoring boys, but it is made clear that he wants to be
fair to the girls. The illustrations (though not the cover)
show Mark as the only black child in the book.

Ages 5-8

Also available in:
Talking Book — *I'll Tell On You*
Library of Congress

L

407

Lingard, Joan

A Proper Place

Thomas Nelson, Inc., 1976.
(159 pages)

CHANGE: New Home
MARRIAGE: Teenage
PREJUDICE: Religious
RESOURCEFULNESS
  Ireland
  Marriage: interreligious

The religious strife in Belfast has driven Kevin and Sadie McCoy, a young married couple of different religious faiths, out of Ireland. They now live with their infant son in a rundown section of Liverpool, and Kevin works as a laborer. His wages are low to begin with, and Sadie resents the small sum he sends home every week to his mother. A visit from Sadie's own mother, who disapproves of their marriage, strains their purse and feelings even further. Their relief at her departure is short-lived, when they learn that Kevin's seventeen-year-old brother, Gerald, is coming to live with them. A sullen boy who has become too much for his mother, Gerald is no better with Kevin and Sadie. The turmoil of Belfast has left him tense and irritable, and when he finally finds a job he soon loses it because of his temper. Sadie finds her own temper growing short with Gerald and the loss of their best friends, Kitty and Bill, to a better job out of town. After much looking, Kevin's own search for a better job turns up one which includes a house, on an estate in Cheshire, and he is hired along with Gerald. Moving to the country brings pleasures and pains. Sadie often finds the solitude uncomfortable, with the nearest store two miles away and her only neighbors an older couple. Lively by nature, she begins making trips to the village, meeting new people, and working part-time housecleaning in the main house in order to buy a puppy she intends to breed. Kevin, on the other hand, loves the country life and farm work. But Gerald's insolence with Mr. Halliday, the head cowman, gets the young man fired. After Sadie speaks to the estate owner about Gerald, things improve. Gerald gives Sadie the last sum needed to buy her puppy, Kevin is promoted to head cowman, and Gerald is hired to do work he loves in the stables. After a weekend trip to Liverpool to celebrate, Sadie is just as happy as Kevin is to return to the country. Gerald, too, is happier now, but decides he belongs in Ireland, working in a stable.

Mainly this story concerns the adjustments a young couple must make to each other and to their surroundings if they are to make a home. Young Kevin and Sadie show a maturity beyond their years in accepting family responsibilities and caring for one another. Raised to hate each other's religions — Kevin is Catholic, Sadie is Protestant — they remain wary of the difference. Sadie, in particular, is unreconciled to having been married in the Catholic church and having the baby christened Catholic — but sees nothing to be done about it, a real difference they will simply have to live with. Nor does Gerald ever become more open or pleasant, but he does grow to care for and trust Sadie and Kevin, and reveals a growing strength of character in resisting a scheme suggested by a troublesome buddy. This book is the fourth in a series of stories about Kevin and Sadie.

Ages 12 and up

Also available in:
Cassette for the Blind — *A Proper Place*
Library of Congress

408

Lionni, Leo

A Color of His Own

Color illustrations by the author.
Pantheon Books, 1975.
(29 pages counted)

SELF, ATTITUDE TOWARD: Feeling Different
   Friendship: making friends

Whether parrot, goldfish, elephant, or pig, every animal has a color of its own, except the chameleon. Against a lemon, he is yellow; against grass, green; and so on. One chameleon, desiring a permanent coloration, hops onto a leaf, hoping to remain green forever. But the leaf turns in the fall, and so does the chameleon — from green to yellow to red. Black as the night during the long winter, he turns green in the spring grass. Dissatisfied with this continual changing, he asks an older, wiser chameleon if he will ever have a color of his own. No, he is told, but might not we two stay together so that we remain the same color as each other? Whatever colors they change to, they remain alike in hue from then on, and live "happily ever after."

An animal that by nature changes colors to accord with his background wants the impossible, a permanent color. His aspiration leads, not to a permanent coloration, but to a permanent friendship. The analogy to children needing to accept their natural selves and to the ways they can do so is clear. Since children are sure to ask the reason for the chameleon's color changes, teachers and parents using the book would do well to have an explanation ready.

Ages 3-5

Also available in:
No other form known

409

Lipsyte, Robert

One Fat Summer

Harper & Row Publishers, Inc., 1977.
(151 pages)

INFERIORITY, FEELINGS OF
WEIGHT CONTROL: Overweight
   Determination
   Fear: of physical harm
   Job

Mr. Marks has no confidence in his fat fourteen-year-old son, Bobby, and neither does Bobby himself. At Rumson Lake, where the family goes in summer, his father wants him to be a counselor at day camp like his older sister, Michelle, but what Bobby really wants to be is an athletic hero like Pete Marino, a college boy who dates Michelle. As things are, Bobby is only the butt of jokes and disapproval. Nagged by his friend Joanie, he takes a caretaking job at Dr. Kahn's. Then Willie Rumson, an ex-Marine and local bully who had the job and wants it back, warns him to quit — or else. It being tortuous physical work for a boy of more than 200 pounds, and Dr. Kahn being a demanding employer, Bobby is not sure himself why he is so determined to stay on. Willie abducts the boy and leaves him naked on an island, but Bobby is rescued by Willie's friend, who is trying to keep Willie out of trouble. Still Bobby stands firm. That he is losing weight and gaining strength from the work adds to his confidence — even when Willie comes after him with a rifle. The same friend talks Willie out of shooting, but Michelle's boy friend leaps on Willie. A fight ensues in which Bobby almost drowns

L

Willie, but Willie's friend breaks that up too. Remorseful, Bobby begins to see that the boy friend Pete's swaggering toughness and Willie's bullying are alike poses. Being a man means something else.

This well-paced and sensible first-person narrative traces the formation of "a miserable fat boy into a fairly presentable young man," as Bobby's employer smugly puts it. But the job, though a catalyst for the change, is hardly its cause. As Bobby tells Dr. Kahn, "You didn't do it. I did it." Overweight children could find in this thoroughly credible story the link between overeating and undervaluing oneself.

Ages 12-14

Also available in:
Cassette for the Blind — *One Fat Summer*
Library of Congress

Paperbound — *One Fat Summer*
Bantam Books, Inc.

410

Lisker, Sonia Olson and Leigh Dean

Two Special Cards

Black/white illustrations by Sonia Olson Lisker.
Harcourt Brace Jovanovich, Inc., 1976.
(48 pages counted)

DIVORCE: of Parents

Little Hazel Cooper worries about her parents' continual arguing. Not only miserable with each other, her mother and father scold Hazel and her little brother too, sometimes unjustly. One night Hazel hears her parents arguing about divorce. In the morning her father is gone. Hazel misses him terribly and wonders if her mother, too, will go off, leaving the children alone. Then Mother explains that Daddy will not be living with them anymore, but the children will see him on weekends. The following Friday Daddy takes the two to his new apartment. They love the bunk beds and enjoy drawing pictures for the walls. Later, while shopping with her mother, she tries to find an appropriate card for her parents. Finally she makes a card for each, expressing her love to each.

Grieved by her parents' divorce, a little girl finds she can love each parent individually — and that both still love her. Readers faced with divorce in their families may find this book reassuring.

Ages 6-9

Also available in:
No other form known

411

Litchfield, Ada Bassett

A Button in Her Ear

Color illustrations by Eleanor Mill.
Albert Whitman & Co., 1976.
(32 pages counted)

DEAFNESS

Young Angela has trouble hearing people clearly. When her teacher says, "Tomorrow we're going to learn our letters," Angela thinks she has said, "Tomorrow we're going to burn our sweaters." Angela thinks people mutter. But her parents think otherwise and take her to an ear doctor. Unable to find a physical defect in her ears, he sends her to an audiologist. After testing, she goes to a hearing-aid dealer and is fitted with a hearing aid. Because the device helps so much, she does not mind wearing it. Her teacher, comparing the aid to glasses, asks her to show it to the class. Soon Angela is both accustomed to her "magic button" and hears almost every word spoken to her.

In this first-person narrative, a child talks about misunderstanding others because of poor hearing. The smooth movement of events, from discovery of the hearing loss to its correction, may skate over a child's fears of wearing an aid, of being "different." But this calm and clear exposition should reduce such fears while explaining to other children what a hearing aid is and does.

Ages 5-8

Also available in:
Cassette — *A Button in Her Ear*
Instructional/Communications Technology, Inc.

Cassette for the Blind — *A Button in Her Ear*
Library of Congress

Filmstrip — *A Button in Her Ear*
Westport Communications

412

Litchfield, Ada Bassett

A Cane in Her Hand

Color illustrations by Eleanor Mill.
Albert Whitman & Co., 1977.
(32 pages counted)

VISUAL IMPAIRMENT

Very few fifth or sixth graders have to wear glasses as thick as Valerie has worn for years, and so when her vision worsens, her parents rush her to the doctor. He says he can hope to prevent blindness but cannot promise more. Meanwhile, although schoolwork is harder and harder for her, Valerie yearns to stay with her class. At last a specially trained teacher arrives to help her with her studies and to show her some ways her other senses can aid her more. She learns to differentiate

sounds and to use a cane to prevent herself from bumping into things. Eventually, while still sensitive to people's comments about her handicap, she on the whole accepts the fact of it. "Seeing with your eyes is important, but it isn't everything."

The kindness and understanding of friends and family, as well as skilled professional help, all assist a little girl in coping with a severe visual impairment. As pointed out in the preface, children in similar situations will be able to identify with Valerie. Children with normal vision will better understand the feelings and difficulties of those who are visually impaired.

Ages 6-9

Also available in:
Filmstrip — *A Cane in Her Hand*
Westport Communications

Talking Book — *A Cane in Her Hand*
Library of Congress

413

Little, Jean

Listen for the Singing

E. P. Dutton & Company, Inc., 1977.
(215 pages)

VISUAL IMPAIRMENT
  Blindness
  Canada
  Family: unity
  Friendship: making friends
  Sibling: love for
  War

The time is 1939, the place Canada, and Anna Solden expects trouble in the ninth grade. Since coming with her family from Germany in 1934, she has attended a special class for children with limited vision. Now she fears her transfer to a new school, there to have new teachers, no special tutoring, and no friends. Normally she would confide in her father, but now he is preoccupied with political developments in Germany — his homeland still, though he has had to uproot his family to come to a place where people are "free to speak their thoughts aloud without fear." Soon enough, Britain declares war on Germany. The news distresses Anna's parents and her older brother, Rudi; the war seems remote to Anna. School begins with pleasant surprises: she likes several of her teachers and almost immediately makes new friends. Even a notoriously harsh teacher treats her kindly, and later Anna learns that he has a visual handicap similar to her own. Anna's major obstacle is mathematics. Rudi, a genius in math, tutors her, and a special kinship grows up between brother and sister. But as war spreads through Europe, Rudi determines to fight the Nazi regime. At the end of the school year he enlists — and while still in basic training is blinded in an accident. He returns home polite, bitter, aloof. Anna hears him pacing his room at night, weeping. She recalls her own retreat "into some safe secret place where nobody can reach," and her sense that at the same time a handicap is "like being shut up inside a shell with no way out." She consults with her friends Dr. and Mrs. Schumacher, who had helped her sight, brings home records for Rudi, and learns Braille in order to teach him. With her encouragement, Rudi slowly returns to an almost normal life.

As a child, Anna had been stubborn and clumsy, afraid of school and all things new. Yet she becomes a young woman of determination, compassion, and confidence. Understanding so well the world of the visually impaired, she is able to help Rudi feel whole again. The whole family is portrayed with subtle sensitivity. This book is a sequel to *From Anna*.

Ages 10-14

Also available in:
Talking Book — *Listen for the Singing*
Library of Congress

414

Little, Jean

Stand in the Wind

Black/white illustrations by Emily Arnold McCully.
Harper & Row Publishers, Inc., 1975.
(247 pages)

FRIENDSHIP: Making Friends
SIBLING: Relationships
  Canada
  Maturation
  Self, attitude toward: accepting

The night before Martha Winston is to leave for a week at camp, she breaks her arm. Martha, who has for weeks anticipated this first time at camp, is forced to stay home. Meanwhile, the Winstons, who live in Canada, expect a visit from the Swanns, an American family. The Swanns have two daughters, Kit and Rosemary, who are about twelve and sixteen — the same ages as Martha and her older sister, Ellen. The two sets of sisters have never met, but Martha thinks it would be fun for all four girls to spend the week at the Winston's beach cottage, which she now calls "Camp Better-Than-Nothing." The parents agree, but when the girls finally meet, their differences in outlook and experience cast doubt on the plan. They go anyway. During their stay at the cottage, each girl gains a better understanding of herself and, after some pleasant and painful experiences, learns to appreciate and enjoy the others. For Martha, the other girls turn the last day at the lake into a typical day at camp. All have a wonderful time, and when the girls separate to go home, they realize that their week together has woven a strong friendship.

Living for a time on their own resources, the girls gain a new maturity. Martha and Kit become especially close friends when Martha helps Kit overcome her shyness and fear of new experiences. Though Martha has missed the real camp, she finds what she might have found there, the joy of mutual friendship in a group.

Ages 8-11

Also available in:
Talking Book — *Stand in the Wind*
Library of Congress

415

Little, Lessie Jones and Eloise Greenfield

I Can Do It by Myself

Color illustrations by Carole Byard.
Thomas Y. Crowell Company, Inc., 1978.
(39 pages counted)

DEPENDENCE/INDEPENDENCE
   Fear: of animals
   Pride/False pride

Young Donny resents the help that older people continually press on him — as if they can do everything and he nothing. On his mother's birthday he awakens determined to walk to a nearby florist shop alone and buy a plant he has already picked out as her present. He turns down his older brother's offer of help and walks on, towing a wagon. Belatedly, Donny remembers a frightening bulldog ahead but vows not to walk another way and be laughed at. The dog barks at Donny, briefly scaring him, but is behind a fence, and the boy arrives at

the store with his "cool" intact. Pleased that the storekeeper treats him like a grown-up customer, Donny confidently sets off for home with the plant. But this time the bulldog is outside the fence. Forgetting his vow to be brave, the boy cries and yells for Mama. He does remember not to run from a dog, but backing away, he falls. Now he is truly frightened — but the dog merely looks at him, turns, and goes back inside his yard. Donny quickly latches the gate and walks on home. There he gives Mama the plant and proudly tells his brother, "I told you I could do it by myself."

A young boy's self-reliance outweighs his courage, and his encounter with a dog shows the limits of that. Neither the boy nor the book draws lessons therefrom, but readers should be able to. The book features some Black English; the only difficulty for readers unfamiliar with it might be a sentence in which "bad" means "good": "You think you bad, don't you?"

Ages 5-7

Also available in:
Talking Book — *I Can Do It by Myself*
Library of Congress

416

Long, Judy

Volunteer Spring

Dodd, Mead & Co., 1976.
(126 pages)

MENTAL RETARDATION
   Determination
   Helping

Fourteen-year-old Jill Berger, recruited at school as a volunteer, eagerly looks forward to working at Overton State Hospital for the Mentally Retarded. The hospital is fifty miles away, but Jill and two friends who have also volunteered will be driven by their teacher, Mr. Harris, another volunteer. On their first day, Jill and her friends are given a tour of Overton by Miss Robinson, a therapist. But once inside the building, its bed-ridden residents "drooling, screaming, or lying there vacant-eyed," Jill is assailed by a "nauseating stench." Overpowered by the sights and smells, Jill feels terribly sick and rushes blindly out-of-doors. There she is approached by a resident asking for a cigarette, and she panics and runs off again, aimlessly. Although Miss Robinson soon finds her and guides her to an office to compose herself, and although the rest of the tour is uneventful, Jill still remembers the morning — and wishes that she had not volunteered. All the way home, while her friends talk excitedly, Jill remains silent, pondering her experience. Her distress is evident to her mother, who urges her to give up the job. But Miss Robinson, sensing Jill's dilemma, pays a call and encourages Jill and her mother to give the work one more chance. The next week, Jill assists the residents' band and begins working privately with Lisa, a young child with Down's Syndrome. Jill finds that helping the less handicapped residents is not only challenging but downright fun. Her greatest pleasure and trial comes in teaching Lisa about colors and shapes. Weeks later, Miss Robinson remarks on Lisa's increased attention span and improved coordination, and Jill knows that her work makes a difference. By the end of the school year she is at ease with even the most severely handicapped residents. Lacking the necessary ride to work in the summer, Jill consoles herself with the thought that both ride and job will be there for her in the fall.

This book graphically portrays an adolescent's progress from fear of mentally retarded people to understanding and acceptance of them. Her earliest experience is shown as vividly disquieting. But with persistence she learns to look beyond handicaps and to see people's needs.

Ages 11-14

Also available in:
Paperbound — *Volunteer Spring*
Pocket Books, Inc.

417

Love, Sandra

But What About Me?

Black/white illustrations by Joan Sandin.
Harcourt Brace Jovanovich, Inc., 1976.
(152 pages)

PARENT/PARENTS: Mother Working Outside Home
  Responsibility: accepting

Lucy Hoffman, almost eleven, resents her mother's return to working at a full-time job. Though her mother explains that her career is deeply important to her, Lucy fears that she and her mother will have no more good times together. Worse, the first few days her mother is at the office prove unlucky ones for Lucy. Together with Mike and Janet, the children next door, Lucy accidently breaks a garage window. At school she spills paint on another girl's new jumper. To console her when her mother must be out of town on Lucy's birthday, her father takes her out to buy a birthday gift: a desk and chair for her room. That same week, working up a puppet show, Lucy and Janet and Mike try making use of Lucy's closet and accidentally start a fire with candles. Although the children escape uninjured, Lucy's clothes and her new desk chair are ruined. When her mother returns and learns what has happened, she blames her own absence and announces that she will quit her job. Lucy objects, saying that she has gotten used to her mother being gone, and that she wants her to be happy. Both parents admire the child's ambition to be more self-reliant. The following Saturday, Mike and Janet give Lucy a belated birthday surprise. Mike has installed a pully system between the two girls' bedroom windows so that they can send messages to each other. Lucy decides that life is good after all.

A little girl learns that her mother's job need not undermine her own sense of well-being, that being more independent and taking on more responsibilities can even be fun. Though slow, this story rings true in all respects but one: Lucy's feelings suggest (though nothing else does) a child either previously overindulged or else younger than eleven.

Ages 9-12

Also available in:
Paperbound — *But What About Me?*
Xerox Publishing Company

418

Love, Sandra

Melissa's Medley

Harcourt Brace Jovanovich, Inc., 1978.
(137 pages)

COMPETITION
SPORTS/SPORTSMANSHIP
  Goals
  Maturation
  Parent/Parents: remarriage of

At fourteen, Melissa "Moe" Hayes is already swimming on the senior swim team, preparing for the Indianapolis meet, where she hopes to beat Ferlinghetti Brown, a long-time rival. If Moe does well, moreover, she will qualify for the Junior Olympics, a meet to be held later that summer. Though she loses a couple of Indianapolis events to Ferlinghetti, she wins several medals and the trophy for the most total points. Moe's parents are divorced and each has remarried, but it is her father she secretly longs to do well for; she is still wary of her

stepfather, though he is as kind as everyone else in his interest in her swimming. She calls her father long-distance (he lives in another town) to report her success, and he is delighted. All summer Moe practices for the Junior Olympics. Again she competes against Ferlinghetti Brown, and this time her performance is heroic: she sets a record and wins several medals. Both she and Ferlinghetti qualify for the National Junior Meet, where they will swim on the same team. The last day of the meet, her father comes to watch her, as do her mother and stepfather. Moe realizes how important both families are to her, and she can love them both. She goes home feeling triumphant.

In this story of swimming meets and competitors, a teenage girl must handle the ambiguous pleasure of beating the top male swimmer in her own school, must choose between an important swim meet and a visit to her adored father, and must resist her mother's worries over a rigorous training schedule which (swimmers take note) this somewhat patly resolved book makes no bones about.

Ages 10-13

Also available in:
No other form known

419

Low, Joseph

Benny Rabbit and the Owl

Color illustrations by the author.
Greenwillow Books, 1978.
(56 pages)

FEAR: of Darkness
  Bedtime
  Communication: parent-child
  Imagination

When Benny Rabbit is told it is bedtime, he begs to look at the stars, tries to count them, brushes his teeth with painstaking care and performs a headstand. When his father questions these delaying tactics, Benny tells him of the fearsome owl "with furry feathers and long, sharp claws" that is perched in his bedroom closet. Conceding that such a creature would scare anyone, Mr. Rabbit looks in the closet and confirms the imagined owl's presence. But, he assures Benny, the owl is little, hungry, and frightened. Father gives it a left-over supper carrot and allows it to perch on his right paw. Then, with fatherly aplomb, he escorts Benny — now sympathetic to the owl's plight — and the owl to the edge of the woods, where the little creature can find its way home. Benny and Father then return to the house, and Benny snuggles contentedly under his covers.

This engaging read-alone book portrays a widely held children's fear: that of a frightening creature in the darkness of the bedroom. A sympathetic parent calms the fear by accepting it and its imaginary cause and giving the child a new feeling about it. Though the illustrations clearly show that the father is pretending, the reader senses the concern that gives rise to make-believe. As a bedtime story this book might calm imaginative and fearful readers or listeners.

Ages 4-7

Also available in:
No other form known

420

Low, Joseph

Boo to a Goose

Color illustrations by the author.
Atheneum Publishers, 1975.
(38 pages counted) o.p.

FEAR: of Animals
PROBLEM SOLVING

Six-year-old Jimmy loves the animal world down to the bugs on his parents' farm, and the animal world loves Jimmy — except for Gus the goose. On every occasion the old bird pounces on Jimmy — nipping, hissing, and flapping his mighty wings — and each time Jimmy runs away. His mother points out that running away excites Gus to chase him the more. The only thing to do, she advises, is to say "boo." As Jimmy sets out on his chores the next day, Gus rushes him; the boy opens his mouth to say boo, but nothing comes out. Again he runs away. To help him practice booing, Jimmy enlists other animals to play Gus. Rabbit is first, and at Rabbit's charge, Jimmy emits a "small-sized boo." Mouse is next, and Jimmy's boo is louder. Then Rooster, so magnificently like Gus, swoops on Jimmy, whose boo is a roar. Practice over, Jimmy walks to the house, and suddenly Gus is upon him. Initially frightened, the boy boos long and loud, driving Gus away. Now he knows he can chase Gus any time. But in bed that night, he thinks: "Maybe I won't scare Gus after all. Maybe he can't help being just what he is."

Resolving to stand up to someone is one thing, doing it another; this story follows a boy's progress from resolution to action. And yet another resolution follows: seeing the irascible goose as what he is, the boy decides to forgo scaring him. In using his new knowledge in human relationships, however, Jimmy might also need to determine the difference between a bluffed attack and one that is real.

Ages 5-8

Also available in:
No other form known

421

Low, Joseph

My Dog, Your Dog

Color illustrations by the author.
Macmillan Publishing Company, Inc., 1978.
(32 pages counted)

PETS: Love for
PETS: Responsibility for
  Blame

Jimmy grandly informs Nancy that his dog is better than hers. His dog sleeps all night, learns new tricks all the time, fetches the newspaper, and eats neatly. Hers, on the other hand, barks at the moon, will not learn anything, shreds the paper, and spills his food. Jimmy is likewise proud that his dog helps Mom in the garden, never pulls against the leash, guards the house, and sits in the car quietly. That dog of Nancy's digs in the garden, strains the leash, cares nothing for the house, and barks in the car. Finally Nancy must remind her brother: "You know perfectly well... there is only one Bowser. Sometimes he does what we want. Sometimes he doesn't." Jimmy loves him anyway.

In this slight first-person narrative, children with pets can recognize their own dislike of their pet's misdeeds but, like the main character, learn to accept their pet as it is. They may also want to talk about it.

Ages 4-6

Also available in:
No other form known

422

Lowry, Lois

Find a Stranger, Say Goodbye

Houghton Mifflin Co., 1978.
(187 pages)

ADOPTION: Feelings About
ADOPTION: Identity Questions
  Boy-girl relationships: dating
  Love, meaning of

Seventeen-year-old Natalie has everything but an idea of who she really is, for the Armstrongs adopted her soon after she was born. Toward the end of her high school senior year, Natalie decides she must find her "real" mother. The Armstrongs are hurt by her decision, but they give her money and such information as they have, for Natalie's was a "blind" adoption. Only Natalie's sister, Nancy, and her grandmother encourage the quest. That June, Natalie takes several days off from her father's medical clinic, where she has a summer job, and drives to the small town where she was born. There she manages to see Dr. Therrian, who had delivered her. Now old and dying of cancer, he tells her that her mother, Julie Jeffries, had been an unwed girl of fifteen. The Jeffries, however, have long since moved, and it takes Natalie weeks to trace Julie to New York City, where she is now a married woman with two small sons. Afraid to meet her mother, yet irresistibly drawn to her, Natalie goes to the city and finds that Julie is also a famous fashion model, with few interests other than in remaining beautiful and well-known. The two, although they look alike, have only a biological tie in common. Natalie does find, on reading a diary Julie had kept back then, that she loved her baby but had to put her up for adoption out of the conviction that a girl her age could not possibly care for a child. Natalie then departs, knowing that Julie will be simply a memory, something that happened. Only one task remains: one last visit to Dr. Therrian, whose son, killed long ago in an accident, had been her father.

An adopted girl is driven to seek out her origins, but once she has found her biological mother, she feels her a stranger, only one more item in her past. Natalie's sleuthing in tracing her mother holds some narrative interest, but it is the characterizations and not the simple plot which distinguishes this book. Few adopted young people will have as many resources as Natalie: a generous checking account, a leased car, and free time each week, all provided by her parents. It is also the rare person who is able to go about such a search with so few obstacles. But some readers will likely enjoy, not balk at, so idealized a quest.

Ages 12 and up

Also available in:
Braille — *Find a Stranger, Say Goodbye*
Library of Congress

Film — *Find a Stranger, Say Goodbye*
NBC Special Treat: Daniel Wilson Productions, Inc.

Paperbound — *Find a Stranger, Say Goodbye*
Pocket Books, Inc.

423

Lowry, Lois

A Summer to Die

Black/white illustrations by Jenni Oliver.
Houghton Mifflin Co., 1977.
(154 pages)

FAMILY: Unity
SIBLING: Relationships
    Death: of sibling
    Illnesses: terminal
    Leukemia

The Chalmers family has temporarily moved to a farmhouse in the country. Mr. Chalmers has been given a year's sabbatical from the university to finish writing his book. Thirteen-year-old Meg, plain and intellectual, hates being away from her painting class and her photography club, while fifteen-year-old Molly, pretty and popular, misses her boy friends and cheerleading. But before long, Molly has a new boy friend, and Meg has a new friend of a different kind. Will Banks is the elderly owner of the house the Chalmers rent, and lives nearby. Interested in photography, he allows Meg to photograph him, and, later in the winter, when Meg and her father build a darkroom, Meg teaches Will how to make photographic prints. Meanwhile, Molly has been ill, her frequent nosebleeds keeping her away from school. Briefly in the spring the nosebleeds stop, but one night she awakens to profuse bleeding. During a hospital stay her illness is diagnosed and an effective medication found. But back at home she is listless and depressed. Meg tries to cheer her, but Molly's illness troubles the whole family. When Will rents the third house on his land to a young couple about to have a baby, Meg and Molly befriend the new renters and enjoy them. But one day Molly is taken back to the hospital. Meg suddenly realizes that her sister will not get better — she is going to die. Her parents confirm her suspicion: Molly has leukemia. At first Meg avoids visiting Molly; but soon she goes to tell her of the birth of the neighbor couple's baby. Molly, connected to machines and heavily drugged, barely responds. Two weeks later she dies. The grieving Chalmers family leaves the farmhouse to return home.

Set in the rustic New England countryside, this book is at once refreshing and sad. It portrays the warmth of both family life and friendships. The narrator, Meg, who has always envied Molly's poise and prettiness, finally understands that she is beautiful too in her own way. Molly's illness and death are described with a realism and sympathy that avoid sentimentality.

Ages 10-14

Also available in:
Braille — *A Summer to Die*
Library of Congress

Paperbound — *A Summer to Die*
Bantam Books, Inc.

424

Luger, Harriett Mandelay .

The Elephant Tree
The Viking Press, Inc., 1978.
(115 pages)

FRIENDSHIP: Meaning of
MATURATION
  Delinquency, juvenile
  Lost, being
  Peer relationships
  Values/Valuing: moral/ethical

Dave Starr, a ninth grader and chronic truant, finds himself unwillingly enrolled in a program for unruly boys. Chaperoned by two men, the fatherly Pop Sloan and the younger, athletic Ted, Dave is taken on a hiking trip in the California desert with a group of strangers he is all but determined not to like. It is not long before Louie, once a student at a rival high school, insults Dave's own high school and Dave. He also carries a knife. The other boys, bored and sensing the simmering antagonism, begin to choose sides. When Louie decides to steal Ted's new jeep and invites the others to go for a ride, Dave alone is made to feel he must, to prove he is not afraid to cross the authorities. Louie and Dave do not get far before the jeep bogs down in the sand and the two have to admit defeat and walk back to camp. But finding their way in the desert is harder than they have expected: soon they are hopelessly lost. For two days they wander aimlessly without food or warm clothing, fighting the while over who is to blame for all this. They take shelter in a cave of rocks, but it is only after Dave nearly drowns in a flash flood and is saved by Louie that both boys realize how silly their bickering has been, and how much they have needed and depended on each other. Talking out their feelings about each other and past events, they become friends — and are found by Ted and Pop. Unaware of this new friendship, the boys back at camp are eager to know which one of them has bested the other in the fight that had been brewing. Louie is briefly tempted to renew the grudge until he recalls the experiences of the past few days. The two explain how being lost in the desert affected them: "This whole goddam earth could fall into the sun and no one would notice till they got their butts singed, because everybody is too busy fighting and screwing each other . . . the damn fools . . . all they have is each other . . . ." Now, as Dave says, "Louie and me hang around together."

In Dave's tense first-person narrative, delinquency is a way of life for the characters, until Dave and his unwelcome companion face grave danger and learn something about the interdependence of people. Sharing

L

their thoughts brings about friendship, and explaining this to the rest of their group brings the two pride and a hope that there is a better way to live. Street talk and profanity, prevalent throughout the story, add realism but may offend some readers.

Ages 12 and up

Also available in:
Cassette for the Blind — *The Elephant Tree*
Library of Congress

425

Lutters, Valerie

The Haunting of Julie Unger

Atheneum Publishers, 1977.
(193 pages)

DEATH: of Father
  Communication: parent-child
  Fantasy formation
  Grandparent: living in home of
  Reality, escaping

Julie Unger, an eighth grader living with her mother and younger sister in her grandmother's house in Maine, refuses to mourn the death of her father. While he had lived, Julie had enjoyed family vacations in Maine, although just before her father's fatal heart attack she had stopped working on photographic projects with him and had said she would not go to Maine that year. Now, living in Maine year-round, Julie is enduring her mother and grandmother's advice and solicitude morning to night. For that reason, Julie conceals the fact that she has resumed one of her and Papa's projects — photographing Canadian geese in a nearby cove. Neither does she mention the darkroom she constructs with her father's equipment in a little-used corner of the basement, nor the imaginary conversations she holds with her father while photographing the geese. As Julie's visits to the cove become frequent, encouraged by the cordiality of its owner, Mrs. Seeley, so does her father's presence become more vivid to her — until she is certain he lives. Meanwhile, the friction at home continues, with Julie refusing to talk seriously with her mother and arguing over unimportant matters. When school begins, Julie knows that the geese will soon migrate. Fearing that her father will depart with them, she takes to feeding them to keep them around. Not until she witnesses the death of two geese during the hunting season does she see the seriousness of her error. Shaken by what she has done, Julie tries to frighten the other geese away. She sees her father standing quietly in their midst. Angered by his apparent indifference, she hurls a camera at him. It drops into the water; she tries to retrieve it, and accidentally submerges another. Gazing at the ruined camera, she sobs convulsively — not over it but over her father. At this point Mrs. Seeley guides the sobbing girl indoors and helps her to give vent to her grief. With time and much talking, Julie uncovers her own remorse for acting as she had before her father's death and, at last, accepts the fact of that death. Only then does she begin to patch things up with her mother and plan her immediate future.

Unable, out of remorse, to accept the death of her father, a young girl withdraws from her family and begins to believe a fantasy. By contrast, an older friend is shown accepting the death of her husband and making a life without him. Mrs. Seeley is able to help Julie face things as they are. Strong character portrayals, convincing family relationships, and vivid emotional scenes make this a moving book. Long discussions of photography may put off some readers while delighting camera buffs.

Also available in:
No other form known

426

McGee, Myra

Lester and Mother

Black/white illustrations by the author.
Harper & Row Publishers, Inc., 1978.
(80 pages)

LOVE, MEANING OF

Little Lester and his mother agree that since Lester is growing up fast the two should write a book about themselves now to read two years hence. The first story they relate is of their plane ride. Though Mother is afraid, Lester remains courageous and soon both are enjoying the ride. Another time, the two go shopping in a large department store and become separated. When they finally find each other — going in opposite directions on the escalators — they are so happy they celebrate with ice-cream cones. One day when Mother has a lot of work to do, Lester begs to go fishing. After some persuading, Mother relents and the two hike to a nearby lake, where Mother takes a nap and Lester fishes and hunts for treasure. He surprises Mother with a bright blue bottle, some daisies, and wild raspberries, and Mother is delighted. They even catch a fish.

This pleasant collection of anecdotes is written by a young mother who wants a permanent record of the particularly loving relationship and special moments she has shared with her son.

Ages 5-9

Also available in:
No other form known

427

Mack, Nancy

I'm Not Going

Color photographs by Heinz Kluetmeier.
Raintree Publishers, Ltd., 1976.
(30 pages)

MOVING
Change: resisting

Paul does not want to move with his parents to Baltimore. Unwilling to leave familiar things, he thinks about hiding in a friend's basement so as to be left behind, but sees that cannot work. Paul woefully accepts the move. When the family's belongings are loaded into the van, he goes to his empty room — and leaves when he feels he might cry. But on the way to Baltimore, Paul and his parents stay overnight in a motel, where they not only swim but play Ping-Pong. Once in the Baltimore house, Paul finds that he likes his new room, especially since there will be a place there for his train set.

The anger, sadness, and worry a child experiences when preparing to move are well conveyed in this first-person narrative. Paul's feelings of insecurity are eased by a father who makes the move as pleasant as possible. The photographs complement the text.

Ages 4-8

Also available in:
No other form known

428

Mack, Nancy

Tracy

Color photographs by Heinz Kluetmeier.
Raintree Publishers, Ltd., 1976.
(31 pages)

CEREBRAL PALSY
Handicaps
Wheelchair, dependence on

Still very young, Tracy would like to be able to play hopscotch and jump rope like her friends, but she was born with cerebral palsy. Still, she does "get around" with the help of her wheelchair and crutches, and attends an ordinary school. Sometimes other children tease her about her handicap, but most of the time they help her. Twice a week after school, Tracy goes to a physical therapist to learn to stand and walk by herself. Since writing is difficult for her, she is also learning to type. At home she likes to play in her backyard. Tracy may be handicapped, but she says, "I get around."

Tracy is a true account of a young girl with cerebral palsy. Her simple story, written for young children, tells much that other handicapped children may identify with and that children without handicaps may learn from. It shows that the life of a handicapped child is not vastly different from that of a normal child.

Ages 4-8

Also available in:
No other form known

429

Mack, Nancy

Why Me?

Color photographs by Heinz Kluetmeier.
Raintree Publishers, Ltd., 1976.
(31 pages)

SELF-ESTEEM
Embarrassment

Michelle hates the "choosing up" before a game of kickball, knowing she will be chosen last, as usual. David, angry that his mother forces him to wear his jacket, is sure he will be conspicuous. Despite the fact that she knows she should be "reading along" with her class, Jeanette begins drawing a horse and daydreaming. Not hearing the teacher call on her, she is jolted back to the present by her classmate's laughter. Because he sent his friend Alphonso a teasing note, a young boy finds that his friendship is no longer wanted. A young girl, unable to read at the pace set in her previous reading group, is disconsolate that she must now read with the slowest group.

Each of these short, first-person narratives raises the question "Why did it have to happen to me?" Anger, sadness, and an uncertain self-image afflict each child in his or her embarrassing situation, and each situation invites group discussion.

Ages 5-8

Also available in:
No other form known

430

McKillip, Patricia A.

The Night Gift

Black/white illustrations by Kathy McKillip.
Atheneum Publishers, 1976.
(156 pages)

BOY-GIRL RELATIONSHIPS
FRIENDSHIP: Meaning of
   Cleft lip/palate
   Dropout, school
   Maturation
   School: achievement/underachievement

Claudia, Joslyn, and Barbara, all high school freshmen, are best friends — Joslyn and Barbara outgoing and spirited, Claudia shy and self-conscious because of a cleft palate for which she is still having corrective surgery. Barbara's brother, Joe, has been hospitalized for severe depression after attempting suicide, but now he is coming home, and Barbara decides to fix up a secret place to which he can retreat at difficult moments: "a place for him, just for him, where he could go when he was depressed, that was so beautiful, that just being in it would make him happy." Joslyn and Claudia volunteer to help. The girls know of a run-down, vacant house and begin to clean and decorate one of its rooms. Neil Brown, a boy Joslyn especially likes, also volunteers — but because he's attracted to Barbara. Almost nightly these four meet secretly to paint bright murals on the walls and hang colorful banners; they bring in plants, books, cushions, even an aquarium and a potted fir tree. Joslyn becomes so preoccupied with the room and with Neil's presence that her grades in school drop sharply, and her mother grounds her at home every day after school and pays her older brother, Brian, to tutor her. (Brian is a remorseful dropout, too self-conscious to drop back in; he and Joslyn vow that if through his tutoring she gets all As, he will return to school.) Then comes the blow. Neil asks Barbara to the junior prom, and Joslyn realizes that he has been helping them on account of Barbara. For a while she avoids the others, but then she and Barbara talk, agree that no one is at fault, and Joslyn feels better. At last Joe comes home, and the next day the group and Joe meet at the old house. Joe looks at everything intently and then, expressionless, thanks the friends politely. They are plunged in gloom over wasted effort. For a month, no one mentions the room or returns to it. One day Barbara announces that Joe must return to the hospital: they may as well dismantle the secret room, which must be full of dead plants and dust. But they find the room clean, the plants watered, the books apparently used. Joe has used the room after all. The friends rejoice at having been helpful. They set about the dismantling happily, putting a plant aside to send back to the hospital with their friend.

Joslyn tells this first-person narrative about her fairly unexceptional circle of friends, whose growing up — including her unrequited first love — might be anyone's story. Still, these young people are extraordinary in their compassion for Joe, and in their determination to help him in the only way they can think of. The author has captured the complexity of ordinary human relations — in friendships, in families, especially in Brian and Joslyn — with remarkable, understated sureness.

Ages 11 and up

Also available in:
No other form known

431

McLenighan, Valjean

I Know You Cheated

Color photographs by Brent Jones.
Raintree Publishers, Ltd., 1977.
(31 pages) o.p.

HONESTY/DISHONESTY
  School: classmate relationships
  Shame

The young narrator and his friend David Jones are the "two smartest kids in the class," have always enjoyed the camaraderie in that, and liked to work on projects together. But now the class has been divided into two competing teams with the narrator and David as captains, and things have changed. Vying for points earned in classroom accomplishments, the teams remain close — until a spelling test is given that will decide which team wins. A moment after time is called, the test over, the narrator rewrites one of his answers, thus achieving a perfect score and victory for his team. But David has seen the late change and confronts his friend after school, saying, "I know you cheated." Thereafter, David will not talk to him. The narrator does not know what to do: he could tell David he is sorry, but he might risk discovery by his classmates and teacher.

The "confidential" nature of this confessional narrative may well make children pay close attention, and its open ending should stimulate class discussion.

Ages 6-8

Also available in:
No other form known

432

McLenighan, Valjean

New Wheels

Color photographs by Mark Gubin.
Raintree Publishers, Ltd., 1978.
(31 pages)

STEALING
  Values/Valuing: moral/ethical

The young narrator is impressed by his friend Barry's boldness, ingenuity, and skill with a skateboard, but senses that some of Barry's pranks — his anonymous phone calls, for example — could lead to trouble. The storyteller is trying to earn money for new skateboard wheels, but Barry says, "that's doing it the hard way." One day Barry brings a gift wrapped in a sack — the longed-for new wheels. When the boy asks where the wheels came from, Barry admits he stole them. And when the boy refuses to accept a "stolen gift," Barry turns angry and leaves, taking the wheels with him.

This young first-person narrator, tempted to keep an ill-gotten gift, nevertheless defends his own moral standard, even at the risk of losing a friendship. Photographs capture both boys' emotions, and the text is easy reading for young readers as well as stimulating to discuss if read aloud.

Ages 7-9

Also available in:
No other form known

433

McNulty, Faith

Mouse and Tim

Color illustrations by Marc Simont.
Harper & Row Publishers, Inc., 1978.
(48 pages)

NATURE: Appreciation of
PETS: Responsibility for

When Tim finds her in the barn one April, Mouse is no bigger than a bumblebee. Mother tells Tim he may keep the mouse until she is mature enough to survive in the wild, and so he builds Mouse a cage and gives her nesting materials and food. Soon Mouse gets used to Tim and, as she grows, crawls about in his pockets and on his shoes. Despite Tim's increasing affection for Mouse, however, he does prepare her for a return to her natural habitat by feeding her things she can find to eat in the wild. In August, when the time seems ripe, Tim takes Mouse to the barn at sunset and, sadly, lets her go.

Tim and Mouse take turns telling this story of an experiment children love at least to imagine: raising a wild animal as a pet. Tim's resolve to turn the mouse loose when it is ready is a lesson in humaneness. The pastel tone of the illustrations conveys gentleness, care, and, toward the end, a slight but pleasant sadness.

Ages 5-7

Also available in:
No other form known

434

Madison, Winifred

Becky's Horse

Four Winds Press, 1975.
(152 pages)

FAMILY: Unity
  Daydreaming
  Jewish
  Sharing/Not sharing

It is 1938, and Becky Golden, one of three daughters in a working-class Jewish family, wants a horse so badly she can think of nothing else. Whenever bored or unhappy, she daydreams of galloping away across the countryside. Yet she knows her wish is impossible. The Depression keeps her father, a watchmaker, often out of work, so that Mrs. Golden, a seamstress, must support the family. Worry dogs the household. Even working, Mr. Golden broods about his cousin Bernard, once a boyhood chum in Russia, now a reknowned violinist living in Austria, surrounded by Nazi anti-Semitism. One night, Becky and her two sisters wish on a star. Mimi wishes for blond hair, Dori wishes for a friend, and Becky wishes for a horse. To help her wish along, Becky applies for a job at a stable in a boy's get-up, but the manager sees the ruse and turns her down. Next she notices a contest offer on the back of a cereal box — the first prize being Wonder the Wonder Horse. Becky enters the contest. Soon she turns thirteen, and all through her birthday party tries not to wait for a horse to appear. Weeks later a telegram arrives: Becky has won Wonder, or two hundred and fifty dollars. Her parents fuss about its care and feeding, but she chooses the horse. Then a telegram with more somber news arrives. Bernard and his son, David, have fled Austria across the Swiss border, but Bernard's wife has been killed by the

M

Nazis. Bernard writes from a Swiss hospital that he has pneumonia, and wants to send his son to America. Mr. Golden sets about the all but impossible task of finding the fare. Becky, knowing she is the only hope for little David, renounces the horse and takes the money instead. When David arrives, she enjoys him so much that she no longer thinks of horses.

Becky spends much of her life in a daydream of owning a horse. But when the chance coincides with others' desperate need, she sacrifices her dream to meet that need. Not only Jewish family life but the life of this family in particular is rendered so fully that it keeps the main plot from seeming melodramatic or sentimental.

Ages 10-12

Also available in:
Paperbound — *Becky's Horse*
Scholastic Book Services

Talking Book — *Becky's Horse*
Library of Congress

435

Madison, Winifred

Call Me Danica

Four Winds Press, 1977.
(203 pages)

IMMIGRANTS
  Belonging
  Canada
  Death: of father
  Job

Twelve-year-old Danica Pavelic has grown up in a quiet village in Croatia, Yugoslavia, where her father owns the village inn, renowned for its traditional country atmosphere and good food. In fact, all life in the village is modeled on the traditions of centuries, and Danica and her brother and sister are expected to value their heritage and to conduct themselves much as young people there have done for generations. But Danica wants to live the modern urban life she has heard about. Her dream is to move, like her aunt and uncle, to Vancouver, Canada, a city she imagines as beautiful and exciting. Her family will not hear of such talk. Vesna, a gypsy woman skilled in local medicines, sees in Danica a gift of healing and urges the girl to become her apprentice. Danica is willing, but suddenly life turns over: Papa dies of a ruptured appendix, and a new highway routes business away from the inn, forcing it to close. Then Uncle Ivo invites the family to Vancouver. Danica is elated. But life in the modern city proves disappointing. The family lives in a small basement apartment, and Mama works as a cook in a restaurant where she is cheated and abused. Longing to be a good Canadian, Danica is entrapped by her language, and is friendless and without money for up-to-date clothes. A job walking dogs for some wealthy people helps some, as does friendship with a local girl who wants to form a singing act with Danica. But one day good luck turns bad when Danica, pursuing a dog in her charge which her friend has inadvertently let run into the street, is struck by a car. Hospitalized, though not seriously injured, Danica renews her vow to study medicine. And she returns home to find that Mama has purchased a small restaurant of her own; soon the family moves to a house in a friendly neighborhood.

Danica herself tells this story of family crises in coping with a father's death and the mysteries and barriers of a new culture. Small wonder that the daughter's hold on her own dream is uncertain. A glossary of Croatian names and words is provided, for the story offers many descriptions of Croatian customs and village life.

Ages 10-13

Also available in:
No other form known

436

Madison, Winifred

The Genessee Queen

Delacorte Press, 1977.
(226 pages)

FANTASY FORMATION
  Divorce: of parents
  Parental: unreliability
  Separation from loved ones

Twelve-year-old Monica feels homeless. Her mother, Irina, separated from her violinist husband, Josef, has brought Monica and her little sister, Gabrielle, to an island near Vancouver, British Columbia, where Monica and Irina wait, hoping that Josef will come to take them back to California. Instead, Josef files for and obtains a divorce. Will he take Monica back all the same? She stops practicing the piano, on which she had hoped someday to accompany her father, but tells herself she will pick it up again when he does come. During the next two years Irina, a cultivated woman, fearing that her daughters will "grow up Islander," persuades Monica to apply for a full scholarship to a private girls' school in Vancouver. Sure enough, she wins it. But better still, Josef's chamber music trio comes to play at the Island Festival. Monica and Irina are overjoyed. Things seem to go well, but their joy is shattered when, at the brunch Irina has planned as a reunion, Josef introduces the young pianist of the trio as his fiancée. Angry and disillusioned, Monica accuses him of selfishness and rudeness. The third player of the trio, a young man, takes her aside and helps her see matters honestly: Josef has never wanted to take them back and Monica's certainty that he would has been nothing but intense fantasy. Knowing now that there is no longer a dream to count on, Monica and her mother lay plans to move from the island and to start making their own future.

A girl and her mother build their lives on a delusion and justify their poverty as the price of waiting for it to come true. A parallel to Monica's recognition of the truth behind their fantasy is her realization of the dull materialism behind the glittering facade of a rich boy friend and an appreciation of the worth of a school roommate who visits her. Some readers may find hard to believe the absolute hold their dream of reconciliation exerts over Monica and Irina, but in all other respects they are interesting, resourceful characters.

Ages 11 and up

Also available in:
Paperbound — *The Genessee Queen*
Dell Publishing Company, Inc.

M

437

Madison, Winifred

Getting Out

Follett Publishing Company, 1976.
(288 pages)

IDENTITY, SEARCH FOR
  Boy-girl relationships
  Maturation
  Prejudice: social class
  Talents: artistic

"Dead fast in Steadfast" is seventeen-year-old Maggie Dubois's opinion of her life in her Iowa hometown. She wants to get out. Nothing holds her there, no community or personal involvement. Maggie likes her mother and tolerates her older half sister, but she detests her stepfather, often drunk and always surly, and his son too. Then at a party Maggie helps cater, she meets and falls in love with a geologist, Richard Westcott, who is visiting Steadfast on a field trip. Though older than she, with a wife and family in California, Westcott is attracted to Maggie, but, contrary to her wish, he does not make love to her. Eventually, knowing she wants to go with him, he departs sooner than planned. Heartsick at first, Maggie comes to see that he does not love her. But he has insisted to her that Steadfast is "real," and this idea inspires her to begin a journal — partly for catharsis, partly from love of writing — describing her life "at a certain time in a certain place." And her writing leads to an unexpected opportunity to leave town. A wealthy spinster who has long liked Maggie offers to send her to an eastern college if, afterward, this girl will accept a position as her companion. Unwilling to mortgage her freedom, Maggie declines and takes a summer job waiting on tables. That summer she finds a theme to pull together her writings, but she is otherwise drifting until she learns of a writer's program at a nearby state university. She promptly sends off her writings along with an application.

A young woman finds her hometown no longer a cross but an inspiration as she learns to see it with detached yet interested precision — with a writer's eye. She learns to see it as others do: her best friend, for example, who had hoped to be a model in a large city but acquiesces in her father's demand that she marry early; or Lois, her half sister, a victim of a "caste" system, who leaves for a bigger city and a better job. Indeed, too many characters and sub-plots detract from the story of Maggie's growing up. The dialogue contains some profanity.

Ages 12 and up

Also available in:
Cassette for the Blind — *Getting Out*
Library of Congress

438

Madison, Winifred

Marinka, Katinka and Me (Susie)

Black/white illustrations by Miller Pope.
Bradbury Press, Inc., 1975.
(72 pages)

FRIENDSHIP: Best Friend
 Arguing

Susie, who is just entering fourth grade, has no friends. On the first day of school she meets two newcomers to her class — blond, curly-haired Marinka and red-haired Katinka. The three girls, who live in the same neighborhood, immediately become good friends. None of them has a father. Susie's father died three years earlier, Marinka's parents are divorced, and Katinka's father is in prison. The girls soon spend all their spare time together: Susie has a birthday and invites her new friends; Susie's dog has puppies and each girl gets one; the girls wear matching caps made by Katinka's mother; they even perform in a school play together. But one day Marinka and Katinka have an argument about which one was Susie's friend first. Katinka becomes angry and won't speak to the other two. When Susie is kind to Katinka, Marinka gets mad and so Marinka becomes the outsider. Finally, when Susie and Katinka go to Marinka's house and ask her to jump rope, the three are reunited. They can't even remember what caused the argument, and the friendship continues.

The argument that temporarily separates the girls is probably typical of fourth-grade disputes, as the girls' interests and activities are characteristic of their age group. The illustrations complement and supplement the text, which is written in Susie's first person.

Ages 7-10

Also available in:
No other form known

439

Maher, Ramona

Alice Yazzie's Year

Color illustrations by Stephen Gammell.
Coward, McCann & Geoghegan, Inc., 1977.
(46 pages)

NATIVE AMERICAN
  Grandparent: living in home of
  Grandparent: love for

Eleven-year-old Alice Yazzie lives on a Navajo reservation in the American Southwest, one mile from the school bus stop. Walking that mile every school day — her grandfather stoutly believes in education, even when it is no fun — she passes the ravaged Black Mountain, once a Navajo holy place. Alice hopes her grandfather will live to see the strip-miners, who have pillaged the mountain, depart. In March her class takes a six-day trip to California. There she sees Disneyland, a great female tennis player, Alcatraz, and flowered jeans, all for the first time. But back at home, she admits to her grandfather that she had missed him, missed fried bread, missed having someone to listen to her. But there is excitement in Navajo country, too. In May, Alice rides her horse in the annual rodeo, and afterwards pays a quarter to see a caged buffalo, which she likes almost as much as her pet coyote pup, Jimmy, named after a friend of Alice's who had died the previous June. Then summer is over, and Alice finds she has outgrown last year's school clothes. Halloween approaches, and school, especially sewing class, seems more fun than usual. For Halloween she dresses up as the famous tennis player in the tennis costume she has made for herself. Around Thanksgiving she is sent to the school principal's office for singing a song of her own composition called "We'd Be Glad to See Columbus Sail Away," but the principal, a Kiowa from Oklahoma, only smiles. The year is ending as Christmas nears, and Alice contemplates the Navajo symbols in a rug her grandmother once made. The girl resolves that she will learn to weave so that she too can express the beauty she sees around her.

Alice's twelfth year is described poetically in twelve sections, each titled with a month of the year in English and Navajo. From month to month, the tone and pacing of the text suggest that Alice's life moves with the rhythm of nature. The illustrations of her desert habitat are done in soft earth colors. The book ends with four pages of notes by the Director of Navajo Resources, Navajo Community College, Tsailie, Arizona, who explains the Navajo names of the months, and describes and authenticates briefly some of the Navajo customs and beliefs mentioned in the text.

Ages 9-12

Also available in:
No other form known

440

Majerus, Janet

Grandpa and Frank

J. B. Lippincott Co., 1976.
(192 pages) o.p.

GRANDPARENT: Living in Home of
GRANDPARENT: Love for
  Age: senility
  Determination

It is 1947, and twelve-year-old Sarah cannot recall a time when Grandpa and his son Frank have not quarreled about the farm. They quarreled in 1940, when, both of her parents dead in an accident, she first came to the farm, and seven years later they are still at it. Though weakened by a stroke, Grandpa, who owns the farm, retains the last word. But Frank spreads word that Grandpa has behaved strangely since the stroke and lays plans to have Grandpa declared mentally incompetent and committed to the County Home. Thus Frank can take over the farm. Knowing that Aunt Martha, Grandpa's unmarried sister, will not oppose Frank, Sarah decides to appeal to Aunt Clara's husband, Dr. Richard Hirschman, to vouch for Grandpa's sanity. But there are two obstacles: (1) Frank has made Clara unwelcome at the farm since she married a Jewish man, and (2) the Hirschmans live a journey away in Chicago. Sarah resolves to transport Grandpa to the city — somehow. She snares Joey Martin, thirteen, a boy she ordinarily ignores, and persuades him to fix up an old Model A truck. While Frank is busy showing a prize hog at the state fair, Sarah and Joey take the willing Grandpa on a "picnic" that turns into an almost 200-mile hazardous journey, taking two days. Once in Chicago, they learn the Hirschmans have gone to the farm in response to an urgent message that Sarah and Grandpa are missing. As the three start back, a Chicago policeman stops them for a traffic violation and takes them to the station. There another policeman, hearing Sarah's story, obtains their release and arranges to have her story publicized in a newspaper. Returned to the farm, Sarah sits in on a family conference which concludes little but that Grandpa is in the early stages of *senile dementia*. The real conclusion is Grandpa's: he grants Frank part interest in the farm. Uneasy about this arrangement, Sarah nonetheless leaves for a boarding school that fall. Seven months later, after receiving a letter from Joey that Frank has begun another campaign to portray a now much weaker Grandpa as crazy, Sarah returns home to take on Frank again.

In this first-person narrative, a girl tells of doing battle in behalf of her grandfather against his son, who has designs on the family farm. Her highly original strategy works, but the ending finds things coming more than full circle. The characters here and their idiosyncracies — Frank's obsession with hogs, Aunt Martha's with pickled peaches, Joey's with machines — provide amply for comic situations that ring true for the rural Midwest then and now. Profanity and some barnyard language crop up in the dialogue.

Ages 12 and up

Also available in:
Cassette for the Blind — *Grandpa and Frank*
Library of Congress

Paperbound — *Grandpa and Frank*
Pocket Books, Inc.

441

Mann, Peggy

There Are Two Kinds of Terrible

Doubleday & Company, Inc., 1977.
(132 pages)

DEATH: of Mother
MOURNING, STAGES OF
    Cancer
    Communication: parent-child
    Illnesses: terminal

To fall off your bike on the first day of summer vacation when you are about twelve is perfectly terrible, as Robbie Farley finds out. You miss tennis lessons, baseball, and swimming. But that autumn, his arm healed, Robbie learns that "there are two kinds of terrible." His mother, to whom he is extremely close, tells Robbie she must have a minor operation and will be in the hospital for a few days. That is bad enough. The boy sees little of his always-aloof father, and spends his days and evenings alone. But when his mother does not come home after two weeks, he becomes suspicious. His father seems sad and more remote than ever. Finally his father admits that Mother is dying of cancer. When Robbie is at last permitted to visit her, he cannot believe how thin, pale, and weak his beautiful young mother has become. She dies soon afterward. Devastated, son and father avoid each other, and Robbie feels hurt and angry that his father will not reach out to help him. Then he finds a scrapbook under his father's pillow containing photographs of his parents, photographs his father must be poring over privately. For the first time he glimpses the pain of his father's loss. He writes a note saying as much, and his father answers gratefully. When his father buys Robbie a set of drums, the boy decides that the two of them can make a life together after all.

This sad but not melodramatic first-person story portrays a child's loneliness and grief at the loss of a parent after a frightening illness. Robbie must take a leap toward growing up in order to make a family of himself and his father.

Ages 9-12

Also available in:
Paperbound — *There Are Two Kinds of Terrible*
Avon Books

442

Marshall, James

George and Martha — One Fine Day

Color illustrations by the author.
Houghton Mifflin Co., 1978.
(47 pages counted)

M

FRIENDSHIP: Meaning of
  Anxiety
  Consideration, meaning of
  Privacy, need for

George the hippopotamus is amazed to see his friend Martha, also a hippo, walking a tightrope, and says that he could never do that: he might fall. Right then he notices that Martha is losing her balance — and her confidence. He quickly restores both by complimenting her talent and skill, and soon she is walking smartly, just as before. In a second story Martha notices that George is trying to peek whenever she writes in her diary. George confesses that he does want to read the diary, and Martha says he should ask permission. When he does, Martha refuses it. In a third story George and Martha are eating lunch when George commences to tell an "icky" story. Martha asks him to stop, but George ignores her and finishes the story. That is when Martha tells an "icky" story of her own, causing George to feel queasy and turn green. In the fourth story Martha is working on her stamp collection when George frightens her. Martha vows she will scare George in return and he agrees that is only fair. But Martha says she will not scare him immediately. Thus George spends the day worrying and wondering when Martha will scare him — until she remarks that she has forgotten all about it. In the final story George and Martha spend the evening in an amusement park. They have a wonderful time — until Martha grows strangely quiet in the tunnel of love.

Suddenly she shouts "Boo," frightening George out of his wits. Then she tells him that she had not, after all, forgotten to scare him.

By observing how the main characters behave toward each other, the young reader can discern some of the qualities and actions that go into building a strong friendship. Since Martha decides in two of the stories to teach George a lesson, discussion might be started about alternative ways to reform a friend. The illustrations here are no less delightful than the witty text.

Ages 3-6

Also available in:
Paperbound — *George and Martha — One Fine Day*
Scholastic Book Services

443

Marshall, James

George and Martha Rise and Shine

Color illustrations by the author.
Houghton Mifflin Co., 1976.
(46 pages)

FRIENDSHIP: Best Friend

George and Martha are best of hippopotamus friends, but are not perfect. In two of the five stories in this book, George makes boasts: in one, that he can charm snakes; in the other, that he is not afraid of scary movies. But Martha sees how far he jumps at the sight of a stuffed snake and how white he turns at a scary movie. In two stories, Martha's curiosity embarrasses her: she does experiments with fleas and she disapproves of George's secret club. But the fleas make her itch and the club turns out to be The Martha Fan Club. In the remaining story, Martha pushes a sleepy and abed George, bed and all, to a picnic, which George then enjoys while Martha, exhausted, falls asleep.

These stories show how, when one friend is caught fibbing or being foolish, the other friend handles it in a considerate, often funny way. The drawings form a warm, integral part of the story. This book is one of the popular "George and Martha" series.

Ages 3-7

Also available in:
Paperbound — *George and Martha Rise and Shine*
Houghton Mifflin Co.

444

Marzollo, Jean

Close Your Eyes

Color illustrations by Susan Jeffers.
The Dial Press, Inc., 1978.
(30 pages counted)

BEDTIME
  Fear: of darkness
  Imagination

While getting his little boy ready for bed, a father suggests he imagine sleeping in an apple tree or on a ship, imagine playing with lambs or kittens, pretend to be floating on a cloud. He could imagine cuddling with a panda or watching lightning bugs. What the father has not noticed is that the child is not listening. He is asleep.

A brief, simple text and expressive illustrations tell very young readers the pleasures of fantasy while awaiting sleep — and, though it is not said, one way to handle a fear of the dark.

Ages 2-5

Also available in:
No other form known

445

Mathis, Sharon Bell

The Hundred Penny Box

Color illustrations by Leo and Diane Dillon.
The Viking Press, Inc., 1975.
(47 pages)

AGE: Respect for
  Afro-American
  Relatives: living in child's home

Young Michael loves his Great-great-aunt Dew very much, even though, at one hundred, she sometimes forgets and calls him John, his father's name. Michael likes to listen to her favorite record with her, and to hear her sing. But he especially likes her to tell stories of long ago, while he counts the pennies in her hundred-penny box. To Aunt Dew, each penny represents a year in her life, and the box where she keeps them all means everything to her. As she says, "Anybody takes my hundred penny box, takes me." But the over-tidy Ruth, Michael's mother, wants to burn Aunt Dew's big, scruffy penny box, and replace it with a smaller, prettier one. Michael, who knows how his aunt values the box, cannot understand such insensitivity. Ruth tries to tell Michael that Aunt Dew does not need just that box, but Michael knows she does. Angry with his mother, he begs his aunt to let him hide the box, but she will not let it out of her sight. Then Aunt Dew begins to sing her old gospel song again, and he knows she will not be persuaded. Michael respects her wishes.

Old age and its memories can change a person's perspective on life, as Michael learns. Ruth sees Dew as a childish old woman, partly because Ruth has not listened, as Michael has, partly because Dew forgets things. But at one hundred, one may have one's own idea of what is important to remember. Dew plainly states the source of the misunderstanding: "But me and Ruth can't talk like me and John talk — cause she don't know all what me and John know." This story, told mostly in dialogue, is beautifully written and the character of Aunt Dew skillfully developed.

Ages 8-10

Also available in:
Cassette for the Blind — *The Hundred Penny Box*
Library of Congress

Filmstrip — *The Hundred Penny Box*
Miller-Brody Productions

446

Matthews, Ellen

Getting Rid of Roger

Black/white illustrations by Pat Duffy.
The Westminster Press, 1978.
(96 pages)

SIBLING: Older
  Maturation
  Parent/Parents: single

Nine-year-old Chrissy is mortified at school by the antics of Roger, her six-year-old brother. She is a model student; he is a terror, frequently in need of discipline. At school she can try to ignore him (it does not work), even pretending not to be his sister; but at home he pesters her constantly. She complains to her mother, who points out that Roger is not only younger but different even from most other boys his age: he needs to mature, "to grow inside." Chrissy listens but does not understand, and Mother suggests that both children may need some growing inside. But Chrissy fears that Roger will even ruin her mother's chances to remarry. Divorced, the mother is seeing Mr. Davis, whom they all like. Indeed, the boy causes so much trouble when Mr.

Davis takes them out that Chrissy lies, saying he is adopted. Shamed anew to hear that Roger is to be held back in first grade, Chrissy tries to persuade her father to take him. But events conspire to draw the two children together. They spend a night alone when a snowstorm prevents Mother from getting home from work. Chrissy notices a classmate's little brother misbehaving in school. And it is to his sister that Roger turns for comfort after breaking two teeth in an accident. Chrissy even sees how much she depends on him for help and companionship. In the end she is inclined to say, "I won't get rid of him."

Unable to understand or tolerate her little brother, this youngster tries to ignore him or drive him away. Her mother's advice and her own awakening to the boy's worth gradually change her mind. Roger himself matures, though the book, mainly written from Chrissy's viewpoint, does not dwell on this. Neither child is now troubled by their parents' divorce. The single-parent household, visits to the father, and the mother's new suitor are presented as commonplace. Chrissy thinks her mother and father happier for divorcing.

Ages 8-10

Also available in:
No other form known

447

Mayer, Mercer

Just Me and My Dad

Color illustrations by the author.
Golden Press, 1977.
(24 pages counted)

PARENT/PARENTS: Respect for/Lack of Respect for

A little boy and his father go camping together. Once they are settled in their campsite, the boy sets about launching their canoe — and sinks it. Father and son go fishing, and the boy cooks their catch — which is stolen by a bear. Father and son dine on scrambled eggs. After dinner, the boy roundly frightens his father with ghost stories — but takes care to hug him so he'll feel better. Then they settle in their tent for a good night's sleep.

The illustrations of this little boy's first-person narrative add much to a very simple text. They show, for example, that the characters are whimsical, furry animals. But they show too how understated the child's account is: when, for instance, he tells us, "I pitched the tent," we see him ensnared hopelessly in ropes, poles, and canvas. Above all, they show his adoring admiration for his father, who is a model of patience throughout.

Ages 3-6

Also available in:
Paperbound — *Just Me and My Dad*
Western Publishers, Inc.

448

Mazer, Harry

The War on Villa Street: A Novel

Delacorte Press, 1978.
(182 pages)

ALCOHOLISM: of Father
GANGS: Being Bothered by
INFERIORITY, FEELINGS OF
  Child abuse
  Helping
  Mental retardation
  Perseverance
  Sports/Sportsmanship

Eighth grader Willis Pierce has been an outsider since as far back as he can remember. He is an only child whose family has moved around a lot, his mother working as a waitress to make up the money her alcoholic husband wastes on drink. Wherever they have lived Willis has been taunted by classmates about his quick-tempered father. Willis feels best when he is running — not in competition, just for the fun of it — and he runs wherever he goes. One day the school bully, Rabbit Slavin, after forcing Willis to rescue a handball from the roof of a building, invites Willis to join his gang, a gang that has always tormented the boy. For a fleeting moment, Willis is tempted: at last he would belong somewhere. But when he is told that the next meeting would be at his house and he would have to provide refreshments, he knows the idea is impossible. For he can never tell when his father will be "so out of it he couldn't even say hello . . . staggering around mumbling to himself . . . smelling of puke." Declining to join them, Willis knows he is also guaranteeing their enmity. One night, Mr. Pierce, drunk as usual, beats Willis until the boy can hardly breathe. It is not the first time. The next day, the man is horrified to see the bruises he has inflicted and swears he will never drink again. In fact, he does remain sober for several weeks, and things seem to be looking up. Willis is hired by Mr. Hayfoot to help his retarded son, Richard, train for the school's field day. What with Richard's progress and Mr. Hayfoot's praises for Willis's coaching — Willis admires Mr. Hayfoot greatly — Willis's self-confidence grows. Then one day, Willis is set upon and beaten by Slavin's gang. Tempted at first to quit everything, he resolves instead to continue as if nothing has happened — and,

encouraged by Mr. Hayfoot, he even enters the running events scheduled for the field day. The main contender is one of Slavin's henchmen. Field day arrives, and Richard excels at the broad jump. Willis loses his first race but is leading in the last yards of the half-mile when his drunken father staggers up to the track. The stunned boy slows, loses his lead, and comes in third. He takes his father home and his father becomes abusive. Willis strikes back, hitting his father again and again, then runs from the house. Stealing a ride in the back of a truck he travels for miles and seeks shelter for the night in an abandoned factory. Alone, he reviews the past weeks, considers the future, and decides to go home, but he is determined never again to live in fear of his father. He will be remembered for his speed, not his father's drunkenness.

This perceptive account shows a lonely, besieged, insecure young teenager gradually acquiring self-confidence and resolve to stand up to his alcoholic father and some threatening classmates. For the retarded boy he ends up coaching, Willis at first has only scorn, but as he patiently coaches him, Willis grows proud of Richard's progress and surprised and pleased with his own ability to help. Readers will believe in and identify with this resilient protagonist. Profanity crops up here and there in dialogue, always ringing true.

Ages 11-13

Also available in:
Paperbound — *The War on Villa Street: A Novel*
Dell Publishing Company, Inc.

M

449

Mazer, Norma Fox

Dear Bill, Remember Me? And Other Stories

Delacorte Press, 1976.
(195 pages)

ALCOHOLISM: of Father
DEPENDENCE/INDEPENDENCE
ILLNESSES: Terminal
SELF, ATTITUDE TOWARD: Confidence
    Boy-girl relationships: dating
    Death: attitude toward
    Family: extended
    Inferiority, feelings of
    Love, meaning of
    Parental: overprotection

In this collection of eight short stories, fifteen-year-old Jessie Granatstein, in the first story, experiences first love, yet strives to maintain her individuality. In the second story, fourteen-year-old Zoe Eberhardt, struggling to loosen the protective bonds linking her to mother, grandmother, and aunt, gains a measure of independence by disobeying a parental command. In the third story, Marylee Daniels discovers her mother's infidelity and says nothing. By remaining silent, Marylee judges herself a coward until she prevents a theft. Mimi Holtzer, a high school student in the fourth story, realizes that, despite her mother's hovering protection, she is moving "away from her mother, swimming toward her own life." In the fifth and title story, fifteen-year-old Kathy Kalman begins letter after letter to her sister's former boy friend, trying to confess her love for him. Story six deals with Chrissy's efforts to make a pleasant life for herself while living in a dilapidated trailer with an uncle and father who are alcoholics. The seventh story brings eighteen-year-old Louise, who has had two mastectomies and had a leg amputated, to the realization that she is dying. Although she is in constant pain and bloated from drugs, her mother and sister refuse to confirm her suspicion. When the truth is finally told, Louise feels at peace with herself and what is to come. Fifteen-year-old Zelzah, of the final story, travels from turn-of-the-century Poland to the United States, where she is to marry her cousin. When the groom marries another, Zelzah makes a satisfying life for herself with her training and career as a school teacher.

In this collection of short stories, eight young women come variously to grips with the need for independence, an uncertain self-confidence, paternal alcoholism, serious illness, maturation, and relationships with young men. The first, third, fifth, and sixth stories are first-person narratives. All eight are well written, their protagonists easy to know and care about. Though the name of the disease in the seventh story is not mentioned, it may be cancer.

Ages 12 and up

Also available in:
Cassette for the Blind — Dear Bill, Remember Me? And Other Stories
Library of Congress

Paperbound — Dear Bill, Remember Me? And Other Stories
Dell Publishing Company, Inc.

450

Meddaugh, Susan

Too Short Fred

Color illustrations by the author.
Houghton Mifflin Co., 1978.
(39 pages)

HEIGHT: Short
SELF, ATTITUDE TOWARD: Accepting
  Bully: being bothered by
  Pride/False pride
  Resourcefulness

Fred is so short that he hates going to dances, where all the girls are taller than he. But his height is of no importance when Isabel Robbins, the tallest girl in the class, shows him some new steps. Trying them out, Fred and Isabel are soon the center of the large, appreciative audience. Well then, Fred will try out for the school play, "The Princess and the Frog." It is the King he wants to play, but he is chosen to be the frog — and is hurt, thinking it is because he is short. His friend has to remind him that the Princess kisses the frog in the last act. But what is Fred to do about the school bully who takes away his lunch every day? Fred knows he cannot physically overpower the bully, and so he tricks him, driving him off forever with a worm-on-toast sandwich.

In these short stories, the short main character learns to live with his shortness. Tired of feeling inadequate, he learns all the good things he can do if he forgets about what he cannot change.

Ages 6-8

Also available in:
Braille — *Too Short Fred*
Library of Congress

451

Melton, David

A Boy Called Hopeless

Black/white illustrations by the author.
Independence Press, 1976.
(231 pages)

BRAIN INJURY
  Cooperation: in work
  Education: special
  Family: unity
  Helping
  Love, meaning of
  Perseverance
  Success

Seven-year-old M. J. Rodgers and her younger brother, Josh, are less than thrilled to learn that their mother is pregnant. When Jeremiah is born, the family pronounces him "perfect in every way." But as time passes, they notice that he seems too perfect: sleeping a great deal and crying very little. When Jeremiah cannot crawl by his first birthday, Mrs. Rodgers begins taking him to specialists. Three years later, the family concludes that, beyond the fact that Jeremiah is now walking, the specialists have done little good. At the county medical center, Jeremiah is diagnosed as mentally retarded, but Mrs. Rodgers refuses to accept that finding. While reading a book by a man named Glenn Doman, she sees hope for her son in a place in Philadelphia called The Institute for the Achievement of Human Potential. The family votes to vacation in Philadelphia so that Jeremiah can be tested at the Institute. There the boy is diagnosed as brain-injured and the family is trained in an intensive daily program to treat Jeremiah at home: for twelve hours each day Jeremiah is scheduled through body exercises — crawling, rolling, somersaulting, etc. — eye exercises, reading instruction, tactile

M

experiences, speech drill, and so forth. Volunteers are recruited from the neighborhood to keep up the hectic program. After a time, Jeremiah is showing gradual progress. When he returns to the Institute for a six-month checkup, the family is given a new program to train him in reading simple sentences, running, undressing himself, speaking in short sentences, and printing his name. Soon he is accomplishing these, and the family is told that with another year's training he will be well. When that time comes, Jeremiah enrolls in school.

A journal kept by Jeremiah's older sister tells this simple yet dramatic story of brain injury, its possible causes, and a detailed, concrete method of treating it. The book portrays candidly the emotional strain on the family and the love which holds the family. The Institute in Philadelphia is real and is headed by Glenn Doman, and the author, a parent of a brain-injured child, tells us that "the family in this story is a composite of many families." This powerful book educates without being didactic.

Ages 10 and up

Also available in:
Paperbound — *A Boy Called Hopeless*
Scholastic Book Services

452

Merriam, Eve

Unhurry Harry

Color illustrations by Gail Owens.
Four Winds Press, 1978.
(30 pages counted)

PATIENCE/IMPATIENCE
    Daydreaming

People are always telling young Harry to hurry up. He must hurry out of bed to get ready for school, hurry through breakfast before it gets cold, and hurry to get in line at school. In school, where he might like to think about things or just daydream occasionally, he must work fast, eat his lunch fast so he can play with his friends, and then work fast through the afternoon. Home again, he must hurry setting the table, eating, clearing the table, and getting ready for bed so that father can read him a story. Small wonder that when Harry is finally alone in bed, he takes his own sweet time to ponder and daydream.

What child has not felt rushed by adults when he or she would prefer to contemplate things as they are, or daydream things as they might be? Youngsters in Harry's story can find precious time to slow down in a hurry-up world. The illustrations here show Harry's fleeting daydreams when he is supposed to be doing something else.

Ages 5-8

Also available in:
No other form known

453

Meyer, Carolyn

C. C. Poindexter

Atheneum Publishers, 1978.
(208 pages)

DEPENDENCE/INDEPENDENCE
MATURATION
    Divorce: of parents
    Height: tall
    Parent/Parents: remarriage of

Almost sixteen years old, Cynthia Charlotte "C. C." Poindexter is, at six-feet one-inch tall, taller than the boys she knows and impatient for them to catch up. Although she lives with her mother, her divided loyalties to her recently divorced parents tug at her continually, while her forthright Aunt Charlotte, also divorced, wields ardent feminist arguments to counter the influence of C. C.'s traditionalist mother. C. C.'s best and perhaps only friend, Laura, who is bright and knows exactly what she wants, counsels her to find a sense of direction. To that end, C. C. considers living in a commune where Aunt Charlotte's son lives, where she imagines life must be more exciting. But Aunt Charlotte goes away for the summer before she can take C. C. to the commune on a visit; C. C. agrees to care for her Aunt's house so as to earn bus fare to visit the commune on her own. Laura promptly moves in to get away from *her* parents, recently separated. Meanwhile, C. C. and her younger sister, Allison, worry about the woman their father plans to marry. They do not think much of her and dislike her three children. In time, the girls resign themselves. They do not have to worry about their mother remarrying, but instead she launches a retail fabric business that barely survives the summer. But it rallies — as does C. C. when she begins to find success while working at her mother's store. When her cousin, home on a visit, describes primitive conditions at the commune, C. C. feels herself well out of that.

There is no clear plot to this story but much revelation of characters as they respond to events and each other. C. C. foregoes the commune; her aunt returns with a man, minus her feminist principles; and friend Laura discards her careful plans for the future to enter the commune herself. Readers will enjoy C. C.'s wry, first-person narrative as she discovers one truth after another about herself, her goals, and her relationships. Her maturation is naturally gradual, and on the way, readers will find much they recognize in C. C., in her sister, and in Laura.

Ages 12 and up

Also available in:
No other form known

454

Miles, Betty

All It Takes Is Practice
Alfred A. Knopf, Inc., 1976.
(101 pages)

FRIENDSHIP: Making Friends
   Marriage: interracial
   Prejudice: ethnic/racial
   Shyness

Stuart Wilson, a "smooth and dedicated" basketball player in the fifth grade, finds it easier to make left-handed shots than to make friends, his only close friend being Alison Henning, a neighbor he has known for years. When Peter Baker and his family move into this Kansas City suburb, Stu, on his parents' advice, tries his best to be friendly and is invited to Peter's home. Having met Mr. Baker, who is white, Stu is startled to find that Mrs. Baker is black. Embarrassed by his own surprise, Stu is relieved that it goes unnoticed. Soon the boys are talking happily, even discussing Peter's cultural heritage and the bigotry his older brother is meeting with among classmates. At home Stu excitedly informs his parents that Mrs. Baker is black and is relieved to see their surprise, which seems to excuse his own. The Wilsons are delighted that Stu has found a new friend, but worried, as well, that some people in town may cause trouble for the Bakers. Stu worries too, especially after Alison's father warns him to avoid Peter because "colored" are "better off with their own kind." All the same, Stu gets together with Peter after school, but the two are jumped and beaten by three teenage boys — Peter for being a "nigger" and Stuart for being a "nigger-lover." The bullies are frightened away by a passing motorist, who takes Peter and Stu to the latter's house. While the boys rest up, Mrs. Wilson calls the doctor and the Bakers, who come at once. Peter and Stu are pleased to see how well their parents get along. Back at school, the boys' injuries, though not severe, make them heroes. In time, Stu reflects on how easy it was for him to make friends with Peter. All he had to do was practice.

In this first-person narrative, a boy learns that making friends, like playing basketball, is a skill to be practiced, and from his understanding parents he gains the moral strength to challenge the bigotry directed toward a racially mixed family. If the Bakers and the Wilsons are families almost too good to be true, their perceptions of an ugly and volatile situation are realistic and instructive. A classroom discussion, held after Stu and Peter's beating, explores some causes of racial hostility as well as its effects.

Ages 9-12

Also available in:
Paperbound — *All It Takes Is Practice*
Dell Publishing Company, Inc.

455

Miles, Betty

Around and Around — Love

Black/white photographs from various sources.
Alfred A. Knopf, Inc., 1975.
(42 pages)

LOVE, MEANING OF

Love is everywhere to be seen every day. Sharing flowers with one's grandmother, smiling at a friend, talking over a disagreement, helping someone do something — all show love in action. Caring for pets, sharing a secret,

sometimes even being sad or angry — all may be part of loving. Love is part of everyone's life for as long as one lives.

This photographic picture book suggests how many different ways people express love for each other every day, and how love changes yet endures as people grow. Young children may profit from having the photographs explained by an adult. Probably all children and most adults will find people resembling themselves in these pictures, so various are the classes and ethnic groups depicted. The accompanying rhymed verse considers what love is and how it feels.

Ages 3-8

Also available in:
Paperbound — *Around and Around — Love*
Alfred A. Knopf, Inc.

456

Miles, Betty

Just the Beginning

Alfred A. Knopf, Inc., 1976.
(143 pages)

INFERIORITY, FEELINGS OF
  Embarrassment
  Maturation
  Parent/Parents: mother working outside home
  Pride/False pride
  Responsibility: accepting
  Sibling: rivalry

Thirteen-year-old Cathy Myers is embarrassed over the work her mother is undertaking, but dreads even more telling her parents of her two-day suspension from school; such a thing could never happen to her brilliant sister, Julia. Sure enough, her parents behave as though the whole family has been disgraced, and Julia deepens

Cathy's shame with a thoughtless remark for which she later apologizes. Adding insult to injury, Cathy's parents insist that she spend her two free days cleaning the house and helping her father paint his store. Only too eager to make amends, Cathy pitches in, and to her surprise discovers she likes the housework she had thought demeaning. Even more surprising to her, the clientele in the store treat her with a respect she is not used to. As they work, father tells daughter of some mischief he had made as a youngster and about his mixed feelings toward his more successful, financially secure older brother. That helps Cathy and her mixed feelings toward Julia. Back in school, Cathy finds that housework is not left behind: she must tell her more well-to-do friends that her mother plans to clean houses for extra income. Her friends are not put off — in fact, they seem a bit too understanding, and the girl's morale hits a new low. But life perks up when the Estys, a young couple Mrs. Myers cleans for, ask her — not Julia — to baby-sit. Cathy protests that she may not be up to the job but finally accepts, and the Estys like her so much they ask her again. When one night she calmly handles an emergency, the Estys ask her to go with them on vacation to Maine and look after the baby. This happy news comes on the same day as Julia's letter of acceptance from Yale. The family is as delighted by Cathy's news as by Julia's.

In this realistic first-person narrative, an adolescent feels better about some waywardness and resentment when she discovers that others have been through them, too. And given a chance to apply herself responsibly, she finds that her sister is not the only capable person in the world. With this new confidence, it is easier for her to accept her mother's commonplace job. These characters, in themselves and as a family, are thoroughly convincing.

Ages 10-12

Also available in:
Braille — *Just the Beginning*
Library of Congress

Paperbound — *Just the Beginning*
Avon Books

457

Miles, Betty

Looking On
Alfred A. Knopf, Inc., 1978.
(187 pages)

M

IDENTIFICATION WITH OTHERS: Adults
IDENTITY, SEARCH FOR
  Belonging
  Boy-girl relationships: dating
  Embarrassment
  Height: tall
  Maturation
  Responsibility: accepting
  Weight control: overweight

Fourteen-year-old Rosalie Hudnecker is tall, overweight, and self-conscious. Ever since her father abandoned the family eight years before, Rosalie has lived with her mother, Rita, a beautician, and, until recently, her older brother, Joe Pat, now married and living out of town. Rosalie has a close girl friend, a boy friend, and a regular baby-sitting job. Still, she is not really happy with herself or life. Her dissatisfaction finds some relief when a neighbor, Mrs. Cree, rents the trailer in her backyard to two newly married college students, Tony and Jill. At first, Rosalie watches only curiously while the pair move in, imagining how nice such privacy and independence must be. But when Tony comes over to introduce himself, Rosalie is taken with his beard and sophisticated manner. Suddenly she wants to become part of Tony and Jill's life, even if only in her daydreams. She becomes preoccupied with watching the couple's life day by day. She envies Jill her petite build, and watches out her window as the "perfect" couple play frisbee, go off to classes, have arguments, and prepare for a weekend party. Soon she is turning down invitations from her friends, just to watch Tony and Jill, just to muse on their perfect life together. Desperate to know more, she goes to the trailer one night uninvited while Tony and Jill are having a party. Though they are friendly and seem to like her, Rosalie feels out of place. Very well, she will spend more time with them — even if it means incurring the disapproval of her mother and friends, who have begun to notice how preoccupied she is. She has already missed a chance to work on the school play, turned down a date with her boy friend, and been late for a baby-sitting job, just to keep a date with Jill. But guilt about all this eats away at her until, one day, she irritably hits the child she baby-sits for. That does it. She apologizes to her friends, makes a date with her boy friend, goes on a diet, and cuts her hair. It is fun to talk to Jill, but for feeling easy and at home she will take her own friends and the interests they genuinely share.

Rosalie finds in her almost obsessive curiosity about Tony and Jill that getting married does not spell the end of change, dissatisfaction, or difficulty. She also realizes that she, and no one else, is responsible for directing her own life, but that to do that she must get along with her contemporaries as well as her admired elders, with whom she cannot, finally, have a great deal in common. This introspective story is eventful but leisurely in pace. Rosalie's maturing is natural, at times painful, and at last satisfying. Teenagers will identify with her desire to belong.

Ages 11-14

Also available in:
Paperbound — *Looking On*
Avon Books

Paperbound — *Looking On*
Dell Publishing Company, Inc.

458

Miles, Miska, pseud.

Aaron's Door

Black/white illustrations by Alan E. Cober.
Atlantic Monthly Press, 1977.
(46 pages)

ADOPTION: Feelings About
  Fear
  Loneliness
  Rejection

Aaron, who is about eight years old, and his younger sister, Deborah, had been placed in a children's home by their mother after their father moved out. When a couple adopts them, Deborah takes easily to their new parents, but Aaron, refusing to believe that they want him or love him, locks himself in his room. Safe behind the door, he thinks of all that has happened that could show he has nothing and can expect nothing. And he finds reasons for hating everyone: he hates Deborah for hugging the new parents and calling them Mom and Dad; he hates the new parents, especially the man who, though he has built him a model ship, Aaron is sure wants to beat him. Though they set food outside the door, the parents do not try to force the boy to come out. But he decides that not only the food but the gifts they have given him are meant as bait. So he refuses the food, smashes the model ship, and remains locked in his room through the night and the following day. When the father returns from work, he breaks in the door, picks

Aaron up and, holding him close, carries him toward the dinner table. Fearful of him, Aaron pushes away, and the father releases him. Yet the boy follows him to the table, thinking, "Maybe they want me."

Aaron's encompassing fear, loneliness, and shame are all too real: he is afraid to love or be loved and transforms all possibilities into threats. When the boy is forcibly freed from his own prison, the reader can feel that Aaron has been looking for just this — an active, physical proof of love.

Ages 5-9

Also available in:
No other form known

459

Milgram, Mary

Brothers Are All the Same

Black/white photographs by Rosmarie Hausherr.
E. P. Dutton & Company, Inc., 1978.
(31 pages counted)

ADOPTION: Interracial

Nina, a second grader, has a younger sister, Kim, and a younger brother, Joshie, who is adopted. Rodney, the boy next door, does not consider Joshie a real brother to Nina and Kim, because he did not come from a hospital and he was not even a baby: "He was walking around when they brought him home." Besides, Joshie does not look like Nina or Kim and is even a darker color. But then, Rodney thinks he knows everything — yet he cannot make treehouses or paper airplanes the way Nina and Kim do. And anyway, Nina's friend Joey has a little sister who came on an airplane and was walking around when they got her, too. Nor does she look like Joey's family. Rodney goes on thinking that adopted brothers are somehow fake until he sees that Joshie

does the funny, stupid things that all brothers do: Joshie gets into the bathtub with all his clothes on, even his shoes; he sprays the hose on Rodney, Nina, and Kim as they come home from school; he spills all the cookies. Brothers are all the same after all, Rodney finally agrees.

Taking a loving look at adopted siblings, this book can help children explain these brothers and sisters to their friends. The photographs capture the moments of joy and bafflement that younger brothers and sisters bring. This book has an added attraction: the girls are as active and inventive as the boys.

Ages 4-8

Also available in:
No other form known

460

Miller, Ruth White

The City Rose

McGraw-Hill Book Co., 1977.
(171 pages)

LONELINESS
ORPHAN
PREJUDICE: Ethnic/Racial
RELATIVES: Living in Home of
  Friendship: making friends
  School: transfer
  Shyness

Two weeks after her parents and sisters have died in a fire in their ghetto apartment, eleven-year-old Dee Bristol is en route from Detroit to North Carolina to live with her Aunt Lulu and Uncle George, whom she has never met. Dee, a quiet, shy child, is filled with grief and dread. Aunt Lulu welcomes her lovingly, but Uncle George is puzzlingly cold and distant. Overhearing an argument between the two, Dee learns that Uncle George wishes her gone because she reminds him of a girl named Wendy, whom Dee thinks must be a daughter who has died. In the newly integrated school she is sent to, Dee also meets everything from racist scorn to affectionate friendship. Most of all, she likes playing in the nearby woods, where she finds a little old abandoned church to explore. She asks Aunt Lulu about the church and the mystery of Wendy, and her aunt tells her of a black woman who married a cruel, good-for-nothing white man, how the ostracized couple moved into the vacant church and later had a child there. In time, the woman, abandoned by her husband, hung herself. The church was pronounced haunted. Uncle George and Aunt Lulu had raised the orphaned child — a little girl named Wendy — for nearly nine years. Then the spiteful father, Rick Martin, had returned and taken the child away with him, to punish Uncle George for reporting Martin's illegal still and whisky peddling. Uncle George has been grieving for her for a year. A few days after Dee's talk with Aunt Lulu, she meets a girl in the woods, who claims to be Wendy; she and her father have returned, she says. "Rick says if I let them know we are back he'll make sure I never see them again." Wendy knows Martin has a still hidden somewhere in the woods, and she suspects he has returned to operate it. The girls begin to meet daily to hunt for the still, searching the old church repeatedly. There Martin catches them one night. Dee runs home as fast as she can and tells the waiting Uncle George the whole story. Soon Wendy appears, beaten, her arm broken. Uncle George rushes her to the hospital. During the night, Dee sneaks back to the church, and this time finds a concealed stairway that leads her to the still — and to Martin, who ties her up in the basement and leaves. The next day, Uncle George finds her — the police, whom he had notified, have captured Martin. Wendy will be fine. Uncle George tells Dee he wants to adopt them both.

A city girl, shocked and grieved by the loss of her family, is sent to rural relatives and surroundings where people respond to her in unpredictable ways. Her uncle's remoteness begins as a mystery but is soon enmeshed in other mysteries, each of which she unravels. By the story's end, Dee has found a delightful new friend and won her uncle's love. Any child who has been uprooted will recognize Dee's feelings and applaud her determination.

Ages 11-13

Also available in:
Paperbound — *The City Rose*
Avon Books

461

Moe, Barbara

Pickles and Prunes

McGraw-Hill Book Co., 1976.
(122 pages)

DEATH: of Friend
FRIENDSHIP: Best Friend
  Communication: parent-child
  Illnesses: terminal
  Parent/Parents: single

Thirteen-year-old Anne Carter is suspicious of Dr. Elwood Abrams, the new medical director of Children's Hospital, where Anne's widowed mother, a nurse, has worked for six years. Anne's mother has been acting strange lately — practicing tennis, curling her hair — and has mentioned the name of Elwood Abrams so often that Anne is afraid he is her mother's boy friend. Anne, who will not permit any man to take her father's place, wants to scare Dr. Abrams away. Waiting for her mother one day at the hospital, Anne meets Laurie Burns, a patient about her own age, a bright, daring girl with a serious blood disease. The girls quickly become close friends, and Anne's daily visits keep Laurie from being bored. Then one day Laurie learns that her illness is incurable and tells Anne. The girls discuss it calmly, though inwardly each is upset. Meanwhile, Anne has met Dr. Abrams several times, and though she no longer dislikes the man, she continues to resent his relationship with her mother. Laurie is permanently discharged from the hospital and soon confides to Anne her relief that she and her parents have finally talked openly about her death. Though Laurie is much thinner and paler, she seems very much at peace. She and Anne plan that Anne will visit her at her grandfather's ranch on the way to summer camp. On the day Anne is to leave for camp, Dr. Abrams offers to drive her, and talks kindly and frankly of his interest in her mother. They stop to see Laurie but find her weak and quiet. The following Wednesday, Dr. Abrams returns to the camp and tells Anne that Laurie has died. The two talk briefly, and as he leaves, Anne gives him a big hug. She is sure he will make a fine stepfather.

Both Anne and Laurie must face Laurie's death, and Anne alone the prospect of having a new stepfather. Laurie decides to view death as the start of a new adventure. Both girls exhibit a mature kind of courage. This is a candid presentation of people coping with death. Although Laurie's blood disease is not named, the symptoms and treatment lead the reader to believe it is leukemia.

Ages 10-13

Also available in:
No other form known

462
Mohr, Nicholasa

In Nueva York
The Dial Press, Inc., 1977.
(192 pages)

NEIGHBORS/NEIGHBORHOOD
PUERTO RICAN-AMERICAN
  Friendship
  Homosexuality: female
  Homosexuality: male
  Loneliness
  Love, meaning of
  Poverty
  Stealing

By now, Old Mary has lived in New York almost forty years, having left behind in Puerto Rico a baby. Now William is coming to New York to be with her, and Old Mary is elated, for William is her hope for her old age. To Old Mary's astonishment, William turns out to be a dwarf. But his gentle kindness wins over the neighborhood, and he takes a job at the hub of the neighborhood, Rudi's luncheonette. There he becomes the best friend of Lali, Rudi's young wife, also recently come from Puerto Rico, lonely and homesick. Old Mary's American-born son, Federico, in New York on a visit, also takes a job at the luncheonette when Rudi breaks his leg. Federico and Lali become lovers. Already lovers are two young men in the neighborhood, Johnny and Sebastian. When Johnny is drafted (the time is the late 1960s), he marries a lesbian who will turn over his dependent's allowance to Sebastian — all this with the neighborhood's blessing. Soon Rudi recovers, and Federico plans to move on. Lali begs to go with him. She even takes money from Rudi's savings to buy a car, but Federico leaves one night without her. Lali is heartbroken; Rudi is furious at her deception. Still, life returns to normal, and Lali and William continue to be friends. When the luncheonette is robbed and Rudi shoots one of the thieves, the excitement of a new adventure dims the older ones.

This book is a collection of short stories about everyday life in a poor ethnic neighborhood on New York's Lower East Side. Each character's story is told separately, and Rudi's diner provides the point at which the characters intersect. These accounts combine wry humor and pathos in a persuasive way. Mature readers will probably take street language and passages on sex in stride, though others may not.

Ages 13 and up

Also available in:
Paperbound — *In Nueva York*
Dell Publishing Company, Inc.

463

Moncure, Jane Belk

A New Boy in Kindergarten

Color illustrations by Dan Siculan.
Childrens Press, Inc., 1976.
(32 pages counted)

BELONGING
SCHOOL: Transfer
  Friendship: making friends

David is entering a kindergarten class where he does not know anyone. He wants to play with the children using the playhouse, but no one invites him. In fact, he is ignored by everyone — until he shows a boy named Ron how to skip. After that, Ron and David work on puzzles together and, during recess, figure out a way to get some other children to share a make-believe boat they say is leaking: Ron and David simply "fix" it.

This book "stresses the need to belong and to help others feel that they belong," as the introduction tells us. It is one in a series on values, and the introduction offers suggestions for its use. The book's ending may strike an adult as pat — children often fail to fit into a new group this fast — but it may prompt useful discussion.

Ages 4-7

Also available in:
No other form known

464

Montgomery, Elizabeth Rider

The Mystery of the Boy Next Door

Color illustrations by Ethel Gold.
Garrard Publishing Co., 1978.
(48 pages)

DEAFNESS
FRIENDSHIP: Making Friends

Joe Gold, the new boy in the neighborhood, does not even turn around when May, Dick, and Bill call to him to come play ball. They begin without him, but accidentally hit the ball into his yard. Joe, busy playing with his dog, does not answer when they ask for the ball back. Rather, he glances up at his porch light and goes inside. Bill decides to get the ball himself, but Joe's big dog stops him. The three friends then go knock on the Gold's front door; no one answers. The next afternoon they try again. No answer, although they can see Joe inside watching television. The following afternoon, when Joe gets off his school bus, May approaches him and asks for the ball, but Joe does not seem to understand; he gestures, makes strange sounds, and runs into his house. While May is telling the other two what happened, Joe returns with the ball. He then signals for his dog to stop barking. Suddenly, May notices the American Manual Alphabet printed on Joe's T-shirt and realizes he is deaf. Mrs. Gold comes out and, like her son, touches her ears and lips, indicating she is also deaf. Now they know why no one had answered the door. This time when Joe is asked to play ball he "hears" the invitation and, after checking with his mother, goes off with his new friends.

This straightforward beginning reader shows some of the difficulties deaf children have in making friends. Because Joe cannot hear the invitation to play, he seems unfriendly. The three children are implausibly persistent in trying to make contact with him, but their open acceptance of his handicap and enthusiastic determination to learn the hand alphabet — shown on the last page — are entirely believable in young children. However idealized, this story may stimulate instructive discussions.

Ages 5-8

Also available in:
No other form known

465

Morey, Walter

Year of the Black Pony

E. P. Dutton & Company, Inc., 1976.
(152 pages)

FAMILY: Relationships
STEPPARENT: Father
  Animals: love for

In the early 1900s Ma and Pa Fellows and their children, Chris and Ellie, take up ranching in Oregon. Twelve-year-old Chris is troubled that Ma, stubborn and practical, so often loses patience with her impulsive husband, who himself so often slips off to carouse with

bad company in town. On one such day the sheriff comes to the ranch and tells Ma that Pa has provoked a fight with Frank Chase, whose punch has knocked him into the creek. Pa has drowned. Ma accepts the news with resignation. After Pa's funeral, Frank Chase apologizes to Ma, telling her he will do anything he can to help her and the children. After struggling alone, the hard-pressed widow remembers his words, and after long thought she confronts Mr. Chase with a blunt marriage proposal. By combining their ranches and resources, both can prosper; alone, she will lose everything. Feeling responsible for her husband's death, the stunned rancher reluctantly agrees. The children learn to love Frank, and Chris finds a bond with him the boy had never had with his father. Aloof, designedly a wife "in name only," Ma surprises Frank as both a resourceful homemaker and a successful rancher. Selling her own holdings, she buys more stock to add to Frank's herd. The prospering Frank presents Chris with a black pony the boy has been longing for. Wild and untrained, it seems to the boy's mother a useless investment, but with time and his customary gentleness, Frank breaks the black pony, and Chris becomes the envy of all the boys in the valley. At Christmastime, Ellie is assured of a teddy bear, Chris a .22 rifle. But just before Christmas, Ellie falls seriously ill. Chris, hoping to cheer her, rides his pony to town to get the teddy bear. Returning, the boy loses his way in a blizzard, but the black pony carries him safely home to the ranch. By morning, the pony is deathly sick with pneumonia. Through the following night, Frank, Ma, and the children nurse the animal, and on Christmas morning he rallies; he will live. Ellie, cheered by her teddy bear, also improves. Best of all, Ma has finally warmed to Frank. Chris is elated by the finest Christmas present ever: four people have become a family.

Ma's courageous proposal to a man she scarcely knows saves her home, her family, and their future. But she refuses to acknowledge the love of her exemplary husband until the two work side by side to save the black pony one child adores. In this poignant but fast-moving story, plot springs naturally from credible characters.

Ages 10-13

Also available in:
Braille — *Year of the Black Pony*
Library of Congress

Paperbound — *Year of the Black Pony*
Scholastic Book Services

466

Morrison, Bill

Louis James Hates School

Color illustrations by the author.
Houghton Mifflin Co., 1978.
(32 pages)

EDUCATION: Value of
　　School: Achievement/Underachievement
　　School: Truancy

Louis James hates school, skips it whenever possible, and fails to learn to read and spell. Finally he throws his books away altogether and goes to an employment office to seek a job. To get a good one, he says he can read and spell — and is given a job as a skywriter. After misspelling his first day's work, he is fired. Louis tells Mr. Klinker, the "head job-person" at the employment office, that flying does not agree with him, and is then given a job as an ambulance driver. Unable to read signs directing him to the hospital, he loses that job too. This time, he confesses to Mr. Klinker that he cannot read or spell. He is given jobs successively as a night watchman in a haunted house, as a spinach taster, as a snake snuggler, and as a tooth and fang brusher in the zoo. Disliking all of them, he tells Mr. Klinker he will return for a good job later, and rushes to retrieve his books from the trash.

In this funny and fanciful story, Louis finds that learning to read and spell is necessary if one is to find a good job. There is no moralizing here, and none needed.

Ages 5-7

Also available in:
Film — *Louis James Hates School*
Learning Corporation of America

467

Murphy, Barbara Beasley

No Place to Run

Bradbury Press, Inc., 1977.
(176 pages)

DELINQUENCY, JUVENILE
GUILT, FEELINGS OF

Billy Janssen and his family, small-town people, have lived in New York City only two years and in crowded, bustling Manhattan only two months. Now fifteen, Billy has recently become friends with "Milo the Cougar," a prankster whose latest enthusiasm is spray-painting graffiti on buildings, fences, anything. Their neighborhood being gang-controlled "turf," Milo must go afield to find surfaces. One night he leads Billy to a park, where they find a tramp lying on a bench, seemingly drunk. Milo gives Billy spray paint and orders him to paint the man. Billy is reluctant but agrees, and soon the two of them have coated the man with orange and green paint. When they paint his face, the tramp suddenly awakens and begins to cry. Ashamed of what he has done, Billy apologizes to him and runs away. Later that night the boy returns, but the tramp is not there. Billy stays in the park all night and in the morning, heavy with remorse, he vows he will never speak again. Thus he can guard his ugly secret and defy Milo as well. ("Then he wouldn't be saying 'yes' to him when he should have said 'no.'") At home Billy finds his parents frantic about his absence, more so when he will not speak. Several days later he hears that a tramp, painted orange and green has been found dead on a bench near the subway. He is sure that he and Milo are to blame. Billy now lives in silent despair, his only care to avoid Milo. But at a school art exhibit Milo finally catches up with him and insists that he see the canvas Milo has entered. There Billy sees a likeness of himself spray-painting a man lying on a park bench. Horrified, furious, Billy attacks Milo, but the principal stops the fight and suspends both boys. Later, Billy tells Milo of the tramp's death and accuses him of killing the man once Billy had gone. Milo denies it. That same day, his remorse intolerable, Billy confesses everything to Pastor Esselius, a friend of his parents. The pastor urges Billy to find out what actually happened to the tramp before declaring himself guilty. That night Milo calls and insists Billy meet him in an abandoned building. Billy takes a friend along and finds Milo hiding in the dark. He tries to talk sensibly with Milo, but Milo rushes at him with a paint can, accidentally hitting him in the eye with purple paint. Billy's friend hurries Billy off to a hospital and calls Billy's father. After a doctor treats the eye and tells him he will be fine, Billy goes home with Mr. Janssen, who comforts him and reports that Pastor Esselius has learned that the tramp died in a diabetic coma, not from the paint. Though Billy vows he must still be punished for his misdeed, he is relieved that the worst did not happen. Now he most wants his family.

Eager to learn about the street life of the big city, Billy allows himself to be goaded by an unprincipled friend into harming a defenseless stranger, ignoring his own decency and common sense. Billy is amazed to glimpse the capacity for evil in himself, finally confesses, and discovers he is somewhat less culpable than he thought. Without denying the boy's guilt, his family stands by him. There is ample street language in this candid portrayal of urban delinquency, and the passages on the painting of the tramp and Billy's eye injury could distress some readers.

Ages 12 and up

Also available in:
Paperbound — *No Place to Run*
Pocket Books, Inc.

468

Myers, Bernice

A Lost Horse

Color illustrations by the author.
Doubleday & Company, Inc., 1975.
(31 pages counted)

COMMUNICATION: Lack of
LOST, BEING

Imagine: a horse is lost in the city. Since he cannot talk and so ask for help like a lost child, he could wander around aimlessly for some time. His presence on the subway or in a department store would certainly attract attention, but no help. A man looking for the horse would probably be ignored or misled. The man and the horse could continue just missing each other, or even bump into each other without realizing it. Still, the horse might meet someone who knows how it feels to be lost, and that person would surely help the horse find his way home.

A horse lost in the city stands little chance of finding his way out without help. Perhaps the only person who can or will help him is someone who knows what it feels like to be lost. This humorous tale suggests how bewildering it is to know no one and be unable to explain yourself. Wonderfully silly drawings adorn this book, but the youngest readers may not understand the ironies in the text. Any readers who have ever been lost, however, will understand the horse's feelings. This book should start a good discussion of what to do if one gets lost.

Ages 4-7

Also available in:
No other form known

469

Myers, Walter Dean

Fast Sam, Cool Clyde, and Stuff

The Viking Press, Inc., 1975.
(190 pages)

FRIENDSHIP: Meaning of
MATURATION
   Afro-American
   Clubs
   Empathy

At twelve-and-a-half years old, Francis moves to 116th Street, a black neighborhood in New York. Two days later he meets a bunch of local children: Cool Clyde, Fast Sam, Gloria, and others. They accept him immediately and nickname him "Stuff." But Stuff has barely time to get acquainted when he and others land in jail for trying to do good: during a fight between Binky and Robin, Robin has bitten a piece off Binky's ear. The kids take Binky to the hospital to have the piece sewn back on, and the police come and arrest them all for fighting. Soon after that, Clyde's father dies. Times look rough. The crowd decides to form a club to help one another out in time of need — to "dig each other's problems." They call themselves "The 116th Street Good People." But before long they are in trouble again, this time falsely accused of being thieves after recovering a woman's stolen purse and preparing to return it. Luckily, a witness exonerates them. Throughout the school year the club sticks together — through parties, basketball games, and troubles with school and parents. Everyone feels especially close when, together, they save Carnation Charlie from a drug overdose. (Later Charlie is shot to death in an attempted store robbery.) When Sam and Clyde graduate from high school, the club begins gradually to dissolve. Eventually, time separates the Good People, but Stuff will always remember the happy, rewarding times they had together, and he knows the others will remember too.

Stuff's tender, funny first-person narrative recaptures his life of five years earlier and conveys the warmth and safety friendship provides. The discussion here of premarital sex is both frank and unexceptional, and the dialogue is at all times natural without being coarse. If anything, the plot and style may be thought prim by some readers.

Ages 11-14

Also available in:
Paperbound — *Fast Sam, Cool Clyde, and Stuff*
Avon Books

Talking Book — *Fast Sam, Cool Clyde, and Stuff*
Library of Congress

470

Myers, Walter Dean

It Ain't All for Nothin'

The Viking Press, Inc., 1978.
(217 pages)

CRIME/CRIMINALS
VALUES/VALUING: Moral/Ethical
  Afro-American
  Alcoholism: adolescent
  Decision making
  Deprivation, emotional
  Guilt, feelings of
  Honesty/Dishonesty
  Parental: unreliability

Black, twelve-year-old Tippy, whose mother died when he was born, has lived with his kind, proud, religious maternal grandmother all his life. Now she has been sent to a nursing home, and he is sent to live with Lonnie, his father, whom he has scarcely seen. The two live in dirt and clutter, their meals irregular, and Tippy sleeps on a cot. He mistrusts Lonnie's friends, Bubba and Stone, and he notices that Lonnie, despite having no job, always has enough cash for food and liquor. One evening Lonnie confides that he steals for a living. Then he forces Tippy to take part in a robbery. For days afterward, the boy is tormented by guilt. No Catholic, he nevertheless goes into a church one day, finds a priest, and begins to unburden himself. The priest asks him to wait and makes a telephone call which Tippy overhears. Frightened, the boy makes for home. When he tells Lonnie what he has done, Lonnie beats him. Soon Tippy is drinking to forget the trouble he is in. One day he becomes so belligerently drunk that he starts a fight

and blacks out. He comes to in the house of a man named Roland Sylvester, who, with his wife, shows genuine concern for Tippy, giving him their phone number and address, and telling him to reach them should he ever need help. When Lonnie, Bubba, and Stone involve him in an armed robbery, during which Bubba is wounded, concern for Bubba (and his own complicity should Bubba die) drives Tippy to brave a beating from Lonnie and Stone's drawn gun in order to make straight for Mr. Roland. He tells Mr. Roland all, and the police are called: Lonnie and Stone are arrested, and Bubba is taken to a hospital, where he later dies. Meanwhile, after eight days in a detention home, Tippy is cleared of all charges and becomes Mr. Roland's ward. Just before Lonnie is sent to the state prison, Tippy visits him in jail. Father and son promise to keep in touch, and Lonnie assures Tippy that he was right to go to Mr. Roland. As time passes, Tippy finds himself able to look forward to his father's release and a good life for both of them.

In this somber but melodramatic first-person narrative, Tippy learns that no one avoids choosing between right and wrong. With that knowledge, he begins to spurn the liquor he has started to depend on and tries to depend on his conscience. As a character, Tippy is perceptive and remarkably rounded, a basically honest young man caught and gradually strengthened by rapidly changing circumstances and events, all during one summer vacation. The other characters are well-realized and the black dialect will not prove difficult for readers unfamiliar with it.

Ages 11-13

Also available in:
Paperbound — It Ain't All for Nothin'
Avon Books

471

Nakatani, Chiyoko

My Teddy Bear

Translated from the Japanese.
Color illustrations by the author.
Thomas Y. Crowell Company, Inc., 1976.
(29 pages) o.p.

TRANSITIONAL OBJECTS: Toys

We meet a little boy and Teddy Bear, who are the best of friends. They often play together, sometimes fight, go on walks on fine days, and keep each other safe from the big dog next door. They share meals and get messy. Thanks to Mother, Teddy Bear gets a bath, which he enjoys; but he does not enjoy hanging by his ears from the clothesline to dry. When he is ready to play again, it is the boy's turn for a bath. The day over, they go to sleep together.

This first-person narration of a day in the life of a small boy and his stuffed companion is told in few words. The full-color paintings make this a book to be treasured.

Ages 2-5

Also available in:
No other form known

472

Nardine, Elisabeth

Daydreams and Night

Color photographs by Heinz Kluetmeier.
Raintree Publishers, Ltd., 1976.
(31 pages)

DAYDREAMING
NIGHTMARES

A little girl begins her first ballet class, but she is so absorbed in a daydream of being a famous dancer that she cannot pay attention to instructions. Another little girl, having spilled milk at the dinner table, immediately imagines running away from her scolding parents. But she is brought back to reality fast when ordered to clean up the mess. Still another child is snooted by her friends and imagines herself being just as unpleasant toward them. Fantasy is less fun when a young boy, reading a frightening story in bed, is later attacked in a nightmare by a shadowy creature. But the boy is rescued when his father wakes him. Lastly, a little girl constructs a cardboard airplane and dreams she is flying through the clouds.

Young children often try to escape unpleasant situations by daydreaming control over them. Such daydreams figure in most of these brief stories, along with pleasant daydreams for their own sakes. This book does not encourage daydreaming, although its photographs are lovely. Children may want to talk about their own daydreams and what the children in the book could have done instead.

Ages 4-7

Also available in:
No other form known

Naylor, Phyllis Reynolds

Walking Through the Dark

Atheneum Publishers, 1976.
(212 pages)

MATURATION
PRIDE/FALSE PRIDE
  Boy-girl relationships
  Empathy
  Poverty
  Values/Valuing: materialistic

Driving by shacks where victims of the Depression live, Mr. Wheeler admonishes his daughters — Ruth, fourteen, and Dawn, five — "This is hard times. Don't ever forget it." But the Depression has not yet hit the Wheelers, and Ruth cannot see why people like their former maid, the impoverished Annie Scoats, cannot help themselves. Determined the Depression will not prevent her from going on to college and a teaching career, Ruth feels hard times only in attracting Clyde, a boy in her class, about whom she constantly seeks advice from her best friend, Kitty, who has never had a boy friend. But early in 1932, Mr. Wheeler loses his job, and by the end of the year Ruth can no longer hide their poverty from Clyde or from herself. Not only is her father without work but her mother takes in laundry and rents out a room. Yet another casualty of the Depression is Ruth's infatuation with Clyde. After he backs out of a dance date with her to take a richer girl, Ruth recognizes he dated her only because he could not afford a richer girl. Rather than moon about losing him, Ruth attends the dance with Kitty and the Wheelers' young boarder — a date Ruth has arranged. Later, Ruth pleads with her father's former employer to give her father another job. Though turned down, she nonetheless knows she will,

like Annie, keep on going. Just how much she has changed Ruth understands when Annie comes to the house bringing vegetables. Divided between proudly sending her away and sincerely hugging her, Ruth winds up hugging her while pouring out her troubles. For Ruth, "the wall has gone, and she was so glad."

A self-absorbed girl intent on maintaining appearances gradually drops them and accepts her family's sudden poverty. A teacher helps her comprehend that the Depression's hardships, rather than being a waste of time, are chances to learn. Though the ending hardly promises that Ruth will realize her plans, the striking changes in her outlook, especially a newfound empathy, promise she will no longer settle for gentility and dreams. She has learned what is important to her.

Ages 12 and up

Also available in:
No other form known

474

Neigoff, Mike

Runner-Up

Black/white illustrations by Fred Irvin.
Albert Whitman & Co., 1975.
(128 pages)

INFERIORITY, FEELINGS OF
  Expectations
  Self-esteem
  Sports/Sportsmanship
  Talents: athletic

In junior high school Gary Gets feels the pressure of family and friends to take part in sports, but thinking himself a born loser, he resists. His best friend, Tubby, training for the track team, joins the coach in persuading Gary to try running "just for the fun of it." Gary proves to be a naturally gifted runner — but finding himself in a practice race one day, and, fearing he will lose, quits trying and comes in last. Tubby calls him a quitter. Bridling, Gary joins the track team to prove himself. But in his first meet he loses both events he enters, and again he wants to quit. The coach encourages him to stay on, to study running strategy and practice hard, and soon Gary can imagine himself a winner. He works like a Trojan. In the next meet he wins a race, and, crossing the finish line, sees his father in the stands cheering his proud, happy son.

Convinced he is a born loser, young Gary is persuaded by a loyal friend and a wise coach to "give winning a try." He learns that trying is more important than winning — and that wholehearted effort can make him a winner. The happy ending is achieved without falsifying situations or characters. This story provides appealing easy reading for the slow reader.

Ages 9-11

Also available in:
No other form known

475

Neigoff, Mike

Soccer Hero

Black/white illustrations by George Armstrong.
Albert Whitman & Co., 1976.
(128 pages)

LEADER/LEADERSHIP
  Glasses, wearing of
  Perseverance
  Resourcefulness
  Sports/Sportsmanship

Specs Conn is a popular fellow, a good student, a skillful organizer, and a third-rate athlete who yearns to excel at a sport, any sport. Thus when he comes across the relatively little-known game of soccer he decides to organize a soccer team at his junior high school. In this he faces all sorts of obstacles, but one by one he overcomes them: he finds players; he finds a teacher to sponsor them and a friend's grandfather, Mr. Suski, who knows the game cold, as the teacher does not. Specs even arranges for equipment, money, and a field to practice on. All is in readiness excepting Specs' own ability as a player. Worse than his awkwardness on the field is the skepticism he meets off it. Stas, his best friend and Mr. Suski's grandson, tells Specs that however good a manager he is, he is not a proficient player and will harm the team if he insists on playing. So Specs enlists Mr. Suski to teach him after practice and mornings before school, and Stas, a skilled player, joins them. On the day of their first game, the coach tells Specs he can play but broadly hints that another player is better. Would Specs withdraw? Instead of deciding, Specs puts the question to the team, and — with Stas speaking out strongly in his favor — they vote him in. Specs makes errors, but his teammates grin at them, as they do at their own. Games, Specs recognizes, are not only about winning, but also about having fun. By combining a trick play and a good kick, he manages to score the winning goal.

Here is a familiar situation with familiar characters: a boy who is a good student and a leader is too small and too unskilled to be the athlete he wants to be. The ending is no great surprise: by determined application of what he has, the boy scores the winning goal in a soccer match. What is unusual is that winning is seen here as by no means all-important; what one brings to a team may be much more than what one does during a game. This book would be a good choice for slow or reluctant readers, especially those who care about sports.

Ages 9-11

Also available in:
No other form known

476

Nelson, Mary Carroll

Michael Naranjo: The Story of an American Indian

Black/white photographs (collection).
Dillon Press, Inc., 1975.
(66 pages)

BLINDNESS
TALENTS: Artistic
  Courage, meaning of
  Native American

Michael Naranjo, a Pueblo Native American, moved with his family to Taos when he was a child, growing up among the customs of the Taos pueblo. After graduation from high school, Michael enters college, but after one semester finds it uninteresting. He also attends the Institute of American Indian Art but finds the rigid schedule too confining. Leaving the Institute, Michael makes another attempt at college but flunks out. He then works as an aide in the Bureau of Indian Affairs until he is drafted into the Army in June of 1967. After basic training, Michael is sent to Vietnam where, during combat, he is blinded by a grenade explosion. In an Army hospital, Michael begins fashioning clay figures. When he is released from the hospital, he continues with sculpture, now to be cast in bronze. Because of his talent and desire to succeed, he gains prominence as a sculptor, honored with an exhibition of his work in Washington, D.C. He also serves on the Arts Commission for the State of New Mexico. But Michael does not want to be known as a blind sculptor or an Indian sculptor. "Rather, he wants to be known simply as a sculptor," for he does not measure his work against that of the blind or Native Americans; he compares it with other sculptors'.

Much of this biography, one in a series concerning Native Americans, tells of Naranjo's childhood and youth, prior to his blindness. Another section describes the processes one of his figures goes through to become a completed bronze sculpture. We learn little of Naranjo's sense of his blindness until the closing chapter. Emphasis is placed, rather, on his successes and drive to succeed as a sculptor; in short, he does not dwell on his blindness and neither does this biography, which offers an example, not an inspiration. Its prose is awkward, often departs into geography, a description of customs, and history of the Southwest.

Ages 9-12

Also available in:
No other form known

477

Neville, Emily Cheney

Garden of Broken Glass

Delacorte Press, 1975.
(215 pages)

FRIENDSHIP: Making Friends
  Alcoholism: of mother
  Animals: love for
  Family: unity
  Ghetto
  Sibling: relationships
  Weight control: overweight

Summer in a poor part of St. Louis is long and hot, especially for thirteen-year-old Brian Moody. Brian is withdrawn and friendless, living with his divorced,

N

alcoholic mother, his younger brother, Andy, and older sister, Eve. To escape the quarrels and jealousies at home, Brian wanders the streets. There, he is noticed by three neighborhood teenagers — Fat Martha, whose heart is big, like the rest of her, Dwayne, who is regarded as a "cool dude," and Dwayne's hard-working girl friend, Melvita — and they try to bring him out of his loneliness. Dwayne and Martha invite him to their homes — to eat, to work, sometimes just to talk. Brian cannot imagine having so loving a home of his own so filled with love and caring as theirs are. But he makes friends with a dog he calls Slanty, who belongs to an old woman, and is soon spending every free minute with him. When Brian's mother collapses in a drunken stupor one night and is rushed to the hospital, the Moody children are drawn together for the first time, like a family. Brian's mother comes home, on medication to keep her from drinking, but one day breaks down, goes on a binge, and hits Brian. The boy runs from the house, finds Slanty, and makes plans to live on the old woman's back porch. It is Fat Martha who finds Brian and convinces him that running away will not fix anything. Brain returns home to find his mother a little hungover, but sober. He, Andy, and Eve see that the only way to improve their life is by working together as a family. Although the summer is nearly over, Brian, his family, and his new friends plan to make the most of what is left.

The author poignantly describes the loneliness and need for friendship of a boy who cannot connect with his mother, his family, or other children. In general, the lives of young people in a poor part of town are convincingly portrayed, not only through Brian (who is white) but through his new friends (who are black). Martha, for example, struggles to lose weight and Dwayne takes part in a prank that ends in burglary and the beating of an old woman. Some dialogue in this colorful story is written in Black English.

Ages 11-14

Also available in:
Paperbound — *Garden of Broken Glass*
Dell Publishing Company, Inc.

478

Newfield, Marcia

A Book for Jodan

Black/white illustrations by Diane de Groat.
Atheneum Publishers, 1975.
(41 pages)

DIVORCE: of Parents
 Separation from loved ones

The world of nine-year-old Jodan is happy, secure, and full of love. She and her father have long, grown-up conversations, and on Saturday mornings they make surprise-filled pancakes for her mother. Jodan helps her mother build bookshelves, and the two of them gather a leaf collection. The family goes on vacations, hikes, and picnics. Then Jodan's parents begin to argue — yelling at each other over things Jodan thinks are silly. When her parents decide to get a divorce, Jodan moves with her mother to California, and her father remains in Massachusetts. The moving is exciting, but Jodan desperately misses her father and their living together as a family. Although Jodan's mother tries to explain the separation, Jodan cannot see how a divorce will be good for anyone. At Easter Jodan visits her father. They go for walks, visit the zoo, have conversations, and just enjoy each other. When, all too soon, it is time for Jodan to go back to California, her father presents her with a surprise. It is a scrapbook full of pictures, souvenirs, bits of advice, and above all, love. Jodan realizes that although she is separated from her father, she is still deeply important to him.

This perceptively written story realistically portrays the troubles children and parents face in a divorce — separation, loneliness, anger, frustration, guilt, and self-doubt. The sensitively drawn black-and-white illustrations add to the vividness of the story.

Ages 8-12

Also available in:
No other form known

479

Nicholson, William G.

Pete Gray: One-Armed Major Leaguer

Color illustrations by Ray Abel.
Prentice-Hall, Inc., 1976.
(32 pages counted)

AMPUTEE
  Accidents: automobile
  Determination
  Sports/Sportsmanship
  Teasing

At the age of six, Pete Gray has a badly mangled forearm amputated after he falls from a truck. The time is the 1920s, his hometown a tough coal-mining town in Pennsylvania. Pete resents his disability and fumes at having to watch baseball games from the sidelines. He begins to practice hitting rocks with a stick, and before long is so good at it that he is working out with the other boys. By fourteen, he is the best hitter, runner, and fielder on his team. A semiprofessional player a few years later, he turns professional in 1942, a hero of handicapped youth all over the country; a three-year-old amputee travels from California to see Pete play and afterward leaps into his lap and kisses him. For a year, Pete plays in the major leagues with the St. Louis Browns, the acclaimed "One-Armed Wonder." But he is

forced to retire when pitchers discover his weakness: he cannot easily adjust his swing after the ball is thrown. Retired to his hometown, Pete remarks, "I never considered myself handicapped. All I ever wanted to do was play baseball."

Pete's determination to perfect his skill only becomes stronger when he is taunted while standing at the sidelines. Although shy, he advances his career to handle teammates, manager, and fans alike. He also keeps in touch with other handicapped people: his visits to the amputees in Walter Reed Hospital and elsewhere encourage them, and his story, more forceful in theme than in characterization, may well inspire readers.

Ages 9-12

Also available in:
Paperbound — *Pete Gray: One-Armed Major Leaguer*
Scholastic Book Services

480

Nolan, Madeena Spray

My Daddy Don't Go to Work

Black/white illustrations by Jim LaMarche.
Carolrhoda Books, Inc., 1978.
(31 pages counted)

FAMILY: Unity
  Afro-American
  Parent/Parents: unemployed

The father of a young black girl has been unable to find a job. Fortunately, her mother is employed, and certainly the little girl is glad to find her father at home when she herself gets home from school. But one afternoon she comes in to find her parents upset. It seems that Daddy is thinking of leaving home to seek work elsewhere. It is only after a family conference that he decides to stay, considering it more important for the family to stay together. Until he does find work, Daddy says he will stop worrying and become "the best cook there ever was."

The little girl tells this story of a strong, loving family tested both personally and financially by the father's unemployment. In the end, the father agrees for now to shoulder family domestic duties and be content with his wife's income so as to keep the family intact.

Ages 4-7

Also available in:
No other form known

481

Nöstlinger, Christine

Fly Away Home

Translated from the German by Anthea Bell.
Franklin Watts, Inc., 1975.
(134 pages) o.p.

COURAGE, MEANING OF
WAR
  Fear: of physical harm
  Grandparent: love for
  Maturation

Eight-year-old Christel Göth is used to war and bombs; it is her grandmother she worries about. Even in March, 1945, with the Russian Army daily advancing on Vienna, no one should shout, "To hell with Hitler," as Grandma does. Then Christel, her older sister, and her parents are bombed out of their apartment; her father, a wounded soldier, simply leaves the hospital to join them. They all move to a villa outside town, at the behest of the fleeing owner. Christel's grandparents remain in the city. Soon the widowed daughter-in-law of the villa's owner moves in with her two children. In this very unordinary setting, the children live ordinary wartime lives — looting, stealing, always in fear of what the Russians will do. But the Russians prove not so fearsome, and their commanding officer chooses the villa for his headquarters, extending his protection to all within. Mr. Göth comes out of hiding, and the Russians accept his story that his crippled legs have kept him out of the Army. The war simply passes on elsewhere, and other concerns come to occupy Christel's mind. Anxious to see her grandparents, she steals a ride from Cohn, a Russian cook, when he must travel to Vienna. Once there, Christel wishes she had never come. Her grandparents live a bitter, frightened existence. When Cohn fails to return, she must stay overnight. Her father, with no authorization but the commanding officer's paper permit, must spirit her back past the Russian checkpoints. Soon the Russian troops themselves move on, and the Göths, somewhat later, return to the city.

This story, based on the author's own experience, is a first-person narrative about how civilians survive in wartime. Of special interest is how different people behave differently in war, and how Christel herself changes her mind about them as she herself changes. This is a well-written book whose resolution is no more than a family's survival.

Ages 10-13

Also available in:
No other form known

482

Nöstlinger, Christine

Girl Missing: A Novel

Translated from the German.
Franklin Watts, Inc., 1976.
(139 pages)

SIBLING: Love for
    Communication: parent-child
    Honesty/Dishonesty
    Loneliness
    Loyalty
    Maturation
    Running away
    Stepparent: father

Erika Janda, twelve, lives in Vienna with her mother, Lotte, and her stepfather, Kurt — hence an aggregation of half-brothers, half-sisters, and unrelated grandparents — and her very beautiful fourteen-year-old sister, Ilse. Lotte is insensitive, domineering, given to sudden rages, and so inspires much of the constant bickering that plagues the family. Ilse is fed up and confides in Erika that she and a girl friend plan to run away to England to work as domestics. Sworn to secrecy, Erika watches her sister slip off in a car with a stranger. A few days later, she sees the friend with whom Ilse had supposedly gone to England. Knowing, now, that her sister has lied — she has always lied — and terrified that her sister may be in danger, she turns detective and questions all of Ilse's friends. Spotty, a younger boy with a crush on Ilse has followed her everywhere, and points out a local pub she was frequenting, accompanied by a man in a white leather coat. Afraid to investigate the pub alone, Erika is joined by Ali Babba, an eccentric friend of Spotty's who volunteers to spy with her. Jovial and intelligent, Ali Babba proves a good friend. From neighbors in the vicinity of the pub, he learns that Ilse has run off with Erwin, the twenty-two-year-old brother of the pub's landlord. Erika herself learns that the two have gone to Florence, Italy. Afraid to tell her parents for fear of being called an accomplice, Erika seeks her grandmother's help. Granny Janda comforts her and agrees to tell Lotte and Kurt herself. Shocked but relieved, mother and stepfather drive to Italy and retrieve Ilse, whom Erwin has abandoned after finding out how young she is. Back at home, Ilse continues to lie, telling Erika she had been offered a role in a film while in Italy, and plans to return.

In Erika's first-person narrative, a mystery is solved and Erika's love is sorely tried. Hurt by her sister's lies, she feels unloved in return, yet behaves loyally, and in doing so finds good friends to help her. She also glimpses lives happier than her own has been and learns to value clear-sighted honesty over deception and self-deception. This story has no pat ending and so remains true to its strong characterizations.

Ages 11 and up

Also available in:
No other form known

483

Numeroff, Laura Joffe

Amy for Short

Color illustrations by the author.
Macmillan Publishing Company, Inc., 1976.
(48 pages)

FRIENDSHIP: Best Friend
HEIGHT: Tall

Seven-year-old Amy is the tallest girl in her class, and her schoolmates call her "stringbean" and "treetops." Her very best friend is Mark, a classmate and the tallest boy. Amy and Mark spend lots of time together: they live on the same block, have matching sweaters and hats, and are saving money to buy a Captain Crunchy Secret Decoder Ring. But during summer vacation they are separated, and when Amy comes home in the fall, she finds she has grown an inch — an inch taller than Mark. Now he calls her "treetops," and Amy worries that he will not be her best friend anymore. Amy invites him to her eighth birthday party, but he declines because he has to pitch in an important baseball game against Waynie Phillips, the biggest boy in their grade. Disconsolate Amy wants to cancel the party. On the morning of the party, she is surprised to find a box on her doorstep, a box containing a Captain Crunchy Secret Decoder Ring and a message which, when decoded, says, "If it isn't too late, am I still invited? I can beat Waynie Phillips any old time. Mark."

This beginning reader treats with good humor the self-consciousness one girl feels about being tall. A child who is very sensitive about his or her height may not find this story comforting, but most readers will enjoy eavesdropping on Amy and Mark's lively friendship.

Ages 6-9

Also available in:
Paperbound — *Amy for Short*
Xerox Publishing Company

484

Numeroff, Laura Joffe

Phoebe Dexter Has Harriet Peterson's Sniffles

Color illustrations by the author.
Greenwillow Books, 1977.
(32 pages counted)

ILLNESSES: Being Ill
Imagination

Phoebe Dexter has a cold and must miss a day of kindergarten. That means missing a puppet show, oatmeal cookies with raisins, and "show and tell." Her mother suggests ways to pass the time, but Phoebe will not be comforted. At the peak of her boredom, she leaps out of bed, snatches off her socks, puts them on her ears, and assumes the identity of a floppy-eared dog. Her mother, grandmother, and father gladly go along with the act. The next morning Phoebe has no fever, feels much better, and goes off to school, short-eared and socks afoot.

Thoroughly disappointed, Phoebe uses her imaginative sense of humor to make the most of a boring day. Children who are ill may find this entertaining book a pleasant way to pass a little time.

Ages 4-7

Also available in:
No other form known

485

O'Dell, Scott

Kathleen, Please Come Home

Houghton Mifflin Co., 1978.
(196 pages)

DRUGS: Abuse of
RUNNING AWAY
VALUES/VALUING: Moral/Ethical
  Crime/Criminals
  Death: of fiancé/fiancée
  Dependence/Independence
  Judgment, effect of emotions on
  Peer relationships: peer pressures
  Pregnancy

When fifteen-year-old Kathy meets Sybil, a new girl at school, she is attracted by Sybil's glamour and boldness.

Sybil uses drugs — marijuana, uppers, downers, even heroin — and she teases the inexperienced Kathy for being "chicken." Still, she invites Kathy and two other girls to go into the California desert for a weekend camp-out, and while the others are getting high, Kathy goes for a walk. She meets a young Mexican named Ramón, who has illegally entered the United States from Mexico. Kathy speaks fluent Spanish and offers him a ride back to town, where she helps him find a place to live and takes him to Mr. Diaz, who finds him a job for a percentage of the wages. Kathy and Ramón fall in love, and Ramón proposes. When Kathy tells her mother, her mother quietly says she would like to think it over. Secretly, her mother notifies the immigration authorities, and Ramón and several other illegal immigrants are arrested and returned to Mexico. Kathy gives Mr. Diaz money to bring Ramón back, but the truck is ambushed by the authorities as it crosses the California line: Ramón is shot and dies a few days later. Kathy is grief-stricken. In time, she questions her mother about Ramón's capture, and her mother admits to giving Ramón's name to the authorities. She had felt Kathy too young to marry, especially someone she hardly knew. Kathy runs away to Tijuana with Sybil and there gets a waitress job. Her mother locates her there a few days later, but Kathy flees again, sticking with Sybil, earning her living by waitressing. She visits Ramón's family, who receive her warmly. By now Sybil has persuaded Kathy to try uppers and downers, even heroin. Then Kathy learns she is pregnant. Thrilled to be carrying Ramón's child, she is told by a doctor that she cannot take heroin. Sybil is going to another part of Mexico to buy a load of heroin to sell back in the States, but Kathy stays behind to avoid Sybil's influence. Later she does agree to drive back to California with her $10,000 worth of heroin in the car. On the way, there is a terrible accident, and Sybil is killed. Kathy is not seriously injured, but she loses the baby. She is also arrested for possession of some heroin that is found in her purse, and she is sent to Tranquility House, a detoxification facility. Confused and uncertain about what to do with herself, Kathy takes a job to pass the time. Months later, she has decided to go home and see her mother, but she finds their house sold and her mother gone in search of her daughter. Kathy and a girl friend go to the ocean and throw in the remaining heroin; it is washed out to sea.

In this thought-provoking story a teenage girl is so influenced by a peer that, in the name of friendship, she loses all common sense and all regard for the values she has grown up with. Though the story's open ending implies that she will go straight, the attraction to heroin is still with her. The book is written in three parts: the first and third from Kathy's diary, and the second is a first-person narrative by her mother.

Ages 12 and up

Also available in:
Braille — *Kathleen, Please Come Home*
Library of Congress

Cassette for the Blind — *Kathleen, Please Come Home*
Library of Congress

Paperbound — *Kathleen, Please Come Home*
Dell Publishing Company, Inc.

486

O'Dell, Scott

Zia

Houghton Mifflin Co., 1976.
(179 pages)

DETERMINATION
  Autonomy
  Change: resisting
  Mexican-American

It is the 19th century, and Zia Sandoval, fourteen, has come from her home far to the South to a California mission, where she hopes to set sail to the Island of the Blue Dolphins, to find an aunt who has lived there alone for eighteen years. When a longboat from a whaling ship washes ashore, Zia resolves to sail to the Island herself. She and her younger brother, Mando, make repairs and set off on the sixty-mile journey, but soon meet the whaling ship whose longboat they have taken. The boat is reclaimed and Zia and Mando are made captive and forced to work on the ship. They flee at night and row back to the mission, where soon Zia persuades a local hunter, Captain Nidever, to look for her Aunt Karana on his next hunting trip to Blue Dolphins. He decides to take along Father Vincent from the mission, to reassure Karana of their intentions. While the two are gone, some Indians who live at the mission, tired of white men's ways, decide to return to the place where they were born. Sympathetic, Zia helps them escape but stays behind to wait for her aunt. But the girl is questioned about the escape and thrown into prison, released only after Captain Nidever and Father Vincent return — with Karana, at last. But Zia's aunt speaks an unknown dialect, perhaps her own language, formed during years of living alone. Father Vincent coaxes back the runaway Indians, promising reform, and Karana too gets along at the mission at first, until a new priest takes charge and forbids her to sleep on the floor and to keep her dog indoors. Karana moves to a cave, falls ill, and dies — of homesickness, Zia is sure. With the new priest in charge, the Indians are again plotting an escape. Zia knows now that mission life is not for her. In broad daylight, she walks out by the front gate and heads for her home, far to the South.

Zia's strong will and her faith in herself and her origins respond alike to an aunt she has never seen, to that same aunt's misery when she cannot live where and how she likes, and to the plight of some Indians living unwillingly as white men dictate. Eventually Zia must set off to live her own way in her own home place. This story, told in Zia's first person, is a sequel to *The Island of the Blue Dolphins*.

Ages 10 and up

Also available in:
Braille — *Zia*
Library of Congress

Cassette for the Blind — *Zia*
Library of Congress

Paperbound — *Zia*
Dell Publishing Company, Inc.

Talking Book — *Zia*
Library of Congress

487

O'Hanlon, Jacklyn

Fair Game

The Dial Press, Inc., 1977.
(94 pages)

FEAR: of Physical Harm
  Alcoholism: adult
  Communication: parent-child
  Stepparent: father

Fourteen-year-old Denise and her twelve-year-old sister, Leaf, live with their mother, Janice, an artist, and the mother's new husband of four months, Ray. All Denise knows of her father is overheard whispers that he is in a sanitarium. Without knowing why, Denise has always vaguely disliked Ray. One day when she is preparing to shower, Ray suddenly opens the bathroom door, leers at her for a few moments, and is gone. Denise is too shocked and repelled to act. Later, when Ray begs her not to tell anyone, claiming to have had too much to drink, the issue is further beclouded. From then on, Denise's mind is in tumult. She is nauseated by

Ray's presence. At school her usually good grades fall, and her teachers note her inattentiveness. Worse yet, her best friend, Diane, begins to avoid her. Has she inherited whatever hospitalized her father? Did she only imagine what her stepfather did? No less puzzled than her teachers, neither her mother, her sister, nor her aunt can discover what is on her mind. And her mother seems not to see Ray's heavy drinking and the effects upon others of his erratic behavior. At wit's end, Denise steals a book on alcoholism, and sees at once that Ray is an alcoholic. When she confronts her mother, she finds that Janice is aware of Ray's drunkenness but ignores it to keep the peace. Encouraged that her mother sees at least this much, she can buckle down to her schoolwork again and try to rescue her grades. She also asks Diane straight out why she has been avoiding her. To Denise's horror, Diane explains that after the last time they had seen each other, Ray had forced her into his car, driven her to his office, and made advances to her. Now Denise knows she must tell her mother the truth. But before she can take Janice aside, Leaf is left alone in the house with Ray. At the library, Denise receives an hysterical phone call from her sister and rushes home to protect her. Janice, too, returns — to find Ray drunk and the two girls fear-stricken. The secret out, Ray packs up and goes to live with relatives. Denise learns more about her father: he had responded to his stressful job by taking drugs to calm down. He had an auto accident after taking a drug dose and had never been the same. Finally it was necessary to place him in a sanitarium, where he has remained, not even recognizing his wife. This knowledge lays to rest Denise's fear that she might inherit his illness. Afraid no more, a more mature Denise picks up her life where she had left off.

This is a credible first-person narrative about people ignoring danger signals to avoid unpleasantness. Until she can be honest with her family, Denise is unable to live or work normally. Denial of the facts on both sides nearly destroys what had formerly been a solid mother-daughter relationship.

Ages 11-13

Also available in:
Paperbound — *Fair Game*
Dell Publishing Company, Inc.

488

O'Hanlon, Jacklyn

The Other Michael

The Dial Press, Inc., 1977.
(109 pages)

IDENTITY, SEARCH FOR
LONELINESS
   Grandparent: love for
   Rejection: parental
   Talents: musical

Michael, about eleven, is a lonely, quiet boy who likes music. His parents quarrel often — his father stiff, demanding, angry; his mother busy, impersonal — and show Michael scant warmth or affection. Father's business requires that the family move to Greenville, where Michael's maternal grandmother lives. In fact they move right next door to her, and right away Father interferes with a budding friendship. Grandmother, a loving free spirit, is a painter, and her modern house is filled with plants, paintings, and friends. She and Michael love one another on sight; Father thinks her eccentric. She encourages the boy's interest in music, giving him a silver flute; Father will permit him no music. Michael plays his guitar at Grandma's, his flute at the river bank; Father enrolls him in Little League baseball. But Michael reports to the team each Saturday, then leaves to practice his flute. When father discovers the deception, he forbids Michael to see Grandma at all. Meanwhile, the old lady has been suffering dizzy spells and hallucinations. When she reports seeing an elephant in her yard, Father begins arrangements to send her to an institution. But before he can do so, Grandma has left on an "extended vacation." Michael is grieved to lose his only friend, but determines to pursue his music in secret. One day he receives a gift in the mail from her, a small carved elephant. The gift cheers him so much that he takes out his flute within Father's earshot and commences to play.

This is the touching story of a lonely boy's struggle to find and maintain his own identity in the teeth of terrible parental coldness. It is the mutual love between himself and his grandmother that inspires and sustains his self-confidence.

Ages 10-12

Also available in:
No other form known

489

Ominsky, Elaine

Jon O.: A Special Boy

Black/white photographs by Dennis Simonetti.
Prentice-Hall, Inc., 1977.
(30 pages counted)

DOWN'S SYNDROME

Jon O. was born to a life filled with scary words: "Down's Syndrome," "retarded," "not normal." Reality is less scary. True, Jon has taken longer learning to walk and talk than other babies, but he has learned and is very proud of it. Now he attends school, learning how to color and listening to stories. At times he forgets which color is which, and he is slow to comprehend; but he is no less eager. When other children ask why he is different, his teacher tells them Jon is retarded and explains what this means: "Jon O. has a special problem. He will not grow the way most children do. He will not be able to learn the way most children do. He is retarded." But nothing prevents Jon from doing a lot that other children do, or from playing with his brothers. Jon is aware he is different and is sometimes unhappy about it. But always he helps his family and friends, and they help him. He is important to them.

Here is a book that describes mental retardation and Down's Syndrome in simple terms for beginning readers. It shows what a young boy with Down's Syndrome can and cannot do in daily life. The candid photos are helpful. But the author's placid tone may lead readers to assume that retardation can be overcome, and thus mislead them.

Ages 4-7

Also available in:
No other form known

490

Orgel, Doris

A Certain Magic

The Dial Press, Inc., 1976.
(176 pages)

FEAR: of the Unknown
MAGICAL THINKING
REFUGEES
 Foster home
 Guilt, feelings of
 Relatives

A diary her Aunt Trudl kept in 1938 draws eleven-year-old Jenny into a fearful world of a lonely young Jewish refugee. Having discovered the book by accident in her aunt's apartment, Jenny secretly follows Trudl's account of having been sent for safekeeping to an English foster home by her Viennese parents, and there being teased and taunted by Pam and Mark, her foster sister and foster brother. To retaliate, Trudl wishes on an emerald ring, a family heirloom said to have magical powers. First she wishes for ownership of dolls belonging to the two; not receiving them, she wishes that ill befall the children. Later she regrets her wishes and tries to destroy the ring. Here Jenny's reading is interrupted by a long-awaited family trip to London. Deeply troubled by the diary, which lays a curse on strangers who read it, Jenny goes with her father to visit the English village where Trudl stayed. Just like young Trudl, Jenny is sure that the magic is turning against her when they find the house torn down and cannot trace the foster family. Remembering that Pam liked to ride horses, Jenny finds her at a riding stable, where Pam and her husband live. Jenny's worst fear — that the ring had somehow killed Pam — vanishes. Pam, who had broken a promise to give Trudl a doll, now gives the doll to Jenny. Inside it, just as she thought, Jenny finds the emerald. But she fears the jewel will bring evil with it. Back in New York, Aunt Trudl dispels the girl's fears for good by allowing her to read the last few pages of the diary. In them, Jenny finds that Trudl's parents arrive from Austria to take her to America, and the fears that beset Trudl end too.

The diary of a girl who believes that magic solves her difficulties convinces an impressionable girl in quite different circumstances that a similar magic works on her. Guilt at reading her aunt's diary compounds the girl's confusion and prevents her from discussing it with either her aunt or her parents. Told partly from Jenny's viewpoint, partly from young Trudl's (in the diary), this story realistically conveys both girls' odd feeling that something outside the normal is at work in their lives. In fact, as we see, circumstances and coincidences are at work upon lively imaginations.

Ages 11-13

Also available in:
Cassette for the Blind — *A Certain Magic*
Library of Congress

Paperbound — *A Certain Magic*
Dell Publishing Company, Inc.

P

491

Palay, Steven

I Love My Grandma

Color photographs by Brent Jones.
Raintree Publishers, Ltd., 1977.
(30 pages)

GRANDPARENT: Love for
  Grandparent: living in child's home

An unnamed young girl lives with her parents and grandmother, but when her parents are out during the day, the grandmother takes care of her. The grandmother picks her up at school and takes her to the playground to play. Sometimes they visit Mrs. Daniels, who has a nice garden and often gives them flowers. Other times, they'll go to the park with Grandma's friend Mr. James and his dog, Alf. The girl says, "I can tell my grandma anything. She always understands. I love my grandma, and she loves me."

The little girl has fun with her grandmother and learns from her, too. They understand and love each other. The girl feels at ease as well with her grandmother's older friends. The full-page photographs help describe this as a mutually satisfying relationship.

Also available in:
No other form known

492

Pape, Donna Lugg

Snowman for Sale

Color illustrations by Raymond Burns.
Garrard Publishing Co., 1977.
(40 pages)

RESOURCEFULNESS
  Sibling: youngest

Terry and Jerry, Todd's older sister and brother, are building a large snowman in the hope of selling it to earn money for a present for their mother. Little Todd wants to help, but they tell him he is too little. Since he cannot work with his brother and sister, Todd decides to build and sell small snow people. Terry and Jerry have no luck selling their snowman, but many people buy Todd's more portable people to keep in their freezers. Noticing how much money Todd has made, Terry and Jerry warm up to Todd, inviting him to play. He refuses, but tells them that they may pull him on the sled to buy a present.

In this beginning reader, two older children snub their brother as being too young to be of use. Seeing him more resourceful — and successful — than themselves, they court his friendship, but find they cannot bribe his pride. This book could seem just right to any family youngest who has not quite "belonged" in his siblings' activities.

Ages 5-7

Also available in:
No other form known

493

Paterson, Katherine Womeldorf

Bridge to Terabithia

Black/white illustrations by Donna Diamond.
Thomas Y. Crowell Company, Inc., 1977.
(128 pages)

DEATH: of Friend
FRIENDSHIP: Best Friend
  Imagination
  Ostracism
  Prejudice: social class
  Sibling: relationships

Fifth grader Jesse Aarons, a quiet, introspective farm boy in a rural community, plans on being the fastest runner in his school, but on the first day of the new term, he is bested by a girl — his new neighbor and classmate, Leslie Burke. Shunned by the class because she wears jeans to school and sports a short haircut, Leslie tries to make friends with Jesse, but he avoids her at first. Soon, though, they are riding home on the bus together, Leslie confiding that she and her parents moved to the country to escape the pressures of city living. Several days later while they are playing, Leslie suggests they stake out a secret place in the woods behind her house. Leslie names their magical kingdom Terabithia. They must enter it by swinging on an old rope swing across a dry creek bed and into the woods. They build a castle in Terabithia from old boards; Leslie teaches Jesse how to speak and act like a ruler, and tells him stories from the many books she has read. The two become close friends. Jesse helps Leslie and her father fix up their old farm house; Jesse persuades Leslie to put aside her own sense of isolation to befriend an unhappy, belligerent seventh-grade girl; and Leslie, whose parents do not attend church, goes with Jesse and his family to church on Easter Sunday. During Easter vacation it rains heavily, and the creek bed bordering Terabithia becomes a deep, fast waterway. Leslie swings fearlessly across, but Jesse follows cautiously. In the following days the rain continues and Jesse's fear mounts with each crossing, until he privately decides they should give up their kingdom for a time. Then his music teacher invites him to spend the day with her in Washington, D.C., touring the National Gallery. Jesse returns home full of news after a wonderful day — and is told that Leslie is dead. The rope has broken over the stream and she has drowned. Dazed, angry, grieving, and feeling somehow responsible, Jesse withdraws for several days. One morning he returns to Terabithia. Crossing the creek on a fallen branch, he makes a funeral wreath for his departed queen and places it in their sacred grove. He hears his younger sister, May Belle, crying for help, and rescues her from the branch on which she has tried to follow him. A few days later he leads her into Terabithia across a bridge he has built and crowns her its new queen.

A friendship flourishes between a country boy and a girl from the city as each opens new experiences to the other. Leslie introduces Jesse to the world of imagination and books, and Jesse teaches Leslie compassion and regard for other people. As the only boy in his family Jesse has learned to live with others by avoiding conflicts; Leslie inspires him to assert himself. The girl's death is as much of a shock to the reader as it is to Jesse. His recovery, while fairly abrupt, shows the legacy of strength and resourcefulness Leslie has left him. This beautifully written, moving story won the 1978 Newbery Award.

Ages 9-12

Also available in:
Cassette for the Blind — *Bridge to Terabithia*
Library of Congress

Filmstrip — *Bridge to Terabithia*
Miller-Brody Productions

Paperbound — *Bridge to Terabithia*
Avon Books

Record — *Bridge to Terabithia*
Miller-Brody Productions

494
Paterson, Katherine Womeldorf

The Great Gilly Hopkins
Thomas Y. Crowell Company, Inc., 1978.
(148 pages)

P

FOSTER HOME
  Deprivation, emotional
  Hostility
  Love, meaning of

At eleven, Gilly Hopkins scarcely remembers her mother, who left her eight years earlier. But she is obsessed to rejoin a lovely, gracious mother she imagines. Now at her third foster home in less than three years, the ramshackle house of Maime Trotter (called simply "Trotter"), Gilly confidently sets out to establish supremacy over her latest foster parent, over seven-year-old William Ernest (another foster child), and over Mr. Randolph, an aged, blind man who lives next door. She thinks herself too tough and too clever for them. But Trotter effortlessly handles her worst sallies as though her great bulk absorbed them. Gilly then replies to an almost impersonal postcard from her mother that she must be rescued from mistreatment. Aware of her mother's long inattention, however, she steals money from Mr. Randolph and Trotter and buys a transcontinental bus ticket for San Francisco, where her mother lives. The police, alerted by a clerk, stop her. Trotter refuses to press charges for theft but lays down her own law — return the money and help William Ernest with his schoolwork. Gradually Gilly realizes Trotter's goodness to her, to the boy, to Mr. Randolph, and comes to love her foster family. Then out of the blue arrives the girl's unknown maternal grandmother, encouraged by her estranged daughter to take Gilly home to Virginia. Once there, Gilly has a visit from her mother, and a final disillusionment — her mother will not take her back. Heartbroken, the girl begs Trotter on the phone to let her return. But they lovingly agree that it is her grandmother who both loves and needs her, who will otherwise be all alone.

Each time Gilly has offered love, she has seen the other person withdraw. Better to square off against the world reserving "soft and stupid" feelings for an unknown mother far away. Yet Gilly's separations from those she does come to love do not break her. Recognizing that "life has no happy endings," as Trotter points out, she begins again, without fantasies. The theme of this book is serious; the telling and the characters are richly humorous. Gilly uses mild profanity for pungency — and to annoy people.

Ages 10-13

Also available in:
Cassette for the Blind — *The Great Gilly Hopkins*
Library of Congress

Filmstrip — *The Great Gilly Hopkins*
Miller-Brody Productions

Paperbound — *The Great Gilly Hopkins*
Avon Books

Record — *The Great Gilly Hopkins*
Miller-Brody Productions

495
Paulsen, Gary

The Foxman

Thomas Nelson, Inc., 1977.
(125 pages)

MATURATION
  Death: of friend
  Friendship: meaning of
  Nature: respect for
  Relatives: living in home of

Abused by alcoholic parents, an unnamed fifteen-year-old boy is remanded to the custody of his Uncle Harvey and family, who live in the Minnesota north woods. As the summer and fall pass, the boy almost feels like a member of the family, especially with his teenage cousin, Harry. Often at night they all sit around the wood-burning stove, listening to the war stories of Harvey's father and uncle. The old men find humor in every tale, but the boy sees nothing funny in discomfort and death. One day, while tracking deep into the woods on a weekend hunting trip, the young cousins seek shelter from an approaching snowstorm and come upon an isolated cabin inhabited by a man with a frighteningly deformed face. Wearing a mask to put the boys more at ease, the Foxman, as they come to think of him, shelters the two until the storm passes. Returning home, they tell no one of the recluse — sensing that he does not want to be found. Alone, the protagonist makes a return visit to the Foxman, and senses the pleasure this second visit brings. The boy and the man speak of science and how it "kills beauty," of war and how it destroys life. When the boy expresses his distaste for the war stories he has heard, the Foxman, his own face a casualty of battle, excuses the old men for "trying to find some use in all that waste." The boy returns again and again, learning how to hunt foxes and partaking of long and searching discussions. Then, on one such visit, the boy becomes snow-blind and hopelessly lost — and the Foxman rescues him from certain death. As a result, the Foxman falls mortally ill. To seal his anonymity, even in death, he instructs the boy that when he is dead the boy is to burn the cabin, his body, and all his belongings except some valuable hides and books, which the boy is to keep. The boy complies, but in the end saves only one fox pelt, to remind him of his friend.

In this haunting first-person narrative, a teenage boy experiences with an adult an abiding friendship precious to both, a bond forged in free-ranging conversation, in which the boy learns to trust his own mind.

Ages 11-14

Also available in:
No other form known

496

Pearson, Susan

Everybody Knows That!

Color illustrations by Diane Paterson.
The Dial Press, Inc., 1978.
(29 pages counted)

GENDER ROLE IDENTITY
  Friendship: best friend
  School: entering

Herbie and Patty are best friends, and they sometimes play with trains, sometimes with dolls; sometimes they play cops and robbers, and sometimes they bake cookies. But when they start kindergarten, the boys Herbie plays with tell Patty that girls should not play with trucks. The next day, when the class plays airplane, Patty wants to be the pilot but is told she must be a stewardess or a passenger. Later, when Herbie and his

new friends are playing airplane, Patty asks to be the pilot, and the boys say flatly that girls are not pilots. The same thing happens the following day. But on Saturday when Herbie is at Patty's house, Patty turns the tables — she refuses to let Herbie help make cookies because "only girls can bake cookies." "This is dumb," Herbie declares, and Patty agrees, adding that she has been trying to tell Herbie that all week.

Through humor and logic — humor *through* logic — this book lets children see how arbitrary are notions about what is appropriate to boys and to girls. Both subject and treatment may well stimulate discussion.

Ages 4-7

Also available in:
No other form known

497

Pearson, Susan

Izzie

Color illustrations by Robert Andrew Parker.
The Dial Press, Inc., 1975.
(37 pages counted)

TRANSITIONAL OBJECTS: Toys

Cary is three-and-a-half years old when she receives a stuffed-cat doll from a friend of her father's. She names the cat Izzie, after the friend, and takes Izzie everywhere she goes for the next year. In the summer, Cary takes Izzie to the camp where her mother teaches and then to Maine. In the fall, Cary helps her parents pick grapes from their arbor, and Izzie gets a purple bottom from sitting in a half-filled bucket. Cary also brings Izzie along to help rake the leaves in her friend's yard. They play in the big leaf pile and Izzie gets a torn foot, which Mother patches with red and white polka-dot material. To Cary, Christmas is a time for helping make

P

Jülbröd and for celebrating her birthday with friends and Izzie. After the party, they go sledding, and Izzie gets so wet that Mother puts him in the dryer. In the spring, Cary and Izzie have fun making mud pies and getting muddy. Then the whole family, including Grandfather, paint the house: Dad paints the top, Mother the middle, Cary and Grandfather the bottom, and Izzie just watches. By this time, Izzie is very worn and past repairing. Deciding to fix him like new, Mother and a friend of hers sew a new body, paint a new face, and put the old Izzie inside the new one. But when Cary starts school, she leaves Izzie at home on her bed. One fall day she and a friend prepare to rake the leaves in his yard and he asks if Cary is going to bring Izzie. "No," she tells him. "He's too clean to carry around now. He'd just get dirty again. Besides," she adds, "I'm in school now."

This story delightfully chronicles a little girl's attachment to her stuffed doll, highlighting a year's happy moments. It shows her eventual laying aside of the doll as a natural event. As Cary grows up, she wants to be on her own and leaves the doll at home — realizing, however, that she may miss him for a while. The illustrations handsomely capture the warmth of this story.

Ages 2-7

Also available in:
Cassette for the Blind — *Izzie*
Library of Congress

498

Pearson, Susan

Monnie Hates Lydia

Black/white illustrations by Diane Paterson.
The Dial Press, Inc., 1975.
(31 pages counted)

SIBLING: Rivalry
SIBLING: Younger

Monnie's big sister, Lydia, will be ten on Saturday, and all week Monnie has been making birthday preparations: wrapping a present, helping to bake a cake, and planning a surprise picnic at Uncle Jake's. But Saturday morning, Lydia gets up crabby. She ignores Monnie's special tablesetting and does not thank Monnie for her gift. At Uncle Jake's, Lydia's friends are waiting to surprise her — and Lydia is even ruder to Monnie. Retiring to help Daddy build a fire, Monnie complains to him that Lydia is being a creep, but Daddy says to be a good sport. After lunch Monnie proudly brings out the cake — and Lydia remarks that Monnie could not possibly have baked a cake by herself. The younger girl pushes the cake squarely into her sister's face. The tension is broken, and soon everyone — even Lydia — is laughing and eating chocolate cake by the handful.

An ungrateful older sister gets her comeuppance from the younger sister she has slighted. Readers who have felt similarly about older siblings will especially relish the rowdy conclusion to this story. In group discussion, readers may air some of their own grievances and consider ways to settle them. The full-page, emphatic illustrations show the father, but no mother, yet the text says nothing on this score.

Ages 7-10

Also available in:
No other form known

499

Pearson, Susan

That's Enough for One Day, J. P.!

Color illustrations by Kay Chorao.
The Dial Press, Inc., 1977.
(29 pages counted)

PARENTAL: Interference

Engrossed in books about ladybugs and dragonflies, young John Philip stays in his room reading. His mother finally orders him outside to get fresh air, and he joins a baseball game. When he smashes a home run through a garage window, his mother angrily orders him to play elsewhere. He and his friends climb to a treehouse but lose interest when, on the mother's orders, his younger brother comes to join them. And so it goes. J. P. helps a neighbor paint a house, and his mother tells him to let the woman alone. He and a friend dig in the garden for worms, and his mother, mindful of bulbs she has planted there, orders them off. J. P. quietly confides to his friend, "I wish *she'd* go somewhere else," and away they go to help a neighbor wash her car. Wet, bedraggled, and happy, J. P. goes home for lunch, but his mother sends him upstairs at once; "You've had enough fresh air for one day, and I've had enough of you!" Back in his room the little boy happily settles down to read a book about spiders.

Though the boy obeys his mother, he does not understand her constant carping. Young readers will see the humor in his coming full circle to what he was doing — and enjoying — in the first place.

Ages 5-7

Also available in:
Talking Book — *That's Enough for One Day, J. P.!*
Library of Congress

500

Peck, Richard

Are You in the House Alone?

The Viking Press, Inc., 1976.
(156 pages)

P

RAPE
  Boy-girl relationships: dating
  Fear: of physical harm
  Sex: premarital

Gail Osburne, seventeen, lives comfortably with her parents in Oldfield, Connecticut, a gracious town, some of whose families have lived there since early colonial times. Gail's best friend, Alison, dates Phil Lawver, son of one of the most distinguished families. Gail dates Steve Pastorini, also from an old family, but less eminent for Mr. Pastorini's being a plumber. On some of their dates, Gail and Steve have met secretly at the Pastorini lake cottage for sex. Gail takes birth-control pills. One day she finds an obscenely threatening note on her school locker. Shaken, Gail tells Alison, who dismisses it as a prank. But Gail is soon getting nasty phone calls at home and at the house where she regularly baby-sits. When a second note is left on her locker, she is frightened enough to tell the school counselor, who offers little help or comfort. More and more terrified and wary of men, Gail is nevertheless ashamed to tell anyone else about the notes, which mention her secret meetings with Steve. Finally determined to tell her father, she goes to his New York office, only to find that he has been fired, and her parents have not told her. Clearly, she cannot confide this new worry to him.

Yet while doing her usual Saturday-night baby-sitting for Mrs. Montgomery, she gets another threatening call, this time an eerie voice intoning, "Are you in the house alone?" Desperate, she leaves a message at Steve's house for him to come over, and when the doorbell rings, rushes to open the door. Instead of Steve, she finds Phil Lawver, saying he is looking for Alison, wanting to use the phone. "Are you in the house alone," he asks, once inside. He assaults her, and she resists; he knocks her unconscious. She awakens in the hospital with a concussion. She has been beaten and raped. Later, under questioning, Gail is told by the police chief that she deserved what she got, and that accusing Phil Lawver is asking for trouble. Worse, her lawyer explains all too clearly what will happen in the courtroom should she decide to prosecute. Concluding that violation of another kind lies ahead if she presses charges, she finally decides not to. Phil remains at large, and, in time, rapes and nearly kills another girl. He is not convicted — but is sent away by his parents for psychiatric treatment.

This honest, harrowing story is told by Gail herself, with sharp characterizations and impressive detail — down to the medical examination following the rape. The victim, the victim's family, the social and legal ramifications of the crime, and police and judicial procedures apt and otherwise are all scrutinized candidly but without sensationalism. Much is to be found here for thoughtful discussion.

Ages 12 and up

Also available in:
Cassette for the Blind — *Are You in the House Alone?*
Library of Congress

Paperbound — *Are You in the House Alone?*
Dell Publishing Company, Inc.

501

Peck, Richard

Father Figure: A Novel

The Viking Press, Inc., 1978.
(192 pages)

COMMUNICATION: *Parent-child*
  Death: of mother
  Gender role identity: male
  Maturation
  Parental: absence
  Responsibility: accepting
  Sibling: older
  Suicide: of parent

Jim's mother, terminally ill and in increasing pain, has committed suicide by carbon monoxide poisoning. At seventeen, Jim must somehow surmount this second blow, the first having been his father's abrupt departure eight years earlier, never quite explained, never quite forgiven. Since that time, Jim has assumed the role of father to his brother, Byron, now eight; they live with their grandmother. As Jim struggles with his own feelings about his mother's death, he is also concerned about his brother. The night before the funeral, Byron comes to him, embarrassed and frightened at his sudden regression to bed-wetting. Jim talks reassuringly, helps him change the bed, and invites Byron to sleep with him. At the funeral Jim notices a tanned stranger, whom Grandmother acknowledges as their father. Later Jim introduces himself, aware first of his father's curious lack of excuses for his "eight-year coffee break." Jim also physically positions himself between his brother and father to prevent their talking. The following day, Dad is gone again and routine is restored — until Byron is hurt by a street gang while walking home from school. Jim's self-reproach at not having somehow prevented the incident and his pain at seeing Byron injured bring him to the point of tears for the first time since his mother's death, but he explodes in anger instead during a confrontation with Byron's principal. The episode is witnessed and reported to Grandmother who, unwilling to assume parental responsibility for the boys, calls upon their father to take them for the summer. In Florida, Jim and his father manage to sidestep a showdown until Jim awakens one night to find his father caring for the still healing Byron, and he explodes in anger. Seeing no tolerable summer but in coexistence, Jim and his father agree on ground rules for future conversations. The agreement avoids conflict, but it also prevents Jim from asking the lingering questions about the past. Suffering tension with his father that polite conversation cannot resolve, and angered by the growing rapport between his father and Byron, Jim verbally strikes out at a woman who has been a good friend to them all. Ashamed, he seeks out his father for the discussion so long overdue. His father's honest explanation of why he left eases them into a more trusting relationship, although that is soon tested by Byron's wanting to stay in Florida with his father. Jim decides to allow Byron some responsibility for his own life and to allow their father to be a father to Byron. He goes back to New York, to school, to his grandmother's house. For the first time, he can tend his own needs, grieve for his mother, and begin to form relationships with people his own age.

In the eight years since his father's departure, Jim has been a father figure to his little brother, Byron, trying tirelessly to provide Byron a security he himself never knew. Jim's attempt to protect Byron is shattered by his inability to prevent their mother's death, and Byron's misfortune further questions the idea that Jim, or anyone, can successfully shield another person from all pain. During the summer with their father, Jim learns to accept the people around him as they are, and in so doing, is free to accept himself as well. His father was not a "family man," yet he cares for his sons; Byron is not simply his little brother but a person with distinct opinions and needs, and one who has now developed his own unique relationship with his father. In deciding to allow Byron to stay with his father, Jim also chooses to renounce both the security and the confinement of his own role as a substitute parent, and begins assuming greater responsibility for his own life.

Ages 11 and up

Also available in:
Paperbound — *Father Figure: A Novel*
New American Library

502

Perl, Lila

Dumb, Like Me, Olivia Potts

The Seabury Press, Inc., 1976.
(181 pages)

SCHOOL: *Pupil-Teacher Relationships*
   Communication: parent-child
   Inferiority, feelings of
   School: achievement/underachievement
   Sibling: relationships

Ten-year-old Olivia Potts rues the day she entered Miss Kilhenny's fifth-grade class, where her older brother, Greg, and older sister, Meredith, were superior students. Miss Kilhenny expects excellent work from Olivia, who, in her turn, is certain she is "too dumb" to be part of the "Potts brain train" — even her mother attends college — and refuses to work hard. Miss Kilhenny, vowing to improve Olivia's scores, overloads her with assignments. Just as determined to prove her own point, Olivia ignores them, drawing moral support in her uneasy rebellion from Anita Brunelli, a new friend who has trouble with school herself. Olivia cannot talk to her mother, so busy with her own classwork that she brushes aside the idea that a child of hers could have difficulty in school. Olivia's parents depart suddenly to attend a funeral in Florida. The day before their return, Olivia is caught passing notes in class, and Miss Kilhenny demands a parent conference. Feeling surrounded, Olivia skips school the next day — only to encounter a hunted thief whom she assists the police in capturing. A known truant, she must face her mother and tell her of the conference Miss Kilhenny wants. At that conference, the girl at last speaks her mind about her mother's going to college, and requests, and receives, a transfer to the other fifth-grade class, where she will be judged on her own ability.

In this amusing first-person narrative, a girl rebels against being forced to compete with an older brother and sister. Her revolt is fanned by a stubborn, insensitive teacher, an intellectually pretentious sister, and a mother engrossed with her own concerns. Olivia herself proves sensitive to the feelings and needs of others, and displays enough ingenuity and common sense to leave no doubt of her intelligence.

Ages 9-12

Also available in:
Paperbound — *Dumb, Like Me, Olivia Potts*
Dell Publishing Company, Inc.

Talking Book — *Dumb, Like Me, Olivia Potts*
Library of Congress

503

Perl, Lila

The Telltale Summer of Tina C.

The Seabury Press, Inc., 1975.
(160 pages)

INFERIORITY, FEELINGS OF
  Appearance: concern about
  Clubs
  Grandparent: living in home of
  Parent/Parents: remarriage of

Tina Carstairs, in her "thirteenth year on this planet," is intensely aware of her height, her thinness, and her nose — which "twitches" uncontrollably when she is nervous. She and her friends belong to the Saturday Sad Souls, a club Tina has founded for members' mutual personal aid. But during the summer Tina's worries multiply to include the club itself: her divorced mother has married someone a little puzzling; her father is planning to remarry too; and a new girl, Karla, with whom the other girls seem to be smitten, has become a probationary club member over Tina's objections. When Tina's grandmother, with whom she and her father and younger brother, Arthur, live, begins an extended European vacation, Tina declines an invitation to stay in New York City with her mother. She wants neither to leave the club under Karla's sway nor live with her mother and the new husband, Peter, who keeps house while his wife has a job. Arthur accepts and is soon gone. After an argument with her girl friends and telling her father she dislikes the woman he intends to marry, Tina goes to New York too. There, in a museum with Arthur, Tina meets sixteen-year-old Johann, a visitor from Holland. The three agree to meet at the museum the next day. But on the way, Tina has second thoughts: Johann is not like the American boys she knows, her hair is a frizzy disaster, and her nose is twitching. She sends Arthur on alone, promising to meet him later. In fact she meets Johann later, but neither can locate Arthur. After a frantic search, Tina becomes panic-stricken and calls her mother. Sobbing too hard to talk, she gives Johann the phone, whereupon the news comes that Arthur is with his mother. Walking back with Johann, Tina realizes that she has not once thought of her appearance, nor has her nose twitched.

This life-like, sometimes funny first-person narrative takes us inside a twelve-year-old's intense self-concern without making it seem unnatural. Tina exaggerates her least favorite features, is swift to disapprove of her parents, and thinks little of others' feelings. Only when she must concern herself with the very welfare of another does she accept herself unquestioningly and see what is important. A secondary theme, the remarriage of divorced parents, is dealt with instructively.

Ages 10-13

Also available in:
Paperbound — *The Telltale Summer of Tina C.*
Scholastic Book Services

504

Perry, Patricia and Marietta Lynch

Mommy and Daddy Are Divorced

Black/white photographs by the authors.
The Dial Press, Inc., 1978.
(30 pages counted)

DIVORCE: of Parents

Ned and his little brother, Joey, live with their divorced mother and are awaiting their father's regular Wednesday morning visit. Daddy arrives and they play awhile, then work on Ned's model airplane. But when Daddy must leave, Ned loses his temper, shouting that he never wants to see him again. Daddy reassures the boy that he loves him and will see them again Saturday. Later, no longer angry but still unhappy, Ned questions his mother about the divorce. She reminds him about the arguments she and Daddy used to have and how they decided that a divorce would make them happier. Saturday arrives and once again the boys are with their father. And once again they are sad to have him say good-bye — but know that they will soon see him again.

Very young children enduring the aftermath of their parents' divorce will recognize Ned's feelings — his anger, his divided loyalties — through this candid first-person narrative and the accompanying large photographs. Children whose absent parents do not visit regularly may, however, be confused or envious.

Ages 3-6

Also available in:
No other form known

505

Peter, Diana

Claire and Emma

Color photographs by Jeremy Finlay.
The John Day Company, Inc., 1977.
(29 pages counted)

DEAFNESS

Emma, two, and Claire, four, are sisters; they are deaf. With difficulty, the two are learning to speak and to lipread. Though neither girl yet speaks clearly, both can be understood by a patient, helpful listener. Emma and Claire sometimes ignore people they are not looking at, and sometimes misunderstand others' speech. Nevertheless, they like to play with hearing children, are glad to be talked to, and in general want to be included.

The author is the mother of Emma and Claire. Her emphasis on how hearing children can help deaf children and on the difficulties arising from this handicap makes hers a valuable book for "mainstreaming" classes that include deaf children. Lively photographs illustrate what the text describes. This book does not touch on sign language, an important skill in the education of many deaf people.

Ages 5-8

Also available in:
No other form known

506

Petersen, Palle

Sally Can't See

Translated from the Danish.
Color photographs by the author.
The John Day Company, Inc., 1977.
(24 pages counted)

BLINDNESS

Twelve-year-old Sally lives in Denmark and is blind. At a residential school, together with other blind people, she learns to compensate for not seeing by using her other senses: she reads by feeling patterns of bumps on pages, the Braille system; she listens carefully to recorded stories and music; she recognizes objects, too, by feeling them; and she learns to tell from all kinds of sounds what is going on around her. What never fails to upset her is over-solicitous or curious people making her feel she is strange.

Sally is not strange, only blind, and this book cautions children not to treat blind people artificially or patronizingly. Both photographs and text describe the skills Sally learns at school and how she uses them at home.

The Braille notation system is carefully shown and explained, and readers are invited to try using it as they would a code. No information is given on guide dogs.

Ages 5-8

Also available in:
No other form known

507

Peterson, Jeanne Whitehouse

I Have a Sister — My Sister Is Deaf

Black/white illustrations by Deborah Ray.
Harper & Row Publishers, Inc., 1977.
(32 pages counted)

DEAFNESS
Sibling: older

The girl who narrates this story has a little five-year-old sister who loves to leap and roll and swing like other children but never hears a warning shout. She loves to play the piano but never hears the tune. She is deaf. The two usually — but not always — understand each other; the hearing sister speaks slowly and uses her hands, face, and eyes to show what she is saying; the deaf sister can have trouble speaking, but she "speaks" too, in facial expressions and in sign language. The hearing girl plugs her ears and wonders if the effect is the same as being deaf. (It is not, for her sister will never hear noises of any kind.) The littler girl even sleeps on when thunder frightens her sister. When friends ask if it hurts to be deaf, the older sister replies, "No, her ears don't hurt, but her feelings do when people do not understand."

In telling about her deaf sister in this perceptive first-person narrative, a hearing girl shows the ways in which a deaf child differs from a hearing one. Perhaps the most puzzling difference to a hearing child is that a deaf child never reacts to noises, as is shown here several times. Numerous tips are given on how to act toward a deaf child: speak slowly and expressively; stamp the ground or else wave to attract their attention; and so on. The author writes from experience, for she has a younger sister who is deaf. Since this is not an instructional book, and its text resembles verse, discussion will likely be needed to emphasize these lessons.

Ages 4-7

Also available in:
Talking Book — *I Have a Sister — My Sister Is Deaf*
Library of Congress

508

Pevsner, Stella

And You Give Me a Pain, Elaine

The Seabury Press, Inc., 1978.
(182 pages)

SIBLING: Relationships
  Boy-girl relationships
  Death: of sibling
  Love, meaning of
  Maturation
  Running away

The only way thirteen-year-old Andrea Marshall can cope with her sixteen-year-old sister, Elaine, is by retreating to another room to practice gymnastics. Her mother tries to change Elaine, but her efforts end in furious bickering. Elaine remains Elaine — willful, contentious, sarcastic, and selfish. Finally, Andrea turns to Joe, her loving and beloved older brother now in college, for advice. He tells her to leave Elaine to their parents. For a time Andrea's work on a school play and her worries about Joe's girl friend, Cassie, who is cooling towards him, divert her attention from Elaine. She is further distracted by the attentions of a boy named

Chris, also involved with the play. Her mother, however, continues to worry about Elaine and becomes frantic after the girl withdraws her bank savings and refuses to say why, asking only to be left alone. Shortly after that, Elaine runs away, and soon telephones from Arizona, where she is living with her boy friend, who has moved there. The news does not disturb Andrea unduly. It is Elaine's return several weeks later that upsets her, all the more so because her parents then refuse to let Andrea date Chris, after the example Elaine has set. Yet relations improve, perhaps because of the professional counseling Elaine and her parents take. Elaine begins to change and even does small favors for Andrea. Andrea learns of the pressures on her sister, especially Mom's desire that the younger girl emulate the elder's high school successes. Then Andrea's life is shattered when Joe, driving home on a motorcycle to see the play, is killed. For a time, Andrea drops everything, including Chris, and even blames herself for Joe's death: had she not made so much of the play, he would not have made the trip. But, reminded by Cassie of how highly Joe thought of her, Andrea resolves to set aside her grief: "Step by step, move by move, I'd make it."

This first-person narrative shows the effects of a girl's maturing on her relations with a troublesome sister. As Andrea becomes confident in herself, she sees that Elaine must also work things out her own way. There are numerous subplots here — school activities, the vagaries of Joe's romance — that contribute to the realism of the story as well as show the experiences that inform Andrea's growing awareness of herself and others. The Marshall family, though troubled, is a close one, and their dialogue rings true. Humor leavens the whole.

Ages 10-13

Also available in:
Paperbound — *And You Give Me a Pain, Elaine*
Pocket Books, Inc.

P

509

Pevsner, Stella

Keep Stompin' Till the Music Stops

The Seabury Press, Inc., 1977.
(136 pages)

LEARNING DISABILITIES
  Age: respect for
  Great-grandparent
  Self-esteem

Richard, entering seventh grade in the fall, suffers from dyslexia and cannot follow complicated reading matter or conversation. When his family attends a reunion at his great-grandfather's home, Richard's cousin, Alexandra, tells him that she suspects the overbearing Great-aunt Violet of having some secret plan up her sleeve. To discover that plan, Richard — concentrating as never before — learns by eavesdropping that Aunt Vi, convinced that Great-grandpa Ben is too old to go on living in his large house, wants to take her father to Florida. This and additional clues gathered over days persuade the cousins that their great-aunt plans to deposit Grandpa Ben in a senior citizens' trailer court. Richard tells all to his father, extracting his promise to stand up for Grandpa Ben. But when family discussion concerning his welfare becomes heated, Ben announces that he will not be made to move and has made arrangements to rent part of his house to the local historical society, which will allow him to go on living there and help maintain the place. Richard is both relieved that his great-grandfather has thwarted Aunt Violet and more hopeful, after his detective work, that he can conquer his learning disability.

Richard's dyslexia has made him extremely sensitive to criticism, real or imagined, and generally unsure of himself. His father, ambitious and demanding, resents his son's disability. Sensing this, the boy has difficulty trusting or even liking his father. Tempering her husband's impatience, Richard's mother tries to help the boy. Vivid characterizations enliven this leisurely narrative, not least Richard's courage in bewilderment — courage which readers who share his disability may well identify with. Other readers will come away knowing more about dyslexia than before.

Ages 9-12

Also available in:
Paperbound — Keep Stompin' Till the Music Stops
Scholastic Book Services

510

Pevsner, Stella

A Smart Kid Like You

The Seabury Press, Inc., 1975.
(216 pages)

DIVORCE: of Parents
SCHOOL: Pupil-Teacher Relationships
STEPPARENT: Mother
  Maturation

Twelve-year-old Nina Beckwith's parents are recently divorced, and she still has difficulty accepting their separation. She resents her father's remarriage even more. Nina is also worried about starting junior high school. Her first school day goes well, until she enters the mathematics class and finds that her teacher is her father's new wife. Nina wants to transfer to a different class, but her friends convince her to try another approach — to force the teacher to quit. For several days the students harass Mrs. Beckwith until she finally puts her foot down. In a private talk, Mrs. Beckwith and Nina agree to work together as best they can. Meanwhile, Nina has other troubles. Her mother works as a secretary and has little time to talk with her. Nina is even more annoyed when her mother starts dating Phil. On Saturdays, Nina goes out with her father; slowly she learns to understand him as an individual with needs of his own. She begins to warm toward his new family and accept his new wife. When communication with her mother improves and Nina comes to know Phil better, she starts to feel that things may work out after all.

Nina not only faces the usual adolescent worries — school, boys, clothes, relationships with parents — she must also learn to accept her parents' divorce. Her initial feelings of resentment, fear, and loneliness give way to an understanding of her parents' desires to make new lives for themselves, apart from each other, but not excluding her.

Ages 10-13

Also available in:
Paperbound — *A Smart Kid Like You*
Scholastic Book Services

511

Pfeffer, Susan Beth

Kid Power

Black/white illustrations by Leigh Grant.
Franklin Watts, Inc., 1977.
(121 pages)

JOB
   Friendship: best friend
   Resourcefulness
   Responsibility: accepting
   Values/Valuing: materialistic

Eleven-year-old Janie Golden has never given much thought to money — nor held onto it long. Just when her mother loses a job, she and her sister, Carol, at thirteen a junior miser, find they need money to buy new bicycles. Carol already has a newspaper route, and Janie decides to advertise for odd jobs under the name of "Kid Power." Soon she is so busy working and so fascinated by making money that she is neglecting her best friend, Lisa, who accuses her of forsaking everything for the almighty dollar. In fact the dollar is plaguing the whole household. When Mrs. Golden stops looking for a new job, she and her husband stop talking to each other. When Mr. Golden and Carol blame Janie for the family disruption, she worries that they may be right. The glitter of all her new money dims. Matters only worsen when a newspaper article about Janie and her business brings in many more job offers than she can fill — babysitting, gardening, walking dogs, helping at yard sales. Soon she is sharing jobs with friends, asking for 10% of their earnings as her agent's fee. Janie has found her true calling, management, and Mrs. Golden employs herself by starting her own agency — a Kid Power for adults.

This first-person narrative shows the delights and pitfalls of making money. Inventive at solving problems on the job, Janie is not prepared for the stress her work causes her family and friends. By becoming an agent, she finds time for them and takes 10% to boot. Children bent on summer jobs should enjoy this story, filled with interesting characters, humor, unexpected troubles, and intelligent, believable solutions.

Ages 9-12

Also available in:
Cassette for the Blind — *Kid Power*
Library of Congress

Paperbound — *Kid Power*
Scholastic Book Services

P

512

Pfeffer, Susan Beth

Marly the Kid

Doubleday & Company, Inc., 1975.
(137 pages)

MATURATION
  School: pupil-teacher relationships
  Self, attitude toward: accepting
  Stepparent: mother

Wanting no more of her divorced mother's sarcasm, fifteen-year-old Marly Carson runs away from home to live with her father and his wife, Sally. Marly fears her stepmother will send her back to her mother, but soon enough finds her stepmother a friend who will listen and offer sound advice. Then, at her new school, Marly "falls in love" with her English teacher, Mr. Hughes. This special attachment for a teacher is a wholly new experience for the quiet, studious Marly, who has always suppressed any feeling, good or bad, toward teachers. Her enforced neutrality fails her again with her history teacher, Mr. Marshall — whom she finds dogmatic, boring, and cruel to students who disagree with him. One day Marly voices an opinion in history class and Mr. Marshall rudely announces that she is "plain, plump, and pimply," and should not speak unless called on. Incensed by his crudeness, Marly demands an apology, arguing that "teachers shouldn't make uncalled for remarks" that are rude and offensive. At that, Mr. Marshall ushers her to the vice-principal's office, where *he* demands an apology, in writing. When Marly staunchly refuses it, she is suspended. Both her father and Sally agree that Marly was maltreated, but Sally adds some dispassionate, practical advice: Marly may have to compromise with Mr. Marshall, because school rules, even distasteful ones, must be followed. Soon Marly learns that fellow students, her mother, and some of Mr. Marshall's colleagues have all come to her defense. Gratified by such backing, and with Sally's advice in mind, Marly agrees to make a verbal apology, and Sally convinces the vice-principal to erase the suspension from Marly's record. Even after apologizing, Marly feels she has won a victory: she has made others see that she is someone to reckon with and that changes should be made in school regulations.

This story portrays a teenage girl gradually becoming aware of both the force of her feelings and the worth of her beliefs. The characters are sharply and plausibly drawn, and the time is very much the present. This is a sequel to *The Beauty Queen*.

Ages 11-13

Also available in:
Paperbound — *Marly the Kid*
Dell Publishing Company, Inc.

Talking Book — *Marly the Kid*
Library of Congress

513

Pinkwater, Manus

Wingman

Black/white illustrations by the author.
Dodd, Mead & Co., 1975.
(63 pages)

REALITY, ESCAPING
  Chinese-American
  Fantasy formation
  Poverty
  Prejudice: ethnic/racial
  School: classmate relationships
  Talents: artistic

Chen Chi-Wing, or Donald Chen, as he is known at school, is the poorest child in his class, and the only Chinese-American at P.S. 132 in New York. At Thanksgiving his teacher presents him with some holiday food — and Donald is so humiliated that he decides to quit school. To keep his father from discovering his truancy, he packs his schoolbag full of comic books and spends his days reading amid the beams of the George Washington Bridge. Donald loves comics, lives through them, and has collected over two thousand of them; he even dreams in brightly colored squares. One day while reading on the bridge, Donald sees something in the sky that looks like a huge bird. Then he sees that it is a man wearing shining armor and a cape of gray feathers — and the man is Chinese. To Donald, he is Wingman, a Chinese super-hero. At home that night Donald wants to tell someone, but he knows no one would believe him, and so he draws pictures of Wingman instead. The next morning Donald is caught by the truant officer, and forced to go back to school for one terrible day. Happily, the next ten days are Christmas vacation, and Donald plans to spend them at the bridge waiting for Wingman. The first day, Wingman takes him on a spectacular flight over old China. Alas, the weather for the rest of vacation is colder, making the bridge too icy to climb. Inevitably, classes resume, but Donald finds that a new teacher, Mrs. Miller, has taken over his class. She is kind, patient, and pleased at Donald's above-average reading ability. Since most of his classmates are poor readers, she asks Donald to bring his comics to stimulate them to read more. To the class, this is a whole new side to Donald, and he is soon looked up to. He likes Mrs. Miller and wants to tell her about Wingman, yet cannot seem to tell her in words. He shows her his drawings of him instead. Impressed, she rounds up some art supplies and asks Donald to paint her a picture. His painting takes first place in a local art contest, and is displayed in the school lobby, whereupon the school starts regular art classes for all the children.

For Donald, one teacher changes school from intolerable to wonderful. Allowed to express himself, he not only gains new self-respect but proves a good influence on his classmates. Many children will understand the boy's hurt when he is offered charity and teasingly called a "Chink." His escapes into isolation and the fantasy of Wingman last only until life itself offers a welcome to his real interests and talents. Then Wingman recedes to his rightful place in imagination.

Ages 9-12

Also available in:
Paperbound — *Wingman*
Dell Publishing Company, Inc.

Talking Book — *Wingman*
Library of Congress

514

Piper, Watty

The Little Engine That Could

Retold from The Pony Engine by Mabel C. Bragg.
Color illustrations by Ruth Sanderson.
Platt & Munk Publishers, 1976.
(39 pages)

DETERMINATION
  Consideration, meaning of
  Problem solving

A small train is carrying dolls, toys, books, and good food for boys and girls who live on the other side of the mountain. Suddenly, at the foot of the mountain, the engine breaks down. Worried that the children will be disappointed, the toys and dolls look for another engine to pull their train. A large, shiny new engine refuses because he pulls only passenger trains. A freight engine will carry only cargo for adults. An old rusty engine is too weary to pull anything over a mountain. The dolls

P

and toys are about to lose hope when a pretty, new engine comes down the tracks. She does not know if she can pull so heavy a load over a mountain, but is eager to help. She is hitched to a train and starts slowly up the slope repeating, "I think I can — I think I can...." Just in time, and barely, she gets over the mountain. The children are delighted with the joyous freight.

This 50th-anniversary edition of a classic is larger than the original and has been reillustrated in the style of the 1920s. The larger size is convenient to use with read-aloud groups. The unchanged text will continue to satisfy youngsters with its message of consideration, perseverance, and willingness paying off.

Ages 3-7

Also available in:
Braille — *The Little Engine That Could*
Library of Congress

Filmstrip/Cassette — *The Little Engine That Could*
Society for Visual Education

Paperbound — *The Little Engine That Could*
Scholastic Book Services

Talking Book — *The Little Engine That Could*
Library of Congress

515

Platt, Kin

Chloris and the Freaks

Bradbury Press, Inc., 1975.
(217 pages)

DIVORCE: of Parents
  Sibling: relationships
  Stepparent: father
  Suicide: of parent

Twelve-year-old Jenny Carpenter is worried: her four-teen-year-old sister, Chloris, claiming to be in contact with the spirit of their dead father, has predicted that the girls' mother and stepfather, Fidel, will soon divorce. Jenny would hate this to happen; she thinks of Fidel as her father, her parents having divorced when she was two, the father having then committed suicide five years later. Realizing that Chloris actively wants this second divorce, Jenny, a devotee of astrology, daily consults her family's horoscopes for signs of its coming to pass. The signs are there. Noticing too that her mother is working longer hours than necessary, Jenny consults her best friend, Kathy, whose parents are divorcing, in an attempt to learn ways of averting divorce in her own family. She and Kathy also discuss the subject of divorce with Fidel, who cautions them that without "genuine concern for other individuals, and very little concern for oneself" a marriage has scant hope of lasting. Before long, Jenny notes flaws in the once-loving relationship between her mother and Fidel. Jenny's mother brings home a male friend, Duane Turner, while Fidel is out of town. Chloris, who had always shunned the suitors of their mother's widowhood, welcomes Duane warmly. Jenny knows all too well that her mother courts Chloris's approval and may act in accord with it. When Fidel returns, the mother demands a divorce, accusing him of not giving her the attention and security she needs. Fidel quietly assents, and tells Jenny, when she begs him to reconsider, that he cannot stop his wife when her mind is clearly made up. Not until the household has broken up, the girls and their mother having moved to an apartment, does Chloris reveal to Jenny that she loathes Duane and intends to get rid of him just as she did Fidel.

This candid first-person narrative chronicles the dissolution of a marriage and its effect on a twelve-year-old girl. The reader is witness to her anger and helplessness to preserve a comfortable and loving past. Her stepfather speaks for an adult view of marriage and divorce. The main character is fearful of her ruthless sister, who had required psychiatric care in the face of an earlier divorce, her father's suicide, and her mother's remarriage. (The main character tells us her own thoughts on suicide.) There is no happy ending to this sequel to *Chloris and the Creeps*. The narrator perceptively recognizes and reluctantly accepts human frailty and difference. Touches of humor prevent the book from becoming morbid.

Ages 11 and up

Also available in:
Braille — *Chloris and the Freaks*
Library of Congress

Paperbound — *Chloris and the Freaks*
Bantam Books, Inc.

516

Platt, Kin

Chloris and the Weirdos

Bradbury Press, Inc., 1978.
(230 pages)

COMMUNICATION: *Parent-Child*
PARENT/PARENTS: *Single*
  Arguing
  Autonomy
  Boy-girl relationships: dating
  Judgment, effect of emotions on
  Sibling: relationships

Thirteen-year-old Jenny Carpenter is delighted to be dating Harold Osborne, despite the judgment of her fifteen-year-old sister, Chloris, that Harold is a "weirdo." Harold and Jenny discuss many things, including Harold's belief that divorced mothers like theirs have the right to lead social lives. With this new perspective, Jenny defends her mother's right to date when Chloris adamantly insists that their mother stay at home and tend to her daughters. In fact, Chloris tells her mother the same thing, hinting that if disobeyed, she might run away. Worse, when Jenny finds fault with her mother's latest date, her mother's hurt and anger startle the girl so much that she seeks more advice from Harold. Harold has learned from a television talk show that daughters often object to their mother's suitors out of fear of losing their mother's love to someone else. Jenny carries this news first to Chloris, who scoffs at it, and then to her mother, who takes it into account in deciding to take a weekend trip with a male companion. When Chloris hears of the trip, she becomes irate, and a violent argument ensues. She storms out of the house, vowing to take her own weekend trip. Vowing that Chloris will not, however, ruin her weekend, Jenny's mother departs — but returns after calling home and finding that Chloris has not yet returned. When Chloris does return, shortly after her mother, arguments and apologies fly. But as all three sit down to breakfast, much else has gone unsaid.

In this first-person narrative (the third in a series about Jenny and her sister) the reader watches the narrator learning to judge questions independently of her controlling sister, whose own inclination is to use guile and veiled threats to run others' lives. But neither of these teenage girls finds it easy to accept their single parent's desire to be an independent person with a social life of her own. This open-ended story also gives an honest view of dating among young teenagers and their view of divorce in their own families.

Ages 11 and up

Also available in:
Braille — *Chloris and the Weirdos*
Library of Congress

Paperbound — *Chloris and the Weirdos*
Bantam Books, Inc.

P

517

Platt, Kin

Headman

Greenwillow Books, 1975.
(186 pages)

DELINQUENCY, JUVENILE
DETENTION HOME, LIVING IN
GANGS: Being Bothered by
    Gangs: membership in

Owen Kirby has been committed for a two-year sentence at Camp Sawyer, a youth correction center in northern California, far from his native Los Angeles. Though only in his mid-teens, Owen has already been convicted of several offenses, among them robbery, auto theft, and assault with a dangerous weapon. Camp Sawyer has no guards and no fences, and the boys there are taught to work and play hard, to try to change attitudes and learn to live with a purpose. At first Owen cannot believe the freedoms given him. Outwardly, at least, he is cooperative, and with the aid of the counselor, Johnson, he learns to garden and play tennis. He learns which of the boys to avoid and which to respect. But secretly he decides that when he is released, if he is to survive in the filth, noise, and corruption of his home neighborhood, he must join a gang. When Joey Hawkins and Caroma, two one-time gang leaders, almost kill each other in a fight at the camp, Owen is even more firmly convinced of the need for a gang's support. After some eight months, he is told that his mother is sick, and that he is being released to go home and try to help out. Owen has mixed feelings about returning to the old neighborhood and his drunken mother, and wonders which gang to join when he gets there. Once home, he is robbed. He and three friends form their own gang, with Owen as headman. One night Owen sees the boy who had robbed him. He approaches the boy, sure of victory, only to find that he has once more ended up on the bottom side of a bloody fight. What is the sense of it all, he wonders as he loses consciousness.

Owen's story tells of the hopelessness of gang life in the back streets of Los Angeles. The encouragement and instruction given him at the camp seem almost useless in his own neighborhood. The open ending, which leaves the reader wondering if Owen is dead or only injured, promotes discussion. The profanity characteristic of street gangs is used profusely throughout the book. This fast-paced book will appeal to readers who need high-interest, low-vocabulary materials.

Ages 13-19

Also available in:
Cassette for the Blind — *Headman*
Library of Congress

Paperbound — *Headman*
Dell Publishing Company, Inc.

518

Platt, Kin

Run for Your Life

Black/white photographs by Chuck Freedman.
Franklin Watts, Inc., 1977.
(95 pages)

DETERMINATION
    Competition
    Sports/Sportsmanship
    Stealing

Fifteen-year-old Lee Hunter runs almost everywhere, even though he has been dropped from the track team. He works after school to help out his mother, a widow trying to support four children, and for that reason he cannot get to practice on time — but he practices on the track every chance he gets, hoping to persuade the coach to take him back. Still, his speed does not improve, and soon he has a new worry. Someone using a key has robbed the newspaper boxes on his route, and Lee, sure he has the only key, is equally sure his supervisor will suspect him. But he can do nothing except continue working and hope the thief stops. Meanwhile, encouraged by Connie, a girl he admires, and Ross, a miler on the team, Lee undertakes more rigorous training. His speed picks up, and the coach asks him back. One day soon after, the thief robs the boxes again, and Lee's supervisor takes away his key, just "to check." Dejected, Lee walks away, wondering who could want to make trouble for him — and is stunned to see Connie's brother, Mike, a teammate, robbing a box. Although he follows Mike, he cannot — thinking of Connie — confront him or turn him in. Instead, he vows to beat Mike at an upcoming race. But Connie discovers that her brother has been stealing from boxes: he has worked for the newspaper himself, and duplicated a key. And it is Connie who tells the supervisor that Mike is stealing to get back at the company for firing him. Reinstated in his job, Lee goes on to finish ahead of Mike at the race.

A youth succeeds in returning to a sports team by hard training and determination, but his success in solving some incriminating thefts comes from his girl friend's efforts. The girl confronts the ethical issue while the boy settles for a competition in a race. Written in simple language, this book relies on numerous photographs and a straightforward, quick-moving plot to interest readers with limited vocabularies and little reading interest.

Ages 9-12

Also available in:
Paperbound — *Run for Your Life*
Dell Publishing Company, Inc.

Cassette for the Blind — *Run for Your Life*
Library of Congress

Pollowitz, Melinda

Cinnamon Cane

Harper & Row Publishers, Inc., 1977.
(154 pages)

P

CHANGE: *Resisting*
GRANDPARENT: *Love for*
  Age: aging
  Death: of grandparent
  Grandparent: living in child's home
  Illnesses: of grandparent
  Maturation
  School: pupil-teacher relationships

Despite protests from twelve-year-old Cassie Bennison, her parents move her Grandfather Joshua from his beloved farm to an apartment in the city. To assure herself that he will not be lonely, Cassie visits frequently. When school begins, Cassie joins the school poetry club and the Sub-Debs, an exclusive service organization, but with Cassie so busy, her visits to Joshua become less frequent. Shortly after Thanksgiving, Joshua suffers a massive stroke. When he is released from the hospital and settles in a room in their house, Cassie renounces friends and school activities to take care of him. All the same, upon returning from school one afternoon, Cassie discovers that Joshua has collapsed in the yard. She summons an ambulance and her parents and then goes to the hospital, where she learns he has had another stroke. He returns home, but Joshua is slipping in and out of reality. One day he frightens Cassie by insisting that she is his dead wife. That same evening while Cassie is with him, Joshua dies, and she prepares to say good-bye for the last time.

This touching story explores a spirited girl's social maturation and, more private, her love and concern for her fragile grandfather. The deterioration of the grandfather's health, and its effect on the family, is convincingly portrayed. So is Cassie's mistaken belief that her parents' wish for Joshua to be safe and cared for in town implies a callous disregard for his love of the farm. Cassie also reproaches herself for pursuing extracurricular activities instead of visiting her grandfather. After so much misunderstanding and cross purposes, her mature acceptance of Joshua's death seems abrupt. But her story provides a realistic view of aging nevertheless. Cassie's love for a teacher is a secondary theme.

Ages 10-12

Also available in:
No other form known

520

Polushkin, Maria

Bubba and Babba

Color illustrations by Diane de Groat.
Crown Publishers, Inc., 1976.
(30 pages counted)

RESPONSIBILITY: Avoiding

Bubba and Babba are two very lazy bears who always argue about the housework. Bubba says Babba should make the beds, but Babba says that is pointless since they will only muss them again at night. When Babba says Bubba should sweep the floors, Bubba declines, saying they will only get dirty again. While out walking one day, they are offered a dozen eggs by a farmer if they will help with his mowing. They both decline, saying that should they break the eggs on the way home, all that work would have been for nothing. Instead, they sit under a tree and watch the farmer work. At suppertime, because they cannot think how to avoid it, they chop wood for a fire and prepare some porridge. At the end of the meal, however, they have a loud, long argument over who should do the dishes. Finally Babba suggests that they leave the dishes and go to bed — and whoever gets up first will do them. They agree. But in the morning, both bears stay in bed feigning sleep. Most of the day passes and neither gets up. In the late afternoon, their raccoon friend comes by for a visit, and is appalled by the awful mess in the kitchen. He decides to surprise the bears by cleaning it up. Hearing noise, both bears leap out of bed and run into the kitchen, where Raccoon is so startled he drops a bowl. At that Bubba and Babba laugh and laugh. They see their own silliness and promise to try to be less lazy in the future.

Young children will get the point of this funny story, based on an old Russian folk tale, and see how laughing at oneself can be the beginning of change. The book is especially fun when read aloud.

Ages 3-8

Also available in:
No other form known

521

Pomerantz, Charlotte

The Mango Tooth

Color illustrations by Marylin Hafner.
Greenwillow Books, 1977.
(32 pages counted)

TOOTH, LOSS OF
Imagination

Biting into the pit of a mango fruit, young Posy loses a tooth, which she names "the mango tooth." Her mother writes a verse about it and tells Posy she will find a dime beneath her pillow in the morning. Posy loses her next tooth while eating a chicken leg at school. Again her mother composes a tooth verse and promises that

Posy will find another dime. Losing teeth is such fun and so profitable that Posy pretends to lose a third, but her mother recognizes it as only a grain of rice and Posy gets no dime. The real third tooth falls to candy that Posy and her friend Jenny collect on Halloween. The fourth tooth, she promises her mother, will fall out because of elephants. If that happens, her mother replies, "two dimes for an *elephant* tooth." While at Jenny's birthday party, Posy trades her animal crackers for elephant crackers. Once home, she eats the crackers until she loosens a tooth. Her mother laughs and says the two dimes will be under her pillow in the morning.

This story, with its homely but adequate drawings, shows how imagination, a handful of dimes, and humor can make light of losing teeth. Gaiety about the subject could, however, bewilder children unaware that permanent teeth grow in to replace the primary ones. The book does not dispel belief in the tooth fairy; the source of the dimes is not explained. The rhythmic text lends itself to reading aloud.

Ages 4-7

Also available in:
No other form known

522

Prather, Ray

New Neighbors

Color illustrations by the author.
McGraw-Hill Book Co., 1975.
(30 pages counted) o.p.

FRIENDSHIP: Making Friends
  Change: new home
  Moving

Once at the new house, young Rickey is so eager to get acquainted in his new neighborhood that he races outdoors immediately. But the children he sees offer not so much as a hello. They only stare. With nothing else to do, Rickey goes back inside and explores the new house. He discovers an assortment of left-behind toys, including marbles under a radiator, an old baseball glove in the basement, and a skate in the attic. The baseball glove reminds him of his pals in the old neighborhood, what good times they all had, how he will never see them again. He recalls in particular a store they used to hang around. Suddenly Rickey decides to become a storekeeper himself. He sets his discoveries out on cardboard boxes, makes a sign, and waits for the other children to appear. He hears them talking behind a hedge but stays where he is. One by one they approach and silently crowd around — then begin to mimic his movements, folding their arms when he folds his, blinking when he does, standing still when he does. Then he and they begin to laugh. Amid chatter and introductions, Rickey is offered a swap for the skate and is invited to join the group, a gang calling themselves the Penguins. Rickey and the others walk away doing "the penguin wobble."

Making new friends is, to a child, the test of a new neighborhood. Rickey's first attempt at getting acquainted falls flat, but he does not give up. His second plan is original, economical, and successful. This story suggests that sometimes making the first move and going more than half way to make friends can pay off handsomely.

Ages 4-7

Also available in:
No other form known

P

523

Pursell, Margaret Sanford

A Look at Adoption

Black/white photographs by Maria S. Forrai.
Lerner Publications Co., 1978.
(34 pages counted)

ADOPTION

Sometimes a married couple adopts a child, one who was born to someone else. They can love such a child exactly as if he or she were their own. Some adoptive parents may not be able to have their own children, but others, who can, may want to adopt a child anyway. Children are made available for adoption for varied reasons: their parents may be unable to raise them; the parents may have died; young mothers without husbands may hope to ensure sound, happy homes for their offspring. Adoptive children are often placed in foster homes until arrangements for their adoption can be made. But whatever the case, parents and legally adopted children are considered by law to be just like other families. "Adopted children understand that their adoptive parents are 'real parents.' They are the people who love and care for them, who share their lives with them."

This is a clear, reassuring presentation of a complicated, often confusing subject, a book young children will listen to and may want to discuss. It is one of the titles in the Lerner Awareness Series, intended to present complex subjects to very young children.

Ages 3-7

Also available in:
No other form known

524

Pursell, Margaret Sanford

A Look at Divorce

Black/white photographs by Maria S. Forrai.
Lerner Publications Co., 1976.
(34 pages counted)

DIVORCE

Even though a husband and wife divorce, one or both seeking a better life, they remain bound to their children in a special, lasting way. Children frequently do not understand their parents' divorcing, and become frightened and angry. But they should remember that divorce is meant to replace an unhappy family life with a new and happier one. True, the new life calls for difficult changes in living and working; the absent parent, though wanting to visit the children often, may be unable to. But the difficulties can be gotten over if parents and children both address them. And children may end up being "closer to Dad or Mom than ever before."

After first describing the normal permanence of family ties, the author takes up the consequences of their failure: divorce. This short, simple book sees divorce as a solution to unhappiness, leading in most cases to happiness. That view may seem superficial or over-simplified and is best suited to starting up discussion. This book is one of the titles in the Lerner Awareness Series, intended to present complex subjects to very young children.

Ages 3-7

Also available in:
No other form known

Pursell, Margaret Sanford

A Look at Physical Handicaps

Black/white photographs by Maria S. Forrai.
Lerner Publications Co., 1976.
(34 pages counted)

HANDICAPS

People who lose the use of a part of the body through illness, injury, or an accident at birth are physically handicapped. They must learn to do some things differently from other people in order to pursue the kinds of goals we all pursue. They may recover some use of a damaged part of the body, or learn to compensate for a loss: blind people, for example, read by touching raised dots in the Braille system. Handicapped persons, given help and encouragement, can participate purposefully in everyday life.

One can learn here about the most widespread physical handicaps and how various are the means of rehabilitation and adjustment. The author does not introduce more complex topics, such as the psychological difficulties attendant on handicaps. This book is one of the titles in the Lerner Awareness Series, intended to present complex subjects to very young children.

Ages 3-7

Also available in:
No other form known

Rabe, Berniece Louise

The Girl Who Had No Name

E. P. Dutton & Company, Inc., 1977.
(149 pages)

IDENTITY, SEARCH FOR
REJECTION: Parental
  Communication: lack of
  Guilt, feelings of
  Sibling: relationships

R

Twelve-year-old Girlie Webster, motherless and the youngest of ten sisters, wants to stay with her Papa, but he takes her to stay with her married sister Lil. Girlie is certain this new home is temporary, and that her father will get over being distant and mean. But in the coming year she is sent from one sister to another. By her third home, she has a part-time job working in a dry-goods store. There, a dress manufacturer for $25 borrows the dress she is wearing to copy the pattern. But Girlie's delight at her newfound fortune causes her to be sent to yet another sister's home, where Girlie discovers a sex magazine. Appalled, she tells her father — who takes her back to Lil's. She sees that these are no temporary separations. At her next home, Girlie learns that her mother had been warned she would die if she had a tenth child; yet she had died twelve years after Girlie's birth. Lil provides one answer: Papa does not think Girlie is his, because he was out of town nine months before she was born, and she does not resemble the other daughters. Girlie is stunned. At the store she again sees the man who bought the dress pattern from her. Something he says about inherited talent makes her think *he* might be her father. In a library book about birth she makes an important discovery: overdue babies are often large, with much hair. She had been a thirteen-pound baby with five inches of hair. This is the proof she needs to show her father. He is not convinced. She pleads with him, saying that even if she is not really his, maybe he could just adopt her, because she is not really a bad person. Again he takes her to Lil's. Lil explains that their father knew the consequences of another child, cannot accept the blame for his wife's death, and so has chosen to believe that Girlie is not his. He suspects the dress manufacturer, who frequently bought patterns from her mother. That is why he never gave Girlie a name. But after thinking about what Girlie has said about adoption, and knowing that people who adopt a baby give it a name, he will give her, if she likes it, the name Glencora, and have the records changed. Going home with her father, Girlie notices what a wide handspan he has — even wider than hers, which people have always teased her about. Girlie starts to tell him, then realizes that this will not ease her father's sense of guilt.

A bright, inquisitive girl, renounced by her father after her mother's death, tries to uncover the reason. Her tough independence despite the often unfeeling responses of her sisters is admirable, if sometimes unbelievable. Some readers may feel the author has stacked the odds too heavily against a twelve-year-old. But the setting is the Depression, when money and food were a daily worry to many who had little time for tact or hurt feelings. Information on birth and unwanted pregnancy is given as integral to the story.

Ages 12 and up.

Also available in:
Paperbound — *The Girl Who Had No Name*
Bantam Books, Inc.

Talking Book — *The Girl Who Had No Name*
Library of Congress

527
Rabe, Berniece Louise

Naomi

Thomas Nelson, Inc., 1975.
(192 pages)

AUTONOMY
MATURATION
 Expectations
 Family: relationships
 Fear: of death
 Puberty

Eleven-year-old Naomi lives in rural Missouri in the late 1930s. Her father is a poor farmer, her mother a hard-working, religious woman whose aim in life is to see her two daughters married. Her mother berates Naomi's tomboy behavior: it will get her no husband and leave her a burden on the family. As for Naomi's dream of becoming a rich lady preacher, God, her family warns, forbids women to speak in public. One day Mrs. Jeno, a fortune-teller, tells the girl she will die before she is fourteen. When the family learns Naomi has consulted her, another scolding follows: they pronounce Mrs. Jeno a fraud. God, says older brother, Abe, adds years to one's life for good behavior. With that as her only hope, Naomi gives up her preacher dreams and vows to mind her parents. But when a copperhead snake bites her, Mrs. Jeno's prediction seems to be coming true. It is Mrs. Sarah Mitchell, a nurse viewed with suspicion for being an educated woman, who treats Naomi and brings her back to health. Then Naomi is thrown from a horse — and again she lives, for again Sarah Mitchell comes daily, over several months, to care for her. Since Naomi's mother does not like Sarah's influence, she forbids the girl, once well, to see her.

Months pass, and Naomi, interpreting her first menstrual period as cancer, goes to Sarah anyway. The two go on the nurse's house calls, and Sarah's praise of Naomi's gentle ways with the afflicted gives the girl confidence and self-esteem. She is relieved, too, when Sarah explains that menstruation is normal. It is an incident on an overnight stay with two girl friends that brings things to a head between Naomi and her family. When word reaches her parents that some boys watched the girls trying on clothes through a carelessly unshaded window, they charge her with disgracing the family and ruining all chances of ever getting married. Suddenly Naomi is not ashamed or afraid, but angry. She vows to hereafter ignore small-town gentility, superstition, and warnings of bad ends. She will decide her life and let "fate" go hang. On her fourteenth birthday she sees Mrs. Jeno for what she is. Naomi goes to work for a local doctor and will live to serve people. She thinks about becoming a doctor herself someday.

In Naomi's experience, the belief that a woman's only proper hope is to marry, and that any sacrifice is proper to that end, goes hand in hand with superstition, suffocating religiosity, and fear. She decides that fate does not have the final say about her life, and she dares to make her own plans for the future. Her story is told candidly and with spirit.

Ages 12 and up

Also available in:
Paperbound — *Naomi*
Bantam Books, Inc.

Talking Book — *Naomi*
Library of Congress

528

Raynor, Dorka

Grandparents Around the World

Black/white photographs by the author.
Albert Whitman & Co., 1977.
(46 pages)

R

GRANDPARENT: Love for
  Age: respect for

Love for grandparents is universal around the world. A French child confidently holds Grandfather's hand as they walk through the village. An Indonesian grandmother lovingly feeds her grandchild. A German grandmother teaches her grandchild how to swim. In Tokyo, a child and grandmother share a meal, eating with chopsticks. A little Swiss girl accompanies Grandmother to the hayfield, and a Jordanian boy helps his grandfather tend his shop. Children everywhere share both special and everyday moments with their grandparents — in cities and towns, in hamlets and rural areas. Geography is various but the quality of love remains the same.

This book presents forty-six full-page photographs of grandparents and children, taken in twenty-five countries. In these scenes, children lovingly care for or are cared for by grandparents. A brief text identifies the location in which each picture was taken. The author is well known for her photographs of children. An admirer, A. Hyatt Mayor, says of her work: "You find the same tenderness, the same exquisite communion in all costumes and all lands." This is a beautiful sampling of love between generations throughout the world.

Ages 4 and up

Also available in:
No other form known

529

Rees, David

Risks

Thomas Nelson, Inc., 1977.
(92 pages)

DEATH: of Friend
HITCHHIKING
MATURATION
RISK, TAKING OF
    Boy-girl relationships
    Death: murder
    Guilt, feelings of
    Loss: feelings of
    Mourning, stages of

When Derek's older brother invites him to London for the weekend, the fifteen-year-old and his best friend, Ian, decide to hitchhike from their hometown of Exeter. Their parents agree, though Derek's mother only grudgingly. After several hours, a car finally does stop for them, but the driver will take only one. Ian insists Derek take the ride, saying, "Anyway, I'll beat you there." But, Derek arrives first and finds his brother's party in his new apartment well under way. Derek feels out of place among these older people and impatiently awaits Ian's arrival. The evening wears on with no sign of Ian, and Derek wants to call the police. But his brother waits until the following morning to call in a description. Several hours later, the police arrive to tell Derek that a boy matching Ian's description has been found dead, evidently strangled. Derek keeps his emotions in check during most of the police questioning, but near the end of the interview, remembering the first time he had seen his friend in school, the boy breaks down. Back at home, Derek is disheartened to learn that the one and only lead he has given the police has turned up nothing.

Now he avoids all discussion of Ian and is particularly terse with his mother. School is dreadful, for he feels everyone is watching him; he cannot concentrate on anything. Derek keeps wondering why Ian was killed, who the killer is, and whether he ever will be caught. The one bright spot in his life is Yvonne, his first girl friend, with whom he feels so comfortable that he can talk about anything — even Ian. A few days after the funeral, Derek forces himself to call on Ian's mother and is relieved to hear her say, "Derek, don't ever think of it as your fault." As a memento of his friend, she gives him a picture of the two boys together. As the weeks go by, Derek realizes that things are smoothing out at home and school. He even brings Yvonne home to meet his parents. One evening his brother calls and invites him up for another weekend, suggesting he bring Yvonne. His father agrees, but forbids hitchhiking. When Derek goes to invite Yvonne, he begins talking to her about Ian. "It's awful how easily everything goes on," he muses. Yet he sees that his interest in Yvonne has changed him; he knows his life cannot stand still, not even for Ian. Together they go to ask Yvonne's parents about the weekend.

In this book a teenage boy, impatient to assert his independence, finds that anticipating hitchhiking, drinking, and partying is more exciting than the reality. But all minor disappointments give way to grief and feelings of guilt when Derek learns of his friend's violent death. He progresses through the stages of mourning: first feeling anger at the faceless killer, then sorrow for the loss of a friend. Only when he realizes that his own life will go on, that he cannot change Ian's death by dwelling on it, does he move to the final acceptance.

Ages 11 and up

Also available in:
No other form known

530

Reiss, Johanna

The Journey Back

Thomas Y. Crowell Company, Inc., 1976.
(212 pages)

CHANGE: Accepting
  Belonging
  Jewish
  Maturation
  Stepparent: mother
  War

A young Jewish girl, Annie de Leeuw, and an older sister, Sini, have spent the last two-and-a-half years of World War II hidden in the upstairs bedroom of Johan and Dientje Oostervel's farmhouse in Usselo, Holland. With the war over, Annie, now thirteen, and Sini rejoin their father and another sister, a convert to Christianity, in their home village. (Their mother had died early in the war.) Annie, who has grown to love Johan, his mother, and Dientje, is unhappy at home. Everyone and everything has changed. Her two older sisters have other interests and eventually move to the city. Father is gone much of the time, trying to rebuild his business. None of Annie's pre-war friends return to the village, and Annie is slow to make new friends. Even physical recovery comes slowly, with daily visits to the masseur to strengthen legs weak and painful from her long confinement. She longs to return to Johan and Dientje. Her father remarries, and her stepmother brings to the household, along with many lovely possessions, a critical eye for whether Annie is behaving "like a lady." Annie longs for her stepmother's approval, but that seems reserved for her own daughter, away at boarding school. At last Annie is allowed to visit Johan and Dientje — but once there she is bored by the routine of farm life. Though Johan and Dientje still love her, she feels like a misfit. Returning home, she can only hope one day to win her stepmother's favor.

In this first-person account, a Jewish girl describes the spiritual hardships of rebuilding one's life after war has destroyed all that was familiar and secure. Annie's own quiet struggle is complicated by her father's remarriage. But after repeated disappointments, she waits patiently for signs that she has come to where she belongs. This sequel to the autobiographical *The Upstairs Room* is a bittersweet picture of the aftermath of war, with its reunions, fragmented families, shortages, ravaged villages, determination, and hope.

Ages 10-14

Also available in:
Filmstrip — *The Journey Back*
Miller-Brody Productions

Record — *The Journey Back*
Miller-Brody Productions

Talking Book — *The Journey Back*
Library of Congress

531

Renner, Beverly Hollett

The Hideaway Summer

Black/white illustrations by Ruth Sanderson.
Harper & Row Publishers, Inc., 1978.
(134 pages)

ANIMALS: Responsibility for
SIBLING: Relationships
  Cooperation: in work

Addie Carter, twelve, and her nine-year-old brother, Clay, are on their way to summer camp when their bus passes by Grandmother Carver's land, where Addie has spent every summer of her life until this one. Gram has recently died, and the children's father has sold her farmhouse and part of the land, keeping only a stretch bordering the river, on it an old cabin Addie calls the Hideaway. The girl feels she must visit the old place, and so, when the bus stops at Groten's Crossroads Grocery, she and Clay grab their luggage and hop off, intending to board a later bus to camp. But they discover that Gram had repaired, redecorated, and furnished the Hideaway before her death. They decide to stay for the summer. First they cancel their camp reservations, then buy groceries at Groten's with camp money, and from then on phone their father each Sunday, pretending to be calling from camp. They love living in the woods and being together, for until recently, Clay has lived with their mother. They make a schedule and share the chores. No one seems to have found them out. When they rescue two orphaned raccoons, their worry about two hunters they have seen deepens. But the raccoons thrive under their care, and the children are too busy to worry long. Several weeks pass, and a bad rainstorm floods the river, leaving the children stranded for a few days. After the water subsides, Clay finds fresh footprints in the sand near the cabin: someone knows. They wait, but no one appears. One afternoon Addie spies the hunters on Carver land. Knowing that the men think the property haunted, she and Clay scare them off once and for all. But summer is over. The children close the cabin and say good-bye to the by now self-sufficient raccoons. Before boarding the bus for home, they stop at Groten's Grocery to say good-bye. Mrs. Groten confesses that she has been watching over them all summer; thus the footprints. She promises to check on the raccoons and says she hopes to see the children next summer.

A brother and sister spend a marvelous summer learning to live in the woods and getting to know each other again. While this story will satisfy any child's fantasy of secret, independent living, these children's self-reliance seems a bit overdrawn. It is also unlikely that an adult, aware of them, would not report their presence to anyone.

Ages 10-13

Also available in:
Paperbound — *The Hideaway Summer*
Scholastic Book Services

532

Resnick, Rose

Sun and Shadow: The Autobiography of a Woman Who Cleared a Pathway to the Seeing World for the Blind
Atheneum Publishers, 1975.
(274 pages) o.p.

BLINDNESS
EDUCATION: Special
TALENTS: Musical
  Courage, meaning of
  Dependence/Independence
  Perseverance
  Pets: guide dog
  Resourcefulness

In 1918 the doctors tell two-year-old Rose's parents that their child will grow to see only light and shadow. Appalled, Rose's mother nevertheless continues to treat Rose just like the other seven children, sending her to public school with them (they are a poor family), but grateful that blind students can learn Braille there. Through the New York Association for the Blind, known as the Lighthouse, Rose joins the Campfire Girls, with whom she learns to rollerskate, takes piano lessons, and acts in plays. At the Lighthouse-sponsored camp called Mossyledge, Rose expands her world still farther, learning to swim and to ride and understand horses. At school, she discovers she has a talent for languages, and soon decides to go to college and become a French teacher. Successful in college and in her student teaching, she finds to her dismay that blind people are barred from teaching in New York (they were, but are no longer). Luckily, Rose has exceptional musical talents too, and she wins a scholarship to study at the Fontainebleau Conservatory in Paris. Upon returning to New York she gives a piano concert at Carnegie Hall to excellent reviews, and soon she enters a piano competition in San Francisco, but does not win. Still in San Francisco, she takes a job accompanying a singing group in an organization called Blindcraft. The work pays well, but Blindcraft is mismanaged and seems dedicated to perpetuating clichés about blind people. Rose begins playing in honky-tonks and night clubs, but one day, while performing at a psychiatric hospital, she meets Nina, a psychiatric nurse, and they become friends. Rose tells Nina about her longing to create a Lighthouse in San Francisco. They decide to collaborate on the project, the first step being to raise enough money to start a camp similar in spirit to Mossyledge. Once the camp is established, Rose allows herself to be persuaded that by merging their fledging organization with Blindcraft and the Buchanan Street Center, the creation of the new Lighthouse will be facilitated. Nina doubts this and is proved right. The two lose all executive control over their camp and are ordered about like newcomers. Then Rose is fired, and the project she had worked so hard for is ruined. But she goes back to school for a master's degree and a certificate to teach exceptional children. Soon, with the help of some teacher friends, she sets up the California League for the Handicapped, an agency to help multihandicapped children. She has seen at last part of her dream fulfilled.

Few autobiographies describe two careers, and Rose's music is no less interesting than her detailed accounts of the formation of her agencies. Her major achievements are lightened with candid, sometimes funny descriptions of good times with friends, dating, and her life with one or another of three guide dogs. The behavior of sighted people toward the blind is also examined in detail and set beside the latter's capacities, limitations, and right to aspire.

Ages 12 and up

Also available in:
Braille — *Sun and Shadow: The Autobiography of a Woman Who Cleared a Pathway to the Seeing World for the Blind*
Library of Congress

Talking Book — *Sun and Shadow: The Autobiography of a Woman Who Cleared a Pathway to the Seeing World for the Blind*
Library of Congress

R

533

Reynolds, Pamela

Will the Real Monday Please Stand Up

Lothrop, Lee & Shepard Co., 1975.
(184 pages)

DEPRIVATION, EMOTIONAL
SIBLING: Relationships
    Boy-girl relationships: dating
    Marijuana

Monday Holliday's sixteen-year-old brother, Johnny, has just been arrested for illegal possession of marijuana, and fourteen-year-old Monday and her parents are on their way to see Dr. Muriel Aarons, a family-court investigator. Two days earlier, Monday herself had telephoned family court, asking to be placed in a foster-home. Now she is reluctant to be questioned in front of her parents, and so Dr. Aarons asks her to make a tape recording telling all the events leading to Johnny's arrest and what family life at the Hollidays' has been like. Through this recording and accompanying flashbacks, we learn that Monday's parents are wealthy people who have given Monday and Johnny everything but attention. Johnny, the favorite, has always teased Monday cruelly, and she feels inferior. Thus when he had been sent away to private school, Monday breathed easier — until, suspended for smoking marijuana, Johnny had returned home. Bribed with a new car, he agrees to enroll in the same school Monday attends. Worse, Monday finds a box of marijuana in Johnny's room, and is frightened. When she finally tells her mother, Mrs. Holliday simply refuses to believe her. Meanwhile, Monday has been happily dating a nineteen-year-old boy named Mano, though she has deceived him about her age. When Mano fails to appear one evening, Monday learns that Johnny, to repay her for telling on him, has told Mano that Monday is only fourteen and is sneaking out to see him. Monday is furious. Eavesdropping as Johnny talks on the telephone of an upcoming "pot" party, Monday herself is caught on the phone telling her best friend, whose father calls the police. Johnny and the other partygoers are arrested. Monday's parents are furious with her. She is numb and locks herself in her room. So ends her tape recording for Dr. Aarons, which has cleared her mind considerably about Johnny and her parents. Now she feels a need to talk to someone so as to find out "which is the real me." But she will not leave her family. With Dr. Aarons' help, perhaps the Hollidays can get through this difficulty together.

Monday muses: "I guess the real Monday is part of this family and it wouldn't do any good to run away." Monday's parents, who are more interested in their social lives than in their children, have never seriously considered Monday's feelings. Johnny has learned to manipulate the parents, but he guesses wrong when he destroys the one relationship that gives Monday self-esteem: she feels justified in reporting him to the authorities. Later she regrets what she has done. Each chapter of this first-person narrative begins with a short excerpt from Monday's tape, on which she then comments and elaborates at some length.

Ages 11-14

Also available in:
Paperbound — *Will the Real Monday Please Stand Up*
Pocket Books, Inc.

534

Rice, Eve

Ebbie

Color illustrations by the author.
Greenwillow Books, 1975.
(32 pages counted)

NAME, DISSATISFACTION WITH
  Tooth, loss of

After young Edward loses two front teeth, he begins to call himself "Ebbie" because he cannot say "Eddie." His family picks this up. Though still lacking his front teeth, he learns to say "Eddie" and resents being called "Ebbie" anymore. But his family continues to call him "Ebbie" even though he corrects them. Eddie is frustrated and does not know what to do. He sees a solution when his uncle comes to visit: Eddie hides. The family looks for "Ebbie" and cannot find him; they find only "Eddie" written on a paper in the hall, spelled out in toothpicks in the kitchen, and written on a wall in his room. His father shouts "Ebbie" and there is no answer. Then someone under the bed yells "Eddie." After that, everyone calls him "Eddie" except for his little sister, who has lost *her* two front teeth.

In this story a young child shows great ingenuity in teaching his family to call him by the name he prefers.

The story illustrates that little things can matter a great deal to children and that a child, no matter how young, needs to be heard and respected.

Ages 3-7

Also available in:
Paperbound — *Ebbie*
Penguin Books, Inc.

535

Rice, Eve

New Blue Shoes

Color illustrations by the author.
Macmillan Publishing Company, Inc., 1975.
(32 pages counted)

DECISION MAKING
DEPENDENCE/INDEPENDENCE
  Encouragement

One day Mother takes Rebecca downtown to buy her a new pair of shoes. Rebecca insists the shoes be blue. Mother objects at first, then relents. After searching throughout the store, the clerk finds one pair of blue shoes in the right size. But on the way home with the shoes Rebecca begins to doubt her choice. With playful impatience her mother suggests that "maybe we should get a different pair of feet." The shoes, she says, will be fine, but the little girl is still uncertain. At home, Mother suggests she wear her shoes around the house. Rebecca puts them on and soon decides they will be just fine after all. "I like my feet the way they are," says Rebecca. Mother answers that she herself likes "all of you the way you are — right down to your very own feet in your new blue shoes."

A little girl is trying her wings by making a choice independent of her mother. When misgivings follow, she is soothed by her mother's faith in that choice. But she finally must, and does, decide herself that the choice was right. Pictures and text portray a young child's normal swings between independence, self-doubt, and need for reassurance.

Ages 3-5

Also available in:
Paperbound — *New Blue Shoes*
Penguin Books, Inc.

536

Rich, Louise Dickinson

Summer at High Kingdom

Franklin Watts, Inc., 1975.
(112 pages)

PREJUDICE: Social Class
  Commune
  Family: relationships
  Freedom, meaning of

Thirteen-year-old Dana Chadwick has always thought his family's prosperous farm in Maine "the best in the whole area," his peaceful, well-ordered life there with his parents, sister, and grandfather the nicest to be found. But this summer, the long-deserted King farm, nearby, known as High Kingdom, has been rented by a group of "hippies," and most valley residents, Dana and his parents included, distrust them. When Gramps begins visiting the newcomers, Dana cannot understand the old man's tolerance of their shiftless ways. Gramps even goes so far as to lend them his prize cow, help them rebuild their ramshackle barn, and teach them farming. To further puzzle Dana, his older brother, Whit, on leave from the Army, also lends a hand to the newcomers. Dana and his parents continue to be wary. But when the Chadwicks' crop of beans —

R

on consignment to a cannery — threatens to go unpicked because half the regular harvesters are ill, a word from Gramps and Whit brings the High Kingdom commune flocking. Many hours of tiring work bring the harvest in on time. And as their new neighbors chat about their hopes, their disappointments, and their desire to live free of conventional constraints, the entire Chadwick family begins to like and understand them. Finding them entertaining and honest, Dana and his parents visit their new friends and defend them to others. That is why, when the group moves on, Dana says good-bye with regret, knowing how much of tolerance, freedom, and individuality he has learned.

A teenage boy, brought up to suspect people who live differently from himself, looks down on the members of a nearby commune. The book airs the boy's prejudice candidly, showing how it derives from his parents. Life in the commune itself, as he sees it and as the members do, is fully set out. Also explored is the grandfather's advancing age and his inability to accept modern labor-saving devices and farming techniques.

Ages 12 and up

Also available in:
Paperbound — *Summer at High Kingdom*
Dell Publishing Company, Inc.

537

Richard, Adrienne

Into the Road

Atlantic Monthly Press, 1976.
(206 pages)

MATURATION
Freedom, meaning of
Life style
Self, attitude toward: confidence
Sibling: relationships

As he nears high school graduation, orphaned Nathaniel "Nat" Combs, who has known only school, sports, and the delicatessen where he works for his uncle, is undecided about his future. When his older brother, Cy, returns to town after not being heard from for six years, Nat lets himself be persuaded to buy a used motorcycle and come travel with Cy for the summer. Nat's introduction to Cy's life is hard, for his brother is an impatient and demanding teacher. Nat soon learns he must follow Cy's rules — go where and when Cy wants, camp and live the way Cy does — if he wants to keep up. On their first night out they encounter Cy's friends, the notorious Hell's Angels, who invite them to ride with them in a funeral procession the following day. Afterwards, finding themselves tagged as part of the gang, the brothers leave town quickly. During the summer they travel up and down the New England coast, meeting and joining other bikers for rallies and races, enjoying the comaraderie of the road. As Nat gains confidence in his own riding skill, he also gains respect for his brother's knowledge and care of his "machine." But Cy is adventurous where Ned is cautious, and that makes for strain. When a biker, a girl named Gage, joins them, competition for her attention increases the strain. But Gage refuses to align herself with either one, although toward the end of summer, she does travel with them to a nationally famous road race in New Hampshire. There they meet Cy's friend and mentor from California, the Duke of the Road, the man who had sent Cy back to find Nat in the first place. One day while trying to disperse some rowdy bikers, the Duke is hit on the head with a beer bottle, and Cy is wrongly arrested for the assault. Gage has gone with the Duke to the hospital, and Nat goes to the jail to persuade the hostile police to release his brother. He soon sees that his only hope is to bring the Duke himself in to testify. Fortunately, he catches Duke on his way out of town — and Cy is set free. But the summer is over. As they ride out of town, Cy asks Nat if he plans to sell his bike when he gets home. Nat says no, that he likes it. But he adds that he is only "a guy who has a bike — you know what I mean?" Cy answers, "Yes, I know what you mean. You're a guy with a bike. I'm a biker."

In accepting his brother's challenge to try the motorcycling life, Nat broadens his outlook and learns what his own values and limitations are; his journey becomes one of self-discovery and self-acceptance. At first equating life on the road with freedom, he soon learns that even so free a life is hedged by rules, standards, and some hard times. As he learns how he differs from his brother, Nat gains a new understanding and respect for his brother. This book naturally includes much technical information about motorcycles, but all of it can be understood by the novice.

Ages 12 and up

Also available in:
Cassette for the Blind — *Into the Road*
Library of Congress

Paperbound — *Into the Road*
Dell Publishing Company, Inc.

538

Riley, Susan

What Does It Mean? Afraid

Color illustrations by Collateral, Inc.
The Child's World, Inc., 1978.
(32 pages)

FEAR
   Emotions: accepting
   Emotions: identifying

A small boy hides behind a big door, refusing to come out because he is afraid. He fears many things: the dark in his room at night; falling out of a tall tree when climbing; getting a shot from the doctor; storms, thunder, and lightning; doing things for the first time. He remembers his fright about the first day of school and at the first parade he saw. But after talking about his fears to us, he is no longer afraid and is ready to come from behind the door.

This simple first-person narrative, written in verse, could help small children confront and discuss their own fears. The narrator's question at the end of the book, "What makes you afraid?" is followed by the suggestion "If you'll talk about things you're afraid to do, you will feel much better, too." This book is one in a series meant to encourage young children to identify and accept their own feelings.

Ages 3-6

Also available in:
No other form known

539

Riley, Susan

What Does It Mean? Angry

Color illustrations by Collateral, Inc.
The Child's World, Inc., 1978.
(32 pages)

ANGER
   Emotions: accepting
   Running away

A little boy is running away from home because everyone seems angry about everything he does. Mom scolds when he spills his milk, and when he gets muddy playing outdoors. Of course he gets angry, too — when no one listens to him; when he is not allowed to play with his friends; when a building he has carefully built of blocks comes tumbling down; and when he may not go shopping with his mother. His friend becomes angry

R

when he pulls her pigtails; he admits he is wrong to tease her this way. After thinking all this over, the boy concludes: "Anger is OK but no reason to run away." Instead, he smiles and will go home and "work this thing out."

The young narrator contemplates anger in himself and others, concluding that anger is both real and acceptable. This simple account is written in verse and is part of a series meant to encourage young children to identify and accept their feelings.

Ages 3-6

Also available in:
No other form known

540

Riley, Susan

What Does It Mean? Help

Color illustrations by Collateral, Inc.
The Child's World, Inc., 1978.
(32 pages)

HELPING
  Giving, meaning of

A small boy high up in a tree and afraid to climb down alone calls for help. The fire department arrives to bring him down safely. Help is a good thing to get, but it is also a good thing to give. He helps younger children cross the street and wash dishes; he also sets the table and cleans his room. On the other hand, he needs help putting on shoes and boots, untying a knot, and reaching for things on a high shelf. He explains that "helping people makes me feel GOOD," and suggests: "Let us all help each other in all that we do."

The young narrator describes in verse some thoughts and experiences having to do with helping. He never forgets to mention the happiness that comes from giving and receiving help. This book is part of a series meant to encourage young children to identify and accept their feelings.

Ages 3-6

Also available in:
No other form known

541

Riley, Susan

What Does It Mean? I'm Sorry

Color illustrations by Collateral, Inc.
The Child's World, Inc., 1978.
(32 pages)

CONSIDERATION, MEANING OF
EMOTIONS: Identifying

A little boy apologizes for being late. But he is not just sorry for things he does — he also feels sorry for other people when they are sick or unhappy. Among other things he regrets are hitting others, spilling his milk, or splashing a friend; when he does those he always apologizes. That lets people know he is sorry and trying to improve. That "makes everyone feel better."

A child may feel sorry when he regrets his own actions or when he sympathizes with others' unhappiness or misfortune. This simple first-person verse narrative could be used to start a discussion on the value of expressing regret. It is part of a series meant to help young children recognize and cope with emotions.

Ages 3-6

Also available in:
No other form known

542

Riley, Susan

What Does It Mean? Sharing

Color illustrations by Collateral, Inc.
The Child's World, Inc., 1978.
(32 pages)

SHARING/NOT SHARING

The little narrator says he will share his candy with his friend. He goes on to explain that almost anything can be shared: books, apples, toys. Sharing is evidence of kindness and caring for others. Jokes and riddles, hugs, kisses, and handshakes are all to be shared. Sadness, too, can be shared, and that can make people feel better.

Written in verse, this simple first-person narrative provides examples of sharing objects as well as feelings, and explains how satisfying such sharing can be. This book is one in a series meant to encourage young children to identify and accept their feelings.

Ages 3-6

Also available in:
No other form known

543

Riley, Susan

What Does It Mean? Success

Color illustrations by Collateral, Inc.
The Child's World, Inc., 1978.
(32 pages)

SUCCESS
  Perseverance
  Pride/False pride

A little boy tells what it takes to be a success. "I am me. That's really much more than you see." For he has learned how to do many things by always doing his best. Through them, he is a success. He no longer rides a tricycle but a two-wheeler bike. He ties his own shoes after much practice. He is able to stand on his head, climb a tree, recite the alphabet, zip his jacket, whistle, and hum — all because he has tried hard. "And I'm proud of my success, of what I can do. You should be proud of what you can do, too."

This simple first-person verse narrative offers one meaning of success: everyone has things he or she does best, and these make one successful. This book is one in a series meant to encourage young children to identify and accept their feelings.

Ages 3-6

Also available in:
No other form known

544

Rivera, Geraldo

A Special Kind of Courage: Profiles of Young Americans

Black/white illustrations by Edith Vonnegut.
Simon & Schuster, Inc., 1976.
(319 pages)

COURAGE, MEANING OF
  Accidents: airplane
  Adoption
  Amputee
  Cancer
  Cerebral palsy
  Ghetto
  Little League
  Mental hospital, living in
  Multiple sclerosis
  Poliomyelitis
  Prejudice: ethnic/racial
  Prejudice: sexual
  Responsibility: accepting

The eleven young people portrayed in this collection are not heroic in stature — their ages range from six to twenty-one — and their heroism is not always dramatic. Put simply, they "have chosen to act on their own, with honor and dignity, at moments of individual crisis." Sometimes the crisis reflects a larger social crisis. Six-year-old Gail Etienne, scarcely comprehending that she is one of four black children chosen to desegregate the New Orleans schools in 1960, nonetheless endures the spite and insults of enraged whites. Maria Pepe, twelve, fights another kind of discrimination, and her court case against the Little League Association opens the way for girls to play Little League baseball. At other times the crisis is individual and lasts for years. Erwin Ponder, a

black youth brought up in a slum, drifts into a street gang and petty thievery but, aided by his parents and a summer school for "lost causes," breaks with his peers and wins a college scholarship. Mark Gaither takes over the family farm after his father dies and his older brother is paralyzed, and still does so well in high school that he earns a scholarship to Harvard. A young Vietnamese girl, Thu Van, severely crippled by polio, survives a wretched life to be adopted by an American couple. The crises are sometimes medical. Stephen Baltz, sole, temporary survivor of a plane crash, suffers with immense dignity before his death. Bernard Carabello, a Puerto Rican suffering multiple sclerosis (misdiagnosed as mental retardation) had spent most of his twenty-one years in the notorious Willowbrook school and helps to expose that institution in news stories. Teddy Kennedy, twelve, is determined to continue a normal life despite losing a leg to cancer. And Joey Cappelletti, ill most of his life, first from encephalitis, then from leukemia, insists on living cheerfully. The other two crises are more dramatic. Sixteen-year-old Bob Hernandez, a Chicano explorer scout on a police training program, though seriously wounded, helps rescue two wounded policemen. A New York teenager, Henry Schwartz, dismayed by six others' apathy, tries to stop a bicycle thief and is stabbed to death.

Courage and heroism are not of a piece, as these true stories illustrate. The author, a well-known television reporter, writes in crisp journalistic style, adding social background where relevant. These are not only inspiring stories: some are an implicit criticism of society; others raise questions, not about youth's courage, but about its wisdom.

Ages 12 and up

Also available in:
Paperbound — *A Special Kind of Courage: Profiles of Young Americans*
Bantam Books, Inc.

545

Roberts, Willo Davis

Don't Hurt Laurie!

Black/white illustrations by Ruth Sanderson.
Atheneum Publishers, 1978.
(166 pages)

CHILD ABUSE
  Guilt, feelings of
  Loneliness
  Mental illness: of parent
  Stepbrother/Stepsister
  Stepparent: father

Eleven-year-old Laurie Kolman lives with her mother, Annabelle, and her stepfather, Jack, and Jack's son, Tim (nine), and daughter, Shelly (five), by an earlier marriage. Annabelle's first husband had deserted her when Laurie was three, and the mother has been physically abusing Laurie ever since. Tim knows this, knows that Laurie is not "clumsy," as Annabelle insists to friends, neighbors, and hospital staff, every time Laurie "bumps herself." Neither Tim nor Laurie will tell anyone about the abuse for fear of Annabelle taking revenge. Besides, Laurie feels that no one would believe her. Annabelle is always on her best behavior when Jack is home, and always lies so convincingly about Laurie's injuries that Laurie thinks her mother really believes them to be accidents. Laurie has no friends to talk to; every time she finds one, and every time someone in the hospital emergency ward notices the frequency of her visits, Annabelle moves to a new neighborhood. In a rage one day, Annabelle threatens to kill Laurie, and as usual the girl can tell no one, feeling that somehow these rages are her own fault. It is not until Annabelle attacks Amigo, the puppy Laurie and her only friend have been secretly keeping, that Laurie turns on her mother. Annabelle is so infuriated that, forgetting Tim is watching, she beats Laurie unconscious with a poker. When Laurie comes to, she knows she cannot live with her mother anymore. Tim, who had feared his stepsister was dead, insists they tell his grandmother, Nell. All three children make the long bus trip across town, and Nell is told the shocking story. To Laurie's amazement and relief, Nell believes every word. Jack and Annabelle come, but Nell refuses to let the children go back with Annabelle, and urges Jack to get help for his wife. For the first time in her life, Laurie is free of fear. While Laurie's mother receives treatment, the children stay with Nell. Laurie learns both to trust and to love.

This tense story untangles the inner lives of an abused child, including her reasons for not seeking help. Sometimes Laurie tries to escape with books, without which she would have no idea what normal families are like. Her fantasy about her real father coming to save her only prolongs her silence to others. Each time she does decide to tell someone, her own fear or circumstances beyond her control stop her. Such incidents are so convincingly told that we come to share Laurie's bafflement and despair. But we come as well to believe Jack: Annabelle's derangement is connected with her having been beaten herself as a child, and never having told. Jack will stay with her and help her get well.

Ages 10-14

Also available in:
No other form known

R

Roberts, Willo Davis

The View from the Cherry Tree

Atheneum Publishers, 1975.
(181 pages)

COMMUNICATION: Lack of
PROBLEM SOLVING
   Death: murder

Eleven-year-old Rob Mallory, seeking refuge from the happy tumult at home — his sister Darcy will be married in two days — sits in a cherry tree, only descending for necessities like food, sleep, and satisfying his curiosity. Occasionally he throws cherry pits on Mrs. Calloway's windowsill next door, to annoy the old woman, whose complaints about his cat, named S.O.B., annoy Rob in turn. Down for lunch, he finds two of Darcy's former suitors have come: Max already interested in Rob's sister Teddi; and Derek, Mrs. Calloway's nephew. The next day again finds Rob in the tree, determined to avoid the wedding hysteria by remaining there all day. Suddenly he sees someone push Mrs. Calloway out the window. The strap of her binoculars catches on a limb, and she dies by hanging. Rob tries to convince people of what he saw, but no one will listen. He even begins to doubt himself — until someone tries to kill him, first by shooting, then by dropping a flower pot that just misses him. Again Rob tries to tell people, even phoning the police, and again no one will listen. After an attempt is made to poison him, he narrows his suspects to Max and Derek. But how to tell which one? Easily — S.O.B. has scratched the killer's arm. Later the police come and Rob, fearing they will arrest him for the phone call, dashes over to search Mrs. Calloway's house for evidence. He finds nothing conclusive and is about to leave when Derek enters. Rob rips open Derek's sleeve, and the scratch reveals him as the killer, Derek chases Rob upstairs and eventually corners him. Rob, hurling a spider at him, distracts Derek long enough to slip past him. By this time Mr. Mallory and the police have entered the house, and they capture Derek.

A boy who witnesses a murder convinces only the killer that he has actually seen it and from then on is busy ducking attempts on his own life. Readers will almost surely second-guess Rob's tactics, but his character is so well done that a reader can also see why he could not have acted otherwise. This book dramatizes all too well the futility children feel when adults ignore or disbelieve the truth.

Ages 9-12

Also available in:
Paperbound — The View from the Cherry Tree
Atheneum Publishers

Talking Book — The View from the Cherry Tree
Library of Congress

Robinet, Harriette

Jay and the Marigold

Color illustrations by Trudy Scott.
Childrens Press, Inc., 1976.
(48 pages)

CEREBRAL PALSY
   Determination
   Friendship: making friends

Eight-year-old Jay, who has cerebral palsy, wishes he could play and get about like his twin sister, Janie, but all he is able to do is roll on his outdoor mat, sit in his wheelchair, and speak a few words. One day, outdoors, he spies a marigold shoot trying to grow in a crack in the concrete steps. From then on, with Janie's help, Jay waters the small plant faithfully. But the same things still make him angry, chief among them his being ignored by the other neighborhood children, who think his limited speech means he is stupid. Small wonder he welcomes the friendship offered by a new boy in the neighborhood named Pedro. It is with Pedro's help that Jay is soon included in neighborhood games. But though Jay is busy, he does not forget his marigold. In fact, when he overhears his father speaking of his son's limitations, he thinks of his new friendship and his sturdy plant — both growing despite limitations — and resolves to open up more in school when it starts in the fall and to use the aids available to him there. When, on the first day of school Jay sees his marigold's first blossom, he is "sure that one day — in spite of his limitations, in spite of handicaps, in his own way, in his own time — he, too, would bloom."

This story is no less touching for making the reader aware of the anger and loneliness felt by a child with cerebral palsy. Readers with cerebral palsy may find inspiring the hope and determination Jay finds in himself when chance provides gates through his isolation. The author, we are told, brings an intimate knowledge of cerebral palsy to this story, having a son who suffers from this brain dysfunction.

Ages 6-9

Also available in:
Cassette — *Jay and the Marigold*
Childrens Press, Inc.

Large Print — *Jay and the Marigold*
Childrens Press, Inc.

548

Robinson, Charles

New Kid in Town
Color illustrations by the author.
Atheneum Publishers, 1975.
(29 pages counted) o.p.

R

BULLY: *Being Bothered by*
  Friendship: making friends
  Problem solving

A young boy, new in town, is asked by a neighbor boy of about the same age to play. They build a tree fort, the neighbor doing only the easy work. They plan a garden, and the neighbor does all the planting, leaving the new boy all the digging. Whatever they play, the new boy gets the worst of it. Finally, he runs home and tells his mother the other boy is a bully. But when they see the neighbor fall off his homemade car and begin to cry, the boy's mother says: "My, he's not a very good driver is he? You wouldn't cry like that! I don't think he's so great!" The boy agrees and that night dreams of getting even. The next day, playing the horse to his cowboy neighbor, he bucks him off. When the neighbor pretends to be a king, the new boy spills His Majesty's root beer over him. The boys have a tussle which ends with the neighbor suggesting a game of checkers. They walk off, arm in arm.

This book is a good beginning reader, perhaps for reading aloud. The boy resents the way his neighbor acts, and his sympathetic mother helps him to see he is being bullied and what to do about it. He returns every slight in kind, until the two reach a mutual understanding and respect.

Ages 4-7

Also available in:
No other form known

549

Robison, Nancy

On the Balance Beam

Black/white illustrations by Rondi Anderson.
Albert Whitman & Co., 1978.
(64 pages)

SELF-DISCIPLINE
  Hostility
  Sports/Sportsmanship
  Talents: athletic

Andrea, a sixth grader, shows natural ability at gymnastics and just as native a gift for carelessness. Her mother uses one against the other by letting her take gymnastics lessons on condition that she keep up with her homework. Though Andrea progresses rapidly under the careful coaching of Trudy (called Trudy the Terrible by class members), her pleasure is marred by Cynthia, star of the team, who taunts and tricks her maliciously. Andrea ignores her for the most part but vows to show Cynthia up. Proud when Trudy names her to compete in an upcoming meet, Andrea soon sees her dreams brought low — her mother grounds her for undone homework. Downcast, the girl vows to concentrate on studying as she does for gymnastics, and soon completes the work. At the meet, she gloats when Cynthia, disconsolate that Andrea receives all the attention, withdraws to the stands, refusing to take part. But Andrea takes no pleasure in her own routine and finds she cares about the team's performance more than getting back at Cynthia — whom she passionately persuades to return and compete.

A girl with talent learns the value of concentration, foresight, and cooperation — to underpin talent and much else — as she trains and competes as a gymnast. She also learns the reason for a classmate's baffling hostility — an ambitious mother who drives her daughter to excel. The ending of this story is as conventional as the characters, but readers may be held by the sports background.

Ages 8-10

Also available in:
No other form known

550

Rock, Gail

Addie and the King of Hearts

Black/white illustrations by the author.
Alfred A. Knopf, Inc., 1976.
(86 pages)

MATURATION
  Boy-girl relationships
  Love, meaning of
  School: pupil-teacher relationships

It is 1949, the day after the Christmas-New Year's holiday, and Addie Mills and her friends are amazed to find that their new seventh-grade teacher is a man. Young, easy-going, and handsome, Mr. Davenport quickly wins the favor of the class. Paid some extra attention for her artwork, Addie is hopelessly infatuated. Soon, she and Mr. Davenport are having frequent after-school chats about art, and these talks feed Addie's daydreams. She yearns to be older so that Mr. Davenport would take her seriously. Theirs would be an ideal relationship, not at all like that between her widowed father and the loud, earthy Irene, whom Addie thinks common. Feigning sophistication, Addie tells her friends and Mr. Davenport that she does not plan to attend the "childish" Valentine's Day dance, and she discourages her lifelong friend, Billy, from inviting her. But as the day of the dance approaches, her father and grandmother persuade her to go after all, without a date. Determined to look older, Addie sets out for the beauty shop, only to be stopped by Mr. Davenport, who offers her a ride and himself urges her to come to the dance, because he has a surprise for her. From that moment she prepares for the dance as though it were a royal ball. Uncomfortable at first about going alone, once at the school gym she is soon at ease with her friends. She apologizes to Billy for having acted superior — and too soon discovers that Mr. Davenport's surprise, standing by his side, is his fiancée, Kathy. Feeling hurt and abandoned, Addie turns on some boys who are teasing her and hurls a basketball at them. An impromptu basketball game begins, and Addie, her first pair of high heels abandoned, is soon in the middle of it; the dance is disrupted. Unfortunately, it is Mr. Davenport who breaks up the fun, calling Addie childish. Burning with embarrassment, she rushes out. Her father, who is present with Irene, follows Addie out. On the way home, they discuss boys, marriage, and finding the right person. Addie's father explains that relationships are not always ideal, and adds that though Irene could never replace Addie's mother, she is nonetheless a warm and loving person who is fun to be with. Touched by her father's honesty, Addie thinks she understands a little better how relationships begin. Back home, Irene arrives to join them for ice cream and cake. Seeing her father relaxed and laughing with Irene, Addie sees too that Irene is good for her father. Addie has been jealous, but no longer. Billy arrives with a Valentine box of candy for Addie. Remembering all that she and Billy have shared growing up, she sees her friend in a different light. She decides to give Billy the elaborate valentine she had designed for Mr. Davenport.

In this first-person narrative, a high-spirited, uncompromising girl discovers that the movie portrayal of love and marriage is not necessarily true to life. Addie begins to mature when she reflects upon the probable feelings of a friend and apologizes to him, and when she can accept her father's right to decide what is best for him. This is the author's fourth book about Addie Mills. All four have been dramatized on television.

Ages 9-12

Also available in:
Paperbound — *Addie and the King of Hearts*
Bantam Books, Inc.

Talking Book — *Addie and the King of Hearts*
Library of Congress

551

Rock, Gail

A Dream for Addie

Black/white illustrations by Charles C. Gehm.
Alfred A. Knopf, Inc., 1975.
(90 pages)

FRIENDSHIP: Meaning of
  Alcoholism: adult
  Expectations
  Talents: artistic

It is 1948 and twelve-year-old Addie Mills lives in Clear River, Nebraska, with her father and grandmother. The most exciting event in Addie's life to date has been the return to Clear River of hometown-girl Constance Payne, now a Broadway actress, come back to sell the family home after her mother's death. Against her father's wishes, Addie and some friends go to the star's house for her autograph. To impress a highfalutin friend, Addie invites Constance to Saturday-night dinner at the Millses'. Addie's father, who scarcely knows the actress, rebukes the child for making people (including Constance) think he is Constance's old friend. But Addie's grandmother is as thrilled as her granddaughter is to have a star to dinner, and so the invitation stands. The dinner, however, has its tense moments. Constance herself seems nervous and asks several times for cocktails or wine, although the Mills family does not serve liquor. When Addie speaks of wanting to be an artist and live in New York, her father dismisses the idea as nonsense and recommends a safe, quiet life in Clear River. But Constance comes to Addie's defense, saying that dreams give one something to look forward to; and as if to seal her approval, agrees to award the prizes at a 4-H Club Style Show. But on the awards night, Constance arrives late, and to everyone's embarrassment is drunk. Unable even to read the winners' names, she makes a hasty and awkward exit. Feeling sorry for her, Addie visits her the next day and arranges to take acting lessons. Those, too, begin well enough, but when Addie arrives early for the second one, she finds Constance drunk again. She insults Addie and tells her to leave. The girl is hurt and ready to give up on Constance until her grandmother remarks that true friends help out when someone is in trouble. Addie and her father go to visit Constance and find her so ill that Mr. Mills invites her to spend a few days with them. Suddenly Constance tells them that she has never been a Broadway star. Her vaunted career has been with small acting companies for little money. Clear River gossip has so exaggerated her success that she has been afraid to come home and be found out. Constance continues to encourage Addie to pursue her own dream, but warns her never to be afraid to admit the truth, or be ashamed to come home. Constance never quite fits in with the safe, quiet life in Clear River, but she does stay, teaching acting and piano. Addie does become an artist and moves to New York.

A young adolescent learns how to give and receive friendship, and how important it is to be honest with oneself. A little contrived, her story benefits from sound characterizations and believable relationships. Written in Addie's first person, the book is based on the television play "The Easter Promise" and is one of several books about Addie.

Ages 9-12

Also available in:
Paperbound — *A Dream for Addie*
Bantam Books, Inc.

Talking Book — *A Dream for Addie*
Library of Congress

552

Rockwell, Harlow

My Dentist

Color illustrations by the author.
Greenwillow Books, 1975.
(32 pages counted)

DENTIST, GOING TO

A little girl describes a routine visit to her dentist — the chair that goes up and down, the X-ray camera, his little mirror on a handle, the tools for taking tartar off her teeth, and his drill and its attachments. She has no cavities today, but she has her teeth cleaned and explains how that is done. After the dentist has brushed her teeth with a special drill attachment, he has her rinse her mouth, then polishes her teeth, and tells her to rinse again. Afterwards he checks each tooth, even the loose one and the space where she had lost one a week before. She is finished. The dentist lowers the chair, removes the plastic bib, and reminds her to take care of her teeth. The girl chooses a prize from the prize drawer and goes home.

This book is an informative preparation for a child's first visit to the dentist. Both the text and the illustrations are straightforwardly factual. No mention is made of a dental assistant, who in life often does the dentist's preliminary work. But the detailed drawings accurately show the tools and equipment.

Ages 4-7

Also available in:
Braille — *My Dentist*
Library of Congress

553

Rockwell, Harlow

My Nursery School

Color illustrations by the author.
Greenwillow Books, 1976.
(24 pages counted)

NURSERY SCHOOL

A little girl takes the reader along for a typical day at her nursery school. After introducing the two teachers and the nine other children, she describes the materials in the room and how the children use them: Susan builds a tower with blocks; Olly works on a puzzle; the girl herself molds clay; and so on. The children are also shown playing games, exercising, and reading.

Vivid pictures combine with a simple text to show what nursery school is like. The tone throughout is one of enjoyment and interest, and will encourage children approaching nursery school for the first time.

Ages 3-5

Also available in:
No other form known

554

Rockwell, Thomas

The Thief

Black/white illustrations by Gail Rockwell.
Delacorte Press, 1977.
(81 pages)

LONELINESS
  Friendship: making friends
  Guilt, feelings of
  Sibling: relationships
  Stealing
  Vandalism

Since his choice is usually between being with his bullying older brothers or playing alone, nine-year-old Tim is pleased that newcomer Dwayne wants to be his friend. But about as often as Dwayne comes over, family possessions and money disappear. Tim refuses to believe, as his family does, that Dwayne is the thief, and continues to play with him. There is an old man they like to spy on, and one day when he is out the boys enter his house. In mounting terror of discovery, Tim watches Dwayne vandalize the place. Tim bolts, and minutes later Dwayne joins him as the old man returns. He spots them hiding behind a wall and yells threats as they run away. The next morning, Tim can think only about the vandalism, and only slowly does it dawn on him that the money missing from his own bank has, in all probability, been taken by Dwayne. Then his mother is speaking with a visitor — the old man come to collect recompense for his losses. Tim's mother gives him twenty dollars, then storms into her son's room, demanding a full confession. When his father hears the news, he tells Tim in no uncertain terms that he should have stopped Dwayne or found someone who could: he is as guilty as his friend. He says that Tim may no longer play with Dwayne and must work to earn back the

R

money his mother gave the old man. By evening, Tim has concluded that Dwayne is no better than the bullying older brothers, but also that his parents, knowing Dwayne to be "a very troubled little boy," should have known too that he needed help.

A friendless boy beleaguered by unkind brothers, wants companionship so desperately that he is willing to accept a suspected thief as a friend. His parents, morally right about his eventual complicity, only make him feel more isolated by offering no defense against his brothers and no concern for his disturbed friend. There is no resolution to this brief story. A group discussion could consider ways which the other characters could have helped Dwayne.

Ages 8-10

Also available in:
Paperbound — *The Thief*
Dell Publishing Company, Inc.

555

Rodowsky, Colby F.

P.S. Write Soon

Franklin Watts, Inc., 1978.
(149 pages)

BRACES ON BODY/LIMBS
REALITY, ESCAPING
  Attention Seeking
  Boasting
  Honesty/Dishonesty
  Inferiority, feelings of
  Sibling: youngest

Tanner McClean, a sixth grader, is the youngest of three children in a successful, talented, and busy family, and she wears a waist-to-ankle brace on her paralyzed leg, the result of an auto accident four years earlier. But Tanner writes her pen pal, Jessie Lee, none of this — preferring to fabricate tales of her athletic ability. When Tanner's older brother, Jon, elopes, she writes Jessie of being a bridesmaid at Jon's beautiful wedding, and neglects to tell her that she dislikes her new sister-in-law, Cheryl. She also dislikes the fact that Jon and Cheryl have settled in the third-floor apartment of the family home while Jon continues law school. When Tanner visits the apartment, she learns that Cheryl has inherited a small house in Virginia from which she has brought some things with her. In Tanner's next letter to Jessie this fact becomes Cheryl owning a very grand house indeed, from which she has brought precious antiques. In ensuing letters, Tanner brags that Jon and Cheryl have bought a house and are remodeling it with her help and that Cheryl is pregnant. But Cheryl accidently discovers what Tanner has written and confronts her. She reminds Tanner that she is not pregnant and that they have bought no house — in fact she and Jon will be moving to the small house in Virginia. She then encourages Tanner to tell Jessie the truth, to let her meet the real Tanner. But Tanner does this only after Jessie writes that she and her parents will be taking a vacation trip and would like to drop in on the McCleans for a visit. When at last Tanner receives a reply to her confessional letter, she happily shows it to Cheryl: her pen pal still wants to visit and wants Tanner to visit her during the summer.

A handicapped youngster improves reality in letters to a pen pal, while her feelings of inferiority and anger go unrecognized by her otherwise considerate, understanding family. To compensate, Tanner lies, falls down on purpose, speaks rudely to her sister-in-law, even steals to impress a friend. Only her new sister-in-law has the insight to recognize Tanner's unhappiness and help her do something about it. Despite the predictability of the plot, readers will empathize with Tanner and may want to discuss similar feelings and experiences.

Ages 10-12

Also available in:
Cassette for the Blind — *P.S. Write Soon*
Library of Congress

556

Rodowsky, Colby F.

What About Me?

Franklin Watts, Inc., 1976.
(136 pages)

DOWN'S SYNDROME
JEALOUSY: Sibling
   Ambivalence, feelings of
   Death: of sibling
   Guilt, feelings of
   Talents: artistic

Dorie, fifteen, lives in New York City with her parents and her eleven-year-old brother, Fred, who has Down's Syndrome. Dorie is a talented artist planning to make art her career. She has always gotten along well with her parents and liked her brother, but lately it seems to her that the older Fred gets, the harder he is to manage, and the more often her mother asks her to change her plans and "help out" with him. The boy's heart condition requires particular caution in the choosing of baby-sitters. Dorie has to miss a party because of him, and her parents miss seeing art shows where Dorie's works are displayed, because there is no one to baby-sit for Fred. Usually affable and well-received even by strangers, Fred is nevertheless becoming an embarrassment to Dorie. She tells us, "I hated him Honest-to-God hate. Not all the time, not every day, but enough to scare me sometimes." Just when she thinks her life could not possibly be worse, her father tells her that the family will be moving to Maryland so that he can join his brother's law firm — but primarily to be near relatives who can lend a hand with Fred. Dorie sees her career plans going up in smoke. She is so desperate to stay in New York that she gives up an internship teaching art so that she can teach at Fred's school, hoping that her show of interest in her brother will make her parents want to stay. But they are steadfast in their decision. After several explosive scenes with her parents and an unfortunate incident in which Fred breaks her best ceramic piece, Dorie's mother and father arrange for her to stay with Guntzie, her art teacher, mentor, and friend, while Dorie finishes her last two years of high school. With that settled, Dorie begins to soften toward her brother. She agrees to baby-sit one night while her parents go to dinner. But when she looks in to check on Fred, she sees that his lips are blue and he is gasping for air. She calls the doctor, and an ambulance takes Fred to the hospital, where he dies. Dorie is amazed to find that her parents had been worried about her being alone in so frightening a situation. She sees they do think of her. Fred's funeral is held in Maryland, and on her way back to New York, having watched her mother grieving, Dorie realizes how much a part of their lives Fred has become, and how much she will miss him.

In this first-person narrative, a girl, jealous of the attention given her handicapped brother, alternately loves and hates him. Because she never fully expresses her feelings, including her guilt about those feelings, she becomes increasingly confused, resentful, and lonely. The relationship with her teacher affords her some opportunity to vent emotions and, toward the end of the story, she has gained some insight into her family's relationships. But it is not until Fred's death that she understands what her brother has meant to all of them and that she loved him. The stress of a family coping with a retarded child is dramatized realistically here, and Dorie's confusion is of a kind readers will sympathize with.

R

Ages 11-13

Also available in:
Paperbound — *What About Me?*
Dell Publishing Company, Inc.

557

Rogers, Helen Spelman

Morris and His Brave Lion

Color illustrations by Glo Coalson.
McGraw-Hill Book Co.; 1975.
(45 pages counted)

DIVORCE: of Parents
 Courage, meaning of

His daddy takes four-year-old Morris to the zoo, where the boy sees a live lion for the first time. He and his father have a wonderful afternoon, and Morris goes home thinking about the lion's strength and courage. He notices that his mother looks sad. That night, he awakens to hear his parents fighting and is frightened. In the morning his father is loading the car with boxes and suitcases. He tells Morris he will not be living with him and Mama anymore because Daddy and Mama are getting a divorce. He gives Morris a huge toy lion, but Morris says he wants his daddy instead. His mama tries to comfort his tears, telling him to be strong and brave like the lion. Waiting day after day for Daddy to come for a visit, Morris has bad dreams at night. He does not understand why, if his father really loves him, he does not come to see him. Mama explains that Daddy needs time to compose himself. Then Mama and Morris move to a new neighborhood, and Morris must say good-bye to his old friends. By the time he has his fifth birthday, his deepest wish is for his father to come to his party. He decides to send his father the toy lion along with his party invitation — to help Daddy be brave too. On the day of the party, while Morris and his guests are playing games, the doorbell rings. It is Daddy. Morris is thrilled, especially when Daddy offers to take him and his friends to the zoo, where they all look at the brave lion. But Morris knows that Daddy is home only for a visit; he will have to leave again.

This is a tender story of a little boy's sorrow over his parents' divorce. His father's gift of the lion helps Morris to find his own courage. His mother's explanations of divorce and people's emotional changes are clear enough for children to understand. The illustrations' use of color conveys Morris's emotions as he tries to understand the change in family relationships.

Ages 4-7

Also available in:
No other form known

558

Rogers, Pamela

The Stone Angel

Thomas Nelson, Inc., 1975.
(96 pages)

ATTENTION SEEKING
IDENTITY, SEARCH FOR
 Communication: parent-child
 Friendship: meaning of
 Jealousy: sibling
 Maturation

Susan, an English girl, feels that everything in her life is changing. Rosemary, her older sister, is now married and pregnant, no longer around to be "her ally and protector." Her father has grown older, unable to do the work he did before, and works now as a gravedigger, which embarrasses Susan. She also resents her parents' affection for Rab, her "shadow," a boy from Uganda. Somehow, she is no longer the center of things. One day, with Rab in the graveyard, she looks up at her favorite statue, a white stone angel, waiting for a sign. The stone angel says "Go!" and Susan tells Rab what that means: she is to be a saint, to love people and do good. But her attempts at sainthood bring unexpected results. Trying to tame a fierce dog, she ends up taking refuge in a tree. Wishing to help someone pathetic, she undertakes to care for Mrs. Briggs's baby without Mrs. Briggs's knowledge, and, upon returning the baby, is met with hysteria and allegations of kidnapping. She tries to make friends with Serena, one of the "popular" girls in school, but even that ends in anger. Pressing on, Susan and Rab together plan to do good for the most horrible person they can think of: Mrs. Anstruther. Their efforts are admirable, but end with Rab spitting on the woman's floor and Susan saying that she would too if her throat were not so dry. Mrs. Anstruther follows Rab and Susan home, and Susan's mother asks her daughter to apologize. Still, she says she understands and that she and Dad think Susan "all right as she is." The girl's last attempt at sainthood is to agree to "walk on water" for Serena and her friends — in reality, on boulders just below the surface. But Rab tries it and nearly drowns, and Susan herself escapes narrowly in trying to save him. Later, home in bed, the center of her parents' attention, Susan realizes her error: "The other way was best, with give and take and good and bad, and dark and light all through the days." To atone, she goes to the statue and sacrifices her prettiest feature by cutting off her braids. Rab is going away and in his going she realizes what a good friend he has been. At home, she finds her sister's baby has been born. Seeing the infant for the first time, Susan gladly relinquishes sainthood for the love she feels for her new niece.

Growing up is hard for Susan. She sees other people getting her family's attention — attention she once thought all belonged to her. It is difficult not to resent the intrusions of Rosemary's husband and expected baby as well. Unhappy, unpopular, and overweight, Susan decides to show everyone how special she is: she will be a saint. When her attempts fail and her best friend leaves, Susan re-evaluates what she has been, and what she has lost. Experiencing the touch of the hand of her newborn niece, Susan realizes that being an aunt is special indeed — and her own. This is a perceptive, often funny book, in which some painful lessons are learned.

Ages 10-12

Also available in:
Talking Book — *The Stone Angel*
Library of Congress

559

Rose, Anne K.

Refugee

The Dial Press, Inc., 1977.
(118 pages)

JEWISH
REFUGEES
Loneliness
War

Twelve-year-old Elke is Jewish and lives in Antwerp, Belgium. The year is 1939, the onset of World War II, and if war comes to Belgium, Elke's parents, themselves unable to get passports, plan to send her to America to live with an uncle. Elke is heartsick to think of leaving her beloved country, her parents, and her two best girl friends. But in January of 1940 she departs for New York City to live with Uncle Jacques and Aunt Elise. Overcome with homesickness, she hates New York, hates the cramped apartment that is now her home, hates the school where she is a stranger. Time passes, and she receives word that her parents have finally been permitted to enter Brazil. Just days after their departure from Belgium, the country falls to the Nazis. Two more years pass, and the War in Europe continues. Elke turns sixteen. Sometimes she wants to forget the War and her homeland, wants only to be American and dance the Lindy and go to the drugstore with her friends. Then at long last, Maman and Papa join her in America. The family reunion, though joyous, is shadowed with sadness. The War has aged Maman and Papa; and Elke is no longer the little girl they sent away. Another year passes, and just before the War ends, Elke learns that both her girl friends have died in concentration camps. Then the War is over, and the family travels to Antwerp to seek news of friends and relatives. The trip only increases their awful sense of loss. Feeling homeless in Europe, they return to America to stay.

This novel, based on the author's own experience, is a first-person narrative written in diary form, with letters and newspaper excerpts filling out a story of world war and its effects on the lives of one family. Separation, loss, fear, uncertainty, loneliness all touch Elke's family, but they find inner resources to meet them.

Ages 10-14

Also available in:
No other form known

560

Rosen, Winifred

Henrietta, the Wild Woman of Borneo

Black/white illustrations by Kay Chorao.
Four Winds Press, 1975.
(45 pages counted)

SELF, ATTITUDE TOWARD: Feeling Different
  Belonging
  Sibling: rivalry

"Pretty she is, Nice she's not." Henrietta, about six, thus sums up Evelyn, her older sister, whom everyone but Henrietta likes. Henrietta considers herself the reverse: "nice but not pretty." Her teeth stick out, and her hair is bushy, and her mother calls her "the Wild Woman of Borneo." Evelyn, so often angry with Henrietta's antics, also calls her wild, among other things. One day Henrietta brings home to her mother a misshapen clay horse she has made. Expecting criticism from Evelyn, she is unruffled by it; but when her mother asks what the sculpture is, Henrietta becomes angry. Scolded for her outburst, she then decides, "I AM the Wild Woman of Borneo." Sure that everyone is disparaging her, she dreams of riding a wild horse through the uncritical jungles of Borneo. Unable to buy a bus ticket to Borneo, Henrietta has Evelyn box her in a crate for mailing there. While in the box, she dreams of Borneo, and wakes to someone opening the crate. Borneo already? No, home and family. She asks them what they see, and Evelyn replies, "just what we want." Henrietta knows they love her after all.

In the shadow of a model sister and frequently called down by very proper parents, a girl tells in this first-person narrative how she tries to escape into a world where she can be accepted "as is." The resolution, showing Henrietta accepted by her family, pops up without preparation. This, and Henrietta's flippant remarks, may puzzle young readers, but it can be inferred that the girls' parents have been startled into second thoughts at seeing the length their daughter will go to find acceptance. Henrietta has also imagined more favoritism than her parents have actually shown toward Evelyn.

Ages 4-7

Also available in:
No other form known

561

Rosenblatt, Suzanne

Everyone Is Going Somewhere

Black/white illustrations by the author.
Macmillan Publishing Company, Inc., 1976.
(32 pages counted)

DEPENDENCE/INDEPENDENCE
   Pride/False pride

For the first time, young Alvin is going to school by himself. On so important an occasion, it follows that he notices everyone and everything is going somewhere: people rushing to work or setting off shopping, the fruit vendor pulling his heavy cart and fruit flies swarming after its delicious contents, an ant climbing a garbage pail and hungry dogs sniffing after food, a busy street-cleaner washing the dirty pavement, and a speeding fire engine roaring past. Alvin notes that even the newspaper blowing past his feet seems to be going somewhere. "And I'm going somewhere too!" he thinks proudly. "I'm going to school. By myself!"

Delightful sketches and a simple text exactly catch a little boy's pride to be walking to school by himself. Alvin's observations could reassure other children who will be walking to school alone for the first time.

Ages 4-6

Also available in:
No other form known

562

Ross, G. Maxim

When Lucy Went Away

Black/white illustrations by Ingrid Fetz.
E. P. Dutton & Company, Inc., 1976.
(29 pages counted)

PETS: Love for
   Loss: feelings of

While preparing to leave their summer home, a family discovers their cat, Lucy, is missing. They search the house and the woods thoroughly, and wait another day for the rain to stop. The children think Lucy's leaving means she no longer loves them. Their mother says no, Lucy is only independent and needs her freedom. Back in the city, the children continue to worry. Lucy is no longer lost, no longer alone in the woods, but has found a nice family to live with. Sometimes they can scarcely believe she is really gone. There is always the hope she will reappear one night and jump into bed with them like old times.

This first-person narrative describes the painful experience of losing a pet, the children's feelings of abandonment, fear, and grief. The end of the story offers no false hope that the cat will return, nor do the children try to replace her with another. Instead, they remember what she did that made them happy.

Ages 3-7

Also available in:
No other form known

R

563

Roth, Arthur J.

The Secret Lover of Elmtree

Four Winds Press, 1976.
(165 pages)

ADOPTION: Feelings About
  Boy-girl relationships
  Communication: misunderstandings
  Communication: parent-child
  Love, meaning of
  Suicide: attempted

Seventeen-year-old Greg Yardley does not believe what his parents have told him, that unlike his younger brother and sister, he is adopted. One day while working in his father's gas station, he is approached with a number of questions by a stranger who says he is doing a survey. After several more such visits, Greg suspects that the questioner is hiding his true identity. Sure enough, the man admits he is Peter Marsh, Greg's biological father. The boy is not particularly excited by this. But when the wealthy Marsh announces that he wants Greg to take over his very successful construction business, to come live with him at his seaside home, and to be put through college, Greg has serious doubts. Although he will not admit it, he loves his hometown of Elmtree, hopes one day to run the gas station, and has no wish to leave his family and girl friend to go off to a new career with someone he scarcely knows. When his family encourages him to accept this seemingly bright future, Greg thinks that Marsh is paying them off. So content do they seem at the prospect of losing him that Greg tries to kill himself; instead of sleeping pills he accidently takes caffeine tablets. But the suicide attempt

forces his parents to admit their real reluctance to see him go. He in turn admits how badly he wants to stay and run the gas station.

Greg learns that it is important for people to express what they feel about important things. Marsh understands the boy's decision and respects it. Greg tells his story with candor and wit, and the other characters are richly believable.

Ages 12 and up

Also available in:
No other form known

564

Ruby, Lois

Arriving at a Place You've Never Left

The Dial Press, Inc., 1977.
(149 pages)

DEATH: Attitude Toward
DEATH: Murder
MENTAL ILLNESS: of Parent
PREJUDICE: Ethnic/Racial
RESPONSIBILITY: Accepting
STEALING
UNWED MOTHER
  Child abuse
  Illnesses: terminal
  Love, meaning of
  Rejection: parental

In the first of seven stories, sixteen-year-old Ellen tells of the anger she feels toward her mother for having a mental breakdown. But she tells, too, of her struggle to overcome her anger and to assist her mother in recovering. In the second story, sixteen-year-old Shana Miller has accepted her pregnancy, has made up her mind to give up her baby, and understands that David, her boy friend, wants neither herself nor his unborn child. After the baby is born, though, David visits Shana in the hospital, and at one and the same time Shana realizes she has never loved David, while he realizes he cannot wholly dismiss Shana or his child from his mind. In the third story, Zeke Cassidy, till now a happy-go-lucky senior, falls in love with Ruth Bellini. Once graduated, Zeke decides to join the Army so as to learn a trade that will support his future marriage to Ruth. In the fourth story, fourteen-year-old Jonah Edwards, arrested for the murder of his father, confides to his attorney that he killed his father after seeing him beat his younger brother. The attorney, knowing that Mrs. Edwards may allow Jonah to be convicted just to protect her husband's reputation, persuades her to reveal the truth. Jonah is then released to the custody of his mother — though he views her as a stranger. In the fifth story, seventeen-year-old Daniel, hospitalized with a terminal illness, burns with bitterness that he is being cheated of a full life. Only after meeting fifteen-year-old Molly, similarly doomed, who shares her thoughts with him, does Daniel accept his impending death. In the sixth story, a dormitory advisor, puzzled by a series of thefts, suspects that the thief may not realize what she is doing. When finally caught, the thief, horrified to discover her guilt, begs for help. The school authorities advise psychiatric treatment, but the girl's mother rejects any thought of professional counsel. In the final story, sixteen-year-old Rosalie wonders why her grandfather, a former concentration camp inmate, ignores the anti-Semitism directed at him. But when Rosalie herself is molested because she is Jewish, her grandfather at once sells the store where they both have worked — the center of his life — to take her out of harm's way.

All of these perceptive stories about adolescents have open endings or endings conducive to discussion. The first, fifth, and sixth are first-person narratives. In the story concerning child abuse, it is apparent that the mother's refusal to help her son is itself a form of child abuse. All seven are told with clarity and force.

Ages 12 and up

Also available in:
Paperbound — *Arriving at a Place You've Never Left*
Dell Publishing Company, Inc.

565

S

Sachs, Marilyn

A December Tale

Doubleday & Company, Inc., 1976.
(87 pages)

IMAGINARY FRIEND
  Deprivation, emotional
  Foster home
  Loneliness
  Rejection: parental
  Sibling: relationships

Ten-year-old Myra Fine cries a good deal, and with reason: her remarried father seems interested only in his new wife and family. He allows Myra and her six-year-old brother, Henry, to be crowded out of their own home. The two are taken in by Mrs. Singer, an elderly neighbor genuinely concerned about their welfare. But with her ailing husband, the two children prove too much for Mrs. Singer to handle indefinitely. After being turned out of several other foster homes because of Henry's bad behavior, the two are sent to the foster home of Mr. and Mrs. Smith. Mr. Smith ignores them; Mrs. Smith controls them. When Myra tells Mrs. Singer how miserable she is, and Mrs. Singer tells the social worker, home life at the Smiths' becomes intolerable. Mrs. Smith forbids Myra to see Mrs. Singer, saying that if she does not like her foster home she has only the orphanage to go to. Soon Mrs. Smith is giving Henry severe beatings. Frantic and friendless, Myra one day discovers in the library a book about Joan of Arc, a radiant young woman who stood up to her powerful enemies and defeated them. Myra identifies so strongly with Joan that she begins conducting imaginary conversations with her. In Joan she finds a friend who accepts her as she is, sees what trouble she is in, and believes Myra can overcome it. In the end, Myra draws on the strength derived from these conversations. She rescues Henry from Mrs. Smith and runs with him to Mrs. Singer's house. There they can be safe for a time.

Myra aches with conflicting emotions: love and hatred for the trouble-making Henry; liking for Mrs. Singer, but hatred for her inability to provide a permanent home; hating Mrs. Smith but needing to please her so as to keep what little security Myra and Henry have. Torn as Myra is, her imagination of a great and brave leader fires her own courage to save herself and her brother from immediate danger. But their refuge is temporary, of a piece with a story that avoids sensationalism and sentimentality.

Ages 9-12

Also available in:
No other form known

566

Sachs, Marilyn

Dorrie's Book

Black/white illustrations by Anne Sachs.
Doubleday & Company, Inc., 1975.
(136 pages)

CHANGE: Resisting
SIBLING: New Baby
  Change: new home
  Communication: parent-child
  Only child

Choosing to write a short book for an English assignment, eleven-year-old Dorrie proceeds to record the recent changes in her life. Previously Dorrie had been an only child, enjoying her parents' undivided love and attention, living in a beautiful two-bedroom apartment in San Francisco. Then her mother announces she is pregnant. At first Dorrie feels important, running errands and helping her mother do the shopping. She is fascinated when the doctor says her mother is going to have twins, and she helps her father cheer her mother up during discomfort. She is even more fascinated when her mother gives birth to triplets, two boys and a girl. Dorrie's fascination ends a month later when the babies come home and take over the apartment! They demand constant attention, and one of the boys is especially fussy. Everything changes: Dorrie has to help with the babies; the apartment is a mess; her parents never seem to have time for her; and worst of all, they are moving into an old shabby house. Dorrie argues against moving, but to no avail. The first few days in the new house she spends sulking and refusing to go to school. Although her mother sympathizes with her, she still seems to have little time for Dorrie. It is Mrs. Cole, a neighbor who helps her mother with the babies, who comforts Dorrie when Genevieve, the girl next door, calls Dorrie names and kicks her. Mrs. Cole explains that the fatherless Genevieve and her brother, Harold, are neglected by their mother — who eventually deserts them. The two children move in with Dorrie's family, and soon, with Dorrie's grudging consent, her parents agree to keep them as foster children. At this point in her autobiography, Dorrie cannot decide on the ending. Her parents and her teacher suggest that she conclude by having the main character take an interest in one of the family members. Seeing Genevieve pick on Harold one night, Dorrie defends him and decides to try taking an interest in him. She does not yet know the end of her story.

This book looks clearly at the fears and resentments a long-time only child can feel with the arrival of other children in the family. The main character narrates her own story with humor and an awareness of her often unhelpful behavior. Considering the many changes she experiences in one short year, she copes well even while resisting.

Ages 9-12

Also available in:
Cassette for the Blind — *Dorrie's Book*
Library of Congress

567

Sachs, Marilyn

A Secret Friend

Doubleday & Company, Inc., 1978.
(111 pages)

FRIENDSHIP: Making Friends
FRIENDSHIP: Meaning of
    Parental: interference
    Rejection: peer
    School: classmate relationships

Jessica Freeman and Wendy Cooper, fifth graders, have been best friends for many years. Now something has gone wrong, for reasons unknown to Jessica. Wendy says she is not Jessica's friend any more, but has chosen to be best friends with a classmate named Barbara. Jessica hopes a note written to herself, signed "A. S. F." will make Wendy curious, even jealous. And Wendy is curious — the note says Jessica has a better friend in the class than Wendy — but she is not jealous and refuses

Jessica's plea to renew their friendship. Jessica confides in her mother. Finding no way to reconcile the two girls, Mother advises Jessica to find a new friend. Despite this advice and despite her dislike for Wendy's cruelty, Jessica desperately pursues the reconciliation by writing herself more notes from "a secret friend." She even sets up a meeting with the "friend" at the library, across from Wendy's house, but Wendy sends her new friend, Barbara, to tell her to stop spying on them. At a loss to find another friend among her classmates, Jessica asks Helen, her teenage sister, how friendship is made. Reciting the things that go into it, Helen remarks that she and Wendy share none of these: their mothers have pushed them into being friends. Yet even after a talk with Barbara about Wendy's meanness, Jessica returns to her quest of her former friend, who is such fun to be with. One day, failing to prevent Wendy from going home with Barbara, and then mistaking Wendy's mockery of Barbara for mockery of herself, Jessica stops her pursuit abruptly and begins to look seriously elsewhere. Her next friend turns out to be Barbara, who has seen Wendy for what she is.

A girl's quest to restore friendship after a friend has scorned her ends when she understands what a friend really is. Her realization that her goal is "disgusting" marks not only her new wisdom about friendship but her recognition of her mother's interference. Previously Jessica has accepted her mother's advice indiscriminately, but she now sees that her mother tries to impose her own values and wishes on others.

Ages 10-12

Also available in:
Paperbound — *A Secret Friend*
Xerox Publishing Company

S

Samuels, Gertrude

Adam's Daughter

Thomas Y. Crowell Company, Inc., 1977.
(209 pages)

PAROLE
  Crime/Criminals
  Justice/Injustice
  Rejection
  Values/Valuing: moral/ethical

Seventeen-year-old Robyn Adams has been told to regard her father as dead. Eight years earlier the father, Robert Adams, drunk and jealous, had killed his stepfather in a fight. Now he is to be paroled, and against the wishes of her mother and stepfather, Robyn arranges to meet him on the day of his release and plans to help him get re-established. Her only ally is Johnny, another ex-con, the manager of the halfway house for parolees (though her stepsister, Joyce, tries to smooth things with the family). But Robyn's mother and stepfather finally demand that she cease helping Robert or move out. Robyn moves in with her father. Her steady boy friend, disapproving of her father, breaks up with her. For a time, Robert gains confidence, but as he senses the obstacles facing released prisoners and runs afoul of his tough, seemingly unjust parole officer, he starts drinking heavily. Beset by doubts herself, Robyn fears he may lose control again. And one evening he does. The parole officer, searching the apartment, finds some marijuana hidden there by a friend, unbeknownst to father and daughter, and arrests the two. Robert pummels the man before Robyn can stop him. He is jailed. Robyn, vowing never to give up on him, seeks out a friendly parole officer for help.

Based on true incidents (and smacking a little of the case history), this book dramatizes how the parole system and unthinking social scorn can break parolees and severely try the families and friends aiding them. Robyn ends up determined to save her father but with very different ideas of who is right and who wrong; she sees that right can be on both sides, and neither. Shelly, a character from the author's *Run Shelly Run* and a parolee herself, is a friend to Robyn. There is bitterness and profanity in the dialogue here; the book could hardly be authentic without it.

Ages 13 and up

Also available in:
Paperbound — *Adam's Daughter*
New American Library

Sargent, Sarah

Edward Troy and the Witch Cat

Black/white illustrations by Emily McCully.
Follett Publishing Company, 1978.
(144 pages)

FRIENDSHIP: Best Friend
MATURATION
  Afro-American
  Change: accepting
  Friendship: keeping friends
  Goals
  Loss: feelings of
  Money: earning
  Parent/Parents: single
  Resourcefulness

Nine-year-old Edward Troy finds a black cat that his mother's friend Juanita says is a witch cat; it belonged to a woman, now dead, who was rumored to be a witch. When some children who have stolen Edward's ball give it back out of fear of the cat, Edward starts thinking this animal can be of great use. He takes it to school the next day hoping to frighten away some older boys who always push him around. They push him around anyway. But that afternoon, Edward's best friend, Howard, reports that the bully who touched the cat has broken out in spots and is warning everyone to stay away from Edward's cat. Edward's faith in his pet is restored, even though he too breaks out. Recovered from the chicken pox, Edward is stunned and disbelieving when his mother tells him that Howard will probably move when Howard's father receives his engineering degree that summer. Later, at Howard's house for dinner, he learns that the family is indeed hoping to move out of the housing project they all live in and into a house of their own. Edward thinks he and his mother should do the same. She says that is out of the question. Immediately, Edward lays plans to travel to his long-absent father in Chicago and ask him for help. Edward and Howard set up a club and begin earning money for the four-hour bus trip. At one club meeting they are saddled with Juanita's eight-year-old cousin, Peaches, living with Juanita while the girl's mother is temporarily in jail. Both Howard and Edward dislike Peaches, but she soon proves herself trustworthy and they take her into the club. Edward leaves for Chicago. His father seems delighted to see him, takes him to lunch, and buys him new clothes and toys. Then he slips out, leaving Edward alone in the apartment to contend with an angry, threatening caller. Edward's uncle comes to the rescue, and, seeing Edward's surprise at his father's behavior, says, "Some things you can't take somebody else's word for; some things you have to find out for yourself...." Back home, Edward feels less dismayed by Howard's moving away: Edward and Peaches and his cat can find lots to do. But Howard has not given up on getting the money for the Troys to move too. Maybe the dead witch woman left some money behind. Howard and Edward go to search her shack, and are joined by a neighborhood vagrant. After two days of finding nothing, the man says, "We still no closer to figuring her out than we were yesterday," and speculates idly that her cat may have good-luck power to bring money. Edward returns the next day to show his cat to the man, but he is gone. About the cat, the man had also said, "It's got to figure out for itself where it's going." So Edward tells the cat it is free to go. The cat waits a few minutes, then follows Edward home.

In this story of maturation, a boy learns that there are some things he cannot change, no matter how hard he tries. Yet his own mind changes and grows, as he learns new things about Peaches, Juanita's little boy, Mr. Troy, Howard's move, and even his cat. He recognizes that the "witch cat," like people, is not his to use, and that both he and the cat must choose their own way in life. Several incidents show that Edward and other black people must still take racism into account. The adults around Edward also show that keeping a child out of trouble in a housing project such as the one they live in is a daily concern. Edward's mother, a realist, has high ambitions for her son. These are firmly drawn characters whose dialogue one believes.

Ages 9-11

Also available in:
No other form known

S

570

Sawyer, Paul

Mom's New Job

Color photographs by Roald Bostrom.
Raintree Publishers, Ltd., 1978.
(31 pages)

PARENT/PARENTS: Mother Working Outside Home
  Change: accepting
  Dependence/Independence

Mary, age nine, cannot understand why her mother is looking for a job. She wonders if her mother is angry with her or wants to get away from her. She is also worried about being home alone when her mother is working. Her parents reassure her that she will only be by herself a few minutes a day, after school, and that her best friends' mothers will be handy if needed. The first day her mother is gone, Mary quails at entering the empty house, but a note and some cookies from Mom cheer her. Mom calls her, and two friends come to play, and before Mary has time to feel lonely, Mom arrives. Mary takes pride in her new independence.

A young girl faced with a frightening change in her life gains new confidence in the realization she can take care of herself. Color photographs help tell the story, which could be read by primary-age children.

Ages 7-10

Also available in:
No other form known

571

Sawyer, Paul

New Neighbors

Color photographs by Mark Gubin.
Raintree Publishers, Ltd., 1978.
(31 pages)

REJECTION: Peer
  Friendship: meaning of
  Loneliness

Seven-year-old Billy Fowler and eight-year-old Tom Davis are close friends. When Kevin Kramer, nine, moves into the neighborhood, Billy and Tom make him welcome — in fact are proud to be the friends of so talented an athlete and game player. But Billy soon learns that Kevin takes quite a different and belittling view of him. For his part, Tom just ignores Billy and plays exclusively with Kevin. One more snub sends Billy to his room to cry. But with time he gets over the hurt, finds new interests, and makes new friends, though none as close as Tom had been. A year later, Kevin moves away and Tom apologizes to Billy, offering him his friendship as it had been before. Billy accepts, but tells Tom that they cannot be the same as before, because each boy is different now.

When a boy is dropped by his best friend, the wound runs deep. To counteract his sadness, he becomes more self-reliant. Billy's sensitive and compassionate father assists him in accepting and adjusting to his situation. Large, expressive photographs complement the text.

Ages 5-8

Also available in:
No other form known

572

Schalebin-Lewis, Joy

The Dentist and Me

Color photographs by Murray Weiss.
Raintree Publishers, Ltd., 1977.
(30 pages)

DENTIST, GOING TO

At first, young Adam shrinks from his first dental exam-ination, but the dentist and his assistant calmly explain every step, and so put the boy at ease. The dentist begins by taking X rays of Adam's teeth. The assistant shows him the correct ways to brush and use dental floss, then cleans and polishes his teeth. Then the dentist, using a long tool called the explorer, looks for cavities. Finding none, he gives Adam encouraging advice about caring for his teeth, and the boy leaves. Another dentist asks his young patient Nikki to "help" when he finds she has a cavity to be filled. Nikki complains, "I didn't ask for the dumb cavity," but complies. The dentist puts a mask over her nose and asks her to think about her favorite sport while breathing the gas. He then numbs her gums, cleans the cavity, and fills it. Meantime, the assistant removes excess silver chips with a suction tool and keeps the tooth clean by squirting it with water and air. The dentist thanks Nikki for helping, tells her how to keep her teeth healthy, and invites her to select a toy to take home.

These straightforward, first-person accounts would answer many children's questions and anticipate some of their fears about going to the dentist. Both the boy and girl in this book are reassured by their dentists' explain-ing things. Those sights and sounds of dental tools, which can frighten adults as well as children, go unmentioned, as does pain. The omission seems delib-erate. But the accompanying photographs are as accu-rate as the text.

Ages 4-7

Also available in:
No other form known

573

Schick, Eleanor Grossman

Neighborhood Knight

Black/white illustrations by the author.
Greenwillow Books, 1976.
(64 pages)

FANTASY FORMATION
IMAGINATION
  Parent/Parents: single

A young boy who lives in a city apartment with his mother and older sister imagines himself to be a knight protecting the castle for his long-absent father, the king. Describing the urban view from his room in the castle, the boy tells how even the sun and moon respond to his commands. He defends the princess (his sister) and queen (his mother) from harm, and every morning rides his imaginary horse to school. The boy does not share his secret identity with his classmates or teacher; they do not know why he is so interested in building castles and painting battle scenes. One day a castle he has built of blocks falls down, some children laugh, and he begins fighting with them. Punished for the commotion along with the others, the boy reflects that the king would never have been so unfair as his teacher. Still angry when he gets home, he retreats to his room and lets off steam by battling an invading army, shouting and knocking over furniture. Victorious, he gallops happily in to dinner. At bedtime he sleeps content, knowing his castle is secure.

In this first-person narrative, a young boy employs fantasy to cope with the loneliness and uncertainties of growing up fatherless. But his imagining of knights and kings helps him face, not evade, reality. The soft pencil sketches show an everyday urban environment from a young child's wonder-filled perspective.

Ages 5-7

Also available in:
No other form known

574

Schlein, Miriam

The Girl Who Would Rather Climb Trees

Black/white illustrations by Judith Gwyn Brown.
Harcourt Brace Jovanovich, Inc., 1975.
(29 pages counted)

GENDER ROLE IDENTITY: Female
 Resourcefulness

Melissa is an active little girl who lives in Brooklyn — a puzzle-doer, a cook, a reader, a ballplayer, and a tree climber. One day, when Melissa's mother's best friend is visiting, the little girl is presented with a big, fancy, curly haired doll complete with carriage. Melissa does not care for dolls but does not want to hurt anyone's feelings either. Traipsing dutifully around the house with the doll in her arms, she delights her mother, her grandmother, and the visitor alike. But there is not much else one can do with a doll, she reflects, beyond carrying it around, pretending it is a real baby. Melissa's doll does not remind her of a real baby at all; it is not interesting, and she will not spend the rest of the day in the house with it. Taking the doll and the carriage into

her room, she re-emerges, tiptoeing, and says, "Shhh! Dolly's asleep." Everyone is pleased, and Melissa can now go outside and climb trees.

A child's imaginative, if deceiving, maneuver can gently outwit grownups' misguided assumptions. Although oversimplified, the point that not all little girls like dolls is made clear. The illustrations of a scruffy, busy little girl are delightful.

Ages 4-8

Also available in:
Paperbound — *The Girl Who Would Rather Climb Trees*
Xerox Publishing Company

575

Schlein, Miriam

I Hate It

Color illustrations by Judith Gwyn Brown.
Albert Whitman & Co., 1978.
(32 pages counted)

ANGER
 Emotions: accepting

What children hate: snow melting, people who take your toys, seeing Mother cry, dressing up, saying goodbye to a best friend who moves away, meeting a big dog. And it is all right to dislike such things: all right to dislike it when someone grabs your toy car, or when Mother cries, or when someone is bossy. And after all, such things only happen sometimes, and even when they do, things get better: "Most days I would say things are really OK."

Children should find at least one of their pet hates here, and a discussion among readers or listeners will reveal the author's perspective on dislikes: no need to feel guilty about them — and no point in exaggerating them.

In short, it is better to express one's anger than to swallow it. The illustrations lend a light, often humorous tone to a book well suited to reading aloud.

Ages 4-7

Also available in:
Filmstrip — *I Hate It*
Westport Communications

576

Schulman, Janet

The Big Hello

Color illustrations by Lillian Hoban.
Greenwillow Books, 1976.
(32 pages)

FRIENDSHIP: Making Friends
   Moving
   Transitional objects: toys

The little girl who tells this story is moving to California with her parents and her doll, Sara. By reassuring the doll, the girl is able to convince herself that the plane ride is all fun and California an ideal place to live. But she wonders if she will find new friends. Two days after the family arrives, she loses Sara, with whom she has always slept. As a surprise, her father gives her a dog, which she names Snoopy. That night, Snoopy sleeps with her. The next day is doubly happy. She finds Sara and meets her first new friend.

The young narrator finds that moving to a new home brings her adventures and new friendships. Color illustrations add to this cheerful story, which young readers can read alone easily.

Ages 3-7

Also available in:
Paperbound — *The Big Hello*
Dell Publishing Company, Inc.

577

Schulman, Janet

Jenny and the Tennis Nut

Color illustrations by Marylin Hafner.
Greenwillow Books, 1978.
(56 pages)

EXPECTATIONS
   Self, attitude toward: accepting
   Talents: athletic

S

Young Jenny loves gymnastics, and her father loves to play tennis. One day Daddy presents Jenny with a tennis racket and says he will teach her to play. Bored with the lesson and the sport, Jenny puts on an acrobatic display then and there. Daddy ignores her and goes on with the lesson. Finally Jenny objects, and insists that he watch the really difficult feats she has mastered. Amazed, Daddy agrees that Jenny has found her own sport — and it is not tennis. She will have gymnastics lessons; he will buy and set up her equipment; and if the other is ever interested in learning, Jenny will teach her father gymnastics and he will teach her tennis.

A father tries to force his daughter into playing his sport but learns that she is happiest and best at her own. This read-alone book offers a good lesson for parents in recognizing individual differences, and likewise encourages children to cultivate their own interests and talents.

Ages 7-9

Also available in:
Paperbound — *Jenny and the Tennis Nut*
Dell Publishing Company, Inc.

Talking Book — *Jenny and the Tennis Nut*
Library of Congress

578

Scoppettone, Sandra

Happy Endings Are All Alike

Harper & Row Publishers, Inc., 1978.
(202 pages)

HOMOSEXUALITY: Female
RAPE
SELF, ATTITUDE TOWARD: Accepting
  Courage, meaning of
  Differences, human
  Loyalty

Jaret Tyler and Peggy Danziger, two very attractive, popular high school senior girls, are lovers. They have tried to keep their lesbianism a secret, but Jaret's mother knows, as does Peggy's older sister, who repeatedly threatens to expose the two. The girls go often to a secluded spot in a woods near Jaret's house, where one day Mid Summers, a boy who hates Jaret (he is a friend of her brother) and has been planning to "teach her a lesson," discovers Jaret and Peggy making love. His awful plan takes shape: when Jaret is alone he will rape her; then he will warn her that if she exposes him, he will tell everyone about her and Peggy. Shortly afterwards he finds Jaret alone in the woods. He beats her, rapes her, and leaves her unconscious. On a tip from a friend of the girls, Jaret's family finds her there a few hours later. The next day, in the hospital, Jaret gives the police Mid's name; he is arrested, and he confesses. He tells the police he raped Jaret because he saw her and Peggy having sex and went crazy. Despite the accusing, doubting police interviews, Mid's threat, and the police chief's warning that a trial will make the newspapers and expose the girls' relationship, Jaret decides to press charges. Then, Mid goes to the press and tells his story, but not before a frightened Peggy has told Jaret (who is not ashamed of her lesbianism) that they are through. Reporters spread the story quickly. Both girls' parents support their daughters. Lonely and sad, Jaret waits for the passing of summer, after which she will go away to college. The day before she is to leave, Peggy appears. She tells Jaret she still loves her and wants to be with her though she does not know what the future holds. "So what if happy endings didn't exist? Happy moments did."

A courageous young woman defends her right to be a lesbian, though she finds that in practice there are consequences to pay. The people in her small town prove almost vicious in their prejudice against her and her lover, and an unfair system of justice may hand a rapist a light sentence for having raped a lesbian. This bold story draws moral issues clearly, yet is handled everywhere in good taste. The rape scene is no more brutal than it must be. Some chapters are taken from the rapist's diary, thus keeping the reader informed of the boy's feelings and intentions.

Ages 12 and up

Also available in:
Paperbound — *Happy Endings Are All Alike*
Dell Publishing Company, Inc.

579

Scoppettone, Sandra

The Late Great Me

G. P. Putnam's Sons, 1976.
(256 pages)

ALCOHOLISM: Adolescent
  Boy-girl relationships: dating
  Mental illness: of parent
  Peer relationships: peer pressures

Seventeen-year-old Geri Peters has always been a lonely, quiet girl, with only two girl friends, until Dave Townsend becomes her boy friend and introduces her to drinking. Geri discovers that drinking gives her the social confidence her mother has always preached. By mid-May of her junior year, Geri cannot complete a school day without a drink of milk and vodka from the thermos in her locker or the bottle in her purse. Blackouts assail her; periods of time blank in her memory; she cannot concentrate in class; she keeps a bottle of Scotch in her closet at home. Her older brother notices changes in her, but the family ignores him: Mrs. Peters's mind is failing, and that and his work absorb Geri's father. It is Kate Laine, a non-drinking alcoholic who is Geri's humanities teacher, who, observing Geri, candidly suggests to her that she may be an alcoholic. Worried that Kate may be right, Geri limits her drinking. But when her mother is institutionalized, Geri again drinks heavily. While drunk she takes her mother's car and some time later, having blacked out, recovers from her blackout in a rented room where she is beaten by a stranger whose sexual advances she has resisted. Geri now sees her severe drinking problem and calls on Kate for help. At the teacher's urging, Geri attends meetings of Alcoholics Anonymous and, to better understand Geri's illness, Mr. Peters and his son attend meetings of Ala-non. By December of her senior year, Geri has gone without drinking for ninety days and is learning to like and understand herself.

In this first-person narrative, a teenage alcoholic graphically describes her blackouts and the physical discomfort and mental anguish of withdrawal from alcohol dependence; her sexual encounters are only touched on. Kate Laine, a non-drinking alcoholic, is contrasted with Dave Townsend's mother, an alcoholic whose drinking leads directly to her own death. Mrs. Peters's mental illness is portrayed convincingly but from her alcoholic daughter's perspective. More attention is given to Geri's perilous drinking than to her recovery and consequent self-knowledge; this, then, is an account of teenage alcoholism more vivid than moralizing.

Ages 12 and up

Also available in:
Paperbound — *The Late Great Me*
Bantam Books, Inc.

Film — *The Late Great Me*
ABC Afterschool Special

580

Screen, Robert Martin

With My Face to the Rising Sun

Harcourt Brace Jovanovich, Inc., 1977.
(106 pages)

IDENTITY, SEARCH FOR
PREJUDICE: Ethnic/Racial
  Afro-American
  Fantasy formation
  Grandparent: living in home of
  Ostracism
  Self, attitude toward: accepting

In a Southern town during World War II, thirteen-year-old Richard Sadler, a light-skinned Negro,* occupies a precarious position between the white and Negro communities. His mother, long dead, his father, unknown, Richard lives with his grandparents, who are light-skinned themselves. In fact, his grandfather tends to side with the whites. Except for his girl friend, Reeny, Richard is mistrusted by Negroes his own age. Their attitude deepens to open hostility after Richard, under orders from his grandfather, refuses to identify the white killers of a Negro boy whose drowning he has witnessed. Villified by his classmates, Richard is trans-

---

*This term, and not "black," is used in the book.

ferred to a private school. In his misery he turns to High Papa, his great-grandfather, who tells him his father is a white from a nearby town, now in the Army. From hating whites, Richard suddenly moves to wanting to pass for white. He builds an elaborate fantasy, including a fictitious correspondence, about his father claiming him. His aunt says flatly that passing for white is no cure for his troubles, but she cannot dislodge Richard's fantasy. What does is his father's death in battle. Spurned by his white grandparents when he introduces himself, Richard learns that his father denied him, too: his military records show no wife and no son. Before running away to start over, Richard attends his father's funeral. Reeny, his grandmother, and his aunt come looking for him and Richard, knowing what they want, agrees "to go home again."

A youth of mixed parentage, caught between two communities, finds neither will accept him. At first he tries to resolve his dilemma by declaring allegiance to the Negro community, then to the white community. Thrown back by both, he thinks of running away but in the end accepts his circumstances. Basing this intense story partly on his own experiences, the author dramatically demonstrates the finer distinctions of racial prejudice.

Ages 11 and up

Also available in:
No other form known

581
Seuling, Barbara

The Great Big Elephant and the Very Small Elephant

Color illustrations by the author.
Crown Publishers, Inc., 1977.
(40 pages counted)

FRIENDSHIP: Best Friend

In the first of three short stories, Big Elephant must take a trip. His best friend, Small Elephant, does not want him to go and so feigns a headache, a cold, and a stomachache to prevent it. Only after assurances from his friend that he will return soon, does Small Elephant agree to his friend's departure. In the second story, Small Elephant is worried about an impending visit by his great-aunt: he doubts he can be a proper host. When he voices his fears to Big Elephant, the latter volunteers to help make the visit pleasant. Taking the proffered help, Small Elephant discovers there is no reason to worry. As the third story begins, Big and Small Elephant are playing in the jungle. When Big Elephant finds that he is not as adept at games as his friend, he refuses out of shame to play. It is only after he defends Small Elephant from a bully that he realizes his friend likes him the way he is.

These three stories show that friendship works through sensitivity to the feelings of another. Children can readily recognize each character's fears, as well as the bond that dispels them.

Ages 4-7

Also available in:

Paperbound — *The Great Big Elephant and the Very Small Elephant*
Scholastic Book Services

Talking Book — *The Great Big Elephant and the Very Small Elephant*
Library of Congress

582

Shanks, Ann Zane

Old Is What You Get: Dialogues on Aging by the Old and the Young

Black/white photographs by the author.
The Viking Press, Inc., 1976.
(110 pages)

AGE: Aging
  Death: attitude toward
  Fear
  Friendship
  Grandparent
  Life style
  Loneliness
  Marriage
  Money
  Nursing home, living in
  Sex: attitude toward

Sixty-nine-year-old John Howard counts on the daily calls he receives from a Telephone Reassurance Program to keep in touch with the outside world. But Hope Bagger who, at eighty-four describes herself as a "defiant person," is unready to become inactive merely because she is growing older. In the same vein, eighty-seven-year-old Dr. Louis Kushner finds himself "more aware of life today," and wishes he had had the same awareness when young. Other elderly people long to be less isolated from life than they are, feel prepared to accept change around them, want to remain as physically active as possible, and, as in sixty-eight-year-old Fred Wolly's case, "hope young people are going to be kind to you." Young people, such as sixteen-year-old Anthony Shanks and fifteen-year-old Kim Caughman, worry about becoming burdens in their old age. But twelve-year-old Dewey Thom seems to have "an inborn sense and acceptance of the life cycle," for he feels that growing old is part of it. In all cases, the young express some trepidation about growing old, hope that they will be treated with respect in their old age, want to remain physically active and mentally alert, and agree that the elderly have valuable wisdom and advice to offer.

A series of interviews sets before the reader many ideas about aging and its relation to sex, death, money, retirement, and health. Young and old alike talk about growing old; the elderly bring up other subjects, including widowhood and remarriage. A short biography of each person interviewed is offered, and in a preface the author explains why she compiled this book and how she collected the interviews. In his own interview, a Pulitzer-Prize-winning author and gerontologist, Dr. Robert N. Butler, says of the state of the elderly: "We have a massive cultural problem on our hands, and one which all of us very soon will have to solve." With its many large photographs, often as eloquent as the text, this book could hardly be better suited to inspire discussion of its subject.

Ages 10 and up

Also available in:
No other form known

S

583

Sharmat, Marjorie Weinman

A Big Fat Enormous Lie

Color illustrations by David McPhail.
E. P. Dutton & Company, Inc., 1978.
(32 pages counted)

HONESTY/DISHONESTY

It begins as the smallest of lies, the little boy telling his father, then his mother, then his sister, that he did not eat all the cookies in the jar. If he tells the truth, he is sure, they will all be angry. He certainly regrets having eaten the cookies, but that is no help. However much he pretends that the lie is nothing, it remains monstrously with him. He is stuck with it. He wonders how a boy as smart as he is could be so stupid as to lie. Finally, unbearably oppressed by the lie, he confesses to his parents and is instantly loosed from its hold. Wherever it has gone, it has gone forever. And that, we are told, is "the absolute and total truth."

The lie is first depicted as a small, harmless, snouted green creature. As the boy continues to worry about it, the monster grows and grows and finally sits on him. Once the boy confesses, the monster grows smaller and smaller, and finally disappears. This first-person narrative whimsically shows how one thing leads to another. Seemingly harmless at first, the lie eventually affects the boy terribly. The humorous illustrations accompanying this story text make this a fine book for reading aloud.

Ages 3-7

Also available in:
No other form known

584

Sharmat, Marjorie Weinman

Burton and Dudley

Black/white illustrations by Barbara Cooney.
Holiday House, Inc., 1975.
(46 pages counted)

FRIENDSHIP: Best Friend
FRIENDSHIP: Meaning of

Dudley Possum invites his friend Burton Possum to go for a walk, but Burton does not care for exercise. Only after a good sit around the house to prepare himself does Burton pack a shoulder bag with supplies — magazines, bandages, flea powder, and tea — and they are off. Dudley announces that their destination is a tree by the brook some twenty miles away. During the first part of their journey Dudley gives vigorous, inspiring leadership, while Burton remains indifferent, stopping often to rest and complain. But soon Burton begins to notice the beauty of the landscape, then both become tired, then Dudley becomes exhausted. "Then I'll help you," says Burton. "I've been saving my energy all these years." He pushes his friend up hill after hill, but Dudley stops short of their goal and wants to go home. "I don't want to see the whole world without you," announces Burton, and he pushes Dudley all the way home. While Burton chatters on about all the places he now wants to see, Dudley sits in his friend's chair, gazing out the window, savoring the comforts of home.

This easy reader is a delightful story of friendship, change, and understanding. The lightly conversational dialogue includes banter without sarcasm and reveals sensitivity without sentimentality. Unusual words and occasional poetic phrasing make this an enjoyable read-aloud book. The engaging pen and ink drawings are whimsical and compassionate, a perfect complement to the text.

Ages 5-8

Also available in:
Braille — *Burton and Dudley*
Library of Congress

Paperbound — *Burton and Dudley*
Avon Books

585

Sharmat, Marjorie Weinman

I Don't Care

Color illustrations by Lillian Aberman Hoban.
Macmillan Publishing Company, Inc., 1977.
(30 pages counted)

EMOTIONS: *Accepting*
LOSS: *of Possessions*

His blue balloon is one of the delights of young Jonathan's life — until one day the string holding it slips from his hand, and the balloon floats out of sight. The boy sits alone for a long, long time, and then goes home, where he tells his father that the "dumb balloon" blew away. Wandering back outdoors, Jonathan tells himself over and over that losing the balloon does not bother him. He tells his friend and his parents the same thing, even shouts it at the sky. Later in the day, again looking at the sky, he suddenly yells, "My balloon is gone," and begins to cry. He cries for a long time, then tells his parents that he has finished crying. They hug him, and then the whole family sits down to supper.

This little boy discovers that expressing grief over a loss can make him feel better. By extension, this book encourages children to accept and express all of their feelings.

Ages 3-6

Also available in:
Paperbound — *I Don't Care*
Dell Publishing Company, Inc.

586

Sharmat, Marjorie Weinman

I'm Not Oscar's Friend Anymore

Color illustrations by Tony DeLuna.
E. P. Dutton & Company, Inc., 1975.
(29 pages counted)

FRIENDSHIP: *Best Friend*
Anger

A young boy argues with his friend Oscar and decides that they are not friends anymore and never will be again. He imagines they will never make up. Oscar will miss him a lot, he thinks. He pictures Oscar getting up in the morning, remembering they are not friends anymore, then sliding back under the covers and having a nightmare. Then he imagines Oscar being unable to get dressed correctly and sitting glumly in front of the television set watching cartoons. He even imagines Oscar moping around the house so much that his mother thinks him sick and takes him to the doctor. The boy visualizes Oscar as a sinking ship and decides he has been too hard on him. He walks past Oscar's house to give him a chance to make up, but Oscar does not see him: a lost last chance. But thinking through the list of friends he could play with, he decides to give Oscar another last chance. He calls him, and Oscar doesn't even remember the argument, invites him over to see his new train, and they are friends again.

This story shows how imagination both invents and surmounts disagreements. Oscar himself had forgotten their argument, but the young boy could think of nothing else. As it turned out, his need for Oscar's companionship was greater than his desire for a lonely revenge.

Ages 3-7

Also available in:
Cassette for the Blind — *I'm Not Oscar's Friend Anymore*
Library of Congress

587

Sharmat, Marjorie Weinman

I'm Terrific

Color illustrations by Kay Chorao.
Holiday House, Inc., 1977.
(30 pages counted)

PRIDE/FALSE PRIDE
  Boasting
  Identity, search for

Jason Everett Bear is a little bear who lives in a tidy house in the forest with his mother. Jason thinks himself "terrific" and awards himself with gold stars for especially superior deeds. His friends Raymond Squirrel and Marvin Raccoon see him differently. Marvin thinks Jason a goody-goody and calls him a "mama's bear." One day a new bear moves into the forest. Jason decides he will make the new bear his friend. He goes to her house and introduces himself: "I'm Jason Everett Bear. I suppose you've heard of me." When he goes on bragging, the new bear, Henrietta, calls him a show-off and slams the door in his face. Jason is depressed, doubtful about himself, and decides that he wants to try acting entirely different. The next day, not to seem a goody-goody, he acts mean. He ties knots in Marvin's hair and kicks over Raymond's pile of nuts. Then he goes over and tells Henrietta what he has done. Once again she calls Jason a show-off and slams the door in his face.

Jason broods about his behavior some more. He goes back to Marvin and Raymond and apologizes. He brings a flower to Henrietta. But he is still unsure who he is and spends the rest of the day thinking. The next day he throws away all the gold stars. Jason's friends decide they like him when he is just Jason, not trying to impress anyone.

Jason's effort of self-discovery is long and painful. He finds that by being vain and boastful he loses friends, just as he does when acting mean. Only when he starts thinking about others more than himself does he discover who he is.

Ages 4-7

Also available in:
Paperbound — *I'm Terrific*
Scholastic Book Services

588

Sharmat, Marjorie Weinman

Maggie Marmelstein for President

Black/white illustrations by Ben Shecter.
Harper & Row Publishers, Inc., 1975.
(122 pages)

LEADER/LEADERSHIP
  Revenge
  School: classmate relationships

Hurt and angry, Maggie Marmelstein has decided to run for sixth-grade class president because her friend, Thad Smith, has bluntly refused her offer to be his campaign manager. Maggie feels that her speaking ability, coupled with the brain power of Noah Moore, her own campaign manager, makes her a sure winner over Thad. He is "not a terrific speaker," and *his* campaign manager and best friend, Henry, "couldn't manage an ice-cream cone from dripping." Neither Maggie nor

Thad has any thoughts about what the president could do to serve the sixth grade. They are concerned with defeating each other. When Maggie, campaigning, becomes tongue-tied while answering questions, Noah steps in, voicing opinions he credits to Maggie. This intervention soon has students remarking that "Noah would make a terrific president." The day before the election a debate is held between the two candidates. It soon degenerates into a shouting match, with Maggie accusing Thad of sending her a cruel, anonymous note. Thad denies doing it and unmasks the real culprit. Maggie, realizing that he has saved her chance to be president, sincerely wishes him good luck. She also begins to realize that she has never thought about what she would do as class president — only what she would be, a winner over Thad Smith. When the votes are tallied the next day, the winner is Noah Moore, a write-in candidate. He accepts the office, and both Thad and Maggie bow to the choice of their classmates, realizing that Noah, who has ideas which may help his class, is a real winner.

A girl's drive to be class president is fueled by a desire for revenge. The desire brings feelings of jealousy, anger, and distrust into play against feelings of long-standing friendship. The argument during the debate brings these feelings to the fore, where they can be dealt with. This humorous account subtly points out the qualities and importance of true leadership.

Ages 9-12

Also available in:
Paperbound — *Maggie Marmelstein for President*
Harper & Row Publishers, Inc.

Talking Book — *Maggie Marmelstein for President*
Library of Congress

589

Sharmat, Marjorie Weinman

Mitchell Is Moving

Color illustrations by Jose Aruego and Ariane Dewey.
Macmillan Publishing Company, Inc., 1978.
(46 pages)

MOVING
  Friendship: best friend

Mitchel the dinosaur has decided to move as far away as he can walk in two weeks' time. Marge, his best friend and next-door neighbor, begs him to stay, but he staunchly insists he wants to change old routines by moving. Afraid that Mitchell no longer likes her, Marge threatens him with ingenious methods of imprisonment. He, insisting that he still likes Marge, counters with equally clever means of escape. And so Mitchell leaves, walks for two weeks, and builds himself a house. But he finds life lonely and writes Marge a letter, inviting her to visit. When she arrives, both decide that, since they are neighborless and miss each other very much, Marge will build a house next door.

Two friends, in this humorous and easy-to-read story, decide to remain together despite a move by one, something that does not usually happen in life. For moving need not signal the end of a friendship, nor does it mean the friends do not like each other.

Ages 5-8

Also available in:
Paperbound — *Mitchell Is Moving*
Scholastic Book Services

590

Sharmat, Marjorie Weinman

Mooch the Messy

Color illustrations by Ben Shecter.
Harper & Row Publishers, Inc., 1976.
(64 pages)

CONSIDERATION, MEANING OF
PARENT/PARENTS: Respect for/Lack of Respect for

Mooch is a rat who enjoys a mess and keeps the hole he lives in very disorderly. Learning that his father is coming to visit, he looks forward to showing off his quarters. But when his father arrives, the elder rat is not impressed. After looking the home over, with all its tunnels, the father suggests Mooch try putting something away. Obligingly, Mooch puts two shoes in the closet. Again to please his father, that evening he cleans the clutter off his bed. The next morning his father praises him for his neatness. Mooch packs a picnic breakfast and they set off for the field — but his father declines Mooch's jam sandwiches, which have ants in them. At home, Mooch promises to put lids on his jam jars. Still his father finds discomfort everywhere and finally goes to bed. That night Mooch cleans up his entire hole and his father is happy for the rest of his visit. Before leaving, the proud father makes his son a new tunnel as a good-bye present. Alone again, Mooch throws the clothes out of his drawers and everything back where it had been.

In this "I Can Read" book, Mooch respects his father's feelings by temporarily changing his housekeeping habits, although the change is short-lived. The illustrations capture the gentle, poetic tone of the story.

Ages 6-8

Also available in:
Paperbound — *Mooch the Messy*
Random House, Inc.

591

Sharmat, Marjorie Weinman

Walter the Wolf

Color illustrations by Kelly Oechsli.
Holiday House, Inc., 1975.
(32 pages counted) o.p.

SELF, ATTITUDE TOWARD: Accepting
  Decision making

Walter the Wolf is a perfect fellow: he works hard, he always obeys his mother, and never uses his fangs on anyone. Peace is everything to Walter. One day Wyatt the Fox persuades Walter to stop being perfect. He advertises Walter as a "professional biter." Regina the Beaver hires Walter to bite her neighbor Naomi for stealing from Regina's woodpile. When Walter arrives to carry out his assignment, Naomi denies the accusation. She thereupon bites Walter in the tail to show him what a dreadful profession he has fallen into. Walter quits the business and goes home to soak his tail.

This witty fable points to a moral: one should put one's talents to a good as well as a profitable use.

Ages 4-7

Also available in:
No other form known

Shaw, Richard

The Hard Way Home

Thomas Nelson, Inc., 1977.
(127 pages)

RESPONSIBILITY: Neglecting
RUNNING AWAY
   Commune
   Job
   Maturation
   Self, attitude toward: pity
   Work, attitude toward

When sixteen-year-old Gary Hutt's father stalks into Gary's room and, without a word, cuts the cord to the amplifier on his blaring hi-fi, Gary, an only child, decides to leave home. He writes a note saying he is going "to a place where I'll be loved and appreciated." Indeed, on looking back he sees a history of unfair treatment ever since he was twelve, when his father had begun cutting his allowance for chores he had left undone. Recently, Gary had been working after school one day each week at his father's newspaper, but after weeks of repeated warnings his father had fired him for not doing his share. Now his parents plan to send the boy to a rugged summer camp where everyone must work together to survive. Instead, Gary takes the camping equipment and runs away the week before final exams. He sells some equipment to get money, hitchhikes to a nearby town, rents a room, and waits for his parents to search for him, find him, and beg him to come home. But nothing happens. He checks with the police, but no one has reported him missing; he combs the "personals" column of his father's newspaper, but there is no notice having to do with him. Meanwhile, his parents know right where he is, and they hire an off-duty policeman to keep an eye on him. But they allow him to continue on his own, in hopes he will do some growing up. He gets a job as a busboy when his money runs low and moves to a commune, where he is to donate his earnings and help with the work. But at his job he spends more time talking and eating than working, and is fired. And at the commune is soon asked to leave for avoiding chores and breaking rules. He decides to go west, but is crushed when a girl from the commune answers his invitation to go with him by saying, "You're awfully nice, Gary, and I sort of love you, but you're just not grown up enough to take care of anybody — not even yourself." When Gary finally goes home, his parents act as if nothing has happened. But when he tells them he plans to make up his school exams, they know that Gary has finally grown up.

A charming, utterly immature boy tells how he resents being "hassled" by everyone: first his parents, then a landlady, an employer, commune dwellers — even a girl friend. His account is alternated with chapters narrated by these people themselves, describing their experience with him. This is a perceptive, often wittily exaggerated account of a boy who cannot recognize his own irresponsibility but at length does succumb to maturity. The clever exaggeration prevents the story from being preachy.

Ages 11-13

Also available in:
Talking Book — The Hard Way Home
Library of Congress

S

593

Shaw, Richard

Shape Up, Burke

Thomas Nelson, Inc., 1976.
(142 pages)

COMMUNICATION: Parent-Child
FEAR
MATURATION
  Camp experiences
  Peer relationships
  Self-esteem

Teenage Pat Burke, a retiring, fear-ridden boy, lives in the New York suburbs with his mother, Martha, and his father, "Beagle" Burke, a retired New York City police officer who runs a private detective agency. Disappointed that his son shines neither in sports nor in school, Beagle plans to send him to Shiloh, a military academy. Hating the idea, Pat begs his mother to intervene, but she cannot argue with her husband or the facts: Pat is a poor student, friendless, and at a loss in the outdoors. To prepare him for Shiloh, Beagle sends the boy to Camp Atlas, a "survival camp." Terrified, Pat tries to run away. An injury lands him in the camp infirmary, where he begins thinking about himself in relation to his fellow campers. He particularly admires Gil, a small, confident boy from the Bronx, who means to learn to take care of himself in his tough neighborhood. Pat sends Gil a note saying he is "ready to start getting ready." Gil obligingly sneaks him out of the infirmary several times to practice climbing on the big net; after his initial fright, Pat enjoys newfound confidence in his own body. Discharged from the infirmary, Pat continues learning wilderness survival with the group, his fears gradually abating. On his difficult three-day "solo" in the wilderness, he does fine, but

misses sharing it all with Gil. After surviving a near-snakebite, he at last concludes that he wants to live his life his own way — and can do without military school. Leaving a note to that effect for the camp counselor, he spends several days hiking through New England to New York, sees his mother, then goes back to Camp Atlas. His father, much impressed by his son's new strength and confidence, decides that Pat need not go to Shiloh after all.

Pat and Beagle tell this story in alternating chapters, enabling the reader to see the father-son conflict from both sides — and how much the two have in common. Pat matures over the summer from a "mama's boy" to a self-confident young man. Beagle changes too, finally acknowledging his son's strength and Martha's good sense and perceptiveness. The story also contains episodes of adventure and descriptions of wilderness survival techniques. The brief last chapter is told by Martha, a sign that she will henceforth have her say in family decisions.

Ages 10-14

Also available in:
No other form known

594

Sheffield, Janet N.

Not Just Sugar and Spice

William Morrow & Company, Inc., 1975.
(192 pages)

DIVORCE: of Parents
PARENT/PARENTS: Remarriage of

Eleven-year-old Lani Huston resents her parents' divorce. Though it has been two years since she moved to California with her mother and little brother, Luther, Lani wants more than ever to move back to Connecticut with her father, whom she remembers as dignified and wealthy. An angry, rude child, Lani disapproves of her mother's relationship with a bearded art teacher, Tony Brown. Tony, whom Lani calls "Beast," is patient and gentle, and teases Lani about her grouchy disposition. When Lani learns that her father will be in San Francisco on business, she secretly takes a bus there to see him. He greets her with polite surprise, but little warmth. He gets her a hotel room, then leaves to attend a meeting. Feeling confused and lonely, Lani begins to think that Mama and even Beast are not so bad after all. The next morning, her father drives her home, and after politely greeting her mother and brother, leaves. Lani puts him out of her thoughts. Shortly afterward, her mother is hospitalized with appendicitis, and Lani and young Luther spend much time with Beast and his son, Clay. At last Lani begins to warm to Beast's friendship. But when her mother, home from the hospital, tells the children they plan to be married, Lani becomes angry all over again, and accuses Beast of wanting to take her father's place. Finally Clay explains that, at first, the idea of marriage upset him too, but that serious thought has shown him that he likes Luther and Lani's mother a lot, and he thinks being in a family would be fun. Then he admits that he would like Lani as a sister.

Lani makes no effort to conceal her feelings about her parents' divorce. In her rebellion, she lashes out at anyone who tries to befriend her. Eventually, she lets go of the unrealistic picture she has held of her father, and learns to trust Beast.

Ages 9-12

Also available in:
No other form known

595

Shimin, Symeon

I Wish There Were Two of Me

Color illustrations by the author.
Frederick Warne & Company, Inc., 1976.
(30 pages counted)

IMAGINATION

A little girl goes to bed wishing there were two of her, and dreams of all the special things she and her double could do. With two pairs of eyes, and ears, two noses, and two mouths, two girls could see and hear and smell and taste twice as much. Two bodies with four pairs of limbs could do twice as much. When one body slept the other could stay up. Awake, the girl ponders: "Where am I? Where are you? Am I — me?... I wish there were two of me."

Watercolor and ink illustrations and poetic language provide a dream-like setting for this story, which will appeal to the imaginative young reader.

Ages 4-7

Also available in:
No other form known

596

Showers, Paul

A Book of Scary Things

Black/white illustrations by Susan Perl.
Doubleday & Company, Inc., 1977.
(31 pages counted)

FEAR

S

A little boy tells us that all sorts of things, including spiders and slamming doors, can be frightening. Everyone "is afraid of some things some of the time." His grandmother fears airplane flights; the man next door fears cats; his mother fears snakes; and his father is afraid of climbing tall ladders. In fact, we are told, it is good to take fright at such things as the warning blast of a car horn, tornadoes, wild animals, and being out in the open during a thunderstorm. Some things we do well just to be careful of, as the little boy is careful of his dog when it is eating, even if the dog does nothing frightening. It is sometimes nice to help someone else feel less frightened, as when the boy comforts his dog during thunderstorms and when the dog investigates darkened rooms to assure the boy they are safe.

The little boy in this first-person narrative enumerates and distinguishes between many of the things people fear, showing that fear is natural and sometimes even beneficial. Some common safety tips are offered along the way. Children may want to discuss the fears mentioned here as well as others they have felt.

Ages 3-6

Also available in:
Paperbound — *A Book of Scary Things*
Xerox Publishing Company

597

Shura, Mary Frances Craig

The Season of Silence

Black/white illustrations by Ruth Sanderson.
Atheneum Publishers, 1976.
(123 pages)

COMMUNICATION: *Importance of*
MATURATION
   Boy-girl relationships
   Death: of grandparent
   Nature: appreciation of
   Trust/Distrust

Susie Spinner, a young adolescent, spends the beginning of a strange spring in her room with a strep throat, then with complications that keep her confined to bed several more weeks. When she emerges, thin, pale, and weak, her family has changed: her baby brother has begun to walk; her mother and father have private conferences; her older sister, Carrie, stays locked up in her room, then one day disappears. Moreover, her best friend, Lindy, now has a boy friend, Trevor Howard, the neighborhood bully. Susie has no one to walk home from school with, or play with, and her parents are too busy worrying about Carrie to notice Susie's loneliness. But Susie finds refuge in a quiet, secluded grove on the old nearby Clary estate. She thinks the place almost magical, and sits there for hours in complete silence. A fox and an owl wander in, and she studies the birds and wildflowers. One day an angry boy appears in the grove saying Susie is trespassing. She is so startled she says nothing, and as he berates her, it comes to him that she is mute. After that, he comes often to the grove and tells her all about himself: he is Derek Born, Mrs. Clary's grandson. Mrs. Clary is dying, and Derek and his father are nursing her despite the fact that Mrs. Clary and her late husband refused to allow Derek's runaway mother,

Angelica, to return home when Angelica was dying. Throughout his musing confidences, Susie remains silent. Derek gives her a book on "Country Simples" that his grandmother had written about herbs native to the region. It is full of descriptions of wildflowers and their healing properties, interspersed with a journal of Angelica's life. One day Lindy's boy friend, Trevor, beats Susie up, erroneously thinking she has caused trouble between Lindy and himself. She is rescued by Carrie's former boy friend, Martin, and seeks refuge in the grove. Derek is already there, crying. Mrs. Clary has just died. Trevor bursts in on the scene and again attacks Susie, but Derek intervenes. Trevor pulls out a knife and Susie yells to warn Derek. He wheels around, amazed that she can speak, and Trevor slashes his leg. Derek stares at her with complete disdain and limps away. It is Martin who at last explains to Susie why Carrie has run away. Her life had come to seem wholly confusing, not least the part involving a man who wanted to marry her. Carrie has gone to San Francisco to try to think things out. As Martin says, "She ran away from all of us — him and me *and* your folks, all of us." Martin and Susie drive to San Francisco and find Carrie, who consents to return home with them. The two sisters are wholly reunited, and at last, too, Susie can explain her "season of silence" to Derek and return the journal to him. He explains that she had thought he needed someone to confide in, and who better than someone who could not repeat what he said? Once they had begun, she did not want to discourage his trust by admitting she could talk. Derek gives her a wooden swan he has carved but must go home to the East. He promises to write.

Susie grows up during a spring full of sadness, violence, and discovery. At the end of this book, she is satisfied that she has renewed her relationship with her sister and has salvaged a friendship with Derek. She is happily aware that her body is maturing, and she knows she has learned something about life, love, and death. The author tells the story from Susie's point of view and we share her bewilderment about the sudden changes that have happened to her family and friends. There are hints of sexual encounters in the lives of both Carrie and Lindy, but we understand only what Susie does. The most dramatic story here is that of Angelica, who had run away, married, been denounced by her parents, had a baby, tried unsuccessfully to return home, and died. Mrs. Clary's journal is heartbreaking. The eight full-page, black and white illustrations delicately chronicle Susie's adventures, particularly her encounters in the grove.

Ages 10-14

Also available in:
No other form known

598

Shyer, Marlene Fanta

Welcome Home, Jellybean

Charles Scribner's Sons, 1978.
(152 pages)

MENTAL RETARDATION
  Sibling: love for

Geraldine Oxley is one year older than her twelve-year-old brother, Neil, but has only now been toilet-trained and learned to tie her shoes. Gerri is mentally retarded. After a stay in a residential training center, she is moving back home, though Mr. Oxley, wary of her return, tells Neil it is not going to be easy living with her. Sure enough, she disturbs and angers other tenants in their apartment house, when, out of anger or disappointment she beats her head against the wall at night. And she makes messes of her parents' and Neil's belongings. She even causes Neil trouble at school. New there and without close friends, the boy sees a chance to be befriended by some popular fellow students by playing the piano for a show; Gerri continually interrupts not only his practicing but also his homework. Eventually he is near to being expelled, until his father explains the home situation to the principal. Mr. Oxley maintains that Gerri's actions make no sense, but by now Neil thinks they do; he begins to understand and protect his sister, encouraging her to learn. Mr. Oxley, however, moves out, unable to tolerate Gerri any longer. Neil refuses to leave with him. Then Gerri creates chaos during the school show, and he feels he *must* leave, though Gerri piteously tries to stop him. Only when Mr. Oxley arrives to pick him up does Neil reconsider. He realizes that Gerri is his sister no matter what she does. His father has quit, and one quitter in the family is enough.

A retarded girl tries to show her love for her family, but her misunderstood efforts — often noisy and disruptive — anger and bewilder others, and thus herself. But when her brother, who narrates this story, learns to perceive the intentions behind what she does, he can genuinely like and accept her. Readers will learn from the logic he discovers in Gerri's actions and can share his joy in her accomplishments. Good humor is by no means the least of virtues in this sympathetic, realistic story.

Ages 10-13

Also available in:
No other form known

599

Silman, Roberta

Somebody Else's Child

Black/white illustrations by Chris Conover.
Frederick Warne & Company, Inc., 1976.
(64 pages)

ADOPTION: Feelings About
LOVE, MEANING OF

Peter, a fourth grader, is an adopted child. He strikes up a friendship with a school-bus driver, an older man called Puddin' Paint. One day a snowstorm stalls the bus, and Puddin' Paint comes to Peter's house to call the garage. As they wait there for help, Peter learns that Puddin' Paint has no children, and the boy suggests that he adopt one. Not realizing Pete is adopted, the man says he has always wanted children, but could not accept "somebody else's child." Peter hides his hurt, but later, when his mother tries to explain why some people shy away from adoption, Peter angrily announces that he should have come from his mother the way his sister did. His mother replies, "When people take care of a child the way your father and I have taken care of you, they are the child's parents. You are ours because we love you with that special love that parents have for children." Some weeks later, Puddin' Paint tells Peter that his two dogs are missing and Peter volunteers to help look for them. Soon enough, Peter sees how worried his friend is, realizes how much he must love the dogs, and begins to understand what his mother meant about the special kind of love people have for their children. Peter tells Puddin' Paint that he is adopted, and the man apologizes for what he had said. Peter helps find the dogs, who were caught in traps, and at the veterinary he faints from exhaustion, awakening to hear that the dogs will recover. The veterinarian's wife congratulates Puddin' Paint on having such a fine son. The man replies that Peter is not his, but he wishes he were. They are several hours late returning to Puddin' Paint's house, where Peter's father anxiously awaits his son.

In this first-person narrative the boy and the old man come to share a special friendship and begin to understand the bond between parents and their children — a bond that is just as strong for adopted as for other children. When Peter and his mother talk about adoption, she answers his questions clearly and truthfully, including the difficult question of why his biological mother gave him up. The winter setting dramatizes the conflicts of the story.

Ages 9-11

Also available in:
Paperbound — *Somebody Else's Child*
Dell Publishing Company, Inc.

Talking Book — *Somebody Else's Child*
Library of Congress

600

Simmons, Anthony

The Optimists of Nine Elms

Black/white illustrations by Ben F. Stahl.
Pantheon Books, 1975.
(62 pages)

FRIENDSHIP: Meaning of
PETS: Love for
SIBLING: Relationships
  Age: respect for

The nine-year-old narrator and her younger brother, Mark, live in Nine Elms, a poor industrial area of London. Their father works from dawn until late night to save enough money to move them all to a larger apartment. Mother is grouchy and preoccupied with a new baby, with no time to spare. The children make friends with an equally grouchy, eccentric old man named Old Sam, a "busker" who makes a living playing a small hand organ while his aged dog, Bella, collects money in a cup. Old Sam takes the children "busking" with him into London and shows them the pets' cemetery in Hyde Park, where he wants Bella one day to be buried. A dog, he says, is the only true friend, and he leads them to a shelter for strays, where Mark chooses a small dog they name Battersea. During the following week Old Sam helps them earn enough money to pay for Battersea. Meanwhile, Father has found the larger apartment. When the children surprise their parents with the dog, both the father and mother are angry. Dogs are not permitted in their new apartment building. Grabbing Battersea, the children run away to Old Sam's — where they find Sam drunk and Bella dead. When Sam staggers off to buy more liquor, the children take Bella in her basket, trudge across town to the Hyde Park cemetery, and hold a funeral for her. By the time they complete the burial, it is dark, and they hear the approaching voices of their father and Old Sam. They stay hidden in the bushes and fall asleep. Father finds them in the morning, but instead of scolding them, he hugs them. The three go home together, leaving Old Sam and Battersea standing by Bella's grave.

This is a tender story of two children who enjoy an unusual companionship with a lonely, gruff old man and his dog. His disposition aside, Old Sam has a feeling for the children's needs and interests that even their parents lack.

Ages 8-11

Also available in:
Talking Book — *The Optimists of Nine Elms*
Library of Congress

S

601

Simon, Marcia L.

A Special Gift

Harcourt Brace Jovanovich, Inc., 1978.
(132 pages)

COURAGE, MEANING OF
GENDER ROLE IDENTITY: Male
PREJUDICE: Sexual
   Perseverance

Peter, in junior high school, leads a double life. At school he is a star basketball player, and after school — without any of his friends knowing it — he takes ballet lessons. When his dance teacher announces that auditions are soon to be held for a production of the ballet *The Nutcracker,* the boy must make a choice. If he appears in the ballet, his classmates will know his secret, and many of them will tease him. Furthermore, rehearsals may interfere with basketball practice. Peter decides to audition anyway — and is thrilled when he gets a part. He finds no conflicts at first. Then one Saturday, he has to miss a basketball game for a dress rehearsal. His father, who does not entirely approve of the boy's dancing and wants him to develop his athletic prowess, is angry. The following week, Father insists Peter miss part of another rehearsal so as to make another game. Early in that game, Peter badly twists his ankle. Unable to play, he leaves and goes to rehearsal. But he further injures the ankle by dancing. A doctor tells him he must not dance for two weeks; he will have to miss the first few Nutcracker performances. At school the following week a gang of bullies teases Peter about his dancing and pelts him with snowballs. Encouraged by his older sister (also a dancer), his director, and the many new friends he has made, Peter waits impatiently for his ankle to heal. At last, at his first performance, he is transported by the music and the beauty of the dance, and is profoundly proud to be a dancer. His family — including his father — and his best friend are in the audience, deeply proud of him too.

A promising young male dancer faces down the opposition of his father and friends, who think dancing sissified. Landing a role in an elaborate production, meeting several accomplished performers, and making friends with other male dancers all help Peter accept his love of dancing as "a special gift," certainly not something to be ashamed of. This book, both sympathetic and realistic, could encourage boys interested in dance and make their case to readers without such an interest.

Ages 10-13

Also available in:
Film — *A Special Gift*
ABC Afterschool Special: Martin Tahse Productions

602

Simon, Norma

All Kinds of Families

Color illustrations by Joe Lasker.
Albert Whitman & Co., 1976.
(37 pages counted)

FAMILY: Relationships
FAMILY: Unity
   Belonging
   Family: extended
   Life style

Almost everyone is a member of a family. Families share good and bad times. They may have any number of children, or none at all, and may have one, two, or no parents. Families gather from far-apart places to celebrate or mourn together. In any case, families — some including grandparents, aunts, uncles, and cousins —

are a unit. That unit is added to by births, adoptions, and marriages and is subtracted from by death, separation, and divorce. The members of some families are not close and do not communicate with each other. Others when apart, keep in touch through letters, visits, and telephone calls. These latter families share stories, work, visits, sadness, and fun. In fact, the thing that makes a family unit is not its size, but the care and love members show one another.

This story, speaking directly to the reader, discusses the differences and similarities in families. Through illustrations and text, the reader learns that families vary but are to be found everywhere. We also learn that the family unit is steady and fertile, nurturing the emotional and physical growth of the child.

Ages 5-8

Also available in:
Talking Book — *All Kinds of Families*
Library of Congress

603

Simon, Norma

Why Am I Different?

Color illustrations by Dora Leder.
Albert Whitman & Co., 1976.
(31 pages)

DIFFERENCES, HUMAN
  Autonomy

Children of the most varied backgrounds, and with the most varied appearances and skills, talk about the ways they are different. Some are tall, others short. One child is the only one in his family with red hair. Another is allergic to chocolate, shrimp, and clams, and dislikes the difference that makes. As for skills, one is good at drawing, another at writing. Having no TV set at home,

one child wonders why his parents should be different. Another child's family owns no car: he and his mother take the bus to "lots of places." Parents differ too in their occupations. And having a grandmother living at home makes a delightful difference to a boy who likes his grandmother. Some children are adopted. One boy is an only child. One youngster sums it up: "We're different, but alike, too. We eat and play and wear clothes and live in houses. But I'm not you, and you're not me. I think different things, I feel different things. I know different things, and I do different things. I look different. I *am* different. That's good!"

This book encourages young children to recognize and accept differences in themselves and others. The author's introductory note speaks of helping "children feel pride in the specialness of 'Being me!'" Questions scattered throughout the text encourage thought and promote discussion. The last page is written for adults, and offers suggestions on how the book may be most helpfully used.

Ages 4-8

Also available in:
Cassette — *Why Am I Different?*
Instructional/Communications Technology, Inc.

604

Singer, Marilyn

It Can't Hurt Forever

Black/white illustrations by Leigh Grant.
Harper & Row Publishers, Inc., 1978.
(186 pages)

SURGERY: Heart
  Death: attitude toward
  Friendship: making friends
  Hospital, going to

Eleven-year-old Ellie Simon is to enter the hospital, where she will have tests to confirm and surgery to repair a "patent ductus arteriosus" — an open duct on her heart. Though her parents and physician have thoroughly explained the procedure, and her mother has promised that she will not die, Ellie is deeply worried. Admitted to the hospital, Ellie meets another patient, Sonia, a girl about her own age who takes her to meet the other children in the ward. This helps Ellie to relax and to stop feeling alone — but then she meets May, who terrifies her with wild stories about her own heart catheterization and surgery. Sure enough, Ellie is badly scared when she is taken for her heart "cath," but finds that, though painful, the procedure is not debilitating. In any case, surgery approaches, and the team that will operate on Ellie comes to her to discuss it. Despite honest answers from all concerned, Ellie remains fearful all the way into the operating room. She survives as promised, but in the recovery room finds she is in extreme pain. Mercifully, shots relieve that. When the pain lessens and she is again allowed to walk through the ward, Ellie meets Melissa, a girl also scheduled for heart surgery. Melissa is so frightened that she has bitten a doctor and repeatedly attempted to run away. Ellie persuades her to have mock surgery — a kind of rehearsal — in the recreation room. Having learned what is ahead, Melissa is far less frightened and Ellie is pleased that she, like Sonia, was able to help someone be less afraid.

This first-person narrative, based on the author's own experience with heart surgery at eight, is filled with candid observations concerning serious surgery and lengthy hospital stays. When the main character meets other patients in the children's ward, they display a multitude of feelings about surgery and serious illness. Truthfulness is shown to be the best antidote to children's fears about surgery. Because the main character candidly expresses her own feelings, this book could be of great use and comfort to children facing surgery, and to those friends and siblings who want to understand what a hospital stay and an operation are like.

Ages 9-12

Also available in:
No other form known

605

Singer, Marilyn

No Applause, Please

E. P. Dutton & Company, Inc., 1977.
(122 pages)

FRIENDSHIP: Best Friend
MATURATION
  Boy-girl relationships
  Loyalty

Ruthie Zeiler is fourteen and a high school sophomore, but her interests are by no means typical. Her best friend, Laurie, plays a guitar, and the two girls enjoy singing together, as they will do shortly in the high school talent show. As things turn out, the girls take second place to Lonnie, a junior, and his magic act. Afterward Laurie begins acting snobbish and worldly and, prompted by her mother, takes piano and voice lessons and has her hair styled. She has no time for Ruthie, who is disgusted by her affectations anyway. Then Lonnie surprises Ruthie by inviting her to his house for an evening. So begins her first friendship with a boy. When she manages to arrange an audition for herself and Laurie with an agent, the latter will work only with Laurie. Hurt and angry, Ruthie stops speaking to Laurie. Yet she does go to hear her sing in a local night club, only to find her performance disappointing. Soon enough Ruthie learns that the agent is a confidence man who has taken all of the money Laurie's mother had advanced to him and left town. Knowing how humiliated Laurie must feel, Ruthie goes to see her, comforts her, and promises they will always be friends.

In this first-person narrative, a young adolescent, unready for change, resents her best friend's new ambition and defensive airs. But a pleasant friendship with a boy causes changes in Ruthie, too. Putting aside her hurt feelings, she rediscovers and declares her friendship with Laurie.

Ages 10-12

Also available in:
No other form known

606

Skorpen, Liesel Moak

Bird

Color illustrations by Joan Sandin.
Harper & Row Publishers, Inc., 1976.
(41 pages)

ANIMALS: Love for
ANIMALS: Responsibility for

A young farm boy wandering listlessly around the yard finds a small bird in the grass. Fetching a ladder, he places it back in its nest. Several times he finds it, several times replaces it until, deciding the bird's mother is gone, he asks his father what to do. A book his father consults says not to keep a baby bird if you can help it. Willy-nilly, the boy cannot help it. He names his little charge Bird. Soon Bird, perched on his shoulder, accompanies the boy everywhere. However much the boy tries to teach Bird to fly, Bird does not. The boy concludes that Bird is stupid and looks in his father's book on birds for ideas. Finding one, he pushes Bird off a branch, and Bird flies in a halting way. The boy is very proud, even though, while the bird can fly, it now still

prefers to ride on his shoulder. In the fall, Bird disappears, and the boy is miserable. One fine spring day the boy is wandering listlessly around the yard when he almost steps on an egg hidden in the grass. He replaces the egg in a nest, thinking the mother pretty stupid to lose an egg. Perched on a branch above the nest is the mother; it is Bird. "I was right," the boy says to the egg. "Your mother's dumb." He expects he will need to teach her children to fly. Though he tries not to show it, the thought pleases him.

A withdrawn boy tries to conceal his attachment to a bird by calling it "dumb," but his sorrow at its disappearance and joy at its return show his true feelings. This story shows how responsibility for Bird enlivens the boy, though not how or if he applies the experience to his relations with people.

Ages 6-8

Also available in:
No other form known

607

Skorpen, Liesel Moak

His Mother's Dog

Color illustrations by M. E. Mullin.
Harper & Row Publishers, Inc., 1978.
(46 pages)

PETS
SIBLING: New Baby
  Jealousy

A little boy is at last told by his parents that he can have a longed-for dog of his own. He wants a Newfoundland; his parents buy him a cocker spaniel, the kind his mother used to have. Still, he likes it, and he names it Moose. But the puppy becomes attached to the boy's mother, who calls him Puck. This is most depressing, and the boy comes to think of the dog as his mother's. Then a baby girl is born to the family. The boy resents her — and becomes unhappier still. Puck, too, is jealous of her, growls at her, and is exiled to the yard. The boy goes for a walk and Puck follows him. Later, when the boy is lying in his room depressed after a scolding, the dog comes in, sits by the bed, and then, when the boy cries, climbs up and licks his tears; a new bond is forged. The boy and dog become best friends and do everything together. The boy calls him Moose.

A little boy's jealousy when his mother becomes the object of his pet's attachment, and his resentment of a new baby sister, are both dispelled when the dog suddenly offers his devotion to him. This quiet, perceptive story makes understandable the joy, dismay, jealousy, and hurt any child might feel in similar circumstances.

Ages 5-8

Also available in:
Talking Book — *His Mother's Dog*
Library of Congress

608

Skorpen, Liesel Moak

Mandy's Grandmother

Color illustrations by Martha Alexander.
The Dial Press, Inc., 1975.
(32 pages counted)

GRANDPARENT: Love for
  Gender role identity: female

Little Mandy is a tomboy. She likes horses, forts, and frogs. When her grandmother comes to visit, expecting to find a little dear in lace and frills, Mandy's boyish appearance and interests offend her. Indeed, Mandy thinks her grandmother hates her. One morning she takes Grandmother a cup of tea, and finding her feeling sad, climbs onto her lap. A friendship is born. From that morning on, the two have a lot to share. Mandy shows Grandmother the barn, her pony, her pirate ship, and Grandmother tells Mandy stories. When it is time for Grandmother to leave, the two tell each other, "I love you."

When Mandy and her grandmother can each accept the other as she is, the two find each other both interesting and loving. This brief, sometimes funny account shows both how and why loving friendships can suddenly start.

Ages 4-7

Also available in:
Film — *Mandy's Grandmother*
Illumination Films

609

Skorpen, Liesel Moak

Michael

Color illustrations by Joan Sandin.
Harper & Row Publishers, Inc., 1975.
(40 pages)

FEAR: of Storms
  Animals: responsibility for
  Communication: parent-child

Young Michael, who lives with his family on a farm, is afraid of thunderstorms. Whenever one strikes, he and his dog, Mud, hide under a quilt, and Michael counts to one hundred and back and feels less afraid. One morning, after being scolded by his father for carelessness, Michael leaves the house angrily. While roaming with Mud, he finds a young rabbit whose nest has been destroyed and takes it home. Michael's father is mowing the lawn and snaps at him not to take the rabbit in the house. Michael builds a nest for the rabbit outside, and his mother shows him how to feed it with a baby bottle. During the night another storm strikes. Michael is afraid and wonders if the little rabbit is afraid, too, and if she misses her mother. He goes outside to find her, but she is not in the nest. Returning to the house, he finds his father feeding the little rabbit. His father says, "That's too much weather for anyone," and tells Michael to take her upstairs with him. Later, the father comes to Michael's room, tells him, "I love you," and kisses him goodnight.

Michael is deeply afraid of thunderstorms, but his affection for the rabbit overcomes his fear in this warm, believable story. The rabbit also brings him closer to his father, because his father understands Michael's affection for it, remembering the pet rabbit he had had when he was young.

Ages 4-8

Also available in:
Talking Book — *Michael*
Library of Congress

610

Slote, Alfred

The Hotshot

Black/white photographs by William LaCrosse.
Franklin Watts, Inc., 1977.
(87 pages)

SPORTS/SPORTSMANSHIP

Ninth grader Paddy O'Neill wants desperately to be named to the all-city Bantam hockey team. From there he could count on a position on the varsity hockey team when he enters high school in the fall. In an effort to be noticed by the nominating committee during a championship play-off, Paddy endeavors to score an unlikely goal. Knowing that passing to his teammate would bring a sure goal, Paddy attempts the shot himself and loses the puck to an opponent, who scores the winning goal. Now Paddy's team will have to play another game tomorrow to decide the city champion. After the game, Paddy is berated by the coach; the other boys agree that they will play as a team tomorrow and win the championship. The next day Paddy has no opportunity to score until the final period. He sees an opening and decides to take it, even though he knows the shot to be risky. The next moment, he is hit and loses the puck. Rather than going to an opponent, the puck skims over the ice to the waiting stick of his teammate. When the teammate scores the winning goal, Paddy resigns himself in disgust to the fact that the all-city team is now beyond him. But to his amazement, he finds that the nominating committee has mistaken his fumble for a timely pass to his teammate, and has placed him on the all-city team after all. On the way home Paddy confesses to his father that the lucky shot had started as a solo attempt at a goal and in so confessing, realizes that a winning pass is just as important as a winning goal.

Paddy's self-seeking in this first-person narrative is clear and convincing. The reader sees how it affects the boy's relations with his teammates, coach, and family. Paddy's understanding that teamwork can be essential in sports alters his feelings about himself and others. A glossary of hockey terminology has been included. The large print photographs and fast-paced story here will appeal to the reluctant reader.

Ages 8-11

Also available in:
Paperbound — *The Hotshot*
Dell Publishing Company, Inc.

611

Slote, Alfred

Matt Gargan's Boy

J. B. Lippincott Co., 1975.
(158 pages)

PARENT/PARENTS: Single
Little League
Prejudice: sexual

Eleven-year-old Danny lives in Arborville, Michigan, with his divorced mother. Danny's father, Matt Gargan, is a well-known catcher for the Chicago White Sox, and Danny pitches for a recreational league baseball team in Arborville. Against all his mother says to the contrary, Danny believes his parents will reunite when his father retires in another year. Pitching his first game of the season, Danny notices that in the stands his mother is enjoying the company of a new escort. Distracted, he pitches badly — recovering only when the man leaves early. The man is Herb Warren, his mother's new boss at the library, a widower with two daughters. Susie, the eleven-year-old, plans to try out for Danny's baseball team. Against all the boys' efforts to keep a girl from qualifying, Susie passes — and Danny quits the team just before a tough game. He reasons that with no games to attend together, Mr. Warren will leave his mother available for his father. When he tells her this, Danny's mother responds that she is going to the big game anyway. Danny calls his father for advice — and Matt Gargan tells his son that he is getting married. He dons his uniform and bikes over to the game. The team is doing badly. Finally, after explaining everything to the coach, Danny gets to pitch. He strikes two players out; then he and Susie execute another play for a third out and victory. Later that evening, Danny tells his mother

of his talk with his father: "I admire him, Mom. I'm his son. I'm always going to be his son, aren't I?" His mother replies, "Of course you are. You always will be."

This believable first-person narrative perceptively describes a boy's resentment of his parents' divorce and his unfounded hope for reconciliation. His father's planned remarriage shocks Danny into seeing clearly that his parents are individuals with their own lives. Even if both parents remarry, Danny won't lose his identity; he will always be "Matt Gargan's boy."

Ages 9-11

Also available in:

Braille — *Matt Gargan's Boy*
Library of Congress

Paperbound — *Matt Gargan's Boy*
Avon Books

612

Smith, Doris Buchanan

Dreams & Drummers

Thomas Y. Crowell Company, Inc., 1978.
(180 pages)

MATURATION
Ambivalence, feelings of
Boy-girl relationships
Friendship: meaning of
Parental: overprotection
School: achievement/underachievement

Stephanie is beset with an unusual problem for a fourteen-year-old: the absence of problems. As her mother says, Stephanie was born old — no adolescent turmoil for her. Yet Stephanie worries that her life has perhaps been too smooth, ruffled only by her annoying younger brother, Simon. Does she need more "growing up hard," like her rebellious older brother, Seth? Whatever she needs, she is weary of being a placid model student. But she cannot explain this uneasiness to anyone, not even to Easter, her best friend. It only deepens when Jase, a fellow band-member whom she has flirted with, professes love for her. At times infatuated with him, at other times wanting to break off their friendship, Stephanie wonders what to do. For there are two other boys who are attracted to her, and there is a friend, black, who unseats her as the band's first-chair drummer — unfairly, she thinks. How should she respond? Stephanie wants to be honest with these people, yet avoid hurting their feelings, and she finds the two courses are not easily combined. She falls into a depressed mood but soon realizes that these doubts and dubious surprises hardly threaten what she is, her real self. That weekend she and Jase go bicycling, and she enjoys the outing thoroughly — until he asks her to be his girl friend. Aware that they have little in common and that she is in any case not ready to have a boy friend, Stephanie says she cannot be his girl friend but does want to be his friend.

A girl whose life is not as uncluttered as she thinks it is becomes aware of just how tenuous and fragile are the bonds between herself and friends when she enters a stage of changed relationships and interests. Yet she loses neither her sense of values nor her zest for trying new things. Underscoring Stephanie's moves toward maturity and the sensible way her parents treat her is a subplot showing how an overprotective mother reduces a daughter to meekness and a son to unthinking rebellion. In fact, it is the subplots which enliven this otherwise static first-person narrative.

Ages 10-12

Also available in:
No other form known

613
Smith, Doris Buchanan

Kelly's Creek
Black/white illustrations by Alan Tiegreen.
Thomas Y. Crowell Company, Inc., 1975.
(71 pages)

LEARNING DISABILITIES
  Self-esteem

Nine-year-old Kelly O'Brien is worried. For two months he has been in the special class for children with learning disabilities, but his progress report shows no progress: his hands and feet will not obey his brain. Knowing his parents will be disappointed, he escapes to the one place where no one thinks him clumsy or slow, the marshland down the bluff from his home. There he meets his friend Phillip, a biology student who has taught Kelly much about the science of the marsh life they both love so much. Sure enough, Kelly's mother is angered by his absence and rules Phillip and the marsh off limits. Kelly must stay home and practice drawing basic shapes. But the next day Kelly sneaks off to the marsh, on his way finding an empty ice-cream container. He traces its roundness over and over, only to find Phillip watching him. He feels more stupid than ever. At home he tries drawing the circle on paper unaided — and for the first time draws not only a circle but a square. His parents, his teacher, even his schoolmates are happy for him. Phillip comes to Kelly's house and offers a suggestion: that the boy share with his classmates what he has learned about the marsh. The next day Kelly takes two pairs of fiddler crabs to class and talks about them. His classmates are astounded by how much he knows, and for once, Kelly feels the warm self-respect of having excelled in front of others.

The author has created a charming, vigorous little boy, whose spirit is not suffocated by all those who expect too much of him too quickly. Kelly's disability is described only as "an eye-to-hand problem."

Ages 8-13

Also available in:
No other form known

614

Smith, Nancy Covert

Josie's Handful of Quietness

Black/white illustrations by Ati Forberg.
Abingdon Press, 1975.
(143 pages)

RESPONSIBILITY: Accepting
  Expectations
  Friendship: meaning of
  Mexican-American
  Migrant workers
  Prejudice: social class

Josie Garciá, twelve, is the daughter of Mexican-American migrant farm laborers. During the summer, while her parents are working in the fields, she looks after her younger sister, Mariá, and baby brother, Carlos. She goes to school when they are staying near one and when there is enough money so her mother doesn't have to work but can stay home with the younger children. But more than anything, Josie wants to live in one place, finish school, and become a teacher. She has little hope of that, however. When she mentions her ambition to her father, Ramón, he bridles at the idea that she disdains the life he provides. With constant moving, Josie has never had a friend her own age, but one day she does meet elderly Mr. Curtis on the next farm over. He is the only farmer in the area who tends his own orchard; Ramón's employer, Mr. Welter, has bought all the other small farms. Josie likes Mr. Curtis and is impressed with his permanence: the kitchen appliances, the furniture, the carpets. Mr. Curtis lives alone, enjoys having Josie and the children visit him, and, even deciding that Josie should have a girl friend, introduces her to Mr. Welter's daughter, Lydia. A much-indulged child, Lydia hurts Josie with her mysterious moodiness and with remarks that betray her prejudice. Finally, envious of Josie's friendship with Mr. Curtis, Lydia steals the bicycle he has given to Josie. Confronted with this, Mr. Welter calls Josie a troublemaker and forbids her to see his daughter again. He eventually learns the truth, and apologizes, but Josie's father has been so outraged by Welter's accusation that he quits his job in the fields for one in a factory — so that Josie can finish school in one place. Mr. Curtis can see that Ramón hates the thought of the routine factory work, and he himself wants neighbors badly. He offers Ramón the job of managing his orchard, and talks Welter into letting the Garcias stay where they are through the winter. Josie likes school, and hears of scholarships available for college. Her dream is finally within her reach.

Josie, a Mexican-American, has been treated as an inferior outsider by Americans native-born, whiter, or more monied. Having one good "gringo" friend, Mr. Curtis, makes her feel as if she belongs where she is and gives her more confidence. Josie finds that although Lydia appears to have everything, Mr. Welter's huge farm keeps him so busy that he has no time for his daughter. Mr. Curtis is satisfied with his small orchard, and also has time for his friends. This uncomplicated story is given to pat resolutions, but still provides information on the lives and hopes of migrant workers.

Ages 9-11

Also available in:
Paperbound — Josie's Handful of Quietness
Xerox Publishing Company

615

Snyder, Anne

First Step

Holt, Rinehart and Winston, Inc., 1975.
(128 pages)

ALCOHOLISM: of Mother
  Boy-girl relationships
  School: classmate relationships

Senior high student Cindy Stott is not only embarrassed by her divorced mother's drinking, but also fearful that her mother, who often loses her temper when drunk, will hurt her younger brother, Brett. One night Cindy invites her best friend, Sherrie, to sleep overnight, but Sherrie's mother knows that Mrs. Stott drinks too much and refuses to give permission. Furious, Cindy stops speaking to Sherrie. Soon Cindy has isolated herself from all her friends. Then Mitch, a popular senior, tells her that his own mother and father are alcoholics and invites her to attend a meeting of Alateen, an organization for the children of alcoholics. Cindy emphatically denies that her mother is an alcoholic, but she does attend the meeting, where she hears other young people explain how they have learned to handle their feelings about their parents' drinking. Meanwhile, Cindy is to play the lead in the school play. The night of its presentation, Cindy's mother mortifies her by staggering onto the stage in front of everyone and handing her a bouquet of roses. Now Cindy is desperate, and seeks the support of the members of Alateen. At the next meeting she admits aloud to the group her own grief and confusion — and goes home reassured and fortified by new friendships.

Though this story seems contrived — almost a promotion for Alateen — it rings true, and the information given could be useful for young people whose parents are alcoholics.

Ages 11-13

Also available in:
Paperbound — *First Step*
New American Library

616

Snyder, Anne

My Name Is Davy — I'm an Alcoholic
Black/white illustrations by the author.
Holt, Rinehart and Winston, Inc., 1977.
(128 pages)

ALCOHOLISM: Adolescent
DECISION MAKING
  Boy-girl relationships
  Loneliness
  Responsibility: accepting
  Responsibility: avoiding
  Sex: premarital

Lacking friends or interested parents, fifteen-year-old Davy has been drinking steadily for the past year to ease his loneliness. While sneaking a drink at school one day, he is discovered by Mike — the leader of the crowd Davy most envies — and invited to join a lunchtime drinking party. That evening the glow of being accepted deserts him when Mike and his friends, finding that Davy is sexually inexperienced, get him drunk and force him on Maxine, a girl whose willingness to share herself and her liquor have earned her a reputation as "everybody's pal." Overcome by embarrassment and drink, Davy passes out and later cannot remember what, if anything, happened. The next day Davy learns that Maxine had been beaten by her alcoholic father for coming home late, and he apologizes to her. They become friends, spending many hours at her secret hideaway, a dried-up creek in a park, talking and drinking. During a party at Maxine's house, Mike and his friends trick Maxine into losing a game of strip poker. She protests and looks to Davy for help, but he stands by mutely while they rip her clothes off. Then he comforts her and tells the others to leave. After this the two stay away from the group, needing only each other and the bottle. Soon, however, Maxine's liquor supply runs out. They drive to a liquor store and give three tough-looking men some money to buy them a bottle of Scotch, but the men keep both the bottle and the change. Davy angrily demands both and is brutally beaten. Shunning the police or an ambulance, Maxine takes him to her father's camper to recuperate. Frightened and disgusted with themselves, Davy and Maxine decide to quit drinking. The first few days of withdrawal are painful for both of them, but Maxine, a heavier drinker than Davy, experiences frightening convulsions. That settles it: Davy decides to attend Alcoholics Anonymous meetings with her. Maxine accepts the A.A. program wholeheartedly, but Davy is more skeptical. Increasingly bored with the meetings, and seeking to regain their former closeness, he persuades Maxine to skip a session and go with him to the beach, where they meet Mike and his crowd. Davy joins their drinking party; Maxine protests, but eventually gives in. From a drunken stupor Davy watches as Maxine and the others go swimming nude and thinks himself dreaming when he sees Mike carry a girl's body out of the water. The next morning when he regains consciousness he finds it was not a dream — Maxine is dead. He goes home, fights with his parents, and runs away when they threaten to send him to an institution. Too guilty to go on living and afraid to die, he retreats to the hideaway, drinking himself to oblivion. When he runs out of money and is unable to beg any more drinks off passing derelicts, Davy sneaks home for clean clothes and money, then heads for a liquor store. There a young boy asks him to buy a bottle of wine for him. Davy explodes. He chases the boy until he can no longer run, then sinks down exhausted and begins to cry. "He couldn't fight any longer. He couldn't think anymore. He could only hurt." Finally, he walks to the A.A. clubhouse, enters, and says, "My name is Davy — I'm an alcoholic."

In this story, a teenage alcoholic goes through many of the well-known rationalizations to avoid the truth about his addiction. His final decision to seek help, precipitated by the death of his girlfriend, affirms the idea that it is necessary for an alcoholic to hit rock bottom before he can begin to change. Much A.A. philosophy is included in this book, often at the expense of plot and characterization. Some readers may be unprepared for the profanity, subject matter, and explicit sex scenes to be found here.

Ages 12 and up

Also available in:
Paperbound — *My Name is Davy — I'm an Alcoholic*
New American Library

617
Sobol, Harriet Langsam

Jeff's Hospital Book
Black/white photographs by Patricia Agre.
Henry Z. Walck, Inc., 1975.
(45 pages counted)

HOSPITAL, GOING TO
  Fear: of the unknown
  Surgery

Young Jeff is going to the hospital for an operation to straighten his eyes, which have been crossed since birth. Even though his mother and his favorite stuffed animal accompany him, he feels lonely and afraid, but the hospital staff understand his fears and carefully explain hospital procedures to him. After being given an identification bracelet and taking a blood test, Jeff goes up to his room, where he meets his nurse, a nurse's aide, and a resident doctor. Jeff's mother plays games with him to cheer him up, but he is still frightened and wants to go home. Another doctor, an anesthesiologist, arrives. He kids with Jeff about the injection he will give him in the morning and tells him not to eat anything after dinner so that his stomach will be empty for the operation. That evening Jeff's own eye doctor comes to visit. Next morning Jeff gets ready for the operation. The nurse gives him medicine to make him drowsy, and an orderly puts him on a long cart and wheels him to surgery. Later, Jeff wakes in his room without any memory of the operation at all. The following day he puts on sun glasses to protect his eyes and gets ready to go home. Everyone at the hospital has been kind to him and the operation has not been so bad, but Jeff is happy to be going home with his mother and father even so.

Telling a little boy's hospital experience from his admittance through his discharge, this book may calm children's fears of hospitals and surgery. But because Jeff's operation is relatively minor, the book could seem superficial for children who will be hospitalized for more serious conditions. The photographs show a lively boy, at once curious and afraid.

Ages 2-7

Also available in:
No other form known

618

Sobol, Harriet Langsam

My Brother Steven Is Retarded

Black/white photographs by Patricia Agre.
Macmillan Publishing Company, Inc., 1977.
(26 pages)

MENTAL RETARDATION
  Ambivalence, feelings of
  Emotions: accepting
  Sibling: relationships

S

Eleven-year-old Beth has an older brother, Steven, who is mentally retarded. Although she knows that the term means "you can't understand things like everyone else," she does get angry with Steven when he breaks things. She feels sorry for him because his condition is permanent, but wishes her parents could spend more time with her. She also knows that mental retardation is not "catching," and that Steven's brain damage is not her mother's fault. During the day, Steven goes to a special school and has friends there. But Beth enjoys her own time with him and they often play a special game of ball. When her own friends come over, she explains Steven's condition to ease their nervousness. Beth says, "I guess I love Steven because he's my brother, but many times I think he's hard to love." In fact, Beth feels relieved that it is Steven who is retarded and not she, but feels guilty about this relief. After examining her feelings about him, though, she realizes that her deepest wish for Steven is that he be happy.

This first-person narrative follows Beth's exploration of her mixed feelings toward her retarded brother. Her self-inquiry shows maturity, frankness, and compassion. The black and white photographs communicate her feelings well and portray Steven as a happy boy.

Ages 7-10

Also available in:
No other form known

619

Spence, Eleanor

The Devil Hole

Lothrop, Lee & Shepard Co., 1977.
(215 pages)

AUTISM
Ambivalence, feelings of
Australia
Change: new home
Responsibility: accepting
Sibling: relationships
Talents: musical

The Devil Hole is a deep chasm where the ocean pounds unstoppably, furiously against one of Australia's ragged reefs. Ten-year-old Douglas Marriner fears it. But soon there are matters closer to home to worry about. His baby brother, Carl, cries a lot and hates to be touched. By the time he is three, his mother is so worried about Carl that she takes him to a specialist in Sydney, who confirms her suspicion: Carl is autistic. The family sells its general store and moves to Sydney, where Carl can attend a special school. In the big city, Douglas's life takes a great turning. A gifted pianist, he is accepted at the Music College and immerses himself in his studies. His only free time he spends helping his mother care for Carl, for whom he feels real responsibility, although the boy is growing more and more difficult, and more galling to Douglas, who can scarcely talk to his mother anymore. One day, when the older boy's room is left unlocked, Carl makes a mess of it. Worse, he destroys Douglas's musical compositions. Douglas is nearing the end of his rope. Soon after, the two boys playing in the park, Carl becomes furious over something trivial and throws a tantrum on the sidewalk. Douglas stares, horrified at the rage in Carl's eyes, and whispers, "You're *not* my brother! . . . You never *were* my brother!" and runs away, leaving Carl on the sidewalk. On his way to a friend's apartment, Douglas calls home to tell his family where Carl is. But at his friend's place, he meets one of Carl's teachers, who explains autism to him as no one else has ever done. He also suggests that Douglas consider the good Carl has brought to the family. For example, their move to Sydney brought Douglas to the Music College. Still somewhat bewildered about autism, Douglas finds he feels better and will strive to accept and live with Carl's condition.

Douglas, unlike his older brother, who has left home with a religious group, feels a deep sense of responsibility toward his other, autistic brother, Carl. At times, Douglas resents his mother's absorption with Carl, but continues to do all he can to ease his mother's load. He must learn that Carl's rages have no personal meaning, that Carl cannot feel kinship toward the family, but that he is none the less part of it. This book is about Douglas and Carl almost exclusively. Other family members are shadowy by comparison, but the impact of an autistic child on a family is clearly drawn.

Ages 10-14

Also available in:
Talking Book — *The Devil Hole*
Library of Congress

620

Stanton, Elizabeth and Henry Stanton

Sometimes I Like to Cry

Color illustrations by Richard Leyden.
Albert Whitman & Co., 1978.
(32 pages counted)

EMOTIONS: Accepting

Young Joey likes to laugh. But sometimes he cries: when he cuts his finger, or feels left out, or grieves for his pet hamster, killed by the cat. In fact, he decides, everybody cries once in a while: his cat, his dog, even grownups, as when his sister got married and his father cried at the ceremony. Sometimes people even cry when they are happy.

A young boy discovers — and his parents agree — that crying is sometimes necessary and right. Both girls and boys can recognize Joey's experiences, and his relief when he accepts his emotions without embarrassment.

Ages 4-7

Also available in:
Filmstrip — *Sometimes I Like to Cry*
Westport Communications

621

Steptoe, John Lewis

Marcia

Color illustrations by the author.
The Viking Press, Inc., 1976.
(81 pages)

SEX: Attitude Toward
 Afro-American
 Boy-girl relationships: dating
 Sex: premarital

Fourteen-year-old Marcia lives in a Brooklyn housing project with her mother. She is dating Danny, and they are deeply fond of each other, but Marcia is worried that Danny wants to make love to her. She feels altogether unready to take that step and to risk becoming pregnant. She worries the matter around, and unable to find a solution, discusses it with her best friend, Millie. To her relief, she finds that Millie is worried about the same thing. The two acknowledge that they eventually want to make love with their boy friends; that seems to them only natural, given their feelings. But when Danny comes to visit while Marica is home alone and wants to make love to her, she rebuffs him. He storms from the apartment and Marcia is sure they are finished. It is then that she discusses the situation with her mother and says fully what she thinks: "There ain't nothin wrong with sex — there ain't nothin wrong with loving somebody — it's just that you have to defend yourself against the stupidity of the world and realize that the *world* is screwed up, not you." *And* she does not want a baby until, as she puts it, "I can give my child the things I want easily." Soon Danny returns and the two are going steady again.

This first-person narrative is told largely in dialogue, mostly in Black English, changing into something nearer standard English when a conversation is serious. Marcia's dilemma lies in wanting to make love with Danny, yet feeling unready for and afraid of pregnancy. The book also airs her mother's views, Danny's, and those of her best friend. The young people in this novel take themselves seriously, plan for success, and scorn drugs. These subjects are discussed along with the central subject of sex. Plot and character run second to ideas here.

Ages 12 and up

Also available in:
No other form known

622

Stevens, Carla McBride

Pig and the Blue Flag

Color illustrations by Rainey Bennett.
The Seabury Press, Inc., 1977.
(48 pages)

WEIGHT CONTROL: Overweight
  Embarrassment
  Self-esteem

Pig, who is fat, likes everything about the elementary school he attends — everything except gym class. In gym class there is nothing he can do well — not somersaults, not catching a ball, not running. One day Otter, the gym teacher, announces that the class will play Capture the Flag. Two teams are chosen; no one wants Pig, but Raccoon's team finally gets him. Each team must try to capture the blue flag from the other's territory while defending its own flag. On this day of days in the final moments of the game, Pig heroically captures the flag and brings his team to victory. "See what happens when

you try?" says Raccoon. When Otter announces that the class will play Capture the Flag again on Monday, Pig is overjoyed.

A clumsy, overweight pig is ashamed of his ineptness in sports. One success in a game, one chance to be a hero, fires him with enough self-confidence to yearn to try again. Children who hate physical education will identify with pig in his embarrassment and will rejoice in his success.

Ages 6-8

Also available in:
No other form known

623

Stevens, Carla McBride

Stories from a Snowy Meadow

Black/white illustrations by Eve Rice.
The Seabury Press, Inc., 1976.
(48 pages)

SHARING/NOT SHARING
  Death: attitude toward
  Death: of friend
  Friendship: meaning of
  Helping

Three friends — Mole, Shrew, and Mouse — are quarreling about who should have the quilt they are making, but they adjourn to deliver soup to Vole, an old lady. Finding her bedridden in a freezing house, they at once light a fire. Vole tells them a story about another old lady vole who gives shelter to a cricket. In return, the cricket sings and gives her a pebble that, when boiled in water, makes a tasty broth. On Vole's birthday, the friends give her the quilt. Vole responds by telling about a lady shrew who finds shoes, clothes, and toys on her doorstep — and finally a large box. A mole, stepping from the box, says he is a gift, and the shrew is delighted. One day, Mouse enters Mole's house to find him bundled up by the fire. Crossly, Mole orders him to leave. Shrew receives the same rude treatment. Bewildered by Mole's behavior, they ask Vole for advice. She tells about a childhood friend, normally kind and gentle, who one day complains about absolutely everything. Next a note arrives from the friend explaining she has the mumps and, as a result, has been very cross. Now understanding Mole's gruffness, Mouse and Shrew return to help him recover from a bad cold. In the spring, Vole dies. Mouse and Shrew regret not having done more for her, but Mole reminds them of her age — it was time for her to die. Mouse wants to cover the body with the quilt, but Mole corrects him: Vole would want the quilt to go to someone in need of it.

This collection of four related stories about the same animals endows them with human qualities like quarrelsomeness and crossness, and generosity and understanding. The elderly Vole's stories, themselves comments on situations in the "real world" of the meadow, may suggest to readers or listeners that lessons from stories can be applied to their own experience. This book lends itself to reading aloud.

Ages 3-7

Also available in:
No other form known

624
Stevenson, James

Wilfred the Rat
Black/white illustrations by the author.
Greenwillow Books, 1977.
(32 pages counted)

FRIENDSHIP: Meaning of
    Values/Valuing: moral/ethical

For as long as he can remember, Wilfred the rat has been on the road — not *to* any place, but *away* from wherever he has been. His current stop is a seacoast resort town in winter that at first look "takes the cake for lonely." Wilfred ducks into an amusement park to sleep and wakes to company: Dwayne, a squirrel, and Ruppert, a chipmunk. Explaining that the park is theirs for the taking until June, they show Wilfred around. As one exciting day of playing on rides follows another, the three become fast friends. But as summer nears, and the amusement park opens to the public, Ruppert and Dwayne choose to move out, lest they end up caught by the owner and his mean dog. Staying to see the park open, Wilfred is trapped on the roller coaster between owner and dog, leaps, and ends up in a popcorn pail. The owner asks if he would repeat this nightly; Wilfred can be a star — the "daredevil rat." One thing, however: Wilfred cannot have his friends join him. "Not a chance," the dog says. "No animals!" Convinced he cannot have fun without his friends, Wilfred forsakes stardom to join them.

A rat, forced to choose between newfound friends and the indulged life of a star, chooses his friends. Youngsters most likely will enjoy this well-illustrated fable for its literal story, but with some direction, they can see its analogy to human values.

Ages 4-7

Also available in:
Paperbound — *Wilfred the Rat*
Penguin Books, Inc.

625

Stevenson, James

The Worst Person in the World

Color illustrations by the author.
Greenwillow Books, 1978.
(32 pages counted)

LIFE STYLE: Change in
  Hostility
  Loneliness

From a messy old house behind a tangle of poison ivy, the worst man in the world looks out and glowers at a lovely spring day. "If there's anything I hate it's spring," he grumbles. After breakfasting on a lemon, he walks out and meets the ugliest creature in the world. Ugly (that is his name) admits this but owns up to having a nice personality. He follows Mr. Worst home and, appalled by the mess, cleans the house for a party. But Worst, finding party decorations everywhere the next morning, states he will have no party in his house — ever. Ugly restores the house to a mess and goes out to play baseball with some children. No longer comfortable at home and struck by an idea, Worst hurries outside, too. The ball game has stopped, the ball having been hit far into the woods. Worst emerges from the woods, clutching the baseball, to announce the game is over. Ugly and the children must come to his house for a party.

Hostility to the world, this story points out, often conceals loneliness. The formidable defenses Mr. Worst has erected cannot withstand the unwavering cheeriness of pastel-spotted, one-horned Ugly and his wisdom in letting Worst stew in his own mess. The illustrations here often stand alone as cartoons, as when Worst finds his one-lemon breakfast too sweet.

Ages 4-8

Also available in:
Paperbound — *The Worst Person in the World*
Penguin Books, Inc.

626

Stolz, Mary Slattery

Cider Days

Harper & Row Publishers, Inc., 1978.
(130 pages)

FRIENDSHIP: Making Friends
FRIENDSHIP: Meaning of
  Mexican-American
  Shyness
  Sibling: rivalry

For all her nine years, it seems, Polly Lewis has been best friends with Kate Willard, always sharing, always talking. When Kate moves to California, Polly finds herself friendless and unable to make friends easily. Her classmates at school seem a dull bunch. She loves her parents and grandmother, who lives with them, but the family cannot take Kate's place, and her younger brother, Rusty, is a nuisance, always quarreling with her. For a time, she hopes to befriend a newcomer, Consuela, but the half-Mexican girl is formal and distant, apparently more interested in riding Polly's horse than in talking to her. Moreover, Consuela is unhappy about the arrangement between her divorced parents whereby she must live during the school year with her mother, a famous and sometimes suffocating painter, far from her Mexican father and the land she was raised in. Her isolation deepens when, offended by some classmates, she runs from school on the opening day. But gradually, by riding horseback with her, by introducing Consuela to the Vermont countryside and culture, Polly wins the girl's confidence. In turn, Consuela reveals her feelings: she likes Polly and wants to stay in Vermont. When she spends Thanksgiving with the Lewises, the two girls talk, yet also share easy silences, confident now in their friendship.

This story proceeds gradually, more by scenes that authentically unfold a growing friendship than by a definite plotline. The girl from Vermont, accustomed to an easygoing, talkative friend, learns to talk less impetuously so as to befriend a shy girl from a more reserved background. Along the way, the author implicitly contrasts the permissiveness (and its effects on parents, children, and schools) afforded children raised in the U.S.A. and the direction of a Mexican upbringing. This is a sequel to *Ferris Wheel*.

Ages 8-11

Also available in:
Paperbound — *Cider Days*
Harper & Row Publishers, Inc.

627

Stolz, Mary Slattery

Ferris Wheel

Harper & Row Publishers, Inc., 1977.
(131 pages)

FRIENDSHIP: Best Friend
SIBLING: Rivalry
  Family: relationships
  Friendship: making friends

The summer before fifth grade is an unhappy one for Polly Lewis. Her best friend, Kate, is moving to California, and acts as if she will not miss Polly at all. Polly and her seven-year-old brother, Rusty, despite the pleas of their parents and grandmother, who lives with them, argue as often as they look at each other. Polly tries to befriend Consuela, a new girl in the neighborhood. But Consuela, her Mexican father and American mother divorced, she herself still a bit new in the U.S. and living with her mother, is shy and unresponsive. Polly and Kate exchange farewell gifts and say good-bye. Some days later, Rusty, while walking through the pasture, is surrounded by a herd of curious cows and is too frightened to move. Polly rides her horse into the huddled herd, and with the help of her father, scatters the cows. Afterward, she feels the stirrings of a wish to get on better with Rusty. The day of the church social, Polly especially misses Kate, for she has no friend with whom to ride the ferris wheel. Again seeking out Consuela, she persuades her to come along. She also tells Consuela she can ride her horse some time — and she hopes in her heart that they will become good friends.

The lonely sadness of losing her best friend leads a girl to attempt to make a new friend and to get on better with her brother. This pleasant, leisurely story rings particularly true in its dialogue and shifting relations between characters. Readers should not be misled by the book jacket, which pictures a girl too young to be Polly or any other character inside. The story of Polly and Consuela continues in *Cider Days*.

Ages 8-11

Also available in:
Paperbound — *Ferris Wheel*
Harper & Row Publishers, Inc.

S

628

Stoutenburg, Adrien

Where to Now, Blue?

Four Winds Press, 1978.
(186 pages)

MATURATION
RUNNING AWAY
  Animals: love for
  Friendship: meaning of
  Parental: weakness
  Poverty
  Risk, taking of

Blueberry, twelve years old, lives with her mother and stepfather in a tarpaper shack in northern Minnesota, where her mother smokes cigarettes and reads romance magazines all day, and her rude stepfather spits tobacco juice on the hot stove, for the noise. Blueberry's brother, Tad, had gone away promising to keep in touch, but Blueberry has only gotten two postcards. She and Tad had patched together a boat, the Victory, and with it she determines to escape her dreary life at Chicksaw Landing and go join her Uncle Stew in Minneapolis. But she and her cat and her parrot (who swears) find an unexpected passenger on board: Tibo, a six-year-old boy from the orphanage, who threatens to tell on her if he is not allowed to come along. They head down river for Minneapolis. Although Blueberry has not heard from her uncle in two years, she thinks he is probably rich and lives in a beautiful house, perhaps with servants.

But on their second day out, a storm strands them on a deserted island. The boat is damaged and unusable, and their food runs out. Just in time they are rescued by a boy named Harley Colter, who is fishing by the island. He takes them all to a resort his family owns, and the Colters treat them to large meals and great kindness. But Blueberry is still determined to reach Uncle Stew. Harley's brother gives the two children a ride to Minneapolis, and there Blueberry's dream collapses: Uncle Steward is dead and was far from rich. A disillusioned Blueberry returns to the resort, searching her mind for a way to avoid going back to Chicksaw Landing. It is Tibo who brings her to realize that there is nowhere else to go. She goes — but while things at home will be just as before, she herself has changed. She knows that someday it will be time to leave again, and when that time comes she wants to be ready. For now, she will work hard in school and make the best of her home life. And she will make a plan.

This is a believable account of the temporary escape of a plucky girl bored and neglected in a squalid home by a spineless mother and a slovenly, bullying stepfather. Although she ends up where she started, she is as determined as ever to find a better life somewhere else. She is more realistic about preparing herself, not only to get away, but to be capable and independent when she does.

Ages 10-12

Also available in:
No other form known

635

Talbot, Toby

Dear Greta Garbo

G. P. Putnam's Sons, 1978.
(91 pages)

DEATH: of Grandparent
DEPENDENCE/INDEPENDENCE
MATURATION
PARENTAL: Overprotection
    Grandparent: living in child's home
    Grandparent: love for
    Love, meaning of
    Mourning, stages of

Miranda, thirteen, and her mother are spending the last few days of summer at their cottage on Long Island when they are summoned home by Father. Grandfather, Mother's father, is dying — in fact is dead by the time they can get back to New York. September is bleak for Miranda. Though she struggles to grow up, her mother seems to have become more strict with her. And though Miranda had looked forward to moving into her sister Sonya's room, Sonya having left for college, now Grandma is staying there and Miranda remains stuck in her old small room. The girl also misses Grandpa and cries easily at remembering him. Grandma is lonely too, but she resists being dependent and, like Miranda, declines to be babied by Miranda's parents. When Grandma, a former librarian, takes a job as ticket seller at a neighborhood theater, Mother is shocked. Grandma explains that she needs to be useful and to have her own life. When Miranda asserts herself and has her

long hair cut short and styled, Mother is downright angry. But one day Miranda finds Mother holding some of Grandpa's clothes she has come across, and very near tears. Miranda reaches to touch her, to comfort her, and in a moment they are both in tears, comforting each other. Suddenly Miranda "could see herself as a woman, a mother, and her own mother as a grandmother. . . . Miranda's mother was Miranda grown-up, and she wasn't always a pillar of strength." Miranda sees, too, that her mother is overly protective of Grandma and herself because she does not want to lose them too. Shortly afterward, Grandma announces she must move back to her own apartment, to her own life, her own memories. Mother, though reluctant, accepts the decision. And Miranda finds a gift from Grandma in her "new room" — a handmade, patchwork quilt for her bed and a note saying, "Thank you for helping me to do what I wanted."

A grandfather dies and the members of his family mourn his death in their different ways. Grandma, though lonely, does not want to grow old feeling useless and sorry for herself. She wants instead to work and be independent. Her daughter, Miranda's mother, unable to express her grief directly, becomes overly solicitous of Grandma and Miranda. Miranda tries to assist Grandma's plans. In time, each one's grief over Grandpa's death is less intense and each can see the others' more truly. This book, without exploring family grief deeply, does show its variousness and the light it casts on generational differences.

Ages 11-13

Also available in:
No other form known

T

636

Taylor, Mildred D.

Roll of Thunder, Hear My Cry

The Dial Press, Inc., 1978.
(276 pages)

AFRO-AMERICAN
PREJUDICE: Ethnic/Racial
  Family: unity
  Justice/Injustice

Like some other black Southern families, eight-year-old Cassie Logan's family raises cotton on a four-hundred-acre farm in Mississippi in 1933. The land, purchased by Cassie's grandfather years before, makes the Logans more secure than the nearby black sharecroppers, but it also arouses the covetousness of Harlan Granger, descendant of the family whose plantation it had been part of before the Civil War. Granger longs to rebuild the original plantation, and would seize any opportunity to force the Logans off. When the Wallaces, owners of the local store, attack and badly burn some sharecroppers, the Logans try to organize a boycott. Able to enlist only a few families, they prove more of an irritation to the Wallaces than a financial threat — but for that, Cassie's father, David, is physically injured by the Wallaces and loses his job with the railroad. It is only with financial aid from his brother up North that David keeps their land out of Granger's clutches. While David is recuperating from his injuries, thirteen-year-old T. J., a friend of Cassie's brother, makes friends with the white, shiftless Simms boys, who are older than he is.

When the Simmses and T. J. rob a store and the Simmses murder the owner, T. J. is recognized while the brothers escape. That night the Wallaces and the Simmses (who have gone undetected) gather a lynching party and storm T. J.'s house. To create a distraction, David sets fire to his own cotton field and the fire threatens the Grangers' adjoining forest. T. J. is saved from the mob and turned over to the sheriff. And as David explains the ways of white justice at that time, the Logan children realize they will never see T. J. again. He and he alone will be convicted, because he is black.

The story Cassie tells shows how her family faces unrelenting humiliation and hardship without compromising their values or losing self-respect. This story, skillfully paced, candid, and rich in characterization, affords discussable lessons in American black history. If persecution of blacks is usually less blatant now, the spirit behind it is by no means dead, and this story will be understood.

Ages 10 and up

Also available in:
Cassette — *Roll of Thunder, Hear My Cry*
Miller-Brody Productions

Cassette for the Blind — *Roll of Thunder, Hear My Cry*
Library of Congress

Film — *Roll of Thunder, Hear My Cry*
Tomorrow Entertainment

Paperbound — *Roll of Thunder, Hear My Cry*
Bantam Books, Inc.

Record — *Roll of Thunder, Hear My Cry*
Miller-Brody Productions

Video Tape — *Roll of Thunder, Hear My Cry*
Tomorrow Entertainment

637

Taylor, Mildred D.

Song of the Trees

Black/white illustrations by Jerry Pinkney.
The Dial Press, Inc., 1975.
(48 pages)

COURAGE, MEANING OF
Afro-American
Nature: appreciation of
Self, attitude toward: respect

Eight-year-old Cassie, who is black, lives in rural Mississippi during the Depression. Her father, David, is working in Louisiana. Her family's home is surrounded by a centuries-old forest her grandmother owns. Cassie loves the trees, and imagines she can hear them singing. One day while playing in the forest, Cassie and her brothers hear some white men saying they are going to cut down all the trees. Upset, the children run home only to find a white man trying to buy the forest from the mother and grandmother for sixty-five dollars. The women are outraged that he would offer such a small sum. But with David away and the white man making threats, they are forced to give in. Cassie's older brother goes to bring her father back from Louisiana. Once home, David sets dynamite charges around the forest, saying he will blow it up if the lumbermen do not leave. The white man tries to frighten him, but David does not back down and the lumbermen depart.

Cassie's family would rather destroy their beloved forest than have it taken from them. David shows his family how to put aside fear of people more powerful than they are. He says that "a black man's gotta be ready to die. And it don't make me any difference if I die today or tomorrow. Just as long as I die right." The book, written in Cassie's first-person, is based on a true story

the author heard as a child. The style is poetic, especially in describing the forest. Although characterization is minimal, the father is portrayed as a strong figure.

Ages 8-11

Also available in:
Film — *Song of the Trees*
Tomorrow Entertainment

Paperbound — *Song of the Trees*
Bantam Books, Inc.

Video Tape — *Song of the Trees*
Tomorrow Entertainment

638

Taylor, Paula

Johnny Cash

Color illustrations by John Keely.
Creative Education, 1975.
(31 pages)

CAREERS: Singer
DRUGS: Dependence on
Giving, meaning of
Self, attitude toward: accepting
Success

Johnny Cash grows up listening to country music on the radio and dreaming of becoming a country singer. He gets his first chance when he and two friends audition for Sun Records and cut a moderately successful first record. Soon "John Cash and the Tennessee Two" are getting bookings on the road with other country performers. After recording "I Walk the Line," they are famous and tour nation-wide. Cash marries, and has four daughters. As the road trips grow longer and recording sessions take more time, Cash begins taking amphetamines to overcome shyness and drowsiness — and then tranquilizers to help him sleep. Soon, little by little, he is taking up to one hundred pills a day. After some seven years of his addiction, a member of the troupe named June Carter tries to help him by destroying his pill supply. Not long after, in 1968, he is given a suspended thirty-day sentence for trying to bring pills across the Mexican border. His wife files for divorce and the Musicians Union threatens to expel him for missing so many shows. Johnny finally admits what has happened, enlists the aid of a psychiatrist, and kicks his drug habit. Since that time, he has stayed away from drugs, married June Carter, and feels he can withstand the pressure of concerts and recording sessions.

This biography of Johnny Cash, the extremely successful country singer, shows him overcoming poverty but succumbing to drugs. His withdrawal from them is not easy. The book is simply written, with a modest vocabulary, and the illustrations are boldly colorful.

Ages 7-10

Also available in:
Cassette — *Johnny Cash*
Creative Education

Paperbound — *Johnny Cash*
Creative Education

639

Terris, Susan Dubinsky

Amanda, the Panda, and the Redhead

Color illustrations by Emily McCully.
Doubleday & Company, Inc., 1975.
(46 pages)

ATTENTION SEEKING
JEALOUSY: Sibling
 Family: relationships

When little Amanda gets up in the morning, she starts chattering to anyone within earshot. This morning her parents are busy with her baby brother and they ignore Amanda. She talks louder; she barrages her parents with questions; she screams. They just go on being busy and ignoring her. Finally Amanda falls silent. She will not talk to her father when he takes her to school, nor to her teacher when she gets there. Her mother cannot make her talk on the way home from school, nor can a woman at the store and a man in the park. At bedtime, Amanda does talk to her Panda Bear. When he does not respond, she beats him up and goes to bed. Later, when her parents walk past her room, she calls out to them in her usual chattering way, firing question after question. They are pleased she is back to normal and give her the attention she wants.

A little girl, annoyed and hurt by her parents' unresponsiveness, gives them and everyone else "the silent treatment" for a day. That night she pummels her teddy bear for not talking to her, and her anger subsides. It is made clear that she is not only angry at not getting attention herself but also at the attention her baby brother does get. An adult may think the parents' lack of response overdone, but small children being read to may well have a lot to say about it.

Ages 5-7

Also available in:
No other form known

Terris, Susan Dubinsky

The Chicken Pox Papers

Black/white illustrations by Gail Rockwell.
Franklin Watts, Inc., 1976.
(124 pages) o.p.

COMMUNICABLE DISEASES: Chicken Pox
  Anger
  Family: extended

Augusta Amy Myers, or Gussie, has been confined to the house with chicken pox on this, her tenth birthday. To make matters worse, she finds she will not be getting the bicycle she wanted, cannot have a party, and cannot return the silver letter-opener she has secretly borrowed from Great-aunt Augusta. Wanting desperately to return the opener, she tries to escape from the house but is caught by her great-aunt and grandmother. To show them how angy she is, she writes letters to both and to her mother as well. She also cuts her long, red hair. When her mother sees her ragged tresses, she accuses Gussie of being like Aunt Augusta, who also cut her own hair when she was ten. This makes Gussie even angrier — she does not want to resemble "that old lady who plays the piano for her ferns." Her mother makes one concession to the girl's seeming restlessness: she allows Gussie to sit on the porch and watch her infant cousin, Baby Natalie. But from there, Gussie makes another ill-fated escape attempt. This so angers her mother that she assigns Gussie the task of amusing Natalie for the rest of the day. And so it is with Natalie in tow that Gussie makes one more dash for Aunt Augusta's house. Just before reaching it, Gussie props Natalie in a curb-side trash basket to keep her out of the way. But Gussie is spotted by Aunt Augusta. Thrusting the letter-opener at the old lady, she runs, realizing halfway home that she has forgotten Natalie, and rushes back to retrieve the screaming baby. Home at last, Gussie endures her mother's scolding for being sneaky, immature, and untrustworthy, agrees roundly, and stomps off to her room with Natalie. When her mother summons them to a family party, Gussie insists on staying put. Soon she discovers in an old desk some childhood keepsakes of Aunt Augusta's and her mother's. Pondering these, she is struck by the thought that her elders too, in their time, must have been angry and misunderstood.

In this funny, first-person narrative, a ten-year-old girl resorts to subterfuge to avoid trouble, but only makes things worse. Fed up and confused, she at last begins to sort out her feelings by realizing that those who disapprove of her must themselves have gotten into scrapes when young. For all its humorous turmoil, this story portrays a warm and loyal family. Since we are left in no doubt of Gussie's itching, scratching misery throughout, this book may console readers confined with chicken pox.

Ages 10-12

Also available in:
Paperbound — The Chicken Pox Papers
Dell Publishing Company, Inc.

641

Terris, Susan Dubinsky

Two P's in a Pod

Greenwillow Books, 1977.
(181 pages)

LEADER/LEADERSHIP
  Communication: rumor
  Friendship: meaning of
  School: classmate relationships

T

One day during school recess, twelve-year-old Pru Phillips encounters Penny Hoffman, a new girl in school. Pru is delighted at Penny's intention that they be good friends. Always together, they look so alike that they are nicknamed "two P's in a pod." Penny proves to be the leader she claims she is, and does the thinking for both of them. She has a "strategy" for everything she does, and does everything with great flair and enthusiasm. But her motives are not always honorable, and she often uses people for her own convenience and pleasure. Pru is a loyal follower and innocently trusts all Penny says and does. When Mr. Harrington, the English teacher, and Mrs. Monzoni, the school principal, chaperone a sixth-grade field trip, Penny starts a rumor that the two are having an affair. Martha, overweight and unpopular, earns money by typing for Mr. Harrington. She is Penny's next victim. One Saturday morning when Martha is to deliver her typing, Penny, accompanied by Pru, goes to Harrington's apartment to spy on him and Martha. Penny peeks in at a window, sees nothing but tells Pru that she saw Harrington seduce Martha. Sickened by Penny's detailed account, Pru runs away. Meanwhile, Penny tells everyone that Pru saw Harrington assault Martha sexually. The following Monday at school, Pru is called into the principal's office and asked to tell what happened. She becomes so upset she vomits and must be sent home. Confused, she reflects on all of Penny's schemes — and realizes what Penny's twisted pranks have done to her and to others. She decides to cut herself off completely from Penny and be her own person again. But a talk with her father reminds her that Penny will still need a friend and perhaps she should resume the relationship using better judgment.

Pru herself tells this shocking story of a girl who uses her imagination in ways that hurt other people. The message that popularity gained at other people's expense is not desirable, is presented without moralizing. The emotions, relationships, and pressures of early adolescence are portrayed realistically.

Ages 9-12

Also available in:
No other form known

642

Tester, Sylvia Root

Billy's Basketball

Color illustrations by Linda Sommers.
The Child's World, Inc., 1976.
(31 pages)

SIBLING: Relationships
  Afro-American
  Perseverance

Young Billy smarts at being ignored by his older brother, Mike, and Mike's friends. One such friend, Jamie, who has no little brother, takes time to play basketball with Billy and coach his shooting. Jamie even gives Billy a birthday present — a basketball of his own. From then on, Billy shoots baskets every day; sometimes with others, but usually alone. In fact, when Billy is practicing alone one day, Mike happens by in time to see him sink a basket. Mike is amazed and asks, "Mind if I join you, Kid?" Billy answers, "You can play if you stop calling me 'Kid,'" and at the end of their session, Mike compliments his brother on his shooting.

A boy is spurned by his older brother, but finds encouragement and companionship with another older boy. Accepting them, his sense of self-worth is bolstered so that, in time, he can accept his older brother on his — not the brother's — terms. The illustrations add expressiveness to Billy's loneliness, joy, determination, and pride, as he finds his way out of a sense of inferiority.

Ages 5-7

Also available in:
Paperbound — *Billy's Basketball*
Child's World, Inc.

643

Tester, Sylvia Root

Feeling Angry

Color illustrations by Peg Roth Haag.
The Child's World, Inc., 1976.
(32 pages counted)

JEALOUSY: Sibling
  Anger
  Sibling: new baby

Young Paula Jean is angry, but is quite certain that her feeling has nothing to do with her new brother, Carl. At the crib, she pats the sleeping Carl on the head and then pinches his tiny fingers — hard. When he cries, Paula Jean becomes so alarmed that she calls her mother and insists that she has been doing nothing — not even pinching — to make him cry. Still, when Momma has calmed Carl, she sits in the rocker with Paula Jean and discusses pinching. Later, when Carl is being fed, Paula Jean asks for and is given a bottle like the baby's, and decides it tastes terrible. Upon this pronouncement, Paula Jean is invited into the rocker with Momma to help feed Carl. There Momma recounts some of the things she did for Baby Paula, and even allows her to hold her brother. Holding him, Paula Jean realizes she is no longer angry.

Young readers will recognize Paula Jean's jealousy at having to compete for her mother's attention, and may also be reassured to see that other children feel so, yet are accepted. What is shown as unacceptable is harming a baby. The foreword to this simple text for very young children, one book in a series on values, suggests ways to explore its subject further.

Ages 3-6

Also available in:
No other form known

644

Tester, Sylvia Root

That Big Bruno

Color illustrations by Helen Endres.
The Child's World, Inc., 1976.
(31 pages counted)

FEAR: of Animals
  Courage, meaning of

When young Jeremy visits Aunt Faye, he ascertains first that her big, frightening dog, Bruno, is locked in the basement. When the dog is inadvertently let out while Jeremy and his younger cousin, Andrea, are playing, Jeremy crouches silently in the middle of a bed until Bruno is back in the basement again. Eventually Aunt Faye insists that Bruno be allowed upstairs — and Jeremy makes for a high kitchen stool. But the excited dog puts his front paws on the stool and licks Jeremy's face. Aunt Faye leads the dog into the living room, but Jeremy is in tears. When Bruno is asleep, Jeremy's mother persuades the boy to stand beside the huge dog, but he will not touch Bruno — not until Andrea calls Jeremy a baby. "That did it! No kid . . . could call Jeremy a baby." He gingerly strokes the sleeping giant and, not wanting to show his fear, allows the now-awakened Bruno to

T

sniff his hand. Suddenly the dog extends his paw, asking for a shake, and Jeremy is so pleased that he laughingly obliges. The next time Jeremy comes to visit, he is not the least bit frightened of Bruno.

This almost pat story stresses the need for courage in overcoming fear. Like the other books in this series on values, this book contains a foreword explaining the series, with suggestions for teachers or parents and questions to use in discussion and in role-playing.

Ages 3-7

Also available in:
No other form known

645

Thiele, Colin Milton

The Hammerhead Light

Harper & Row Publishers, Inc., 1976.
(109 pages)

CHANGE: Accepting
  Age: aging
  Animals: love for
  Loneliness

Axel Jorgenson, an old man living in a hut on the Australian coast, has taught twelve-year-old Tessa Noble about birds and ships and the sea, has been her friend and confidante, and seems to her invincible. When the government announces plans to blow up Hammerhead Light, Axel leads the local protest, claiming that the lighthouse symbolizes enduring strength; it is a sentinel. At first Tessa agrees completely, and when he moves there, she helps him guard the tower. Her mother argues that the tower may as well be destroyed: there is a new automatic beacon in place, and anyway the Light is about ready to crash into the sea. Tessa sees the truth in these arguments but continues to value the Light as a symbol. It survives through that winter and the following summer. But that fall, Tessa recognizes something new: how lonely Axel is. He can scarcely bear to release a bird he has nursed back to health. Winter is coming again, and Tessa feels responsible for the old man. He seems, like the tower, endangered by the winter's storms. Yet both he and the Light work when they are needed. With Tessa's help, the old man operates Hammerhead to guide her family through a storm to the harbor after the new beacon is damaged. But the storm has left the tower ready to crash into the sea. Tessa's father and brother get Axel out in time, but he later takes a bad fall and endures a long convalescence. Unable to live alone, he will be sent to a home for the aged.

This suspenseful story is a working out of symbols. The girl hopes that Axel, like the Hammerhead Light, will endure, for he too is a sentinel. But, like the tower, Axel falls to time's erosion. Only after his injury does Tessa realize the certain loss of things dear to her and "a loneliness that was hers alone." The friendship between Tessa and Axel is touchingly portrayed, and readers should enjoy the Australian setting and the exciting action at the lighthouse.

Ages 10-12

Also available in:
Cassette for the Blind — *The Hammerhead Light*
Library of Congress

646

Thiele, Colin Milton

Storm Boy

Black/white illustrations by John Schoenherr.
Harper & Row Publishers, Inc., 1978.
(63 pages)

NATURE: Respect for
 Death: of pet
 Nature: living in harmony with
 Pets: love for

Since the death of his mother seven years earlier, Storm Boy and his father, Hideaway Tom, have lived in a rough shack near a seaside sanctuary in Australia. Storm Boy's time is spent roaming the dunes and learning nature's ways from an Aborigine friend. Hunters who illegally kill sanctuary birds are the only threat in this otherwise peaceful life. After one such group blunders through the sanctuary, Storm Boy finds three parentless pelican nestlings. Realizing that without care the baby birds will die, he takes them home. He lavishes most of his attention on the weakest baby, grows fond of him, and names him Mr. Percival. When the birds are mature, Storm Boy and his father return them to the sanctuary. Lonely, Storm Boy returns home — and is delighted to find that Mr. Percival has preceded him. With Hideaway's consent, the bird stays, and soon boy and bird are inseparable. Storm Boy even teaches his pet to fetch and carry. This trick becomes lifesaving when a fierce winter storm grounds a tugboat off shore. Fearing that the men on board are doomed, Storm Boy coaxes his bird to carry a lead to the boat. A stout line is attached, drawn to shore, and Tom pulls the crew to safety, one by one. Though the crew offers, as a token of gratitude, to pay Storm Boy's way at boarding school, he refuses to leave his pet. It is only when Mr. Percival is shot dead during hunting season that a grieving Storm Boy informs his father he is ready to attend school. Now, one hundred miles from home, Storm Boy carries the memory of his beloved friend with him, "for birds like Mr. Percival do not really die."

This touching story of a boy and his unusual pet exemplifies man living with nature and respecting it. By contrast, sportsmen are portrayed as sometimes being unable to understand the natural setting they profess to enjoy. The untimely death of Storm Boy's bird is an initiation into loss through death. Though grief pervades the end of this book, it is mitigated by the boy's warm memories of his pet.

Ages 8-11

Also available in:
No other form known

647

Thomas, Ianthe

Eliza's Daddy

Color illustrations by Moneta Barnett.
Harcourt Brace Jovanovich, Inc., 1976.
(61 pages counted)

DIVORCE: of Parents
 Stepbrother/Stepsister

Her parents divorced, young Eliza lives with her mother. Her father, whom she sees on Saturdays, lives across town. Although Eliza knows that his new family includes a daughter and a baby, she has yet to see them. One night, in a dream about her stepsister (for whom she makes up the name Wonderful Angel Daughter), the latter rides up to Eliza on a beautiful black horse and asks if she wants a ride. Eliza, although she cannot ride, answers yes and is given as a mount a "flea-bitten" donkey. Still wanting to meet her stepsister yet fearing to, Eliza finally asks her father to take her to his house. They arrive to find a girl of Eliza's age jumping rope — Mandy, the stepsister. Remembering the dream, Eliza asks her if she knows how to ride horseback. Mandy says no and suggests that they ask their father to take them riding. To their delight, he agrees.

In this simple "Let Me Read Book," a young girl accepts the fact that her parents are divorced but fears losing her father to his new daughter. Eliza resolves her fears after deciding to meet the new daughter. By the end of the story, Eliza seems comfortable with Mandy's calling him "Daddy," too.

Ages 4-7

Also available in:
Paperbound — *Eliza's Daddy*
Harcourt Brace Jovanovich, Inc.

648

Thompson, Jean, pseud.

I'm Going to Run Away!

Color illustrations by Bill Myers.
Abingdon Press, 1975.
(31 pages counted)

RUNNING AWAY

Little Jimmy is having a particularly bad day: his shoe-laces will not tie; his two favorite shirts are dirty; the neighbor's dog has destroyed his sand fort; and his best friend is not at home. Bored, Jimmy asks his mother to take him to Andy's house twenty miles away. When, being in the midst of housecleaning, she refuses, he decides to run away to a place where people are nicer. He packs his things and starts down the block, asking the people in each house if they want a new little boy. By sunset he has asked at every house on the block except one. Summoning up his last bit of courage, he

knocks on the door. He shyly asks the woman who answers — his mother — if he can live there. She says she has always wanted a little boy just like him.

After seeking alternatives, Jimmy sees that his parents are nice after all. And he is glad to find that home is a place you can always go to, even when you have made a mistake.

Ages 4-8

Also available in:
No other form known

649

Tobias, Tobi

Arthur Mitchell

Color illustrations by Carole Byard.
Thomas Y. Crowell Company, 1975.
(33 pages)

AFRO-AMERICAN
CAREERS: Dancer
  Perseverance
  Prejudice: ethnic/racial
  Pride/False pride
  Responsibility: accepting
  Success

Arthur Mitchell is the oldest child in a large, hard-working, poor black family in Harlem in 1934. His father, ashamed of being unable to provide adequately for his family, drinks heavily and eventually deserts them. While still in school, Arthur works part-time and tries to take his father's place with the family. But he thinks of his future too, and, on the advice of one of his teachers, auditions for the High School of Performing Arts. Though he has had no formal dance training, Arthur is accepted and begins to train in modern dance. The hours spent in exercise and rehearsal are torture to his untrained muscles at first, but this only makes him drive himself harder. The results show when eighteen-year-old Arthur accepts a scholarship to train with the New York City Ballet. But he is warned by his sponsor that, because he is black, he will have to try twice as hard as other dancers to succeed. He works diligently, and after only three years of study, he dances a featured role with the company. In the ten years that follow, Arthur dances many featured roles, amazing audiences with his skill and grace. But by 1968, realizing he wants to give more black dancers the opportunity he has had, Arthur founds the Dance Theatre of Harlem. Neighborhood residents become interested in the hard-working group, which trains in an old Harlem garage, and soon they are helping to make costumes and sets. When enrollment grows to 400, the Dance Theatre moves to larger quarters, and Arthur adds other kinds of dance to the curriculum — jazz, native African, modern, and tap. With a Ford Foundation grant, the group converts an old warehouse into a new home for themselves. Even now, though he no longer performs as a dancer, Arthur Mitchell serves the company as a teacher, choreographer, director, and manager.

This biography portrays the determination of the distinguished dancer-director Arthur Mitchell to make a place in an art. The book, written in an easy-to-read style, shows Mitchell overcoming racism by excelling in his work and by giving others the opportunity to do the same. The story might inspire anyone and may especially encourage boys who want to study dance.

Ages 7-10

Also available in:
No other form known

650

Tobias, Tobi

Chasing the Goblins Away

Color illustrations by Victor Ambrus.
Frederick Warne & Company, Inc., 1977.
(32 pages counted)

BEDTIME
FEAR: of Darkness
  Dependence/Independence

T

Regardless of his mother's assurances, young Jimmy knows that goblins invade his room. Sure enough, late that night while his parents sleep, the goblins come. Jimmy yells, and his daddy comes. Jimmy claims there are a hundred — no, a zillion — goblins, but his father sees none. Of course not, Jimmy replies, for goblins can be *thought* easier than seen. The next night the goblins return in force: "Steve. Big Hands. Liar. Swallow. Shock. Filthy. Nail. Mugger. Susan." An appalling lot. Again Jimmy calls out, and this time Mommy comes and sits with him. The next night Daddy answers Jimmy's summons, but only to say that the boy will have to fight the goblins himself. Scarcely is Daddy gone than goblins, heedless of Jimmy's shouts to go away, fill the room. Suddenly angry, the boy throws a pillow at them. Three goblins go down. A quilt follows — a skate, a softball, and comic books. Half the goblins are down, yet one is growing larger and larger. Jimmy orders stuffed Brown Dog to the attack, and the huge goblin breaks up and vanishes. But others without names rise in his stead. Jimmy thinks to yell magic words to ward them off, but knows none. "Jimmy Richard Evan Powell," he yells, for he is real and the goblins are not. When he opens his eyes, the goblins are gone. Dragging

Brown Dog with him, he goes to his parents' room to announce his victory: "If those goblins ever come back, they'll be sorry, because I know just what to do."

Jimmy tells this story. A child who peoples the darkness with fearsome goblins, he takes his father's advice to battle them himself. The goblins, as their names suggest, arise from the boy's experience, and this the parents recognize. The battle with the goblins parodies an epic tale, and the illustrations give the goblins an air of the ridiculous that should prevent young readers from becoming afraid themselves.

Ages 4-7

Also available in:
No other form known

651

Tobias, Tobi

Jane, Wishing

Color illustrations by Trina Schart Hyman.
The Viking Press, Inc., 1977.
(46 pages counted)

FAMILY: Unity
WISHES
Appearance: concern about

For a dreamy, ten-year-old girl, Jane's first wish is modest enough. She wishes for long red hair which Mom would let her wear loose. But Mom says loose hair is for special occasions — otherwise braids. Grandmother remarks that red hair does not run in the family. Margaret, Jane's teenage sister, favors curly blond hair like her own. Daniel, the younger brother, wonders why anybody would care about such a dumb thing as hair. Dad likes Jane's hair as it is. Similarly, Jane's wish to have "sea-green sea-blue" eyes elicits counterarguments, as does her wish for clear, pale skin like a

fairytale princess's; for a mellifluous name like Melissa or Amanda; for a lovely singing voice; and for a silky black kitten she could name Night. Dad says, "Come on, your highness, there's work to be done around here," and she winds up washing their mongrel dog, Sam. Jane continues to wish, and the family continues commenting. She wishes for a room where she could wish on the stars to make all her dreams come true. The bedroom window, Margaret points out, gives a view of McCloskey's yard. Mother tells Jane to stop mooning at the window and do her homework, and Daniel maintains the wish is his since he saw the star first. Jane decides "to be happy anyway."

A little girl's wishes regularly evade the mundane realism of her family's comments upon them. In the illustrations, her wishes are drawn in romantic color, the family responses in flat-footed black and white. Still, the reader is encouraged in the impression that this is a close-knit family. Under the assault of jibes, common sense, and some sympathy, Jane decides to be happy with what she has. Most of this text is dialogue, but the aim of its ironic counterpoint may be lost on some young readers.

Ages 6-9

Also available in:
No other form known

652

Tobias, Tobi

Moving Day

Color illustrations by William Pène du Bois.
Alfred A. Knopf, Inc., 1976.
(28 pages counted)

MOVING
Transitional objects: toys

It is moving day for a little girl and her toy bear. Bear is afraid, she says, but she is not. She tells how she and Bear prepare for their departure. She packs some things and throws some others away — but not Bear, who must always be by her side. She observes how everything in the house is carefully sorted, boxed, and loaded into the moving van. For an unsettling moment, Bear is lost in the shuffle. But he is found, just in time to help his owner say good-bye to the old neighborhood. After a long ride, the little girl and Bear arrive at their new house. It is so big that she worries Bear may get lost in it. She eats her first meal in the new house with Bear beside her. Seeing family objects arranged in the new surroundings, she finds that the big house feels more like home. Next day, the little girl and Bear find a new friend and begin to feel happy in the new neighborhood.

Written in free verse, this book shows a child successfully getting used to a major change in her life by projecting some of her own fears onto her toy, and by holding onto that toy as a friend when other friends must be left behind. The story is told as much in the illustrations as in the simple verse.

Ages 3-6

Also available in:
No other form known

653

Tobias, Tobi

Petey

Color illustrations by Symeon Shimin.
G. P. Putnam's Sons, 1978.
(31 pages)

DEATH: of Pet

Emily takes good care of her pet gerbil, Petey, and plays with him daily. Every day when she comes home from school, he seems to be waiting for her. At night she goes to sleep at the sound of his nocturnal puttering about the cage. One day Emily comes home and Petey does not run across the cage to greet her. Instead he huddles, shivering, in the corner. Emily's father says Petey is sick, and the pet-care books say there is no way to help a sick gerbil. All they can do is wait overnight and see if Petey recovers. Her father tries to prepare her for Petey's death, reminding her that her pet is already five years old, quite old for a gerbil. The next morning Emily finds Petey dead. The whole family is saddened. Tenderly they recollect funny things Petey had done. Then they put his body in a box and bury it in the yard at the spot where the shadow of the swing falls when it swings the highest. Emily feels empty, so much does she miss Petey. When her mother urges her to accept two gerbils offered by a friend, Emily refuses. "It won't be the same," she says. Her mother replies, "It can be different, Em, and still be good." Emily will think it over.

Experiencing the death of a pet helps Emily to see that although things change, life goes on. She tells the story herself, and matter-of-factly. Symeon Shimin's paintings of the family more subtly portray their feelings.

Ages 6-9

Also available in:
No other form known

T

654

Tobias, Tobi

The Quitting Deal

Color illustrations by Trina Schart Hyman.
The Viking Press, Inc., 1975.
(30 pages counted)

HABITS
   Communication: parent-child
   Cooperation
   Helping
   Smoking
   Thumb sucking

Seven-year-old Jenny and her mother both have bad habits they want to break: Jenny sucks her thumb and her mother smokes cigarettes. They decide to help each other quit. First they try the "Holding Hands Cure": when Jenny feels like sucking her thumb, Mommy holds her hands until the feeling passes, and Jenny does the same when Mommy wants a cigarette. This works fine until Jenny needs her hands free to build with her blocks and Mommy needs hers free to fix dinner. Both are so busy they almost forget about thumbs and cigarettes — but alas, not quite. They try other cures — the "Talking Cure," the "Candy Cure," the "Comforting Cure" and the "Nasty Stuff Cure" — with varying degrees of success. Jenny secretly knows her mother keeps cigarettes hidden in a kitchen drawer; she herself sometimes hides in her room and sucks her thumb. When Daddy finds Mommy's hidden supply, Mommy starts to cry, then laughs because he is laughing good-naturedly. She resolves to try again, to really quit — but after a while she finds other hiding places and other "cures." Finally Daddy suggests one more cure: he promises to give each of them something she badly wants if they both quit for good. Jenny wants ballet lessons; her mother wants Sunday breakfast in bed forever. Whenever they feel like cheating, they remind each other of the rewards they are working toward. But sometimes that fails to work. Jenny slips away to her room, and her mother smokes a cigarette in front of Daddy. The prize seems not worth the effort. He is of course disappointed but keeps his promise anyway because he knows they are trying. In the end, Jenny and her mother decide to quit their habits gradually, a little less thumb sucking and a little less smoking each day — until one day they can stop relying on their habits altogether.

There are no recriminations or punishments when either Jenny, who tells this story, or her mother falls back into her old bad habit. Mother and daughter respect each other's right to fail as well as to succeed. Jenny's father, too, treats with compassion and understanding their struggles to reform, praising their achievements and underplaying their failures. The ending may disappoint those who expect will power to triumph, but they will find the ending no less believable. The illustrations are up to date, showing mother and daughter in jeans, a good deal of family clutter, and a scene of the mother smoking while breast-feeding the baby.

Ages 7-9

Also available in:
Paperbound — *The Quitting Deal*
Penguin Books, Inc.

655

Tolan, Stephanie S.

Grandpa — and Me

Charles Scribner's Sons, 1978.
(120 pages)

AGE: Senility
  Empathy
  Grandparent: living in child's home
  Maturation
  Suicide

Eleven-year-old Kerry Warren's grandpa has lived in the Warren home for years, once a good companion to the girl and her brother, Matt, fourteen, but now rather a handful, especially when he goes "crazy." Early one summer morning, Kerry sees him dressed oddly and urinating in the middle of the backyard. Fearing others will see him, she coaxes him inside and does not tell anyone. Kerry begins thinking about how much they have neglected him, and she begins to spend more time with him herself. Two weeks later, Grandpa again acts odd, calling Kerry "Sophie," the name of his long-dead sister, and having her make breakfast for him. A doctor diagnoses his trouble as *senile dementia,* and says that more and more he will imagine himself living in the past. As Grandpa talks more and more about that past, Kerry enlists her intelligent friend, Jeannie, and her own mother in finding out about Grandpa's life. Soon she understands Grandpa in a new light, but she worries that in his old age he has nothing before him but death. Kerry and Matt and their parents sit down to decide what to do with Grandpa, aware that no choice is good but some choice must be made. By himself, they know Grandpa would choose what was best for the family, not for him. But Grandpa has already chosen: he drowns himself in a pool so that he will never lose himself, as Kerry sees. A person must live his own life and make his own decisions. They later find his belongings neatly sorted, packaged, and labeled, with the names of people for whom they are intended, and one box labeled "Discard."

In this first-person narrative, a girl who hasn't done much independent thinking is driven to it by her grandfather's distress. Where previously her love for Grandpa was unquestioning and childlike, her love is now informed by an empathy for his present and for his past, and understanding that extends even to his motive for committing suicide. Written as though spoken into a tape recorder, the book reads easily and well. It seeks to encourage sympathy and fellow-feeling with aged people and with those who live with an aged, senile loved one.

Ages 10-13

Also available in:
No other form known

656

Townsend, John Rowe

Noah's Castle

J. B. Lippincott Co., 1975.
(256 pages)

SHARING/NOT SHARING
VALUES/VALUING: Moral/Ethical
  Communication: lack of
  Communication: parent-child
  Decision making
  Parent/Parents: respect for/lack of respect for
  Secret, keeping

In this novel of some future England, sixteen-year-old Barry Mortimer is puzzled at his father's moving the family into an isolated old mansion across town far larger than the Mortimers' moderate needs require. The mystery deepens: Father takes over the shopping from his wife, spends most of his time locked away in the basement, and discourages all visitors to the house. Barry and his older sister, Nessie, increasingly curious about Father's secret, one day sneak downstairs and discover a room filled with rows and rows of shelves stocked with food. They are shocked and disgusted at this hoarding. When Father catches them, he is not angry but proud to take them into his confidence. He feels the country is headed for thorough economic disaster, and he is preparing to defend his family against starvation. He demands their loyal secrecy, and they grudgingly promise it. Soon Father's prediction seems to be coming true. The newspapers are full of ominous reports of the country's financial crisis. Prices are rising alarmingly — weekly, then daily. As food shortages worsen, money is worthless; there is not enough food at any price. A classmate of Barry's named Wendy spends most of her day standing in food lines to get enough to keep her sickly mother and herself alive. Struggling with his loyalty to his father, Barry steals once for Wendy from his father's supplies and tries also to help the Meals on Wheels program. But these are only temporary solutions to his dilemma. Then it is declared illegal to hoard food, and people are encouraged to report hoarders. Unable to bear the strain of what she knows, Nessie leaves to stay with her boy friend and his mother, and soon Barry's mother and younger sister join Nessie. Things are closing in on Mr. Mortimer, but when Barry and his friends urge him to give the food up, he refuses. Finally, Barry decides to stage a mock food robbery with his friends — but they are intercepted by real looters, who take almost everything. In the end, Mr. Mortimer is reconciled with his family but still cannot understand that they wanted his love more than his food.

This tense first-person narrative takes place in England in some future time, but its themes are appropriate today. Barry's conscience tells him that what his father is doing is wrong, though well meant. There is no clear-cut right and wrong, and it is a more mature Barry who finally realizes that he can only do what feels most right, just as his father had. This is a complex book, thought-provoking in its many sub-themes about parent-child relationships and in its picture of a country whose economy has gone bad.

Ages 11 and up

Also available in:
Paperbound — *Noah's Castle*
Dell Publishing Company, Inc.

657

Uchida, Yoshiko

Journey Home

Black/white illustrations by Charles Robinson.
Atheneum Publishers, 1978.
(131 pages)

CHANGE: Resisting
JAPANESE-AMERICAN
PREJUDICE: Ethnic/Racial
    Family: unity
    Internment
    Security/Insecurity
    War

At the beginning of World War II, the United States government confined Japanese-Americans in internment camps in the West. Yuki Sukane, twelve years old, and her parents have been living in Topaz, a camp in the Utah desert, and when they are released, shortly before the War's end, they take a small apartment in Salt Lake City. Papa, once the manager of a shipping business, finds a job as a shipping clerk in a department store. Yuki's brother, Ken, an enlisted man in the U.S. Army, is stationed in France. One day the Sukanes receive a telegram saying that Ken has been wounded and will be sent to a military hospital in Washington, D.C., for treatment. Next they receive permission to return to their hometown, Berkeley, California. Someone else is living in the house they had lived in, and so they move into a hostel established for returning Japanese. There they meet a reclusive old man, Mr. Oka, and are later joined by Yuki's best friend, Emi, and her grandmother Kurihara. Papa suggests that Mr. Oka and Grandma Kurihara and he pool resources and buy back a small neighborhood grocery store Mr. Oka had earlier sold. The families can live in the apartment above the store. But shortly after they move in, someone sets the building on fire. Firemen quickly extinguish the flames, and a white American neighbor, Mr. Olssen, offers to help repair the damage. Soon the Olssens and the Sukanes are good friends. One day Yuki receives a call from Ken; he is in Berkeley and will be home shortly. She is delighted to see her brother, but cannot understand why he is so sullen and withdrawn, until Mr. Oka talks with him and learns that Ken's best friend had sacrificed himself to save Ken and some other soldiers. Ken is bitter about the War, feeling that too many lives were lost uselessly. The Olssen's invite the families at the grocery store for Thanksgiving dinner, and during it, Mr. and Mrs. Olssen tell the others that their own son was killed at the hands of the Japanese. But they have realized, they say, that they cannot hold hate and bitterness in their hearts. The words work magic upon Ken; even old Mr. Oka is touched. Ken begins to talk of going away to college. But Yuki is bewildered again. Always she sees too much change; always she waits for things to be the same as before the War. Finally, she understands that she must cherish each day for what it is.

A Japanese-American family courageously struggles to overcome the hate and mistrust directed at them during World War II. Their daughter, Yuki, in spite of many disappointments, learns to find joy in the small things of each day. This sequel to *Journey to Topaz* offers a realistic picture of the domestic cruelty governments and people — including the American — have been capable of in wartime. The persecution of the Nesei during the 1940s will open the eyes of many young readers.

Ages 12-14

Also available in:
No other form known

658

Udry, Janice May

How I Faded Away
Color illustrations by Monica De Bruyn.
Albert Whitman & Co., 1976.
(30 pages counted)

INFERIORITY, FEELINGS OF
  Rejection: peer
  Self-esteem

Robbie, a third grader, feels invisible at school. In first grade he had felt all too visible, for everyone criticized him when he made mistakes. In second grade he stopped trying to do things with others, counting the days until summer vacation. This year his teacher has stopped calling on him, and classmates bump him or skip him in line. He decides he does not like feeling invisible. On the day recorders are passed out to the children, and Robbie fails to receive one (the supply has run out), the boy is keenly disappointed: he had been looking forward to playing the recorder. After school he buys one himself with his Christmas money, and begins practicing at home. When he takes the instrument to school and starts playing it, there is no question that he can be seen. His classmates and teacher are amazed at his playing and declare him to be a musician. Robbie is rarely invisible from then on and even when he is, he does not mind.

The young narrator describes his sadness at being ignored at school. Rather than feel further rejection, he has withdrawn into himself. Then, unintentionally, he puts himself in the limelight by excelling on the recorder. Children who have experienced rejection will readily identify with the protagonist. Bold, colorful illustrations help tell this subtle story, showing the boy as a transparent figure with a dotted outline when he feels invisible. But the children pictured appear years older than the primary audience for whom the book was written. Read aloud, the story would be a good lead-in for discussion.

Ages 5-8

Also available in:
Cassette — *How I Faded Away*
Instructional/Communications Technology, Inc.

Filmstrip — *How I Faded Away*
Westport Communications

659

Valencak, Hannelore

A Tangled Web

Translated from the German by Patricia Crampton.
William Morrow & Company, Inc., 1978.
(189 pages)

FANTASY FORMATION
  Anxiety
  Belonging
  Communication: parent-child
  Friendship: lack of
  Guilt, feelings of
  Security/Insecurity

Daydreams come easily to a ten-year-old German girl named Annie. Lonely, teased by her classmates, and criticized by her mother, Annie often seeks comfort in fantasy. One rainy day she becomes engrossed in a legend about an abandoned mill and treasure, and when a classmate, Josepha, helps her during a fight after school, Annie tries to buy the girl's friendship by offering to share the treasure the legend says can be found when the nearby Rannach River runs dry. Annie further says that she knows a spell which will stop the rain, and that her gold ducat necklace — a christening present — is part of the treasure. Lo, the rain stops, and both girls are convinced of Annie's power. Weeks go by, and a dry spell becomes drought; without rain the harvest will fail. Josepha's brother is killed fighting a forest fire abetted by the dry weather. Suddenly Annie's new sense of power is blighted by guilt and fear. When the river does run dry, Annie confesses her fabrications to Josepha, but the latter, angry, threatens her if she does not give up the necklace and obey Josepha's every wish. As Josepha becomes tyrannical, Annie becomes terrified — until one day, she tells all to the village chaplain. Assuring her that rain cannot be regulated by spells, he encourages her to confide in her parents and to get the necklace back from Josepha. Annie summons her courage and demands the necklace back, whereupon she sees Josepha suddenly powerless, but her power had come from Annie herself. And when Annie tells all to her parents, her mother is concerned for her and angry only at Josepha. Outside, a storm has become a gentle rain. Annie goes to bed, convinced that her parents love her, and resting at last in that love.

When, toward the end of this steadily suspenseful story, Annie finds that she can tell shameful secrets to a chaplain and her parents without recrimination, she finds herself free of tormenting conscience and able to look at herself clearly and calmly. In the final pages she reflects on the past months and sorts the fantasy from the facts.

Ages 9-11

Also available in:
No other form known

660

Vestly, Anne-Catharina

Aurora and Socrates

Translated from the Norwegian by Eileen Amos.
Black/white illustrations by Leonard Kessler.
Thomas Y. Crowell Company, Inc., 1977.
(144 pages)

LIFE STYLE: Change in
  Baby-sitter
  Gender role identity: male
  Sibling: relationships

Aurora, a Norwegian girl of about eight, has decided that she and her younger brother, Socrates, are a nuisance to their parents. Their father, who has been studying for his doctorate and caring for the house while their mother works, has been offered a temporary teaching position which he cannot accept unless someone is found to care for Aurora and Socrates. Aurora "solves" everything: she and her brother run away. They get no farther than an elderly neighbor's house before Daddy catches up with them — and assures Aurora that she and Socrates are not a nuisance at all. He then arranges for the neighbor, Gran, and their Uncle Brande to care for the children while he teaches. The children enjoy being with their baby-sitters but find that their favorite time is when Daddy is home during the day. When Daddy goes away for two weeks to study for his final examination, Aurora's own grandmother comes to take care of the children while Mother works. Aurora in turn helps Grandmother care for the house and Socrates. After passing his examination,

Daddy returns and announces that he may not look for a permanent job but stay home, where he can write and do further research.

This genial, contemporary story portrays a family in which the father takes on responsibilities traditionally reserved for a woman and the mother works at a job. When the father takes a job (temporarily), the children feel unwanted, but in time learn to accept the care of outside baby-sitters. Aurora, the older child, finds she can do this more easily than the younger Socrates. The father here is happy to be a "house-husband," and his character could make this sequel to *Hello Aurora* useful in a discussion of the changing roles of men and women. This book is also entertaining when read aloud.

Ages 8-10

Also available in:
No other form known

661

Vigna, Judith

Anyhow, I'm Glad I Tried

Color illustrations by the author.
Albert Whitman & Co., 1978.
(32 pages counted)

REJECTION: Peer
  Ambivalence, feelings of

Irma Jean is the meanest child in her school class and especially mean to the girl, about seven years old, who narrates this story. Irma Jean talks hatefully about her behind her back and is generally such a nuisance that the girl wishes she would get lost. But the narrator's mother advises her to be nice to one so friendless. She tries, is rebuffed, but at the mother's request makes one last try, giving Irma Jean a small cake for her birthday. "I'll bet it's poisoned," Irma Jean says, accepting the cake reluctantly. Yet after the narrator leaves, it is a smiling Irma Jean who skips away singing, "Happy Birthday to me." Fairly sure Irma Jean did not like the cake, the narrator is glad that at least she tried being friends.

The girl telling this story is caught between her mother's advice and her own feelings. She tries to follow the first and takes satisfaction in even a seemingly futile effort. The illustrations and text layout are imaginatively used to show the characters' emotions. Children who have ever encountered an unfriendly, disagreeable child will readily understand the narrator's mixed feelings.

Ages 3-6

Also available in:
No other form known

662

Vigna, Judith

Couldn't We Have a Turtle Instead?

Color illustrations by the author.
Albert Whitman & Co., 1975.
(31 pages counted)

SIBLING: New Baby

Lizzie's mother is going to have a baby. She says Lizzie will have to move her toy box to make room for a crib. Lizzie immediately foresees the baby receiving all available attention. She imagines the door of her room with a very large sign announcing "BABY" and a tiny one reading "Lizzie." She informs her mother firmly that there is no room for a baby. She asks for a turtle, a hamster, or a guppy instead. They, she explains, could sleep under her bed. Lizzie in fact suggests larger animals: a cat, a dog, a donkey, a tiger, a monkey, a bear, a giraffe, even an elephant. She describes just how these

could be made to sleep comfortably in her room, while, on the other hand, baby would not fit. Lizzie's mother points out that feeding and cleaning all those animals would keep them both so busy there would be no time to play. Lizzie abruptly decides she would rather have a baby.

Though broadly oversimplified, this witty book with its rhyming text could promote discussion with children who are apprehensive about a forthcoming sibling. The delightful illustrations show Lizzie's imagined animals disposed casually around the house.

Ages 4-6

Also available in:
Cassette — *Couldn't We Have a Turtle Instead?*
Instructional/Communications Technology, Inc.

663

Vigna, Judith

Everyone Goes as a Pumpkin

Color illustrations by the author.
Albert Whitman & Co., 1977.
(30 pages counted)

SELF, ATTITUDE TOWARD: Accepting

Young Emily looks forward to wearing a very pretty costume at the Halloween party. On the day of the party she takes the costume to show her grandmother and loses it on the bus. Her grandmother suggests that they make another costume, perhaps a pumpkin. Emily objects, "No.... Everyone goes as a pumpkin!" Then her grandmother suggests a skeleton costume, and Emily rejects that because she wants to be beautiful. Finally, the grandmother suggests that the girl go as herself. Emily shakes her head: "No. Everyone has to be someone." Grandmother replies, "You're someone,

Emily. You're *you*." Emily does go as herself and does not miss her costume because she has so much fun just being Emily.

A young girl learns to rely on herself rather than on materials for enjoyment. Children who have feared being different from their peers will readily sympathize with Emily's hesitation at attending the costume party without a costume.

Ages 3-6

Also available in:
No other form known

664

Viorst, Judith

Alexander, Who Used to Be Rich Last Sunday

Black/white illustrations by Ray Cruz.
Atheneum Publishers, 1978.
(32 pages counted)

MONEY: Management
Sibling: relationships

Alexander despairs of ever having money like his older brothers, Anthony and Nicholas. He tries to save, but somehow what little money he gets disappears. Take Sunday — when he receives a dollar from his grandparents. After spending fifteen cents for gum and losing three nickel bets, he decides he will positively save his seventy cents. He does, until he rents a snake for twelve cents, is fined ten cents by his father for saying naughty words, loses three cents in the toilet and five cents between the floorboards, and accidentally eats and must pay for Anthony's eleven-cent candy bar. Again vowing to save what remains, he nevertheless loses some in a magic trick, must pay another parental fine,

and spends the rest buying attractive items at a garage sale. He has no more money to save — only his rummage sale items: a melted candle, an incomplete deck of cards, and a one-eyed bear.

This amusing first-person narrative offers many opportunities to discuss money management and affords a funny look at sibling relationships as well.

Ages 5-9

Also available in:
Paperbound — *Alexander, Who Used to Be Rich Last Sunday*
Atheneum Publishers

Talking Book — *Alexander, Who Used to Be Rich Last Sunday*
Library of Congress

665

Viscardi, Henry

The Phoenix Child: A Story of Love

Paul S. Eriksson, Inc., 1975.
(208 pages)

BIRTH DEFECTS
LOVE, MEANING OF
  Children's home, living in
  Deformities
  Handicaps: multiple
  Surgery

This is the true story of Darren Dilliard, a black boy born with the left side of his head malformed, a hare lip, and a cleft palate. His mother will not keep him. The Human Resources Center, founded by the author, takes four-year-old Darren in when it adds a residence for handicapped children to its day school. There the shy, deprived boy befriends a summer counselor, Stephanie Kaley. Warmed by her love, he shows intelligence and talent. When a fire destroys the residence, the children are sent to temporary homes; Darren goes to the Kaleys.

In time, the Center decides against continuing the residential program, and the child agency handling Darren places him in a permanent home. The Kaleys, having applied, are accepted. Their love and care, along with surgery to correct his deformities, go toward preparing the boy to enter the mainstream of American life.

The author interweaves Darren's story and the Human Resource Center's: an organizational failure and Darren's personal success stemming from this. For his success is not solely thanks to the love and attention shown him; it comes through the opportunity to be in the world and adjust to it, a condition that child-care institutions cannot offer. The case histories of other handicapped children recounted in this book are strong stuff, suitable for mature readers. The whole could prove as inspirational as it is informative.

Ages 13 and up

Also available in:
No other form known

666

Vogel, Ilse-Margret

Dodo Every Day

Black/white illustrations by the author.
Harper & Row Publishers, Inc., 1977.
(42 pages)

GRANDPARENT: Love for
 Emotions: identifying

A little girl cannot explain her sadness to Grandmother Dodo except to repeat, "I am sad." "Be sad for a while," Dodo replies, but gradually cheers her up by singing. Next day, the girl is bored but can describe the sensation only as the absence of feeling: nothing helps. But Dodo gives her a fresh perspective on life by having her imagine herself a ladybug strolling among the familiar objects on a table. Similarly, Dodo resolves the girl's jealousy of Mozart, to the child simply a title on a book absorbing Uncle Karl; Dodo explains who Mozart was and plays one of his minuets on a music box. When the girl throws a stone at the cat, she hides behind a bush out of shame. Dodo coaxes her out and shows her that the cat has forgiven her. "Why can't you forgive yourself?" Dodo asks logically. The usual relationship reverses after the grandmother, frightened by a garter snake, is comforted by the little girl, who is proud of helping Dodo for a change. Although Grandmother's birthday on the final day of the year is a red letter day, the girl knows she does not have to wait for special days to be happy: "I had Dodo. I had Dodo every day."

Six reminiscences tell in the first-person how a girl's grandmother comforts her, explains the world to her, and returns her love. At times the grandmother guides the girl, at times helps the girl understand her emotions, and on occasion lets herself be guided. The setting in an older, slower world justifies the gentle, almost poetic tone of this narrative.

Ages 7-9

Also available in:
No other form known

667

Vogel, Ilse-Margret

My Twin Sister Erika

Black/white illustrations by the author.
Harper & Row Publishers, Inc., 1976.
(54 pages)

SIBLING: Rivalry
TWINS: Identical
 Death: of sibling

Today, seven-year-old Erika tells her twin sister, Inge, I will be you and you me. Wanting to be herself, Inge protests, but gives in as usual. They trick their uncle by exchanging identifying hair ribbons. So successful are the deceptions that occasionally Inge herself wonders: am I me or am I Erika? On another day, jealous that Erika is their neighbor Magda's best friend, Inge outbids her sister for Magda's favor by lending the neighbor a favorite doll for a week. Reclaiming the doll, she eagerly asks if she is not Magda's best friend. "Sometimes," says Magda. Still another day, Erika supervises the building of a house in the woods, and Inge is glad to help. But she leaves in disgust when Erika posts a sign, "Erika's Secret House." The girls are reconciled when Erika changes the sign to "Inge's Secret House," as her birthday gift to Inge. When they welcome Magda to the house, she scorns it and leaves. The twins remain, enjoying it thoroughly, and Inge thinks how good it feels "to feel as one." But Erika suddenly dies after a short illness. Inge feels unusual now; she knows she is Inge, and she is alive, but she also weeps and wonders whether she might not be her sister. In the end she determines to help her parents by being twice as good as she used to be, to make up for the loss of Erika.

The author, an identical twin herself, uses Inge as a first-person narrator to tell five short stories about a younger (by a half-hour) and less aggressive twin's life with and without her "identical" sister. Each story sensitively captures Inge's mixed feelings for Erika — jealousy, rivalry, love, even hatred. At the end, Inge realizes that love was dominant. But her decision to be ideally good to compensate for the loss of her twin could confuse and distress children who have lived through the death of siblings.

Ages 6-10

Also available in:
No other form known

668

Waber, Bernard

But Names Will Never Hurt Me

Color illustrations by the author.
Houghton Mifflin Co., 1976.
(32 pages)

NAME, DISSATISFACTION WITH

Alison Wonderland does not like her name — but it has an interesting history. Her grandparents, the Vonterlants, had come from Europe. When they reached the United States, the man who checked their papers could not pronounce or spell their name, and so he had written "Wonderland" instead. Alison's grandparents had liked the new name and kept it. It is when their daughter-in-law, whose favorite name is "Alison" gives the name to her own daughter that troubles begin. Everyone at school laughs at Alison's name. They warn her to watch out for rabbit holes, and send notes signed by the Mad Hatter inviting her to tea parties. In spite of everything, Alison learns to live with her name, and in the end grows up to be a veterinarian. When a little girl brings her a sick rabbit, Alison tells her not to worry: "I know all about rabbits."

Alison's dissatisfaction with her name is handled humorously, and the illustrations add to the fun. But Alison's trials may be too easily resolved to be of great comfort to a child who is suffering similar teasing because of an unusual name. This book could, however, provide an opening for group discussion to help children understand how hurtful such teasing can be.

Ages 4-8

Also available in:
Braille — *But Names Will Never Hurt Me*
Library of Congress

669

Wahl, Jan

Doctor Rabbit's Foundling

Color illustrations by Cyndy Szekeres.
Pantheon Books, 1977.
(28 pages counted)

LOVE, MEANING OF
  Foster home

Returning from a house call, Doctor Rabbit nearly stumbles over a small bamboo bucket with a tiny tadpole inside. Attached to the bucket is a note saying, "Take care of my child." This the doctor does, with the help of Mother Rabbit and many woodland friends. As the foundling grows into a toad, Doctor Rabbit notices that, though she is happy where she is, Tiny Toad spends much time listening to night sounds, her two eyes wide, rolling moons. This saddens Doctor Rabbit, for he knows that soon she will strike out on her own. When Tiny hops out of sight one evening, the good doctor's mother reminds him that, though it is sad, every child must leave home sometime — even as Doctor Rabbit himself once did.

This beautifully illustrated fanciful story dramatizes two themes: the first, that a foster child can be dearly loved and cared for, and the second, that every creature grows up and seeks his or her individuality and independence.

Ages 4-7

Also available in:
No other form known

670

Wahl, Jan

Jamie's Tiger

Color illustrations by Tomie De Paola.
Harcourt Brace Jovanovich, Inc., 1978.
(45 pages counted)

DEAFNESS

Just recovered from German measles and enjoying his birthday party, Jamie notices his ears feeling "strange," and he can hear nothing but the "growling of the tiger," a stuffed tiger given him, as a present. When he tells his parents he cannot hear them for the tiger's growling, they chide him for acting babyish. The next day, Jamie is sent home from school with a note from his teacher saying he cannot hear her on account of the growling. Jamie's grandmother notices his inattentiveness and suggests that he may have a hearing loss. The doctor diagnoses nerve damage brought on by the German measles. When Jamie's parents explain to him what has happened and assure him that they love him, the tiger stops growling at them. A tutor instructs Jamie in lip reading and finger spelling, but the boy is often lonely for the old friends who no longer play with him. Finally, after receiving a hearing aid and attending special classes, Jamie returns to his old school. His friends accept him and, in so doing, learn of the special talents he has developed since the loss of his hearing. Now the tiger stops growling altogether.

A young grade-school boy is angry and bewildered learning to cope with a hearing loss. The illustrations no less than the text convey these feelings, and the hesitancy, too, of the boy's friends to associate with him. The tiger's "growling" could confuse a reader unaware that it represents Jamie's own anger. When the anger abates, the tiger no longer growls. The brief text, written for the "hearing child as well as the hearing-impaired child," contains a chart of finger spelling, but is "in no way designed to teach lip reading, hand talking, or finger spelling."

Ages 4-8

Also available in:
No other form known

671

Wahl, Jan

Who Will Believe Tim Kitten?

Black/white illustrations by Cyndy Szekeres.
Pantheon Books, 1978.
(55 pages)

ATTENTION SEEKING
HONESTY/DISHONESTY

Tim Kitten would rather help his mother or make up tall tales about himself than have mud fights and play baseball with his sisters. But his tall tales make him unpopular with the other kittens in the neighborhood. When he tells Harold about the time he drove his racecar in a famous race and won, Harold calls him a liar and leaves. When he tells the ball team about a race he won at the North Pole with Santa Claus in attendance, the players laugh at him. Finally his sisters decide to help Tim win some respect. They build a soap-box racer for him. Humiliated because the racer was built by girls, Tim refuses to drive it. But on the morning of the race, Tim's family pulls him out of bed, stuffs him in the racer, and pushes him to the top of Cherry Hill. He wins the race — but for once he tells the truth; he declines the trophy and says his sisters built the car. Everyone is so awed by his honesty that when he starts spinning his next tall tale, they listen eagerly.

A little male kitten seeks attention through exaggeration and boasting, but his reputation with his fellows is saved by one self-sacrificing piece of truth-telling. This Read Aloud/Read Alone book is a sequel to *Great-Grandmother Cat Tales*. It is not especially lively and uses words beyond the vocabulary of the intended reader, but it could invite discussion when read aloud to a group.

Ages 5-8

Also available in:
No other form known

672

Waldron, Ann Wood

The Integration of Mary-Larkin Thornhill

E. P. Dutton & Company, Inc., 1975.
(137 pages)

INTEGRATION
PREJUDICE: Ethnic/Racial
*   School: classmate relationships*

Under an integration ruling, Mary-Larkin Thornhill, a seventh grader in the South, must leave all her school friends and enroll in a largely black school. Unlike her mother and minister father, who strongly favor school integration, Mary-Larkin has misgivings. Sure enough, in the new school she finds her only white contemporary is Critter Kingsley, an unkempt boy with a reputation for trouble, and her classmates speak and dress in ways she is not used to. Several of the boys make off with her lunch money until Vanella, a popular black girl, tells her how to handle them. Back with her old girl friends, she finds the talk is all about cheerleading, and Mary-Larkin decides to try out as a cheerleader at her new school. In the finals, which are to be judged by the applause of the student body, she is greeted by only

W

scattered clapping and some hisses, and runs off in fear and dismay. Her parents sympathize, but insist that she return. In time she makes friends, learns to write poetry in her English class, and makes up for slow periods by reading library books. One day Mary-Larkin invites a new friend, Jimmie-Jo, to sing in her church choir. The rudeness with which many of the choir and congregation treat her friend turns out to be only one of the new differences she sees between herself and her old friends. When more of her black classmates express interest in joining the choir, it is learned that some of the church members, already uncomfortable with Jimmie-Jo's presence, have drafted a new rule that only church members can be choir members. Mr. Thornhill threatens to resign and the new rule is voted down. Mary-Larkin by now understands and shares her parents' belief in racial integration. During Christmas vacation she sees few of her old friends, spending her time instead with Critter, whom she has come to like. Returning to school, she is surprised to win an award at an assembly for one of her poems. Remembering her past failure on that same stage, she hesitates to step forward. But by this time the applause is friendly and unanimous.

This young adolescent's struggle to accept and be accepted by a hitherto black student body is both believable and timely. New friends, new interests, common sense, and some imagination of others, black and white, set her squarely on the side of integration. Her parents' preachments on the subject, however, while staunchly idealistic, prove repetitious.

Ages 10-13

Also available in:
Cassette for the Blind — *The Integration of Mary-Larkin Thornhill*
Library of Congress

673

Wallace, Barbara Brooks

Julia and the Third Bad Thing

Black/white illustrations by Mike Eagle.
Follett Publishing Company, 1975.
(54 pages)

FAMILY: Unity
  Fear: of the unknown
  Russia
  Sibling: relationships
  Superstition

Eight-year-old Julia lives in Russia at the turn of the twentieth century, and since her family is poor, she and her eleven-year-old sister, Katya, attend the charity school. One day when Katya and five-year-old Anicia are visiting Grandmama, their happy day is ruined when Anicia burns her hand on Grandmama's iron. The doctor tells them the burn will heal, but Grandmama warns them that bad things always happen in threes. They must expect two more bad things. Julia waits fearfully. Some days later, in school, she begins to giggle helplessly. Her teacher makes her sit in the corner in shame and embarrassment, but afterwards Julia is relieved too. This punishment is obviously the second bad thing, and now only one more remains. Meanwhile Katya has been chosen from her class to take free piano lessons from a wealthy woman, Madame Demidova. Julia will be permitted to walk the long way to Madame's house with Katya to keep her company. On a cold, windy afternoon a maid greets the girls at Madame's door but refuses to admit them. Have the lessons been cancelled? This, the third bad thing, is surely the worst of all. Sadly the girls walk home. But at home they find that Mama is in the bedroom; the doctor is with her, and they are not permitted to see her. Is this another bad thing? The girls spend the night at Grandmama's, and in the morning go home to be greeted with happy news: baby brother has been born during the night. When Julia can at last talk with her mother, she asks about Grandmama's prediction. Mama tells her that not all sayings are wise. True, many bad things do happen, but many good things happen too. Father believes there will be an explanation about the piano lessons. Shortly afterward, it comes. Madame Demidova herself appears at the door to apologize for her maid's misunderstanding. Piano lessons will begin the following week, and perhaps Julia, too, may have lessons in the future. The girls are overjoyed. Julia thinks more good things happen than bad. Possibly this is the first of a hundred good things.

A little girl believes everything her loving family tells her, until she learns she must separate superstition from wisdom. This story is based on events in the author's mother's childhood in Russia but is no less universally appealing for that (although a present-day child may wonder how an eight-year-old would not be aware of her mother's pregnancy). This is a good book to read aloud.

Ages 8-10

Also available in:
No other form known

674

Wasson, Valentina Pavlovna

The Chosen Baby, 3d ed. rev.

Color illustrations by Glo Coalson.
J. B. Lippincott Co., 1977.
(44 pages counted)

ADOPTION: Explaining
  Sharing/Not sharing

Since Mr. and Mrs. Brown want a baby but are unable to conceive, they decide to adopt one. Mrs. Brown calls an adoption agency, and a caseworker, Mrs. White, after an investigation, approves their request. The Browns are warned, however, that they may have a long wait. Time passes. At last, Mrs. White calls and asks them to come and see a baby boy: if the Browns like him, they can take him home. They like him a lot, adopt him, and name him Peter. When Peter is about four years old, all three Browns decide to call Mrs. White and ask for a sister for Peter. After another long wait, they are given a baby girl, whom they name Mary. Peter is so pleased that he calls the newcomer "Peter's baby" and gladly lets her use his outgrown crib and stroller. When Mary becomes old enough to understand, both children enjoy hearing the story of how they were adopted.

This edition of a 1939 classic is revised in both text and illustrations to appeal to today's children and reflect today's practices. The text is smoother, the dialogue more natural than in its first edition. The soft, warm colored illustrations complement a story whose clarity should reassure adopted children and impart understanding to those who are not.

Ages 3-9

Also available in:
No other form known

675

Watson, Pauline

Curley Cat Baby-Sits

Color illustrations by Lorinda Bryan Cauley.
Harcourt Brace Jovanovich, Inc., 1977.
(27 pages counted)

BABY-SITTING: Involuntary
PROBLEM SOLVING

While his parents go shopping, Curley Cat looks after his younger brother, Baby Cat. Curley Cat takes Baby out walking to divert him from mischief but finds this only gives his mischief greater scope. Scrambling up a tree, Baby Cat refuses to come down. Finally his older brother lures him down by offering him a stone, but before he can stop him, Baby Cat pops the stone into his mouth. Afraid he will swallow it, Curley Cat again resorts to a trick, urging his brother to throw the stone at a tin can. He throws it at a goat instead. And so it goes. Finally, Curley Cat gets his brother home by playing tag. After lunch Baby disappears. Curley Cat retraces their wanderings, looking for his brother, but returns home without him. His parents come home and ask if Baby has taken his nap. Of course! Curley Cat finds Baby sleeping and remarks how good Baby has been. Praising Curley's baby-sitting, his mother rewards him with catnip.

An experienced baby-sitter must concoct various ruses to make his mischievous brother do what he should. This Let-Me-Read book, is designed especially for young readers. Children with younger siblings will find it appealing.

Ages 5-8

Also available in:
Paperbound — *Curley Cat Baby-Sits*
Harcourt Brace Jovanovich, Inc.

676

Watson, Pauline

Days with Daddy

Color illustrations by Joanne Scribner.
Prentice-Hall, Inc., 1977.
(30 pages counted)

COMMUNICATION: Parent-Child
PARENT/PARENTS: Mother Working Outside Home
  Change: accepting

In a house somewhat topsy-turvy — Mother has taken a job while Dad returns to school — Mark, about eight, and his younger sister, Vickie, wonder who will care for them. Dad says he will and that things will be just about as always, except that Mark and Vickie will have a few extra chores to do. Mark finds out what this means the next morning when Dad makes him clear the table after a burnt-pancake breakfast. In school Mark tells the class how Mother and Dad have switched work, and afterwards he chases Vickie home. He thinks it great to have Dad there after school, sitting down with them for a snack and telling stories — great, that is, until Dad gives each child a long list of chores. Mark, told to sweep the kitchen, sneaks outside to play, but Dad brings him back. Mark must help prepare dinner too. Although Mother is surprised how well things have gone, Mark feels they went better when she was in charge.

A young boy tells about a day with a "house-husband" in this humorous first-person narrative. His dad's businesslike scheduling and strict expectations differ considerably from the way his mother used to run the house. The clever illustrations depict an earlier era (say, the 1930s), while the text seems thoroughly up to date.

629

Strete, Craig Kee

Paint Your Face on a Drowning in the River

Greenwillow Books, 1978.
(149 pages)

NATIVE AMERICAN
  Change: accepting
  Change: resisting
  Hostility
  Identity, search for
  Pride/False pride

Tall Horse, a nineteen-year-old Native American orphan, lives on a reservation with his drunken grandfather and his sharp-tongued, quarrelsome grandmother. Tall Horse, embittered, tired of his bleak existence, thinks he can make a better life for himself in the white man's world. When he announces his decision to leave the reservation, his grandfather, though grieved, accepts the boy's need to seek a better life. Grandmother begs him to stay, not to leave them heartbroken; he is their hope, their reason for being alive. Nila, his girl friend, can scarcely believe that his love for her would allow him to go. Will he not stay where he has a place and a people? Tall Horse persists, "If we stay here we're dead! Dead and we don't know it!" Leon Brokeshoulder, Tall Horse's best friend, back from Vietnam having lost an arm, also loves Nila, and Tall Horse is content that his own departure will allow their love to grow. Tall Horse cannot be persuaded to stay. His grandparents will wait for death, resigned.

It seems possible that neither reservation life nor life in the white's world will satisfy a young Indian man whose life has become meaningless to him. But in this story of his last few hours on the reservation, he withstands every warning offered against his leaving. Beneath all the insults and arguments lies a deep bitterness toward white people. The story's simple, tense plot is filled out by recollections of other young people's attempts to combine tradition and modern life, an attempt Tall Horse refuses to make. The prose style, terse and brisk, heightens emotion.

Ages 12 and up

Also available in:
No other form known

630

Sunderlin, Sylvia

Antrim's Orange

Color illustrations by Diane de Groat.
Charles Scribner's Sons, 1976.
(57 pages)

SHARING/NOT SHARING

In wartime England, the only abundance is of shortages. So when Granny, visiting eight-year-old Antrim and his mother, gives the boy an orange, he treasures it like a rare gem. He proudly shows the large orange to friends, saying he will keep it a long, long time. Mr. Grove, an aged gardener, advises against this, lest it rot. But Antrim wants to show it at school before eating it, does so the next day, and loses the orange when the teacher misunderstands and accepts it as a gift. The boy's sense of courtesy will not let him correct her. Later she sees her error and returns the orange. Joyously, Antrim dashes home, tossing the orange high in the air, only to see it crash to the earth as it slips from his grasp. Mother, joking that there is no use crying over split orange, peels it, and Antrim gives a section to Mr. Grove and each of his other friends. While doing this, he drops and steps on the section saved for himself.

Mother suggests he take the piece saved for his teacher, but Antrim staunchly refuses. Remembering the small navel in the orange, Mother gives it to him: "It was a little orange, but every drop was delicious."

The accurate description of wartime shortages here, and the to-do made over Antrim's orange builds a convincing case for the value of the orange at any time and thus for this boy's generosity in sharing it. The illustrations, whose only color is that of the orange, also convey the importance of this once scarce, though now common, fruit and of the exhilaration of sharing when times are hard.

Ages 7-9

Also available in:
No other form known

631

Supraner, Robyn

It's Not Fair!

Color illustrations by Randall Enos.
Frederick Warne & Company, Inc., 1976.
(31 pages counted)

SIBLING: Older

A little girl has a troublesome baby brother named Andrew. Mother explains that he acts as he does because he does not know any better. The difference is that the girl does know better. When Andrew makes a mess eating spinach, Mother calls him a "wonderful little spinach eater"; when the girl accidentally spills cereal, Mother delivers a "two-hour lecture" on not making messes. And so it goes. If Andrew bites the little girl and she hits him, Mother tells her not to hit someone smaller; yet when Mother spanks her, surely that is hitting. Sometimes the girl goes on special outings with

Mother and Father — and Andrew, not understanding "that things aren't always *that* fair," screams his head off at having to stay home with a baby-sitter.

Here is a humorous look at fairness in the family and at how fairness to one member can appear unfairness to another. This little girl, though struck by inconsistencies, sometimes recognizes differing ages and abilities as part of the equation. This book should help both children troubled by seeming unfairness and adults trying to explain the conventions of family life.

Ages 3-7

Also available in:
No other form known

632

Swarthout, Glendon Fred and Kathryn Swarthout

Whales to See The

Black/white drawings by Paul Bacon.
Doubleday & Company, Inc., 1975.
(121 pages)

LEARNING DISABILITIES
Differences, human
Education: special

DeeDee, John, and eight other children are members of Miss Fish's sixth-grade class in San Diego, California. In two days Miss Fish will take them on a boat ride to see whales. This is no ordinary field trip; each child has a disabling neurological impairment. Miss Fish almost cancels the trip the day before because of a classroom fight. Then bad weather threatens to prevent the boat's departure. But at last the children — together with a regular sixth-grade class — are off to sea. The second group, with their teacher, Miss Bellows, is curious about this "special" class, which needs tranquilizers and who will not socialize. They begin calling the others "retards," and a fight breaks out. Soon the boat reaches the open sea, and the children all become seasick. It is when someone throws the lunches belonging to the special class overboard that the teachers decisively intervene. They gather together Miss Bellows's class, explain why the other children act as they do, and urge the children to make the rest of the trip as pleasant as possible. They do. John and DeeDee feel they have made new friends when Todd and Gloria, students from Miss Bellows's class, share their lunches with them. The seas grow quiet, and sure enough, some whales surface and perform. Back home, Todd and Gloria, at Miss Bellows's request, call DeeDee and John respectively and tell them they will be their friends when they enter junior high school the following school year. John and DeeDee are pleased, though Todd and Gloria later confess to one another that they only made the phone calls to please their teacher.

This story provides insight into specific difficulties "retarded" children face, chief among them confusion under stress. A child's difficulties may be further complicated at home: DeeDee is apraxic and hyperkinetic, and from a wealthy family, and John, partially deaf, dyslexic, comes from a poor family.

Ages 10-12

Also available in:
No other form known

Swetnam, Evelyn

Yes, My Darling Daughter

Black/white illustrations by Laurie Harden.
Harvey House, Inc., 1978.
(167 pages)

FOSTER HOME
TRUST/DISTRUST
  Adoption: feelings about
  Inferiority, feelings of
  Love, meaning of
  Orphan
  Security/Insecurity

S

Josephine, an eleven-year-old orphan, has lived in four foster homes before coming to live with the Jensens — Mina, Joe, and son Timmie — in their oceanside home. From the start, Josephine vows that *this* time she will not allow herself to become fond of or dependent on her foster family. But when she meets her foster mother's father, she takes an instant liking to him, calls him Grandpa, and visits him often. She also finds, much to her dismay, that she is growing fond of Mina, Joe, and young Timmie. When she falls off a pier and almost drowns, she takes the remedy into her own hands and starts taking swimming lessons — secretly. Passing from beginning to intermediate swimming, she has the rare feeling of being proud of herself. She has that feeling again and again after she starts preparing dinner successfully once a week. But school begins, and all this is forgotten; a classmate takes pains to point out that Josephine is only a foster child and that, unknown to Josephine, her foster mother is pregnant. Sure that the Jensens will soon have neither time nor space for her, sure they will send her back to the group home she came from, she runs away down the beach, forgets the incoming tide, and, again, almost drowns. Although

Mina and Joe are angry, they vow to her that they love her and want to adopt her. But a skeptical Josephine, who has been promised adoption before, only agrees to stay until the baby is born. It is only after baby Heidi is part of the family that Josephine accepts the offer of adoption — happily, without reservation.

An emotionally bruised girl has built defenses to keep from becoming fond of her foster family. Because she has been let down by so many foster parents before, Josephine is distrustful of other people and thinks little of herself. But her uncertain sense of her own worth is buoyed by a loving, patient foster family. Setting, plot, and characters are convincingly contemporary but, especially by the end, seem needlessly idealized.

Ages 9-12

Also available in:
No other form known

634

Talbot, Charlene Joy

The Great Rat Island Adventure

Black/white illustrations by Ruth Sanderson.
Atheneum Publishers, 1977.
(164 pages)

COMMUNICATION: Parent-Child
  Friendship: making friends
  Running away
  Weight control: overweight

Eleven-year-old Joel Curtis, whose parents are divorced, lives not awfully happily with his mother in New York City. He is overweight from gorging on junk food. Because she must spend the summer in Paris, on business, Mrs. Curtis persuades Joel's father to take him for a couple months. An aloof, hard-working ornithologist, Mr. Curtis has little time for people, Joel included.

Spending the summer on Great Rat Island studying terns, Mr. Curtis puts Joel to work at once. Eggs are disappearing from several terns' nests, and Joel, among other duties, becomes a lookout near the birds' nesting ground. He catches the egg thief — Vicky, a girl about his age who has run away from summer camp and is hiding out alone on a small island nearby. Glad to have a friend his own age, Joel does not betray Vicky, who comes over to see him a number of times during the next days. One day, with a huge storm threatening, Joel boats over to Vicky's island to get her dog and take it to safety, thinking she has gone somewhere else. But he finds her wedged in some rocks on shore. The storm worsens, and the two seek shelter in an abandoned building, but Vicky after hours of buffeting by water and wind, becomes ill. All night the storm rages, while Joel does his best to care for his friend. In the morning, he builds a signal fire on the beach, and the two are rescued by the Coast Guard. Vicky is taken to a hospital; her parents are notified; and Joel is delivered back to Great Rat Island — a hero. His father, thinking Joel drowned in the storm, joyfully welcomes him back. After weeks away from junk food, Joel has even lost weight.

The overweight hero of this exciting story expects to be bored and lonely during his summer stay on an island, but finds friendship and adventure instead. Best of all he gains recognition — even some love and respect — from his father when he heroically saves a friend's life. So absorbing is his life on the island that Joel himself fails to notice his loss of weight. As a bonus, this book offers a good deal of ornithology within an altogether believable narrative.

Ages 10-13

Also available in:
No other form known

the only day Ludell enjoys at all is Friday, when one can buy hot dogs for lunch. Other days, school bores her, and she does not like her teacher. Not at all boring is the day when she learns that her mother, living in New York since Ludell was a baby, is sending a television set. Her grandmother warns the girl not to talk about it to anyone because the set may be a long time coming, but very soon Ludell has told the whole Johnson family next door. The set finally does arrive in time for Christmas, but it has been broken. Once her grandmother settles the claim with the shippers, she and Ludell go shopping for a new set, which the girl likewise expects for Christmas. It does not appear, but some other good presents do, including the blue jeans she has wanted so badly. She surmises that her grandmother needed the money to straighten out some tax problems. A chance to earn money herself arrives that summer, when Ludell joins Ruthie Mae, her older brother Willie, and the two younger Johnson boys on a cotton-picking crew. But during her first week out, as has happened before, she has an asthma attack, and that is the end of her cotton-picking. Instead, she helps with the laundry her grandmother takes in. That fall Ludell and Willie, the latter held back unfairly, are in the sixth grade together, and Ruthie Mae, no luckier than her brother, is in fifth grade again. Soon Ludell is baby-sitting and doing light cleaning for several white women. In seventh grade she has the school principal for her teacher and, finding her less frightening than other teachers, begins to enjoy school. In fact, Ludell finds herself chosen for many favored tasks and becomes known as the teacher's pet. That year, too, she starts going with Willie and experiences the excitement of a boy friend, a first kiss. And her grandmother buys the long-awaited television set. At school Ludell develops skill in writing and finds she wants to become a writer. By the end of seventh grade, she is filled with the twin joys of discovery and promise.

This warm, candid story, based on the author's girlhood in a small Southern town, unfolds the fears, interests, frustrations, and dreams of a young black girl approaching adolescence. While racial prejudice is not a central theme, the author shows how Ludell's experiences differ from other children's because she is black. A skillful use of black dialect adds interest and authenticity to the book, but may also be hard for some readers to follow. Reading the dialogue aloud may both vivify and clarify the more confusing words. Ludell's story is continued in the sequel, *Ludell and Willie*.

Ages 10-14

Also available in:
Cassette for the Blind — *Ludell*
Library of Congress

Paperbound — *Ludell*
Bantam Books, Inc.

681

Wilkinson, Brenda Scott

Ludell and Willie

Harper & Row Publishers, Inc., 1977.
(181 pages)

BOY-GIRL RELATIONSHIPS: Dating
  Afro-American
  Age: senility
  Death: of grandparent
  Grandparent: living in home of
  Parent/Parents: substitute
  Poverty
  Responsibility: accepting

Ludell, a high school senior in the early 1960s, in Waycross, Georgia, plans to marry her boy friend, Willie, after their graduation. Both are from poor, fatherless families, and both realize the importance of finishing high school. Ludell's grandmother, who has cared for her since Dessa, her mother, went to New York to find work, keeps a tight rein on the girl; Ludell has therefore never been to a football game or a dance. She resents such restrictions, but tolerates them because Willie, a thoughtful and patient young man, does not wish to anger his future in-law. On top of all this, Ludell must spend her Saturdays cleaning house for a white woman, a job she finds demeaning. Only the thought of her upcoming marriage and her secret desire to become a writer keep her going. Suddenly, to her surprise and delight, her grandmother begins to ease up and allow her a dance and an evening out now and then. Just as unexpectedly, however, Grandma's health begins to fail and soon Ludell is spending most of her time caring for an old woman both bedridden and incontinent. Burdened by the extra work, Ludell is nevertheless relieved that her now childlike grandmother can no longer boss her around. But she is shocked and grieved when Grandma dies. Helpful neighbors make the sad time bearable — but when Dessa arrives for the funeral and announces she plans to take Ludell back to New York City with her, the girl is plunged into despair. She and Willie try their best to dissuade Dessa, and a kind neighbor offers to house Ludell for the six weeks left before she finishes school; but Dessa stubbornly insists, and Ludell, broken-hearted, goes off to finish school in a strange city. Ludell and Willie write to each other, vowing to be reunited and to marry after graduation.

Two adolescents, forced by the harsh circumstances of their lives to grow up quickly, cling to a love that appears strong enough to survive their separation. Ludell and Willie talk not only about love and marriage but about their families and missing fathers as well. The lively dialogue is written in Southern black dialect, whose phonetic spelling may prove difficult for some readers. This is a sequel to *Ludell,* and, like it, is a sensitively written story based on the author's girlhood, telling of adolescent fears, disappointments, joys, and expectations.

Ages 12 and up

Also available in:
Cassette for the Blind — *Ludell and Willie*
Library of Congress

Paperbound — *Ludell and Willie*
Bantam Books, Inc.

682

Willard, Nancy

Strangers' Bread

Black/white illustrations by David McPhail.
Harcourt Brace Jovanovich, Inc., 1977.
(28 pages counted)

HELPING
SHARING/NOT SHARING
  Honesty/Dishonesty

Young Anatole, about five, likes to watch trucks unload at Roscoe's corner store, and now and then to deliver groceries. Asked to take a loaf of bread to Mrs. Chiba, he weighs the long trip there against treats she has given him, and agrees, putting the bread in his wagon. Hardly started, he meets a fox, "a starving poet," who asks for a slice of bread. The bread, Anatole explains, is for Mrs. Chiba's grandchildren. "Grandchildren cannot live by bread alone," the fox answers. Anatole thinks this a fine sentiment, and one slice will not be missed, so he gives the fox the bread and lets him ride. Next a rabbit, claiming to be a Reverend, begs similar treatment. Anatole agrees; the rabbit rides. Then an enormous Barberry sheep comes, asks for one slice, and takes two. She then hops aboard, and Anatole, wondering what he can possibly say to Mrs. Chiba, struggles to pull the wagon onward. Next a bear, claiming to be a wandering soldier, dances toward them and, without asking, takes the rest of the bread. He too hops in the wagon, but now Anatole cannot budge it. The four animals then pull the boy to the top of the hill, where they depart. Deciding honesty is best, Anatole hands Mrs. Chiba an empty bag and an explanation of who ate the bread. She concludes she should have ordered two loaves, and says, "If you have two loaves, give one to your friends. And if you have one loaf, give one to your strangers."

A boy is gullible and generous enough to fall for implausible tales from small animals, thoughtful enough to bow to the importunate wishes of large animals, honest enough to admit the improbable circumstances to a lady he has disappointed. This story is nicely capped by a folk saying that attests to the wisdom of keeping strangers well-fed and pacific. Dotty animal characters, with dialogue and illustrations to match, make this fanciful book a fine choice for reading aloud.

Ages 3-8

Also available in:
Paperbound — *Strangers' Bread*
Xerox Publishing Company

683

Williams, Barbara Wright

If He's My Brother

Color illustrations by Tomie De Paola.
Harvey House, Inc., 1976.
(29 pages counted)

EGOCENTRISM

Since it is his room, Bill wants to know why he cannot paint it as he wishes. He also questions why he cannot leave his shoe laces untied, put worms in his pockets, take his radio apart, throw his ball in the house, and ride on his dog — since all these things belong to him. But most of all, he would like to know why he cannot punch

his little brother. He finds the answer to this last question when his brother raps him soundly with a teddy bear.

This funny first-person narrative, well suited to the beginning reader, raises the question "If it's mine, why can't I do with it what I want?" The text does not have all the answers, and for this reason, a parent or other adult may wish to be present to guide reader response. The colorful illustrations are essential to the abbreviated text, which reads aloud well.

Ages 3-7

Also available in:
No other form known

684

Williams, Barbara Wright

Jeremy Isn't Hungry

Color illustrations by Martha Alexander.
E. P. Dutton & Company, Inc., 1978.
(32 pages counted)

BABY-SITTING: Involuntary
  Anger
  Sibling: older

Davey is trying to care for his baby brother, Jeremy, while his mother gets ready to go out. When Jeremy cries, Davey tries to put him in his chair, but Jeremy stiffens up and refuses to sit. Mother, dripping from the shower, rushes into the kitchen, seats Jeremy, and tells Davey to get a jar of baby food. This he does, but when he tries to feed Jeremy, he gets nowhere. He has to tell his mother, who is drying her hair, and she comes and heats the food. Still, Jeremy flatly refuses to eat — and finally throws the baby-food jar on the floor. Mama, newly dressed, decides to leave the mess for the sitter to clean up, and suggests that Davey give his brother a

W

banana, which Jeremy promptly mashes and throws at Davey, and a cup of milk, which Jeremy refuses to drink. Davey announces himself fed up and takes the baby out of the chair. Once on the floor, Jeremy heads straight for the spilled food, sits in the middle of it, and begins feeding himself.

Any youngster who has been asked to care for a baby will recognize the trouble Davey has with an obstinate, inarticulate little brother. This is how babies are, and the dialogue between Davey and his mother is completely true to life.

Ages 4-7

Also available in:
No other form known

685

Williams, Barbara Wright

Kevin's Grandma

Black/white illustrations by Kay Chorao.
E. P. Dutton & Company, Inc., 1975.
(30 pages counted)

GRANDPARENT: Love for

Two small boys have much about grandmothers to compare notes on. The narrator's grandma brings him crayons, coloring books, and ice cream when he's sick; his friend Kevin's grandma brings Kevin *Mad* magazine and homemade peanut-butter soup. The narrator's grandma drives an air-conditioned blue station wagon and takes him to Florida; Kevin's grandma drives a Honda 90 and they hitchhike to California. The narrator's grandma belongs to a bridge club, a garden club, and a music club; Kevin's grandma belongs to a karate club, a scuba-divers club, and a mountain-climbing club. Kevin's grandma used to work in a circus and goes skydiving. The narrator is not sure he believes everything he hears about Kevin's grandma.

This delightful story shows one grandma embarked on surprising and exciting adventures which she shares with her grandson. The other grandma leads a more conventional life but is no less prized by her grandson, cheering him when he's sick, treating him on his birthday, taking him on a vacation. The narrator tells the story of his times with his grandmother simply and lovingly. Kevin has obviously embellished the truth. The two grandmothers are presented alternately with charming black and white illustrations contrasting the two from page to page.

Ages 4-7

Also available in:
Paperbound — *Kevin's Grandma*
E. P. Dutton & Company, Inc.

686

Williams, Barbara Wright

Someday, Said Mitchell

Black/white illustrations by Kay Chorao.
E. P. Dutton & Company, Inc., 1976.
(29 pages counted)

GIVING, MEANING OF
SELF-ESTEEM
  Daydreaming

Young Mitchell vows to his mother that, when he is older, he will buy her a large super-efficient vacuum cleaner so she can spend more time talking to him instead of cleaning. His mother says that that would be nice, but she likes right now having help from someone small enough to crawl under the bed to retrieve toys. Mitchell also says that, when he is older, he will buy his mother water beds, pillowy chairs, and a castle full of servants. Mother acknowledges that all those things would be pleasant, but insists that she would rather have someone small help her, as now, dust chair rungs, sweep cobwebs, and unpack groceries. Even so, Mitchell promises his mother that he will buy her a speedy car and a mountain so that she will not have to stay in the house working. Mother appreciates those future presents too, but says that she is happy Mitchell is small enough to pick violets and sit on her lap.

Young readers will recognize this small boy's desire to do something important for his mother and can take reassurance, along with Mitchell, that what they are able to accomplish now is itself important. The illustrations show the chores Mitchell can help with, as well as his daydream gifts for the future.

Ages 3-6

Also available in:
No other form known

687

Windsor, Patricia

Diving for Roses

Harper & Row Publishers, Inc., 1976.
(248 pages)

IDENTITY, SEARCH FOR
LONELINESS
   Alcoholism: of mother
   Dependence/Independence
   Unwed mother

Jean, a young woman not long out of high school, lives with her mother in an old house in the country. For years, Jean has believed her mother to be mad, and has taken care of her — her parents are separated — to the exclusion of any life for herself. As a result, Jean herself

has become reclusive, introverted. One day, while walking in the woods, she meets a young man named Sasha who has set up a camp on the property. Though Jean orders him off the land, she is strangely drawn to him, and later returns to his tent. The two become lovers, but when summer ends, Sasha announces he must return to a job in the city. Jean thinks she has V.D. but finds instead that she is pregnant. Sasha invites her to come away with him — even offers to marry her — but she refuses. She wants to keep the baby, but she cannot leave the big old house, the forest, and most of all, her mother. Sasha tells her she is foolish to dedicate her life to a woman who is not mad at all but is an alcoholic. He has heard this from people in the town, but Jean has been too secluded to hear the universal rumor. She is furious at his accusation and rushes away. Later, she searches her mother's room and finds whiskey bottles hidden everywhere. She is stunned to find she has lived a life based wholly on lies. She confronts her mother, and eventually the woman joins Alcoholics Anonymous. But as her mother becomes more outgoing and confident over time, Jean, left with a virtually purposeless life, must struggle with her own identity. With the help of her doctor, she gradually learns to better understand herself and to make plans. After she gives birth to a baby girl, the three generations of women move out of the old house, where Jean hopes to leave old fears and sorrows.

Before her mother's rehabilitation, Jean's life is a self-imposed imprisonment. Afterwards, she thinks she has not the inner strength to change, and dreads the future. Yet she learns to set aside her bitterness at her mother's deception and to make some decisions for herself. This haunting first-person narrative is made all the more complex by the extreme innocence of the narrator, whose fantasies, sexual and otherwise, we are told. Even her rendering of truth can be suspect for the same reason. Immature readers may have difficulty finding their way through.

Ages 13 and up

Also available in:
No other form known

688

Windsor, Patricia

Mad Martin

Harper & Row Publishers, Inc., 1976.
(119 pages)

COMMUNICATION: Lack of
DEPRIVATION, EMOTIONAL
    Emotions: accepting
    Emotions: identifying
    Foster home
    Loneliness

Orphan Martin Drivic and his grandfather live a quiet, routine life in a small, bare, unkempt house on Mop Street in London. Grandfather does not talk to the neighbors, only rarely talks to Martin, and then only about the most mundane matters. Each day's meals, each day's events are like the day before. At school the boys call Martin "mad," for he never laughs or shows happiness, never frowns or gets angry, no matter how they torment him. One day Martin's routine goes out the window. Upon returning from school, he finds, not his grandfather snoozing in a chair, but two ladies, strangers. Gently they break the news that his grandfather has broken his hip, and that Martin is to stay with Mrs. Crimp until Grandfather has recovered. Arriving at Mrs. Crimp's house, Martin is dazzled by all the pictures, furniture, carpets, dishes, plants, and whatchamacallits. At supper, he meets the five Crimp children, who are fuller of talk than anyone he has ever heard — and questions! Why does he not smile? Martin's question goes unspoken: how do the Crimps find so much to say? (As for smiling, he knows what it is but cannot remember doing it.) When Mrs. Crimp makes Martin bathe and change clothes, he takes it that she thinks him improperly cared for. In fact, with so many people pointing out his oddities, he feels something vague and negative, something he wants to call "hate." Sharing Charlie's room, he asks Charlie about hate — and later about love, but that is harder to grasp. Martin does begin to like the Crimps. Yet when he is accidentally left out of a family discussion, he suddenly, painfully sees that he is not a Crimp, that soon he will have to go back to boredom and Grandfather. Impossible! He will drown himself first. Heading for the canal, he is attacked by schoolboys. In the knick of time, Charlie appears and helps him. Martin is convinced now that Charlie is his friend, and he finally understands what love is. Indeed, he feels wonderfully alive, and life is good. Sometime later, back at home with Grandfather, he determines to talk more. Fresh from his companions at the rest home, Grandfather has decided the same thing. He tells Martin a story. Martin says he wants a dog, a carpet, and a cleaner house. Their life will never be the same again.

The touching story of Mad Martin's transformation from an empty shell to a full-blooded boy is told with wit as well as pathos. Martin has never known what he was missing, and as he thoughtfully labels each new feeling, young readers who take home, family, and friends for granted may see more clearly what they have.

Ages 10-14

Also available in:
Paperbound — *Mad Martin*
Harper & Row Publishers, Inc.

689

Winthrop, Elizabeth

A Little Demonstration of Affection

Harper & Row Publishers, Inc., 1975.
(152 pages)

EMOTIONS: Accepting
SIBLING: Love for
    Death: of pet
    Family: relationships
    Jealousy: sibling
    Maturation

In the spring, sixteen-year-old John devises a plan for an underground hideout. His sister, Jenny, thirteen, knows that she and her brother Charley, fourteen, will have to do all the hard work. For years John has gotten the ideas, she has pitched in, and Charley, who has asthma, has done what he could. But suddenly John, against his parents' wishes, wants to go away for the summer. Jenny and Charley are drawn together when Charley's dog is shot. Together they decide to build the underground room without John. Day after day the two work, and a special kind of love grows up between them. One night Charley reads Jenny a story he has written about his dog's death. Jenny is moved to tears, and Charley holds her close. Both wonder at the sudden feelings physical closeness brings. Soon Jenny is possessive of her brother, even jealous when he shows interest in her friend Lucy. By now the underground room is completed, and Jenny suggests the two celebrate their accomplishment by sleeping out in it. That night, both long to relive the moment of special feeling. Jenny snuggles close to her brother, and for a second he responds. Then he pushes her away, saying a brother and sister should not hug. Lonely and ashamed over the next few weeks, Jenny isolates herself from family and friends. Nothing can cheer her. Guilt and despair depart only when Charley comes to try to comfort her. Finally, Jenny talks it all over with her father. He lovingly explains that her feelings and actions were quite normal. Slowly she warms to her family again, becomes again her old self.

Jenny's whole family has trouble showing feeling, and the moral claims of the Roman Catholicism her mother has raised them in and her father's vague God "with a hand on the steering wheel" confuse Jenny further. When brother and sister awake to feelings about each other as boy and girl, Jenny is incapacitated by guilt. At last she entrusts her feelings to her father, who turns out to be both wise and reassuring. This is a powerful and unsettling novel about a family's deepest feelings.

Ages 12-16

Also available in:
Paperbound — *A Little Demonstration of Affection*
Dell Publishing Company, Inc.

Talking Book — *A Little Demonstration of Affection*
Library of Congress

690

Winthrop, Elizabeth

Potbellied Possums

Black/white illustrations by Barbara McClintock.
Holiday House, Inc., 1977.
(32 pages counted)

FEAR: of Darkness
WEIGHT CONTROL: Overweight
    Emotions: accepting
    Sibling: relationships

Otto is a slim possum whose table manners are impeccable, and Gertrude, his sister, a potbellied possum whose table manners are absent. Gertrude eats directly from the garbage can — voraciously. Despite her resolve to stop eating so much, Gertrude winds up obeying her stomach whenever it hungrily growls. Though Otto continually teases Gertrude about her pot belly, he always tags after her at night. He is afraid of the dark but cannot admit it lest Mama be ashamed and his brothers and sisters laugh at him. One day Gertrude awakens early and leaves the nest so that the sound of her growling stomach will not bother the family. After a good feed at a garbage can, she falls asleep. That night, without Gertrude to follow, Otto intends to stay in the nest, but hunger first forces him out and then into dropping his dainty eating habits to eat garbage from the can. He meets Gertrude there and confesses his fear of the dark. "We all have our problems," Gertrude says. "Have some garbage." After gorging themselves the night through, they drag their pot bellies back to the nest, content in all things.

The resolution to this story is not in altering the characters' habits but in changing their feelings about them. Otto accepts his fear of the dark and Gertrude, after a losing struggle to stop eating so much garbage, accepts her pot belly. Children can learn from this tale that trying to change oneself or others can be a hazardous business.

Ages 4-6

Also available in:
No other form known

691

Winthrop, Elizabeth

That's Mine!

Color illustrations by Emily Arnold McCully.
Holiday House, Inc., 1977.
(30 pages counted)

COOPERATION: in Play

A little girl is building a castle out of building blocks, and, beside her, a little boy is building one too. The girl and boy argue about whose castle is taller and whose blocks are bigger. "Let go of my block," yells the little girl, "or I'll knock down your castle." "If you knock down my castle," yells the boy, "I'll knock down your castle." They each knock down the other's castle, and the blocks get all mixed up. Then the boy and girl discover that together they can build a castle bigger and more beautiful than anything each could build alone.

This short, simple story demonstrates the advantages of playing together cooperatively. The children find that when toys are shared, more can be done with them. The two-color illustrations are delightful.

Ages 2-6

Also available in:
Braille — *That's Mine!*
Library of Congress

Wittman, Sally

Pelly and Peak

Color illustrations by the author.
Harper & Row Publishers, Inc., 1978.
(64 pages)

FRIENDSHIP: Best Friend
  Self, attitude toward: accepting

Peak, a peacock, and Pelly, a pelican, live together and share happy times. They play guessing games, make presents for each other, cook together, and play tricks on each other. One day, at the seashore, Peak is strutting around with his fantail open. Pelly has no beautiful tail to open and when he tries to strut, he can only waddle. He feels bad, so Peak suggests that they go fishing. Pelly swims right out and catches sixteen fish in his bill. Peak wades along the shore, throws a line in the water — and falls asleep; whereupon a fish takes his bait, line, and pole. "You see," says Peak, "we are both good at some things." "Yes," laughs Pelly. "And not so good at others."

Good friends, though playful, are careful not to hurt each other's feelings. They recognize each other's strengths and accept each other's weaknesses. They complement each other. This is an I-Can-Read book of four amusing stories for young readers, with simple sentences but much new vocabulary, carefully introduced and repeated.

Ages 4-8

Also available in:
Talking Book — *Pelly and Peak*
Library of Congress

Wittman, Sally

A Special Trade

Color illustrations by Karen Gundersheimer.
Harper & Row Publishers, Inc., 1978.
(32 pages)

AGE: Respect for
FRIENDSHIP: Meaning of

Bartholomew is an old man when he first meets Nelly, the baby next door. He takes her for daily walks in her stroller, stopping so they can pat friendly dogs and the two of them occasionally racing through the neighbor's sprinkler. When Nelly learns to walk, Bartholomew is careful to offer her help only when she needs it. They are so often together the neighbors call them "ham and eggs." Nelly grows older and goes to school, while Bartholomew grows older and sometimes needs her help crossing the street. One day, while out alone, he falls and is taken to the hospital. Nelly writes to him every day, urging him to come home so they can go for walks again. But he returns in a wheelchair and says to Nelly, "I guess our walks are over." Nelly does not agree. She now takes him for walks, just as he once took her. "Now it's my turn to push," she says, "and Bartholomew's turn to sit . . . kind of like a trade."

This story of friendship through time and change is exceptionally well written and illustrated, and makes for amusing reading at any age. In a few brief pages, the author gives two characters vibrant life, persuades us of their strong friendship, and effects a logical role reversal, all this without affectation or sentimentality. The witty illustrations are consistent with the naturalness of the text.

Ages 2-5

Also available in:
Film — *A Special Trade*
Arthur Barr Productions, Inc.

Filmstrip — *A Special Trade*
Encyclopaedia Britannica Films

694

Wold, Jo Anne

Tell Them My Name Is Amanda

Color illustrations by Dennis Hockerman.
Albert Whitman & Co., 1977.
(30 pages counted)

SHYNESS
  Problem solving

Young Amanda is proud of her name — but not of the nicknames her family and classmates call her. She is just too shy to correct anyone. Instead, she prints her name in large letters on her school papers, wears a name tag, buys a T-shirt with her name printed across the front and back. No one notices. She then makes up her mind. Boldly she goes to each person who does not call her by her name and says, "My name is Amanda." She achieves her aim, and even better, learns how to overcome her shyness.

The predicament here and its solution are broadly depicted, but Amanda's shyness battling with determination seems very real indeed. An introductory note suggests using Amanda's story to start children discussing their own shyness.

Ages 5-8

Also available in:
Filmstrip — *Tell Them My Name Is Amanda*
Westport Communications

695

Wold, Jo Anne

Well! Why Didn't You Say So?

Color illustrations by Unada.
Albert Whitman & Co., 1975.
(31 pages counted)

COMMUNICATION: Misunderstandings

Willie is gone, and Little John, his young owner, goes out to look for him. He asks the first person he comes to, a man raking leaves, if he has seen Willie, and the man asks what Willie looks like. "Mostly brown," Little John answers. No, the man has not seen Willie. Other people Little John asks — girls roller-skating, a woman selling ice cream, a man sitting in a park, an old lady feeding birds — also ask for a description of Willie. To each, Little John gives additional details: Willie has a long tail, eyes of two colors, and a red collar. But no one has seen Willie, and Little John retraces his steps. As he passes, the people inquire if he has found his pony, his goat, his squirrel, or his cat. To each, Little John replies that Willie is a dog, and each says, "Well, why didn't you say so?" The leaf-raker, told Willie is a dog, says he has a dog like that in his garage, and Little John asks, "Well, why didn't you say so?" The man replies, "You didn't ask."

This satirically instructive story shows the importance of asking the right questions. The boy in his search omits to say the obvious — that Willie is a dog — and the people he asks neglect to question their assumptions that Willie is some other animal. They blithely talk past each other. These points are nowhere directly made in the story but can easily be discussed.

Also available in:
No other form known

696

Wolde, Gunilla

Betsy and the Chicken Pox

Translated from the Swedish.
Color illustrations by the author.
Random House, Inc., 1975.
(23 pages counted)

COMMUNICABLE DISEASES: Chicken Pox
    Illnesses: of sibling
    Jealousy: sibling

Betsy's baby brother is cranky, covered with spots, and feverish. When the doctor arrives and examines him, she neglects to say hello to Betsy. Even after she has finished diagnosing chicken pox and prescribing medication for the brother, the doctor says nothing to Betsy. After the doctor has gone, Betsy paints spots on herself. Her parents, busy caring for the baby, ignore Betsy — even with spots. Suddenly Betsy begins to yell, calling her father "mean," her mother "horrible," and her brother "stupid." Everyone gets angry; everyone quiets down; and mother, father, and Betsy care for the baby brother. That evening, when Betsy's painted spots are washed off, Daddy discovers real spots all over her. Now Betsy has the chicken pox — but doesn't want them any more.

A little girl, ignored when her brother falls ill, attempts — through imitation and anger — to gain attention. The anger generates anger in return. But thoughtful parents can recognize jealousy and reassure the child against the fears that cause it. This is one in a series of books about Betsy.

Also available in:
No other form known

697

Wolde, Gunilla

Betsy and the Doctor

Translated from the Swedish.
Color illustrations by the author.
Random House, Inc., 1978.
(23 pages counted)

HOSPITAL, GOING TO
    Accidents
    Doctor, going to
    Sutures

Little Betsy has fallen on her head from the climbing tree on the nursery-school playground. Blood is trickling down her face and she is crying. Robert, a nursery-school employee, comes, picks her up, and says she must see a doctor. When they arrive at the hospital, Robert and Betsy must wait their turn, and Betsy wonders what the doctor will do to her. When her turn comes, a nurse bathes her forehead and the doctor checks for broken bones. The doctor explains that he will close the cut with stitches after he gives her a shot so the stitching won't hurt. After the shot, which pricks a little, Betsy no longer feels any pain at all, and the doctor makes three stitches, applies lotion to them, and bandages the cut. Now Betsy is eager to tell her parents and friends all about what has happened. A week later, when the stitches are removed, she feels only a little tickle on her forehead and sees a tiny red mark where the cut has been.

All young children could benefit from having this simple little book read aloud to them. They would be somewhat prepared and less anxious if an accident someday necessitates an emergency visit to the doctor. The presentation is honest and reassuring, and invites group discussion. This is one in a series of books about Betsy.

Ages 3-7

Also available in:
No other form known

698

Wolde, Gunilla

Betsy's Baby Brother

Translated from the Swedish.
Color illustrations by the author.
Random House, Inc., 1975.
(23 pages counted)

SIBLING: New Baby

Little Betsy has a cute, much littler baby brother. Asleep, he is quiet, but awake he often cries. When he cries to be fed, their mother feeds him. The truth is, Betsy resents the amount of attention her baby brother receives and sometimes wants to give him away, so as to have her mother all to herself. But at other times Betsy likes her baby brother and is glad to be his helpful older sister. She can help give the baby a bath and can change his dirty diaper and put soothing ointment on his bottom. But the baby — like all babies, according to Mother — likes to grab Betsy's hair, and that hurts. But like all babies, this one gets sleepy, too, and when he does, Betsy likes to talk to him quietly until he falls sound asleep. On the whole, Betsy thinks baby brothers are annoying and lovable, mostly lovable.

This simple, colorfully illustrated book shows candidly an older child's feelings when a new baby is brought into the home. It is one in a series about Betsy.

Ages 2-5

Also available in:
No other form known

699

Wolde, Gunilla

Betsy's First Day at Nursery School

Translated from the Swedish.
Color illustrations by the author.
Random House, Inc., 1976.
(24 pages counted)

NURSERY SCHOOL

Although Betsy doubts nursery school will be any fun, she goes along with her mother and baby brother. She does not speak to the man who greets them there, because the other children are staring at her, and she chooses to keep her snowsuit on while the man shows them around. In one room filled with pillows she feels like jumping but is too ill at ease with the other children. Betsy's brother likes the youngest children's room but Betsy goes on to see the bathroom where each child has a specially marked place to keep a towel and toothbrush. Betsy's place is marked with a carrot. In the kitchen a lady is cooking food in large pots, and in the cloakroom there are specially marked hooks, Betsy's marked with a carrot again. The man tells her she can hang up her things, but she takes off only her boots. While her mother is talking to the man, Betsy and another girl make faces at each other. Soon they are laughing and the girl tells Betsy her name. Her coat hook is right next to Betsy's, and Betsy takes off her snowsuit so the two can go to the pillow room to jump.

Playing so long with her friend, Betsy suddenly remembers her mother and brother and runs to find them. The brother has been playing too and is tired, so her mother says it is time to go home until tomorrow. Betsy waves good-bye to her friend and decides that nursery school is fun after all.

This book, one in a series about Betsy, usefully anticipates the new experiences of nursery school. The colorful illustrations show fun-loving, energetic children who often create a happy disorder.

Ages 2-5

Also available in:
No other form known

700

Wolde, Gunilla

This Is Betsy

Translated from the Swedish.
Color illustrations by the author.
Random House, Inc., 1975.
(23 pages counted)

AUTONOMY

Young Betsy is sometimes happy, sometimes sad. Usually, she puts her jeans and sweater on the right way, but sometimes she puts her jeans on her head and her sweater on her legs to be funny. Most of the time she brushes her hair nicely and drinks cocoa from a mug, but sometimes she prefers messy hair and drinks cocoa from a saucer. She enjoys playing with blocks, but gets angry when they fall down. She often shares her teddy bear with her baby brother but may suddenly grab it away from him. Betsy likes to take a bath and get clean all over; she also likes to play in the mud and get dirty all over. She hears her father perfectly when he announces bedtime, but sometimes she pretends she

cannot. When she is sleepy, Betsy puts on her pajamas and gets into bed. True, she sometimes asks for a drink of water or a story. But always, eventually, she falls asleep.

With the aid of colorful pictures the author shows a little girl's often contradictory yet perfectly normal feelings and actions. This is one in a series of books about Betsy.

Ages 2-5

Also available in:
No other form known

701

Wolf, Bernard

Adam Smith Goes to School

Black/white photographs by the author.
J. B. Lippincott Co., 1978.
(48 pages)

SCHOOL: Entering
Pride/False pride

It is Adam Smith's first day of school. After meeting his first-grade teacher, Mrs. Young, Adam and everyone else are given name tags to help them get acquainted, and are told where to keep personal belongings. The rest of the day, Adam listens to a story, reads for his teacher so that she can judge where to start him in his reading workbook, plays a game with a newfound friend, does two pages in his math workbook, and uses the counting board. Next day, Adam is introduced to the metric system and addition, and goes to music-appreciation class, where he acts a little silly. Back in the homeroom, Mrs. Young cautions all the children to be better behaved. On the following day, Adam learns how to root a sweet potato, how to use the "listening center," meets his gym teacher, does some math and reading, and makes a bookmark. The day after that, Adam and

W

the others celebrate the sixth birthday of a classmate named Elizabeth and go to the woodworking shop, where Adam learns to use a coping saw. On the last day of the school week, Adam helps clean up the paint corner, works on the class mural, and paints a self-portrait. When his family sees the portrait, they tell Adam they are very proud of him. So is he.

This photographic essay records Adam's first week at school. Though his doubts and fears are mentioned, the account is almost entirely a happy one. And crowded with interest: the school shown has an abundance of teaching equipment for the children to use and specialists to teach music, physical education, and enough varied, specific activities are shown to encompass just about any typical school day. This book could offer reassurance to children feeling anxious about starting school.

Ages 4-7

Also available in:
No other form known

702

Wolf, Bernard

Anna's Silent World

Black/white photographs by the author.
J. B. Lippincott Co., 1977.
(48 pages)

DEAFNESS

Six-year-old Anna, though she lives in clangorous New York City, is not bothered by noise: she was born deaf and hears only the loudest sounds. Four years' training have taught her to read, write, and talk, and she and her teachers continue to work diligently at this. Anna attends school with hearing children, and ballet classes as well, for two hearing aids help her follow the basic rhythms of music. On Saturday she plays with a hearing friend who does not always understand what she says. Anna's mother explains to the friend how difficult talking is when one has never heard speech; she also shows her the hearing aids and explains lip reading. On Christmas day Anna is delighted to receive a recorder, with which she can make her own music.

This informative book describes a week in a deaf child's life. It also examines one way of teaching the deaf, the aural-oral method. But it says nothing about another way, which depends heavily upon sign language. Since the two methods are in contention among educators, this book might be instructively supplemented by one discussing sign language, as does Edna Levine's *Lisa and Her Soundless World* (See THE BOOKFINDER, Vol. 1, 1977). The present book describes honestly the special needs of a deaf child without dwelling on the child's limitations.

Ages 5-9

Also available in:
No other form known

703

Wolf, Bernard

Connie's New Eyes

Black/white photographs by the author.
J. B. Lippincott Co., 1976.
(96 pages)

BLINDNESS
PETS: Guide Dog

Fifteen-year-old Alison Gooding is the first owner of Blythe, a female puppy she raises for The Seeing Eye, Inc., which trains guide dogs for blind people. Alison herself trains the pup in obedience, and after a year returns Blythe to the agency for three months of intensive training. There, Connie David, twenty-two, a recent college graduate blind from birth, comes to claim her. Fond of each other from the start, Connie and Blythe train rigorously as a team for a month, then set off for Connie's job as a teacher of handicapped children in Iowa. Connie's warmth and charm win quick rapport with the children, who also take to Blythe. One successful year at the school leads to a job in Germany, where Connie will be a counselor at a Girl Scout camp.

This account centers on a young woman whose handicap does not keep her from happiness and useful work. Readers will also get to know the dog, who makes her life easier. Outstanding candid photographs and unsentimental prose combine to make a narrative suitable for a wide range of readers.

Ages 9 and up

Also available in:
Cassette for the Blind — *Connie's New Eyes*
Library of Congress

Paperbound — *Connie's New Eyes*
Pocket Books

Talking Book — *Connie's New Eyes*
Library of Congress

704

Wolitzer, Hilma

Out of Love

Farrar, Straus & Giroux, Inc., 1976.
(147 pages)

DIVORCE: of Parents
MATURATION
  Boy-girl relationships
  Love, meaning of
  Parental: overprotection
  Stepparent: mother

Thirteen-year-old Teddy Hecht can recall incidents leading up to her parents' divorce — quarrels and silences and slammed doors — but she cannot understand how they fell out of love. She lives with her mother and her eleven-year-old sister, Karen, but she regularly sees her father and wonders how his love, shown in letters she has found, could shift from her mother to his new wife, Shelley. Teddy herself is unable to see much to like in Shelley and concludes that Mother simply let her appearance go. She sets out to persuade Mother to lose weight and spruce up. Mother tries but ends up joking about her failure to improve. Teddy's best friend, Maya Goldstein, brings over some boys one day, but the visit only further sours Teddy on the whole boy-girl business. She thinks herself too plain to attract boys anyway. An aunt, finding out about her plans to reconcile her parents, admonishes Teddy that they did not divorce because of looks, that it takes much more to dissolve a marriage than fading good looks. Teddy's earlier resolve to forget about boys weakens when one of the boys who had come over calls her up. Advised by Shelley, Teddy gets a new and attractive haircut. Then friend Maya runs away to protest her parents' overprotection and Teddy successfully negotiates between parents and daughter. But her newfound confidence is shattered when she learns that Shelley is pregnant. How can the family reunite now? But then, she thinks, why pretend? Divorce is divorce. Her mother, even though alone, is "brave and kind and loving," and a person could do worse than to turn out like her.

This first-person narrative records a spirited girl discarding youthful illusions for a more mature assessment of her life and memories. The changes do not come easily, and Teddy sometimes backslides. But in the end she seems to know how things stand and to be looking ahead to future changes. This author's wit and gentle humor should help adolescents take their daily trials less seriously.

Ages 10-13

Also available in:
Paperbound — *Out of Love*
Bantam Books, Inc.

Talking Book — *Out of Love*
Library of Congress

705

Wolitzer, Hilma

Toby Lived Here

Farrar, Straus & Giroux, Inc., 1978.
(147 pages)

EMOTIONS: Accepting
FOSTER HOME
  Mental illness: of parent

Though taken to a mental hospital, Toby's mother lingers with her twelve-year-old daughter in spirit. After her husband's death the mother had lived calmly, uncomplainingly, even cheerfully, doing what she had always done. Her motto: "You just have to live." Toby applies this dictum cheerlessly to living in the foster home where she and her six-year-old sister, Anne, are placed. She does not cry; she does not complain; she only silently yearns for her mother's release and attempts to ignore the present situation. Little Anne, however, takes readily to the Selwyns, a sympathetic older couple whose many foster children love them; but Toby holds back, even concealing from her new friend, Susan, where her mother is, and why. Particularly unhappy on her birthday, Toby blurts out to Mrs. Selwyn that she hates her mother for leaving them. On Mrs. Selwyn's insistent advice, a social worker arranges for the girls' first visit with their mother, who until now was allowed to see no one. At the reunion, the mother explains that she had broken down because, fearing her own emotions, she had bottled them up. Realizing that she, too, has done this, Toby tells all to Susan and calls herself a dope. Several months later, released from the hospital, her mother plans to move back to their former neighborhood. Toby would now love to stay in the new one but accepts her mother's decision, understanding that she will always be a welcome visitor at the Selwyns'.

Toby, like her mother, must learn to express her emotions. The barriers she puts between herself and her foster family are formidable and come down only when Toby stops deluding herself and others about the important things in her life. Her eventual confession to Susan and recognition of what the Selwyns have done for her suggest a healthier acceptance of life. This realistic, perceptive story offers no pat answers. Toby knows life has been painful and will be again. But she will be better prepared to meet difficult times when they arise.

Ages 10-12

Also available in:
Paperbound — *Toby Lived Here*
Bantam Books, Inc.

706

Wolkstein, Diane

The Visit

Color illustrations by Lois Ehlert.
Alfred A. Knopf, Inc., 1977.
(28 pages counted)

DEPENDENCE/INDEPENDENCE
VISITING

To us it is often a small world, but it is a very large one indeed for the little ant who goes to visit a friend. She walks laboriously, "step by step" over a twig and then down a branch to meet her friend, finally. For a while they sail a leaf boat on a puddle, and then they sit together until the little ant must leave. Retracing her steps, she arrives home *"just before dark."*

This story underscores the vast size of an ant's world and the time needed to move around in it despite the actual shortness of the distances covered. The illustrations not only invite youngsters to acquire an ant's perspective as the little creature toils across the solid, brightly-colored shapes that loom all around it; they may also lead listeners or readers to turn this ant's perspective on objects familiar to their own world. Adults could also read aloud this very simple story on the advent of a child's first independent trip to a friend or to the store.

Ages 3-5

Also available in:
No other form known

707

Wood, Joyce

Grandmother Lucy in Her Garden

Color illustrations by Frank Francis.
Collins-World, 1975.
(30 pages counted) o.p.

GRANDPARENT: Love for
  Nature: appreciation of

A young girl brings her grandmother three rose bushes on the first day of spring and shares with us their walk through the garden. Tom the cat watches their preparations from his "yellow saucer" of spring sunshine. Grandmother Lucy fills her basket with the rose bushes, a trowel, and hats with veils for looking at bees. Girl and grandmother walk off hand in hand. They see frogs, yellow butterflies, daffodils, and goldfish, and they plant the rose bushes. They pick pussy willows, and the

girl is reminded of Tom's soft feet. She picks some yellow catkins for her grandmother, is scolded for getting her feet muddy, but knows Grandmother Lucy likes the gift. They put on the veiled hats to watch the bees at work, and look for Eric Bristle the hedgehog, who is still hibernating. Tom appears and follows them now, but Grandmother tells him to go back home so that they can watch the chickadees. Tom is offended. They watch a chickadee build a nest in the birdhouse waiting for him. Then they return home. The girl puts the pussy willows and catkins in a pot and strokes Tom. Grandmother pours him some milk, for he is still angry.

The text and illustrations portray this young girl's love for her grandmother amid the wonder of nature in springtime. The color illustrations, many of them full-page, add much to the child's poetic first-person narrative. This is the first in a British series of books about the little girl, Grandmother Lucy, and Tom.

Ages 4-8

Also available in:
No other form known

708

Wood, Phyllis Anderson

Get a Little Lost, Tia

The Westminster Press, 1978.
(173 pages)

MATURATION
SIBLING: Relationships
  Boy-girl relationships
  Responsibility: accepting

Since the death of his father in a car accident and his mother's taking a job, Jason Hilliard, a high school boy, has been in charge of his thirteen-year-old sister, Tia. But her father's death and her growing pains have left

Tia a bundle of conflicting emotions, and she seems to stir up trouble wherever she goes. One morning Jason is summoned to the high school office by a pretty student aide named Celia. Tia is ill, and she must be taken home. Jason borrows a car, takes Tia home and returns to classes, but coming home after school, he finds Tia chatting and giggling on the phone. He angrily reports her misbehavior to their mother. Meanwhile, he has been attracted to Celia and wonders if he will be able to date her. But she surprises him by inviting him to a family picnic on the following Sunday. Jason is enjoying the picnic when he discovers Tia and her girl friend spying on him from the bushes. He loses his temper, but Celia, instead of sympathizing with him, politely entertains the girls the rest of the afternoon. Next, Tia lies to her home-economics teacher about a sewing project. In fact, she receives deficiency notices in almost all her classes. She hates school and thinks that all her teachers and classmates dislike her. Again Celia comes to her aid. She gives Tia a haircut and helps her choose new clothes and invites both Jason and Tia to another family picnic at a park in the mountains. There Tia meets Celia's cousin Bobby, who keeps her occupied until she decides to go for a hike up the mountain with Celia and Jason. The three split up to hike separate trails, and when Jason and Celia reach the spot where they were to meet, Tia is nowhere around. Jason and Celia search briefly, then return to the picnic grounds to enlist the help of others. Celia's father organizes search parties, but at dusk, Tia has not been found. They build a campfire and sit around it singing and waiting, until Tia — who had slid down the mountainside and gotten hurt and lost — following the light and the music, appears in the clearing. Bobby dresses her wounds and drives her home. A few weeks later, Jason, Celia, and Bobby give a surprise birthday party for Tia. Ladylike as never before, she has a surprise of her own: a thank-you gift for Jason and Celia: two tickets for a concert that they can attend *alone*.

Jason, an exasperated but loyal brother, and his generous, understanding girl friend join forces to help an immature younger sister grow up. Still Jason often wishes Celia would pay less attention to his sister and more to him. Tia, in his view, should "get a little lost." When she does, Jason is heartsick. This is an amusing story, particularly for sorely tried older siblings, but there is little complexity in its characters.

Ages 11-13

Also available in:
Paperbound — *Get a Little Lost, Tia*
New American Library

709

Wood, Phyllis Anderson

Win Me and You Lose

The Westminster Press, 1977.
(137 pages)

BOY-GIRL RELATIONSHIPS
COMMUNICATION: Parent-Child
  Crime/Criminals
  Divorce: of parents

At the custody hearing following his parents' divorce, seventeen-year-old Matt Bristow is asked with which parent he wants to live. Matt chooses to remain in the city with his father rather than move to the country with his mother. Mr. Bristow's job requires a lot of travel, so he and Matt have never spent much time together. Now they are sharing an apartment and Matt feels he barely knows the man; the two, uneasy with each other, quarrel frequently. Then Matt meets Rebecca Javez, who lives down the hall. Her parents, too, are recently divorced, and since her mother works evenings, Rebecca is alone much of the time. One night she calls

Matt for help; someone has tried to get into her apartment. The next day Matt comes by to walk her to school, and Rebecca points out a strange man who she says has been hanging around the apartment building lately. After school the same man follows them. Some nights later Rebecca receives a threatening phone call, and, in the days that follow, both Matt and his father stay as close to her as possible, while the police watch the building. But one afternoon Matt steps out after Rebecca has gone downstairs to do laundry. When he returns, he stops in at the laundry room to tell Rebecca he's going to the store. He walks in on a man holding a knife above Rebecca's head, and as the man lunges forward, Matt grabs the knife. The police rush in; the man is arrested; Rebecca is hospitalized for a shoulder wound. In her absence, Matt realizes how deeply he has come to care for her. He also better understands his father, now, and Mr. Bristow in turn is now willing to respect Matt as capable of making adult decisions. Then Rebecca returns from the hospital, physically healed but frightened, troubled by recurring nightmares, and unwilling to go outside. In time, Matt's gentle reassurance brings her around.

Out of Rebecca's nightmarish experience, three new friendships form. Mr. Bristow learns to love Rebecca as he would a daughter. Matt and Rebecca's friendship deepens into a romance. And Matt and his father, with more acquaintance, gradually develop a mutual respect. This first-person narrative, told by Matt, is tense, low-vocabulary reading. Accomplished readers may find its prose too elementary.

Ages 10-13

Also available in:
Cassette for the Blind — *Win Me and You Lose*
Library of Congress

Paperbound — *Win Me and You Lose*
New American Library

710
Wosmek, Frances

A Bowl of Sun
Color illustrations by the author.
Childrens Press, Inc., 1976.
(47 pages)

BLINDNESS
CREATIVITY
  Love, meaning of
  Peer relationships: avoiding others

Megan, a blind girl, lives with Mike, her father, in the back of Mike's leather store by the ocean. Mike makes belts, sandals, and bags, and Megan helps tidy the store and makes sandwiches and cocoa for the two of them. On Sunday afternoons, they walk on the shore and build sand castles, and later Mike describes the color of the evening sky. One day, at the urging of some of his customers, Mike decides that Megan's world must be enlarged. As a first step, he gives Megan a birthday party and invites all the children in the small coastal town. The girl is overwhelmed by the noise and confusion and wants no more parties. Mike persists, inviting other children to accompany them to the shore. Soon he announces that he and Megan are moving to Boston so that she can attend a school for the blind. Megan is panic-stricken by the city and longs for the comforting sound of the ocean. In Boston she will do nothing for herself and gets nowhere with school. Worried, Mike seeks the help of a neighbor named Rose, who, after rescuing the girl from a fall in the street, tenderly and cheerfully leads her back home. At Rose's pottery workshop, Megan discovers a natural gift for making pots. Remembering the sand castles, she sets to work on a pink bowl the color of the setting sun — "a bowl of sun." Soon she is learning quickly in school. When the bowl is finished, Megan and Rose present it to Mike. He is amazed by his daughter's talent and decides that when she finishes school, they will return to the ocean and open up a new store as partners. Megan asks if Rose can be a third partner, and Mike says yes. To Megan, the room feels "as warm as a friendly hand."

This simple, poetic book shows from the start that while Mike and Megan enjoy a warm and secure relationship, they must move beyond their narrow life. Thereafter, the difference between a small coastal town and a big city are brought home to Megan through sound and touch. Her blindness is made to seem not a disabling condition but a handicap overcome by love. The book ends with Megan much more aware of what life offers: she can read; she has discovered a wonderful talent; and she can open the father-daughter bond to include Rose.

Ages 7-9

Also available in:
No other form known

711

Yep, Laurence Michael

Child of the Owl

Harper & Row Publishers, Inc., 1977.
(217 pages)

CHINESE-AMERICAN
GRANDPARENT: Love for
SELF, ATTITUDE TOWARD: Accepting
 Gambling
 Grandparent: living in home of
 Life style: change in
 Parent/Parents: respect for/lack of respect for

Casey Young, a Chinese-American girl of twelve, and her father, Barney, are constantly moving to avoid Barney's gambling debts. Then, when Barney wins a lot of money, he is beaten, robbed, and hospitalized, and Casey is sent to San Francisco to live with her dead mother's brother. Lonely and ill-at-ease in her wealthy uncle's elegant home, Casey becomes uncooperative and is sent to live with her maternal grandmother, Paw Paw, in San Francisco's Chinatown. Surrounded by so many Chinese-Americans for the first time in her life, she begins to feel intensely aware of her Chinese heritage. Yet she is uncomfortable with her schoolmates, for they speak in Chinese, which she does not understand. Casey begins to explore her heritage with Paw Paw's help, hoping to understand the mother she never knew and to induce the people of Chinatown to accept her. Soon she positively enjoys living in Chinatown. But Paw Paw has an encounter with a thief, who steals her valuable antique owl charm, and in the scuffle Paw Paw's leg is broken and she is hospitalized. Casey suspects that Gilbert, a young neighbor, is involved in the theft. She remains in Paw Paw's apartment, where neighbors occasionally look in on her. It is Gilbert who discovers that Barney, released from the hospital months earlier, is the thief. Barney returns the charm and promises to reform, but Casey wants nothing to do with him. When Paw Paw comes home, she sells the owl charm to a museum in order to pay Barney's debts and her own hospital bills. She also persuades Casey to accept Barney as he is, and Casey goes to telephone him.

The beautiful Chinese legend Paw Paw tells her granddaughter (Chapter 2) explains the supposed origin of the family's owl charm ancestry. Casey herself narrates this moving and complex book, in the course of which she is thrust upon people she hardly knows and must either shoulder or run from an ethnic identity to which she is both an heir and a stranger. Her grandmother offers invaluable guidance, and in the end the girl is not so changed that she cannot forget an errant father and see him more clearly than before. He embodies a secondary theme: compulsive gambling. We are told that Casey's story draws on some childhood experiences of the author.

Ages 11 and up

Also available in:
Cassette for the Blind — *Child of the Owl*
Library of Congress

Paperbound — *Child of the Owl*
Dell Publishing Company, Inc.

712

Yep, Laurence Michael

Dragonwings

Harper & Row Publishers, Inc., 1975.
(248 pages)

CHINESE-AMERICAN
COMMUNICATION: Parent-Child
IMMIGRANTS
PREJUDICE: Ethnic/Racial
   Change: new home
   Creativity
   Maturation

We are in China in 1903; eight-year-old Moon Shadow lives with his mother and has never seen his father, who went to America before Shadow was born. From America comes cousin Hand Clan, and at the end of his visit he takes Moon Shadow back with him to Chinatown in San Francisco in the land of the "white demons." Windrider, Moon Shadow's father, works for Uncle Bright Star at the Company, a family laundry business. Moon Shadow works in the laundry too and goes to school, but lives in constant fear of white demons, who frequently beat and rob Chinese. Then one day Moon Shadow is attacked by one of his own people: Uncle Bright Star's grown son, Black Dog, a

bitter, cruel man, beats him up and steals Company money the boy is carrying. Windrider sets out to avenge his son, wounds Black Dog, and kills another man. Windrider and Moon Shadow leave Chinatown, moving to a white district, where Windrider gets a job as a handyman and mechanic for a kind white man; they live in a stable next door to an elderly white woman, Mrs. Whitlaw, and her niece, Robin, and the four become good friends. Meanwhile, Windrider, who has brought with him from China an expertise in kite-making, has become increasingly interested in the Wright brothers and their flying machines. He begins corresponding with the brothers and, in his spare time, building experimental gliders. Early one morning in 1905, father and son are awakened by a trembling of the earth, and within an hour, the city is destroyed by a great earthquake. After being shuffled from place to place with other Chinese, Windrider and Moon Shadow move across the bay to Oakland, to live in a large vacant barn. There Windrider works on his gliders, until, with the passing of three more years, his dream begins to take visible shape. He has built a large biplane, Dragonwings, which he will launch from a hillside to ride the air currents. On the day of his flight, to his surprise, Windrider's cousins and uncles from the Company, as well as Mrs. Whitlaw and Robin, come to watch. The flight is successful — until a bolt fastening a propeller breaks, and Windrider loses control of the plane and crashes. Dragonwings is ruined; Windrider has broken several bones. But instead of feeling defeated, he makes a sensible decision. His private dream has been fulfilled; now he will work toward bringing his wife to America. Uncle Bright Star tells Windrider there is a partnership available in the Company, and Moon Shadow and Windrider move back to Chinatown.

This is a story of a poor boy's struggle for survival in an alien land and of his father's efforts both to fulfill a private dream and to make his way in the world. It is rich as history, and in its depiction of a culture, but never at the expense of an engrossing plot. In an afterword, the author explains his purpose in writing: to destroy the stereotype of the Chinese who came to America at the turn of the century, to show that these were individuals with fears, dreams, and interesting lives. His book might be a model for such chronicles of emigration.

Ages 12 and up

Also available in:
Cassette for the Blind — *Dragonwings*
Library of Congress

Paperbound — *Dragonwings*
Harper & Row Publishers, Inc.

713

Young, Michael

The Imaginary Friend

Color photographs by Eric Oxendorf.
Raintree Publishers, Ltd., 1977.
(30 pages)

IMAGINARY FRIEND

Young Bobby has no friends. His parents are too busy to play with him. His big brother has gone off with his older crowd. Angry that no one will play with him, Bobby says, "Who needs all of them anyway." He decides to play by himself. He makes a spaceship from some cartons, but his spaceship needs a copilot. Bobby thinks, "But this is not a real spaceship. It's just pretend. Why don't I pretend to have a copilot too? Okay, I'm the pilot and my copilot is named Jim." He and his imaginary friend Jim spend the afternoon checking fuel gauges, life-support systems, and blasting off. When Bobby's mother asks him whom he is talking to, he replies, "No one." She tells him to wash up for dinner. Before he goes into the house, Bobby says, "See you next Saturday, Jim."

In the absence of any real playmates, a young boy creates an imaginary one. He keeps his friend a secret from his mother, suggesting that he may feel Jim is his and no one else's. No resolution of the boy's need for real playmates is suggested. In this spare, brief narrative, the full-page photographs tell as much as the text.

Ages 4-7

Also available in:
No other form known

714

Young, Miriam Burt

Truth and Consequences

Black/white illustrations by Diane de Groat.
Four Winds Press, 1975.
(101 pages) o.p.

FRIENDSHIP: Best Friend
HONESTY/DISHONESTY

On her first day in sixth grade, eleven-year-old Kimberly Jones meets Alison, a new girl in the neighborhood. The two become friends at once. Kimberly has given a lot of thought to lying, both to the little "white lies" people will tell to spare one another's feelings and to her own lies: a book report on a non-existent book, a lie to her teacher that her family has a maid. Close as she has come to getting in trouble with her lies, Kim solemnly promises herself never to lie again. Thus, when her new friend Alison gets her long hair cut short, Kim tells her she looks ugly. Hurt and angry, Alison vows never to speak to Kim again. Christmas vacation starts off lonely indeed. A talk with her parents about truth and tact solves nothing. But in her solitude Kim wonders if her interpretation of "truth" has been too strict. Shortly before Christmas, her little brother, Peter, puts her to the test. He asks her if there really is a Santa Claus. Torn between honesty and an unwillingness to spoil Peter's Christmas, Kim finally answers, "No, there isn't." Christmas caroling with other neighborhood kids cures Peter's sadness for a time, and Kim, spotting Alison in the group, greets her with honest friendliness, to which Alison responds politely. On the way home Kim and Peter visit an elderly neighbor woman. To her, Kim pours out her whole bewilderment about honesty. The neighbor explains how one can be kind and honest at the same time. Thus, Kim tells Alison, at a party the next day, how pretty she looks. When "Santa" arrives to see the younger children, Peter simply decides to believe in him — at least until after Christmas. And just before Kim leaves, Alison gives her a Christmas present. Kim is ecstatic. At home she joyfully plans her gift to Alison: a notebook listing all the good times she and Alison will share in the new year.

Kim reflects, in this first-person narrative, on the irony of her friendship with Alison, that it started with a "lie" and almost ended with a misplaced truth. Through experience Kim learns that raw truth sometimes needs flavoring with imagination and gentleness if friendships are to be maintained and life itself made pleasant. The situations here ring as true as the dialogue.

Ages 9-12

Also available in:
Cassette for the Blind — *Truth and Consequences*
Library of Congress

Paperbound — *Truth and Consequences*
Scholastic Book Services

715

Ziegler, Sandra

At the Dentist: What Did Christopher See?

Color illustrations by Mina Gow McLean.
The Child's World, Inc., 1976.
(32 pages counted)

DENTIST, GOING TO

Z

When Christopher Sangree goes to the dentist for his checkup, his sister, Karina, comes along for her first visit. Knowing that "going to the dentist is not that bad," Christopher encourages the hesitant Karina to enter the reception room. The dentist, Dr. Thompson, has moved to a new office since Christopher's last visit, so he shows the children where everything is. While examining their teeth, Dr. Thompson explains that plaque and sweets cause tooth decay and that proper dental hygiene will prevent cavities. Upon returning home, Christopher, impressed by the dentist's comments draws pictures of "Mr. Plaque," "Sir Sweet," "Ms. Toothbrush," and "Floss."

This simple story will help prepare a child for a visit to the dentist. The primary emphasis is on dental hygiene. This Native American family's interest in sandpainting and rugweaving is depicted incidentally in both text and illustrations.

Ages 4-7

Also available in:
No other form known

716

Ziegler, Sandra

At the Hospital: A Surprise for Krissy

Color illustrations by Mina Gow McLean.
The Child's World, Inc., 1976.
(32 pages)

HOSPITAL, GOING TO
SURGERY: Tonsillectomy

Little Krissy Morgan is going to the hospital for a tonsillectomy. After registering in the admitting office, and with her panda under her arm, she and Mother are shown to Krissy's room. There they meet Ms. Thompson, a nurse, who weighs Krissy, helps her into pajamas, takes her temperature, and shows her how to use the nurse's call button. After having an X ray and a blood test, Krissy meets her roommate, Priscilla. Early the next morning, Krissy, who has been given a shot to make her drowsy, tells Mother to save the surprise she has brought until Krissy returns from surgery. The little girl remembers nothing of her surgery and little of the recovery room, but when she is back in her room she is aware that her throat hurts a lot. That is why she merely nods when Mother displays the surprise — a music box to keep jewelry in. Later, Ms. Thompson gives Krissy a collar of cracked ice and a glass of ginger ale to soothe her throat. And the next morning, Krissy is released, glad to be going home.

This story of a hospital stay glosses over separation from parents, blood tests, and the possible fear of surgery, but it does tell honestly about post-surgery pain. It is a very simple story, to reassure very young children. An adult could elaborate on it in whatever way seems best.

Ages 3-6
Also available in:
No other form known

717

Zindel, Paul

I Love My Mother

Color illustrations by John Melo.
Harper & Row Publishers, Inc., 1975.
(31 pages counted)

LOVE, MEANING OF
Parent/Parents: single

A little boy can have fine times with his mother, whether catching butterflies or going to the zoo. The presents she gives him are also occasions, especially the genuine boa constrictor he got for his birthday. He thinks of the future — of the ring, the collie, the farm, and the flowers he will give to her someday. The two of them comfort each other, too, at times when he has nightmares about gorillas, at times when she is lonely. True, they have differences as well: for instance, she will not let him drive the car. Sometimes the boy wishes his father were back, and his mother assures him that his father misses him, too.

Love is strong between this little boy and his mother, now single. They enjoy each other's company, but there are hard, lonely times as well. No reason is specified for the father's absence. This sensitive first-person narrative is powerfully illustrated in vibrant colors, the illustrations occupying full, sometimes double pages interspersed with brief text. The text appears on two pages at the front of the book. Especially striking are pictures of nightmares and one of the family, with the father drawn in blue to suggest his absence. Read aloud, this book could open up discussion between a single parent and her child.

Ages 3-7

Also available in:
No other form known

718

Zolotow, Charlotte Shapiro

It's Not Fair

Color illustrations by William Pène du Bois.
Harper & Row Publishers, Inc., 1976.
(32 pages)

JEALOUSY: Peer
  Friendship: best friend
  Life style

The girl who tells this story wishes that she had long, black hair like her friend Martha and thinks it unfair that Martha never gets freckles from the sun or gains weight, as she does. She also thinks it unfair that Martha has a homeroom teacher who is witty, a house made to play in, a mother who likes rock and roll, and a grandmother who bakes. Her own homeroom teacher is strict; her house has fancy, breakable furniture and decorations; her mother likes classical music; and her grandmother is a lawyer who lives far away. How puzzling, then, that Martha envies her stern homeroom teacher, her curly hair and freckles, her opera-loving mother, and a grandmother who is a lawyer rather than a cook. Can life have been unfair to *both* of them?

Two good friends in this first-person narrative envy each other's way of life. The fact that the girls in the illustrations appear to be teenagers seems at variance

with the text. Over all, the book is superficial but does make clear how children often feel about each other, their homes, and their family lives.

Ages 5-7

Also available in:
No other form known

719

Zolotow, Charlotte Shapiro

May I Visit?

Color illustrations by Erik Blegvad.
Harper & Row Publishers, Inc., 1976.
(32 pages)

LOVE, MEANING OF
  Consideration, meaning of
  Sibling: younger

A young girl notices that her visiting married sister has changed and now keeps the bathroom neat, talks pleasantly to their mother, and helps Mother make the meals. After the older sister leaves, the girl asks Mother if she, too, may come to visit when she is older — provided that she does not spill powder on the bathroom floor or leave crumbs on the carpet, does not try on all her mother's scarves and necklaces, does not "eat tonight's dessert in the afternoon" or track mud and water into the house, and does not knock over the plants. With that understood, may she come to visit? Her mother tells her she will indeed be welcome and that "it will be fun to have you then, just as it is now!"

Envious of her older sister's competence, a little girl seeks reassurance from her mother that she will herself one day grow up. Her mother gently reminds her not only that she will but that she is loved right now for being just as she is. Children who often yearn to catch up to older brothers or sisters will appreciate this child's relief as much as her apprehension.

Ages 4-7

Also available in:
No other form known

720

Zolotow, Charlotte Shapiro

Someone New

Color illustrations by Erik Blegvad.
Harper & Row Publishers, Inc., 1978.
(32 pages)

MATURATION

A young boy is puzzled by his sense that someone around home is missing. He is surprised, as well, to find that he no longer likes the wallpaper he himself chose for his room. Playing marbles no longer interests him, and he packs his bottle caps and baseball cards and old Bear and Panda away in a box. Then he realizes who is missing — his childhood self. "I am someone new," he muses. He has matured, and that includes outgrowing things.

A boy becomes pensive about his changing feelings, realizing that but for some sentimental attachment to childhood toys he has put away childish things. His experience is told in simple language, partly in verse, and is accompanied by apt illustrations.

Ages 4-8

Also available in:
No other form known

721

Zolotow, Charlotte Shapiro

The Unfriendly Book

Balck/white illustrations by William Pène du Bois.
Harper & Row Publishers, Inc., 1975.
(32 pages)

FRIENDSHIP: Lack of
FRIENDSHIP: Meaning of

Little Judy has lots of friends. She is always ready to see the best in each of them, despite their faults. But Bertha, who has always considered herself Judy's *best* friend, likes none of the other girls. She sees only their faults and therefore has no friends. She criticizes Judy for liking everyone, but Judy sets her straight: she does not like everyone — she likes everyone but Bertha!

The Story, enhanced by the clever illustrations, provides an opportunity for young children to recognize the importance of looking for the good in others. Each friend is pictured first as Bertha sees her, with unattractive traits exaggerated, then as Judy sees her, with the best foot forward.

Ages 4-8

Also available in:
No other form known

Zolotow, Charlotte Shapiro

When the Wind Stops

Black/white illustrations by Howard Knotts.
Harper & Row Publishers, Inc., 1975.
(32 pages)

CURIOSITY
NATURE: Appreciation of
  Communication: parent-child

Sorry to see a splendid day end, a little boy asks his mother: "Why does the day have to end?" Her answer — "so night can begin" — does not satisfy him, and he asks where the sun goes when the day ends. The day never ends, she answers, for the sun always shines somewhere. Nothing ever ends but begins somewhere else or appears in a different form — the wind, a road, a mountain, waves, ships, everything. And falling leaves? The boy's mother explains they fall to the ground in autumn to become food for new trees with new leaves the next spring. Nothing ends. By this time, night has come, ending the day, but soon enough the sun will rise on another day.

This story illustrates a basic ecological principle: everything goes somewhere. Though the principle is rooted in science, the text and the illustrations here — which show the "somewhere" to which everything goes — present the concept in instances familiar to children.

Ages 5-7

Also available in:
No other form known

Zweifel, Frances William

Bony

Color illustrations by Whitney Darrow.
Harper & Row Publishers, Inc., 1977.
(64 pages)

PETS: Responsibility for
  Nature: appreciation of

Z

Young Kim is playing in the yard when a baby squirrel drops at his feet from a tree. Realizing that is is an orphan, Kim gets his mother's consent that he may care for the little creature — he names her Bony — until she is old enough to care for herself outdoors. Bony thrives but, in autumn, when she tries to store her food around the house, she makes a mess. When Mom suggests that Bony had better now live outside, Kim convinces her that the squirrel is still too young; he keeps Bony in his room — until the day she chews his favorite model boat to pieces. Kim berates her until Mom reminds him that "squirrels must gnaw on hard things." Kim realizes that the squirrel is not bad — she is only being true to her nature — and decides that outside is the best place for her. To encourage her to remain outside, Kim and his father build a nest and put it high in a tree. But she does not take to the nest until she meets another squirrel, and they share it. Kim is elated: Bony has become an outdoor squirrel.

Beginning readers will enjoy the simple test and pictures in this I-Can-Read book. They will see that Kim feels responsible for caring for his pet and for encouraging her to return to her natural habitat.

Ages 6-7

Also available in:
No other form known